STATE AND URBAN POLITICS

STATE AND URBAN POLITICS

Readings in Comparative Public Policy

Edited by

RICHARD I. HOFFERBERT *University of Michigan*
IRA SHARKANSKY *University of Wisconsin*

LITTLE, BROWN AND COMPANY *Boston*

LIBRARY OF CONGRESS CATALOG CARD NUMBER: 78-125113

FIRST PRINTING

Published simultaneously in Canada
by Little, Brown & Company (Canada) Limited

PRINTED IN THE UNITED STATES OF AMERICA

PREFACE

In keeping with the interests of many students, this book focuses on those features of politics, economics, and population characteristics that help to shape the policies of state and local governments. This focus is important for the reader who is involved in public affairs as well as for the reader who wants to understand the policy process. The concern here is not "What policies should we have?" but "How do we get the policies that we do?" By understanding how policies come to be we can move some off their present course and reinforce others.

Empirical research is not a fixed science. We show some of its debates — and its excitement — in articles that attack similar problems from different perspectives. In introductory comments before each section, we detail the principal points of agreement and argument and help the reader see how various findings lead us forward in the understanding of policy making in the states.

We owe many thanks. Stefanie Hecht and Deanna Gervasi typed our essays and correspondence. Two conferences sponsored by the Inter-University Consortium for Political Research and the National Science Foundation put us into contact with some of the most creative scholars in the field of state and local politics. Our own research was financed by institutions mentioned in the notes attached to our articles.

The dedication is to our children: Mark and Samuel Hofferbert and Erica and Stefan Sharkansky. We hope their generation will reap some benefits from the empirical analysis of public policy.

CONTENTS

Part 4

POLICIES AND THEIR SOCIOECONOMIC ENVIRONMENTS 373

Conclusion

THE NATIONALIZATION OF STATE POLITICS 463

STATE AND URBAN POLITICS

Introduction

THE ROLE OF STATE AND COMMUNITY POLITICAL SYSTEMS

The studies in this volume share certain common characteristics that have led the editors to believe they are worthy of being brought together in convenient form. Nearly all of the studies adopt one variant or another of a comparative approach. The field of inquiry commonly called "state and local government" for too long has relied upon studies of single communities, single issues, or single actors in the political process. Case studies are interesting and sometimes suggestive; but case studies do not provide the kind of general knowledge that will enable us to move from one situation to another and have some basis for predicting what we will see. G. Theodore Mitau's study of a former governor of Minnesota told of his actions during a strike.[1] Will those who read it know what other governors would do in similar strikes? Robert Dahl has studied how New Haven's mayor went about getting a new school.[2] Can we generalize about mayors and schools from his study?

We can generalize from case studies only to the extent that they manifest characteristics shared by other situations. And we can know these characteristics only if we compare one situation to another. In effect, that is what most authors in this book are doing. Often with the assistance of interesting statistical and observational techniques, they compare aspects of state and community policy making systems in order to make some general statements

[1] G. Theodore Mitau, "The Governor and the Strike," in Robert T. Frost, ed., *Cases in State and Local Government* (Englewood Cliffs: Prentice-Hall, Inc., 1962), 207–218.

[2] Robert A. Dahl, *Who Governs?* (New Haven: Yale University Press, 1961), chapter 11.

about policy systems that will apply to a large number of situations.

This feature of our studies points up another common trait that they share: they all concern, either directly or indirectly, the processes of making public policy in American states and communities. It is in this regard that the study of state and community politics has proven to be most interesting to a wide range of social scientific concerns. Increasingly, as we shall discuss in greater detail later, social scientists have asked why different organizations adopt the policies they do. Political scientists have come to realize that they can fruitfully spend their talents and time in trying to explain the outputs of governmental activity, that is, public policy. Certainly we can understand that attitude toward output of the United Nations or the United States presidency, but why should we be concerned with the fifty states and their several thousand local governments?

Why Study State and Community Policies?

Students of comparative policies start with the assumption that the American states and their communities provide ample bases of comparability for their collective study, although they have sufficient differences in politically relevant characteristics for comparative statements to be possible. Furthermore, they assume that "stateness" or status as a "community" matters sufficiently to warrant dividing up the parcels of the inquiry — the units of analysis — along state and local governmental lines.

Some people argue that state and local political systems are artificial categories for analysis. Unlike various other segments of the polity, they are not "natural," functional entities. They have not evolved out of the basic necessities of the mutual modification of human behavior in the same sense as have other social institutions. Religious institutions, economic structures, and even some other political entities such as primitive tribal councils can have a claim to spontaneity of origin that the subnational American political units may appear to lack. A cultural anthropologist from some extra-terrestrial, more highly developed society seeking to study patterns of culture on earth would not initially divide our collective lives along the lines of the American states or the typical suburb.

We believe, however, that such a visiting scholar would soon discover that there is sociological and political justification for analyzing the constitutional-political categories that exist in the

American governmental situation. Legal forms and political practices, regardless of their initial functional justification, do affect behavior and condition the processes by which political patterns evolve.[3] To be sure, there may have been no reason relevant to initial patterns of social intercourse for drawing the Idaho-Nevada boundary at the 42nd parallel. And it is unlikely that anyone unassisted by maps or legal descriptions would be able to answer the question "Why Oak Park?" There is no "natural" explanation for the boundaries of that suburb. The initial decisions as to what land should constitute which jurisdictions may have been arbitrary and even capricious, having been finally settled on the basis of temporarily relevant or ephemeral considerations of such influences as local politics or family interests. Much of the diversity that exists within the United States and that, for reasons of statistical convenience, is often described in reference to particular states or cities is actually regional in character and is due to factors largely outside the unique attributes or control of a particular local policy system.

We know, for example, that the difference in per capita income between the South and the North is not unique to particular states within each region. In 1963, per capita income ranged from $1,390 in Mississippi to $3,386 in Nevada. Population density ranged from 2.6 persons per mile in Nevada and 0.4 persons per mile in Alaska to 812 per square mile in Rhode Island. And 42.0 per cent of the people in Mississippi were black, compared to only 0.1 per cent in Vermont. These differences could be cited as evidence of the diversity of the states themselves. But we know that they are fairly typical of the regions in which these states are located. Such figures do not make a strong case for studying state politics, although they do point to the possibility of comparative analyses.

A more visual and less statistical examination of individual states goes even further to bear out the regional nature of many of the significant social dimensions of the American polity and the non-sociological nature of some political boundaries. Certainly an east-west drive across Kansas and Colorado does not reveal the state line. The rolling, sparsely populated cattle and wheat country rising from Topeka westward comes to an abrupt halt, not at the Colorado line, but at the foot of the Rocky

[3] This observation is made in a related way by Robert C. Wood with respect to suburban "identity." See his *Suburbia: Its People and Their Politics* (Boston: Houghton Mifflin Company, 1958), 253–255.

Mountains — midway through Colorado. The differences in interaction patterns, social mores, and political belief structures within past and present mining centers such as Cripple Creek, Leadville, and the other mountain communities of Colorado's Western Slope contrast sharply with the semi-arid, irrigated areas of the southern and eastern parts of the state. The differences in life style are strikingly revealed in manners of dress, modes of speaking, forms of political discourse, and a host of other conspicuous behavioral traits.

What is not so readily apparent to the occasional traveler or the casual scholar, however, is the diversity within regions that is due exclusively to the autonomous decision making power of the participants in state and local systems. Many of the differences in life styles of people in the United States are due to the manipulative powers existing in the states as semiautonomous, legal-political entities.

The impact upon individual life styles of state and local policy making cannot be ignored. Nor can one ignore the impact of their legal and political status upon behavior patterns that are of central relevance to understanding the functioning of the larger, national system. The states are significant arenas for much of the consequential political activity that takes place in this country. Although, in many significant ways, the inhabitants of Newark and New York City have more common problems than the people of Buffalo and the Bronx, the fact of separate statehood has major implications for the manner in which solutions to these problems are sought. Newarkites look to Trenton and New Yorkers look to Albany to deal with many of the difficulties that surpass the capabilities of each city. They each pay different taxes and enjoy preferential tuition rates at their own respective state assisted universities and colleges. The price of gasoline, cigarettes, and gin (if it is sold at all) differs across political boundaries because of state and local policies.

The accident of birth in one or another school district can make a tremendous difference in the quality of education a child receives. State residence affects the size of an unemployment check, and whether or not the mentally ill are incarcerated in a custodial institution or receive expert remedial treatment in a technically sophisticated community mental health center. Which state controls legal proceedings makes the difference of life or death in the event of conviction for certain severe crimes. And without reference to the policy making powers and actions of the several states what student of American politics could possibly explain the single most important dimension of current domestic conflict, the problem of accommodating large numbers of white and black people within a single society.[4]

In a host of interesting ways, geographically contiguous states have adopted policies that differ radically from one another and touch the very roots of social organization. It is difficult to believe that such differences in public policy do not have some distinctive impact upon the life style of each state's inhabitants. And if such is the case, then surely the policy making processes and activities of American states and communities are worthy of serious attention by students of politics.

The Social Relevance of State and Local Policies

If we listen to much political oratory or consume the rhetoric of many journalistic critics we may be led to believe that the American states and their local political systems have fallen on idle and evil days. Those on the Right (and some of the New Left) decry the demise of the community as an arena of self-government. To hear the complaints of many state political figures, the states have been denied their birthright. Such constitutional protections of state "sovereignty" as the Tenth Amendment are but tattered shreds of once glorious instruments of liberty. The federal government has so completely entered fields formerly reserved to the states that the latter have been left no significant functions. From the moderate Left come complaints that the continued potency of the states is blocking the arrival of the New Jerusalem. The role of the states is seen as one of obstruction, or inhibition, and of personal exploitation of public substance.

A brief glance at a few aspects of state and community responsibilities will dispel much of the detail in these common caricatures. In the process we shall justify our careful attention to the policy making activities of the states and their communities.

When that much maligned individual, the "typical American" was born, he entered a life intimately and extensively

[4] For example, see Daniel J. Elazar's discussion of the power of the states in the area of racial integration in the schools. "The States and the Nation," in Herbert Jacob and Kenneth N. Vines, eds., *Politics in the American States* (Boston: Little, Brown and Company, 1965), 452.

affected by state and local governmental actions, laws, and processes. His entry into the world was with the aid of a doctor licensed by the state, assisted by a nurse certified by the state, in a hospital inspected by the state. The milk in his bottle was inspected in accordance with state regulations and, in many cases, sold at a price closely controlled by state law. In the normal course of events, this typical American entered a public school, supported by state and local funds, staffed by teachers licensed by the state (and probably educated at a state university or college), and operated by a local school board in accordance with state regulations and under the direction of the state board of education.

If this fictitious, but very familiar, person becomes ill, the druggist who sells him medicine will hold a license from the state. Should his illness be psychosomatic and a manifestation of deep-seated psychic irregularities, needing the facilities of a mental hospital, the chances are high that the unfortunate fellow will enter a state owned or assisted facility.

Everything done by his town, county, city, township, school district, fire department, police force, zoning board, and cemetery authority is subject to the direct impact of state laws. The very existence of local governmental units and the actions taken by them are at the suffrance of states within which they happen to be located.[5]

The man who complains of the denials of "freedom" entailed by the federal social security program or the minimum wage laws should reflect for a moment about the tyranny wrought upon him by local government. He can be prevented from building a garage or installing a wall socket without permission from a local authority. He can be required by a similarly endowed governmental authority to remove a billboard or the family privy, regardless of their sentimental value or the "privateness" of his property.

In recent years, for a variety of reasons (most of which concern the Depression and international conflict), the bulk of public attention seems to have been given to innovations in federal programs. But the innovative role of the states has not yet been eliminated. One of the standard defenses of the federal system has been the usefulness of the states as laboratories for public

[5] For a discussion of the legal relationships between states and their local governments, see Charles R. Adrian, *State and Local Governments* (New York: McGraw-Hill Book Company, 2nd ed., 1967), 122 ff.

policies, although many of those who have complained most vociferously about the demise of states' rights have been the least prone to innovate at home.

While there are glaring examples of states refusing to meet some of the most pressing needs of their citizens, there are equally, if not more dramatic, cases where the states have provided models and valuable experience in new areas of public policy — to the ultimate greater benefit of their own citizens, their fellow states, and the federal government.

The entire structure of primary, secondary, and — outside the East — most higher education in this country has come about through direct state action. Numerous states had enacted civil rights laws long before the federal government got seriously into the act in recent years. Women had the right to vote in Wyoming at the time of statehood in 1890. Minimum wages were set, hours regulated, working conditions supervised by many states long before the Supreme Court decided it was legal for the federal government as well. Louisiana has had a program of widespread medical assistance for older citizens for over three decades. In 1965, Massachusetts moved well ahead of other states and the federal government in passing legislation designed to alleviate racial imbalance in the public schools. The two most significant functions of the states, at least in terms of dollars spent, have perennially been and still are highways and education. Federal involvement in both of these areas has been growing rapidly in recent years, to be sure. Yet the rate of federal expansion hardly challenges the pre-eminent position of the states and their local dependencies.

It is instructive to look at some figures on the state and local share of expenditures in certain major areas of public policy. In 1965, of over $34 billion spent on education, funds raised by state and local governments accounted for 86.89 per cent. The proportion for highways was 69.07 per cent; for health and hospitals, 60.81 per cent; for public welfare, 45.61 per cent. In all cases, these state and local figures exclude federal grants to the state and local governments.

While the trend varies from one policy area to another, the states and their local governments have, for all intents and purposes, paid most of the bill for the "welfare state" as we know it in the United States. Admittedly, there is a hefty federal nudge here and there in the process, but still, the overall rate of expansion of state and local spending compared to federal domestic expenditures has been substantially greater since World War II.

Total domestic expenditures (that is, excluding defense and international spending) increased from $29 billion in 1946 to $149 billion in 1964, or 412 per cent. The federal share increased from $16 billion to $74 billion, or 362 per cent. State and local spending increased, in the same period, by 473 per cent, from $13 billion to $75 billion.

When one considers further that a major portion of the federal domestic spending is channeled through the states and appropriated to specific functions by them (or refused by them), there is hardly an excuse for ringing the death knell on the heirs of the American colonies.

Part

1

THE STUDY OF STATE AND COMMUNITY POLITICS

In recent years the study of American states and communities has experienced changes similar to those of other fields in political science. Past studies featured case studies of single states or localities and the active promotion of reform proposals, but recent studies of states and communities have become increasingly concerned with the use — and development — of scientific techniques. There is an explicit concern for the quality of information collected and the nature of the inferences made from that information. More attention is now given to explanatory than to prescriptive theory. And to make explanatory theories more comprehensive, writers are comparing politics in different states and localities.

Although the case study remains a useful tool for examining particular situations in depth, or developing hypotheses that may be tested on a larger scale, comparative research now receives primary attention. Many recent studies of states and communities are genuinely more comparative than the case studies of foreign governments that appropriate the label of "comparative politics." Studies involving all fifty states or hundreds of localities are not uncommon. The concern is not simply with such questions as "How do politics differ from one situation to another?" More complicated questions are addressed, concerning the elements that are related to differences in politics between systems. Key questions include "What elements about a situation lead to one form of politics rather than another?" and "How do differences in politics influence other features of life in a jurisdiction?" These questions are central to a whole range of human concerns. They deal not only with political phenomena themselves, but with the implications of these phenomena for other features of the economy, life styles, services that individuals receive from their governments, and regulations that governments impose on their citizens.

Strictly speaking, it is inaccurate to say that current research identifies the *influence* that one element exercises over another, or the elements that *cause* certain political developments. The closest it comes to causation is the discovery of relationships that are consistent with likely causal patterns. If we hypothesize that element A brings about condition *B*, we can infer support for that hypothesis if we find element A and condition *B* typically associated together in the same time and place. Of course, we have to determine if the coexistence of A and *B* are not due to some common trait C that might cause both A and *B* to occur together. In other words, we must "control" the relationship between A and *B* to see if it might not simply be a product of C. A tangible example occurs when a political scientist hypothesizes that high levels of political participation produce generous levels of public service. If he finds that states or localities with high levels of participation also have generous levels of public service, the hypothesis has superficial support. The evidence increases in credibility if he determines that likely influences of both high participation and generous services are not actually responsible for the coexistence of participation and generous services. There are several appropriate ways to exercise controls. Most articles in this book employ some kind of control and lead an interested reader to an explanation of the statistical techniques that are used.

States and communities also provide an arena for basic scientific research that has likely application in other fields of politics. This is partly an off-shoot of the new concerns with comparative techniques and with descriptive rather than prescriptive theories. Writers are increasingly asking theoretical questions that are couched in universal terms. They analyze the influence of economic development upon the degree of competitiveness between parties, upon public participation in politics, and upon the generosity of public services. They also analyze the influence of political participation and competition upon the generosity of public services. Findings from domestic studies can be assessed alongside findings from other foreign political systems.

The current approach to state and local politics is not devoid of interest in the proper forms of government activity. Indeed, one of the prominent veins in this literature is its concern with the features of politics that have an important bearing upon the well-being of citizens. These features are called, variously, "policies," "outputs," "outcomes," or "impacts." Research has moved away from emotional—often intellectually sterile—advocacies of policy. The tools of social science can determine which government activities have important implications for citizens and what features of politics or the economy help to shape those activities. Policy-oriented studies of state and local politics promise to link academic political scientists with those persons, both officials and citizens, who formulate and implement public programs. Yet there are barriers to the easy communication between the scholar and the practitioner. Scholars are primarily concerned with understanding the processes by which policies are shaped and by which they influence the behavior of citizens, they seek answers at high levels of abstraction, and they tend to be concerned with what happens *most of the time,* under environmental conditions *most likely* to be encountered. Policy makers, in contrast, work in a particular environment and require specific recommendations for their discrete problems. Yet the scholar's concern with the general can inform their concern with the specific. By knowing the forces that operate under most conditions, policy makers are in a better position to know what is likely to occur in their jurisdiction. Of course, there are deviant cases, but one aim of the sophisticated political scientist is to understand deviant cases and the conditions most likely to provoke them.

The two selections in Part 1 agree in pointing to the virtues of comparison in the recent literature about state and local politics, its focus on policies, and its usefulness in generating ideas for the larger concerns of political science. The article by Herbert Jacob and Michael Lipsky is an intellectual *tour de force* that is highly detailed in its coverage of the recent literature and provocative in its discussion of prominent themes.

Jacob and Lipsky cite several findings that have destroyed, or at least shaken and modified, some shopworn beliefs of political scientists: (1) that the generosity of public services is likely to be increased by equitable apportionments in state legislatures; (2) that services are improved by the intensity of inter-party competition and by the level of public participation in politics; and (3) that services are affected by the majority or minority status of the Republican and Democratic parties. Now we realize that such factors by themselves are unable to affect materially the nature of policies. Some studies find it necessary to modify ancient beliefs by specifying which features of partisanship, participation, or apportionment are important for policies, and under what conditions those features seem to operate; other studies find these elements are subordinate in their influence to the level of "economic development" in a state or locality.

Jacob and Lipsky also find some problems in current literature and urge changes in research interests. They feel that the measurement of partisanship, competition, and participation must accommodate additional aspects of those processes; that measurements of policies should take into account more than simple aggregate levels of expenditures or a limited range of policy benefits in each jurisdiction; and that conceptions of environmental influences should be enriched to include more than aggregate measures for income, education, or industrialization. Further, they urge political scientists to seek better information about the processes by which environmental features (for example, the level of economic development) influence politics and public policies.

It is characteristic of the rapidly developing field of state and local politics that some recommendations of Jacob and Lipsky had been perceived and followed even before their own article was published. We see in later parts of this book how Jennings and Zeigler examine public perceptions of state and local governments; how Sharkansky offers regional location as an influence on politics; how Wilson and Banfield, Wolfinger and Field, and Lineberry and Fowler deal with the influence of a "private-" and a "public-regarding" ethos on policies; how Hofferbert's factor analysis of socioeconomic dimensions finds distinct patterns in the environmental traits that had been measured earlier with discrete variables; and how Walker offers a wholly new conception of policy that does not depend on aggregate levels of government expenditures or public services.

In the second article in Part 1, James Q. Wilson focuses on the "local" element of state and local politics but makes his points at a sufficient level of generality to be relevant for this entire field, and indeed for other arenas of political science. Wilson is concerned with those actions of government that affect citizens. The term he chooses is "outcomes." Wilson's special desire is to understand how the officials of cities, and by extension states and nations, might affect outcomes. He is not satisfied merely to know that certain economic conditions are found with certain kinds of outcomes; he wants to know what elements subject to governmental manipulation can influence outcomes. Only by knowing this can the well-informed policy maker have a predictable impact on his surroundings. By seeking this kind of information, the policy-oriented student of state and local politics can fashion his scientific product to have its greatest impact on policy itself.

Wilson also makes some important comments about widely used indicators of economics, politics, and public policy. Even the student with a tangential interest in this field should be aware of the problems involved in measuring its elements. As Wilson points out, some of the data hide as much as they reveal. Information from municipal budgets is rarely comparable from one city to another because of the different procedures used to categorize revenues and expenditures into one fund or another. Moreover, scholars often assume that total levels of expenditure measure the quantities or qualities of services being provided. Unless scholars make corrections for the support given local services by different governments — state, county, special district — and take account of many nonmonetary elements that also affect the nature of public services, they will provide useless and misleading results.

OUTPUTS, STRUCTURE, AND POWER:

An assessment of changes in the study of state and local politics

HERBERT JACOB
MICHAEL LIPSKY

State and local politics as a field of political science is no longer a "lost world" or the site of "Dullsville." [1] Rather than being the laggard of the discipline that some political scientists perceive it to be, the study of state and local politics has reentered the mainstream of political research. Much of the work in political science which has influenced the drift of the profession has been within its domain. V. O. Key's *Southern Politics* [2] quickly became a classic for the discipline. Robert A. Dahl's *Who Governs?* [3] as well as other community power structure studies have raised significant questions for other spheres of the discipline. *The Legislative System* [4] by John C. Wahlke *et al.* has remained the model for investigations of the roles of political actors; Thomas R. Dye's *Politics, Economics, and the Public* [5] is a landmark in the systematic analysis of public policy.

Although we can confidently say that the state and local politics field is no longer a lost world, we cannot be equally confident that it is a

From Herbert Jacob and Michael Lipsky, "Outputs, Structure, and Power: An Assessment of Changes in the Study of State and Local Politics," in Marian D. Irish, ed., *Political Science: Advance of the Discipline*,

This article also appeared in the *Journal of Politics*, 30 (May, 1968), 510–538.

We are grateful to James Davis, John Gardiner, and Kenneth Vines for comments on an earlier draft.

[1] Lawrence J. R. Herson, "The Lost World of Municipal Government," *American Political Science Review*, 51 (1957), 330–45; Coleman Ransone, "Revolt in Dullsville," *Public Administration Review*, 27 (1967).

[2] V. O. Key, Jr., *Southern Politics in State and Nation* (New York: Alfred A. Knopf, 1949).

[3] Robert A. Dahl, *Who Governs?* (New Haven: Yale University Press, 1961).

[4] John C. Wahlke, Heinz Eulau, William Buchanan, and LeRoy C. Ferguson, *The Legislative System* (New York: John Wiley & Sons, 1962).

[5] Thomas R. Dye, *Politics, Economics, and the Public* (Chicago: Rand McNally, 1966).

unique field of study. Political activity which occurs at these levels of government is not very different from that which occurs at the national level, in other nations, or on the international scene. Because the focus of study has shifted from particular institutions, defined in legalistic terms, recent research has universal implications. Consequently the large body of literature on political phenomena in state and urban political systems has important implications for the understanding of political behavior in general. Conversely, the field must be evaluated by the standards of the discipline rather than by the parochial concerns of a sub-field.

Our focus in the following pages will therefore be on the potential contributions of recent literature to the concerns of the discipline writ large. Further, we shall concentrate on questions which recent research has opened for investigation rather than engage in a laudatory review of settled issues. We shall be concerned with the gaps that remain unfilled and the potential for future research based on the substantial advances of the past quarter century.

We shall focus on problems in four areas: 1) potential for policy analysis; 2) political behavior in institutions where policy decisions are made; 3) utilization of the power structure model of urban politics; and 4) the need for development of pre-theoretical typologies. Our concentration on four areas critical for the advance of the discipline precludes analysis or mention of some studies which would be prominent if we had a different perspective. The recent literature includes studies of the philosophy of federalism, of voting behavior, of parties and elections systems, of particular issues such as urban renewal and of intergovernmental relations, most of which are peripheral to our concern in the following pages. They should be – and are – included in any thorough bibliography of the field.[6]

I Relationship of Policy Outputs to Social, Economic, and Political Variables

The most marked innovation in the study of state and local politics has been the investigation of the relationship of policy outputs to social, economic and political variables as undertaken by Richard E. Dawson

[6] See, e.g. James Herndon, Charles Press, and Oliver P. Williams, *A Selected Bibliography of Materials on State Government and Politics*, Bureau of Government Research, University of Kentucky, Lexington, Kentucky, 1963; Leo F. Schnore and Henry Fagin (eds.), *Urban Research and Policy Planning* (Beverly Hills, Calif.: Sage Publications, Inc., 1967), pp. 603–630; and bibliographical notes in John C. Bollens and Henry Schmandt, *The Metropolis* (New York: Harper and Row, 1965).

and James A. Robinson,[7] Thomas Dye,[8] Richard I. Hofferbert,[9] Lewis A. Froman,[10] and Ira Sharkansky [11] in the state field. Their work follows the earlier efforts of economists, notably Fisher,[12] and Sachs and Harris [13] who were concerned with the relationship of socio-economic variables to the level of governmental expenditure. Similar investigations have examined urban policy outputs.[14]

The investigations at the state level have produced a number of important, indeed startling, results. Three independent investigations, using slightly different analytic techniques, have concluded that legislative malapportionment has not been related to a distinctive pattern of

[7] Richard E. Dawson and James A. Robinson, "Interparty Competition, Economic Variables and Welfare Politics in the American States," *Journal of Politics*, 25 (1963), 265–289.

[8] Dye, note 5 above.

[9] Richard I. Hofferbert, "The Relation between Public Policy and Some Structural and Environmental Variables in the American States," *American Political Science Review*, 60 (1966), 73–82.

[10] Lewis A. Froman, Jr., "Some Effects of Interest Group Strength in State Politics," *American Political Science Review*, 60 (1966), 952–961.

[11] Ira Sharkansky, "Correlates of State Government Expenditures," paper prepared for delivery at the 1966 Annual Meeting of the American Political Science Association, September, 1966 (mimeo.).

[12] Glen W. Fisher, "Determinants of State and Local Government Expenditures: A Preliminary Analysis," *National Tax Journal*, 14 (1961), 349–355; "Interstate Variation in State and Local Government Expenditures," *ibid.*, 17 (1964), 57–64.

[13] Seymour Sachs and Robert Harris, "The Determinants of State and Local Government Expenditures and Intergovernmental Flow of Funds," *ibid.*, 17 (1964), 75–85.

[14] See especially, John H. Kessel, "Governmental Structure and Political Environment: A Statistical Note about American Cities," *American Political Science Review*, 56 (1962), 615–620; Leo F. Schnore and Robert R. Alford, "Forms of Government and Socio-economic Characteristics of Suburbs." *Administration Science Quarterly*, 8 (1963), 1–17; Robert R. Alford and Harry M. Scoble, "Political and Socio-economic Characteristics of Cities," *The Municipal Year Book*, 1965 (Chicago: The International City Managers' Association, 1965), 82–97; Raymond Wolfinger and John Osgood Field, "Political Ethos and the Structure of City Government," *American Political Science Review*, 60 (1966), 306–326; Thomas R. Dye, Charles S. Liebman, Oliver P. Williams, and Harold Herman, "Differentiation and Cooperation in a Metropolitan Area," *Midwest Journal of Political Science*, 7 (1963), 145–155; Lewis A. Froman, Jr., "An Analysis of Public Policies in Cities," *Journal of Politics*, 29 (1967), 94–108; Amos H. Hawley, "Community Power and Urban Renewal Success," *American Journal of Sociology*, 68 (1963), 422–431; Oliver P. Williams, Harold Herman, Charles S. Liebman, and Thomas R. Dye, *Suburban Differences and Metropolitan Policies: A Philadelphia Story* (Philadelphia: University of Pennsylvania Press, 1965).

outputs.[15] Policies which might be heavily favored by the under-represented urban majority are no more in evidence in well apportioned than in poorly apportioned states. The substantial differences in the level of outputs are accounted for by a variety of other variables, not by legislative malapportionment.

Secondly, at least three independent investigations reject the hypothesis that party competition is related to the level of governmental activity.[16] More competitive states are not more liberal in welfare or education expenditures when one holds wealth, industrialization, education, and urbanization constant. In addition, Dye has shown that it makes little difference whether a state is dominated by Republicans or Democrats or whether there is a high or low level of electoral participation.[17] Variations in state policy outputs are principally related to socio-economic variables according to these studies.

These investigations also represent a substantial advance in methodological sophistication. Using simple and multiple correlation techniques, they permit assessment of the relative importance of a large number of variables in accounting for variance in the level of outputs. These techniques also allow truly comparative analysis since there is no technical barrier to the consideration of data from 25, or 50 states or several hundred urban communities. In the near future we shall no doubt see further methodological advances with the use of causal modeling, factor analysis, and time series analysis.

Yet despite the methodological sophistication of these studies, we are troubled by some conceptual simplifications. Each investigator appends a theoretical framework to his study, usually a version of systems theory. The theory, however, rarely guides the research. This is because of the way in which key concepts are operationalized and the manner in which linkages between inputs, the conversion processes, and outputs are conceptualized.

These problems can be illustrated by Dye's work, the most extensive output analysis yet published. Dye outlines a model in which inputs are operationalized as socio-economic variables, the political system is operationalized in terms of the party system, legislative malapportionment, and electoral participation, and outputs are operationalized by levels of ex-

[15] Herbert Jacob, "The Consequences of Malapportionment: A Note of Caution," *Social Forces,* 43 (1964), 256–261; Thomas R. Dye, "Malapportionment and Public Policy in the States," *Journal of Politics,* 27 (1965), 586–601; Hofferbert, note 9 above.

[16] Dawson and Robinson, note 7; Hofferbert, note 9; Dye, *Politics, Economics, and the Public,* note 5.

[17] Dye, *Politics, Economics, and the Public,* note 5.

penditures for a wide variety of programs, impact measures, and measures of the program quality. He then posits linkages which connect inputs to the political variables and then to outputs, and alternatively, inputs to outputs while by-passing the political process.

The first problem with this operationalized model is that income, urbanization, industrialization, and education are not in themselves inputs. The measures have little substantive relationship to the phenomena they are supposed to represent. We might conceive of them as environmental factors which may lead to the articulation of demands and support and their communication to political authorities. Demands are verbalizations or behavioral articulations of satisfaction or dissatisfaction with the status quo.[18] The relationship between demand-behavior and environment may in some circumstances be high but it is certainly neither 1:1 nor constant. We know that in apparently dissimilar environments, political controversy centers around the same issues. Corruption is a controversial and central issue in both Massachusetts and Louisiana.[19] In both Montana and Wisconsin air pollution control was an issue in the 1967 legislatures.[20] Social structure, political culture, political institutions, and elite perceptions intervene between a given environment (as measured by Dye) and the articulation of demands.

Further the operationalization of the political system is generally primitive. In Dye's work, party competition, electoral participation, and legislative apportionment are used; they do not represent the whole of the political system nor perhaps even its most significant elements. In Dye's defense, it must be pointed out that much of his work was intended to test specific hypotheses derived from earlier investigations by Key,[21] and Lockard,[22] on the role of party competition and electoral participation. Dye himself admits that these measures are incomplete representations of the political system.[23] What we need then are synoptic measures of political systems or their most significant elements. Such measures will have to include, as a minimum, consideration of the organization of the

18 David Easton, *A Systems Analysis of Political Life* (New York: John Wiley & Sons, 1965), pp. 38 ff.

19 For Massachusetts, see Edgar Litt, *The Political Cultures of Massachusetts* (Cambridge: MIT Press, 1965); Murray B. Levin, *The Alienated Voter* (New York: Holt, Rinehart, 1960); Duane Lockhard, *New England State Politics* (Princeton: Princeton University Press, 1959), pp. 119–176; for Louisiana, see Alan P. Sindler, *Huey Long's Louisiana* (Baltimore: Johns Hopkins Press, 1956).

20 Douglas C. Chaffey, *Legislative Party Leadership: A Comparative Analysis,* unpublished Ph.D. dissertation, University of Wisconsin, 1967.

21 Key, note 2 above, pp. 298–310.

22 Lockard, note 19 above.

23 Dye, *Politics, Economics, and the Public,* note 5 above, pp. 296–297.

executive branch, the organization of the legislature, the strength of interest groups,[24] the linkages between state systems and their federal and local counterparts. Perhaps the characteristics of party systems should also be considered although their influence is doubtful on the strength of the evidence accumulated thus far.

Considerable further work also needs to be done in conceptualizing the dimensions of policy. Most of the analyses we have cited use measures of several dimensions indiscriminately without showing an awareness that more than one dimension is involved. Most frequently used are measures of the level of expenditure, program quality, and program impact.[25] In addition, we can identify at least one other dimension: the distribution of benefits among a population. The distribution of benefits or sanctions is perhaps the most significant output dimension for political scientists, since much of the conflict preceding adoption of a program is not about whether it should be embarked upon but who will pay and who will benefit. Even programs that apparently benefit most of the population – such as education and highway construction – have a variable incidence of benefits. Thus to understand the politics of education at the state level one must understand how grants-in-aid are distributed to school districts. To comprehend the bitter in-fighting about education in an urban community one needs measures of the inequalities in the distribution of schools, teachers, and teaching aids throughout a city. Measures of distribution unfortunately are rarely available in public records (an interesting political fact in itself). But the lack of data cannot deter political scientists from investigating what may be the most important dimension of policy outputs. Just as it became necessary to spend much money to generate data about voting behavior, it is necessary to allocate resources to collect data about the distribution of program benefits.

Once more adequate measures of the dimensions of outputs have been collected, it will be possible to analyze separately the linkages between these several dimensions and the input and conversion-process variables. It is likely that these linkages will be different for each dimension. For instance, it seems probable that quite different conditions will be associated with the level of expenditure and with the impact of a program. As administrators sadly know, high expenditures may have little impact. The level of expenditures may be closely associated with demands

[24] An early attempt to provide such a measure of interest group strength is in Belle Zeller (ed.), *American State Legislatures* (New York: Thomas Y. Crowell, 1954), pp. 190–191.

[25] The level of expenditure is the most frequently used dimension. Examples of quality measures include teacher/pupil ratios, doctor/patient ratios, and per pupil expenditures. Impact measures include school drop-out rates, literacy rates, and crime rates.

while the impact of a program may be more closely related to structural characteristics of political institutions.

The manner in which Dye infers linkages also raises serious problems and challenges for the future. Dye's method is to account for the variance rather than to use regression coefficients to indicate how much a change in one variable is associated with a change in another variable. Thus for the most part Dye is unable to make causal inferences although he and others often imply causality. He shows convincingly, confirming the findings of others, that socio-economic and political variables are highly correlated. However, because they are highly correlated, by holding one constant, the variance of the other is reduced.[26] Thus he is not able to infer quite as exactly as he claims that one set of variables is more important than another.

Dye also leaves unexplored the nature of the linkages that he asserts exist between economic development and programmatic outs. We conclude from reading his analysis that by some magic a high level of economic development becomes transformed into high levels of expenditure. The processes by which this transformation takes place remain in the shadows although it has been the traditional task of political scientists to illuminate them.

Policy studies which grew out of an entirely different conceptual framework – the process-oriented studies such as *State Politics and the Public Schools*,[27] *Schoolmen and Politics*,[28] and *The Politics of State Expenditures in Illinois* [29] – illuminate some of the linkages which are missing in the statistical studies. Each of these books deals with the immediate as well as distant antecedents of the policy under analysis. Thus, Masters, Salisbury, and Eliot are concerned with interest group structure and activity, the activity of institutions such as the State Department of Education and the legislature, and with the partisan complexion immediately prior to the adoption of a policy decision. The significance of intervening institutions is illustrated by Anton's finding that the rate of growth of governmental expenditure in Illinois is positively related to the budget-cutting norms of the Illinois Budgetary Commission.[30] The rate of growth of educational expenditures in Illinois has

[26] We are indebted to Charles Cnudde and Donald McCrone for making this point to us. In a forthcoming article, they illustrate the use of regression coefficients with Dye's data.

[27] Nicholas A. Masters, Robert H. Salisbury, and Thomas H. Eliot, *State Politics and the Public Schools* (New York: Alfred A. Knopf, 1964).

[28] Stephen K. Bailey, Richard T. Frost, Paul E. Marsh, and Robert C. Wood, *Schoolmen and Politics* (Syracuse: Syracuse University Press, 1962).

[29] Thomas J. Anton, *The Politics of State Expenditures in Illinois* (Urbana: University of Illinois Press, 1966).

[30] *Ibid.*

been related to the norms and functions of the School Problems Commission;[31] where such an articulating agency is absent (as it was in Michigan), the rate of growth will be slower even in the presence of greater environmental resources.[32] What is needed are studies in which the two traditions of analysis reinforce each other. The results of the statistical investigations may provide criteria for the selection of cases for intensive analysis and sensitize case studies to variations in the dimensions of policy outputs. The case analyses may suggest new measures of input, process, and output for further comparative statistical analysis.

Case studies also suggest another conceptual difficulty with the statistical analyses. Researchers generally posit a single political system which operates in the same fashion in the educational, welfare, transportation, recreation, public health, and regulatory areas. As Dahl showed in New Haven[33] and other policy studies imply, policy arenas have quite separate sets of decision makers associated with them. It is probably erroneous to expect that input and process variables are associated in the same way to each policy output. What we need are maps of the subsystems which are responsible for output decisions in various subject areas. The state-wide political system that many have sought to describe may in fact not exist.[34] What we perceive as the ongoing political process may be a series of relatively autonomous processes occasionally linked on the floor of the legislature, in the chief executive's office, and by the fact that political events tend to be concentrated in the capitol and city hall.

Another aspect of the problem of linking the environment, the political process, and outputs is illuminated by Froman's article, "Some Effects of Interest Group Strength in State Politics."[35] Froman related interest group strength in the early 1950's to the characteristics of state constitutions which were written between 1789 and 1965. He finds some slight relationships. The presence of these relationships, however, should

[31] Masters, *et al.*, note 27 above.

[32] *Ibid.*

[33] Dahl, *Who Governs?*, note 3 above.

[34] It is interesting to note that most of the state-wide studies published in the last 20 years are in fact limited to one or two segments of the political system; none deal systematically with outputs. See, for instance, Leon D. Epstein, *Politics in Wisconsin* (Madison: University of Wisconsin Press, 1958) [elections]; Lockard, *New England State Politics*, note 19 above [elections and legislative politics]; Key, *Southern Politics*, note 2 above [elections]; Sindler, *Huey Long's Louisiana*, note 19 above [elections]; William C. Havard and Loren P. Beth, *The Politics of Misrepresentation* (Baton Rouge: Louisiana State University Press, 1962) [legislative apportionment]; John Fenton, *Politics in the Border States* (New Orleans: The Hauser Press, 1957) [elections].

[35] Note 10 above. Cf. recent "Communication" from Thomas L. Thorson, *American Political Science Review*, 61 (1967), 478–479.

not deter us from asking what theoretical justification there is for relating a phenomenon occurring in the mid-twentieth century with outputs spanning nearly two centuries. Sharkansky provides us strong reasons for rejecting this approach. He traces the growth of governmental expenditures and enters into his regression equations the previous level of expenditures. He finds that the level of expenditures in 1962 is closely related to that of 1957 and that of 1957 is closely related to that of 1952.[36] He thus provides supporting evidence for the hypothesis that governmental policy making is incremental in nature; sharply innovative decisions are rarely made. If Sharkansky is correct, then we might expect the same pattern of decision-making to characterize state constitution-making and present day constitutions would be more closely related to input and conversion characteristics of earlier eras than they would be to contemporary phenomena. Sharkansky's investigations initiate the study of the change dimension of political outputs, a subject rarely examined by political scientists.[37]

These problems with output analyses reflect more on the state of the discipline than on the particular investigators. Concerned with a narrow range of problems and utilizing measures at hand, this group of scholars has made a considerable contribution. In part that contribution consists of specific findings which undermine hypotheses long a part of the folklore of political science. But the greater part of their contribution lies in illuminating research gaps which stand in the way of testing more theoretically sophisticated models of the relationship between outputs on the one hand and inputs and the conversion processes on the other.

II Synoptic Indicators of the Political Process

One of the gaps highlighted by policy studies is the lack of synoptic indicators of conversion processes. Concern for these processes characterizes much of the work in state and local politics, but decision-making in institutions has usually been studied as a political process complete in itself. The research is rarely directed to the task of isolating those characteristics of a decision-making process which are essential to understanding the institution's ingestion of inputs or its production of outputs. Thus we have not advanced as far as we might wish in either the task of creat-

[36] Sharkansky, note 11 above.

[37] For a different kind of longitudinal analysis, see H. D. Price, *The Negro and Southern Politics* (New York: New York University Press, 1957), pp. 41–44, who relates Negro registration in 1950 with the percentage non-white in 1900. This is reiterated by Donald R. Matthews and James W. Prothro, *Negroes and the New Southern Politics* (New York: Harcourt, Brace, and World, 1966), pp. 115–120.

ing synoptic measures nor in understanding the relation of behavior in the institutional framework to the larger political world.

These problems can be easily illustrated with the research on legislatures. Scholarly interest in institutions since World War II has been overwhelmingly directed at state legislatures. These studies have several foci. The most widely noted has been the examination of the role perceptions of legislatures in four states, *The Legislative System*.[38] It explicitly adopted role theory as the framework for its research design. Its authors examined the backgrounds of legislators, the formal characteristics of their legislative assemblies, and the significance of the party systems in terms of how legislators perceived their roles. Somewhat akin to this study is James Barber's *The Lawmakers* [39] which more loosely uses the framework of role theory but also studies the activities of Connecticut legislators.

The Legislative System and *The Lawmakers* are both landmarks of political investigation. The former is explicitly theoretical in conception and comparative in its analysis. The latter probes more deeply into the relationship between self-perception and overt behavior. Both studies are careful in operationalizing their key concepts through questionnaire items which permit replication. Both represent the first important studies in political science relying heavily upon role theory.

Yet both leave us considerably short of our objective of understanding legislative behavior. *The Legislative System* is a bit like a hall of mirrors. It permits legislators to observe themselves and see how others perceive them, but it does not tell us how these perceptions affect overt behavior. Its authors fail to link the roles which they identify with behavioral patterns. Barber links his role categories more closely with behavioral patterns and attempts to build a theoretical framework which helps explain why certain legislators choose particular role and activity patterns. However, he fails to take into account the role categories of *The Legislative System*; consequently, his work does not permit that cumulation of observation which would encourage broader generalization.

Other investigations focus entirely on behavior. The one form of behavior that has won most attention has been roll call voting.[40] Research

[38] John C. Wahlke, *et al.*, *The Legislative System*, note 4 above.

[39] James David Barber, *The Lawmakers* (New Haven: Yale University Press, 1965).

[40] Among others, see Duncan MacRae, "The Relationship Between Roll Call Votes and Constituencies in Massachusetts," *American Political Science Review*, 46 (1952), 1046–1055; ————, "Some Underlying Variables in Legislative Roll Call Votes," *Public Opinion Quarterly*, 18 (1954), 191–196; ————, "Roll Call Votes and Leadership," *Public Opinion Quarterly*, 20 (1956), 543–558; R. W. Belker, F. L. Foote, M. Lubega, and S. V. Monsma, "Correlates of Legislative Voting: the Michigan House of

in this tradition has come to a number of findings. In many legislatures most issues are decided without substantial divisions on roll call votes. In many legislatures significant divisions occur at stages other than the final roll call vote; in a substantial number of states, legislative rules are designed to obscure partisan and group differences and to transfer them from the floor of the legislature to committee meetings, committees of the whole, and party caucuses. Constituency characteristics are probably significantly related to deviant voting behavior on roll call votes. Where divisions occur in competitive states, they are usually along party lines and mark the most vital issues rather than routine ones.

What the roll call studies preeminently possess is methodological sophistication, ranging from relatively simple indices of block voting to factor analysis and scalogram analysis of voting behavior. What they almost uniformly lack is a theoretical framework which would place their findings more comfortably into the perspective of other political investigations. Thus roll call studies rarely examine a broad range of outside influences on the voting behavior of legislators [41] and they seldom have been comparative so that the impact of varying institutional arrangements could be assessed.[42]

A third but small set of investigations consists of case studies of legislative decision-making as exemplified by Gilbert Y. Steiner and Samuel K. Gove's *Legislative Politics in Illinois* [43] and Edward C. Banfield's *Political Influence*.[44] Such studies are broader in scope than role

---

Representatives," *Midwest Journal of Political Science*, 6 (1962), pp. 384–396; Malcolm E. Jewell, "Party Voting in American State Legislatures," *American Political Science Review*, 49 (1955), 773–791; W. W. Crane, "A Caveat on Roll Call Studies of Party Voting," *Midwest Journal of Political Science*, 4 (1960), 237–249; and John G. Grumm, "The Systematic Analysis of Blocs in the Study of Legislative Behavior," *Western Political Quarterly*, 18 (1965), 350–362. See also the comprehensive review of this literature in Malcolm E. Jewell and Samuel C. Patterson, *The Legislative Process in the United States* (New York: Random House, 1966), pp. 414–452.

[41] Notable exceptions are MacRae, "The Relationship Between Roll Call Votes and Constituencies," note 40 above, and John G. Grumm, "A Factor Analysis of Legislative Voting," *Midwest Journal of Political Science*, 7 (1963), 336–356. For an excellent example of the focus on this relationship, see Oliver Garceau and Corinne Silverman, "A Pressure Group and the Pressured: A Case Report," *American Political Science Review*, 48 (1954), 672–691.

[42] But see Malcolm E. Jewell, *The State Legislature* (New York: Random House, 1962), pp. 48–76.

[43] Gilbert Y. Steiner and Samuel K. Gove, *Legislative Politics in Illinois* (Urbana: University of Illinois Press, 1960).

[44] Edward C. Banfield, *Political Influence* (New York: The Free Press of Glencoe, 1961).

analyses or roll call studies, but what they gain in scope they lose through theoretical diffuseness and generality. Steiner and Gove, for instance, keep their theoretical framework entirely implicit. Banfield's framework is likewise the examination of influence, although he is more concerned with how various actors exert their influence than with the decision-making process itself. These studies carefully examine the influence of parties, interest groups, and constituencies, and distinguish between one issue area and another in the manner in which the legislative process operates. They are rich in detail and provide us with the flavor of legislative battles. But they are difficult to generalize upon because they fail to operationalize their key concepts. As Dahl and others have made clear, influence and power are elusive concepts; studies which confront influence directly run the risk of stumbling on its operationalization.

The emphasis on legislative behavior and activity reflects the accessibility of legislators and the adaptability of research methods to their arena. Where decision-making is more obscured and where roll call voting and survey research are less applicable, far less work has been done. Consequently, although the mid-twentieth century is par excellence the age of the executive, few researchers have ventured into the cubicles of bureaucrats. Equally few have searched the halls of justice.

The principal study of the states' chief executive is *The Office of Governor in the United States* by Coleman Ransone.[45] Ransone comprehensively describes the politics of gubernatorial selection and the manner in which the chief executives of the states perform their duties. He notes great variations in the selection of governors, their functions, their staffs, and their formal and informal powers over the bureaucracy, but he does not attempt systematically to account for these differences. Although the gubernatorial office is much smaller than the presidential, Ransone stumbles on the same barriers as have scholars of the presidency – neither have developed reliable indicators of influence nor have they been able to isolate the chief executive's role in interactions with bureaucrats which lead to decision-making and policy initiation. Joseph A. Schlesinger's attempt to rank order the formal power of governors is the first at developing the kind of synoptic measures which are needed for comparative research.[46] But as Schlesinger himself recognizes, it is a weak measure because it concerns only formal powers for a position in which many informal functions are very important. Moreover, it is an ordinal scale which yields estimates of power vis-a-vis other governors but not relative to other institutions in the same state or in other political systems.

[45] University, Alabama: University of Alabama Press, 1956.

[46] Joseph A. Schlesinger, "The Politics of the Executive," in Herbert Jacob and Kenneth N. Vines (eds.), *Politics in the American States* (Boston: Little, Brown & Co., 1965), pp. 207–237.

There have been very few studies of the state bureaucracy other than case studies of isolated incidents and investigations of the social backgrounds of key personnel in state agencies.[47] Even though it is generally recognized that most key decisions are initiated or made within executive agencies, the conditions under which they operate, those which are associated with one kind of organizational structure rather than another, and the relationship between executive branch characteristics and legislative and judicial characteristics remain unmapped and challenges for future students of state politics.

The judiciary has been somewhat more frequently studied, but judicial research suffers often from the same insularity as legislative and executive studies. Recruitment patterns and appellate voting behavior have been the principal foci of investigation. The recruitment studies have achieved a preliminary understanding of the results of various judicial selection systems but they have not shown how these recruitment patterns are related to other political behavior – the party system, non-judicial elections, or court decisions.[48] Research on appellate voting behavior [49] has shown that most state appellate court decisions are unanimous, partially as the result of decision-making rules which lead to specialization among judges and limited participation by most judges in decisions before their appellate courts. Stuart Nagel asserts that the party identification of judges distinguishes their voting patterns, but his conclusions are based on extremely limited data for a few states.[50] Sidney Ulmer and Glendon Schubert make a more convincing case for the influential role of party identification among Michigan Supreme Court

[47] Deil S. Wright and Richard L. McAnaw, "American State Executives: Their Backgrounds and Careers," *State Government*, 38 (1965), 146–153; Deil S. Wright, "Executive Leadership in State Administration," *Midwest Journal of Political Science*, 11 (1967), 1–26. See also the case studies published by the Inter-University Case Program.

[48] Herbert Jacob, "The Effect of Institutional Differences in the Recruitment Process: The Case of State Judges," *Journal of Public Law*, 13 (1964), 104–119; see also the forthcoming study of the Missouri selection plan: Richard A. Watson, Randal G. Downing, and Frederick C. Spiegel, *The Politics of the Bench and the Bar*.

[49] Daryl R. Fair, "An Experimental Application of Scalogram Analysis to State Supreme Court Decisions," *Wisconsin Law Review* (1967), 449–467; Edward Ferguson, III, "Some Comments on the Applicability of Bloc Analysis to State Appellate Courts," paper delivered at the Midwest Conference of Political Scientists, 1961, mimeo. One of the few attempts to relate decisions by appellate courts to political behavior elsewhere is in Kenneth N. Vines, "Southern State Supreme Courts and Race Relations," *Western Political Quarterly*, 18 (1965), 5–18.

[50] Stuart Nagel, "Political Party Affiliation and Judges' Decisions," *American Political Science Review*, 55 (1961), 843–851. At the most, he relies on decisions from 13 states; in seven instances he relies on observations from less than five states.

judges.[51] Studies of state trial courts by political scientists are still more scarce.[52] Much interesting work on trial courts, however, has been done by legal scholars and sociologists who have examined the administration of bail,[53] the availability of defense counsel,[54] variability in sentencing,[55] and similar problems of immediate practical importance. But such scholars have not sought to associate these phenomena with other aspects of the political system.

As even this brief review makes clear, the discipline is a long way from providing the statistically-minded comparative analysts the kind of synoptic measures of the political process which they need to optimize the explanatory power of their regression equations. Nor should we define our task as simply providing such measures. Once we recognize the need for such measures, we can be certain that some energies will be devoted to providing them. In the meantime, a great deal of work remains to be done in understanding the legislative, executive, and judicial decision-making processes as they relate to extra-institutional political behavior. Analysis of roles needs to be joined to the analysis of overt behavior. Roll call analyses need to be joined to a more intensive contextual analysis. Much preliminary work remains to be done on the decision-making processes within the executive and judicial branches.

III Community Power Studies

The local community potentially provides political scientists with a natural laboratory in which to examine the dynamics of political and economic resource allocation. This potential has been realized by community power studies which have left open the question of the exercise of influence by focusing attention away from public officials. These studies have

[51] S. Sidney Ulmer, "The Political Party Variable on the Michigan Supreme Court," *Journal of Public Law*, 11 (1962), 352–362; Glendon Schubert, *Quantitative Analysis of Judicial Behavior* (Glencoe, Ill.: The Free Press, 1959), pp. 129–142.

[52] Herbert Jacob, "Politics and Criminal Prosecution in New Orleans," in Kenneth N. Vines and Herbert Jacob, *Studies in Judicial Politics*, Tulane Studies in Political Science, 8 (1962), pp. 77–98, and the study by Kenneth Dolbeare, *Trial Courts in Urban Politics: State Court Policy Impact and Function in a Local Political System* (New York: John Wiley and Sons, 1967).

[53] Charles Ares, Anne Rankin, and Herbert Sturz, "Administration of Bail in New York," *New York University Law Review*, 38 (1963), 67–95.

[54] The most comprehensive study is Lee Silverstein, *Defense of the Poor* (Chicago: American Bar Foundation, 1965).

[55] Edward Green, *Judicial Attitudes in Sentencing* (London: Macmillan, 1961). For a study by political scientists, see Albert Somit, Joseph Tanenhaus, and Walter Wilkie, "Aspects of Judicial Sentencing Behavior," *University of Pittsburgh Law Review*, 21 (1959), 613–620.

shifted research in local politics from prescription of formal-legal arrangements to description of political constellations. They have supplemented other research efforts in American politics by highlighting the importance of the underlying value structure in determining the character of the political system.

Extraordinary energy has been invested in attempting to answer the four questions posed by Harold Lasswell. Debate concerning characterization of American communities as "elitist" or "pluralist" has occupied the attention of many scholars.[56] Yet there remains an unfortunate aridity to the discussion of community politics. This is attributable to at least three factors which will be elaborated here: a confusion of methodology with ideology; limitations of focus; and failures in the utilization of comparative techniques.

The debate between those investigators who discover various shadings of elite and pluralist configurations in American cities, which has encouraged the development of technical and theoretical advances, in some ways has proved unproductive. There has been confusion as to whether the designations "elitist" and "pluralist" refer to methodological approaches, empirical observations, or ideological postures. This confusion is manifested by lumping together investigators with dissimilar techniques and findings, and linking conclusions about influence distribution with a fixed ideological stance. For example, in an otherwise insightful critique of the literature on community power, Agger and his associates give an ideological caste to a variety of empirical research efforts by using phrases such as "Pluralists take the position . . . ," "As one pluralist puts it. . . ."[57] This usage obscures the debate over areas of disagreement and places it in an arena where tentative conclusions are assumed to be fixed,

[56] The literature on community studies is vast. Bibliographical aids to this literature include Charles Press, *Main Street Politics: Policy-Making at the Local Level* (East Lansing: Michigan State University Institute for Community Development and Services, 1962), and Wendell Bell, *et al.*, *Public Leadership* (San Francisco: Chandler Publishing Co., 1961). The elements of the pluralist-elitist controversy are reviewed in Nelson Polsby, *Community Power and Political Theory* (New Haven: Yale University Press, 1963); Robert Presthus, *Men at the Top* (New York: Oxford University Press, 1964), chs. 1–2; Peter Bachrach, *The Theory of Democratic Elitism* (Boston: Little, Brown & Company, 1967); and Wallace Sayre and Nelson Polsby, "American Political Science and Urbanization," *The Study of Urbanization*, Philip Hauser and Leo Schnore (eds.) (New York: John Wiley and Sons, 1965), pp. 115–156. See also Norton Long, "Political Science and the City," *Urban Research and Policy Planning*, Leo Schnore and Henry Fagin (eds.) (Beverly Hills, Calif.: Sage Publications, Inc., 1967), pp. 242–262.

[57] Robert E. Agger, Daniel Goldrich, and Bert E. Swanson, *The Rulers and the Ruled* (New York: John Wiley and Sons, 1964), pp. 76, 91.

where disparate findings are discussed as if they were uniform, and where it seems that men conduct research in order to validate their own ideological stance.

Research may well reflect ideology to the extent that designs are informed by the kinds of questions in which investigators are interested. Indeed, even where alternative empirical formulations are not forthcoming, research has been subject to criticism because of the attributed ideological content of the work.[58] But the debate on community power has tended to ignore the precept of Dahl and others that operational concepts and observable data should characterize future research on community power.

A second difficulty with the studies of community politics has been their almost exclusive focus on elite activity and orientations. Certainly it is obvious that power is distributed unequally in American society, but the task of determining the extent and impact of that inequality (to paraphrase Nelson Polsby) cannot be undertaken by elite studies alone. The literature on community power in political science, whether employing a framework emphasizing decision-making, reputation for influence, or various combinations for assembling panels of potential influentials, has neglected consideration of the influence of other strata on local politics. For example, Dahl experiences considerable difficulty in explaining the linkages between the political behavior of masses and that of influential elites. Sporadic political pressures articulated outside the pattern in which governmental affairs are normally conducted receive little mention in *Who Governs?* or other prominent studies of city politics.[59]

Oliver Williams and Charles Adrian, who distinguished among city political systems by their orientations toward providing governmental services, also neglect the consideration that a city's service may be a func-

[58] For a recent discussion of these matters see Jack Walker, "A Critique of the Elitist Theory of Democracy," *American Political Science Review*, 60 (1966), 285–295, and a reply by Robert Dahl, "Further Reflections on 'The Elitist Theory of Democracy,'" *American Political Science Review*, 60 (1966), 296–305.

[59] See Dahl's discussion of "the case of the metal houses," *Who Governs?*, note 3 above, pp. 192–199, 302. See, e.g., the two studies of Chicago politics: Martin Meyerson and Edward Banfield, *Politics, Planning and the Public Interest* (Glencoe, Ill.: Free Press, 1955); and Banfield, note 44 above. Sayre and Kaufman, in their study of New York City politics, ascribe no role to ad hoc pressure groups. The ephemeral role of protest organizations in New York City politics is reiterated in the introduction to the paperback edition. Wallace Sayre and Herbert Kaufman, *Governing New York City* (New York: Norton and Co., 1965). See p. xlii. Compare the influence attributed to ad hoc neighborhood groups in J. Clarence Davies, *Neighborhood Groups and Urban Renewal* (New York: Columbia University Press, 1966).

tion of its level of demand.[60] A city may provide a relatively high level of services for reasons of civic ethos, protest activity, organized welfare-oriented interest groups, or high income levels. Where the relationship between "demand" and governmental services has been noted, as measured by percentage poor and welfare expenditures per capita, research has not followed to ascertain the reasons for this confluence.[61]

The changes in city politics resulting from the Negro protest movements of the early '60's cannot be accommodated by the community power structure models of urban politics. The failure to trace out the impact of various decisions as they "feed back" to affect the political system has left political scientists with very little to say about Negro political activity in the last half of the decade. The conditions under which quiescence and arousal of relatively deprived groups occur – to use Murray Edelman's terms – and the impact of governmental and elite behavior on these conditions, has emerged as a high priority research focus for the discipline. This is a priority poorly served by previous studies of community politics.

The failure to study non-elite behavior in the literature on community power has not been remedied by research concentrating on urban Negro politics. For the most part, these studies of Negro politics have exhibited the same shortcomings as characterize the literature on city politics. They have focused on elite behavior with little reference to the effectiveness of differential leadership patterns, or they have concentrated on case descriptions without the theoretical insights which would help explain a profusion of observations.[62]

In *Negro Politics*, for example, James Q. Wilson analyzes the relationship of Negro politicians to white politicians in considerable detail but omits consideration of the impact of these relationships on the Negro community.[63] Similarly, leadership studies which promulgate dichotomous

[60] Oliver Williams and Charles Adrian, *Four Cities* (Philadelphia: University of Pennsylvania Press, 1963). The converse, of course, may also obtain. Protest activity may receive encouragement from civic organizations because they provide high service levels. It is precisely the nature of this ambiguity in charting input-feedback flows that requires extensive research.

[61] See Robert Wood, *1400 Governments* (Garden City, N.Y.: Doubleday and Co., 1964), p. 64. Problems with interpretations of "demand" have been previously discussed, Section I.

[62] These remarks on the literature on Negro politics are elaborated in Michael Lipsky, *Rent Strikes in New York City: Protest Politics and the Power of the Poor*, Unpublished Ph.D. dissertation, Princeton University, 1967, pp. 7–16.

[63] See James Q. Wilson, *Negro Politics* (New York: The Free Press, 1960). This study remains surprisingly pertinent in many of its insights, although it was written in the pre-sit-in era.

typologies of Negro leadership in distinguishing between "militants" and "moderates" fail to analyze the impact of differential leadership styles on obtaining rewards.[64]

Like the research on community power, studies of Negro leadership would benefit from consideration of the systems in which political activity takes place. Greater understanding of the context of Negro politics might help account for some of the contradictions in the literature. For example, it might help explain findings that conflict among Negro leaders is functional in some cases, and apparently dysfunctional in others.[65] It might also assist in synthesizing contradictory findings that militant Negro leaders seek "status" goals in Chicago, but "welfare" goals in Atlanta.[66] One hypothesis that might be tested in an analysis of the context of Negro politics is that the efficacy of different patterns of minority group leadership is related to the internal division of local elites. Where fundamental community cleavages emerge as a result of minority group demands, leadership divided among those who demand and those who conciliate may produce favorable results. But where deep community division is absent, and conflict emerges over obtaining greater proportions of community resources, then unified leadership may be more effective in bargaining than one split by internal disputes.

Recently, some efforts have been made to transcend the decision-making approach and elite orientation of studies of urban politics by examining the relationship between political pressure and actual political outcomes.[67] These studies are unified by the fundamental conviction that

[64] This dichotomy pervades the literature, although some writers have preferred "protest leaders" to "militants," and "accommodation leaders" to "moderates." See, e.g., Wilson, *ibid.*, pp. 214 ff.; Gunnar Myrdal, *An American Dilemma* (New York: Harper and Row, 1962), pp. 720 ff.; Lewis Killian and Charles Grigg, *Racial Crisis in America: Leadership in Conflict* (Englewood Cliffs, N.J.: Prentice-Hall, 1964), pp. 81–90; Jack Walker, "Protest and Negotiation: A Case Study of Negro Leadership in Atlanta, Georgia," *Midwest Journal of Political Science*, 7 (1963), 99–124.

[65] Those who have argued that conflict was functional include James Q. Wilson, "The Strategy of Protest: Problems of Negro Civic Action," *Journal of Conflict Resolution*, 5 (1961), 298; Horace Cayton and St. Clair Drake, *Black Metropolis* (revised edition) (New York: Harper and Row, 1962), p. 731; Walker, "Protest and Negotiation," note 64 above, 122; Kenneth Clark, *Dark Ghetto* (New York: Harper and Row, 1965), p. 156. An excellent review of the literature on Negro politics can be found in John Strange, *The Negro in Philadelphia Politics, 1963–65*, unpublished Ph.D. dissertation, Princeton University, 1966, ch. 1.

[66] See Wilson, *Negro Politics*, note 63 above, pp. 214 ff.; Walker, "Protest and Negotiation," note 64 above, 110.

[67] See e.g., James Q. Wilson (ed.), *City Politics and Public Policy* (New York: John Wiley & Sons, 1968). Also Herbert Jacob, "Politics and Crim-

research must be pursued beyond the point that decisions are announced and policies promoted. They attempt to discover what *in fact* happened to those most affected by governmental activity. They assume that only in this way can meaningful study of the relationship between political activity and participation, governmental action, and underlying political attitudes be conducted. In this context it is instructive that studies of political participation and activity conventionally have been pursued by inquiring into partisan preferences and electoral participation. Insight into the behavior of low-income groups might be different if inquiry into participation in welfare systems and perceptions of schools and police behavior were also foci of investigation.

A third difficulty with studies of community politics has been their failure to utilize successfully the opportunities for comparative systems research. Many studies of community power have been pursued in single cities. They have usually presented conclusions accompanied by invitations to other scholars to attempt replication of the studies. This has rarely been done, although some investigators have attempted to synthesize the decision-making approach of Dahl with the reputational approach of Hunter.[68] Some writers have followed their studies of single cities with attempts to generalize from their observations to a larger universe. Their constructs are not so much attempts to develop theory as they are observational frameworks at the pre-theoretical level. These include Banfield's study of Chicago, and Wilson's utilization of bargaining language in understanding protest politics.[69]

A number of studies have recognized the desirability of adopting the comparative case method.[70] However, the cases are selected frequently for

---

inal Prosecution in New Orleans," note 52 above; William Keech, *The Impact of Negro Voting: The Role of the Vote in the Quest for Equality* (Chicago: Rand McNally, forthcoming); Strange, note 65 above; Lipsky, note 62 above.

[68] See Presthus, note 56 above. The structure of Atlanta elites has been studied in order to test some of the conclusions of Floyd Hunter. See M. Kent Jennings, *Community Influentials: The Elites of Atlanta* (New York: Free Press, 1964).

[69] See Banfield, note 44 above; Wilson, "The Strategy of Protest," note 65 above; Norton Long, "The Local Community as a Ecology of Games," in Norton Long, *The Polity*, Charles Press (ed.) (Chicago: Rand McNally and Company, 1962).

[70] By comparative case method we are not referring to the common practice of studying many issues within single cities. See Presthus, note 56 above; Agger *et al.*, note 57 above; Williams and Adrian, note 60 above. See also Wilson, *Negro Politics*, note 63 above; and Wilson, *The Amateur Democrat: Club Politics in Three Cities* (Chicago: University of Chicago Press, 1962).

reasons of convenience, and superficial similarities of size, location, or economic base. The reason for selecting cases has little to do with the subject of inquiry.

A promising development in the comparative study of urban politics is the recent trend toward utilizing aggregate data to try to explain statistically the incidence of governmental forms and policy outputs to various socio-economic community factors.[71] As with output studies, the alternative of integrating quantitative analytic techniques with the comparative case method remains to be explored. Significant variables may be isolated by quantitative techniques, while the case method may be employed to approach greater understanding of the appearance of significant correlations.[72]

IV Classifications in the Study of State and Local Politics

The relative sophistication of theoretical formulations in the field is partially revealed in the schemes used for classifying political phenomena generally designated as "state and local." The classification systems used by state and local scholars are often untested as to their reliability, validity, and utility. Their reliability depends on the existence of operational guides for placing phenomena in exhaustive and mutually exclusive categories. Their validity depends on our knowing what they represent by applying them to actual data. Utility is related to the problem(s) and question(s) under investigation. To be useful, a classificatory scheme must distinguish on theoretical grounds between empirically different phenomena. Both theoretical relevance and empirical differentiation are characteristic of a successful classificatory scheme, but are criteria which are rarely met in state and local studies.

Political scientists continue to distinguish among systems by location and size. While Southern politics, following the investigations of V. O. Key,[73] continue to display unique political configurations related to racial discrimination and franchise limitations, it is by no means clear that other regional configurations are particularly salient. Research efforts subsequent to the publication of *Southern Politics* appear to have accepted regional distinctions for convenience, while actually expressing interest

[71] See note 14 above.

[72] A start in this direction is provided in Martha Derthick, "Intra-State Differences in Administration of the Public Assistance Programs: The Case of Massachusetts," in James Q. Wilson (ed.), *City Politics and Public Policy*, note 67 above; and John Gardiner, *Police Department Policy-Making: The Case of Traffic Law Enforcement* (in manuscript).

[73] Key, *Southern Politics*, note 2 above.

in other phenomena. The most significant aspect of Lockard's *New England State Politics* relates to the impact of varying degrees of interparty competition. John Fenton's *Midwest Politics* was undertaken to explore notions of goal orientations of state government.[74] A recently published collection of readings on state politics, utilizing a sectional framework, testifies to the continued assumed salience of regional patterns.[75]

Another classification which political scientists have adopted uncritically is that of size of city. Students of community power utilizing the comparative case method frequently attempt to "hold things equal" in part by studying communities of the same size. Perhaps one of the reasons that communities of relatively similar size appear so diverse in the literature is that investigators never specify what it is that they think they are holding constant. Controlling for size might mean controlling for resource availability, community heterogeneity, bureaucratic complexity, or frequency of elite social interaction. Failure to specify the meaning of size in community studies has left obscure the importance of size of place.[76]

One area in which classification based upon both size and place does seem fruitful is that of suburban politics. Schnore and Alford have identified three types of suburbs displaying patterns of governmental form and socio-economic characteristics.[77] Williams and his associates also usefully distinguish among three kinds of governmental units in the metropolitan

[74] Lockard, note 19 above; John Fenton, *Midwest Politics* (New York: Holt, Rinehart and Winston, 1966); Fenton, *Politics in the Border States*, note 34 above; Frank Jonas (ed.), *Western Politics* (Salt Lake City: University of Utah Press, 1961).

A different rationale for using region as an independent variable outside the South is provided by Wolfinger and Field, note 14 above. In this study region is thought to "stand for" time of urban settlement. See also Schnore and Alford, note 14.

[75] Frank Munger (ed.), *American State Politics: Readings for Comparative Analysis* (New York: Thomas Y. Crowell Co., 1966). "Sectional differences have declined, but still exist." p. viii.

[76] Size of place does seem related to form of government and the adoption of various reforms associated with a "good government" orientation. Middle-sized cities, for example, have adopted the council-city manager form in much higher proportions than big or small cities. See Alford and Scoble, note 14 above. The limitations of studying the big city as a critical category are revealed in Edward C. Banfield, *Big City Politics* (New York: Random House, 1965), pp. 3–15; and Agger, *et al.*, note 57 above, pp. 760–779. The tendency to classify by size has not infected students of state politics.

[77] Note 14 above. A classificatory scheme based on anything other than governmental form is not explicitly promulgated in this study.

area (excluding the central city).[78] This study is outstanding for its adherence to the standards of inquiry enumerated above. Somewhat similar distinctions are made by Leo Snowiss in his analysis of differences in congressional recruitment patterns in metropolitan areas.[79]

Studies such as these have helped to break down the notion, prevalent in the 1950's, that the metropolitan problem was one of inferior management and inadvertent fragmentation. These studies view metropolitan governmental fragmentation as serving the function of providing different and separate environments for urban area residents.[80] One might speculate that it is the critical functions served by different metropolitan environments, rather than the areal or size dimension, which makes useful the typologies focusing on suburban differentiation.

A second perspective on classifying sub-national areal politics has been sought through a vague and uneven interest in underlying political attitudes. This may be called a focus on political culture, although nothing as systematic as the exploratory investigations of *The Civic Culture* is usually intended.[81] Rigorous research on underlying political cognitions and attitudes has not characterized studies of state or urban politics. Nonetheless, there has been an interest among students of these areas in "the 'internalized' expectations in terms of which the political roles of individuals are defined and through which political institutions (in the sense of regularized behavior patterns) come into being." [82]

Illustrative of this interest, Agger, Goldrich and Swanson propose a

[78] Williams, *et al., Suburban Differences and Metropolitan Policies,* note 14 above.

[79] Leo Snowiss, "Congressional Recruitment and Representation," *American Political Science Review,* 60 (1966), 627–639. For an analysis of public officials' roles based upon the size of constituency in metropolitan areas see Michael Danielson, *Federal-Metropolitan Politics and the Commuter Crisis* (New York: Columbia University Press, 1965).

[80] Also contributing to this reorientation have been the writings of Robert Wood, esp. *1400 Governments,* note 61 above, and *Suburbia* (Boston: Houghton Mifflin Company, 1958). See also recent studies of metropolitan consolidation in Edward Sofen, *The Miami Metropolitan Experiment* (Garden City, N.Y.: Doubleday and Company, 1966); Frank Smallwood, *Metro Toronto: A Decade Later* (Toronto: Bureau of Municipal Research, 1963); Henry Schmandt, *et al., Metropolitan Reform in St. Louis* (New York: Holt, Rinehart and Winston, 1961). Victor Jones anticipated many of the problems of metropolitan reform in *Metropolitan Government* (Chicago: University of Chicago Press, 1942).

[81] Gabriel Almond and Sidney Verba, *The Civic Culture* (Boston: Little, Brown and Company, 1965).

[82] Harry Eckstein, "A Perspective on Comparative Politics, Past and Present," in *Comparative Politics: A Reader,* Harry Eckstein and David Apter (eds.) (New York: The Free Press of Glencoe, 1963), p. 26.

four-fold classification of urban political systems based upon two dimensions: 1) sense of potency among the electorate; and 2) the probability of illegitimate sanctions being employed against incipient efforts to alter the scope of government. These dimensions yield four regime types.[83] Pursuit of these considerations cuts across an areal pattern of observation, points to the similarities between the relatively closed systems of a southern middle-sized city and a small parochial western city, and encourages comparison of city political systems with systems at other levels of government. Further, the concentration of research efforts over a long time span permits the entertaining of possibilities of regime change within recognizable periods.

Political culture considerations are at the foundation of Williams and Adrians' classification of urban government based upon governmental scope. They initially suggest a typology of "local community values" (p. 21) or "roles of local government" (p. 23), although in their discussion of the characteristics of their four cities they shift to classify cities "according to performance" (p. 187). Their typology, based upon the considered judgment of the investigators, yields cities classified as those 1) promoting economic growth; 2) providing or securing life's amenities; 3) maintaining traditional services; and 4) arbitrating among conflicting interests.[84] This presentation provides an excellent example of the utility of typology for organizing findings, although as the authors point out, their work is essentially descriptive and pretheoretical.[85]

The stimulating work of Edward C. Banfield and James Q. Wilson in attempting to demonstrate differential value orientations toward governmental expenditures by analyzing referenda data also suggests an interest in characterizing cities by citizen attitude toward governmental scope.[86] This refinement of the old machine-reform dichotomy has placed questions of ethnic politics again in the forefront of urban studies. Their

[83] Agger, *et al.*, note 57 above. The four regime types are: developed democracy (high, low); guided democracy (high, high); underdeveloped democracy (low, low); and oligarchy (low, high).

There is an implicit reference to political culture in the elitist-pluralist dichotomy, particularly in the sense that citizens are alleged to anticipate the sanctions of those "really in power." Recent studies have abandoned this simplistic dichotomy. See, e.g., Presthus, note 56 above, p. 25.

[84] Note 60 above, p. 23, and *passim*.

[85] *Ibid.*, pp. 312–315.

[86] James Q. Wilson and Edward C. Banfield, "Public-Regardingness as a Value Premise in Voting Behavior," *American Political Science Review*, 58 (1964), 876–887. See also Banfield and Wilson, *City Politics* (Cambridge, Mass.: Harvard University Press and the M.I.T. Press, 1963). The utility of the public-regardingness distinction has been forcefully challenged by Wolfinger and Field, note 14 above. See also the exchange of comments in the *American Political Science Review*, 60 (1966), 998–1000.

further explorations in this area, as promised in their recent "Communication," will be awaited with interest.[87]

Two recent studies of state politics have employed political culture concepts – one implicitly, one explicitly – without providing the reader with the means to evaluate the classifications. John Fenton's study of six midwestern states attempts to explore the distinction between job-oriented and issue-oriented politics, although what in a sense is his major independent variable – issue-job orientation – is an assumption the validity of which is never established.[88] Daniel Elazar has written a mystifying book on American states, utilizing what he calls a "political culture" approach. Unfortunately the data which permit the author to distinguish among Individualistic, Moralistic, and Traditionalistic American political culture patterns are never presented.[89] Elazar is undoubtedly correct when he argues that a regional division of the states is not necessarily the best for political analysis.[90] But he fails to assess the utility of his classification.

The most extensive typological developments in the study of state and local politics have been in areas of research where attempts have been made to confine analysis to some of the structural variables of the political system. This may be observed in reviewing classificatory efforts in the area of state party systems.

Following the seminal research of V. O. Key, political scientists have made considerable attempts to distinguish among states by the degree of party competition. For some purposes, classification has been based upon a combination of factors which accounts for both national and interstate variations in party competitiveness.[91] For other purposes, particularly a concern with testing the relationship between party competition and pub-

[87] *American Political Science Review*, 60 (1966), 999.

[88] *Midwest Politics*, note 74 above.

[89] Daniel Elazar, *American Federalism: A View from the States* (New York: Thomas Y. Crowell, 1966). See esp. ch. 4.

[90] *Ibid.*, p. 114.

[91] Austin Ranney and Wilmore Kendall originally utilized a single index for classification, in *Democracy and the American Party System* (New York: Harcourt, Brace, 1956). See also Lockard, note 19 above. Joseph Schlesinger attempted to account for the distinction between states which experience long periods of one party government, followed by resurgence of the other party, from states in which party control alternates. See "A Two-Dimensional Scheme for Classifying the States According to Degree of Inter-Party Competition," *American Political Science Review*, 49 (1955), 1120–1128. See also Schlesinger, "The Structure of Competition for Office in the American States," *Behavioral Science*, 5 (1960), 197–210. Richard Hofferbert has offered an approach which combines the advantages of accounting for the "cyclical" problem with the statistical desirability of working with a single index, in "Classification of American State Party Systems," *Journal of Politics*, 26 (1964), 550–567.

lic policy outputs, classification has proceeded by concentrating exclusively on inter-state measures.[92] These efforts have thoroughly explored the classificatory problems of cut-off points, selection of time-dimensions, and application to various research problems.[93] The attempts to develop typologies of states based upon party competition serve as the most complete area toward which political scientists have focused systematic attention. The continuing utility of these classifications remains to be demonstrated as other studies challenge the notion that party competition is highly salient to public policy outcomes.

Related to interest in the degree of state party competition has been speculation concerning the structural-functional hypothesis that degree of interest group activity is inversely related to party competition. Where political parties fail to aggregate interest, in other words, this function will be assumed by interest groups.[94] One student of American politics has made an attempt to characterize state politics in terms of interest group activity. He perceives four distinct state patterns.[95] This study forcefully illustrates the wide gaps in basic data availability in the field. It is dependent for an evaluation of interest group strength on the highly undependable characterizations by political scientists in the various states published more than a dozen years ago.[96] Testing of the usefulness of the typology must await basic data collection on various dimensions of interest group activity in the states.

Typological interest in other structural features of state and local politics has been neglected.[97] While the three forms of urban executive

[92] See Robert T. Golembiewski, "A Taxonomic Approach to State Political Party Strength," *Western Political Quarterly*, 11 (1958), 494–513, and Dawson and Robinson, note 7 above. For an attempt to relate party competition to other systemic factors in urban politics see Charles Gilbert and Christopher Clague, "Electoral Competition and Electoral Systems in Large Cities," *Journal of Politics*, 24 (1962), 323 ff.

[93] These difficulties are discussed by Leon Epstein in his evaluation of the applicability of the Ranney-Kendall classification for Wisconsin. See Epstein, *Politics in Wisconsin*, note 34 above, pp. 33–35.

[94] This is an alternative hypothesis to one promulgated by Key, who suggested that where party competition was weak, interest group aggregation increasingly was focused on the dominant party. See, e.g., V. O. Key, Jr., *American State Politics: An Introduction* (New York: Alfred A. Knopf, 1956), pp. 97 ff.

[95] Harmon Zeigler, "Interest Groups in the States," in Herbert Jacob and Kenneth Vines (eds.), note 46 above, pp. 101–147.

[96] Belle Zeller, note 24 above. These characterizations by political scientists – certainly a "reputational" measure – are also utilized by Lewis Froman in "Some Effects in Interest Group Strength in State Politics," note 10 above. See also the classification of nongovernmental groups by scope of activities and frequency of participation in decision-making in Sayre and Kaufman, note 59 above.

[97] An exception is the work on nonpartisanship by Eugene C. Lee, *The*

arrangements – mayoral, council-manager, and commission – are familiar to students of city politics, little systematic research has been conducted on the impact of these executive forms on other aspects of urban politics. Some research has revealed the kinds of cities likely to adopt various executive styles,[98] and in the case of the city manager, some research has suggested various conditions affecting the political behavior of urban executives.[99] These efforts, however, represent exceptions. Without assistance from substantive research, writers on city politics must resort to distinctions, such as the formal-legalistic, strong mayor-weak mayor dichotomy,[100] or the non-operational continuum of Influence Centralization-Decentralization.[101]

Implicit throughout this discussion has been the unwavering focus on the basic areal legal units of analysis – the cities and states. In part this is entirely sensible because the performance and characterization of these units remain critical research problems. But classification of political phenomena in terms of these units alone may obscure links with other categories of political behavior. Theodore Lowi's recent work provides a case in point.[102] By concentrating on three functionally coherent policy areas in city politics – distributive, redistributive, and regulative – Lowi has discerned distinct recruitment patterns which might never have been revealed if he had, say, researched comparative recruitment patterns in three cities. A willingness to transcend the areal, legal units in searching for classificatory meaning may prove fruitful at a time when other typological developments appear unrewarding.

V Conclusions

In this brief survey we have attempted to review the development of the field of state and local politics over the last twenty years. We have concentrated on three areas in which notable contributions toward an

---

Politics of Nonpartisanship (Berkeley, Calif.: University of California Press, 1960); and Charles Adrian, "A Typology of Nonpartisan Elections," *Western Political Quarterly*, 12 (1959), 449–458.

[98] See, e.g., Alford and Scoble, note 14 above.

[99] See Gladys M. Kammerer, Charles D. Farris, John M. DeGrove, and Alfred B. Clubock, *City Managers in Politics: An Analysis of Manager Tenure and Termination* (Gainesville: University of Florida Press, 1962). This limited research on Florida city managers does not, strictly speaking, permit inferring of classificatory divisions.

[100] As does Charles Adrian, *Governing Urban America* (2nd ed.) (New York: McGraw-Hill, 1961), pp. 199–214.

[101] As do Banfield and Wilson, *City Politics*, note 86 above, pp. 104–111.

[102] Theodore Lowi, *At the Pleasure of the Mayor* (New York: The Free Press, 1964). See also his "American Business, Public Policy, Case-studies and Political Theory," *World Politics*, 16 (1964), 676–715.

understanding of political phenomena have been made – the study of outputs, of institutions, and of community power relations. We have focused attention on aspects of these subjects which remain to be explored, clarified, and re-examined, and have tried to highlight these problems through analysis of the adequacy of typological developments.

Political scientists in attempting to divorce themselves from the prescriptiveness and formal-legalism of former generations, have succeeded in taking on, and destroying, a number of clichés about American politics and problems. They have demonstrated that suburban fragmentation serves social functions that could not be easily challenged by purely administrative solutions. They have resurrected the reputation of machine politics by pointing out the integrative function performed by patronage and personalistic politics. They have forced investigators to search deeply to explain relative non-participation in conventional political activity by those segments of the population which would be most likely to benefit from certain public policies. They have substantially discredited two highly regarded precepts of American political life – that malapportionment and low levels of party competition are substantially related to the level of outputs.

In these pages we have reviewed some of the advances in the field, and suggested some of the areas in which research in state and local politics might profitably be initiated. These areas in a sense are mirror reflections of a field devoted to decision-makers and not decision-takers, to elites rather than masses, to the results generated by political stimuli and not the impact of those results on subsequent stimuli. Thus we look forward to future studies which will examine the impact of policies on individual attitudes and behavior. We look forward to studies in non-electoral politics and the impact of non-elite pressures on the policy process. These studies would include basic anthropological investigations of Negro and white lower class incipient political groups, and intensive analysis of police precincts, welfare offices, newspaper city rooms and other lower-level bureaucracies whose effects on the political system are so extensive. We look forward to studies of differential administration, so that we may begin to explain differences in the impact of a variety of public expenditures.

PROBLEMS IN THE STUDY OF URBAN POLITICS

JAMES Q. WILSON

The principal problem in the study of urban politics is less with its means than with its ends. The journals and bookshelves are choked with articles and volumes arguing at white heat and in sometimes strident tones the "methodology" of urban political studies – arguing, in short, the means by which one should seek the answers to questions in this field. At the center of this controversy can be found the bloody but unbowed figure of Floyd Hunter; around him, his sociological defenders trade blows with his political-science attackers. Even to mention the controversy now requires a footnote of staggering length to refer the reader to the endless literature on this subject.[1]

I think this has gone on long enough. The methodological issue – how we study urban politics – is not a trivial issue; but it is not the fundamental one, either. It was a secondary issue when it was first raised, and it is a secondary issue now. The basic issue is not how we answer questions but what questions we want to answer; ultimately, we should be more concerned with where we are going than with how we get there.

We have been in danger for some time, it seems to me, of developing, at least with respect to urban affairs, a kind of "apolitical" political science. This is unfortunate, for I am sufficiently loyal to my own field to believe that political science, to a greater extent than sociology or economics (the disciplines to which we are most in danger of selling out), has had a fundamental preoccupation with the ends of human action. It is because of this preoccupation, indeed, that the study of politics in our universities has always included the study of political philosophy as well as the study of political facts. Although these two wings of the profession are often at war over the claims each makes, both have (or should have) one concern in common: the ends and outcomes of political ac-

Reprinted by permission from James Q. Wilson, "Problems in the Study of Urban Politics," in Edward H. Buehrig, ed., *Essays in Political Science* (Bloomington, Ind.: Indiana University Press, 1966), 131–150.

[1] I will omit the conventional footnote and refer instead to an anthology: Charles Press, ed., *Main Street Politics* (East Lansing, Mich.: Institute for Community Development, 1962).

tion. Just as the political philosopher is properly concerned with systematically inquiring into the moral quality of political action (more than with the history of ideas), so the political empiricist is properly concerned with systematically explaining why political action has one outcome rather than another.

Various analytical concepts can be used to organize (or justify) political inquiry, but almost all of those in common use share this concern for ends. Politics may be the study of power, but a power relationship presupposes a difference in ends that a wielder of influence attempts to overcome. Politics may be the study of conflict; what is in conflict, however, are the goals of the actors. Politics may be the study of political development, modernization, or legitimacy; it is difficult to raise these issues, however, without asking why development, modernization, and legitimacy are important. The answer, it seems to me, is that each implies that government will serve some ends and not others, will distribute goods and services to benefit one group and not another, or will mobilize loyalty for one cause and not for another.

Not every political science study, certainly, need be considered unpublishable if it fails to explain differences in policy outcomes. One can list an imposing number of intellectually interesting questions that have no immediate or obvious connection with ends. Without discounting the value of studying such matters, I would argue that the traditions, the classic literature, and the special competence of our profession have always been, in mood if not in practice, ultimately concerned with the ends of political action. Social science seeks to explain human behavior; political science, whatever else it may do, at the very least seeks to explain why some ends and not others are served by the community and the state. "Who governs?" is an interesting and important question; an even more interesting and more important question, it seems to me, is "What *difference* does it make who governs?"

Norton E. Long called our attention to the importance of such research objectives in his article "Aristotle and the Study of Local Government." [2] Like almost everything else he has written, this essay was widely influential. At least, part of it was, for it now appears that his readers got only half the message. They certainly acted as if they had paid close heed to his suggestions that Aristotle, in addition to being concerned with the formal or legal constitution of the community, was concerned as well with its "economic" or "sociological" constitution – "the actual economic and social structure of the society that underlies and informs the legal con-

[2] Norton E. Long, "Aristotle and the Study of Local Government," in *The Polity* (Chicago: Rand McNally, 1962), pp. 222–41.

stitution."[3] The more important part of the message, which seems to have been forgotten, was that the reason for this concern with the regime (now called the "power structure") was that the "regime exemplifies a particular conception of the good life, be it the wealth of oligarchy, the freedom of democracy, or the martial spirit of timocracy." How a city is governed, in short, should make a difference in what ends that city serves.

It is entirely possible, of course, that the character of the regime makes no difference at all in what ends are served; this would be a discouraging finding, to be sure, but nonetheless one of the greatest theoretical importance. No greater blow to both hot-blooded advocates of "good government" and cool-eyed defenders of machine politics could be delivered than to establish that, after all, procedures make no difference. (How the political philosophers would react is a matter of conjecture, but they are a hardy lot who may admire Socrates for drinking the hemlock but have no intention of trying any themselves.)

Many problems stand in the way of making meaningful inter-city comparisons. Nothing, it seems to me, is clearer than the fact that simple two-by-two tabulations relating easily specified variables will not get us very far. If they could, then performing some rank-order correlations among the tables in the *Municipal Yearbook* (perhaps throwing in material from the *City and County Data Book* for good measure) would answer our questions. Any graduate student could do it. But it is not simply because professors are unlikely to admit that any graduate student could do their work that such procedures are, by and large, blind alleys. Political events are too complex for any single variable (or any two variables) to explain very much, particularly since we are dealing with cities that are all part of one nation and, broadly, one culture. (Cultural uniformity is both a blessing and a curse: on the one hand, it makes it possible to "hold constant" many variables while looking at a few critical ones; on the other hand, it reduces – perhaps eliminates – the variation in those variables we do examine.)

Comparative analyses of urban political systems are hard precisely because it is so difficult to specify outcomes. We have become fairly sophisticated about inputs: we have studied the distribution of influence, forms of government, city ecology, and party organization. But we have only begun to suggest what it is that cities *do* that might be affected by these inputs. James Coleman, Maurice Pinard, and others have begun to analyze the incidence of water-fluoridation among various kinds of cities in a way that suggests that the character of the city's regime may have a considerable influence independently of the distribution of preferences

[3] *Ibid.*, p. 228.

among the citizens.[4] Amos Hawley has offered some data concerning the adoption of urban-renewal programs that have the same implication, although his findings are being questioned by some other sociologists.[5] Oliver P. Williams and Charles R. Adrian, in the most ambitious effort thus far to relate regimes to outcomes, have shown some important policy variations – in four middle-sized cities in Michigan – that depend on community differences.[6]

These efforts have not been completely successful. There are several reasons for this, all of them indicative of the difficulties inherent in comparative analysis. Most importantly, the available data on city "inputs" and "outputs" are not readily comparable without extensive reworking. One might assume, for example, that a city's budget would be the most important and most available source of information about what a city does: the ends it serves and the resources it allocates to attain them. In fact, budgets have so far proved to be a poor source of reliable information. Expenditures are differently classified in different cities; functions performed in one city by the general administration are performed in another by an independent board or commission; state and federal grants-in-aid are a large portion of some cities' expenditures and a small portion of others'; and there are great differences in what money will buy (an old, high-density city may spend much more on school construction or police protection and still buy less education or safety than a newer, low-density city, because the costs of equivalent units of such services are functions of, among other things, land values and land uses). Not only is it difficult to know what the figures in budgets mean, but it is problematical whether the budget allows sufficient freedom of action to the politicians to permit them to make any meaningful decisions about resource allocation.[7] Cities are (or think they are) pinched for revenue, so much of which must go for the maintenance of "essential" services that little, if anything, is left over for new programs. (This fact in itself is important, for in principle many of these services are not "essential" in the sense that government must administer them or; if government does administer

[4] Maurice Pinard, "Structural Attachments and Political Support in Urban Politics: The Case of Fluoridation Referendums," *American Journal of Sociology*, March, 1963, pp. 513–26.

[5] "Community Power and Urban Renewal Success," *ibid.*, January, 1963, pp. 422–31. Hawley's findings have been challenged in Bruce C. Straits, "Community Adoption and Implementation of Urban Renewal," *ibid.*, July, 1965, pp. 77–82.

[6] Oliver P. Williams and Charles R. Adrian, *Four Cities* (Philadelphia: University of Pennsylvania Press, 1963).

[7] Cf. the account of budget-making in New York City given in Lillian Ross, "$1,031,961,754.73," in Oliver P. Williams and Charles Press (eds.), *Democracy in Urban America* (Chicago: Rand McNally, 1961), pp. 418–35.

them, that it must pay for them out of tax revenue. One might have thought that their high degree of local autonomy would have encouraged at least a few cities in America to experiment more than they have with user charges or private management.)

The systematic data on inputs is in only slightly better form. The *Municipal Yearbook*, for example, conceals more than it reveals by its classification of some cities as "partisan" and some as "nonpartisan." (Boston and Chicago are "nonpartisan" in an utterly different sense from Los Angeles or Detroit; many writers have explained why this is so, but there seems as yet to be no way of using better categories for the kind of routine but essential fact-gathering service that the International City Managers' Association performs for us). Election data are in even worse shape. Efforts are now under way to put the collection of local election data on a more systematic basis, but the task that confronts the brave scholars who are trying to effect this change makes the job Richard Scammon did for national and state voting statistics simple by comparison. As long as the citizens of Los Angeles, for example, refuse to accommodate scholars by adopting a small-ward system for tabulating votes, the scholars will have to do electoral analysis by using as the basic unit either one city of 2.5 million or several thousand precincts of a few hundred people each. But at least in Los Angeles you know where the precincts are. In some other large cities, precinct lines change frequently between elections, but nobody in the cities seems to have kept track of what these changes have been.

Even if input and output data could be put into usable form, it is not at all clear what they would show. The most obvious indicators of the quality of life in our cities – per capita income, median school years completed, home ownership, morbidity rates, participation in cultural activities – are not much affected by the form or functioning of city government.[8] The American city is not Aristotle's self-sufficient city-state; the life chances of an American city dweller are much more the function of aggregate national and regional factors (economic growth, the structure of the labor market, national security) than of factors over which local officials and "power structures" have much control. It would be hard to sustain the argument that the distribution of those things *most* important to *most* people is greatly affected by the distribution of power in the community. It is not by any means clear that much can be said even about those things that concern the "attentive elite" in our cities – such as the efficiency of municipal services. The measurement of municipal services has made little progress since Herbert Simon and Clarence Ridley first

[8] Cf. Edward C. Banfield and James Q. Wilson, *City Politics* (Cambridge, Mass.: Harvard University Press, 1963), pp. 329–46.

(unsuccessfully) tried it, the reason being that the services supplied by different cities and the tastes of the consumers in different cities are rarely the same.[9]

In the long run, none of these problems may prove insuperable; and certainly every reasonable effort to develop and refine data sources that are useful in making gross intercity comparisons or helpful as indicators of urban trends ought to be encouraged. Several of my colleagues are energetically pressing the search for gross, "hard data" observables that will make it possible to assert interesting facts about the outcomes of city politics without having, as Norton Long puts it, "to hide under the mayor's bed." It certainly would make for a more efficient and systematic social science of cities if it were possible to answer the important questions by knowing how the data are correlated instead of where the bodies are buried. I am warmly sympathetic to efforts to get the first kind of answers, but I am not optimistic that for the foreseeable future we shall be able to avoid the necessity of disinterring a few political skeletons. A political sociology or even political economy of cities may be the ultimate objective, but a political anthropology is still very much in order.

Input-output analysis in the study of urban politics has made even less progress (if that is possible) than input-output analysis in political science generally. It is still necessary to study the contents of the black box, and not simply to examine what goes in and what comes out. No substitute has yet been found for the intelligent observer who can find the tribal informants and extract from them a rich, complex, and largely subjective account of the lives, values, goals, habits, and methods of the city fathers. We can, however, begin to shift the focus of such research to stress (1) new *objectives* of analysis, (2) new *levels* of analysis, and (3) new *units* of analysis.

The new objectives would emphasize, as I have said before, an effort to explain the outcomes of community politics and government. There are two broad strategies for making this effort. First, one can begin, as Williams and Adrian have done, with a small number of communities that are presumably different in important ways and then seek to understand what differences, if any, in the ends of government action there are among the cities and what aspects of the cities – social, economic, eco-

[9] Clarence Ridley and Herbert Simon, *Measuring Municipal Activities* (Chicago: International City Managers' Association, 1938) and Alice Vendermeulen, "Guideposts for Measuring the Efficiency of Governmental Expenditure," *Public Administration Review*, Winter, 1950, pp. 7–12. Recently, renewed attention has been paid to the problems of criteria, as a result of the effort to apply cost-benefit analysis to municipal services. See the papers in Howard G. Schaller, *Public Expenditure Decisions in the Urban Community* (Washington, D.C.: Resources for the Future, 1963).

logical, or political – account for these differences. Finding the differences, though not simple, is of course the easiest part of the investigation. The harder part lies in attributing causation among the enormous number of possible explanations. Solving the problem of identifying the dependent variables (by intensive study of a few communities that one hopes will provide different outcomes) makes it that much harder to solve the problem of specifying the independent variables. The second approach is to find some measure of an outcome (for example, the adoption of an urban-renewal or fluoridation program, the level of welfare or educational expenditures, or the crime rate) and apply that measure to a very large number of cities. The familiar techniques of multivariate and regression analysis would then be used to discover what "input" factors are associated with the variation in the dependent variable. The problem with this approach, as I hope I have made clear by now, is that for most of the interesting outputs we have no reliable measures. We have lots of "measures" (like the FBI Uniform Crime Reports, educational expenditures per pupil in average daily attendance, and net project costs for urban-renewal projects completed or authorized), but nobody knows for sure what any of these "measures" measure. The crime rates are the most notoriously unreliable, but the others are not much better. Solving the problem of specifying the independent variables (by having enough cities in our sample to make statistical techniques useful) makes it that much harder to solve the problem of specifying the content of the dependent variables. The seemingly inevitable gains and losses associated with these two research strategies make me think that there is at work in social science an equivalent of the Heisenberg Uncertainty Principle, such that success in determining the magnitude of one variable precludes the possibility of determining the magnitude of another.

The easy (and conventional) way out of this Hobson's choice is to say that the method one picks depends on the questions one wants to answer, and then to change the subject. This is of course true, but it never really works that way. The method one chooses rarely depends simply on what questions one seeks to answer; it really depends on the personal research style of the investigator, almost regardless of what method is theoretically best.[10] Recognizing this, I am willing to go a bit further than the easy answer and suggest that, at this stage, although much bolder experimentation with aggregate-data analysis is needed, real progress still requires the intensive study of a small number of communities. This is so not simply because it happens to be my research style, but also because

[10] A brilliant account of the meaning of theory and research is Michael Polanyi, *Personal Knowledge* (Chicago: University of Chicago Press, 1958), especially chaps. IV, VI, X.

intensive "outcome-oriented" research is critically necessary to enable us to learn in detail what the "outcomes" are, how they may be measured (if at all), and what factors *seem* to be causally related to them.

The level, as well as the ends, of analysis should be specified. In principle (and to a considerable extent in practice) there are three possible levels: the individual, the group or organization, and the system. I think it fair to say that almost all the research on urban politics done over the last several years has emphasized the second level.[11] One now can refer to a sizable number of respectable studies on urban party organizations, pressure groups, leadership patterns, "power structures," and the like. These organizations or groups or cliques, however, operate within a system, constrained not only by the character of the system as a whole but by the preferences of the individuals (voters, members of voluntary associations, newspaper readers, and party workers) whose dispensation (or indifference) is required before action can be concerted toward organizational or community goals. Much more needs to be done at the organizational level; I would be the last to urge anyone to abandon studies of this sort. All kinds of institutions have received only the sketchiest study – newspapers, the more important voluntary and civic associations, and municipal bureaucracies, to name only three obvious examples. Nevertheless, the great void exists at the other two levels: that of the individual and that of the urban political system as a whole.[12]

I do not say this in order to open up a sterile controversy about reductionism in social science. I know there are always a few scholastics around who insist on pointing out for the twentieth time why one cannot (or can) explain collective behavior as the consequence of individual attributes. The point I want to make is somewhat different: analysis entirely at one structural level (a) makes explanations of the outputs of whole systems unlikely and (b) reduces the possibility of comparative study. It has the first deficiency because it does not take into account the con-

[11] The same point I am here making with respect to urban political studies has been made with respect to organizational theory in Peter M. Blau, "The Comparative Study of Organizations" (paper delivered at the annual meeting of the American Political Science Association, Chicago, September, 1964).

[12] There are some conspicuous exceptions. Edward C. Banfield, *Political Influence* (New York: Free Press, 1961) not only analyzes the behavior of some of the principal organizations involved in Chicago politics but discusses the consequences for public policy of the distribution of influence in the community as a whole. Robert A. Dahl, *Who Governs?* (New Haven: Yale University Press, 1961) combines an analysis of organizations and elites with a study of voter attitudes and political participation. The forthcoming study of southern Negroes by Donald Matthews and James Prothro uses survey and local-informant data in combination to show the relationship between the distribution of attitudes and the level of organizational activity in various communities.

straints (or, from another perspective, opportunities) facing organizations; it has the second because the study of a single institution or organization almost invariably leads the research deeper and deeper into the organization and farther and farther away from those *gross* characteristics of the organization that distinguish it from others in the same community or indicate its similarity to comparable organizations in other communities. There is no inevitable reason why this should be so except for the very real fact that knowledge tends to come in dissertation-sized chunks; trying to force a graduate student who has learned enough about one organization to satisfy his thesis committee to go out and do the same thing on a similar organization in a different city is widely regarded as an unfair labor practice.

Despite the popularity of survey and electoral research during the last fifteen or twenty years, little of this research has been done on cities. This is not surprising; cities have rarely been the arena in which momentous national issues are fought out. The current civil-rights controversy may change all this. One continuing difficulty, of course, has been that a principal source of funds – the federal government – has not in the past been anxious to sponsor research that had as its major categories ethnicity and religion and that was explicitly directed toward political questions in some congressman's district.

There is reason to believe that some of these constraints will be relaxed or got around. The important thing, however, is to decide what questions are worth asking of local voters. It seems to me that the city is the best place to explore the kinds of attachments citizens have to the polity – their sense of obligation or duty, their conception of the public interest, and the extent to which (or the circumstances in which) their preferences in community programs are the product of rational self-interest or of learned cultural norms.[13] These are difficult questions to answer in any circumstances; but they are doubly so when the question at issue is stated in general terms, resolved in a remote place, and experienced only indirectly – in short, when it is a "momentous national issue." It is the very ordinariness of local concerns – garbage collection, police protection, street repair, school programs – that make them valuable as tools to explore the nature of citizenship and civility. These services are directly experienced, their quality is (in principle) calculable in terms of narrow self-interest, and they are paid for by a variety of interesting tax and revenue procedures that have a very uneven incidence.

Furthermore, survey and electoral analyses done intensively in one or

[13] Edward C. Banfield and I have explored some of these matters, using data from municipal referenda elections, in "Public-Regardingness as a Value Premise in Voting Behavior," *American Political Science Review*, December, 1964, pp. 876–87. We are now testing some of these hypotheses by means of interviewing.

a few cities permit heavy sampling of certain groups that are more thinly dispersed in the national population – Negroes, Italians, Poles, and Jews, for example – and about which our knowledge is largely fragmentary and impressionistic. (Our understanding of middle-class Negroes has not kept pace with our interest in them, in part because they are such tiny portions of random national samples.) Survey research can help us to understand the city in a way that, until now, we have not; but the help will be limited unless some professional constraints are eased. The drive for impeccable technique has progressed at the expense of substantive knowledge, precisely because (among other reasons) the most interesting questions are the most difficult to phrase and code. (One valuable source of survey data about urban politics – the Detroit Area Study – has not fully realized its promise, largely, I think, because it has not asked very interesting questions; and it has not done so, I would guess, in part because the answers to such questions are extraordinarily difficult to handle in a routinized and easily replicable manner.) It has been said before but I will say it again: we need to exploit more fully the techniques of Samuel Lubell and David Riesman before we can decide to what extent the techniques of the Survey Research Center are applicable.

The urban political system is, like the individual, a level of analysis where the need at present is for less rather than more rigor.[14] (The level of organizational analysis is one where *more* rigor – or at least more effort at being systematic – is required.) By "urban political system" I mean something rather simple – for example, in what politically important respects do the growing cities of the Southwest differ from the stagnant or declining cities of the Northeast? What difference to politics do the facts of affluence, a rapid increase in population and land values, and an in-migration of already acculturated, middle-class families (instead of alien, lower-class families) make? [15] What important differences does city size make in the issues that arise and in the manner in which those issues are resolved (or not resolved)? [16] What have been the secular trends for different kinds of cities over the last half-century? (Several fascinating changes suggest themselves, but they have largely been ignored in con-

[14] On the subject of comparative urban studies, see the excellent treatment in H. Douglas Price, "Comparative Analysis in State and Local Politics: Potential and Problems" (paper presented before the annual meeting of the American Political Science Association, New York City, September, 1963).

[15] *Ibid.*, pp. 17–20, and H. Douglas Price, review of *Who Governs?* in *Yale Law Journal*, July, 1962, especially pp. 1094–95.

[16] The subject has been opened up by James G. Coke, "The Lesser Metropolitan Areas of Illinois," *Illinois Government* (published by the Institute of Government and Public Affairs, University of Illinois), no. 15, November, 1962.

temporary research. Not very long ago, in any strike the police were automatically on the side of business; today the police are either neutral or – in some cases – on the side of the unions. Not long ago, known thieves running on pro-thievery platforms could be elected to high municipal office; today, hardly any *known* thieves stand a chance.)

Analyzing urban political systems as systems cannot be done simply by trying to look at the system "whole," for there are always as many "wholes" as there are observers. Furthermore, it may be that not all of urban politics has the character of a "system" – that is, of a set of interdependent variables. Attention must therefore be given to the appropriate *units* of analysis. Most recently, the unit employed by the political scientist has been the *issue*, and that employed by some (though by no means all) sociologists has been the *elite*. As we all know by now, these differences (among others) have led to different research findings. Looking at issues – i.e., at conflict – one is more likely to find pluralism, contention, and bargaining. Looking for elites, one is more likely to *find* elites (i.e., persons who possess a disproportionate share of some resource, such as income, prestige, or putative power). Having recognized this, I do not feel that truth lies in eclecticism. Using both methods simultaneously may only add the errors of one to the shortcomings of the other. I happen to believe that the issue-oriented approach is, in most circumstances, the most fruitful one – in part because American cities, to a greater extent than cities almost anywhere else, are engaged in managing conflict; in part because many of the crucial features of a system are best seen under conditions of strain and conflict; and in part because asking people who they think is "powerful," no matter how carefully the findings are subsequently validated, is at best a waste of time and at worst misleading.

The real difficulty with the issue-oriented approach is not that it is wrong but that it leaves a great deal unsaid. Some communities produce few, if any, obvious issues.[17] In other communities, certain matters do *not* become issues because some group that can influence the civic agenda manages to suppress certain demands; these "nonissues" may be even more interesting than the problems that do find a place on the agenda.[18] Furthermore, in any city, what is of greatest importance to the daily lives of the citizens and most influential in the conduct of American govern-

[17] Cf. Arthur Vidich and Joseph Bensman, *Small Town in Mass Society* (Princeton, N.J.: Princeton University Press, 1958), chaps. V–VIII, and James S. Coleman, *Community Conflict* (Glencoe, Ill.: Free Press, 1959).

[18] See Peter Bachrach and Morton S. Baratz, "Decisions and Nondecisions: An Analytical Framework," *American Political Science Review*, September, 1963, pp. 632–42, especially pp. 641–42, and Banfield, *Political Influence*, pp. 9–10.

ment as a whole may not be issues at all but may instead be certain services and institutions that are largely taken for granted.

I suggest that the most challenging area for new research on cities is to take as the unit of analysis the routine behavior of the city as it provides certain services or as it conducts its political affairs. Three examples of such units are the system of justice, the educational system, and the welfare system.

The system of justice – and my early research suggests that it *is* a system and not simply a collection of institutions such as courts, prosecutors, and police officers – should be examined as a means by which the community exemplifies and enforces its normative codes. The system of justice, I suspect, is best seen not in the highly publicized murder trial but in the routine disposition of drunks, vagrants, shoplifters, auto thieves, and fornicators.

The problem in examining education is not to justify its importance (that, I take it, is obvious) but to find some way of assessing its output. If professional school administrators cannot tell us how to recognize good as opposed to poor education or how to measure how "much" education we are producing, then political scientists concerned with the outcome of urban governmental arrangements cannot be blamed for avoiding the field for so long.[19] Nonetheless, interesting issues remain. How, and by what criteria, are educational resources allocated among various groups and neighborhoods within the community? How is the distribution of influence within the school system related to the kinds of subjects and the types of students taught? If taxable income and teachable children continue to abandon the central city, what alternatives exist for the management of America's great experiment with mass education under public auspices?

The politics of welfare programs in our cities ought to be broadly conceived, to include not only the conventional forms of public assistance and relief but all measures by which the city government, implicitly or explicitly, seeks to redistribute income. The larger and older central cities are, in some cases, well on their way to becoming the urban equivalents of Indian reservations in which perpetual wards of the state are subsidized by a system of "welfare colonialism" that creates serious problems (e.g., subsidizing broken homes) while solving others (e.g., preventing starvation). We know little of how (or by whom) the goals of these programs are set, how politics intervenes (if at all) in the administration of these programs, or how the level of welfare expenditures differs from city to

[19] A fruitful beginning was made almost thirty years ago; but, until the Syracuse studies were begun, no one tried to follow it up. See Nelson B. Henry and Jerome G. Kerwin, *Schools and City Government* (Chicago: University of Chicago Press, 1938).

city. New programs in the welfare field, such as federally sponsored "community action" organizations in lower-class neighborhoods, raise interesting questions about the sort of incentives necessary to mobilize the impoverished; the implications of these incentives for the goals and tactics of the organizations; and the propriety of using public revenues to support a program that, at least in some cities, consists very largely of organized political and civic action directed *against* the governmental institutions that are paying the bill.

Thinking back over all this, I suspect I may have emphasized more than I meant to the need for goal-oriented comparative research on cities. There are, I should like to repeat, many intellectually interesting questions that, if answered, do not necessarily illuminate the question of outcomes. (No one, by the way, has to my knowledge ever proposed a satisfactory set of criteria for distinguishing intellectually interesting from intellectually uninteresting questions. Maybe that is because devising such criteria does not seem intellectually interesting.) Understanding politics, a very difficult subject to comprehend, is intrinsically satisfying; and it needs no other justification than that. I here emphasize the ends of community action, not because there is no other way to do research, but because I feel political science has, in some degree, a peculiar mission and competence: to think simultaneously about the quality of the ends that are served and the reasons why those ends, and not others, are in fact served.[20] But also I feel that a preoccupation with outcomes is the most meaningful way to do comparative research, that it is a preoccupation closest to the subjective states of the principal actors in politics, and that it directs attention to "high stakes" matters rather than "low stakes" matters. Although we have had a number of studies about community conflict that have told us something about how urban renewal or fluoridation programs are enacted or defeated, in the long run these programs may turn out to be trivial, or very nearly so.[21] For most people, the stakes are low (even for the most involved actors, the stakes may be as much the fun of playing a civic game as a real concern with the outcome). Those matters over which the community has any significant control that

[20] The current functionalist approach to comparative government has recently been criticized, in a similar way, for failing to use policy as an explicit variable: Roy Pierce, "Comparative Politics: Liberty and Policy as Variables," *American Political Science Review*, September, 1963, pp. 655–60.

[21] This does not mean that nothing significant can be learned from such issues. Two important "single city" studies have been done on urban-renewal politics: Peter Rossi and Robert Dentler, *The Politics of Urban Renewal: The Chicago Findings* (New York: Free Press, 1961) and Harold Kaplan, *Urban Renewal Politics: Slum Clearance in Newark* (New York: Columbia University Press, 1963).

have high stakes for most of us are few compared to those found at the national level; but they include how our children are educated, how our taxes are levied, how (and to what end) our poor are supported, how the use of our land is controlled, and how (and in whose behalf) our criminal laws are enforced. To a great extent, they include many of the matters that, taken together, make up some magnificent part of what we mean when we speak of civility. And that, I feel, is not an unworthy subject.

Part

2

POLITICS AND PUBLICS

The articles in Part 2 illuminate several features of the relations between citizens and their state and local governments. All use comparison in one form or another. If they do not compare situations in different states or localities, they do compare different kinds of behaviors in individual jurisdictions or present categories of analysis that lend themselves to comparisons. One looks at the decisions of voters in Michigan in four electoral settings, each of which presents different features capable of influencing the outcomes. Another analyzes the responses of a national sample of citizens to questions about state and local governments. By varying the traits of people being examined, the authors identify the characteristics likely to be associated with certain attitudes. Another offers some generalizations about the role of protest in local politics and identifies several of the factors involved in the protest-policy linkages.

The common focus of these articles is the behavior of individuals in their roles as citizens. These are the "publics" that give their support or opposition to candidates for elective office and provide to the incumbents subtle or overt cues about the desired course of public policy. The first selection concerns an elemental feature of citizen-government relations: the level of attention paid to the affairs of state and local governments. Other essays deal with the influence of political parties over the choices made by voters; characteristics of "political culture" that affect the policies supported by citizens; and the choices that officials make in permitting citizens to decide certain policies by means of referenda.

M. Kent Jennings and L. Harmon Zeigler identify the salience of state and local politics for various groups in the population. A "salience map" describes those public affairs that are important to certain individuals. We are not all interested in the same things. For some people, national and international affairs are most prominent, while for others state and local politics are significant. Many others are indifferent to politics and show little interest in governmental decisions, except those having an immediate impact on their own lives. Jennings's and Zeigler's salience maps reflect the economizing we do as citizens. Since we cannot pay equal attention to all issues, we concentrate on a few. Some knowledge of these priorities permits officials to know which segments of their publics are interested in their decisions. Jennings and Zeigler do not tell us a great deal about salience maps, although they do tell us what kinds of people are most interested in state and local — as opposed to national and international — affairs. Still unexamined are questions about the types of state and local issues that attract the attention of various publics. Interests in state and local affairs tend to go together and to attract people who are relatively less interested in national and international affairs. Compared to the rest of the population those interested in state and local affairs tend to be less well educated, members of lower status occupational groups, residents of rural areas and small towns rather than large cities, and disproportionately from the South. We can infer that people interested primarily in state and local affairs are more parochial than cosmopolitan and are less fascinated with the larger issues of the nation and the globe. Before a policy maker acts on the basis of these "salience maps," he should know how people divide on their awareness of various kinds of issues (e.g., civil rights, education, welfare, conservation). He should also know to what extent other people may be attracted to state and local arenas when certain kinds of policy are at issue.

Michael Lipsky examines several features of political protests in urban settings and infers a model of protest that may guide further research into the protest-policy linkages. At the beginning, the protesters are "powerless." To have an impact on policy, they must enlist the support of "third parties" who will support their demands. Lipsky indicates that the features important in enlisting supporters are the role played by communications media, the nature of "material" and "symbolic" rewards associated with the protest activity, and the nature of relationships that develop among protesters, third-parties, and the policy makers themselves. Involved in these relationships is the unstable character of the protest movement and the skill of the protest leadership to maintain a balance among several tensions. Lipsky's model will foster comparative research to the extent that we can use its categories to organize observations about separate protest movements and to show how different aspects of a protest movement affect each other.

The essay by James Q. Wilson and Edward C. Banfield considers complex sets of attitudes and behaviors that characterize distinct groups in the population. Wilson and Banfield describe polar sets of attitudes labeled public- and private-regardingness. The central feature of each is a person's tendency to put the "public interest" or the "welfare of the community" above, or beneath, his own immediate benefit. The authors isolate some evidence of these postures in the voting behavior of ethnic and income groups on local referenda. Upper-income Anglo-Saxon and Jewish groups frequently vote in a public-regarding way for proposals that will not provide them with any direct economic benefits, while other ethnic groups vote in ways that are more consistently private-regarding. The findings suggest how historical experiences can affect a contemporary generation of ethnics. Yet Wilson and Banfield do not examine the status of many large ethnic groups on the public-private-regardingness spectrum, or the process by which attitudes may change under such influences as education, occupational mobility, or residential mobility away from an ethnically homogeneous community.

Ira Sharkansky considers the regional location of states as a likely influence on their politics. He tests the correspondence between region, several indicators for voting participation, and party competition. Not only does he find that states of different regions show distinctive scores on these features, but he finds that regional location is more important for them than a state's level of economic development. Although region is a gross concept that does not clarify the process by which states come to different levels of participation and competition, it does suggest the importance of cultural and historical influences. This selection guides the scholar who would search for the specific events and experiences that comprise "regional" patterns.

Norman C. Thomas tests the importance of several influences on voting patterns in state constitutional referenda. Because the referenda are not overtly partisan in their character, he can compare the influence of party leaders with other voting cues, without a party label on the ballot. Thomas examines four referenda. Although the small number of cases and the limitation to one state makes this study merely an exploration, the findings are suggestive and merit consideration in other contexts. Where an issue received little attention from the customary providers of political cues (the press, interest groups, and parties), citizens appeared to make their decisions on the basis of their social and economic characteristics, particularly education. When non-partisan cue-providers entered an issue (the press, interest groups and reformers), the factors that influenced citizens were altered. In these cases urban and rural residence took precedence over other social and economic traits. On an issue that generated the involvement of party leaders, however, the voters' party affiliation became the strongest single determinant of their vote. These findings show how the context of a decision can affect the factors that influence it. Parties, the press, and interest groups help to shape that context. When they assert themselves to participate, these institutions may alter the social and economic divisions among the voters that would otherwise prevail.

The article by Robert L. Crain and Donald B. Rosenthal helps us to bridge Part 2 and Part 3. It seeks to explain the outcomes of fluoridation decisions. Crain and Rosenthal consider the influence of local political traits, especially voter participation and party strength and the nature of local government structure (whether council-manager, partisan mayor, non-partisan mayor, or commission). Their findings fit together into a persuasive package, even though it is weakened by the small number of cities that responded to some questions. Crain and Rosenthal are less interested in the decision to — or not to — adopt fluoridation than the way in which a locality makes the decision: by action of the government alone or by referendum. Several features help to isolate the decision making arena from intense controversy; where there is little controversy, there tends to be governmental action on fluoridation, without a referendum. Elements that protect a community from a referendum include a governmental structure that is "strong" enough to assert its support of an issue and a local ethos that is not supportive of high popular participation. The governmental structures that are most protective against referenda include council-manager and partisan-mayor forms of government. Where parties are involved in the mayor's selection, the character of local parties also helps determine a governmental or referendum course of action. Parties that involve themselves heavily in local issues yet accept the postures taken by national leaders of their parties are most likely to protect local office holders from pressures to hold a referendum.

THE SALIENCE OF AMERICAN STATE POLITICS

M. KENT JENNINGS
HARMON ZEIGLER

Research emphasizing the correlates of state policy outputs and the performance of particular institutions has overshadowed the role of the citizenry in the drama of state politics. One question of basic concern is the relevance of state government and politics for the inhabitants of a state. At the level of public policy and institutional performance the answer to this is factual and straightforward. The nature, amount, distribution, and to some extent the quality of a state's services and policies can be specified. Since states perform most of the traditional functions of governmental units and since these functions affect the fortunes of the citizens, state politics has an obvious, tangible, objective relevance for a state's inhabitants.[1] At another level, however, the answer is not so clear-cut. Here we are dealing with the idea of what is subjectively relevant. Large numbers of people apparently pass their lives being touched by political institutions in a variety of ways without becoming particularly

Reprinted by permission from M. Kent Jennings and Harmon Zeigler, "The Salience of American State Politics," *American Political Science Review,* LXIV (June, 1970), 523–535.

This is a revised version of a paper originally presented at the 1968 annual meeting of the American Political Science Association, Washington, D.C. The direct and indirect financial support of The Danforth Foundation and the National Science Foundation is gratefully acknowledged. We also wish to thank Bruce Campbell and Paul Beck for their assistance at various stages.

[1] The literature on the correlates of state policy outputs is becoming voluminous. Thomas Dye's *Politics, Economics, and the Public: Policy Outcomes in the American States* (Chicago: Rand McNally, 1966) perhaps represents the zenith of this approach. Other questions are also receiving attention, however. See, for example, some essays in Herbert Jacob and Kenneth Vines (eds.), *Politics in the American States* (Boston: Little Brown, 1965); Samuel C. Patterson, "The Political Cultures of the American States," *Journal of Politics,* 30 (February, 1968), 187–209; Norman C. Thomas, "The Electorate and State Constitutional Reform: An Analysis of Four Michigan Referenda," *Midwest Journal of Political Science,* 12 (February, 1968), 115–129; and Wayne Francis, *Legislative Issues in the Fifty States: A Comparative Analysis* (Chicago: Rand McNally, 1967). Herbert Jacob and Michael Lipsky provide a sound and enlightened discussion of the field in their "Outputs, Structures, and Power: An Assessment of Changes in the Study of State and Local Politics," *Journal of Politics,* 30 (May, 1968), 510–538.

interested in or involved with these institutions. Other people become intensely, purposively related to these same institutions. Still others fall along a continuum between these two poles. If substantial variations exist in the general salience of politics, there is little reason to doubt that the same conditions may be found in particular subsets of political matters. In the case at hand this subset consists of the cluster of institutions, actors, and processes known as state political systems.

I The Concept of Salience Maps

It may be assumed that for every individual at a given point in time some aspects of politics are more salient than are others. These varying degrees of salience result in cognitive maps yielding surfaces with divergent contours and topographies. Analytically, at least two kinds of mapping operations can be visualized. One is laid out according to issue domains. For some people civil rights issues are most salient, for others tax and fiscal issues, for still others questions of foreign affairs predominate, while education may be the prominent part for yet another cluster of people. Some individuals may place equal stress – ranging from high to low – on a host of disparate issues, but given the opportunity costs involved it seems likely that at any point in time the mapping operations result in an ordering of issue salience.

More germane for present purposes is a salience map arranged according to geopolitical units. A variety of investigations have suggested that people do, in fact, develop such maps.[2] Perhaps the most noted shorthand expression of this differentiation is the local-cosmopolitan dimension. Important ramifications for political systems stem from differentiated salience maps. One has only to think of the stresses and strains in the emergent countries or the separatist enclaves in established polities to grasp these possibilities. The difficulties encountered by national governments as a partial consequence of sub-national loyalties are impressive. Proclivities toward independence in the Canadian province of Quebec, the Nigeria-Biafra confrontation, the uneasy federalism of India, and the failure of the American South to be incorporated fully into the mainstream of American politics testify to the magnitude of these difficulties. As with salience maps oriented around issues, the maps dealing with

[2] For an example and references to the literature see M. Kent Jennings, "Pre-Adult Orientations to Multiple Systems of Government," *Midwest Journal of Political Science*, 11 (August, 1967), 291–317. An historical perspective with a different focus is found in Samuel P. Hays, "Political Parties and the Community-Society Continuum," in William Nisbet Chambers and Walter Dean Burnham (eds.), *The American Party Systems* (New York: Oxford University Press, 1967), pp. 152–181.

levels of government could in fact attach equal relevance to the component parts. That is, a person could be equally interested (or uninterested) in international, national, state, and local public affairs and politics. Yet this would seem to be an inefficient mode of operation if nothing else, and as we shall see momentarily it is a deviant pattern.

Upon what basis would a person distinguish among these four levels of politics? Assuming that he had equal information about all of them, or at least access to equal information, two dimensions can be suggested. First, he may arrange them according to his interest in the policy outcomes involved. Whereas some find local outcomes about services and amenities of greatest subjective relevance, others are more intrigued by the results of military encounters and diplomatic skirmishes at the international level. A second dimension rests not so much with outcomes as with the demands and conversion processes at work within a given system. Here the interest comes from watching how the game is played rather than in what the final scores are. Charismatic political leaders, factional fights, and broader societal cleavages are kinds of forces which can lead to differential salience along this dimension. Attention to outcomes and conversions may operate simultaneously and feed upon each other. Interest generated by a strong, personable governor might be combined with concern over a state tax program to produce a heightened salience for state politics. Should such convergences occur, the two types of salience maps begin to merge. That is, the overlay of the issue salience map on the system salience map begins to produce a single topography. Although the question of overlap between issue and system maps is an important one, our major concern is with the system map arrangement.

II The Place of the States Versus Other Levels

For a variety of reasons one could predict that the states generate but a modicum of interest amongst their residents. Many of these reasons are either explicit or implicit in a statement by Dahl, made in the context of a discussion about optimum units for popular democratic government:

> Yet in the perspective I am suggesting the states do not stand out as important institutions of democratic self-government. They are too big to allow for much in the way of civic participation – think of California and New York, each about as large in population as Canada or Yugoslavia and each larger than 80 per cent of the countries of the world. Yet an American state is infinitely less important to citizens of that state than any democratic nation-state to its citizens. Consequently the average American is bound to be much less concerned about the affairs of his state than of his city or country. Too remote to stimulate much participation by their citizens, and too big to make extensive participation possible anyway, these units inter-

mediate between city and nation are probably destined for a kind of limbo of quasi-democracy. . . . It cannot even be said that the states, on the whole, can tap any strong sentiments of loyalty or likemindedness among their citizens.[3]

In a sense the states are caught between the immediacy of the local system and the glamour and importance of the national and international systems. Without wishing to become embroiled in the question of the appropriate units for a democratic polity, we can nevertheless introduce some material which will clarify the location of the states in the salience maps of Americans.

Our data are drawn primarily from the University of Michigan Survey Research Center's 1966 election study, which utilized a national probability sample of the adult population. In order to obtain the interest accorded various levels of politics a series of questions was put to the respondents, beginning with an initial question designed to filter out those people (17 per cent) who barely attend to matters of the body politic.[4] The remainder rank-ordered which kinds of public affairs they follow most closely – international, national, state, and local.[5]

One immediate result of the ranking operations is that it reveals the readiness of Americans to distinguish among the four levels. All but 6 per cent of the sample (excluding the inattentive) gave complete orderings. The ease with which the rankings were obtained as well as the meager proportions declining to give complete orderings indicates that people at least believe they have salience maps characterized by a rugged terrain rather than a smooth plain.

It is apparent that, while some respondents place state affairs above all other levels, the majority share of first rank attention is devoted to national and local affairs, such as Dahl predicted (Table 1). If one wants

[3] Robert A. Dahl, "The City in the Future of Democracy," 61 (December, 1967), p. 968.

[4] This question ran: "Some people seem to follow what's going on in government and public affairs most of the time, whether there's an election going on or not. Others aren't that interested. Would you say that you follow what's going on in government and public affairs most of the time, some of the time, only now and then, or hardly at all?" Those selecting one of the first three alternatives are considered to be members of the attentive public.

[5] After handing the respondent a card showing the four levels of public affairs, he was asked to rank them in this fashion: "Which one of these kinds of public affairs do you follow most closely?" "Which one do you follow next most closely?" "Which one do you follow least closely?" With first, second, and fourth ranks thus determined the residual level automatically occupied the third rank.

TABLE 1. *Rank Order Distributions for Salience of Governmental Affairs at Four Levels*

Level of Governmental Affairs	Rank of How Closely Followed					
	First	Second	Third	Fourth	Total[a]	N
International	20%	16%	22%	42%	100	983
National	32	31	26	10	99	983
State	17	33	27	22	99	983
Local	30	20	25	25	100	983
	99%	100%	100%	99%		
N =	983	983	983	983		

[a]Total percentages do not equal 100% due to rounding. Cases involving tied ranks or missing data have been deleted in this table. Their inclusion in any rows or columns would have a maximum effect of but 1 percent on any cell value. The total number of cases for analysis will be 1,008.

to consider international affairs a mental extension of America's role in world affairs (which some respondents undoubtedly did), then state affairs is even more clearly in last place. Taking only the leading rankings demonstrates that the attentive public for state politics is not particularly large.

The danger in closing the argument on the basis of first ranks is nicely demonstrated in two ways. Looking at fourth ranks, for example, reveals that state affairs has next to the lowest proportions in this category. More compelling evidence is provided by moving to the second ranks. State affairs has strong second-place strength, being in fact the level selected most often at that rank. The contrast with the fate of international affairs is the most striking, since it too (compared with national and local affairs) had abundant opportunity to pick up second place strength. The result of combining first and second ranks finds one-half of the sample placing state matters either first or second, thereby moving it to an equal footing with local affairs, well ahead of international affairs, but still to the rear of national affairs. While the states may not be uppermost in the political thoughts of their residents, they do occupy a secure niche.[6]

[6] It should be recognized that we are not merely playing with numbers in order to make a case for the saliency of state politics. There is no logical necessity, given the nature of the questions used, that state affairs attract any second rankings. All respondents after making their first choice could have ranked state affairs third or even last had they been so inclined.

What are the risks in using the respondents' rank orderings of interest in the four levels of politics as a way of driving their interest in state politics alone? Three immediate justifications for the measure can be offered. First, it should be reemphasized that these orderings reflect those of the national sample *minus* an apolitical stratum, the 17% who avowed they paid no attention to public affairs and politics. Thus we have eliminated at least a substantial proportion of those people who might have contributed idiosyncratic, error-prone estimates of the differential salience of various levels of politics. Second, these kinds of rank-orders have been subjected to a spatial scaling technique which indicates the prominence of at least one major dimension running through the rank orders, *viz.*, that of the geo-political domain encompassed by given governmental levels.[7] Essentially, this means that the ranking of state politics nestles reasonably well within an overall, multi-level salience framework.

A third argument is perhaps the most persuasive. It could be charged that the *relative* salience of state politics bears but little correspondence to its *absolute* salience. Illustratively, a politically passive person ranking state politics first might actually pay less attention to it than a political activist ranking it third or fourth. While the plentiful presence of such inconsistencies could be overlooked on the grounds that one is primarily interested in the workings of individual preference orders regardless of intensities, our concept of salience maps will acquire an extra dimension if it can be shown that this is not the common pattern. The 1966 election study did not ascertain absolute levels of interest in politics at multiple levels, but the 1968 election study did this as well as obtaining the rank orderings of interest.[8] A moderately satisfying result would take the form of little association between relative and absolute salience. This would at least allow for the play of relative salience across a spectrum of people having about the same absolute interest in state politics. A much more gratifying result, of course, would be a clear positive relationship between the two dimensions.

The cross-tabulation of the two measures (Table 2) is unequivocal

[7] See Jennings, *op. cit.*, for an application of the Coombsian unfolding technique to data of this type from a national adolescent sample. Separate analysis with the sample at hand yields similar results.

[8] In the 1968 study the respondents were, as in 1966, first put through a screening question which eliminated the apoliticals. They then replied to questions about their attention to the four levels of politics. For state politics the question read: "And how about affairs here in (STATE WHERE R LIVES); do you pay a great deal, some, or not much attention to state affairs?" Rank orders of relative interest were obtained after these questions.

TABLE 2. *Relative Versus Absolute Levels of Interest in State Politics*[a]

Rank of How Closely State Politics Followed	Attention Paid to State Politics			Row Totals	Marginal Totals	N
	Great Deal	Some	Not Much			
First	58%	39%	04%	101%	15%	(166)
Second	44	50	06	100	38	(407)
Third	27	55	18	100	28	(307)
Fourth	22	56	22	100	19	(204)
Marginal Totals	37	51	12		100%	(1084)

[a]Data are drawn from the Survey Research Center's 1968 national election study.

in demonstrating a moderate correspondence between absolute and relative salience, in terms of self-reports. We can say with some confidence that, on the average, those who attend relatively more often to state affairs also tend to pay more absolute attention. By the same token (if the table is percentaged vertically) it is clear that the attentive public in absolute terms comes disproportionately from the ranks of those for whom the state is relatively more salient. There is little reason to suspect that different results would have been obtained from the 1966 respondents, had they been asked the additional questions. One indirect piece of evidence, for example, is that the marginals for the rank-ordered interest in state politics are remarkably similar across the two samples.[9]

Given previous work with the local-cosmopolitan dimension, a positive association between rank orderings for state and local affairs would be hypothesized. Rank order interrelationships can be demonstrated in a fairly straightforward way without the added refinement of spatial or scaling techniques. The respondents' rankings of state politics were crossed against their rankings of each of the other three levels of politics. From these matrices were extracted the sum of respondents who allocated

[9] Since we have both relative and absolute measures for the 1968 sample, it might be asked why we do not utilize that sample rather than the earlier one. The reasons are two-fold: 1) in order to capture a "purer" reflection of the salience of American state politics it seems desirable to base the analysis on data gathered during a period relatively uncontaminated by the forces of a national election, for much the same reasons that studies of state voting turnout, division of the vote, and party strength often separate the off-year from presidential year statistics; 2) a number of questions of direct relevance for state politics were asked in the 1966 study, but not in 1968. On the other hand, subsequent work in this general area might well utilize both absolute and relative measures of salience in order to arrange people in a multi-dimensional mode.

either a first or second rank to each of the other three levels. These proportions are as follows:

First or Second Rank Given to:	State Affairs Ranked: First	Second	Third	Fourth
International	5	9	30	40
National	43	38	42	37
Local	52	52	28	23
	100%	99%	100%	100%

Without doubt, the higher the salience of state affairs the higher is that of local matters and, on the other hand, the lower is that of international affairs.

An easy transition between and intermixing of state and local politics creates a sizable cluster of people who are state and locally oriented. Another way of viewing these rankings is to think of people living in the same geographical area, but focusing their attention upon different political objects. There is a state public – overlapping in great part with the local – and a more cosmopolitan public. Both cosmopolitan and state-local political processes operate simultaneously within a given area; but the "separate" publics of each level probably filter out to varying degrees the information about processes less relevant for them.

Having set forth the concept of salience maps and the place of the states in such maps, we can now turn to two major sets of questions. First, we are interested in the attitudinal and behavioral corollaries or consequences of differential state salience. Other things being equal, the various psychological theories of balance, congruence, and consonance would suggest a probable linkage between high state salience and the favorable evaluation of objects associated with states, and a negative evaluation of objects foreign to the states. Similarly, high salience should be associated with greater behavioral activity in the domain of state politics.

Second, we are concerned with the determinants of distinctive state salience maps. These may be presumed to flow from two sources, one social and the other political. A variety of social experiences are ordinarily associated with narrower, more provincial perspectives. These lead us to predict that state salience will vary with the nature of these experiential histories. The strictly political factors to be considered are state-specific. Although theoretical underpinnings are less apparent here, we will take as a point of departure the progressive, "good government" model of politics. This model would suggest that the more the state political system conforms to the tenets of progressive democracy, the more interested will be the citizenry in the state as a political institution. That is, salience maps will vary with (good) systemic properties, *ceteris paribus*.

In the analysis to follow we have collapsed the four rankings of state politics into two by combining ranks one and two into "high," and three and four into "low."

III Salience, Attitudes, and Behavior

While one can argue that determining the distribution of differential salience maps is important in and of itself, the subject will be more compelling if it can be shown that certain attitudes and behaviors accompany the different configurations. For instance, it can be demonstrated that there is a connection between salience levels and affective orientations. Those following state affairs could, in fact, be responding to negative impressions about the state's institutions and leaders. Given the need for consonance rather than dissonance in the human psyche, it seems more likely that there would be a "strain toward congruity." [10] Attention and favorable dispositions do, indeed, occur together. One example is that those who pay more attention to state politics accord higher prestige to the occupation of governor than do those paying less attention ($\gamma = .32$).[11] That is, there is greater identification with a symbol (role) connected with the more salient level of government.

By drawing upon data from the 1968 election study it is possible to show more precisely the connection between salience and affect. Respondents rank ordered their faith and confidence in the three levels of the American federal system – national, state, and local.[12] Comparing salience and confidence levels reveals that as the salience of a state's

[10] For experimental evidence see, *inter alia*, Milton J. Rosenberg, *et al., Attitude Organization and Change* (New Haven: Yale University Press, 1960).

[11] The question read: "Now we're interested in learning what kinds of work Americans respect most highly. Which of these occupations do you respect the most?" Three choices were made. The list included, in this order: "U.S. Senator, Bishop or other church official, general or admiral, famous doctor, justice of the U.S. Supreme Court, atomic scientist, professor at a large university, President of the U.S., well-known athlete, president of a large corporation like General Motors, governor of your state." Altogether governor was the fourth-most choice, being tabbed by 29% of the sample. The correlation in the text is based on first choices.

[12] The questions ran: "We also find that people differ in how much faith and confidence they have in various levels of government in this country. In your case, do you have more faith and confidence in the national government, the government of this state, or in the local government around here?" "Which level do you have the least faith and confidence in – the (——) or the (——)?"

politics rises so does the evaluation of that government's performance. Just as people tend to pay more attention to candidates they like, and vice versa, so too they seem to operate in a selective fashion with respect to political units such as the states. Again, there is no particular reason to suppose that this pattern would not hold for the 1966 sample with which we have been dealing.

Inferentially, the relatively more attentive public for state politics would seem to provide sources of political support for the ongoing performance of state officials.[13] While the overlap of attention and support is a pleasing state of affairs for state officials, it also raises the possibility of a tacit exchange between these officials and the supportive public. The convergence between support and favorable perception suggests that the values of the attentive public are echoed and legitimized by the state's elites. In any event, if people for whom state politics is highly salient have socio-political views differing from those of the less attentive public, and if there is meaningful interaction between and among elites and attentive publics, then it should follow that the state's political life would vary according to the mix of people more closely attuned to state affairs. It becomes relevant, then, to assess the political values of this attentive public.

We may begin by noticing that people who pay more attention to state politics are basically less trusting of the world about them. They are more likely than others to say that one can't be too careful when dealing with other people rather than affirming that most people can be trusted ($\gamma = .31$). They are also more inclined to think that their fellow man is primarily looking out for himself rather than trying to be helpful to others ($\gamma = .19$). By ranking state politics higher than national and international affairs an individual has given a hint that he may be suspicious of larger, more remote environments. His more distrustful orientation toward other people rests comfortably in this outlook.

Attitudes more manifestly political give some glimpse into the way state-oriented individuals view national government and its role in their own lives. Those inclined toward state affairs avow more often that what Washington does makes less of a difference in their personal lives ($\gamma = .30$). In one sense this is a confirmation of our earlier speculation

[13] Any further exploration of the linkage between salience maps and support structures needs to take into account such support dimensions as delineated by David Easton, namely, specific-diffuse; overt-covert; and direct-indirect. See his *A System Analysis of Political Life* (New York: Wiley, 1965), pp. 153–340. For an investigation of support processes at the state level see G. R. Boynton, Samuel C. Peterson, and Ronald D. Hedlund, "The Structure of Support for Legislative Institutions," *Midwest Journal of Political Science*, 12 (May, 1968), 163–180.

that a system-level salience map reflects in part an issue salience map, since state-oriented citizens see less subjectively important outcomes at the highest level of the federal structure.

Given the subjectively lesser importance of Washington decisions, it would be anticipated that the special public of the states is concerned about the increasing erosion of state decision-making by the federal government. Such concern is present, though not as visible as might be expected. Those attuned to state matters more often say that the federal government is playing too powerful a role in society ($\gamma = .16$). By the same token they more often oppose Washington's taking a strong role in integrating the nation's schools ($\gamma = .21$). The lack of stronger relationships may proceed from the fact that such people may simply not feel threatened by an actor (Washington) which is of lesser importance to them in general.

It should be noted, incidentally, that the prominent political orientation of party identifications bears almost no overall relationship to state salience: ($\gamma = .08$), using the S.R.C. seven-point party identification measure which runs from strong Democrat to strong Republican. This is so despite the fact that, nationally, the Republican party is often linked with a states' rights position. Actually the only region in which party identification has an observable connection with state salience is the South, where Democrats more often rank state affairs higher ($\gamma = .21$). For the other regions the relationship is nil.

Although virtually all the above relationships persist within each category of the control variables employed,[14] they are more marked among some strata. The prime example is not socio-economic or spatial; rather, it is by political strata. Non-voters in the 1966 general election (and to a lesser extent non-voters in the 1966 primary contests) exaggerate the original correlations. Thus the relationships are heightened for non-voters versus voters when salience is related to a disavowal of Washington's impact (.54 vs .15); belief that the federal government is too powerful (.30 vs .11); and being against federal intervention in school integration (.28 vs .17).[15]

Identification with the state is as much or more symbolic than active for the non-voters. Denying the relevance of a disliked national government, they interpose the state as a symbolic barrier between the national government and themselves. These and other variations denote a multiplicative effect, whereby salience maps are especially linked to views about the federal government among citizens with certain characteristics. Con-

[14] Controls included region, urbanization, education, subjective social class, interest in public affairs, voting regularity, and party identification.

[15] The results obtained when controlling for voting participation are not artifactual of differential turnout rates by region or urbanization.

sequently, the practical, political effects of varying proportions of state-oriented residents in the state depend upon other traits of these residents.

Perhaps the most acute test of the impact of differential attention toward state politics comes in examining overt behaviors. If the concept of diverse salience maps is to have viability, some behavioral manifestations are in order. Should these be found, it would suggest that the fabric of a state's politics is further mediated by or informed by the distribution of interest orderings.

It may be stated at the outset that close followers of state politics are, in many respects, slightly less participative than are those less devoted to state politics. For example, they report following public affairs and politics often ($\gamma = -.20$), they vote less often in presidential elections ($\gamma = -.16$), they had less interest in the 1966 congressional campaign ($\gamma = -.13$), knew a little less about the candidates ($\gamma = -.10$), and were just a shade less likely to vote in the congressional election ($\gamma = -.08$). These relationships seem at first glance to cast doubt on our earlier demonstration (with the 1968 sample) that relative interest in state politics was linked to absolute interest. However, the declining magnitude of these correlations as one moves from a general interest in politics on through to activities reflecting participation in congressional races contains a hint that the closer the activity is to state and local matters the more likely will this pattern be erased or even possibly reversed.

Such proves to be the case. There is absolutely no difference in turnout for the gubernatorial election in those states where that office was at stake. Furthermore, those most interested in state politics more often reported voting in the 1966 primaries ($\gamma = .15$). Finally, an indirect indicator of a linkage between state-level salience and forms of participation is that the more attention paid to state matters the greater is the likelihood of voting a straight party ticket in the 1966 state and local elections ($\gamma = .17$).[16] The general drift of these admittedly modest correlations over a range of behavioral phenomena suggests that a higher focus on state affairs may depress participation within nationally oriented politics but enhance it at state and local levels. Thus the concept of attentive publics is given a behavioral as well as attitudinal dimension.

These overall relationships disguise some fascinating interplay between state level salience and other factors associated with political participation. It is well-known, for example, that education is positively related to both spectator and participatory levels of politicization. Since – as shall presently be demonstrated – education is inversely related to the

[16] This holds true among Democrats and Independents, but not for Republicans.

attention paid state politics, it might be assumed that the generally negative relationships between state level salience and political participation are a function of education. If this were so, it would not account for the absence of a relationship with turnout in the gubernatorial election and the presence of a positive association with turnout in the primary balloting. Nevertheless, it is true that at least some portion of the meager relationships are a function of the confounding influence of educational attainment. What is much more intriguing, though, is that education and the attention directed toward state affairs interact with each other to produce strikingly divergent patterns of political behavior.

This process is best illustrated with three measures: interest in the 1966 congressional campaign, voting in the 1966 general election, and voting in the 1966 primary. It will be recalled that the bivariate correlations between interest in state politics and affirmative responses to these three items were either slightly negative (for the first two) or positive (for the latter). By noting the correlations at each of four educational levels it is possible to see the profound interaction effects between education and state interest. There is considerable deviation around the aggregate bivariate correlations. This is shown in Figure 1, which contains plottings by educational level for each of the three measures. Among the less educated, following state politics is marked by less interest and voting. As education rises these negative relationships either decline or move to the positive side. Finally, among the well-educated being attuned to state politics exerts a very positive effect. A similar pattern holds among the subsample located in states with a gubernatorial contest in 1966.

These changing relationships are not easily accounted for. One line of explanation is that the salience of state politics for the poorly educated and the well educated attentive publics rests upon different bases of psycho-political orientations. For the poorly educated, who have much less factual knowledge about state politics, the attachment is primarily affective, a buffer against a fearsome intruder. For the better educated, high interest in state politics takes a more instrumental form, whereby participation becomes more meaningful. If, indeed, the better educated transform their attention levels into more participation via an instrumental orientation, then it should follow that the participation levels in state (and local) elections would be higher for those paying more attention to state politics. As we observed, this is precisely the case.

It is more difficult to say why the attention level is inversely related to participation among the poorly educated. Perhaps their more affective orientation, when combined with a higher interest in state politics, results in a perspective that voting accomplishes relatively little. High affective symbolic orientations may reduce the need for participation. Inner gratification flows from withdrawal and non-participation.

FIGURE 1. Relationship between Salience of State Politics and State-Level Participation, by Education

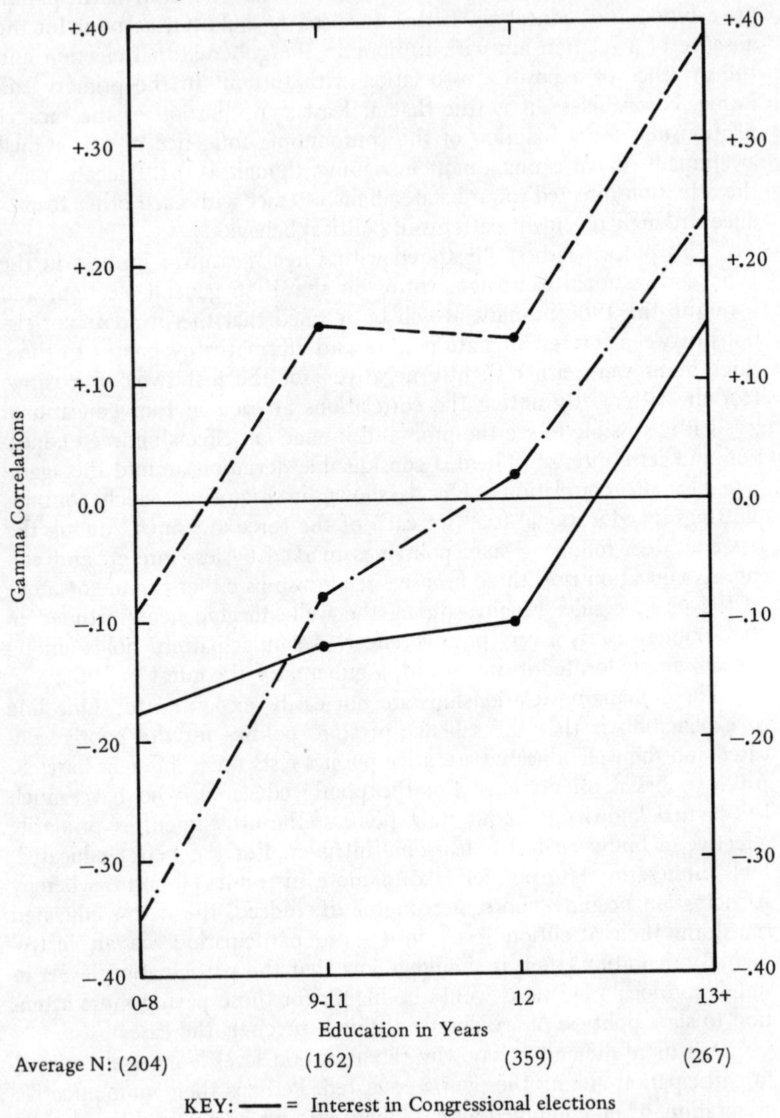

IV Individual and Demographic Bases of State-Level Salience

The place of state politics in an individual's attention frame will be a function of formative experiences – summed up in the term political socialization – as well as more contemporary factors denoting the type of life space occupied by the individual. Here we concentrate on the various "static" characteristics rather than on those reflecting dynamic elements.[17]

Where a person was reared says something, in gross terms, about his family of orientation, the life style around him, and the nature of the surrounding political culture. It is apparent that the more urban a person's upbringing the less likely he is to pay attention to state politics (panel 1, Table 3). A similar pattern may be discerned in terms of contemporary residence. For convenience, we have categorized locations in terms of the twelve largest standard metropolitan statistical areas (SMSA), other SMSA's, and non-SMSA areas. The more urban or metropolitan the area the less compelling are state affairs (panel 2, Table 3).

A third locational factor is that of region. As with the other spatial variables, region is a summary construct. That is, it often captures (imperfectly to be sure) a set of historical experiences, socialization patterns, life styles, and political culture differences which are relevant to certain political phenomena. Two recent illustrations of "regionalism" are the findings that the adoption of policy innovations and the patterns of state expenditures have distinct, independent regional components.[18] It can also be argued that, even if region as a term simply disguises the "real" underlying dimension at work, this still does not alter the fact that the distribution of opinion and behavior within a region – hence the states in that region – is different, and that these differences may

[17] An attempt to look at the nuances of state level salience over the life cycle will be found in an extended version of this article to be published in Edward C. Dreyer and Walter A. Rosenbaum (eds.), *Political Opinion and Electoral Behavior* (rev. edition, Belmont, Calif.: Wadsworth, forthcoming).

[18] Jack L. Walker, "The Adoption of Innovations by the American States," [American Political Science Review], 63 (September, 1969), 880–899; and Ira Sharkansky, "Economic Development, Regionalism, and State Political Systems," *Midwest Journal of Political Science*, 12 (February, 1968), 41–59. See also Samuel Stouffer, *Communism, Conformity and Civil Liberties* (New York: Doubleday, 1955); Norval D. Glenn and J. L. Simmons, "Are Regional Cultural Values Diminishing?" *Public Opinion Quarterly*, 31 (Summer, 1967), 176–193; and M. Kent Jennings and Harmon Zeigler, "Political Expressivism Among High School Teachers: The Intersection of Community and Occupational Values," in Roberta S. Sigel (ed.), *Learning About Politics: Studies in Political Socialization* (New York: Random House, 1970).

TABLE 3. *Social and Demographic Correlates of State Politics Salience*

Proportion of People Paying First or Second Most Attention to State Affairs, by:

Where Reared				gamma[a]
Farm	Small town	Small city	Large city	
65% (323)[b]	50% (256)	42% (169)	40% (240)	–.30
Current Residence				
Non-SMSA	Medium SMSA	Large SMSA		
62% (359)	51% (357)	38% (292)		–.31
Current Region				
South	West	Midwest	Northeast	
62% (288)	54% (167)	46% (310)	43% (243)	–[c]
Education				
0-8 grades	Some high school	High school graduate	Some college or more	
64% (208)	59% (164)	52% (362)	34% (269)	–.32
Subjective Social Class				
Working	Middle			
59% (543)	41% (441)			–.34
Length of Residence in State				
0-19 years	20 years or more, but less than entire life	Entire life		
42% (120)	47% (236)	54% (620)		.17

[a]These represent the correlation between the overall high-low salience dichotomy and the accompanying social and demographic characteristics.
[b]These are the N's upon which the percentages are based.
[c]Gamma computation inappropriate because region is a nominal variable.

either reflect or produce different political processes. In the case at hand it turns out that the salience of state politics does vary among the regions, with Southerners being most attuned to state matters, Westerners next, and Midwesterners and Northeasterners least (Table 3).[19] Similar proportions emerge by taking the individual's region of birth instead of current region.

A slight diversion is necessary here to comment on the possible historical and contemporary reasons for these regional divergencies. In one cluster are the Southern states, bound by the pains, memories, and dislocations of an historical trauma. To say that the states have a unique place in past and present Southern politics is to repeat a commonplace. At the other extreme is the cluster of Northeastern and Midwestern states, those states generally considered most cosmopolitan in outlook, the major repositories of the great economic, cultural, social, and political institutions of the nation. Between these two clusters are those states which may be characterized as Western and hybrid in nature. Settled in large part by immigrants from other states, carved in part out of the former federal territories, ushered into statehood at a time when the trend was toward stronger state government,[20] and physically remote from the centers of national power, these states have neither the high cosmopolitanism of the Northeastern-Midwestern tier, nor the scars and ethnocentrism of the South. It remains to be seen whether these regional patterns persist in the light of various controls which shall subsequently be applied.

To the locational factors may be added those characteristics reflecting a person's social status and life style. The higher a person's formal education and subjective social class the less interest he evinces in state politics (panels 4 and 5, Table 3). This pattern echoes the well-known propensity of the better off and better educated to be more concerned than lower status people with broader environments. In view of this it is not surprising that those from the working class and lower educational strata are more likely to form a portion of the attentive public for state politics.

While the demographic and social strata components supply a substantial amount of differentiation, there are also temporal factors at work.

[19] Regional groupings follow Census Bureau classifications: Northeast = New England and Middle Atlantic states; Midwest = East North Central and West North Central states; South = South Atlantic, East South Central, and West South Central states; and West = Mountain and Pacific states. Other regional combinations were employed, but with less rewarding outcomes.

[20] Daniel Elazar discusses the historical tendencies toward state centralism versus localism in *American Federalism: A View from the States* (New York: Crowell, 1966), pp. 186–193.

One of these is simply the individual's length of residence in his state. The common-sense hypothesis that the longer a person resides in a state the higher the salience of that state's politics for him is borne out by the data (panel 6, Table 3). At this aggregate level the differences are not marked, but are clearly in the hypothesized direction.

We now know that the amount of attention devoted to state affairs differs according to several social and spatial characteristics. Of additional importance is whether the observed patterns hold under a variety of control conditions and whether there are cumulative effects at work. The answer to the first query is unequivocal. With only one exception [21] the original bivariate associations are maintained when controls are exerted for each of several other variables. For example, the basic negative relationship between SMSA size and state level salience persists regardless of rearing site, region, education, social class, and length of state residence. With some confidence one can say that the social and locational factors cited above have an independent impact on the probable occurrence of divergent salience maps.

Although the staying power of the various characteristics constitutes an important aspect of the analysis, it is significant that there are also cumulative processes at work. Two examples will depict what is, for the most part, a common form of behavior when two of the predisposing factors are combined and then related to state politics salience. One instance of this process comes by combining educational attainment and the site where the individual was reared. It was established previously that the higher one's education and the more urban the rearing site environment the less salient is state politics. Now if these two factors operate in an additive fashion when combined it should mean, for example, that the highly educated from urban areas would be especially prone to rank state affairs low. Without doubt this is the case. Only 28 per cent of the college educated persons reared in a city placed state politics high. On the other hand, 74 per cent of the elementary educated respondents who were reared on farms gave high prominence to state affairs. Percentages between these two poles tended to reflect very faithfully the operation of additivity principles.

A second example of the cumulative processes at work merges education and region. In addition to knowing that education is negatively related to following state affairs and that pronounced regional variations exist, we also know that educational differences persist within each of the

[21] The deviant case is that of length of residence controlled by region. Interest in state affairs does not increase with length of residence in the West (−.05), a finding no doubt occasioned by the continued Westward migration of the populace. Correlations for the other three regions are South = .39; Northeast = .26; Midwest = .16.

four regions (a: South = −.32; West = −.34; Midwest = −.34; Northeast = −.23). Under such conditions it should come as no surprise to find that by categorizing people in terms of both education and region the range of high interest in state affairs is elongated. Furthermore, the elongation conforms remarkably well to the predicted values, assuming additivity.

Figure 2 contains two lines, one showing the predicted order of values under an additivity model, and the other showing the actual values attached to those predicted for each region-education combination. While the lines do not follow the same precise path, the actual propor-

FIGURE 2. Predicted and Actual Values of High State Level Salience for Region-Education Combinations

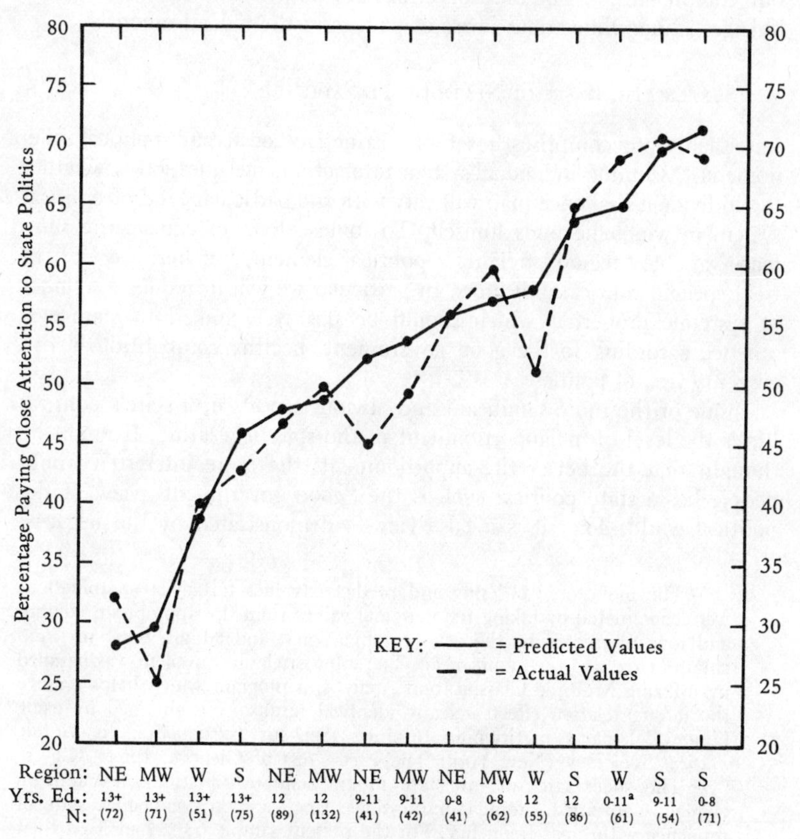

[a] Grades 0-8, 9-11 have been combined because of small N's.

tions adhere rather nicely to the predicted ones.[22] That is, given four overall regional means, the effects of education are roughly similar across each region. Conversely, given different educational strata means, the effects of region are approximately the same across each educational strata.

Because we are dealing with a national sample, none of the foregoing results would apply with certainty to particular states. Yet to the extent that the nationally-based findings provide state-specific clues it is clear that salience maps possess quite different configurations according to some well-defined individual and demographic properties. Short of dramatic events, the states thus seem destined to be populated by unequal proportions of state-attentive publics.[23] How much and in what ways these inequalities affect the state's political life cannot be answered here, nor are they easily solved questions. Their solution, however, should enrich our comprehension not only of intra-state politics but also that of the linkages among the various levels of politics in the federal union.

V Systematic Bases of State-Level Salience

Each state comprises a set of distinctive social and political phenomena. Assuming individual-system interaction, the question is whether the individual's salience map will vary with the particular kind of political system in which he finds himself. To some extent, of course, the summary variable "region" freights a political element; but here we wish to treat specific political indicators. In particular we will introduce a number of systemic properties which should be positively linked to state-level salience according to the good government, healthy competition, active citizenry view of politics.

One of the more significant and obvious aspects of a state's political life is the level of malapportionment in the state legislature. It might be thought that the better the apportionment, the more interested would people be in state politics: such is the "good government" view of the political world. That it is a false view is demonstrated by the negative

22 The monotonic ordering and predicted values for given combinations were constructed by taking the marginal values from the appropriate column and row intersected by the cell (combination), and adding these row and column effects to the grand mean. The intercorrelation problem was handled by utilizing Multiple Classification Analysis, a program which helps remove the intercorrelation effects. Nearly identical results were obtained by using James Coleman's partitioning formulas. See his *Introduction to Mathematical Sociology* (New York: The Free Press of Glencoe, 1964), Ch. 6.

23 The sheer rates of interstate mobility impose a strong restraint on change. Contrary to popular impressions Americans do not change state of residence with great frequency. For the present sample 63% had lived their entire lives in one state and another 24% had spent at least 20 years there.

relationship (−.27) between following state affairs and the fairness of apportionment – using the 1960 David-Eisenberg Index.[24] This association shows a remarkable persistence under a variety of control conditions. Region is an especially critical control to impose here since the South, which is relatively malapportioned, is also the area containing the largest number of state-oriented respondents. Nevertheless, with Southerners removed from the sample, the negative association persists (−.21); and in no region does a positive trend emerge.

Much the same conclusion can be reached about the degree of inter-party competition. Let contests for the governorship and Hofferbert's omnibus inter-party competition index serve as indicators of state-level competition.[25] While it might be expected that the more spirited the competition between the parties the more salient would be the politics of the state, the opposite is true. Regardless of which measure is used the relationships are negative, even though not strong (−.24 and −.22 for the governorship and Hofferbert's index, respectively). Again the pattern tends to persist under a variety of control conditions, including region.

Another common variable used to characterize the states' political culture is that of election turnout. In general it is argued that the higher the turnout the more vigorous the level of politics. Turnout for gubernatorial and U.S. senatorial contests will be used as a safe guide to the state-specific forces activating differential turnout. The common-sense hypothesis is that the higher the voting participation the higher the salience of state politics for the state's inhabitants. Such is not the case, however.

[24] From Paul T. David and Ralph Eisenberg, *Devaluation of the Urban and Suburban Vote,* Vol. I (Charlottesville, Virginia: Bureau of Public Administration, University of Virginia, 1961). Although widespread reapportionment has occurred since the *Baker v. Carr* decision of 1962, most occurred after 1964. Indeed the latest reapportionment of *both* legislative houses occurred as late as 1965–66 for thirty states and 1967–69 for eight states. Given the time lag between legal changes of this sort and their imprint on the mass public, it seems advisable to use the 1960 malapportionment figures for our 1966 sample. To utilize this measure and the ones to follow the respondents have been allocated into roughly equal quartiles or quintiles according to the scores of the state in which they resided. It can be shown that the distribution of the sample across *groups* of states with varying score ranges approaches the distribution for the universe.

[25] The gubernatorial measure is based on contests from 1946–62, and is taken from Dennis Riley and Jack Walker, "Problems of Measurement and Inference in the Study of the American States" (unpublished paper, University of Michigan, 1968). Hofferbert's index is reported in Richard I. Hofferbert, "Classification of American State Party Systems," *Journal of Politics,* 26 (August, 1964), esp. pp. 562–563. More recent single elections were also used in our analysis; these produced results similar to those for the above two measures.

There is, in fact, a small tendency (−.12) for salience levels to decline as turnout rises. Whatever forces are acting to develop a high following for state matters, they are not very well described by the differential participation of the electorate.

It has become apparent that for many people the affairs of government are wrapped up in what a few of the very visible political officeholders do. Accordingly, it might be advanced that the stronger the office the more salient would be the institutions, activities, and processes surrounding that office. While it is obviously true that a personable, aggressive governor can capture a substantial amount of attention regardless of the statutory limitations on his power, it seems reasonable to suppose that the same sort of governor with an arsenal of legal powers could do even more to make himself and the state government topics of conversation. As it turns out people living in states with powerful governors [26] are no more likely to follow state affairs than are people living in a state with weak chief executives. What correspondence exists is actually on the negative rather than the positive side (−.12).

As noted earlier, many of the recent investigations about state politics have treated the determinants of public policy outputs. Because the great share of operational measures so far developed for assessing state policy outcomes are based on expenditure items, we are restricted in examining the connection between salience and state performance. The "good government" advocate would argue that the more active the state government, the more salient it would be for its residents. There is but meager support for that proposition. Trivial, positive relationships (ranging from .02 to .14) exist between high salience and the number of state government employees per one thousand population, state expenditures per $1,000 income, and state expenditures per capita. Slight negative associations are found between salience and state aid to cities and recent (1950–1960) changes in general state expenditures. These are all single indicators. Employing a ranking of the states based on Crittenden's "Scope of Government" factor [27] – which has very high loadings on tax level per capita, tax level per income unit, spending level per capita, and governmental employment – again produces an extremely modest positive correlation (.08). Regional controls reveal the association to be slightly higher in the Midwest and West.

Walker, among others, has argued that it is essential that non-expenditure policies be included in any attempt to explicate the articula-

[26] The rankings come from Joseph Schlesinger, "The Politics of the Executive," in Jacob and Vines, *op. cit.*, Chap. 6.

[27] John Crittenden, "Dimensions of Modernization in the American States," [American Political Science Review], 61 (December, 1967), 989–1001.

tion between state performance and socio-economic and political characteristics. In response to his own admonition he developed a set of policy innovation scores for the several states, stretching from the late nineteenth century to mid-twentieth century.[28] The "good government" position is that the innovative states would command more interest from their residents than would the laggardly ones. This is hardly the case, however, for the association is but slightly above zero. Unfortunately, few other reliable indicators of state performance are at hand. If we are to judge by the innovative pattern, non-expenditure performance measures are no more likely to affect salience maps of state residents than are those based on expenditures.

Most of the associations involving the foregoing political characteristics exhibit an exaggerated mode among non-voters. For better or worse, the less participative citizens react to the political culture in a more severe fashion than the more participative. That is, if a system manifestation such as malapportionment accompanies greater interest in state affairs, it is especially prone to do so among the less participative. One can picture them as less autonomous and self-assured than their more participative fellows. Environmental forces thus come to have more impact on them. There would seem to be a certain perversity about this, but apparently the less active citizens are, in effect, bolstered by these aberrations from what the reformers and democratic theorists see as progressive democracy.

Concluding Remarks

The concept of salience maps has been used to explore the relationship of the citizenry to their state governments as a particular set of institutions in the American political system. People do organize their cognitive views of the political world such that some system levels assume more prominence than others. There are indications that cognitive and affective dimensions of state salience are inter-locked. Attitudinal and behavioral corollaries of differentiated salience maps depend in part upon one's social and political status. One of the most emphatic though somewhat puzzling findings is the degree to which these corollaries are exaggerated among less participative citizens. Correspondingly, the salience of state politics among these less active people varies more according to environmental forces than is true for the more active.

Broadly speaking, the forces which contribute to following state politics can be grouped into two categories. On the one hand, there are those factors which are essentially "given" or uncontrollable. On the

[28] Walker, *op. cit.*, p. 883, Table 1.

other hand, there are other factors which are more subject to elite manipulation and political change. Place of residence, education, social class, and the like are – to a greater or lesser extent – set for the individual. To a similar extent, the states have limited control over these aspects of a person's life.

Asserting that these factors are given is not to adopt a crudely deterministic stance. Rather, it is to hold them in contrast to another set of variables that are substantially more malleable. State outputs, such as program expenditures or policy innovations, are more amenable to the short-run persuasive efforts of elites and the occasional demands of masses. These are the areas of a state's political life that attract a good deal of attention from political scientists and specialized publics, but have precious little positive impact upon the salience maps of individuals. The contours of such maps are determined largely by the individual's life experiences and the characteristics of his immediate life space.

We have suggested (though not demonstrated) that a state's policies are partially determined by the attitudes and behaviors of its attentive public. However, the obverse of this proposition is not necessarily correct: the attitudes and behaviors of the attentive state public reflect dimly, at best, the quality of a state's public policy. Arguments that a vigorous, strong, and innovative state government produces an interested public are open to question. So, too, are the emphases placed on such touch-stones of liberal democracy as inter-party competition, equal representation, and enthusiastic electoral participation.

Whatever the correlates of state-level salience, it is apparent that the states still loom large in the perspectives of the American public. Any attempted juggling of political units involving the states would probably confront a reservoir of mass attachments to the states as political entities. Coupled with the historic traditions, legal preserves, and political utility of the states, this salience helps assure the continued prominence of the several states within the federal system.

PROTEST AS A POLITICAL RESOURCE

MICHAEL LIPSKY

The frequent resort to protest activity by relatively powerless groups in recent American politics suggests that protest represents an important aspect of minority group and low income group politics.[1] At the same time that Negro civil rights strategists have recognized the problem of

Reprinted by permission from Michael Lipsky, "Protest as a Political Resource," *American Political Science Review*, 62 (December, 1968), 1144–1158.

This article is an attempt to develop and explore the implications of a conceptual scheme for analyzing protest activity. It is based upon my studies of protest organizations in New York City, Washington, D.C., Chicago, San Francisco, and Mississippi, as well as extensive examination of written accounts of protest among low-income and Negro civil rights groups. I am grateful to Kenneth Dolbeare, Murray Edelman, and Rodney Stiefbold for their insightful comments on an earlier draft. This paper was developed while the author was a Staff Associate of the Institute for Research on Poverty at the University of Wisconsin. I appreciate the assistance obtained during various phases of my research from the Rabinowitz Foundation, the New York State Legislative Internship Program, and the Brookings Institution.

[1] "Relatively powerless groups" may be defined as those groups which, relatively speaking, are lacking in conventional political resources. For the purposes of community studies, Robert Dahl has compiled a useful comprehensive list. See Dahl, "The Analysis of Influence in Local Communities," *Social Science and Community Action*, Charles R. Adrian, ed. (East Lansing, Michigan, 1960), p. 32. The difficulty in studying such groups is that relative powerlessness only becomes apparent under certain conditions. Extremely powerless groups not only lack political resources, but are also characterized by a minimal sense of political efficacy, upon which in part successful political organization depends. For reviews of the literature linking orientations of political efficacy to socioeconomic status, see Robert Lane, *Political Life* (New York, 1959), ch. 16; and Lester Milbrath, *Political Participation* (Chicago, 1965), ch. 5. Further, to the extent that group cohesion is recognized as a necessary requisite for organized political action, then extremely powerless groups, lacking cohesion, will not even appear for observation. Hence the necessity of selecting for intensive study a protest movement where there can be some confidence that observable processes and results can be analyzed. Thus, if one conceives of a continuum on which political groups are placed according to their relative command of resources, the focus of this essay is on those groups which are near, but not at, the pole of powerlessness.

using protest as a meaningful political instrument,[2] groups associated with the "war on poverty" have increasingly received publicity for protest activity. Saul Alinsky's Industrial Areas Foundation, for example, continues to receive invitations to help organize low income communities because of its ability to mobilize poor people around the tactic of protest.[3] The riots which dominated urban affairs in the summer of 1967 appear not to have diminished the dependence of some groups on protest as a mode of political activity.

This article provides a theoretical perspective on protest activity as a political resource. The discussion is concentrated on the limitations inherent in protest which occur because of the need of protest leaders to appeal to four constituencies at the same time. As the concept of protest is developed here, it will be argued that protest leaders must nurture and sustain an organization comprised of people with whom they may or may not share common values. They must articulate goals and choose strategies so as to maximize their public exposure through communications media. They must maximize the impact of third parties in the political conflict. Finally, they must try to maximize chances of success among those capable of granting goals. The tensions inherent in manipulating these four constituencies at the same time form the basis of this discussion of protest as a political process. It is intended to place aspects of the civil rights movement in a framework which suggests links between protest organizations and the general political processes in which such organizations operate.

I "Protest" Conceptualized

Protest activity as it has been adopted by elements of the civil rights movement and others has not been studied extensively by social scientists. Some of the most suggestive writings have been done as case studies of protest movements in single southern cities.[4] These works generally lack

[2] See, e.g., Bayard Rustin, "From Protest to Politics: The Future of the Civil Rights Movement," *Commentary* (February, 1965), 25–31; and Stokely Carmichael, "Toward Black Liberation," *The Massachusetts Review* (Autumn, 1966).

[3] On Alinsky's philosophy of community organization, see his *Reveille for Radicals* (Chicago, 1945); and Charles Silberman, *Crisis in Black and White* (New York, 1964), ch. 10.

[4] See, e.g., Jack L. Walker, "Protest and Negotiation: A Case Study of Negro Leadership in Atlanta, Georgia," *Midwest Journal of Political Science*, 7 (May, 1963), 99–124; Jack L. Walker, *Sit-Ins in Atlanta: A Study in the Negro Protest*, Eagleton Institute Case Studies, No. 34 (New York, 1964); John Ehle, *The Free Men* (New York, 1965) [Chapel Hill]; Daniel C. Thompson, *The Negro Leadership Class* (Englewood Cliffs, N.J., 1963) [New Orleans]; M. Elaine Burgess, *Negro Leadership in a Southern City* (Chapel Hill, N.C., 1962) [Durham].

a framework or theoretical focus which would encourage generalization from the cases. More systematic efforts have been attempted in approaching the dynamics of biracial committees in the South,[5] and comprehensively assessing the efficacy of Negro political involvement in Durham, N.C. and Philadelphia, Pa.[6] In their excellent assessment of Negro politics in the South, Matthews and Prothro have presented a thorough profile of Southern Negro students and their participation in civil rights activities.[7] Protest is also discussed in passing in recent explorations of the social-psychological dimensions of Negro ghetto politics [8] and the still highly suggestive, although pre-1960's, work on Negro political leadership by James Q. Wilson.[9] These and other less systematic works on contemporary Negro politics,[10] for all of their intuitive insights and valuable documentation, offer no theoretical formulations which encourage conceptualization about the interaction between recent Negro political activity and the political process.

Heretofore the best attempt to place Negro protest activity in a framework which would generate additional insights has been that of James Q. Wilson.[11] Wilson has suggested that protest activity be conceived as a problem of bargaining in which the basic problem is that Negro groups lack political resources to exchange. Wilson called this "the problem of the powerless." [12]

While many of Wilson's insights remain valid, his approach is limited in applicability because it defines protest in terms of mass action or response and as utilizing exclusively negative inducements in the bargaining process. Negative inducements are defined as inducements which are not absolutely preferred but are preferred over alternative possibil-

[5] Lewis Killian and Charles Grigg, *Racial Crisis in America: Leadership in Conflict* (Englewood Cliffs, N.J., 1964).

[6] William Keech, "The Negro Vote as a Political Resource: The Case of Durham" (unpublished Ph.D. Dissertation, University of Wisconsin, 1966); John H. Strange, "The Negro in Philadelphia Politics 1963–65" (unpublished Ph.D. Dissertation, Princeton University, 1966).

[7] Donald Matthews and James Prothro, *Negroes and the New Southern Politics* (New York, 1966). Considerable insight on these data is provided in John Orbell, "Protest Participation among Southern Negro College Students," [*American Political Science Review*], 61 (June, 1967), 446–456.

[8] Kenneth Clark, *Dark Ghetto* (New York, 1965).

[9] *Negro Politics* (New York, 1960).

[10] A complete list would be voluminous. See, e.g., Nat Hentoff, *The New Equality* (New York, 1964); Arthur Waskow, *From Race Riot to Sit-in* (New York, 1966).

[11] "The Strategy of Protest: Problems of Negro Civic Action," *Journal of Conflict Resolution*, 3 (September, 1961), 291–303. The reader will recognize the author's debt to this highly suggestive article, not least Wilson's recognition of the utility of the bargaining framework for examining protest activity.

[12] *Ibid.*, p. 291.

ities.[13] Yet it might be argued that protest designed to appeal to groups which oppose suffering and exploitation, for example, might be offering positive inducements in bargaining. A few Negro students sitting at a lunch counter might be engaged in what would be called protest, and by their actions might be trying to appeal to other groups in the system with positive inducements. Additionally, Wilson's concentration on Negro civic action, and his exclusive interest in exploring the protest process to explain Negro civic action, tend to obscure comparison with protest activity which does not necessarily arise within the Negro community.

Assuming a somewhat different focus, protest activity is defined as a mode of political action oriented toward objection to one or more policies or conditions, characterized by showmanship or display of an unconventional nature, and undertaken to obtain rewards from political or economic systems while working within the systems. The "problem of the powerless" in protest activity is to activate "third parties" to enter the implicit or explicit bargaining arena in ways favorable to the protesters. This is one of the few ways in which they can "create" bargaining resources. It is intuitively unconvincing to suggest that fifteen people sitting uninvited in the Mayor's office have the power to move City Hall. A better formulation would suggest that the people sitting in may be able to appeal to a wider public to which the city administration is sensitive. Thus in successful protest activity the *reference publics* of protest *targets* may be conceived as explicitly or implicitly reacting to protest in such a way that target groups or individuals respond in ways favorable to the protesters.[14]

It should be emphasized that the focus here is on protest by relatively powerless groups. Illustrations can be summoned, for example, of activity designated as "protest" involving high status pressure groups or hundreds of thousands of people. While such instances may share some of the characteristics of protest activity, they may not represent examples of developing political resources by relatively powerless groups because the protesting groups may already command political resources by virtue of status, numbers or cohesion.

[13] *Ibid.*, pp. 291–292.

[14] See E. E. Schattschneider's discussion of expanding the scope of the conflict, *The Semisovereign People* (New York, 1960). Another way in which bargaining resources may be "created" is to increase the relative cohesion of groups, or to increase the perception of group solidarity as a precondition to greater cohesion. This appears to be the primary goal of political activity which is generally designated "community organization." Negro activists appear to recognize the utility of this strategy in their advocacy of "black power." In some instances protest activity may be designed in part to accomplish this goal in addition to activating reference publics.

It is appropriate also to distinguish between the relatively restricted use of the concept of protest adopted here and closely related political strategies which are often designated as "protest" in popular usage. Where groups already possess sufficient resources with which to bargain, as in the case of some economic boycotts and labor strikes, they may be said to engage in "direct confrontation." [15] Similarly, protest which represents efforts to "activate reference publics" should be distinguished from "alliance formation," where third parties are induced to join the conflict, but where the value orientations of third parties are sufficiently similar to those of the protesting group that concerted or coordinated action is possible. Alliance formation is particularly desirable for relatively powerless groups if they seek to join the decision-making process as participants.

The distinction between activating reference publics and alliance formation is made on the assumption that where goal orientations among protest groups and the reference publics of target groups are similar, the political dynamics of petitioning target groups are different than when such goal orientations are relatively divergent. Clearly the more similar the goal orientations, the greater the likelihood of protest success, other things being equal. This discussion is intended to highlight, however, those instances where goal orientations of reference publics depart significantly, in direction or intensity, from the goals of protest groups.

Say that to protest some situation, A would like to enter a bargaining situation with B. But A has nothing B wants, and thus cannot bargain. A then attempts to create political resources by activating other groups to enter the conflict. A then organizes to take action against B with respect to certain goals. *Information concerning these goals must be conveyed through communications media* (C, D, and E) to F, G, and H, which are B's *reference publics*. In response to the reactions of F, G, and H, or in anticipation of their reactions, B responds, *in some way*, to the protesters' demands. This formulation requires the conceptualization of protest activity when undertaken to create bargaining resources as a political process which requires communication and is characterized by a multiplicity of constituencies for protest leadership.

A schematic representation of the process of protest as utilized by relatively powerless groups is presented in Figure 1. In contrast to a simplistic pressure group model which would posit a direct relationship between pressure group and pressured, the following discussion is guided by the assumption (derived from observation) that protest is a highly indirect process in which communications media and the reference publics

[15] For an example of "direct confrontation," one might study the three-month Negro boycott of white merchants in Natchez, Miss., which resulted in capitulation to boycott demands by city government leaders. See *The New York Times*, December 4, 1965, p. 1.

of protest targets play critical roles. It is also a process characterized by reciprocal relations, in which protest leaders frame strategies according to their perception of the needs of (many) other actors.

In this view protest constituents limit the options of protest leaders at the same time that the protest leader influences their perception of the strategies and rhetoric which they will support. Protest activity is filtered through the communications media in influencing the perceptions of the reference publics of protest targets. To the extent that the influence of reference publics is supportive of protest goals, target groups will dispense symbolic or material rewards. Material rewards are communicated directly to protest constituents. Symbolic rewards are communicated in part to protest constituents, but primarily are communicated to the reference publics of target groups, who provide the major stimuli for public policy pronouncements.

FIGURE 1. Schematic Representation of the Process of Protest by Relatively Powerless Groups

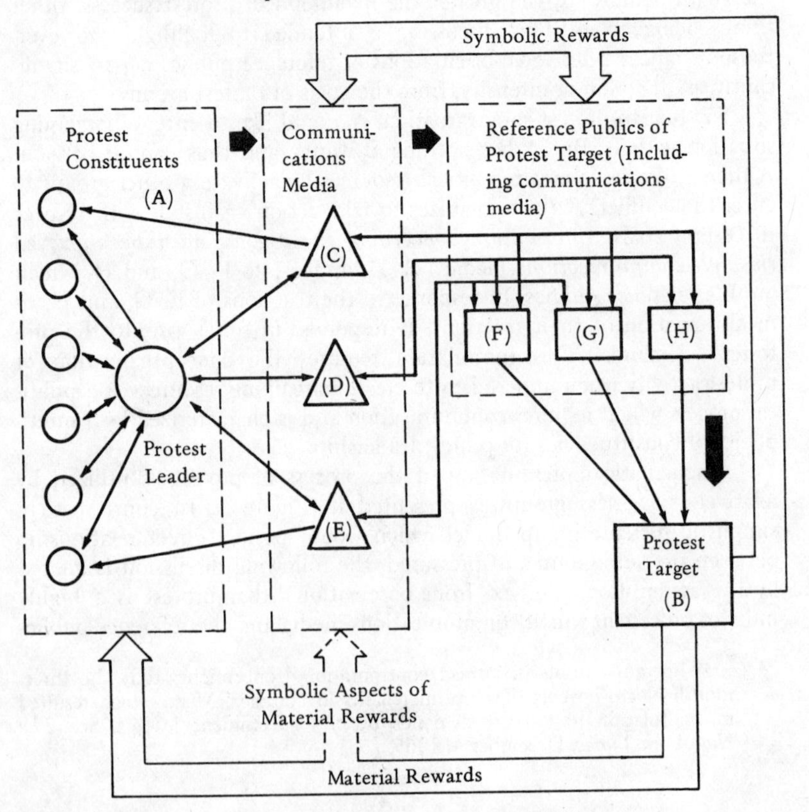

The study of protest as adopted by relatively powerless groups should provide insights into the structure and behavior of groups involved in civil rights politics and associated with the "war on poverty." It should direct attention toward the ways in which administrative agencies respond to "crises." Additionally, the study of protest as a political resource should influence some general conceptualizations of American political pluralism. Robert Dahl, for example, describes the "normal American political process" as

> one in which there is a high probability that an active and legitimate group in the population can make itself heard effectively at some crucial stage in the process of decision.[16]

Although he agrees that control over decisions is unevenly divided in the population, Dahl writes:

> When I say that a group is heard "effectively" I mean more than the simple fact that it makes a noise; I mean that one or more officials are not only ready to listen to the noise, but expect to suffer in some significant way if they do not placate the group, its leaders, or its most vociferous members. To satisfy the group may require one or more of a great variety of actions by the responsive leader: pressure for substantive policies, appointments, graft, respect, expression of the appropriate emotions, or the right combination of reciprocal noises.[17]

These statements, which in some ways resemble David Truman's discussion of the power of "potential groups," [18] can be illuminated by the study of protest activity in three ways. First, what are the probabilities that relatively powerless groups can make themselves heard effectively? In what ways will such groups be heard or "steadily appeased"? [19] Concentration on the process of protest activity may reveal the extent to which, and the conditions under which, relatively powerless groups are likely to prove effective. Protest undertaken to obstruct policy decisions, for example, may enjoy greater success probabilities than protest undertaken in an effort to evoke constructive policy innovations.[20]

Second, does it make sense to suggest that all groups which make noises will receive responses from public officials? Perhaps the groups

[16] A *Preface to Democratic Theory* (Chicago, 1956), pp. 145–146.
[17] *Ibid.*
[18] *The Governmental Process* (New York, 1951), p. 104.
[19] See Dahl, A *Preface to Democratic Theory*, p. 146.
[20] Observations that all groups can influence public policy at some stage of the political process are frequently made about the role of "veto groups" in American politics. See *ibid.*, pp. 104 ff. See also David Reisman, *The Lonely Crowd* (New Haven, 1950), pp. 211 ff., for an earlier discussion of veto-group politics. Yet protest should be evaluated when it is adopted to obtain assertive as well as defensive goals.

which make noises do not have to be satisfied at all, but it is other groups which receive assurances or recognition. Third, what are the probabilities that groups which make noises will receive tangible rewards, rather than symbolic assurances?[21] Dahl lumps these rewards together in the same paragraph, but dispensation of tangible rewards clearly has a different impact upon groups than the dispensation of symbolic rewards. Dahl is undoubtedly correct when he suggests that the relative fluidity of American politics is a critical characteristic of the American political system.[22] But he is less precise and less convincing when it comes to analyzing the extent to which the system is indeed responsive to the relatively powerless groups of the "average citizen."[23]

The following sections are an attempt to demonstrate the utility of the conceptualization of the protest process presented above. This will be done by exploring the problems encountered and the strains generated by protest leaders in interacting with four constituencies. It will be useful to concentrate attention on the maintenance and enhancement needs not only of the large formal organizations which dominate city politics,[24] but also of the ad hoc protest groups which engage them in civic controversy. It will also prove rewarding to examine the role requirements of individuals in leadership positions as they perceive the problems of constituency manipulation. In concluding remarks some implications of the study of protest for the pluralist description of American politics will be suggested.[25]

[21] See Murray Edelman, *The Symbolic Uses of Politics* (Urbana, Ill., 1964), ch. 2.

[22] See Dahl, *Who Governs?* (New Haven, 1961), pp. 305 ff.

[23] In a recent formulation, Dahl reiterates the theme of wide dispersion of influence. "More than other systems, [democracies] . . . try to disperse influence widely to their citizens by means of the suffrage, elections, freedom of speech, press, and assembly, the right of opponents to criticize the conduct of government, the right to organize political parties, and in other ways." *Pluralist Democracy in the United States* (Chicago, 1967), p. 373. Here, however, he concentrates more on the availability of options to all groups in the system, rather than on the relative probabilities that all groups in fact have access to the political process. See pp. 372 ff.

[24] See Edward Banfield, *Political Influence* (New York, 1961), p. 263. The analysis of organizational incentive structure which heavily influences Banfield's formulation is Chester Barnard, *The Functions of the Executive* (Cambridge, Mass., 1938).

[25] In the following attempt to develop the implications of this conceptualization of protest activity, I have drawn upon extensive field observations and bibliographical research. Undoubtedly, however, individual assertions, while representing my best judgment concerning the available evidence, in the future may require modification as the result of further empirical research.

II Protest Leadership and Organizational Base

The organizational maintenance needs of relatively powerless, low income, ad hoc protest groups center around the tension generated by the need for leadership to offer symbolic and intangible inducements to protest participation when immediate, material rewards cannot be anticipated, and the need to provide at least the promise of material rewards. Protest leaders must try to evoke responses from other actors in the political process, at the same time that they pay attention to participant organizational needs. Thus relatively deprived groups in the political system not only receive symbolic reassurance while material rewards from the system are withheld,[26] but protest leaders have a stake in perpetuating the notion that relatively powerless groups retain political efficacy despite what in many cases is obvious evidence to the contrary.

The tension embraced by protest leaders over the nature of inducements toward protest participation accounts in part for the style adopted and goals selected by protest leaders. Groups which seek psychological gratification from politics, but cannot or do not anticipate material political rewards, may be attracted to militant protest leaders. To these groups, angry rhetoric may prove a desirable quality in the short run. Where groups depend upon the political system for tangible benefits, or where participation in the system provides intangible benefits, moderate leadership is likely to prevail. Wilson has observed similar tendencies among Negro leaders of large, formal organizations.[27] It is no less true for leadership of protest groups. Groups whose members derive tangible satisfactions from political participation will not condone leaders who are stubborn in compromise or appear to question the foundations of the system. This coincides with Truman's observation:

> Violation of the "rules of the game" normally will weaken a group's cohesion, reduce its status in the community, and expose it to the claims of other groups.[28]

On the other hand, the cohesion of relatively powerless groups may be strengthened by militant, ideological leadership which questions the rules of the game and challenges their legitimacy.

Cohesion is particularly important when protest leaders bargain directly with target groups. In that situation, leaders' ability to control protest constituents and guarantee their behavior represents a bargaining

26 As Edelman suggests, cited previously.
27 *Negro Politics*, p. 290.
28 *The Governmental Process*, p. 513.

strength.[29] For this reason Wilson stressed the bargaining difficulties of Negro leaders who cannot guarantee constituent behavior, and pointed out the significance of the strategy of projecting the image of group solidarity when the reality of cohesion is a fiction.[30] Cohesion is less significant at other times. Divided leadership may prove productive by bargaining in tandem,[31] or by minimizing strain among groups in the protest process. Further, community divisions may prove less detrimental to protest aims when strong third parties have entered the dispute originally generated by protest organizations.

The intangible rewards of assuming certain postures toward the political system may not be sufficient to sustain an organizational base. It may be necessary to renew constantly the intangible rewards of participation. And to the extent that people participate in order to achieve tangible benefits, their interest in a protest organization may depend upon the organization's relative material success. Protest leaders may have to tailor their style to present participants with tangible successes, or with the appearance of success. Leaders may have to define the issues with concern for increasing their ability to sustain organizations. The potential for protest among protest group members may have to be manipulated by leadership if the group is to be sustained.[32]

The participants in protest organizations limit the flexibility of protest leadership. This obtains for two reasons. They restrict public actions by leaders who must continue to solicit active participant support, and they place restraints on thé kinds of activities which can be considered appropriate for protest purposes. Poor participants cannot commonly be

[29] But cf. Thomas Schelling's discussion of "blinding oneself," *The Strategy of Conflict* (Cambridge, Mass., 1960), pp. 22 ff.

[30] "The Strategy of Protest," p. 297.

[31] This is suggested by Wilson, "The Strategy of Protest," p. 298; St. Clair Drake and Horace Cayton, *Black Metropolis* (New York, 1962, rev. ed.), p. 731; Walker, "Protest and Negotiation," p. 122. Authors who argue that divided leadership is dysfunctional have been Clark, p. 156; and Tilman Cothran, "The Negro Protest Against Segregation in the South," *The Annals*, 357 (January, 1965), p. 72.

[32] This observation is confirmed by a student of the Southern civil rights movement:

> Negroes demand of protest leaders constant progress. The combination of long-standing discontent and a new-found belief in the possibility of change produces a constant state of tension and aggressiveness in the Negro community. But this discontent is vague and diffuse, not specific; the masses do not define the issues around which action shall revolve. This the leader must do.

Lewis Killian, "Leadership in the Desegregation Crises: An Institutional Analysis," in Muzafer Sherif (ed.), *Intergroup Relations and Leadership* (New York; 1962), p. 159.

asked to engage in protest requiring air transportation. Participants may have anxieties related to their environment or historical situation which discourages engagement in some activities. They may be afraid of job losses, beatings by the police, or summary evictions. Negro protest in the Deep South has been inhibited by realistic expectations of retribution.[33] Protests over slum housing conditions are undermined by tenants who expect landlord retaliation for engaging in tenant organizing activity.[34] Political or ethical mores may conflict with a proposed course of action, diminishing participation.[35]

On the other hand, to the extent that fears are real, or that the larger community perceives protest participants as subject to these fears, protest may actually be strengthened. Communications media and potential allies will consider more soberly the complaints of people who are understood to be placing themselves in jeopardy. When young children and their parents made the arduous bus trip from Mississippi to Washington, D.C., to protest the jeopardizing of Head Start funds, the courage and expense represented by their effort created a respect and visibility for their position which might not have been achieved by local protest efforts.[36]

Protest activity may be undertaken by organizations with established relationship patterns, behavior norms, and role expectations. These organizations are likely to have greater access to other groups in the political system, and a demonstrated capacity to maintain themselves. Other protest groups, however, may be ad hoc arrangements without demonstrated internal or external relationship patterns. These groups will have different organizational problems, in response to which it is necessary to engage in different kinds of protest activity.

The scarcity of organizational resources also places limits upon the ability of relatively powerless groups to maintain the foundations upon which protest organizations develop. Relatively powerless groups, to en-

[33] Significantly, southern Negro students who actively participated in the early phases of the sit-in movement "tended to be unusually optimistic about race relations and tolerant of whites [when compared with inactive Negro students]. They not only *were* better off, objectively speaking, than other Negroes but *felt* better off." Matthews and Prothro, *op. cit.*, p. 424.

[34] This is particularly the case in cities such as Washington, D.C., where landlord-tenant laws offer little protection against retaliatory eviction. See, e.g., Robert Schoshinski, "Remedies of the Indigent Tenant: Proposal for Change," *Georgetown Law Journal*, 54 (Winter, 1966), 541 ff.

[35] Wilson regarded this as a chief reason for lack of protest activity in 1961. He wrote: ". . . some of the goals now being sought by Negroes are least applicable to those groups of Negroes most suited to protest action. Protest action involving such tactics as mass meetings, picketing, boycotts, and strikes rarely find enthusiastic participants among upper-income and higher status individuals": "The Strategy of Protest," p. 296.

[36] See *The New York Times*, February 12, 1966, p. 56.

gage in political activity of any kind, must command at least some resources. This is not tautological. Referring again to a continuum on which political groups are placed according to their relative command of resources, one may draw a line somewhere along the continuum representing a "threshold of civic group political participation." Clearly some groups along the continuum will possess some political resources (enough, say, to emerge for inspection) but not enough to exercise influence in civic affairs. Relatively powerless groups, to be influential, must cross the "threshold" to engage in politics. Although the availability of group resources is a critical consideration at all stages of the protest process, it is particularly important in explaining why some groups seem to "surface" with sufficient strength to command attention. The following discussion of some critical organizational resources should illuminate this point.

Skilled professionals frequently must be available to protest organizations. Lawyers, for example, play extremely important roles in enabling protest groups to utilize the judicial process and avail themselves of adequate preparation of court cases. Organizational reputation may depend upon a combination of ability to threaten the conventional political system and of exercising statutory rights in court. Availability of lawyers depends upon ability to pay fees and/or the attractiveness to lawyers of participation in protest group activity. Volunteer professional assistance may not prove adequate. One night a week volunteered by an aspiring politician in a housing clinic cannot satisfy the needs of a chaotic political movement.[37] The need for skilled professionals is not restricted to lawyers. For example, a group seeking to protest an urban renewal policy might require the services of architects and city planners in order to present a viable alternative to a city proposal.

Financial resources not only purchase legal assistance, but enable relatively powerless groups to conduct minimum programs of political activities. To the extent that constituents are unable or unwilling to pay even small membership dues, then financing the cost of mimeographing flyers, purchasing supplies, maintaining telephone service, paying rent, and meeting a modest payroll become major organizational problems. And to the extent that group finances are supplied by outside individual contributions or government or foundation grants, the long-term options of the group are sharply constrained by the necessity of orienting group

[37] On housing clinic services provided by political clubs, see James Q. Wilson, *The Amateur Democrat: Club Politics in Three Cities* (Chicago, 1962), pp. 63–64, 176. On the need for lawyers among low income people, see e.g., *The Extension of Legal Services to the Poor,* Conference Proceedings (Washington, D.C., n.d.), esp. pp. 51–60; and "Neighborhood Law Offices: The New Wave in Legal Services for the Poor," *Harvard Law Review,* 80 (February, 1967), 805–850.

goals and tactics to anticipate the potential objections of financial supporters.

Some dependence upon even minimal financial resources can be waived if organizations evoke passionate support from constituents. Secretarial help and block organizers will come forward to work without compensation if they support the cause of neighborhood organizations or gain intangible benefits based upon association with the group. Protest organizations may also depend upon skilled non-professionals, such as college students, whose access to people and political and economic institutions often assist protest groups in cutting across income lines to seek support. Experience with ad hoc political groups, however, suggests that this assistance is sporadic and undependable. Transient assistance is particularly typical of skilled, educated, and employable volunteers whose abilities can be applied widely. The die-hards of ad hoc political groups are often those people who have no place else to go, nothing else to do.

Constituent support will be affected by the nature of the protest target and whether protest activity is directed toward defensive or assertive goals. Obstructing specific public policies may be easier than successfully recommending constructive policy changes. Orientations toward defensive goals may require less constituent energy, and less command over resources of money, expertise and status.[38]

III Protest Leadership and Communications Media

The communications media are extremely powerful in city politics. In granting or withholding publicity, in determining what information most people will have on most issues, and what alternatives they will consider in response to issues, the media truly, as Norton Long has put it, "set . . . the civic agenda."[39] To the extent that successful protest activity depends upon appealing to, and/or threatening, other groups in the community, the communications media set the limits of protest action. If protest tactics are not considered significant by the media, or if newspapers and television reporters or editors decide to overlook protest tactics, protest organizations will not succeed. Like the tree falling unheard in the forest, there is no protest unless protest is perceived and projected.

[38] An illustration of low income group protest organization mobilized for veto purposes is provided by Dahl in "The Case of the Metal Houses." See *Who Governs?*, pp. 192 ff.

[39] Norton Long, "The Local Community as an Ecology of Games," in Long, *The Polity*, Charles Press, ed. (Chicago, 1962), p. 153. See pp. 152–154. See also Roscoe C. Martin, Frank J. Munger, *et al.*, *Decisions in Syracuse: A Metropolitan Action Study* (Garden City, N.Y., 1965) (originally published: 1961), pp. 326–327.

A number of writers have noticed that the success of protest activity seems directly related to the amount of publicity it receives outside the immediate arena in which protest takes place. This view has not been stated systematically, but hints can be found in many sources. In the literature on civil rights politics, the relevance of publicity represents one of the few hypotheses available concerning the dynamics of successful protest activity.[40]

When protest tactics do receive coverage in the communications media, the way in which they are presented will influence all other actors in the system, including the protesters themselves. Conformity to standards of newsworthiness in political style, and knowledge of the prejudices and desires of the individuals who determine media coverage in political skills, represent crucial determinants of leadership effectiveness.

The organizational behavior of newspapers can partly be understood by examining the maintenance and enhancement needs which direct them toward projects of civic betterment and impressions of accomplishment.[41] But insight may also be gained by analyzing the role requirements of reporters, editors, and others who determine newspaper policy. Reporters, for example, are frequently motivated by the desire to contribute to civic affairs by their "objective" reporting of significant events; by the premium they place on accuracy; and by the credit which they receive for sensationalism and "scoops."

These requirements may be difficult to accommodate at the same time. Reporters demand newsworthiness of their subjects in the short run, but also require reliability and verifiability in the longer run. Factual accuracy may dampen newsworthiness. Sensationalism, attractive to some newspaper editors, may be inconsistent with reliable, verifiable narration of events. Newspapers at first may be attracted to sensationalism, and later demand verifiability in the interests of community harmony (and adherence to professional journalistic standards).

Most big city newspapers have reporters whose assignments permit them to cover aspects of city politics with some regularity. These reporters, whose "beats" may consist of "civil rights" or "poverty," sometimes develop close relationships with their news subjects. These relationships may develop symbiotic overtones because of the mutuality of interest between the reporter and the news subject. Reporters require

[40] See, e.g., Thompson, *op. cit.*, p. 134, and *passim;* Martin Oppenheimer, "The Southern Student Movement: Year I," *Journal of Negro Education*, 33 (Fall, 1964), p. 397; Cothran, *op. cit.*, p. 72; Pauli Murray, "Protest Against the Legal Status of the Negro," *The Annals*, 357 (January, 1965), p. 63; Allan P. Sindler, "Protest Against the Political Status of the Negroes," *The Annals*, 357 (January, 1965), p. 50.

[41] See Banfield, *op. cit.*, p. 275.

fresh information on protest developments, while protest leaders have a vital interest in obtaining as much press coverage as possible.

Inflated reports of protest success may be understood in part by examining this relationship between reporter and protest leader. Both have role-oriented interests in projecting images of protest strength and threat. In circumstances of great excitement, when competition from other news media representatives is high, a reporter may find that he is less governed by the role requirement of verification and reliability than he is by his editor's demand for "scoops" and news with high audience appeal.[42]

On the other hand, the demands of the media may conflict with the needs of protest group maintenance. Consider the leader whose constituents are attracted solely by pragmatic statements not exceeding what they consider political "good taste." He is constrained from making militant demands which would isolate him from constituents. This constraint may cost him appeal in the press.[43] However, the leader whose organizing appeal requires militant rhetoric may obtain eager press coverage only to find that his inflammatory statements lead to alienation of potential allies and exclusion from the explicit bargaining process.[44]

News media do not report events in the same way. Television may select for broadcast only thirty seconds of a half-hour news conference. This coverage will probably focus on immediate events, without background or explanatory material. Newspapers may give more complete

[42] For a case study of the interaction between protest leaders and newspaper reporters, see Michael Lipsky, "Rent Strikes in New York City: Protest Politics and the Power of the Poor" (unpublished Ph.D. dissertation, Princeton University, 1967), pp. 139–49. Bernard Cohen has analyzed the impact of the press on foreign policy from the perspective of reporters' role requirements: see his *The Press and Foreign Policy* (Princeton, N.J., 1963), esp. chs. 2–3.

[43] An example of a protest conducted by middle-class women engaged in pragmatic protest over salvaging park space is provided in John B. Keeley, *Moses on the Green*, Inter-University Case Program, No. 45 (University, Ala., 1959).

[44] This was the complaint of Floyd McKissick, National Director of the Congress of Racial Equality, when he charged that ". . . there are only two kinds of statements a black man can make and expect that the white press will report. . . . First . . . is an attack on another black man. . . . The second is a statement that sounds radical, violent, extreme – the verbal equivalent of a riot. . . . [T]he Negro is being rewarded by the public media only if he turns on another Negro and uses his tongue as a switchblade, or only if he sounds outlandish, extremist or psychotic." Statement at the Convention of the American Society of Newspaper Editors, April 20, 1967, Washington, D.C., as reported in *The New York Times*, April 21, 1967, p. 22. See also the remarks of journalist Ted Poston, *ibid.*, April 26, 1965, p. 26.

accounts of the same event. The most complete account may appear in the weekly edition of a neighborhood or ethnic newspaper. Differential coverage by news media, and differential news media habits in the general population,[45] are significant factors in permitting protest leaders to juggle conflicting demands of groups in the protest process.

Similar tensions exist in the leader's relationships with protest targets. Ideological postures may gain press coverage and constituency approval, but may alienate target groups with whom it would be desirable to bargain explicitly. Exclusion from the councils of decision-making may have important consequences, since the results of target group deliberations may satisfy activated reference publics without responding to protest goals. If activated reference publics are required to increase the bargaining position of the protest group, protest efforts thereafter will have diminished chances of success.

IV Protest Leadership and "Third Parties"

I have argued that the essence of political protest consists of activating third parties to participate in controversy in ways favorable to protest goals. In previous sections I have attempted to analyze some of the tensions which result from protest leaders' attempts to activate reference publics of protest targets at the same time that they must retain the interest and support of protest organization participants. This phenomenon is in evidence when Negro leaders, recognized as such by public officials, find their support eroded in the Negro community because they have engaged in explicit bargaining situations with politicians. Negro leaders are thus faced with the dilemma that when they behave like other ethnic group representatives they are faced with loss of support from those whose intense activism has been aroused in the Negro community, yet whose support is vital if they are to remain credible as leaders to public officials.

The tensions resulting from conflicting maintenance needs of protest organizations and activated third parties present difficulties for protest leaders. One way in which these tensions can be minimized is by dividing leadership responsibilities. If more than one group is engaged in protest activity, protest leaders can, in effect, divide up public roles so as to reduce as much as possible the gap between the implicit demands of different groups for appropriate rhetoric, and what in fact is said. Thus divided

[45] Matthews and Prothro found, for example, that in their south-wide Negro population sample, 38 per cent read Negro-oriented magazines and 17 per cent read newspapers written for Negroes. These media treat news of interest to Negroes more completely and sympathetically than do the general media. See pp. 248 ff.

leadership may perform the latent function of minimizing tensions among elements in the protest process by permitting different groups to listen selectively to protest spokesmen.[46]

Another way in which strain among different groups can be minimized is through successful public relations. Minimization of strain may depend upon ambiguity of action or statement, deception, or upon effective inter-group communication. Failure to clarify meaning, or falsification, may increase protest effectiveness. Effective intragroup communication may increase the likelihood that protest constituents will "understand" that ambiguous or false public statements have "special meaning" and need not be taken seriously. The Machiavellian circle is complete when we observe that although lying may be prudent, the appearance of integrity and forthrightness is desirable for public relations, since these values are widely shared.

It has been observed that "[t]he militant displays an unwillingness to perform those administrative tasks which are necessary to operate an organization. Probably the skills of the agitator and the skills of the administrator . . . are not incompatible, but few men can do both well." [47] These skills may or may not be incompatible as personality traits, but they indeed represent conflicting role demands on protest leadership. When a protest leader exhausts time and energy conducting frequent press conferences, arranging for politicians and celebrities to appear at rallies, delivering speeches to sympathetic local groups, college symposia and other forums, constantly picketing for publicity and generally making "contacts," he is unable to pursue the direction of office routine, clerical tasks, research and analysis, and other chores.

The difficulties of delegating routine tasks are probably directly related to the skill levels and previous administrative experiences of group members. In addition, to the extent that involvement in protest organizations is a function of rewards received or expected by individuals because of the excitement or entertainment value of participation, then the difficulties of delegating routine, relatively uninteresting chores to group members will be increased. Yet attention to such details affects the perception of protest groups by organizations whose support or assistance may be desired in the future. These considerations add to the protest leader's problem of risking alienation of protest participants because of potentially unpopular cooperation with the "power structure."

In the protest paradigm developed here, "third parties" refers both to the reference publics of target groups and, more narrowly, to the inter-

[46] See footnote 31 above.
[47] Wilson, *Negro Politics*, p. 225.

est groups whose regular interaction with protest targets tends to develop into patterns of influence.[48] We have already discussed some of the problems associated with activating the reference publics of target groups. In discussing the constraints placed upon protest, attention may be focused upon the likelihood that groups seeking to create political resources through protest will be included in the explicit bargaining process with other pressure groups. For protest groups, these constraints are those which occur because of class and political style, status, and organizational resources.

The established civic groups most likely to be concerned with the problems raised by relatively powerless groups are those devoted to service in the public welfare and those "liberally" oriented groups whose potential constituents are either drawn from the same class as the protest groups (such as some trade unions), or whose potential constituents are attracted to policies which appear to serve the interest of the lower class or minority groups (such as some reform political clubs).[49] These civic groups have frequently cultivated clientele relationships with city agencies over long periods. Their efforts have been reciprocated by agency officials anxious to develop constituencies to support and defend agency administrative and budgetary policies. In addition, clientele groups are expected to endorse and legitimize agency aggrandizement. These relationships have been developed by agency officials and civic groups for mutual benefit, and cannot be destroyed, abridged or avoided without cost.

Protest groups may well be able to raise the saliency of issues on the civic agenda through utilization of communications media and successful appeals or threats to wider publics, but admission to policy-making councils is frequently barred because of the angry, militant rhetorical style adopted by protest leaders. People in power do not like to sit down with rogues. Protest leaders are likely to have phrased demands in ways unacceptable to lawyers and other civic activists whose cautious attitude toward public policy may reflect not only their good intentions but their concern for property rights, due process, pragmatic legislating or judicial precedent.

Relatively powerless groups lack participation of individuals with high status whose endorsement of specific proposals lend them increased legitimacy. Good causes may always attract the support of high status individuals. But such individuals' willingness to devote time to the promotion of

[48] See Wallace Sayre and Herbert Kaufman, *Governing New York City* (New York, 1960), pp. 257 ff. Also see Banfield, *op. cit.*, p. 267.

[49] See Wilson, *The Amateur Democrats*, previously cited. These groups are most likely to be characterized by broad scope of political interest and frequent intervention in politics. See Sayre and Kaufman, *op. cit.*, p. 79.

specific proposals is less likely than the one-shot endorsements which these people distribute more readily.

Similarly, protest organizations often lack the resources on which entry into the policy-making process depends. These resources include maintenance of a staff with expertise and experience in the policy area. This expertise may be in the areas of the law, planning and architecture, proposal writing, accounting, educational policy, federal grantsmanship or publicity. Combining experience with expertise is one way to create status in issue areas. The dispensing of information by interest groups has been widely noted as a major source of influence. Over time the experts develop status in their areas of competence somewhat independent of the influence which adheres to them as information-providers. Groups which cannot or do not engage lawyers to assist in proposing legislation, and do not engage in collecting reliable data, cannot participate in policy deliberations or consult in these matters. Protest oriented groups, whose primary talents are in dramatizing issues, cannot credibly attempt to present data considered "objective" or suggestions considered "responsible" by public officials. Few can be convincing as both advocate and arbiter at the same time.

V Protest Leadership and Target Groups

The probability of protest success may be approached by examining the maintenance needs of organizations likely to be designated as target groups.[50] For the sake of clarity, and because protest activity increasingly is directed toward government, I shall refer in the following paragraphs exclusively to government agencies at the municipal level. The assumption is retained, however, that the following generalizations are applicable to other potential target groups.

Some of the constraints placed on protest leadership in influencing target groups have already been mentioned in preceding sections. The lack of status and resources that inhibit protest groups from participating

[50] Another approach, persuasively presented by Wilson, concentrates on protest success as a function of the relative unity and vulnerability of targets. See "The Strategy of Protest," pp. 293 ff. This insight helps explain, for example, why protest against housing segregation commonly takes the form of action directed against government (a unified target) rather than against individual homeowners (who present a dispersed target). One problem with this approach is that it tends to obscure the possibility that targets, as collections of individuals, may be divided in evaluation of and sympathy for protest demands. Indeed, city agency administrators under some circumstances act as partisans in protest conflicts. As such, they frequently appear ambivalent toward protest goals: sympathetic to the ends while concerned that the means employed in protest reflect negatively on their agencies.

in policy-making conferences, for example, also helps prevent explicit bargaining between protest leaders and city officials. The strain between rhetoric which appeals to protest participants and public statements to which communications media and "third parties" respond favorably also exists with reference to target groups.

Yet there is a distinguishing feature of the maintenance needs and strategies of city agencies which specifically constrains protest organizations. This is the agency director's need to protect "the jurisdiction and income of his organization [by] . . . [m]anipulation of the external environment." [51] In so doing he may satisfy his reference groups without responding to protest group demands. At least six tactics are available to protest targets who are motivated to respond in some way to protest activity but seek primarily to satisfy their reference publics. These tactics may be employed whether or not target groups are "sincere" in responding to protest demands.

1. Target groups may dispense symbolic satisfactions. Appearances of activity, and commitment to problems substitute for, or supplement, resource allocation and policy innovations which would constitute tangible responses to protest activity. If symbolic responses supplement tangible pay-offs, they are frequently coincidental, rather than intimately linked, to projection of response by protest targets. Typical in city politics of the symbolic response is the ribbon cutting, street corner ceremony or the walking tour press conference. These occasions are utilized not only to build agency constituencies,[52] but to satisfy agency reference publics that attention is being directed to problems of civic concern. In this sense publicist tactics may be seen as defensive maneuvers. Symbolic aspects of the actions of public officials can also be recognized in the commissioning of expensive studies and the rhetorical flourishes with which "massive attacks," "comprehensive programs" and "coordinated planning" are frequently promoted.

City agencies establish distinct apparatus and procedures for dealing with crises which may be provoked by protest groups. Housing-related departments in New York City may be cited for illustration. It is usually the case in these agencies that the Commissioner or a chief deputy, a press secretary and one or two other officials devote whatever time is necessary to collect information, determine policy and respond quickly to reports of "crises." This is functional for tenants, who, if they can generate enough concern, may be able to obtain shortcuts through lengthy agency procedures. It is also functional for officials who want to project images of action rather than merely receiving complaints. Concentrating

[51] Sayre and Kaufman, *op. cit.*, p. 253.
[52] See *ibid.*, pp. 253 ff.

attention on the maintenance needs of city politicians during protest crises suggests that pronouncements of public officials serve purposes independent of their dedication to alleviation of slum conditions.[53]

Independent of dispensation of tangible benefits to protest groups, public officials continue to respond primarily to their own reference publics. Murray Edelman has suggested that:

> Tangible resources and benefits are frequently not distributed to unorganized political group interests as promised in regulatory statutes and the propaganda attending their enactment.[54]

His analysis may be supplemented by suggesting that symbolic dispensations may not only serve to reassure unorganized political group interests, but may also contribute to reducing the anxiety level of organized interests and wider publics which are only tangentially involved in the issues.

2. Target groups may dispense token material satisfactions. When city agencies respond, with much publicity, to cases brought to their attention representing examples of the needs dramatized by protest organizations, they may appear to respond to protest demands while in fact only responding on a case basis, instead of a general basis. For the protesters served by agencies in this fashion it is of considerable advantage that agencies can be influenced by protest action. Yet it should not be ignored that in handling the "crisis" cases, public officials give the appearance of response to their reference publics, while mitigating demands for an expensive, complex *general* assault on problems represented by the cases to which responses are given. Token responses, whether or not accompanied by more general responses, are particularly attractive to reporters and television news directors, who are able to dramatize individual cases convincingly, but who may be unable to "capture" the essence of general deprivation or of general efforts to alleviate conditions of deprivation.

3. Target groups may organize and innovate internally in order to blunt the impetus of protest efforts. This tactic is closely related to No. 2 (above). If target groups can act constructively in the worst cases, they will then be able to pre-empt protest efforts by responding to the cases which best dramatize protest demands. Alternatively, they may designate all efforts which jeopardize agency reputations as "worst" cases, and devote extensive resources to these cases. In some ways extraordinary city efforts are precisely consistent with protest goals. At the same time extraor-

[53] See Lipsky, *op. cit.*, chs. 5–6. The appearance of responsiveness may be given by city officials *in anticipation* of protest activity. This seems to have been the strategy of Mayor Richard Daley in his reaction to the announcement of Martin Luther King's plans to focus civil rights efforts on Chicago. See *The New York Times,* February 1, 1966, p. 11.

[54] See Edelman, *op. cit.*, p. 23.

dinary efforts in the most heavily dramatized cases or the most extreme cases effectively wear down the "cutting-edges" of protest efforts.

Many New York City agencies develop informal "crisis" arrangements not only to project publicity, as previously indicated, but to mobilize energies toward solving "crisis" cases. They may also develop policy innovations which allow them to respond more quickly to "crisis" situations. These innovations may be important to some city residents, for whom the problems of dealing with city bureaucracies can prove insurmountable. It might be said, indeed, that the goals of protest are to influence city agencies to handle every case with the same resources that characterize their dispatch of "crisis" cases.[55]

But such policies would demand major revenue inputs. This kind of qualitative policy change is difficult to achieve. Meanwhile, internal reallocation of resources only means that routine services must be neglected so that the "crisis" programs can be enhanced. If all cases are expedited, as in a typical "crisis" response, then none can be. Thus for purposes of general solutions, "crisis" resolving can be self-defeating unless accompanied by significantly greater resource allocation. It is not self-defeating, however, to the extent that the organizational goals of city agencies are to serve a clientele while minimizing negative publicity concerning agency vigilance and responsiveness.

4. Target groups may appear to be constrained in their ability to grant protest goals.[56] This may be directed toward making the protesters appear to be unreasonable in their demands, or to be well-meaning individuals who "just don't understand how complex running a city really is." Target groups may extend sympathy but claim that they lack resources, a mandate from constituents, and/or authority to respond to protest demands. Target groups may also evade protest demands by arguing that "If-I-give-it-to-you-I-have-to-give-it-to-everyone."

The tactic of appearing constrained is particularly effective with established civic groups because there is an undeniable element of truth to it. Everyone knows that cities are financially undernourished. Established civic groups expend great energies lobbying for higher levels of funding for their pet city agencies. Thus they recognize the validity of this constraint when posed by city officials. But it is not inconsistent to point out that funds for specific, relatively inexpensive programs, or for the expansion of existing programs, can often be found if pressure is increased. While constraints on city government flexibility may be extensive, they

[55] See Lipsky, *op. cit.*, pp. 156, 249 ff.

[56] On the strategy of appearing constrained, see Schelling, *op. cit.*, pp. 22 ff.

are not absolute. Protest targets nonetheless attempt to diminish the impact of protest demands by claiming relative impotence.

5. Target groups may use their extensive resources to discredit protest leaders and organizations. Utilizing their excellent access to the press, public officials may state or imply that leaders are unreliable, ineffective as leaders ("they don't really have the people behind them"), guilty of criminal behavior, potentially guilty of such behavior, or are some shade of "left-wing." Any of these allegations may serve to diminish the appeal of protest groups to potentially sympathetic third parties. City officials, in their frequent social and informal business interaction with leaders of established civic groups, may also communicate derogatory information concerning protest groups. Discrediting of protest groups may be undertaken by some city officials while others appear (perhaps authentically) to remain sympathetic to protest demands. These tactics may be engaged in by public officials whether or not there is any validity to the allegations.

6. Target groups may postpone action. The effect of postponement, if accompanied by symbolic assurances, is to remove immediate pressure and delay specific commitments to a future date. This familiar tactic is particularly effective in dealing with protest groups because of their inherent instability. Protest groups are usually comprised of individuals whose intense political activity cannot be sustained except in rare circumstances. Further, to the extent that protest depends upon activating reference publics through strategies which have some "shock" value, it becomes increasingly difficult to activate these groups. Additionally, protest activity is inherently unstable because of the strains placed upon protest leaders who must attempt to manage four constituencies (as described herein).

The most frequent method of postponing action is to commit a subject to "study." For the many reasons elaborated in these paragraphs, it is not likely that ad hoc protest groups will be around to review the recommendations which emerge from study. The greater the expertise and the greater the status of the group making the study, the less will protest groups be able to influence whatever policy emerges. Protest groups lack the skills and resource personnel to challenge expert recommendations effectively.

Sometimes surveys and special research are undertaken in part to evade immediate pressures. Sometimes not. Research efforts are particularly necessary to secure the support of established civic groups, which place high priority on orderly procedure and policy emerging from independent analysis. Yet it must be recognized that postponing policy commitments has a distinct impact on the nature of the pressures focused on policy-makers.

VI Conclusion

In this analysis I have agreed with James Q. Wilson that protest is correctly conceived as a strategy utilized by relatively powerless groups in order to increase their bargaining ability. As such, I have argued, it is successful to the extent that the reference publics of protest targets can be activated to enter the conflict in ways favorable to protest goals. I have suggested a model of the protest process which may assist in ordering data and indicating the salience for research of a number of aspects of protest. These include the critical role of communications media, the differential impact of material and symbolic rewards on "feedback" in protest activity, and the reciprocal relationships of actors in the protest process.

An estimation of the limits to protest efficacy, I have argued further, can be gained by recognizing the problems encountered by protest leaders who somehow must balance the conflicting maintenance needs of four groups in the protest process. This approach transcends a focus devoted primarily to characterization of group goals and targets, by suggesting that even in an environment which is relatively favorable to specific protest goals, the tensions which must be embraced by protest leadership may ultimately overwhelm protest activity.

At the outset of this essay, it was held that conceptualizing the American political system as "slack" or "fluid," in the manner of Robert Dahl, appears inadequate because of (1) a vagueness centering on the likelihood that any group can make itself heard; (2) a possible confusion as to which groups tend to receive satisfaction from the rewards dispensed by public officials; and (3) a lumping together as equally relevant rewards which are tangible and those which are symbolic. To the extent that protest is engaged in by relatively powerless groups which must create resources with which to bargain, the analysis here suggests a number of reservations concerning the pluralist conceptualization of the "fluidity" of the American political system.

Relatively powerless groups cannot use protest with a high probability of success. They lack organizational resources, by definition. But even to create bargaining resources through activating third parties, some resources are necessary to sustain organization. More importantly, relatively powerless protest groups are constrained by the unresolvable conflicts which are forced upon protest leaders who must appeal simultaneously to four constituencies which place upon them antithetical demands.

When public officials recognize the legitimacy of protest activity, they may not direct public policy toward protest groups at all. Rather, public officials are likely to aim responses at the reference publics from which they originally take their cues. Edelman has suggested that regulatory policy in practice often consists of reassuring mass publics while at the same time dispensing specific, tangible values to narrow interest groups. It is suggested here that symbolic reassurances are dispensed as much to wide, potentially concerned publics which are not directly affected by regulatory policy, as they are to wide publics comprised of the down-trodden and the deprived, in whose name policy is often written.

Complementing Edelman, it is proposed here that in the process of protest symbolic reassurances are dispensed in large measure because these are the public policy outcomes and actions desired by the constituencies to which public officials are most responsive. Satisfying these wider publics, city officials can avoid pressures toward other policies placed upon them by protest organizations.

Not only should there be some doubt as to which groups receive the symbolic recognitions which Dahl describes, but in failing to distinguish between the kinds of rewards dispensed to groups in the political system, Dahl avoids a fundamental question. It is literally fundamental because the kinds of rewards which can be obtained from politics, one might hypothesize, will have an impact upon the realistic appraisal of the efficacy of political activity. If among the groups least capable of organizing for political activity there is a history of organizing for protest, and if that activity, once engaged in, is rewarded primarily by the dispensation of symbolic gestures without perceptible changes in material conditions, then rational behavior might lead to expressions of apathy and lack of interest in politics or a rejection of conventional political channels as a meaningful arena of activity. In this sense this discussion of protest politics is consistent with Kenneth Clark's observations that the image of power, unaccompanied by material and observable rewards, leads to impressions of helplessness and reinforces political apathy in the ghetto.[57]

Recent commentary by political scientists and others regarding riots in American cities seems to focus in part on the extent to which relatively deprived groups may seek redress of legitimate grievances. Future research should continue assessment of the relationship between riots and the conditions under which access to the political system has been limited. In such research assessment of the ways in which access to public officials is obtained by relatively powerless groups through the protest process might be one important research focus.

The instability of protest activity outlined in this article also should inform contemporary political strategies. If the arguments presented here are persuasive, civil rights leaders who insist that protest activity is a shallow foundation on which to seek long-term, concrete gains may be judged essentially correct. But the arguments concerning the fickleness of the white liberal, or the ease of changing discriminatory laws relative to

[57] Clark, *op. cit.*, pp. 154 ff.

changing discriminatory institutions, only in part explain the instability of protest movements. An explanation which derives its strength from analysis of the political process suggests concentration on the problems of managing protest constituencies. Accordingly, Alinsky is probably on the soundest ground when he prescribes protest for the purpose of building organization. Ultimately, relatively powerless groups in most instances cannot depend upon activating other actors in the political process. Long-run success will depend upon the acquisition of stable political resources which do not rely for their use on third parties.

PUBLIC-REGARDINGNESS AS A VALUE PREMISE IN VOTING BEHAVIOR

JAMES Q. WILSON
EDWARD C. BANFIELD

Our concern here is with the nature of the individual's attachment to the body politic and, more particularly, with the value premises underlying the choices made by certain classes of voters. Our hypothesis is that some classes of voters (provisionally defined as "subcultures" constituted on ethnic and income lines) are more disposed than others to rest their choices on some conception of "the public interest" or the "welfare of the community." To say the same thing in another way, the voting behavior of some classes tends to be more public-regarding and less private-(self- or family-) regarding than that of others. To test this hypothesis it

Reprinted by permission from James Q. Wilson and Edward C. Banfield, "Public-Regardingness as a Value Premise in Voting Behavior," *American Political Science Review*, 58 (December, 1964), 876–887.

This is a preliminary report of a study supported by the Joint Center for Urban Studies of M.I.T. and Harvard University and the Rockefeller Foundation. The writers wish to acknowledge assistance from Martha Derthick and Mark K. Adams and comments from James Beshers, Anthony Downs, Werner Hirsch, Hendrik Houthakker, H. Douglas Price, and Arthur Stinchcombe. This paper was originally presented at the Second Conference On Urban Public Expenditures, New York University, February 21–22, 1964.

is necessary to examine voting behavior in situations where one can say that a certain vote could not have been private-regarding. Local bond and other expenditure referenda present such situations: it is sometimes possible to say that a vote in favor of a particular expenditure proposal is incompatible with a certain voter's self-interest narrowly conceived. If the voter nevertheless casts such a vote and if there is evidence that his vote was not in some sense irrational or accidental, then it must be presumed that his action was based on some conception of "the public interest."

Our first step, accordingly, is to show how much of the behavior in question can, and cannot, be explained on grounds of self-interest alone, narrowly conceived. If all of the data were consistent with the hypothesis that the voter acts as if he were trying to maximize his family income, the inquiry would end right there. In fact, it turns out that many of the data cannot be explained in this way. The question arises, therefore, whether the unexplained residue is purposive or "accidental." We suggest that for the most part it is purposive, and that the voters' purposes arise from their conceptions of "the public interest."

I

We start, then, from the simple – and admittedly implausible – hypothesis that the voter tries to maximize his family income or (the same thing) self-interest narrowly conceived. We assume that the voter estimates in dollars both the benefits that will accrue to him and his family if the proposed public expenditure is made and the amount of the tax that will fall on him in consequence of the expenditure; if the estimated benefit is more than the estimated cost, he votes for the expenditure; if it is less, he votes against it. We assume that all proposed expenditures will confer some benefits on all voters. The benefits conferred on a particular voter are "trivial," however, if the expenditure is for something that the particular voter (and his family) is not likely to use or enjoy. For example, improvement of sidewalks confers trivial benefits on those voters who are not likely to walk on them.

Insofar as behavior is consistent with these assumptions – *i.e.*, insofar as the voter seems to act rationally in pursuit of self-interest narrowly conceived – we consider that no further "explanation" is required. It may be that other, entirely different hypotheses would account for the behavior just as well or better. That possibility is not of concern to us here, however.

No doubt, our assumptions lack realism. No doubt, relatively few voters make a conscious calculation of costs and benefits. Very often the voter has no way of knowing whether a public expenditure proposal will benefit him or not. In only one state which we have examined (Florida) do ballots in municipal referenda specify precisely *which* streets are to be paved or *where* a bridge is to be built. Even if a facility is to serve the whole city (*e.g.*, a zoo, civic center, or county hospital), in most cities the ballot proposition is usually so indefinite that the voter cannot accurately judge either the nature or the amount of the benefits that he would derive from the expenditure. Similarly, it is often difficult or impossible for the voter to estimate even the approximate amount of the tax that will fall upon him in consequence of the expenditure. Some states (*e.g.*, Illinois and California) require that the anticipated cost of each undertaking be listed on the ballot (*e.g.*, "$12,800,000 for sewer improvements"). Of course, even when the total cost is given, the voter must depend on the newspapers to tell, or figure out for himself – if he can – how much it would increase the tax rate and how much the increased tax rate would add to his tax bill. Ohio is the only state we have studied where the voter is told on the ballot how the proposed expenditure will affect the tax rate ("17 cents per $100 valuation for each of two years"). Almost everywhere, most of the expenditure proposals are to be financed from the local property tax. Occasionally, however, a different tax (*e.g.*, the sales tax) or a different tax base (*e.g.*, the county or state rather than the city), is used. In these cases, the voter is likely to find it even harder to estimate how much he will have to pay.

We may be unrealistic also both in assuming that the voter takes only *money* costs into account (actually he may think that a proposed civic center would be an eyesore) and in assuming that the only money costs he takes into account are *taxes* levied upon him (actually, if he is a renter he may suppose – whether correctly or incorrectly is beside the point – that his landlord will pass a tax increase on to him in a higher rent).

The realism of the assumptions does not really matter. What does matter is their usefulness in predicting the voters' behavior. It is possible that voters may act *as if* they are well informed and disposed to calculate even when in fact they are neither. If we can predict their behavior without going into the question of how much or how well they calculate, so much the better.

II

On the assumptions we have made, one would expect voters who will have no tax levied upon them in consequence of the passage of an expenditure proposal to vote for it even if it will confer only trivial bene-

TABLE 1. *Relationship between Percentage of Ward Voting "Yes" and Percentage of Dwelling Units Owner Occupied; Various Issues in Cleveland and Chicago*

Issue and Date	Simple Correlation Coefficient (r)
Cleveland (33 wards):	
Administration Building (11/59)	−0.86
County Hospital (11/59)	−0.77
Tuberculosis Hospital (11/59)	−0.79
Court House (11/59)	−0.85
Juvenile Court (11/59)	−0.83
Parks (11/59)	−0.67
Welfare Levy (5/60)	−0.72
Roads and Bridges (11/60)	−0.77
Zoo (11/60)	−0.81
Parks (11/60)	−0.57
Chicago (50 wards):	
County Hospital (1957)	−0.79
Veterans' Bonus (1957)	−0.49
Welfare Building (1958)	−0.67
Street Lights (1959)	−0.83
Municipal Building (1962)	−0.78
Urban Renewal Bonds (1962)	−0.79
Sewers (1962)	−0.79
Street Lights (1962)	−0.81

fits on them. Having nothing to lose by the expenditure and something (however small) to gain, they will favor it. In the *very* low-income [1] wards and precincts of the larger cities a high proportion of the voters are in this position since most local public expenditures are financed from the property tax and the lowest-income people do not own property. We find that in these heavily non-home-owning districts the voters almost invariably support all expenditure proposals. We have examined returns on 35 expenditure proposals passed upon in 20 separate elections in seven cities and have not found a single instance in which this group failed to give a majority in favor of a proposal. Frequently the vote is

[1] Median family income under $3,000 per year. Needless to say, most voters in this category are Negroes.

75 to 80 per cent in favor; sometimes it is over 90 per cent. The strength of voter support is about the same no matter what the character of the proposed expenditure.[2]

In all of the elections we have examined, non-homeowners show more taste for public expenditures that are to be financed from property taxes than do homeowners. Table 1 shows by means of product-moment (Pearsonian r) coefficients of correlation the strength and consistency of this relationship over a wide variety of issues in several elections in Cleveland and Chicago.[3] As one would expect, when an expenditure is to be financed from a source other than the property tax the difference between homeowner and non-homeowner behavior is reduced. This is borne out in Table 2 in which we have compared wards typical of four major economic groups in Cook County (Illinois) in their voting on two issues: first, a proposal to increase county hospital facilities and, second, a proposal to construct a state welfare building. The measures were alike in that they would benefit only indigents; they were different in that their costs would be assessed against different publics: the hospital was to be paid for from the local property tax, the welfare building from state sources, largely a sales tax. Middle-income homeowners showed themselves very sensitive to this difference; the percentage favoring the state-financed measure was twice that favoring the property-tax-financed one. Low-income renters, on the other hand, preferred the property-tax-financed measure to the state-financed one.

Let us turn now to the behavior of voters who do own property and whose taxes will therefore be increased in consequence of a public expenditure. One might suppose that the more property such a voter has, the less likely it is that he will favor public expenditures. To be sure, certain expenditures confer benefits roughly in proportion to the value of property and some may even confer disproportionate benefits on the more valuable properties; in such cases one would expect large property owners to be as much in favor of expenditures as the small, or more so. Most expenditures, however, confer about the same benefits on large properties as on small, whereas of course the taxes to pay for the expendi-

[2] The cities and elections examined are: Cleveland-Cuyahoga County: Nov., 1956; Nov., 1959; May, 1960; Nov., 1960. Chicago-Cook County: June, 1957; Nov., 1958; Nov., 1959; April, 1962. Detroit-Wayne County: August, 1960; Feb., 1961; April, 1961; April, 1963. Kansas City: Nov., 1960; March, 1962. Los Angeles: Nov., 1962. Miami: Nov., 1956; May, 1960. St. Louis: March, 1962; Nov., 1962; March, 1963.

[3] The degree of association was also calculated using a nonparametric statistic (Kendall's *tau*). The relationship persists but at lower values. Since we are satisfied that the relationship found by r is not spurious, we have relied on it for the balance of the analysis because of its capacity to produce partial correlation coefficients.

TABLE 2. *Voting Behavior of Four Major Economic Groups Compared in Cook County*

Group	Percent "Yes" Vote	
	County Hospital (1957)	State Welfare Building (1958)
	(%)	(%)
*High Income Homeowners**		
Winnetka	64	76
Wilmette	55	70
Lincolnwood	47	64
Middle Income Homeowners†		
Lansing	30	54
Bellwood	21	55
Brookfield	22	51
Middle Income Renters‡		
Chicago Ward 44	65	71
Chicago Ward 48	61	72
Chicago Ward 49	64	74
Low Income Renters§		
Chicago Ward 2	88	73
Chicago Ward 3	87	76
Chicago Ward 27	87	78

*Three suburbs with highest median family income ($13,200 to $23,200) among all suburbs with 85 percent or more home ownership.

†Three suburbs with lowest median family income ($8,000 to $8,300) among all suburbs with 85 percent or more home ownership.

‡Three wards with highest median family income ($6,200 to $6,800) among all wards with less than 15 percent home ownership (none of the three wards is more than 4 percent Negro).

§Three wards with lowest median family income ($3,100 to $4,100) among all wards with less than 15 percent home ownership (Negro population of wards ranges from 59 to 99 percent).

ture are levied (in theory at least) strictly in proportion to the value of property. The owner of a $30,000 home, for example, probably gets no more benefit from the construction of a new city hall or the expansion of a zoo than does the owner of a $10,000 one; his share of the tax increase is three times as much, however. Very often, indeed, there is an inverse relation between the value of a property and the benefits that

FIGURE 1. Relation between Percentage Voting "Yes" on Proposition to Provide Increased County Hospital Facilities (November 1959) and Percentage of Dwelling Units Owner-Occupied in the 33 Wards of Cleveland

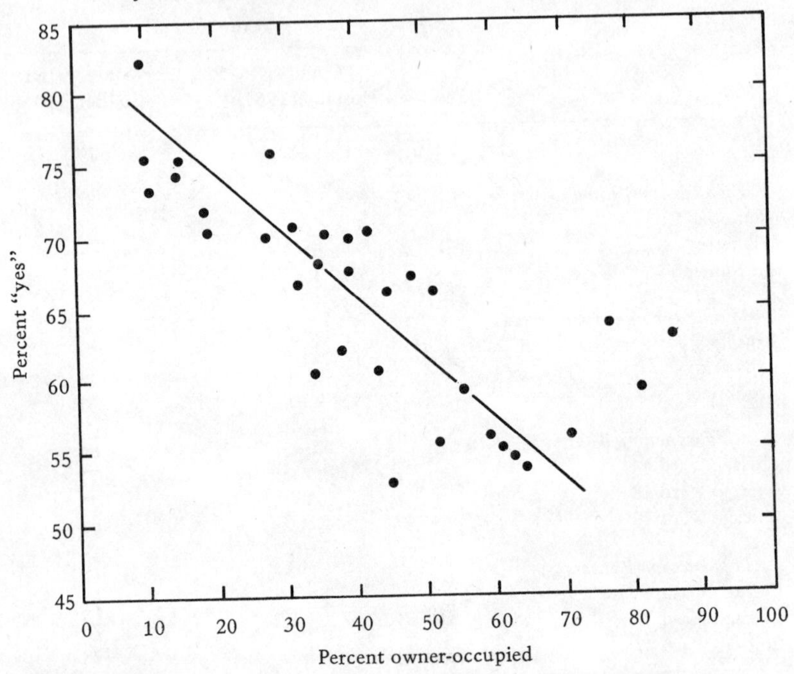

Source of housing data: U.S. Census of housing, 1960. Figure reprinted from Edward C. Banfield and James Q Wilson, *City Politics* (Cambridge: Harvard University Press, 1963), p. 238.

accrue to its owner from a public expenditure. The probability is certainly greater that the owner of the $10,000 house will some day use the free county hospital (patronized chiefly by low-income Negroes) than that the owner of the $30,000 house will use it. Since normally the *ratio* of benefits to costs is less favorable the higher the value of the property, one might expect to find a positive correlation between the percentage of "No" votes in a neighborhood and the median value of homes there.

This expectation is not borne out by the facts, however. Table 3 gives partial correlation coefficients relating the per cent voting "Yes" in the wards of Cleveland and the suburban wards and towns of Cuyahoga County to the median family income in those wards and towns.[4] It shows

[4] Only two measures of tax liability can be got from the Census: median home value and median family income. We have used the latter for the

TABLE 3. *Partial Correlations between Median Family Income of Ward and Percentage "Yes" Vote on Various Measures, Cleveland and Suburbs*

Area and Issue	Partial Correlation*
Cleveland (33 wards):	
Administration Building	+0.49
County Hospital	+0.64
Tuberculosis Hospital	+0.57
Court House	+0.49
Juvenile Court	+0.66
Parks	+0.48
Welfare Levy	+0.70
Roads and Bridges	+0.61
Zoo	+0.59
Cuyahoga County Suburbs (90 wards and towns):	
Administration Building	+0.47
County Hospital	+0.54
Tuberculosis Hospital	+0.43
Court House	+0.60
Juvenile Court	+0.59
Parks	+0.52
Welfare Levy	+0.35
Roads and Bridges	+0.60
Zoo	+0.62

*Controlling for proportion of dwelling units owner-occupied.

that the higher the income of a ward or town, the more taste it has for public expenditures of various kinds. That the ratio of benefits to costs declines as income goes up seems to make no difference.[5]

most part. The Census classifies all homes valued at over $25,000 together, thereby collapsing distinctions that are important for us. We think, too, that people are more likely to know their incomes than to know the current market value of their homes, and that therefore the Census information on incomes is more reliable. Finally, in neighborhoods populated mostly by renters, median home values are likely to be unrepresentative of the class character of the neighborhood: this is so, for example, where a few owner-occupied slums exist in a district of luxury apartments.

[5] Other studies which suggest that upper-income groups may have a greater preference for public expenditures than middle-income groups include Oliver P. Williams and Charles R. Adrian, *Four Cities: A Study in*

The same pattern appears in a 1960 Flint, Michigan, vote on additional flood control facilities. This is shown graphically in Figure 3. Although there is a considerable dispersion around the line of regression, in general the higher the home value – and accordingly the more the expected tax – the greater the support for the expenditure.[6]

It may be argued that because of the phenomenon of the diminishing marginal utility of money these findings are not really anomalous. The richer a man is, perhaps, the smaller the sacrifice that an additional dollar of taxation represents to him. Thus, even though the well-to-do voter may get no more benefit than the poor one gets and may have to pay a great deal more in taxes, an expenditure proposal may nevertheless be more attractive to him. He may be more willing to pay a dollar for certain benefits than his neighbor is to pay fifty cents because, having much more money than his neighbor, a dollar is worth only a quarter as much to him.

Differences in the value of the dollar to voters at different income levels account in part for the well-to-do voter's relatively strong taste for public expenditures. They can hardly account for it entirely, however. For one thing, they do not rationalize the behavior of those voters who support measures that would give them only trivial benefits while impos-

---

Comparative Policy Making (Philadelphia: University of Pennsylvania Press, 1963), ch. v; Alvin Boskoff and Harmon Zeigler, *Voting Patterns in a Local Election* (Philadelphia: J. B. Lippincott Co., 1964), ch. iii; Richard A. Watson, *The Politics of Urban Change* (Kansas City, Mo.: Community Studies, Inc., 1963), ch. iv; and Robert H. Salisbury and Gordon Black, "Class and Party in Non-Partisan Elections: The Case of Des Moines," [*American Political Science Review*], Vol. 57 (September, 1963), p. 591. The Williams-Adrian and Salisbury-Black studies use electoral data; the Boskoff-Zeigler and Watson studies use survey data. See also Otto A. Davis, "Empirical Evidence of 'Political' Influences Upon the Expenditure and Taxation Policies of Public Schools," Graduate School of Industrial Administration of the Carnegie Institute of Technology, January, 1964 (mimeo), and William C. Birdsall, "Public Finance Allocation Decisions and the Preferences of Citizens: Some Theoretical and Empirical Considerations," unpublished Ph.D. thesis, Department of Economics, Johns Hopkins University, 1963. A difficulty with the Davis and Birdsall studies is the size (and thus the heterogeneity) of the units of analysis – entire school districts in one case, entire cities in the other.

[6] Michigan is one of the few states which restricts the right to vote on expenditures to property owners and their spouses. Because the Flint returns were tabulated on a precinct basis, demographic data had to be obtained from block rather than tract statistics; since median family income is given only for tracts, median value of owner-occupied homes had to be used.

Possibly the flood control benefits would be distributed roughly in proportion to the value of properties; about this we cannot say. However, it is worth noting that the vote in Flint on other expenditures which presumably would *not* distribute benefits in proportion to the value of properties (*e.g.*, parks) followed the same pattern.

FIGURE 2. Relation between Percentage Voting "Yes" on Proposition to Provide Additional Sewer Facilities (1962) and Percentage of Dwelling Units Owner-Occupied in Wards of Chicago

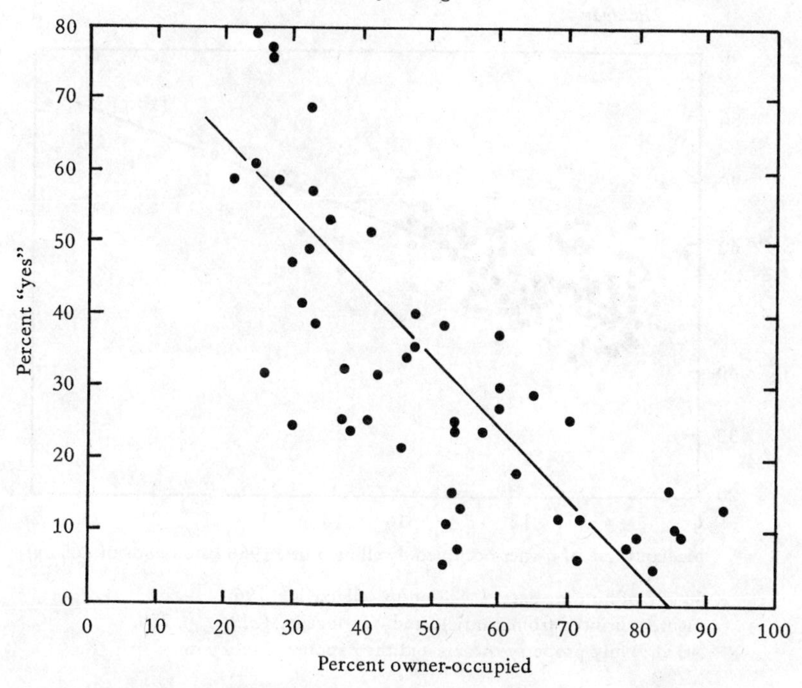

ing substantial costs upon them. The suburbanite who favors a county hospital for the indigent which he and his family will certainly never use and for which he will be heavily taxed is not acting according to self-interest narrowly conceived no matter how little a dollar is worth to him.

Moreover, if the well-to-do voter places a low value on the dollar when evaluating some expenditure proposals, one would expect him to place the same low value on it when evaluating all others. In fact, he does not seem to do so; indeed, he sometimes appears to place a *higher* value on it than does his less-well-off neighbor. Compare, for example, the behavior of the Cook County (Illinois) suburbanites who voted on a proposal to build a county hospital (an expenditure which would confer only trivial benefits on them and for which they would be taxed in proportion to the value of their property) with the behavior of the same suburbanites who voted on a proposal to give a bonus of $300 to Korean War veterans (an expenditure from which the well-to-do would benefit about as much as the less-well-to-do and for which they would not be taxed disproportionately, since the bonus was to be financed from state,

FIGURE 3. Relation between Percentage Voting "Yes" on Proposition to Provide Additional Flood Control Facilities (November 1960) and Median Value of Owner-Occupied Dwelling Units in the Precincts of Flint, Michigan

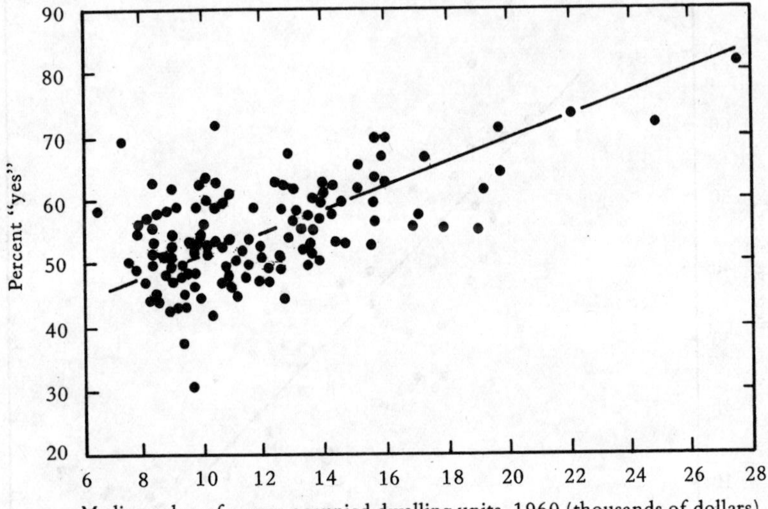

Source of housing data: U.S. Census of Housing, 1960.
Figure reprinted from Banfield and Wilson, *City Politics,* p. 239.
NOTE: Only property owners and their spouses could vote.

not local, revenues, and the state had neither an income tax nor a corporate profits tax). As Figures 4 and 5 show, the higher the median family income of a voting district, the larger the percentage voting "Yes" on the welfare building (the rank-order correlation was +0.57), but the *smaller* the percentage voting "Yes" on the veterans' bonus (the rank-order correlation was −0.71).

In Cuyahoga County, Ohio, the same thing happened. There the higher the median family income, the larger the percentage voting for all the expenditure proposals except one – a bonus for Korean War veterans. On this one measure there was a correlation of −0.65 between median family income and percentage voting "Yes."

Thus, although it is undoubtedly true that the more dollars a voter has, the more he will pay for a given benefit, the principle does not explain all that needs explaining. When it comes to a veterans' bonus, for example, the opposite principle seems to work: the more dollars the voter has, the fewer he will spend for a given benefit of that sort.

FIGURE 4. Relation between Percentage Voting "Yes" on Proposition to Provide Increased County Hospital Facilities (1957) and Median Family Income in the Suburban Cities and Towns of Cook County, Illinois, in Which Two-Thirds or More of the Dwelling Units are Owner-Occupied

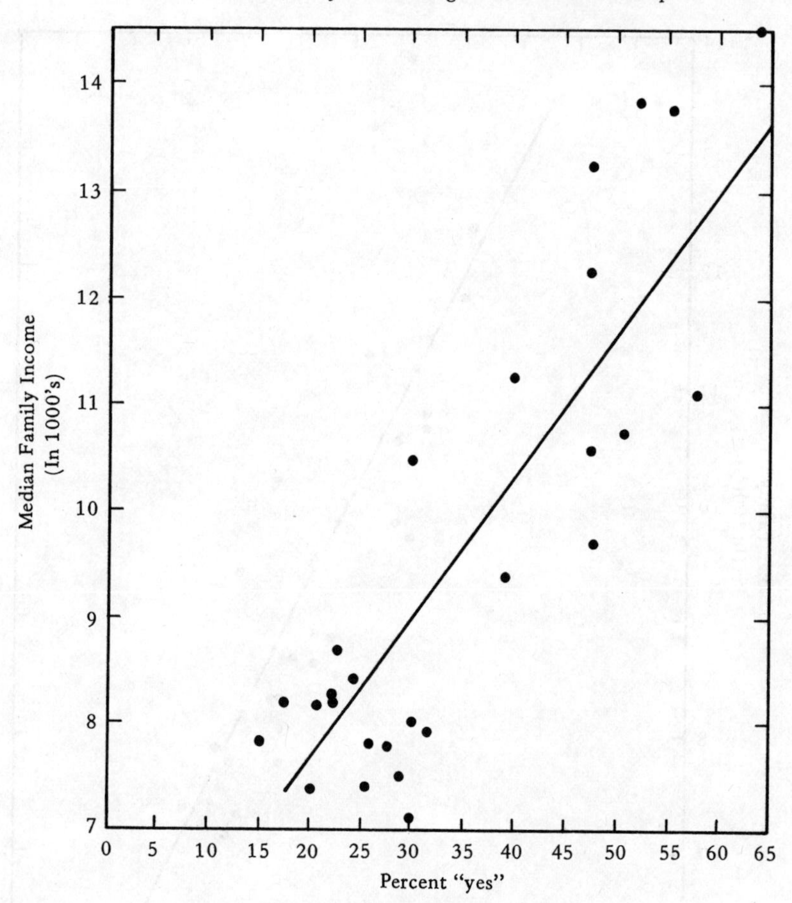

That there is a positive correlation between amount of property owned (or income) and tendency to vote "Yes" does not, of course, imply that a majority of property owners at *any* income level favors expenditures: the correlation would exist even if the highest income voters opposed them, provided that at each lower level of income voters opposed them by even-larger majorities. In fact, middle-income homeowners often vote against proposals that are approved by both the very poor (renters) and the very well-to-do (owners). Table 4 gives a rather typical picture

FIGURE 5. Relation between Percentage Voting "Yes" on Proposition to Approve a $300 Bonus for Veterans of Korean War (1958) and Median Family Income in the Suburban Cities and Towns of Cook County, Illinois, in Which Two-Thirds or More of the Dwelling Units are Owner-Occupied

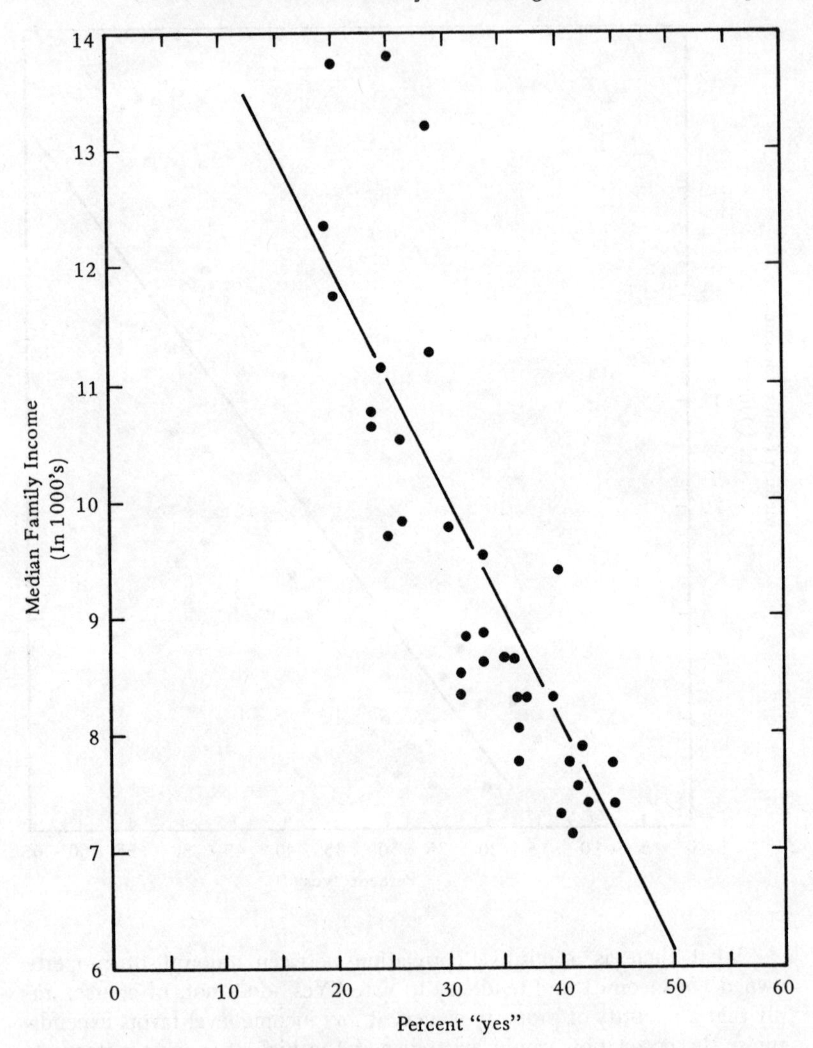

of the response of the various income groups to proposals that are to be financed from the property tax in Cuyahoga County (Ohio).

Not infrequently the highest-income districts support expenditure

TABLE 4. *Voting Behavior of Four Major Economic Groups Compared in Cuyahoga County*

Group	Percent "Yes" Vote	
	County Hospital (1959)	County Court House (1959)
	(%)	(%)
*High-Income Homeowners**		
Pepper Pike	69	47
Beachwood	72	47
Middle-Income Homeowners†		
Olmstead Township	51	28
Garfield Heights (Ward 4)	48	29
Lower-Middle-Income Renters‡		
Cleveland Ward 31	76	66
Low-Income Renters§		
Cleveland Ward 11	73	63
Cleveland Ward 17	74	62

*Two suburbs with highest median family income ($15,700 and $19,000) of all suburbs with 85 percent or more home ownership.

†Two suburbs with lowest median family income ($6,800 and $7,000) of all suburbs with 85 percent or more home ownership.

‡The one ward with less than 15 percent home ownership and which is less than 10 percent Negro (median income: $4,700).

§Two wards with lowest median family incomes ($3,400 and $3,600) of all wards with less than 15 percent home ownership (Negro population of wards was 90 and 97 percent).

proposals by very large majorities – indeed, sometimes by majorities approaching those given in the propertyless slums. Table 5 compares the percentage voting "Yes" in the high-income, high-home-ownership precints of three city-county areas with the percentage of all voters in these areas who voted "Yes." [7] Except for Detroit and Dade County, where only property owners and their spouses may vote on expenditures, the city-county totals include large numbers of renters. Even so, the high-

[7] We isolated all precincts in Census tracts having median family incomes of at least $10,000 a year, with at least 70 per cent home ownership (the central city of Chicago was excepted here), and at least 70 per cent of the population third- (or more) generation native born.

TABLE 5. *Percentage Voting "Yes" on Expenditures in Home-Owning, Upper-Income "Old-Stock" Precincts in Various Counties*

County, Issue, and Date	Percent "Yes" Vote in Upper-Income Precincts (%)	Percent "Yes" Vote in County as a Whole (%)
Detroit-Wayne County		
Sewers (8/60)	83.6	64.3
Increase school tax limit	52.0	39.0
Build schools (4/63)	52.0	33.4
Increase sales tax (11/60)	78.6	47.8
Kansas City—Jefferson County		
Increase school taxes (11/60)	68.6	54.9
Build jails (3/62)	86.3	78.0
Sewage treatment plant (11/60)	93.2	81.6
Miami-Dade County		
Highways (5/60)	71.2	53.0
Schools (1955)	90.8	92.1

income precincts are comparatively strong in their support of all expenditures.

III

When we hold constant the percentage of home ownership, percentage of nonwhites, and median family income, a negative correlation appears between the percentage of voters in the wards of Cleveland who are of foreign stock and the percentage of the total vote in those wards that is "Yes." This is shown in Column 1 of Table 6.[8] Of the many foreign stocks in Cleveland, the Poles and Czechs have the strongest distaste for expenditures. Column 2 of Table 6 shows how markedly the presence

[8] A person is of "foreign stock" if he was born abroad or if one or both of his parents was born abroad. We believe that the reason why a significant relationship does not appear for the suburbs is that there is a considerable number of Jews among the foreign stock of the suburbs. In the central city, there are practically no Jews. Like other Jews, Jews of Eastern European origin tend to favor expenditures proposals of all kinds. Their presence in the suburbs, therefore, offsets the "No" vote of the non-Jews of foreign stock.

TABLE 6. *Partial Correlations between Selected "Ethnic" Variables and Percentage Voting "Yes" on Expenditures in Cleveland and Cuyahoga County Wards and Towns**

	Foreign Stock		Polish-Czech		Negro	
Issue	City	Suburbs	City	Suburbs	City	Suburbs
Admin. Building	−0.40	ns†	−0.54	−0.17	ns	ns
County Hospital	ns	ns	−0.79	−0.40	ns	ns
TB Hospital	ns	−0.22	−0.74	−0.46	ns	ns
Court House	−0.47	ns	−0.58	−0.28	ns	ns
Juvenile Court	−0.46	ns	−0.74	−0.40	ns	ns
Parks (1959)	−0.41	ns	−0.62	−0.31	−0.49	ns
Welfare Levy	−0.58	ns	−0.71	−0.49	ns	ns
Roads and Bridges	−0.48	ns	−0.66	−0.40	ns	ns
Zoo	−0.62	ns	−0.71	−0.40	ns	ns
Parks (1960)	ns	ns	ns	−0.50	ns	ns

*These are partial correlation coefficients derived from a regression analysis in which home ownership, median family income, and two "ethnic" variables have been held constant.

†If the correlations were not significant at the .05 level (Student's t), "ns" is entered in the table. The critical values were based on 27 degrees of freedom for the city data and 84 degrees of freedom for the suburban data.

of Poles and Czechs in a voting district affects the "Yes" vote.[9] In the suburbs the correlation is only slightly weaker, but significant at the .001 level in all but two cases and in these at the .01 level. The complete

[9] Since no home-owning ward or town in Cuyahoga County is more than 25 per cent Polish-Czech according to the 1960 Census, it may be that no inferences can be drawn from the voting data about Polish-Czech behavior. Three considerations increase our confidence in the possibility of drawing inferences, however. (1) Only first- and second-generation Poles and Czechs are counted as such by the Census, but third- and fourth-generation Poles and Czechs tend to live in the same wards and towns; thus the proportion of the electorate sharing Polish-Czech cultural values (the relevant thing from our standpoint) is considerably larger that the Census figures suggest. (2) When other factors are held constant, even small increases in the number of Poles and Czechs are accompanied by increases in the "No" vote; nothing "explains" this except the hypothesis that the Poles and Czechs make the difference. (3) When we take as the unit for analysis not wards but precincts of a few hundred persons that are known to contain very high proportions of Poles and Czechs, we get the same results. Because we are using ecological, not individual, data, we are perforce analyzing the behavior of ethnic "ghettos" where ethnic identification and attitudes are probably reinforced. Poles in non-Polish wards, for example, may behave quite differently.

correlation table shows that in all but three cases the percentage of Poles and Czechs is a more important influence on voting than median family income, and is second in influence only to home ownership. In two of the three exceptional cases, indeed, it was *more* important than home ownership.

The findings in Column 3 of Table 6 are surprising. We expected a positive correlation between percentage of Negroes and the strength of the "Yes" vote. Deficiencies in the data may possibly account for the absence of any correlation: there are not enough home-owning Negroes or enough very low-income whites in Cleveland to make a really satisfactory matching of wards possible.

In order to get a closer view of ethnic voting it is necessary to forego general correlations and instead to examine individual precincts known to be predominantly of a single ethnic group. In Tables 7 and 8 we show how selected "ethnic" precincts belonging to two income and home-ownership classes voted in several elections in the Chicago and Cleveland areas.[10] There is a remarkable degree of consistency in the influence of both ethnicity and income or home-ownership, whether viewed on an intra- or inter-city basis. In Chicago, for example, the low-income renters in *every* case voted more favorably for expenditures than did the middle-income home-owners of the same ethnic group. Within the same economic class, however, ethnicity makes a striking difference. Low-income Negro renters are in *every* case more enthusiastic by a wide margin about public expenditures than low-income Irish or Polish renters. Middle-income Negro home-owners are in *every* case more enthusiastic about the same proposals than middle-income Irish or Polish home-owners. (In passing it is worth noting that Negroes are two or three times more favorable toward urban renewal – despite the fact that they are commonly the chief victims of land clearance programs – than Irish or Polish voters.)

Essentially the same relationships appear in Table 8 for Cleveland-Cuyahoga County. With one exception (Italians voting on the welfare levy), low-income renters in an ethnic group are more favorable to expenditures than middle-income home-owners in the same ethnic group. Low-income Negro renters are the most favorable to all proposals and middle-income Negro home-owners are more favorable to them than are the other middle-income ethnic groups. Aside from the veterans' bonus

[10] The method by which these precincts were selected is given in the Appendix. Unfortunately, it proved impossible to identify relatively homogeneous precincts typical of other ethnic groups at various income levels and degrees of home-ownership. For example, middle-income Jews tend to be renters, not home-owners, and there are practically no low-income Jewish precincts in either city. A complete list of these precincts is available from the authors.

TABLE 7. *Percentage of Various "Ethnic" Precincts Voting "Yes" on Selected Expenditures in Chicago*

Ethnic Group and Number of Precincts	Percent Voting "Yes" On: Co. Hosp. (6/57)	Vet's Bonus (11/58)	Urban Renewal (4/62)	City Hall (5/62)	School (4/59)
	(%)	(%)	(%)	(%)	(%)
*Low-Income Renters**					
Negro (22)	84.9	80.2	88.6	82.3	97.8
Irish (6)	61.3	55.3	45.7	46.3	79.4
Polish (26)	60.1	54.6	57.1	53.8	81.8
Middle-Income Home-Owners†					
Negro (13)	66.8	54.9	69.6	49.8	88.9
Irish (6)	54.6	44.1	22.0	27.2	64.2
Polish (38)	47.4	40.0	14.6	15.2	58.3

* Average median family income under $6,000 per year; at least two-thirds of all dwelling units renter-occupied.

† Average median family income between $7,500 and $10,000 a year for whites; over $6,000 a year for Negroes. At least 80 percent of all dwelling units owner-occupied.

(a special case), both the "Anglo-Saxon" and the Jewish upper-income home-owners are more favorable to expenditures than any middle-income groups except the Negro.

IV

We have shown both that a considerable proportion of voters, especially in the upper income groups, vote against their self-interest narrowly conceived and that a marked ethnic influence appears in the vote. Now we would like to bring these two findings together under a single explanatory principle.

One such principle – but one we reject – is that the voters in question have acted irrationally (either in not calculating benefits and costs at all or else by making mistakes in their calculations) and that their irrationality is a function of their ethnic status. According to this theory, the low-income Polish renter who votes against expenditures proposals that would cost him nothing and would confer benefits upon him and the high-income Anglo-Saxon or Jewish home-owner who favors expenditures

TABLE 8. *Percentage of Various "Ethnic" Precincts Voting "Yes" on Selected Expenditures in Cleveland and Cuyahoga County*

Ethnic Group and Number of Precincts	Percent Voting "Yes" on: Co. Hosp. (11/59)	Court House (11/59)	Parks (11/59)	Welfare Levy (5/60)	Vet's Bonus (11/56)
	(%)	(%)	(%)	(%)	(%)
*Low-Income Renters**					
Negro (16)	78.6	67.3	52.6	85.9	89.9
Italian (10)	68.8	53.3	43.5	49.9	74.8
Polish (6)	54.9	39.9	28.1	33.7	71.6
Middle-Income Home-Owners†					
Negro (8)	68.1	54.0	39.6	73.2	79.2
Italian (7)	59.3	49.7	41.1	56.8	66.8
Polish (12)	52.9	35.8	34.3	46.4	61.7
Upper-Income Home-Owners‡					
Anglo-Saxon (11)	70.6	51.4	57.2	64.8	53.7
Jewish (7)	71.7	47.1	48.4	64.5	56.8

* Average median family income less than $6,000 per year; at least two-thirds of all dwelling units renter-occupied.

† Average median family income between $7,000 and $9,000 a year for whites; over $6,000 a year for Negroes. At least 75 percent of all dwelling units owner-occupied.

‡ Average median family income over $10,000 per year; over 85 percent of all dwelling units owner-occupied.

proposals that will cost him heavily without benefitting him would both behave differently if they thought about the matter more or if their information were better.

A more tenable hypothesis, we think, is that voters in some income and ethnic groups are more likely than voters in others to take a public-regarding rather than a narrowly self-interested view of things – *i.e.*, to take the welfare of others, especially that of "the community" into account as an aspect of their own welfare.[11] We offer the additional hypothesis that both the tendency of a voter to take a public-regarding view and the content of that view (*e.g.*, whether or not he thinks a Korean

[11] *Cf.* Anthony Downs, "The Public Interest: Its Meaning in a Democracy," *Social Research*, Vol. 29 (Spring 1962), pp. 28–29.

war veterans' bonus is in the public interest) are largely functions of his participation in a subculture that is definable in ethnic and income terms. Each subcultural group, we think, has a more or less distinctive notion of how much a citizen ought to sacrifice for the sake of the community as well as of what the welfare of the community is constituted; in a word, each has its own idea of what justice requires and of the importance of acting justly. According to this hypothesis, the voter is presumed to act rationally; the ends he seeks are not always narrowly self-interested ones, however. On the contrary, depending upon his income and ethnic status they are more or less public-regarding.[12]

That his income status does not by itself determine how public-regarding he is, or what content he gives to the public interest, can be shown from the voting data. As we explained above, generally the higher a home-owner's income the more likely he is to favor expenditures. This is partly – but only partly – because the value of the dollar is usually less to people who have many of them than to people who have few of them. We suggest that it is also because upper-income people tend to be more public-regarding than lower-income people. We do not think that income *per se* has this effect; rather it is the ethnic attributes, or culture, empirically associated with it. It happens that most upper-income voters belong, if not by inheritance then by adoption, to an ethnic group (especially the Anglo-Saxon and the Jewish) that is relatively public-regarding in its outlook; hence ethnic influence on voting is hard to distinguish from income influence.

In the three scatter diagrams which comprise Figure 6 we have tried to distinguish the two kinds of influence. For this figure, we divided all wards and towns of Cleveland and Cuyahoga County in which 85 or more per cent of the dwelling units were owner-occupied into three classes according to median home value. Diagram 6a shows the voting where that value was more than $27,000; diagram 6b shows it where it was $19,000–27,000, and diagram 6c shows it where it was less than $19,000. The horizontal and vertical axes are the same for all diagrams; each diagram shows the relationship between the percentage of voters in the ward or town who are Polish-Czech (vertical axis) and the percentage of "Yes" vote on a proposal to expand the zoo (horizontal axis). In the group of wards and towns having the lowest median home value (diagram 6c) the presence of Polish-Czech voters made little difference; these wards and towns were about 65 per cent against the proposal no matter how many Poles and Czechs lived in them. In both groups of higher home-value wards and towns, however, Poles and Czechs were conspicu-

[12] The proposition that "subculture" can be defined in ethnic and income terms is highly provisional. We are looking for other and better criteria and we think we may find some. But so far as the present data are concerned, ethnic and income status are all we have.

FIGURE 6. Relation between Percentage Voting "Yes" on Proposition to Provide Additional Zoo Facilities (1960) and Proportion of Ward or Town Population Which is of Polish or Czech Foreign Stock in Cuyahoga County, Ohio; at Three Median Home Value Levels (Only Wards and Towns with 85 Percent or More Owner-Occupied Dwellings Used)

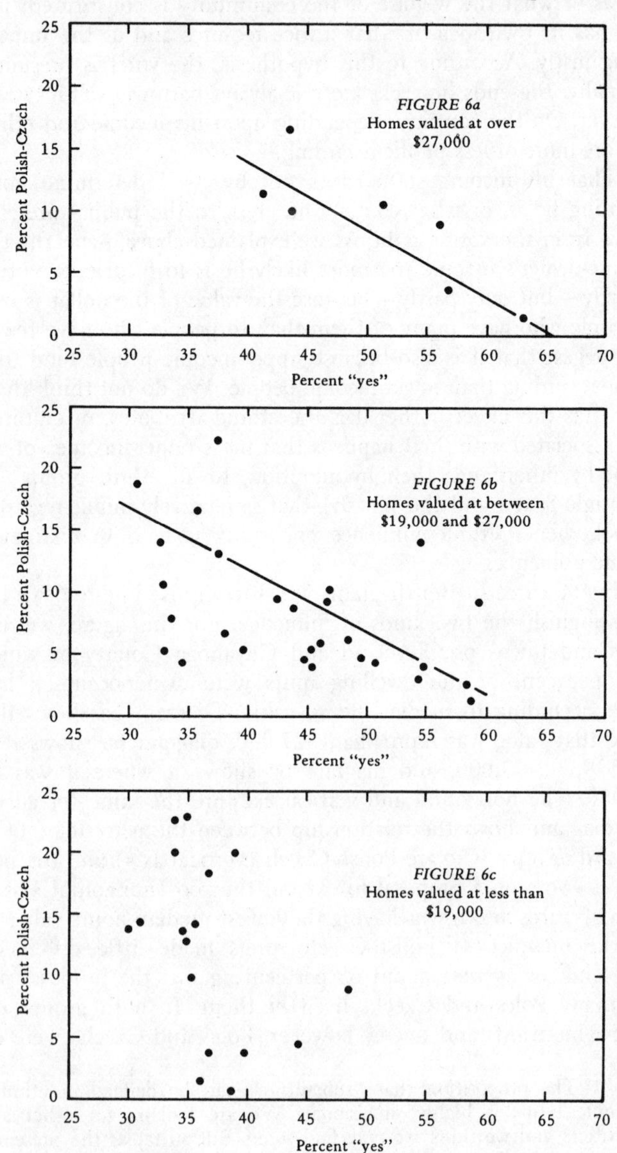

ously less favorable to the proposal than were the rest of the voters. Among the non-Polish-Czech voters in these higher home-value wards and towns, Anglo-Saxons and Jews were heavily represented; therefore it seems plausible to conclude that, as compared to Poles and Czechs in these two income groups, the Anglo-Saxons and Jews were decidedly public-regarding.

Another interpretation of the behavior of the Poles and Czechs is possible, however. It may be that they had the welfare of the community in view also but defined it differently than did the Anglo-Saxons and the Jews. They may have thought that the particular expenditure proposed, or for that matter all public expenditures, would do the community more harm than good. (This would rationalize the behavior of those low-income renters – see Table 8 – who voted against proposals giving them benefits without any costs.) [13] Whatever may be true of the Poles and Czechs, it seems clear that upper-income Anglo-Saxons, and to a somewhat lesser degree Jews, tend to vote on public-regarding grounds *against* some proposals (notably those, like veterans' bonuses and city employees' pension benefits and pay increases) that they regard as serving "special interests" rather than "the community as a whole."

When we know more about each of the various subcultures – especially about the nature of the individual's attachment to the society, his conception of what is just, and the extent of the obligation he feels to subordinate his interest to that of various others (*e.g.*, the community) – we should doubtless be able to make and test more refined hypothesis about voting behavior.

Appendix

We chose the "ethnic" precincts for Tables 7 and 8 by inspecting census tract data and then visiting the precincts that appeared to be predominantly of one ethnic group to get confirmatory evidence from well-informed persons and from a view of the neighborhoods. We could have used a less impressionistic method (*e.g.*, counting the proportion of

[13] Two other explanations are possible and, in our opinion, plausible. One is that the low-income renters may have taken into account costs to them other than taxes – *e.g.*, the cost (perhaps monetary) of changes in the neighborhood that would ensue from expenditures. (Irish objections to urban renewal in Chicago may have been due, not to a fear of higher taxes, but to fear of neighborhood "invasion" by Negroes displaced from land clearance projects.) The other is that in these precincts a much higher proportion of renters than of home-owners may have stayed away from the polls. In Cleveland (though not, interestingly, in Chicago) voter turnout is highly correlated with home ownership and almost all white renter precincts have at least a few home-owners in them. Conceivably – we think it unlikely – all those who voted in some "renter" precincts were actually owners.

ethnic names on voter registration lists), but since we wanted only to identify precincts that are predominantly of one ethnic group, not to place them on a scale of ethnicity, this did not appear necessary.

Having identified the "ethnic" precincts, we divided them into two (sometimes three) income groups on the basis of census data. As we indicate on the tables, with one exception we used the same cutting points to separate the income levels of all ethnic groups. The exception was the Negro. The income distribution among Negroes is so skewed to the low end of the scale that "middle-income" has to be defined differently for Negroes than for whites. We identified "middle-income Negro" precincts by selecting from among all precincts that were at least 85 per cent Negro and had an owner-occupancy rate of at least 80 per cent those few with the highest median family incomes. Some of these precincts turned out to have median incomes as low as $6,000 a year, which is about $1,000 less than any of the "middle-income white" precincts had. If we had made the cutting point higher, however, we would not have had enough middle-income Negro precincts to work with. In our opinion, Negroes with incomes of $6,000 are about as likely to "feel" middle-income as are whites with incomes of $7,000.

ECONOMIC DEVELOPMENT, REGIONALISM AND STATE POLITICAL SYSTEMS

IRA SHARKANSKY

Introduction

In recent years a number of scholars have examined the relationships between the economic characteristics of American states and the political characteristics of voter turnout, inter-party competition and the equity of legislative apportionment. Their findings have provided compelling

Reprinted from Ira Sharkansky, "Economic Development, Regionalism, and State Political Systems," *Midwest Journal of Political Science*, 12 (February, 1968), 41–61, by permission of the Wayne State University Press.

Grants from the Social Science Research Council: Committee on Governmental and Legal Processes, and the University of Georgia Office of General Research provided necessary financial assistance for this study.

evidence for the proposition that the nature of a state's economy may exercise considerable influence over state politics. There are significant positive relationships between measures of "economic development," voter turnout and party competition. Where citizens are relatively wealthy and concentrate in urban areas there seem to be the least inhibitions imposed on political participation and the most intense levels of competition between the candidates of each party. Of the three aspects of state politics considered most frequently in the literature, only the equity of legislative apportionment seems to escape the influence of state economics.[1]

Despite the statistical and theoretical support for economic-political linkages, it is premature to conclude that economics more than other characteristics of states provides an explanation for state political phenomena. Even when economic measures show significant relationships with measures of political characteristics, the relationships are not so strong as to preclude the influence of non-economic variables. In *Politics, Economics and the Public*, for example, Thomas R. Dye reports no instance where a measure of income, education, urbanization or industrialization accounts for more than 44 per cent of the interstate variation in a measure of party competition, voter turnout or legislative apportionment.[2] It is apparent that states frequently surpass or fail to attain the levels of political characteristics that are associated with their levels of economic activity. Although most economically developed states tend to show the highest levels of party competition and voter turnout, several low-income, rural states in the Rocky Mountain area show high scores on these political traits. And the highly urbanized states of Florida and Texas show the low scores on party competition and voter turnout that prevail throughout the more rural states of the South. Such deviations

[1] See, for example, Thomas R. Dye, *Politics, Economics and the Public: Policy Outcomes in the American States* (Chicago: Rand McNally, 1966); Richard I. Hofferbert, "The Relation Between Public Policy and Some Structural and Environmental Variables in the American States," *American Political Science Review*, LX (March, 1966), 73–82; and Richard Dawson and James Robinson, "Interparty Competition, Economic Variables, and Welfare Politics in the American States," *Journal of Politics*, 25 (May, 1963), 265–89. Although the main emphasis of these publications has been upon the impact of economic and political characteristics in public policy, they have made important secondary statements about the relationships between economic and political characteristics of the states. Dawson and Robinson, and Dye have reported positive relationships between measures of economic development and interparty competition and voter turnout. Dye and Hofferbert have failed to find consistent strong relationships between measures of economic development and the equity of legislative apportionment.

[2] *Op. cit.*, pp. 58–68.

from usual economic-political relationships may reflect the historical experiences of states that stimulated their citizens to adopt and then transmit to later generations certain attitudes about the tolerance of dissent or the value of political participation. Some of these historical experiences may have been economic in nature. Thus, the nature of state politics may reflect previous accommodations to economic needs or resources that have become "outmoded" with alterations in agriculture, industry or commerce.

It seems likely that a consideration of regionalism will add to the understanding of interstate differences in the political characteristics of party competition, voter turnout and legislative apportionment. Because neighboring states in the various regions of America have experienced in-migrations, economic crises and political trauma at similar points in history, they may have acquired regional patterns in political attitudes, forms or processes that have remained more prominent than their economic affinities.[3]

Insofar as neighboring states tend to resemble one another economically, it is no simple task to decide whether the political traits of a region reflect current economic characteristics of the states, or if they reflect other episodes in the history of the region. However, there are enough intra-regional economic differences to permit a test of the relative importance of current economics and regional location as correlates of political traits. The three states of northern New England, for example, resemble several southern states in their levels of personal income and urbanization more than they resemble Massachusetts, Rhode Island and Connecticut. Yet all the New England states have common ethnic and religious backgrounds as well as early settlement and statehood that may be critical for certain political developments. In the South, Texas and Florida show several economic discontinuities with their neighbors; but the common background of Civil War, Reconstruction and racial tensions may have produced uniform political characteristics that have resisted more recent economic changes. In the Plains region, Missouri and South Dakota show great differences in their present economic characteristics, but they both had a frontier experience with "wide open" towns, grazing and then an agricultural economic base. And in the Mountains the neighboring states of Colorado and New Mexico now exhibit markedly different levels of personal income and urbanization, but they had similar experiences with trapping, mining and a relatively late acquisition of statehood.

[3] For a discussion of the "geology" of political culture in the United States, see Daniel J. Elazar, *American Federalism: A View from the States* (New York: Thomas Y. Crowell, 1966), Chapter IV.

This article seeks to define the relative importance of current economy and regionalism as influences on the political characteristics of American states. It employs simple, partial and multiple correlation techniques to define the economic-political relationships. And by an analysis of covariance using state scores on economic and political measures, together with three demarcations of American regions, it assesses the relative weight of economics and regionalism on political processes.

Although the concept of regionalism promises some help in the explanation of state political systems, it does not offer a great deal of specificity. The statistical techniques employed here show strong relationships between the regional affiliation of states and their political traits. However, a common regional identification is a diffuse attribute that may include a variety of social or ideological characteristics, and/or responses to common historical experiences. It will be necessary to go beyond the analysis of covariance in order to identify the specific attributes of regional neighbors that seem to account for their distinctive political traits.

Techniques

This study employs twelve measures of inter-party competition, voter turnout and legislative apportionment as its dependent variables. Although these variables do not assess all of the behavior that might be labeled as components of state political systems, they do encompass traits that have been studied as important attributes of state politics. By showing the relative importance of regionalism and current economics with respect to these components of state politics, this article will be helping to explain those phenomena that several important political scientists have taken as salient ingredients of politics. The specific measures of the political characteristics are:

Inter-Party Competition

a) percentage of votes received by winner in 1962 (or 1960) gubernatorial election
b) percentage of state legislature's lower house seats occupied by major party, 1962 [4]
c) percentage of state legislature's upper house seats occupied by major party, 1962
d) number of years in 1952–62 period major party held Governor's office

[4] In recording variables *b* and *c* for Nebraska and Minnesota it was assumed that minimum distortion would occur from the substitution of scores from comparable competition measures for the office of Governor.

e) number of years in 1954–62 period major party held control of the lower house of the legislature
f) number of years in 1954–62 period major party held control of the upper house of the legislature
g) percentage of votes received by major party in 1962 elections for U.S. Representative

Voter Turnout

h) percentage of voting age population voting in the 1962 (or 1960) election for Governor
i) percentage of voting age population voting in the 1962 elections for U.S. Representative

Legislative Apportionment

j) Schubert-Press index [5]
k) Dauer-Kelsey index [6]
l) David-Eisenberg index [7]

Within each group of dependent variables, each measure assesses a different aspect of state politics. Four of the measures for party competition (*a, b, c, g*) assess the percentage of the vote received by the major party in a recent election, or the percentage of seats held during a recent session of the state legislature. The three other measures (*d, e, f*) assess competition over a span of recent years by calculating the length of the time that the major party has had control of certain offices in state government. *In each case, high scores on these variables (a-g) indicate the dominance of state politics by one party; it is the low scores (approaching 50 per cent of each scale) that indicate intense inter-party competition.* The two measures of voter turnout (*h, i*) are similar conceptually, but differ in the electoral contexts that they assess. In each case, high scores indicate high levels of participation by the state electorate in major contests. The three indices of equity in the apportionment of state legislatures are slightly different in their concepts of "equitable" apportionment. The most complex of these (Schubert-Press) assesses apportionment by combining inverted coefficients of variability for district populations with measures of skewness in the distribution of district populations and

[5] Glendon Schubert and Charles Press, "Measuring Malapportionment," *American Political Science Review*, LXIII (June, 1964 and December, 1964), 302–27 and 966–70.

[6] Paul T. David and Ralph Eisenberg, *Devaluation of the Urban and Suburban Vote* (Charlottesville: Bureau of Public Administration, University of Virginia, 1961), p. 5.

[7] *Ibid.*, p. 15.

kurtosis (peakedness of their distribution): thus, this index considers several dimensions of the deviation from the state-wide population norm shown by legislative districts. The Dauer-Kelsey index adds the residents in the smallest-population districts until it finds the minimum percentage of a state's population that can elect a majority of legislators in each house. The David-Eisenberg index shows the equity of apportionment by computing the relative value of a vote cast in the most populous urban county of each state; it determines the inverted ratio of this constituency's population to that of the average constituency's population for each house, and then averages the ratios for both houses. In the case of each apportionment index, the states with the highest scores are most equitably apportioned.

Although each dependent variable assesses a separate aspect of state politics, they tend to cluster together in the categories of party-competition, voter turnout and legislative apportionment. Their coefficients of simple correlation (product moment), shown in Table 2, indicate that states scoring high (or low) on one measure of each category tend to score high (or low) on the other measures. Moreover, there is a tendency for states showing intense (or weak) party competition, high (or low) turnout or equitable (or inequitable) legislative apportionment to score consistently on the other dimensions of politics. Thus, states that enjoy high party competition also tend to show the traits of high voter turnout and equitable apportionment in the legislature. However, the correlations within categories tend to be higher than those between categories. Thus, it appears that variables *a-l* measure three principal dimensions of a coherent phenomena; in the words of this study, they are those components of state politics labeled party competition, voter turnout and the equity of legislative apportionment.

The indicators of current economic characteristics assess three aspects of individual welfare, living conditions and state resources that previous studies have used in assessing "economic development." [8] The specific measures are:

I) per capita personal income, 1962
II) percentage of population living in urban areas, 1960
III) personal income, 1962

Each of these characteristics may affect the resources of individuals and state and local governments within each state, plus the needs that citizens feel for public services and their willingness to tolerate widespread participation in politics and competition for the control of public policies.

[8] See the sources cited in note #1, plus Harvey S. Perloff *et al.*, *Regions, Resources and Economic Growth* (Baltimore: Johns Hopkins University Press, 1962).

TABLE 1. *Coefficients of Simple Correlation among Measures of Inter-Party Competition, Voter Turnout and Legislative Apportionment*

	a	b	c	d	e	f	g	h	i	j	k	l
Inter-party Competition												
a) gubernatorial competition	1.00	.61[3]	.51[3]	.41[2]	.24	.24	.63[3]	–.67[3]	–.62[3]	–.25	–.12	–.39[3]
b) lower house competition		1.00	.85[3]	.46[3]	.57[3]	.45[2]	.78[3]	–.75[3]	–.82[3]	–.32[1]	–.20	–.43[2]
c) upper house competition			1.00	.41[2]	.52[3]	.49[3]	.43[2]	–.75[3]	–.78[3]	–.23	–.04	–.36[1]
d) gubernatorial tenure				1.00	.18	.27	.43[2]	–.43[2]	–.55[3]	–.12	–.07	–.19
e) lower house tenure					1.00	.61[3]	.38[2]	–.38[2]	–.45[2]	–.19	–.04	–.14
f) upper house tenure						1.00	.23	–.37[2]	–.48[3]	–.23	–.08	–.24
g) U.S. Representative competition							1.00	–.64[3]	–.75[3]	–.20	–.09	–.33[1]
Voter Turnout												
h) gubernatorial turnout								1.00	.89[3]	.32[1]	.08	.43[2]
i) U.S. Representative turnout									1.00	.30[1]	.05	.38[2]
Legislative Apportionment												
j) Schubert-Press index										1.00	.52[3]	.65[3]
k) Dauer-Kelsay index											1.00	.45[2]
l) David-Eisenberg index												1.00

[1] significant at the .05 level
[2] significant at the .01 level
[3] significant at the .001 level

NOTE: High scores in the measures of party competition indicate *weak* competition.

Generally speaking, states scoring high (or low) on one measure of economic activity also score high (or low) on the others. However, as the coefficients of simple correlation in Table 2 indicate, there is considerable "slippage" among the characteristics. For this reason, the following analysis employs both simple and partial correlation techniques to determine the relative importance of each economic characteristics upon each measure of state politics.

The dependent and independent variable of this study meet the requirements of the statistics employed: each variable is an interval scale, their distributions approach normality, and there are linear relationships between variables taken two at a time.

It is no simple task to define the regions of America. In any single demarcation there are likely to be disputes about the assignments given to "border states." To cope with the problem of regional definition this study employs three demarcations of the states. The first two are used by Perloff *et al.* in their study of regional economic development.[9] Demarcation #1 divides the 48 states into three regions, principally along the Ohio and Mississippi Rivers. Because of economic affinities, however, Arkansas and Louisiana are placed in the *Southeast* rather than in *Transmississippi*. East of the Ohio River, Demarcation #1 follows the northern borders of West Virginia and Virginia in dividing the *North* from the *Southeast*. Demarcation #2 subdivides two major regions of the first grouping: the North becomes *New England, Mid-Atlantic* and *Great Lakes;* the *Southeast* remains as is; and *Transmississippi* becomes the *Plains, Mountains, Southwest* and *Far West*. Demarcation #3 employs

TABLE 2. *Coefficients of Simple Correlation among Measures of Economic Development*

	Per Capita Personal Income	Urbanization	Personal Income
I) Per capita personal income	1.00	.44[2]	.69[3]
II) Urbanization		1.00	.58[3]
III) Personal income			1.00

[1] significant at the .05 level
[2] significant at the .01 level
[3] significant at the .001 level

[9] *Ibid*. While the component states of Perloff's regional demarcations remain unchanged, his "West" is called "Transmississippi" here to eliminate confusion with other designations. For a similar reason, the region that the Census Bureau names "West" is called "Transplains" here.

the principal divisions of the U.S. Census Bureau: the *Northeast* includes New England plus the urban-industrial states of New York, New Jersey and Pennsylvania; *North Central* includes the Great Lakes and Plains states; the *South* includes the eleven states of the Confederacy plus the border states of Delaware, Maryland, West Virginia, Kentucky and Oklahoma; and *Transplains* includes the remaining states of the mountain, desert and Pacific coastal areas. The states included in each regional grouping are listed below. Because this is part of a larger study extending over the twentieth century, the states of Alaska and Hawaii are excluded. [See Regional Groupings of American States, p. 139.]

Simple correlations and a comparison of means show the relationships between political characteristics and both economics and regions considered individually. Secondly, a limited effort is made to speculate about historical experiences that have contributed to the distinctive political traits of several regions. Finally, an analysis of covariance permits the assessment of relative associations between measures of state politics, economics and regionalism. The technique shows the relationships between a dependent variable (a measure of politics), and a nominal variable (region) and interval variables (economic characteristics) while controlling successively for each likely influence. The tables below show the relationship between economics and politics while controlling for region, and then the relationship between regions and politics while controlling for economics.[10] Each analysis of covariance is performed three times: once with each of the three regional demarcations of the states.

Economics and Politics. As expected, the measures of inter-party competition and voter turnout show numerous significant relationships with the measures of economic activity.[11] The coefficients of simple correlation in Table 3 indicate that high scores on voter turnout and intense inter-party competition occur in states that have high levels of personal income per capita and a high proportion of the population living in urban areas. These findings resemble those reported by Dawson and Robinson and Dye, and reinforce their contention that levels of personal well-being and urbanization support political activism and political competition. Coefficients of partial correlation, also reported in Table 3, indicate that the level of personal well-being (measured by personal in-

[10] The analysis of covariance proceeds according to the procedures described in Hubert M. Blalock, *Social Statistics* (New York: McGraw-Hill, 1959), Chapter 20. The essential computations are provided by "Analysis of Covariance with Multiple Covariates: BMD04V," in *Biomedical Computer Programs* (Los Angeles: University of California Health Sciences Computing Facility, 1965).

[11] The test for statistical significance does not, strictly speaking, apply to the data: the subjects represent a universe (the 48 contiguous states) rather than a sample drawn to represent a larger universe. Nevertheless, the test for significance is useful for denoting relationships that are "sizable."

Regional Groupings of American States

Demarcation #1

North
Maine
New Hampshire
Vermont
Massachusetts
Rhode Island
Connecticut
New York
New Jersey
Pennsylvania
Delaware
Maryland
Ohio
Michigan
Indiana
Illinois
Wisconsin

Southeast
Virginia
West Virginia
North Carolina
South Carolina
Georgia
Florida
Kentucky
Tennessee
Alabama
Mississippi
Arkansas
Louisiana

Transmississippi
Minnesota
Iowa
Missouri
North Dakota
South Dakota
Nebraska
Kansas
Oklahoma
Texas
Montana
Wyoming
Idaho
Colorado
New Mexico
Utah
Arizona
Nevada
Washington
Oregon
California

Demarcation #2

New England
Maine
New Hampshire
Vermont
Massachusetts
Rhode Island
Connecticut

Mid-Atlantic
New York
New Jersey
Pennsylvania
Delaware
Maryland

Southeast
Virginia
West Virginia
North Carolina
South Carolina
Georgia
Florida
Kentucky
Tennessee
Alabama
Mississippi
Arkansas
Louisiana

Great Lakes
Ohio
Indiana
Michigan
Illinois
Wisconsin

Plains
Minnesota
Iowa
Missouri
North Dakota
South Dakota
Nebraska
Kansas

Southwest
Arizona
New Mexico
Oklahoma
Texas

Mountains
Montana
Idaho
Wyoming
Colorado
Utah

Far West
Washington
Oregon
Nevada
California

Demarcation #3

Northeast
Maine
New Hampshire
Vermont
Massachusetts
Rhode Island
Connecticut
New York
Pennsylvania
New Jersey

South
Delaware
Maryland
Virginia
West Virginia
North Carolina
South Carolina
Georgia
Florida
Kentucky
Tennessee
Alabama
Mississippi
Arkansas
Louisiana
Oklahoma
Texas

North Central
Ohio
Indiana
Michigan
Wisconsin
Illinois
Minnesota
Iowa
Missouri
North Dakota
South Dakota
Nebraska
Kansas

Transplains
Montana
Wyoming
Colorado
New Mexico
Idaho
Utah
Arizona
Washington
Oregon
Nevada
California

come per capita) is the economic characteristic that bears most directly on the state political system. Perhaps the relative wealth of citizens permits a tolerant attitude toward the participation in politics by minority social-economic groups, and encourages politicians to solicit popular support actively by offering attractive packages of programmatic and symbolic appeals. The findings of little relationship between a measure of total state resources (personal income) and the political variables suggests further that the relative position of individuals, rather than the economic potential of the state seems to have the most to do with political activity. Consistent with the findings of Dye and Hofferbert, the measures of equity in legislative apportionment show relatively little relationship with economic characteristics; and those relationships that are of significant mag-

TABLE 3. *Coefficients of Simple Correlation, Partial Correlation[a] and Multiple Determination (R^2) Between Measures of Economic Development and Measures of State Political Characteristics*

	Simple Correlation			Partial Correlation[a]			(R^2)
	Income/ capita	Urban- ization	Income	Income/ capita	Urban- ization	Income	
Competition							
a) gubern comp	–.39[2]	–.25	–.12	–.31[1]	.01	.05	.15
b) lower house comp	–.62[3]	–.38[2]	–.27	–.53[3]	.09	–.03	.39[3]
c) upper house comp	–.62[3]	–.38[2]	–.17	–.58[3]	.14	.07	.41[3]
d) gubern tenure	–.40[2]	–.22	–.08	–.36[1]	.04	.08	.17[1]
e) lower house tenure	–.29[1]	–.24	–.19	–.17	–.04	–.05	.09
f) upper house tenure	–.25	–.24	–.05	–.13	–.13	.12	.09
g) U.S. Rep comp	–.54[3]	–.34[1]	–.28[1]	–.45[2]	.10	–.09	.31[3]
Turnout							
h) gubern turnout	.52[3]	.21	.06	.54[3]	–.17	–.13	.33[3]
i) U.S. Rep turnout	.59[3]	.27	.08	.59[3]	–.15	–.17	.40[3]
Apportionment							
j) Schubert-Press	.08	.00	.06	.12	–.11	.07	.02
k) Dauer-Kelsay	–.24	–.28[1]	.07	–.09	–.28	.30[1]	.16[1]
l) David-Eisenberg	.34[1]	.26	.25	.22	–.01	.11	.13

[a]controlling for each of the independent variables
[1]significant at the .05 level
[2]significant at the .01 level
[3]significant at the .001 level

NOTE: High scores on the measures of party competition indicate *weak* competition.

nitude do not consistently indicate whether equitable apportionment shows positive or negative relationships with economic development.[12]

By themselves, the three economic characteristics considered here leave unexplained much of the interstate variation in political characteristics. This is evident from the coefficients of multiple determination reported in Table 3. For only four of the twelve dependent variables do the aggregate of economic measures account for at least thirty per cent of the interstate variation: these are two measures of party competition (*b* and *c*) and both measures of voter turnout (*h* and *i*). For five of the dependent variables (*a*, *e*, *f*, *k* and *l*) the economic measures do not account for enough of the interstate variation to produce a significant coefficient of multiple determination. There remain substantial components of the political variables that are not explained by economics alone. As the following analysis will show, the concept of regionalism is helpful in the understanding of state politics.

Regions and Politics. There are clear regional differences in the components of the state political system that are considered in this study. Table 4 reports the mean scores of states, by region, on each dependent variable. On variables *a-g*, states in southern regions show the least interparty competition, while northern and western states are the most competitive. In particular, the sharpest contrast is found in a comparison of the Southeast with the Mountain and Great Lake regions. The findings for the Southern states reflect the characteristic that V. O. Key and many others have long described: an overwhelming prominence of the Democratic Party in non-Presidential races, and the restriction of political competition to intra-party factionalism.[13] While a measurement more recent than 1960–62 would show greater inroads of two-party competition in Southern state politics, the change would be insufficient to alter the basic finding that the South contains less two-party competition than any other American section. The intense competition within the Mountain region may reflect, in part, the relatively late date of that area's settlement. After the Civil War the Mountain states received settlers from both North and South who brought their party attachments with them. Since that time there has been no party-realigning trauma that has had a primarily sectional impact, so the citizens of the Mountain region have had no reason to replace their family heritages with a new-found sectional partisan tie.[14] The competitiveness of the Great Lake states reflects a

[12] The relevant works of Dye, Dawson and Robinson and Hofferbert are cited above in note 1.

[13] V. O. Key, *Southern Politics: In State and Nation* (New York: Alfred Knopf, 1949).

[14] Frank Munger, *American State Politics: Readings for Comparative Analysis* (New York: Thomas Y. Crowell, 1966), pp. 285–86.

TABLE 4. *Regional Means of State Scores on Measures of Political Characteristics*

	Demarcation #1			Demarcation #2								Demarcation #3			
	North	South-east	Trans-missis-sippi	New England	Mid-Atlantic	South-east	Great Lakes	Plains	South-west	Moun-tains	Far West	North-east	South	North-central	Trans-plains
Competition															
a) gubern comp	52.9	68.8	54.4	52.1	53.3	68.8	53.3	53.2	54.3	54.7	56.1	52.4	65.2	53.3	55.0
b) lower house comp	62.8	90.0	64.5	68.9	62.9	90.0	55.4	63.8	79.5	59.4	57.1	64.1	87.8	60.3	60.8
c) upper house comp	65.2	90.7	68.0	69.9	63.4	90.7	61.5	66.0	89.9	56.6	63.9	66.9	88.1	64.1	64.7
d) gubern tenure	8.5	11.7	8.6	8.7	8.8	11.7	8.0	8.3	8.5	9.2	8.5	8.9	11.0	8.1	8.5
e) lower house tenure	9.1	10.0	8.6	9.7	9.2	10.0	8.4	8.9	10.0	7.2	8.5	9.3	10.0	8.7	8.2
f) upper house tenure	9.1	10.0	8.4	8.3	10.0	10.0	9.2	8.6	10.0	7.6	7.5	8.9	10.0	8.8	8.0
g) U.S. Rep comp	54.0	71.1	57.5	57.4	52.0	71.1	51.7	56.5	60.6	54.4	59.9	55.1	68.2	54.5	56.8
Turnout															
h) gubern turnout	59.8	35.2	57.6	59.3	56.6	35.2	63.5	59.4	42.4	65.8	59.1	58.3	38.3	61.1	59.8
i) U.S. Rep turnout	55.4	25.8	52.9	57.7	51.4	25.8	56.7	54.2	40.1	61.3	52.9	56.4	29.7	55.3	55.3
Apportionment															
j) Schubert-Press	59.4	40.7	42.6	59.7	56.3	40.7	62.0	36.8	28.8	56.5	49.3	62.1	38.8	47.3	49.3
k) Dauer-Kelsay	66.7	68.8	66.4	67.4	60.2	68.8	72.5	70.8	63.0	65.0	63.7	68.9	65.6	71.5	62.9
l) David-Eisenberg	83.3	52.0	54.8	88.0	78.2	52.0	82.6	54.6	38.8	58.8	66.0	86.1	52.5	66.3	58.3

NOTE: High scores in the measures of party competition indicate *weak* competition. For the specific definition of each variable, see the text above.

marked change from the Republicanism that marked the region in past decades. Even Austin Ranney's 1946–63 composite index of inter-party competition places Illinois, Michigan, Indiana, Ohio and Wisconsin below 0.4 on a scale that ranges from 0.0 (one-party Republican) to 1.0 (one-party Democratic).[15] With its emphasis on more recent data, this study finds that the Lake states show the highest levels of inter-party competition. The change over time reflects, in part, the ascendance of the Democratic-labor union alliance in such states as Michigan, Ohio, Wisconsin and Indiana, plus the Democratic Party's capture of the Progressive Party's base in Wisconsin.[16] Perhaps the underlying ingredients of these changes include the industrialization of the Great Lakes area, and the attraction of industrial cities for Democratically-inclined migrants from the rural South. New England lies between the regions that score highest and lowest on inter-party competition; this finding does not reflect a consistent regional trait as much as it reflects intra-regional variation in party strength. While the three states of southern New England (Massachusetts, Rhode Island and Connecticut) are highly competitive or lean toward the Democratic Party, their neighbors of Maine, New Hampshire and Vermont adhere to the strong Republicanism of that region's past. These northern New England states also show the greatest adherence to the social and economic traits of their Yankee heritage: rural patterns of settlement, low industrialization and a majority of Protestants. These states have remained in the backwaters of migration and industrialization, and their Republican loyalists have not faced severe challenges from new settlers with alien cultures.[17]

Generally speaking, the regions that show intense (or weak) party competition also show high (or low) scores on voter turnout. This is evident both from the regional means shown in Table 4 and the coefficients of simple correlation shown in Table 1. On voter turnout the Southeast shows the lowest scores and the Mountain region scores highest. Intense party competition may provide a stimulus to citizen involvement in politics; or an active citizenry may provoke politicians to compete for popular support with alternative candidates. Other data about Southern states show that white elites have excluded Negroes from the electorate and have limited competition to intra-party factional disputes.[18]

[15] Austin Ranney, "Parties in State Politics," in Herbert Jacob and Kenneth N. Vines, *Politics in the American States* (Boston: Little, Brown and Company, 1965), p. 65.

[16] See John H. Fenton, *Midwest Politics* (New York: Holt, Rinehart and Winston, 1966).

[17] See Duane Lockard, *New England State Politics* (Princeton: Princeton University Press, 1958).

[18] Key, *op. cit.*

However, the high voter turnout in New England belies the usual relationship between levels of party competition and turnout. New England scores second only to the Mountain region on one measure of turnout (*i*), although it scores relatively low on several measures of competition. This finding of high turnout may reflect the liberal posture toward individual freedom that has characterized much of New England's history; and it suggests that the low inter-party competition of the region is more a reflection of historic loyalties than any effort to exclude certain groups from the polls.

On the measures of legislative apportionment, the sharpest contrast lies between the most equitably apportioned states of the Northeast and the poorly apportioned states of the Southwest. This difference may reflect the operation of an underlying political characteristic that is not measured in this study: the strength of party organizations. Political parties in the Northeast appear to be well organized, with relatively tight-knit structures extending throughout urban areas and into the state legislatures.[19] In the Southwest, in contrast, party organizations appear weak.[20] This contrast in party organization may affect legislative districting insofar as citizens in urban areas of the Southwest do not have spokesmen in the legislature who may use strong party mechanisms to work for equal representation.[21]

REGIONS, ECONOMICS, AND POLITICS. The question remains: *Does the current level of economic development or region have the greater impact on characteristics of state political systems?* The discussion above should prepare the reader for two observations. First, the multidimensionality of the state political system may preclude any easy answer to the question; economics may provide the better explanation for interstate differences in some political characteristics while region better explains others. And secondly, there is considerable overlap between region and current economics. Table 5 portrays the average scores of each region on the three measures of economic development. Much of what stands as "regionalism" may be nothing more than the resemblance of neighboring states' economies. The South takes its customary place at the bottom of personal income per capita and urbanization, the Mountain region scores lowest on total personal income, and the Middle Atlantic region scores

[19] See Thomas R. Dye, "State Legislative Politics" in Jacob and Vines, *op. cit.*, pp. 185–86.

[20] Samuel C. Patterson, "Dimensions of Voting Behavior in a One-Party State Legislature," *Public Opinion Quarterly*, XXVI (Summer, 1962), 185–200. While Patterson's findings pertain to the Oklahoma Legislature alone, they may be similar for the other state legislatures in the low party competition states of Texas, New Mexico and Arizona. See the score of this region on variables *b*, *c*, *e* and *f* in Table 4.

[21] This interpretation of regional differences on the indices of apportionment was suggested by my colleague, Thomas R. Dye.

TABLE 5. *Regional Means of State Scores on Measures of Economic Development*

	Demarcation #1			Demarcation #2								Demarcation #3			
	North	South-east	Trans-missis-sippi	New England	Mid-Atlantic	South-east	Great Lakes	Plains	South-west	Moun-tains	Far West	North-east	South	North-central	Trans-plains
I) Income/capita	$ 2533	1699	2260	$2393	2793	1699	2457	2229	1960	2153	2749	$ 2504	1880	2324	2335
II) Urban-ization	70.9%	50.0	62.0	66.1%	76.7	50.0	60.4	53.0	69.5	60.6	71.8	71.3%	54.7	60.4	66.4
III) Income	$14195	5833	6889	$4743	21184	5833	18547	5055	7512	2049	15525	$13818	6565	10677	7033

highest on each of the economic measures. As it is noted above in the introduction, however, the regions are not economically homogeneous. In the face of intraregional economic variations, it may be the non-economic aspects of regions that produce marked peculiarities in state political systems. An analysis of covariance provides a means for separating the influences on politics from the economic attributes of states and from those regional attributes that are not economic in character. The coefficients on the left side of Table 6 show the economic-political relationships while controlling for region, and the coefficients on the right side show the strength of regional differences in politics while controlling for economic development.[22]

It is evident from Table 6 that the concept of region makes a statistically important contribution to the explanation of state politics. For nine of the twelve dependent variables, region shows a significant relationship with a political characteristic while controlling for economic development. And in the case of most measures of party competition and one measure of turnout (*l*), region appears to be a more salient independent variable than economic development. Moreover, a comparison of Tables 3 and 6 suggests that an economic-apportionment relationship is more apparent when region is a control variable than when no control variable is employed.

A comparison of the coefficients in Table 6 by regional demarcation suggests that demarcation #3 provides the sharpest statement of regional differences in state political systems. Nine of the twelve dependent variables show significant region-political relationship in that demarcation, whereas only six and seven of the variables show such relationships in demarcations #1 and #2. It will be remembered from the discussion above that demarcation #3 includes four regions: the *Northeast* of Pennsylvania to Maine; the *South* of the Confederacy and Border states; the *Northcentral* of the Great Lakes and Plains states; and *Transplains* of the Mountain and Far Western states. Although it is possible that further experimentation with other groupings of states will yield even sharper regional findings, the present data suggest that subsequent inquiries into the political regions of America should consider the regional boundaries of demarcation #3.

Summary and Conclusions

By examining measures of inter-party competition, voter turnout and legislative apportionment, this study has found evidence that the regional location of states has a relationship with political characteristics that is

[22] See note 10 above.

TABLE 6. *Analysis of Covariance: Intraclass Correlations*[a]

	Between Economic Development and Political Characteristics while Controlling for Region			Between Region and Political Characteristic while Controlling for Economic Development		
	Regional Demarcation			Regional Demarcation		
	1	2	3	1	2	3
Competition						
a) gubernatorial comp	.005	.009	.035	.063	.054	.061
b) lower house comp	.115[1]	.033	.201[2]	.371[3]	.337[2]	.491[3]
c) upper house comp	.154[2]	.081	.227[3]	.126	.297[2]	.236[2]
d) gubernatorial tenure	.014	.015	.041	.276[2]	.144	.149[1]
e) lower house tenure	.046	.079	.045	.138	.297[2]	.216[2]
f) upper house tenure	.028	.110[1]	.013	.101	.266[2]	.143[1]
g) U.S. Rep comp	.071	.088	.138[1]	.243[2]	.173	.140[1]
Turnout						
h) gubernatorial turn	.109[1]	.066	.157[2]	.201[1]	.183[1]	.217[2]
i) U.S. Rep turnout	.135[1]	.089	.213[2]	.530[3]	.538[3]	.530[3]
Apportionment						
j) Schubert-Press	.051	.101[1]	.037	.144	.135	.082
k) Dauer-Kelsay	.205[2]	.183[2]	.214[2]	.012	–.085	.055
l) David-Eisenberg	.008	.040	.032	.316[3]	.286[2]	.162[1]

[a]The analysis of covariance is performed three separate times: once with each demarcation of the states. The procedures followed in computing the intraclass coefficients and the levels of significance are reported in the citation given in note #10.

[1] significant at the 0.5 level

[2] significant at the .01 level

[3] significant at the .001 level

independent of state economic characteristics. The saliency of the regional phenomena is most apparent with respect to inter-party competition and voter turnout, but it is also present in the case of legislative apportionment. Of all attempts to explain interstate variations on these indices of apportionment equity,[23] this study of regional location seems to have borne the strongest relationships.

Along with the claims for the regional approach to comparative state political analysis, it is necessary to mention qualifications: 1) the com-

[23] See the works of Dye and Hofferbert, cited above in note 1.

ponents of state political systems identified here make no claim to cover the field of politics; and 2) "region" as an explanatory variable has only intermediate value. With respect to the first qualification, it is evident that potentially important aspects of state political systems were not included among the dependent variables. Such features as citizens' attitudes toward public officials and the proper role of government, the political inclinations of major newspapers, the political involvement of religious leaders and the recruitment of new participants into public affairs may show relationships with economic development and region that are basically different from the traits considered here. With respect to the second qualification, it is evident that regional location alone does not indicate why some states show high party competition, voter turnout or equitable legislative apportionment. The regional variable only provides a clue to underlying historical experiences, shared by neighboring states, that may explain current political characteristics. The explanations for regional traits that are included in this study may be found wanting in the face of more thorough historical inquiries. Yet the available literature suggests that racial tensions in the South, the lateness of the immigration to the Mountain region, the social-economic isolation and resilient loyalties of northern New England, industrialization and developing unionism during recent decades in the Great Lakes states, and the differing strength of party organizations in the Northeast and Southwest may have a great deal to do with the distinctive traits of those regions with respect to party competition, voter turnout and legislative apportionment.

While the focus of this study has been on static relationships between economics, regions and politics in the American states, it has potential application for a broader range of experience. In an examination of "political development" among nations, Seymour Lipset has argued for democracy's dependence upon prior economic development.[24] But this study finds that historical experience of regions may have greater impact upon current political traits than latter-day economic characteristics. If regional cultures have worldwide holding power over political characteristics such as is suggested by these findings for the American states, the strength of regional cultures should temper the enthusiasm of those who hope for political change to follow economic development in simple fashion. Once established, certain political traits seem capable of withstanding the influence of subsequent economic changes. Voter turnout and party competition may be critical ingredients of any society's maintenance of democratic procedures. Yet several measures of these traits, in the United States, show closer correspondence with region than with eco-

[24] Seymour Martin Lipset, *Political Man* (Garden City: Doubleday, 1960), Chapter II.

nomic development. Here, developments in turnout and competition within the most lagging states may depend upon the police powers of the Federal Government. Because sovereign nations lack developmental opportunities similar to those of our Civil Rights Acts, their road to democratic procedures may be even more lengthy and difficult than that followed in this country.

THE ELECTORATE AND STATE CONSTITUTIONAL REVISION:

An analysis of four Michigan referenda

NORMAN C. THOMAS

In a series of four elections beginning in 1958, voters in the state of Michigan confronted the question of constitutional revision in a statewide referendum. The first three referenda, held in 1958, 1960, and 1961, led to the calling of a constitutional convention. The convention, meeting from October, 1961 to May, 1962, drafted a proposed constitution which the electorate ratified in 1963.[1]

Reprinted from Norman C. Thomas, "The Electorate and State Constitutional Revision: An Analysis of Four Michigan Referenda," *Midwest Journal of Political Science*, 12 (February, 1968), 115–129, by permission of the Wayne State University Press.

Research for this paper was aided by a grant from the Horace H. Rackham School of Graduate Studies of the University of Michigan to the Department of Political Science for a study of the politics of constitutional revision referenda in Michigan between 1958 and 1963. I am especially indebted to J. Merrill Shanks of the Survey Research Center who guided me in analyzing the data. Responsibility for what is said here is, however, mine alone.

[1] The steps leading to the calling of the convention which drafted the 1963 Michigan Constitution and the politics of the convention-making process have been carefully examined in: Albert L. Sturm, *Constitution-Making in Michigan, 1961–1962* (Ann Arbor: Institute of Public Administration, The University of Michigan, 1963); James K. Pollock, *Making Michigan's New Constitution* (Ann Arbor: George Wahr Publishing Co., 1962); and, Robert S. Friedmann, *The Michigan Constitutional Convention and Administrative Organization* (Ann Arbor: Institute of Public Administration, 1963).

The major voting studies have focused on partisan elections primarily because such contests have the most immediate effects and are the most visible aspects of the American electoral system. These studies have led to the development of a model which explains the voting decision in terms of the direct effect of psychological variables, e.g., party identification and political attitudes, and the more indirect effects of socio-economic variables such as class.[2] In contrast, much less interest has been manifested in the analysis of referendum elections.[3] Some recent studies of local politics, however, have examined the effects of social and political

[2] See especially Angus Campbell, Philip E. Converse, Warren E. Miller, and Donald E. Stokes, *The American Voter* (New York: John Wiley and Sons, 1960). The development of voting research is succinctly reviewed in Alvin Boskoff and Harmon Zeigler, *Voting Patterns in a Local Election* (Philadelphia: J. B. Lippincott Co., 1964), Chapter 1.

[3] The most systematic analyses have been of referenda at the local level. See, for example, Clarence Stone, "Local Referendums: An Alternative to the Alienated Voter Model," *Public Opinion Quarterly*, Vol. 29 (1965), pp. 213–222; E. L. McDill and J. C. Ridley, "Status, Anomia, Political Alienation and Political Participation," *American Journal of Sociology*, Vol. 48 (1962), pp. 205–213; John E. Horton and Wayne E. Thompson, "Powerlessness and Political Negativism: A Study of Defeated Local Referendums," *American Journal of Sociology*, Vol. 47 (1962), pp. 485–493; William A. Gamson, "The Fluoridation Dialogue: Is It An Ideological Conflict?," *Public Opinion Quarterly*, Vol. 25 (1961), pp. 526–537; Thomas A. F. Plaut, "Analysis of Voting Behavior in a Fluoridation Referendum," *Public Opinion Quarterly*, Vol. 23 (1959), pp. 213–222. In most of these studies, the principal focus is not on the referendum as an important vehicle of policy-making but rather on the political consequences of such social tendencies as alienation and anomie. Plaut departs from this posture in his analysis of a fluoridation referendum in Cambridge, Massachusetts. He attempts to relate support for fluoridation to certain political variables.

Research on statewide referenda is generally less systematic than that dealing with local elections. See, for example, Eugene C. Lee (ed.), *The California Governmental Process* (Boston: Little, Brown and Co., 1966), Chapter V; Andrew R. Baggaley, "Religious Influence on Wisconsin Voting, 1928–1960," *American Political Science Review*, Vol. 56 (1962), pp. 66–70; John S. Radabaugh, "Tendencies of California Direct Legislation," *Southwestern Social Science Quarterly*, Vol. 42 (1961), pp. 66–78; James W. Vander Zanden, "Voting on Segregation Referenda," *Public Opinion Quarterly*, Vol. 25 (1961), pp. 92–105; Thomas Pettigrew and Ernest Q. Campbell, "Faubus and Segregation: An Analysis of Arkansas Voting," *Public Opinion Quarterly*, Vol. 24 (1960), pp. 436–447; Joseph La Palombara and Charles Hagan, "Direct Legislation: An Appraisal and a Suggestion," *American Political Science Review*, Vol. 45 (1951), pp. 400–421; James K. Pollock, *The Initiative and Referendum in Michigan* (Ann Arbor: University of Michigan Press, 1940); and Winston W. Crouch and V. O. Key, Jr., *The Initiative and Referendum in California* (Berkeley: University of California Press, 1939).

factors on voting patterns in referenda.[4] They have found, *inter alia*, that progressive and reform issues tend to receive proportionately more support from Republican and higher status voters than from Democratic and lower status voters. In addition, two of these studies which compare referenda with other types of elections conclude that social and political variables do not affect outcomes in a similar manner.[5]

This paper is an attempt to fill a part of the gap in the literature of voting patterns in state elections through an analysis of the effect of party, socio-economic factors, and urbanization on the outcomes of the four Michigan constitutional revision referenda.

Background

A summary of the steps leading to the adoption of Michigan's 1963 constitution and of the political circumstances surrounding them will provide a background for the analysis. In 1958 the question of calling a state constitutional convention appeared on the general election ballot pursuant to the requirement of the 1908 Constitution that it be submitted to the electorate every sixteen years.[6] The vote was favorable to a convention, 821,282 to 600,365, but because a majority of the persons *voting in the election* (as determined by the total vote cast for governor) did not support the proposal, it lost. Those voters who failed to express themselves on the issue in effect voted no.

In 1960 the Michigan electorate approved a constitutional amendment which: (1) changed the requirement that a constitutional convention referendum secure a majority of the votes cast in the election to a majority of the votes cast on the question; (2) changed the basis for electing delegates to the convention; and, (3) provided for another constitutional convention referendum in the 1961 Spring election. In April, 1961, the electorate approved the proposal to call a convention.

[4] See Robert H. Salisbury and Gordon Black, "Class and Party in Partisan and Non-Partisan Elections: The Case of Des Moines," *American Political Science Review*, Vol. 57 (1963), pp. 584–592; Oliver Williams and Charles R. Adrian, *Four Cities: A Study of Comparative Policy-Making* (Philadelphia: University of Pennsylvania Press, 1963), Chapter 5; James Q. Wilson and Edward C. Banfield, "Public-Regardingness as a Value Premise in Voting Behavior," *American Political Science Review*, Vol. 58 (1964), pp. 876–887; and, M. Kent Jennings and Harmon Zeigler, "Class, Party, and Race in Four Types of Elections: The Case of Atlanta," *Journal of Politics*, Vol. 28 (1966), pp. 391–407.

[5] Salisbury and Black, pp. 590–591; and Jennings and Zeigler, pp. 400–401.

[6] Michigan Constitution of 1908, Article XVII.

The election of delegates to the convention, in September, 1961 resulted in a surprising Republican victory with the party winning 99 of the 144 seats. The convention convened on October 3, 1961 and worked steadily until May 11, 1962 after which date it recessed until August 2 when it reconvened to adjourn *sine die*. The proposed constitution which the convention produced bore a strong Republican imprint, and Democratic delegates and party leaders announced their determination to oppose its ratification.

If maximum participation in the referendum were desired the electorate would have voted on the ratification of the proposed document at the 1962 general election when a heavy turnout could be expected. The state attorney general ruled, however, that the 1908 Constitution required a vote in the 1963 Spring election. Those elections, which have been abolished by the 1963 Constitution, were traditionally characterized by a low rate of voter participation. The only way in which a vote could have been held in 1962 would have been for the convention to have adjourned prior to April 1, 1962. Between the convention's adjournment on August 2 and the ratification referendum in April, 1963, George Romney became Michigan's first Republican governor in 14 years.

The campaign for ratification of the proposed constitution occupied the center of Michigan's political stage during the first three months of 1963. The question of ratification quickly became a partisan issue. Democrats attacked the constitution as a conservative document which, on balance, was worse than the one it would replace. They charged that Governor Romney had sold out to Republican conservatives at the convention in order to further his personal political ambitions. Romney responded to the challenge by personally campaigning throughout the state in support of the proposed constitution. He made ratification a test of his leadership among Republicans and appealed for voters to support the document in the interest of good government. These partisan postures with respect to constitutional revision contrasted sharply with the stands which the parties took in the pre-convention referenda.[7] In 1958 the Democrats voiced mild opposition and the Republicans were split. In 1960 the Democrats and the Republicans were both divided. In the 1961 referendum which resulted in the successful call of the convention, Democrats supported the proposal and Republicans were officially neutral.

In 1963, after a bitterly fought campaign which overshadowed contests for elective office, the electorate ratified the proposed constitution by the narrow margin of 811,098 to 803,269. The proportion of persons of voting age participating in the election, approximately 36 per cent,

[7] For a discussion of partisan and interest group positions in the pre-convention referenda, see Sturm, *op. cit.*, pp. 17–28.

was well below the normal figure for a general election. However, it was considerably greater than the 27 per cent participation rate in the 1961 referendum to call the convention.

The partisan elections held concurrently with the four referenda were closely contested but consistently Democratic. The party's candidates won every major statewide electoral contest in 1958, 1960, 1961, and 1963, but with winning margins of less than 55 per cent of the two-party vote. George Romney's victory in the 1962 gubernatorial election reflects the strong competitive position of the Republican party during this period. That election is not included in our analysis, however, because it did not involve a constitutional revision referendum.

Research Strategy

The data were obtained from a stratified random sample of 100 of Michigan's 5,200 precincts.[8] The use of precincts rather than counties as analytical units provided the advantage of greater homogeneity with respect to size, partisan tendency, and various demographic characteristics. However, the employment of aggregate data precluded the adoption of analytical techniques similar to those used in the Survey Research Center and the Lazarsfeld studies and suggested instead the use of techniques patterned after those employed by Salisbury and Black and Jennings and Zeigler in their analyses of Des Moines and Atlanta.[9]

The outcome of the four elections for the 100 precincts in the sample constitute the dependent variables and are expressed in terms of the percentage of yes votes in each referendum. The independent variables include party, various socio-economic indicators, and urbanization.

The best measure of party is party registration, which was used by Salisbury and Black in their Des Moines study. However, in Michigan as

[8] I am indebted to Ralph Bisco of the Survey Research Center who designed and drew the sample. The 5,200 precincts were divided into 100 relatively homogeneous strata according to political characteristics as determined by the Democratic gubernatorial vote in 1960, turnout as measured by the percentage of registered voters who participated in the 1960 gubernatorial contest, and whether voting machines or paper ballots were used. (85 per cent of the precincts use voting machines.) One precinct was then selected at random from each stratum.

[9] The dangers involved in using aggregate data for the analysis of voting behavior are those involved in making inferences from any ecological correlations to individual-level phenomena. Such data cannot explain or predict individual behavior but they can suggest behavior patterns and reveal relationships among variables. See Austin Ranney, "The Utility and Limitations of Aggregate Data in the Study of Electoral Behavior," in Ranney, ed., *Essays in the Behavioral Study of Politics* (Urbana: University of Illinois Press, 1961), pp. 91–102.

in Georgia, voters are not required to register by party. Therefore, it seemed appropriate to adopt the measure used by Jennings and Zeigler, the Democratic Vote Index. This index is the average of the Democratic vote percentage in each precinct in the four elections and is "simply a mean party vote over time." [10]

Socio-economic status can be measured in a variety of ways. Salisbury and Black employed a scale based on the "type and quality of housing." [11] Jennings and Zeigler constructed an index based on census data. For each precinct they took an average of the percentage of persons twenty-five years of age and over with less than nine grades of education, the percentage of families with incomes of $5,000 or less, and the percentage of males over fourteen years of age employed in unskilled occupations and then subtracted the average from 100.[12] Because the data were more readily obtainable, the socio-economic status (SES) index developed by Jennings and Zeigler was used.

The third major independent variable employed in this study is urbanization. The employment of urbanization as an independent variable seemed appropriate primarily because the issue of state constitutional revision has traditionally been regarded as an urban-rural conflict over institutional and structural reform with urban interests supporting it and rural interests opposed. This certainly appears to have been the case in Michigan in the three pre-convention referenda [13] and also in a 1960 Iowa constitutional convention referendum.[14] Furthermore, judging from the nature of the highly partisan campaign and the pattern of voting, the 1963 ratification referendum did not appear to fit the urban-rural model.[15]

The measure of urbanization employed was an ordinal-level scale based on census definitions of urban and rural, census population cate-

[10] *Loc. cit.*, p. 393.

[11] *Loc. cit.*, p. 585.

[12] *Loc. cit.*, p. 392.

[13] See John P. White, *Voting Machines and the 1958 Defeat of Constitutional Revision in Michigan* (Ann Arbor: University of Michigan, Institute of Public Administration, 1960). In the 1961 referendum, the proposal to call a convention won a narrow victory, 596,433 to 573,612. It received a favorable vote in only four of the state's 83 counties, all of which are heavily urbanized and located in the Detroit metropolitan area. These counties, Macomb, Oakland, Wayne, and Washtenaw, provided 64.4 per cent of the affirmative vote cast in the state.

[14] Salisbury and Black, *op. cit.*, pp. 590–591; and George B. Mather, *Effects of the Use of Voting Machines on Total Votes Cast* (Iowa City: University of Iowa, Institute of Public Affairs, 1964), pp. 53–55.

[15] Similarly, Boskoff and Zeigler argue that place of residence is "of some importance" as a predictor of voting. They cite a metropolitan reform referendum in St. Louis in which the plan was more consistently opposed in the county than in the city. *Op. cit.*, p. 27.

gories, and manifest ecological characteristics. Five categories of urbanization were established and the precincts classified accordingly. In descending order of urbanization, the categories include: (1) the city of Detroit; (2) suburban, located within the Detroit Standard Metropolitan Statistical Area; (3) outstate (non-metropolitan area) cities with population over 50,000; (4) outstate cities and towns between 50,000 and 2,500; and (5) rural, including communities with populations below 2,500.[16]

The objectives of the analysis were to determine how much of the variance in the four constitutional revision referendum elections can be explained by the independent variables. The expectation was that partisanship would not be strongly related to the vote in the three pre-convention elections. It seemed probable that support for constitutional revision in those contests would be related most strongly to the socio-economic indicators, especially education. To the extent that constitutional revision was an urban-rural issue it also seemed likely that in the pre-convention referenda, the more urbanized precincts would be more supportive than the less urbanized precincts. Inasmuch as Republicans controlled the convention by a two-to-one ratio and the proposed constitution received strong Republican support and Democratic opposition in the ratification campaign it seemed likely that in the final referendum relationships between the independent variables and the vote would be somewhat similar to those manifested in partisan elections.

Analysis

In analyzing the referendum voting patterns, partisanship as measured by the Democratic Vote Index and the socio-economic indicators could easily be correlated with the dependent variable. In relating urbanization

[16] The census defines the rural population as all persons living on farms or in places of less than 2,500 inhabitants. All other persons are classified urban. In establishing additional categories of the urban population according to the degree of urbanization, special recognition was given to the importance of the Detroit metropolitan area in the political and economic life of Michigan. The central city itself presented the most manifestly urbanized area. The suburbs located in the Detroit Standard Metropolitan Statistical Area, including Wayne, Oakland, and Macomb counties, quite clearly seemed to constitute the next most heavily urbanized area. The outstate cities and their environs which the census defined as Standard Metropolitan Statistical Areas (such an area includes a city of at least 50,000 population) represented a third level of urbanization while outstate cities with populations between 50,000 and 2,500 provided a distinct fourth level. These categories in some respects are arbitrary and they are not separated by equal intervals. But they are not so gross that they fail to provide a measure of the urban-rural dimension which is more meaningful than the simple basic census dichotomy.

TABLE 1. *Mean Yes Vote in Referendum Elections by Urbanization Category*

	Detroit	Suburban	Outstate Over 50,000	Outstate 2,500-50,000	Rural
1958	56%	63%	62%	62%	48%
1960	69	69	52	52	40
1961	75	70	46	43	25
1963	35	50	47	52	50
N	(22)	(22)	(9)	(11)	(36)

to the referendum vote the problem of an ordinal-scale variable presented itself. This problem appeared to be further complicated because the yes vote varied considerably between the five urbanization categories from year to year. (See Table 1.)

However, a comparison of correlation coefficients (Pearsonian r's) and E coefficients [17] revealed that the two measures of association were sufficiently close in magnitude to justify considering urbanization as having the characteristics of an interval scale and to undertake a correlation and regression.[18] These data indicate that urbanization was only moderately related to support for constitutional revision in the initial and final referenda, but that it was very strongly related in the 1960 and 1961 elections. In all three pre-convention contests, urbanization as a precinct characteristic tended to be associated with yes voting whereas in the ratification contest it initially appeared that there was a mild reversal in the direction of the relationship.

[17] The E coefficient is the square root of the correlation ratio. The correlation ratio is a measure of association which makes use of the sums of squares generated in an analysis of variance. Its interpretation is analogous to the interpretation of the Pearsonian r in that r^2 and E^2 indicate the proportion of variance in the dependent variable that is explained by the independent variable. See Hubert M. Blalock, *Social Statistics* (New York: McGraw-Hill Book Co., 1960), pp. 267 and 298.

[18] In each election, E showed a somewhat stronger relationship between urbanization and the referendum vote than r:

	E	r
1958	.44	.28
1960	.75	.73
1961	.89	.88
1963	.36	—.27

The gap between E and r was greatest in 1958 and 1963 when voting within the urbanization categories was irregular and the relationship was weakest. The negative sign of r in 1963 is not accompanied by a corresponding sign for E because the latter statistic can only have a positive value due to the manner in which it is defined and calculated. See Blalock, *ibid.*, pp. 267 and 298.

The correlations between the independent variables and the yes vote further amplify the nature of the relationship between the yes vote and urbanization. [See Tables 2A, 2B, 2C.] These data also reflect the effects of the other independent variables, party and socio-economic factors.[19] The relationship between urbanization and support for constitutional revision changed somewhat after partialling out the effects of party and the various socio-economic indicators. Most interesting is the change in the direction of the relationship in the final referendum. The partial correlation coefficients obtained after holding constant party and the various socio-economic indicators all carry a positive sign whereas the simple correlation between the two variables was negative. This sign reversal indicates that urbanization was positively related to support for constitutional revision in the ratification contest although not as strongly as it had been in the two previous elections.[20] Apparently the overwhelming impact of party on the referendum voting in 1963, as revealed in the data and discussed below, obscured the fact that the final contest still carried tones of an urban-rural conflict.

Urbanization emerges from these data, then, as a variable with a considerable range in its explanatory value. In 1958, when the issue of constitutional revision was new, relatively unpublicized, and apparently not particularly salient for many voters, it explained less than one per cent of the variance in the voting. In 1960 it explained approximately one-fourth of the variance and in 1961 well over half.

This suggests that as the issue became more sharply defined and more widely publicized it assumed the characteristics of an urban-rural conflict. In fact, interest groups promoting the cause of good government, reformers, political liberals, and the metropolitan press all supported and publicized constitutional revision in those elections. In 1961 it was particularly stressed that a convention would permit the state's cities to throw off the yoke of rural domination and set about the business of

[19] The effect of the socio-economic factors is illustrated by presenting the data in three sections showing the separate indicators of education, occupation, and income; education with income and occupation excluded, and the combined SES Index. This format permits an extensive analysis of the impact of education as well as socio-economic status.

[20] The discovery of the sign reversal in the partial r between urbanization and the referendum vote, indicating that urbanization worked in the same direction in 1963 as in the previous elections, is a positive return from treating urbanization as an interval-scale variable. Assumptions based on fiat can provide a handsome payoff provided they are not too far-fetched.

The low b coefficient of .24 obtained in the regression analysis provided a useful check on the conclusion, based on the partial r between the yes vote and urbanization, that the strength of the relationship dropped sharply in 1963.

TABLE 2A. *Correlations Between Yes Vote and Urbanization, Democratic Vote Index, and Socio-Economic Indicators*

	Urbanization		Democratic Vote Index		Median Years Education		Percent Skilled		Median Family Income		Multiple Correlation
	Simple r	Partial r	Simple r	Partial r	Simple r	Partial r	Simple r	Partial r	Simple r	Partial r	R
1958	.28	.05	−.04	.02	.56	.37	.23	−.03	.49	.07	.57
1960	.73	.53	.34	.15	.47	.19	.16	.24	.46	.04	.79
1961	.88	.71	.53	.41	.41	.11	.05	.31	.46	.21	.91
1963	−.27	.30	−.85	−.80	.37	.06	.52	.09	.41	.09	.89

TABLE 2B. *Correlations between Yes Vote and Urbanization, Democratic Vote Index, and Education with Occupation and Income Excluded*

	Urbanization		Democratic Vote Index		Education		Multiple
	Simple r	Partial r	Simple r	Partial r	Simple r	Partial r	Correlation R
1958	.28	.09	–.04	.00	.56	.47	.57
1960	.73	.50	.34	.08	.47	.42	.77
1961	.88	.74	.53	.27	.41	.36	.90
1963	–.27	.36	–.85	–.84	.37	.17	.89

modernizing state government.[21] The rural areas became increasingly apprehensive about the prospect of constitutional change so that by 1961 they tended to view the drive for a convention as a Detroit-based conspiracy bent on selling them a constitutional Mackinac Bridge. In the ratification election, after the partisan stakes were made clear, there was still a tendency of the more urbanized precincts to favor constitutional revision although urbanization only explains about 10 per cent of the variance in the voting.

The data presented in [Tables 2A, 2B, 2C] also reflect the relationship between support for constitutional revision and partisan tendency as measured by the Democratic Vote Index. The impact of partisanship increased gradually during the three pre-convention referenda and then jumped dramatically in the ratification contest. This was undoubtedly a consequence of the increased salience of the revision issue for the parties, especially in the final election. The relationship between party and the yes vote was virtually non-existent in 1958. In 1960 a very weak associa-

TABLE 2C. *Correlations between Yes Vote and Urbanization, Democratic Vote Index, and SES Index*

	Urbanization		Democratic Vote Index		SES Index		Multiple
	Simple r	Partial r	Simple r	Partial r	Simple r	Partial r	Correlation R
1958	.28	.15	–.04	–.06	.50	.39	.52
1960	.73	.56	.34	.06	.49	.37	.77
1961	.88	.75	.53	.29	.44	.42	.90
1963	–.27	.37	–.85	–.84	.33	.18	.89

[21] See Sturm, *op. cit.*, pp. 20–28.

tion developed which became somewhat stronger in 1961. The sharp increase in the strength of the relationship and the reversal of its direction, with Democrats opposing ratification, confirmed the hypothesis that the final election was a highly partisan contest. After partialling out the effects of urbanization and the three socio-economic indicators, partisanship explains 65 per cent of the between precinct variance in the 1963 voting. Over 70 per cent of the variance can be explained when a single socio-economic measure, either education or the SES Index, is employed in the analysis.

The highly partisan character of voting in the ratification election can be explained primarily as a consequence of the work of the constitutional convention. The convention proposed a document which the Democratic Party regarded as a threat and which the Republicans saw as a marked improvement. Ratification would redound to the credit of the Republicans and Governor George Romney. In the pre-convention referenda, constitutional revision was only a remote probability, the substance of which was unknown. It did not affect either party strongly enough to produce a distinctive pattern of party-like voting in the referenda. In the ratification contest, constitutional revision was an imminent prospect, clear in substance and containing provisions which pleased most Republicans and upset most Democrats. The stakes were clearly perceived and the two parties conducted their campaigns and the electorate responded much in the manner of a partisan election.

Except for the initial referendum, the various socio-economic factors do not appear to possess the explanatory power of urbanization or party.[22] In 1958, the proportion of the variance in the referendum voting ac-

[22] A limitation in the technique employed to control for socio-economic factors must be acknowledged at this point. The problem is that turnout was not constant through the four elections. The general elections of 1958 and 1960 produced a substantially greater turnout than the Spring elections of 1961 and 1963. There is a strong probability that the latter two elections produced electorates of higher socio-economic status than the two earlier elections. Unfortunately, data on turnout were not obtained by precinct and it was not possible to control for turnout along with socio-economic factors.

The elections in which the socio-economic variables had the strongest relationship to the yes vote were the two high turnout elections in which the proportion of lower status voters was presumably greatest. Even then, however, their impact on the vote was modest compared with the effects of urbanization in 1960 and 1961 and of party in 1963. Also, the strength of the relationship between socio-economic factors and the referendum vote was less in the presidential election of 1960 than in the gubernatorial contest of 1958. (71 per cent of the Census Bureau's estimate of 4,564,000 persons of voting age in Michigan in 1960 voted in the presidential election of that year as compared with 62 per cent in 1958). Finally, an analysis of the partisan elections held concurrently with the four referenda revealed a consistently weak relationship between socio-economic factors and the party vote regardless of turnout. Therefore, even if data had been available on

counted for by the Democratic Vote Index and by urbanization is, in each instance, less than one per cent. In that election, median years of education appear to have been the only one of the three socio-economic indicators with significant explanatory value. After partialling out all other variables, it accounts for 13 per cent of the variance. When the separate measures of income and occupation are excluded from the analysis, education gains in explanatory value to the point where it accounts for 22 per cent of the variance. The lack of any strong effect on the part of party or urbanization seems to reflect the newness of the issue and the lack of knowledge regarding it. Apparently only the better educated voters supported constitutional revision in any discernible pattern in 1958.

After the initial election, the strength of the relationship between education and support for constitutional revision declined and education accounted for progressively less of the variance. As the issue became more widely publicized, voting patterns based on urban-rural conflict and party loyalty tended to establish themselves. The impact of education was, however, considerably greater in all three pre-convention elections than it was in 1963. The reformist character of those initial contests gave way to partisanship in the final struggle.

Neither of the two other separate socio-economic indicators seems to add any additional insights or to help in testing the hypotheses. Income behaves somewhat like education. An examination of occupation reveals a very mild tendency of higher occupational status to be associated with affirmative referendum voting. This phenomenon was most pronounced in 1960 and 1961, the two elections in which the reformist spirit was most predominant. The combined measure, the SES Index, revealed that class was moderately related to support for constitutional revision. In all four referenda, higher status precincts tended to be more supportive of revision than lower status precincts, but with a much stronger relationship in the pre-convention contests than in 1963. Class voting was most evident in 1961, the election in which urban-rural conflict was most manifest. This was not surprising since urbanization is positively correlated with education and the other measures of status.

Conclusion

The findings of this study have implications for our general understanding of statewide referendum voting behavior. They indicate that while some of the principal factors which influence voting in partisan elections are also operative in referenda, their impact in referendum elections

---

turnout differentials among SES categories it does not seem likely that any substantial changes would be required in the findings which follow.

varies considerably from year to year. Here, this was the case even though the issue remained constant. Political circumstances surrounding a particular election, such as the salience of the issue, appear to account for this phenomenon. In contrast, the major voting studies have consistently concluded that the impact of such variables as party and socio-economic status does not vary greatly from one election to the next.

This analysis suggests that in statewide referendum voting, socio-economic factors, especially education, provide the attitudes and values which constitute a basic cognitive mechanism for ordering electoral choice. In a referendum involving a low salience issue, they explain whatever pattern in the vote that exists beyond randomness. When non-partisan forces, e.g., interest groups, reformers, and the press, intervene to give the issue some salience, they are able to influence voting patterns significantly. In these elections, urban-rural identification became an important mechanism. Once activated it exerted more influence than socio-economic factors. Its impact, however, dropped precipitously once partisanship exerted itself as the principal ordering mechanism for the electorate.

In the background of referendum voting, then, is the potential power of party. The voting studies have effectively demonstrated the commanding importance of party identification in partisan elections. These findings strongly suggest that party identification has a similar capacity to influence referendum voting if parties choose to structure the alternatives for the electorate. Party can cut across other cleavages in the political system and reduce their significance to the point where they have only a small effect on referendum outcomes.

Whether the Michigan experience with constitutional revision referenda as reflected in the data analyzed here would characterize similar contests in other states is a question which must await additional analyses elsewhere. Caution must be used in generalizing from this particular case since both institutional and political circumstances vary considerably between states. If the Michigan experience is a valid guide, it would seem that certain conditions and developments might be anticipated. Support for constitutional revision will initially be strongest among voters with higher levels of education and socio-economic status. As the drive for revision mounts, interest groups and other non-partisan forces are likely to influence referendum voting, especially if the issue is cast in terms of a traditional mode of conflict in the state political system, e.g., urban-rural or perhaps liberal-conservative. Finally, if at any point the parties develop a strong interest in the issue, it can be expected that referendum voting patterns will to a considerable extent resemble those operative in partisan elections.

STRUCTURE AND VALUES IN LOCAL POLITICAL SYSTEMS: *The case of fluoridation decisions*

ROBERT L. CRAIN
DONALD B. ROSENTHAL

Emulating developments in the study of national political systems, recent treatments of local politics have moved from an emphasis on the politics and government of specific cities to the development of concepts to permit comparative analysis of the structure and political style of American municipalities.

Williams and Adrian, for example, classify four middle-sized Michigan cities according to their differing "local political values."[1] Such values are manifested in the conceptions held by citizens and decision-makers of the purposes which their local government should serve. These may range from simply operating a "caretaker" government maintaining certain traditional community services to acting as an "arbiter" among competing groups and interests in the city.

Similarly, Banfield and Wilson distinguish among cities on the basis of the "ethos" which they exhibit. Communities adhering to a "Protestant ethos and middle-class political style" are said to act differently from communities having an ethos derived from immigrant and working-class values. The former, it is asserted, are more likely to reject partisanship and to treat local decision-making as a consensual process from which all group or ethnic considerations ought to be banished.[2]

Reprinted by permission from Robert L. Crain and Donald B. Rosenthal, "Structures and Values in Local Political Systems: The Case of Fluoridation Decisions," *Journal of Politics*, 28 (February, 1966), 169–195.

The research on which the present article is based was made possible by a grant from the United States Public Health Service to National Analysts, Inc., of Philadelphia. We wish to thank Aaron J. Spector of National Analysts for his cooperation throughout the many phases of the study. Our special thanks also go to Elihu Katz, for the major part he played in the larger survey, and to him, John Crittenden, Morris Davis, and James Q. Wilson for comments on an earlier draft of the present paper.

[1] Oliver P. Williams and Charles R. Adrian, *Four Cities: A Study in Comparative Policy Making* (Philadelphia: University of Pennsylvania Press, 1963), esp. pp. 21–39.

[2] Edward C. Banfield and James Q. Wilson, *City Politics* (Cambridge: Harvard-MIT Press, 1963), esp. pp. 38–44.

On the basis of research in a number of Florida council-manager cities, Kammerer and her colleagues draw a distinction between communities which have monopolistic and competitive "styles" of politics. They relate these differences to such factors as demographic qualities in the municipalities themselves.[3]

In a related undertaking, Agger, Goldrich, and Swanson differentiate "power structures" and "regimes" at the local level. The former term points to the distribution of power in the community and the ideology of the political leadership; the latter to the "rules of the game" or values prevalent throughout the system. They have then proceeded to develop typologies for both of these dimensions.[4]

Whatever the specific shortcomings of each of these approaches, they have yielded suggestive answers to the question which *should be* central to any study of local decision-making: What are the factors which account for the observed difference among local political systems in handling demands made upon them? [5]

Obviously, all of the aforementioned works point to the importance of a common set of *values* in accounting for variations in the decision-

[3] For some of their ideas see Gladys M. Kammerer, Charles D. Farris, John M. DeGrove, and Alfred B. Clubock, *City Managers in Politics* (Gainesville: University of Florida Press, 1962) and Kammerer and DeGrove, "Urban Leadership During Change," *Annals of the American Academy*, CCCLIII (May, 1964), 95–106. Kammerer and her co-workers are talking only about one form of government – the council-manager system – in one state: Florida. The same limitation operates in another study where variations within one form of government in one state – the manager system in California – were investigated by Eugene C. Lee, *The Politics of Non-Partisanship* (Berkeley: University of California Press, 1960).

[4] Robert E. Agger, Daniel Goldrich, and Bert E. Swanson, *The Rulers and the Ruled* (New York: John Wiley, 1964), esp. pp. 40–51; 69–124.

[5] By "local political systems" we mean throughout, the legally described but community-influencing decision-making structures which exist in a given municipality. The social context of such structures is of considerable importance as our discussion indicates. Our usage follows the model developed by David Easton in his "An Approach to the Analysis of Political Systems," *World Politics*, IX (April, 1957), 383–400. Neither Easton nor any of those writers drawing upon his work have systematically attempted to apply his model to the local level, although Agger, Goldrich, and Swanson make some effort in this direction. Admittedly, there are many problems involved in such an application. Membership in a local political system in the United States involves very little commitment to a consensual system of values allegedly brought into play where the national political system is involved. For present purposes, however, it is sufficient to consider local decision-making as occurring within subordinate or truncated political systems where the values of the locality may only be significant for those who *choose* to be influenced by them.

making process. In addition, we find considerable support in the same literature for the suggestion that such values are expressed in different forms of government and in the acceptance of political practices like non-partisanship and at-large elections. However, this relationship is rarely spelled out. Williams and Adrian indicate that a connection exists between "local political values" and political structure, but they do not make a systematic linkage except in a brief discussion of the built-in conflict between the manager plan and minimal "caretaker" governments.[6] Agger, Goldrich, and Swanson, on the other hand, suggest that the structure of decision-making and the local value system may operate independently. For example, they argue, the "regime" may undergo considerable change over time, while the power structure remains the same.[7]

We will proceed on the assumption that political forms *are* an expression of community values. It is almost impossible to establish, however, once political practices have become legitimized over time, what the direction of causality actually is. Rather, it must simply be recognized that once it is established a particular political structure may permit certain kinds of demands to become more salient and more legitimate than another would. As Charles Adrian has put it:

> Structural arrangements do have an effect on government, but they neither guarantee good government nor prevent it. The forms are important because they affect the pattern of influence of various groups upon policy-making. The specific structure in any given case helps to establish behavior patterns and attitudes toward power that definitely affect the process whereby decisions are made.[8]

Analytically, at least, we are suggesting that electoral practices and forms of government (the "political structure" of a community) express (or cause) varying political values. This assumption is exceedingly important in developing a method of studying local politics which will permit large-scale comparison, rather than the small-scale study which is part of the current stage of comparative analysis.

[6] Williams and Adrian, *op. cit.*, pp. 282–87.

[7] Their discussion of "regime" resembles our consideration of the role of values. Their "power structures," however, bear little relationship to a traditional consideration of formal political structures. Indeed, the amount of attention given to forms of government is meager; where structural factors are brought in, the major concern is with parties, but even then the emphasis is not on distinguishing communities on the basis of the nature of their partisan structures.

[8] Charles R. Adrian, *Governing Urban America* (New York: McGraw-Hill, 2nd ed., 1961), p. 197.

Fluoridation as a Test Variable

As a test of the importance of political structure for differentiating decisional results, we turned to one of the most controversial subjects in the experience of many American cities: fluoridation.[9]

The subject of fluoridation has received considerable attention from social scientists since shortly after World War II. Because of the "extremist" tone of much of the opposition to fluoridation – proposals to reduce tooth decay by adding minute quantities of fluoride to the municipal water supplies – a striking amount of space has been given to the issue both in popular magazines and in scholarly journals, particularly with reference to the heated referenda battles which have taken place.

For the most part, these studies have stressed the social and psychological processes at work in American cities. This has been done through analyses of *public* reaction to fluoridation proposals (by sampling public opinion or by looking at the results of voting behavior on referenda or through investigations of the attitudes and actions of the issue partisans). With the single exception of an unpublished case study by Ravenna Helson and Donald Matthews,[10] political scientists have given only passing attention to the fluoridation phenomenon and no one has tried to develop an understanding of the political systems within which these peculiarly volatile decisions have been made.[11]

Previous studies of fluoridation controversies have been limited to

[9] It is problematic how much controversy arises on any given issue discussed in the power structure literature. One reason that non-political "influentials" may figure so prominently in decisions such as those discussed by Floyd Hunter and, more recently, by Robert Presthus in his *Men at the Top* (New York: Oxford University Press, 1964) may be due to the small number of issues on which there are meaningful differences in ideology between the non-governmental "elites" and the "politicians," on the one hand, and the "elites" and the "public" on the other. Even Robert Dahl, whose approach is considerably at variance with that of Hunter, does not choose for discussion "issues" which are essentially at controversy. For a more sophisticated treatment of local decision-making which does take controversy and ideology into consideration, see the Agger-Goldrich-Swanson volume.

[10] Ravenna Helson and Donald R. Matthews, "The Northampton Fluoridation Referendum: A Case Study of Local Politics and Voting Behavior" (Unpublished paper, Smith College, 1959).

[11] Students of community power structure have been concerned about distinguishing among communities on the basis of the locus of decision-making, i.e., whether a particular decision was made within the formal government structure or by some non-governmental elite either for subsequent private associational performance or for governmental ratification. In this connection, on any political continuum of decisions made at the local level, fluoridation must be treated as one issue handled through *public* mechanisms rather than *private* ones.

analysis of only one city or at most a small number of cities. The research reported here was designed to complement these earlier studies with an analysis which was (1) frankly political in approach, and (2) based on a large number of cases.

Questionnaires were mailed to the local public health officer, the city clerk, and the publisher of the largest newspaper in each of 1,186 cities; 1,051 of these were cities between 10,000 and 500,000 population which (a) did not have fluoride naturally present and (b) were the primary consumers of their water supply. (This excludes many suburbs.) The remaining 75 cities were cities between 5,000 and 10,000 population which had held referenda. These cities bias the sample, but their presence does not affect the direction or magnitude of any of the correlations reported here. Where they do have an effect, they are excluded. Other data were taken from the census and from the *Municipal Yearbook*.[12]

Response rates varied from 35 per cent to 57 per cent for the three questionnaires. (Since a small number of cities – less than a fifth of the cities in our sample – have never considered fluoridation at all, this deflates the response rates below their true figures.) In the analysis that follows, the number of cases varies sharply, depending upon which, if any, of the questionnaires are used in each table. (One table, which requires responses to all three questionnaires for each city, has a very small number of cases, and must be used gingerly for this reason.) We realize, of course, that a complete analysis of political values cannot depend upon an analysis of only one issue, and we hope that other writers will undertake similar studies of other types of decisions.

From the responses to our questionnaires, we conclude that fluoridation has the following political properties: (1) It has almost unanimous support among the elite. (2) Very few members of the elite have a strong interest in seeing it adopted. (3) The opposition comes from an organized minority, usually including chiropractors, Christian Scientists, natural food faddists, and, in a few cases, the radical right. (4) The public at large is uninformed but is cautious because of the possible side-effects of any medical innovation. (5) The medical profession is virtually unanimous in support of fluoridation.

While each of these statements requires a slight qualification, the general implications seem clear to us. Fluoridation can be adopted only by cities in which the political and civic elite's mild support is sufficient to offset the virulent opposition of a minority of ordinary citizens, and only

[12] A complete discussion of the methodology and findings of the study reported here may be found in Robert L. Crain, Elihu Katz, and Donald B. Rosenthal, *The Fluoridation Decision: Community and Innovation* (Philadelphia: unpublished report to National Analysts, Inc., 1964). A monograph covering this material is forthcoming.

when it is possible to keep bounds on the level of public discussion so that the argument does not escalate into a confused debate involving large numbers of the general public.

Form of Government and the Fluoridation Decision

Since we are interested in governmental decision-making, our main variable is *not* whether the city adopted fluoridation or not, but how the city council decided the issue. The council has three choices: to adopt fluoridation (*administrative adoption*); to *hold* a *referendum,* which occasionally may be required if citizens take advantage of provisions for local initiative; (We are not here concerned with whether the referendum leads to adoption or rejection of fluoridation.) or to reject fluoridation without a public vote (*no action*).

In Table 1, we pause to look at the 16 cities which are too large to be included in our study. A single factor – whether the city is *legally* non-partisan in its council elections or not – tells us a good deal about the actions taken by that city in regard to fluoridation. By 1965 *all* of the partisan cities had adopted the policy of fluoridation; the non-partisan cities were divided among the various alternatives for action on fluorida-

TABLE 1. *Partisanship and Fluoridation Outcome for 16 Large Cities: As of January, 1965*

Outcome	Partisan	Non-Partisan
Administrative Adoption	Baltimore Buffalo New York Philadelphia Pittsburgh St. Louis	Chicago Cleveland Minneapolis
Held Referenda		Cincinnati Milwaukee San Francisco
No Action		Boston Detroit Los Angeles New Orleans

NOTE: Two cities are omitted. Houston has natural fluoridation while Washington, D. C., has a Commission government appointed by Congress. (Fluoridation was adopted by Congress for the District of Columbia.)

tion. If we had a more sensitive measure of true partisanship, we might be able to account for Chicago and Cleveland, where strong partisan organization exists behind non-partisan facades. Cincinnati, with its traditions of non-partisan "good government" under influential managers, has held three referenda campaigns on fluoridation. That the issue has come up several times is a tribute to the persistence of "good government" forces.

The present analysis is concerned with reporting the relationship between governmental structure and actions taken on fluoridation. It should be recognized, however, that fluoridation – which has had a rather lackluster history under almost any conditions is in some ways a "hard case" by which to test variations in community styles. In absolute terms, the differences we are actually describing are rather small. Thus, out of all the cities which have acted on fluoridation, only 35 per cent had adopted administratively. Similarly, most referenda have led to fluoridation's defeat.

As to the role of particular actors in the local political system, the mayor and manager appear to play exceptionally important parts in the decision a city makes both administratively and on a referendum. When the mayor favors fluoridation, it has a sixty per cent chance of adoption; when he opposes the measure, or takes no public position, its chances of acceptance are minimal.[13]

Americans are continually experimenting with forms of local government. Lately they have turned from city government to metropolitan government as an outlet for this propensity, but a study of municipal government at any time in this century indicates the success of reformers in introducing new ideas: the commission system; the council-manager plan; election of councilmen on a city-wide basis; nonpartisan elections. Old forms, like the bicameral council, which once flourished, have either disappeared or been severely modified.

The adoption of new forms of city government in the United States has followed a definite geographical trend so that at the present time certain parts of the country show a predilection for one form at the expense of the others. The N's in Table 2 indicate the number of cities using each type of government by region for the cities which are included in our 10,000–500,000 population.

The Northeast and West provide the most contrast in terms of response to proposals for innovation in governmental forms. The older cities

[13] Our findings with respect to the influence of the system's executive are reported in Donald B. Rosenthal and Robert L. Crain, "Executive Leadership and Political Innovation: the Fluoridation Experience," unpublished paper.

TABLE 2. *Outcome on Fluoridation by Form of Government and Region*

	Manager %	Mayor-Council: Partisan %	Mayor-Council: Non-Partisan %	Commission %
Northeast				
Administrative adoption	24	15	9	5
Held referenda	15	5	25	11
No action	62	80	66	84
Total	101	100	100	100
N	(68)	(130)	(32)	(73)
South				
Administrative adoption	44	35	30	30
Held referenda	23	12	21	7
No action	33	52	48	63
Total	100	99	99	100
N	(127)	(40)	(33)	(43)
Midwest				
Administrative adoption	45	36	33	33
Held referenda	19	12	35	13
No action	35	52	32	54
Total	99	100	100	100
N	(110)	(94)	(72)	(39)
West				
Administrative adoption	9	—	8	—
Held referenda	26	—	24	—
No action	64	—	68	—
Total	99		100	
N	(151)	(4)	(25)	(10)

Sources: *Municipal Yearbook;* Public Health Service Data

of the Northeast are primarily partisan, tend not to use the city manager form, and sometimes employ the commission or town meeting forms. The West, in contrast, is heavily non-partisan and managerial. The difference can probably be traced in part to the greater enthusiasm with which the West greeted Progressivism, to the relative youthfulness of its cities, and also to the higher economic level of its population. The other two regions fall in between, both in extent of partisanship and in the percentage of cities utilizing the council-manager plan. Thus, the use of the council-manager form ranges from a high of 80 per cent in the West to 22 per cent in the Northeast, with the South closer to the West, 52 per cent, and the Midwest closer to the Northeast, 32 per cent.[14]

The fluoridation decisions illustrated in Table 2 – whether a city made an administrative decision or decided to hold a referendum – are consistent with our hypothesis that forms of government relate to different styles in processing issues. Despite the small number of cases in some of the cells, the pattern is almost exactly the same in each region. In all regions, administrative adoptions are most frequent in council-manager cities, followed by partisan mayor-council cities. Referenda are more characteristic of non-partisan systems like the non-partisan mayor-council and manager cities. In general, partisan mayor-council cities and commission towns are more likely to fall in the "no action" category, and in all three test cases, the commission government is the higher of the two.

Interpretation

The fluoridation literature gives us few clues as to why the relationship between governmental structure and decision-making appears in Tables 1 and 2. Only one writer – James Coleman, in his important monograph, *Community Conflict*[15] – develops a theory – linking community structure to the presence of conflict, though he is not concerned with governmental structure. His paper seems to suggest the possibility of developing predictions about governmental structure, since he argues that conflict is more likely to occur when the government is remote from the public. But, our research indicates that this argument may be incorrect.

In order to develop an explanation for Tables 1 and 2, we consider it desirable to develop a typology using forms of government as *illustrative*

[14] To the extent that the adoption of the council-manager system represents a consensual approach to local politics, it would seem proper to assume that the heavily white Protestant-governed South should be more like the West in its formal proclivities. Of course, the bases of political diversity exist in the South because of the presence of the Negroes, but for many years Southern politics at the local level proceeded *as if* the Negroes were not participants in the political process. It should be noted, however, that the South has never been peculiarly resistant to governmental innovation. The commission system originated in Galveston, the manager system in Staunton, Virginia.

[15] James S. Coleman, *Community Conflict* (Glencoe: Free Press, 1957). For a consideration of the literature on fluoridation see Donald B. Rosenthal, "The Politics of Community Conflict" (unpublished Ph.D. dissertation, Department of Political Science, University of Chicago, 1964), esp. pp. 89–179.

of differing value systems and political structures. This does not mean we assert a clear relationship between form of government and every other aspect of the political system. Rather, what we are saying is that if it is valid to treat a municipality as a political system, then one of the ways in which the values of that system are expressed is through the political structure (including form of government) which that system uses.

First, for the purposes of analysis, communities which place a high value on wide-spread public participation in decision-making will be called "participative." Such political systems are distinguished from others which restrict decision-making to formal political agencies. We will say that these cities have adopted a "non-participative" political value or style.

Along with this normative or stylistic dimension, we shall also be concerned with one particular structural aspect of the local political system: the extent to which there is executive centralization. Dahl has written of New Haven as an "executive-centered coalition"; we suggest that the degree to which power is centralized in the hands of the administrative and political leadership of a city is an important index of the decision-making *control* exercised. In the literature discussing differences between the "strong mayor" and "weak mayor" systems we find some support for this point, but there has been little systematic effort to trace the relationship between degree of formal governmental centralization and policy decisions. "Strength," of course, is a summary of many factors, but we will mainly be concerned with *control* of decision-making.

The material in Figure Ia traces the hypothesized connection between executive centralization and the "participativeness" of the system. The assumption is that the empirical manifestation of the latter value is the holding of many referenda in the municipality. On the other axis, a strongly centralized decision-making structure would favor actions at the administrative level. Furthermore, our proposition is that it would be *able* to act because there are fewer actors who must give their approval to the recommendations, and because the centralization of authority would be insulated from the anti-fluoridationists either through the use of an appointed executive or the use of strong political parties controlling recruitment to office and protecting the incumbent from defeat.[16]

A city of Type I would be one in which action on proposed innovations is high at both levels: government is centralized, but the public participates heavily. Whether the city prefers to follow the route of administrative adoptions or the holding of referenda, it would be highly disposed to action of some kind. Because of a disposition to encourage public par-

[16] Given the general values of American society, we would further contend that the *ability* to act would lead to innovations under most contemporary conditions.

FIGURE 1a. System Dimensions and Predictions of Community Actions on Fluoridation

Executive Centralization	Participativeness of System	
	Participative (Many Referenda)	Non-Participative (Few Referenda)
Strong Structure (Many Administrative Actions)	I.	II.
Weak Structure (Few Administrative Adoptions)	III.	IV.

ticipation, the referendum is a readily accepted device for attempting to reach a decision. The presence of a strong executive, however, would encourage a decision to be taken through established decisional structures. As we shall suggest below, the actual form of government most closely resembling this type exhibits a marked split-personality on the issue of fluoridation.

Cities of Type II, on the other hand, might be less readily activated in response to proposals for innovation, but having determined to act would do so through established political channels, generally disdaining use of the referendum.

Cities of Type III, with a poorly articulated political center, and operating in a wide-open governmental milieu, would have difficulty preventing the holding of referenda. The lack of a strong executive might mean an effort to shirk responsibility for action in an area of controversy – again a factor working for the holding of a referendum.

Finally, in Type IV cities there is neither an urge towards participation built into the system, nor a locus of executive responsibility. Such systems might be more readily inclined toward inaction.

While these types are "ideal," for present purposes they will be treated *as if* they were embodied in the four forms of government most common in the United States: the council-manager; partisan mayor-council ("Strong mayor"); non-partisan mayor-council ("weak mayor"); and the commission. The most interesting empirical question is how closely these "fit the typology we have outlined. [Figure 1b] indicates the hypothesized relationship between real forms and the typology. Because published materials do not offer standardized measures of the degree of executive centralization in American cities, we have built into our analysis the dimension of partisanship as a part of "political structure."

Gabriel Almond has suggested that one of the major functions performed by political parties in most political systems is the aggregation of

FIGURE 1b. System Dimensions and Related Forms of Government

	Participative	Non-Participative
Strong Structure	I. (Council-Manager)	II. (Partisan Mayor-Council)
Weak Structure	III. (Non-Partisan Mayor-Council)	IV. (Commission)

demands. This function reduces the pressures playing directly on the decision-making machinery. Such an "insulation" effect, we hypothesize, occurs at the local level in the presence of strong political parties. To the extent that decision-makers are secure in their position, they are able to act on the basis of criteria which might not be immediately acceptable to certain vocal segments of the public.[17] For the purpose of argument, therefore, we assume that partisan mayor-council systems are more likely to have strong mayors than non-partisan mayor council systems. Many of the former may appear to be formally weak mayor systems, but even where this is the case, the presence of a party system may help to overcome the formal weakness of the local executive, as it has done in Chicago.[18]

The city manager form of government, on the other hand, is accompanied in its classical version by non-partisanship and a political formula which favors the referendum, thereby weakening formal political authority. However, the system is favorable to innovation (at least in theory) and the manager is vested with considerable administrative authority. Thus, we would expect the system to favor fluoridation and the manager to seek some action on the subject, but the participative bias of the system means that *if any controversy is raised on fluoridation,* the system will have considerable difficulty in resolving the issue. This flows from the "consensual" style which is built into manager systems i.e., they have a capacity for acting where issues *can be defined* as administrative or non-controversial, but situations of real political conflict strain the

[17] Gabriel Almond, "Introduction," in Gabriel A. Almond and James S. Coleman (eds.), *The Politics of the Developing Areas* (Princeton: Princeton University Press, 1960), pp. 38–45. This point is further developed throughout Myron Weiner, *The Politics of Scarcity* (Chicago: University of Chicago Press, 1962).

[18] For a portrait of the ways in which party organization can overcome the forces of decentralization see Edward C. Banfield, *Political Influence* (New York: Free Press, 1961).

structure. A problem of disorganized, but disruptive, participation may arise. It is partly, for this reason, that many matters may be referred to the public for decision or called from the hands of the government by public demands for a referendum.

In the remainder of this paper we will develop additional data to support the argument that these two variables – participativeness and executive centralization – are reasonable explanations of the correlation between the form of government and a fluoridation decision. We cannot, unfortunately, develop very pure measures, nor can we disprove all the possible alternative explanations. However, we can show in a variety of ways that our data are consistent with our interpretation, though we must leave some questions open for further research.

Executive Leadership and Structural "Strength"

Let us first take a closer look at the effect of partisanship, with a somewhat better measure than simply the presence of party names on the ballot. Two questions were addressed to publishers of the leading newspapers in the cities we surveyed. "How important are political parties in the elections for city council and mayor?" and "Do these tend to be local or nationally affiliated parties?" We assume that the more "local" a party is, the less it will act like a strong Republican or Democratic Party is assumed to do, and that local candidates will be less able to depend upon coattail effects to guarantee their election.

The local party is more likely to be fluid in its memberships, better able to enter coalitions with other groups, and more amenable to reform and subversion. In all these respects, the local party is "weaker" than the sort of organization we hoped the publisher would identify as "national" in orientation. In Tables 3 and 4 we look, not at the decision itself, but

TABLE 3. *Party Influence and Mayor's Stand**

Mayor's Stand	Very Influential %	Moderately or Not Very Influential %	Not at All %
Favor	70.8	55.4	54.9
Oppose	4.9	3.6	8.0
No stand	24.4	41.1	37.1
Total	100.1	100.1	100.0
N	(41)	(56)	(62)

*Two categories combined.

TABLE 4. *National and Local Parties and Mayor's Stand*

Mayor's Stand	National Parties %	Local or Mixed Systems* %
Favor	70.6	51.4
Oppose	2.0	7.7
No stand	27.5	41.0
Total	100.1	100.1
N	(51)	(39)

*Two categories combined.

at the health officer's report of whether the mayor publicly endorsed fluoridation.

Tables 3 and 4 illustrate a pattern which we anticipated: the more local politics are influenced by political parties and the more national the identification of the parties, the more favorable the mayor will be to fluoridation – the mayor's freedom to follow the lead of the elites and his bureaucracy reflects the "strength" of the political order. The few mayors actually opposed to fluoridation come from cities whose parties are locally based or completely non-partisan. These results, furthermore, are not merely the consequence of regional distribution of governmental forms. Indeed, controlling for region *increases* the correlation. For example, if we remove the effects of region (by the technique of standardization), we find that in mayor-council cities where the publisher considers parties to be highly influential in elections, 69 per cent of the mayors were favorable towards fluoridation; in mayor-council cities where parties have no influence the percentage drops to 48 per cent. Most of the difference occurs in relation to the willingness of the mayor to take any stand at all. In a system that demands leadership from the mayor, the chances appear greater that he will assume that policy-leadership on fluoridation under conditions of partisanship. In a non-partisan system, we suggest, the mayor is much less likely to feel responsibility for upholding the claims for support made by the local bureaucracy.

The finding that mayors in partisan towns are more favorable to fluoridation than in non-partisan towns is interesting not only in itself but because it was the thesis of the early reformers of local government that non-partisanship would attract to office men likely to work for "good government" measures. While we are reluctant to classify mayors' attitudes towards good government by their stands on fluoridation alone, there does seem to be some support here for those who argue that non-partisanship has not lived up to the promises made for it. Furthermore, the weakness of the non-partisan mayor-council system in this respect cannot be compensated for. At least in the council-manager system, there is an alternate policy leader available.

Charles Adrian, drawing upon material from two city councils and two state legislatures, has proposed some general principles concerning the effects of non-partisanship. He argues, for example, that non-partisanship can attract the successful businessman into local government, as the system was intended to do, but at the same time it encourages the perennial office-seekers, or anyone who has had the opportunity to make his name familiar to the voters, even if it is merely because of a history of oppositionism.[19]

Following this reasoning, we might hypothesize that the non-partisan office-holder would be more reluctant to support fluoridation than the partisan, since he must retain his office solely on the impression he has given the voters and without party support. It seems reasonable that he would want to avoid touching a sensitive nerve in even a small portion of the population by supporting fluoridation. On the other hand, a marginal candidate, a relatively unknown alderman in a large council, or a mayor whose powers are so limited that he is unable to get much attention from the newspapers, all might see opposing fluoridation as a possible way to gain attention. (Supporting fluoridation, on the other hand, does not seem to guarantee the electoral support of pro-fluoridationists, most of whom are not strongly interested in the issue the way the "antis" appear to be. In addition, supporting fluoridation is not an unconventional position and hence not as newsworthy.) In contrast, the partisan official might concern himself with the attitude of the party slating committee and the party's financial supporters toward him, for he might require such support to be renominated and re-elected.[20] This might lead the official who is more tightly structured into a political role to avoid "irresponsible" opposition (though this is no assurance he would favor fluoridation).

Throughout our discussion of the relationship between political structure and fluoridation decisions, we have emphasized both the types of people who are recruited by the several systems and the kinds of restraints

[19] Charles R. Adrian, "Some General Characteristics of Non-Partisan Elections," *American Political Science Review*, XLVI (September, 1952), 766–776.

[20] Given the large number of instances in which mayors do not support fluoridation, this consideration should not be over-stated. It should be stressed that even in partisan towns the intra-party primary provides an opportunity to a candidate to use the support of the public to undermine the party organization. In broad terms, however, it remains a tautology that strong party organizations are able to exercise control over their members' actions.

placed upon their behavior by the contexts in which they find themselves. The manager is frequently a professional with a commitment to the application of scientific principles to administration. The partisan mayor is perhaps more "responsible" – not so much because of his personality or training – but because of the system in which he is functioning. He is, therefore, less likely than a "loner" non-partisan figure to take a radically negative stand on an issue like fluoridation. Indeed, he is *more* likely to take a positive position by virtue of his party's support, or if he feels central to the operations of the system as a spokesman for the city's health department. On the other hand, even the commitment of the non-partisan mayor to "good government" may not give him enough strength to take a stand against the opinion of any sizable (or noisy) group.

If it is true that the differential allocation of power to the executive is a major variable in determining the actions taken by each city in dealing with fluoridation, we should be able to see it by comparing the positions of "weak" and "strong" mayors on fluoridation on other dimensions besides partisanship. The former should be less favorable to fluoridation than the latter. This quality can be approached through two crude measures of mayoral power: his length of time in office (arguing that a mayor's term of office is an indirect correlate of his independence and power) and whether or not he has a veto over the council's decisions. Both indices were applied to 140 cities for which both the health officer and publisher had returned questionnaires. We find in Table 5 that mayors with longer terms of office are noticeably more favorable, as predicted by the hypothesis. Short terms of office tend to occur in non-partisan cities, so the relationship is as expected. The nature of the mayor's veto power, however, does not appear to be an important influence on mayoral action.

Additional material, much of it anecdotal, suggests that systems in which policy-making is concentrated in a few hands are better able to cope with the controversy which surrounds fluoridation. In particular, cities which must deal with an independent water supply, either privately owned or operated by a regional authority, are less likely to adopt, because the water supplier is an additional actor with a partial or complete veto to override. The fight to eliminate decentralization of existing city gov-

TABLE 5. *Term of Office of the Mayor and His Stand*

Term of Office	Percent of Mayors Favorable	N
1 year	36	11
2-3 years	59	75
4-5 years	70	54

ernments has been going on for a long time, but many governments still have a collection of appointive and elective officials only vaguely responsive to other officials.[21]

Fluoridation is the kind of issue which is peculiarly vulnerable in a decentralized decision-making structure. It is an issue likely to attract headlines; at the same time, it is not the typically "important" issue to which civic groups and leading businessmen will flock. In many cities, it is easy for officials to ignore fluoridation as not worth the noise and the opposition liable to arise. But fluoridation is the kind of unpleasant issue in which opposition can generate headlines about "encroaching socialism" or "putting the bureaucrats in control of men's minds."

The more decentralized the system, the greater the number of decision-makers who must make the difficult decision in favor of fluoridation. Given this situation, opposition by one official can often stop adoption; decentralization would thus appear to have particularly unfortunate consequences for fluoridation. We can even argue that doubling the number of decision-makers will more than double the chance for opposition. Each of these leaders is competing for the scarcest of resources in the political game: public attention and personal influence. If the rewards of conformity must be divided many ways (and divided unequally at that) then the unsuccessful politician may find that he can reap more benefit from opposition than from support. If the opponent has a veto, he can often set a high price for his consent. Even if it is legally and institutionally possible to override the objections of the minority, to do so may require considerable expenditure in time, energy, or political capital. It is part of our findings that fluoridation does not have many friends with this amount of power and the willingness to use it. The reader may recognize this argument as similar to the one made by Amos Hawley in his study of urban renewal adoptions: cities with many *influentials* will have power more widely distributed and thus be less able to act.[22]

[21] For discussion of this problem see Banfield and Wilson, especially chapters 6 and 8. The study by Helson and Matthews also is an excellent example of how a system in which there are a great number of institutionalized participants complicates the decision-making process. This same sort of problem appears to be at work in the case of the Jacksonville, Florida, school system where so many governmental actors have their fingers in the making of school budgets and school policy that the system has reached near collapse and has recently lost its national accreditation.

[22] Amos Hawley, "Community Power and Urban Renewal Success," *American Journal of Sociology*, LXVIII (January, 1963), 422–31. Hawley implies that middle-class communities have more difficulty instituting urban renewal plans because they are likely to allow more scope for participation in the making of the decision under the style which we have described as "participative." Data gathered in connection with the fluoridation study in-

TABLE 6. *Mean Number of Elective Officials for Cities Surveyed and Fluoridation Action in Four States**

Action	State: Michigan	Ohio	N. Carolina	Minnesota
Administrative adoption	9.9 (19)	12.8 (11)	8.7 (12)	11.0 (4)
Held referenda	10.1 (11)	14.6 (8)	8.8 (8)	12.0 (6)
No action	8.7 (9)	12.0 (36)	7.8 (9)	10.1 (9)

*The number of cities in each category is indicated in parentheses.

If too many cooks spoil the fluoridated broth, cities which have the most difficulty in obtaining action on fluoridation should be those with the largest number of elected officials. In a quick test of this rather extreme hypothesis, four large states from the Midwest and South were selected at random and the mean number of elected officials, as given by the United States Census of Governments, was compared against fluoridation action where we had sufficient information. The result is shown in Table 6; in all four states, the rank order was identical (There is only one chance in 216 of this occurring by chance): the cities which held referenda had the largest number of officials. After this surprisingly easy confirmation of our hypothesis, however, we find that in every case cities which have adopted administratively have more elected officials than cities which have not taken any positive action on fluoridation. The reasons for *not* acting, however, are so diverse that it is difficult to provide an explanation for this except to indicate that it runs contrary to our initial expectations.[23]

Participativeness

Turning to the dimension of system values or style, we have suggested that "local political values" vary in the importance given to public participation and the attention to be paid to minority opinion. One mea-

dicates that there is a relationship between status variables and participative systems, but the materials are not sufficiently clearcut to be of much value in developing a consistent support for our differentiation among system styles.

23 While the data merits only a note, we should report that in three of the four states, the cities which *won* referenda tended to be cities which had few elected officials. Of course, the number of cases involved is very small.

sure, as previously indicated, is the number of referenda that the system holds. Thus, the commission system is a low user of fluoridation referenda, but it is also a poor adopter, so that the lack of referenda may also mean that this particular form of government is incapable of any sort of action on fluoridation. Of the remaining systems, it is the non-partisan systems which hold the bulk of the referenda, and number of referenda held is a key factor in the failure of fluoridation.

Table 7 demonstrates the differences among the various political systems based on information provided by the health officer in each city. We asked him whether the possibility of holding a referendum was ever discussed in the city and whether one was actually held. As Table 7 shows, partisan cities were less likely to discuss the possibility of holding a referendum and, even if one were discussed, they were relatively unlikely to hold one. Non-partisan mayor-council cities, on the other hand, were most likely to consider holding a referendum and most likely to hold one; in both of these respects, the manager cities were not far behind.

The city with a participative style is likely to develop political practices over time which revolve around the public meeting, the citizens' committee, and the referendum. Fortified by non-partisanship, any group of citizens can agree to find a candidate for office and support him and his chances for election will be meaningful. In such a system any vocal group must be recognized as part of the legitimate opposition.

Sometimes this participative style works in favor of fluoridation. The manager system, for example, is most likely to have the proposal for fluoridation introduced by a civic group, rather than by the public health professionals. Thus, the greater willingness or ability of citizens to partici-

TABLE 7. *Variation between Community "Talk" of Referendum Being Held and Actual Holding by Form of Government*

	Form of Government			
		Mayor-Council		
	Manager	Partisan	Non-Partisan	Commission
	%	%	%	%
Was there ever talk of holding a referendum? (Per cent "Yes")	46	35	54	47
	N (223)	(147)	(82)	(81)
Was one held? (Per cent "Yes")	48	29	52	25
	N (104)	(49)	(44)	(36)

pate means that fluoridation will have more supporters as well as more opponents. In addition, if the participative system rejects fluoridation, it is more likely to have the issue come up again, so that fluoridation gets more chances to be adopted. On the other hand, the same is true if fluoridation is once adopted; participative cities are more likely to cancel the program later. The top line of Table 8 demonstrates that the more participative systems are more likely to reconsider their decision. The high tendency of commission governments to reconsider is an artifact of their initial tendency to take "no action," which is the easiest decision to reconsider. Therefore, in line two, we have presented the expected percentage of reconsideration if the forms did not vary in the probability of reconsidering a particular kind of action, but only varied in the type of initial action they took.[24] Then line three, which is the difference between line one and line two, shows the net effect of form of government on the chances for reconsideration, independent of the effect of initial type of action. As anticipated, the manager and non-partisan mayor-council cities are more likely to reconsider than would be expected, the partisan mayor-council cities less likely.

It is worth noting that citizen participation has a rather surprising effect on reconsideration. Not only are those cities which involve the citizens in decision-making least able to make a stable decision but adoption by referenda is less likely to "stick" than adoption by administrative fiat. One would think that resorting to a majority vote of all the eligible citizens would be a way to settle an issue once and for all. Such is not the case.

One would also expect that if the conventional wisdom about democracy is valid, that the community which over the years encourages its citizens to participate in decision-making would educate its citizens to take more rational actions. In this case, we know from the work of Gamson [25] and others that the voters reject fluoridation primarily because they are afraid of medical side effects. We know from our own work that they are more likely to vote "yes" if fluoridation is endorsed by the mayor and the local medical organizations. We also know that Americans gen-

[24] If the above explanation is unclear, we have simply computed for each form of government

$$\Sigma_a = \sum_{x=1}^{x=4} \left(\begin{array}{c}\text{proportion of all cities}\\ \text{reconsidering action “x”}\end{array}\right) \left(\begin{array}{c}\text{percentage of type “a” cities}\\ \text{taking initial action “x”}\end{array}\right)$$

where Σ_a is the expected percentage reconsidering for cities with type "a" form of government, and x=1, 2, 3, 4 represents four types of initial action (adopt, win referenda, lose referenda, no action).

[25] William Gamson, "The Fluoridation Dialogue: Is it Ideological Politics?" *Public Opinion Quarterly*, 1962, 26, pp. 526–537.

TABLE 8. *Percentage of Cities Reconsidering Initial Action on Fluoridation, by Type of Government, with Effect of Type of Initial Action Removed*

	Form of Government			
		Mayor-Council		
	Manager	Partisan	Non-Partisan	Commission
Percentage reconsidering	36.7%	29.6%	40.7%	41.1%
Expected percentage, based on distribution of initial actions taken	34.2	36.0	35.6	41.1
Difference, between lines 1 and 2: the net effect of form regardless of type of initial action	+ 2.5	−6.4	+ 5.1	0.0
N	(215)	(142)	(76)	(73)

erally have high respect for medical science. Thus, it follows that the citizen's rational decision is to accept the advice of the medical profession. Now let us look at cities which have a tradition of citizen participation in referenda. In Table 9, we look at the referenda results in cities which have held over five referenda in the past 12 years compared to those which have held fewer.

At this point, what we find is no longer surprising. The cities with participative governments behave no more rationally than those without. In addition, they are less likely to be able to settle the issue with a single decision and they are as likely to have controversy (even though these cities do not need controversy as a pretext for holding referenda). Finally, they are not more likely to vote for fluoridation despite the fact that their mayor is more likely to support it. We can't present the cross-tabulation controlling for mayor's stand since the reports are from different cities. However, if we could, we would probably find that "controlling" for mayor's position, the more experience a community had with referenda, the more likely it would be to reject fluoridation.

The reader may notice another rather complex interaction effect here. Non-partisan cities have mayors who are less likely to support fluoridation. But Table 9 indicates that in the cities which hold many referenda the mayors are more likely to support fluoridation during the referenda. The explanation is simple, but interesting. If a mayor in a partisan city sup-

TABLE 9. *Behavior of High and Low Referenda Systems: Referenda Cities Only*

	Cities Holding Five or More Referenda In Past 12 Years	Cities Holding Less Than Five Referenda In Past 12 Years
Percent of referenda leading to adoption	26 (77)	27 (56)
Percent of referenda actions "complex"*	39 (77)	21 (56)
Percent of referenda hotly debated**	53 (34)	57 (30)
Percent of mayors favorable	62 (26)	41 (22)

* "Complex" actions involve at least two actions: either two referenda, an administrative adoption preceding a referendum or some other combination.

** Derived from a question to publisher: "Compared to other issues with which you are familiar, would you say that fluoridation was: very calmly discussed; calmly discussed; warmly discussed; hotly debated?"

ports fluoridation, it will be adopted administratively in most cases. The referendum is used when the administration wants to be neutral. In the non-partisan city, however, the referendum must often be used by a mayor who supports fluoridation, since he lacks the power or party discipline to get it adopted administratively.

When we turn from the process of decision-making to the mechanics of the battle itself, we see some interesting differences in the extent of public participation in partisan and non-partisan systems. Since non-partisan systems hold more referenda, they should be expected to display more of the pre-conditions of high controversy. However, even when we compare *only* cities which held referenda, the non-partisan mayor-council and manager systems are more likely to have held many public meetings. We asked health officers to indicate how many meetings were held on fluoridation. In non-partisan mayor-council systems 58 per cent of the cities reporting indicated that many meetings were held during referenda campaigns. In partisan mayor-council systems, however, only 47 per cent of the campaigns were marked by many meetings.

Some of the difference in political action can also be traced to the interaction between the system and the opposition. In the course of the study, the characteristics of persons who were regularly identified as leading proponents and opponents were analyzed. In general, we found that proponents were more likely to have a college education, a high status occupation (especially that of physician or dentist) and to be well-known in the community (on the basis of the judgment of the publisher of the leading newspaper); in two cases out of three, however, they had no past political experience.

The opponent leader, typically, was older, was not a college graduate and was somewhat less high-status in occupation (though not as distinct from the proponent leaders as one might have pre-supposed).[26] He was less well-known than the proponent, and also less politically experienced. Out of 269 opponents who were characterized, only eighty-seven had some prior activity in political life. As Table 10 indicates, the political inexperience of these opponents may account for a difference in outcome.

Table 10 also offers a comparison of the relative effectiveness of politically experienced and inexperienced leaders in terms of the partisanship of the community in which they operate. Contrary to what we might expect, there is no difference in administrative adoptions, but there are striking differences in the number of referenda held. The partisan systems hold fewer referenda but when they do hold them the opponents are more likely to have political experience. In contrast, the non-partisan system seems to hold its referenda in response to the non-political opponent. This suggests the possibility that the referendum may serve different functions in the two systems: in the partisan system it might be used to relieve a stalemate within the government itself, whereas in the non-partisan system it may reflect a situation where the structure is more vulnerable to the politically "unsocialized" opponent, i.e. the "radicals" of the community.

While we have mentioned the partisan system as providing "insula-

TABLE 10. *Political Experience of Opponent Leader and Outcome by Partisanship*

Outcome:	Strong Parties		Weak Parties	
	Opponent Experienced	Opponent Inexperienced	Opponent Experienced	Opponent Inexperienced
	%	%	%	%
Administrative adoption	31	29	23	22
Held referendum	33	15	38	49
No action	36	55	40	29
Total	100	99	101	100
N	(36)	(65)	(48)	(96)

[26] For a further discussion of the activities of the proponents and opponents of fluoridation, see Crain, Katz, and Rosenthal, esp. pp. 93–95.

tion" from public participation, we have not specified any of the factors working towards this effect. One such element is the function performed by a minority party. When the minority party refuses to champion opposition to fluoridation, persons opposing fluoridation are left without any *easy way* to present their case. On most issues, the minority party may consider whether opposition will cost them support from their own party, from the "good government" elements, or from financial supporters. These possibilities appear likely in the case of fluoridation. In addition, they may estimate that the anti-fluoridationists are not a lasting source of political backing. Table 11 seems to demonstrate the superiority of the two-party system as far as administrative action on fluoridation is concerned. For both mayor-council and manager forms of government, the two-party system is marked by the largest proportion of administrative adoptions (and, in the case of mayor-council cities, the smallest proportion of referenda held). Next best, in both cases, is the system of local parties where structural competition may still exist. The two non-partisan systems lag far behind.

Our findings suggest that fluoridation ideally has a better chance of consideration and possible adoption where the following conditions are met: a local political structure which is characterized by decision-making authority centralized in a relatively strong executive, like a manager or partisan mayor; a political structure which provides the mechanisms through forms of government and strong parties that insulate partisan mayors and managers from the "irregular" pressures likely to arise on this issue; and, finally, a political system which has a low level of direct citizen participation, both as a general rule and specifically on the fluoridation decision.

Broad popular participation, particularly in the absence of strong executive leadership and an institutionalized channel for confining the expression of opposition, spells defeat to fluoridation. We have elsewhere argued that it does so because fluoridation is a technical issue, the advantages of which are rather small from the citizen's point of view and equally minor from the viewpoint of the politician as far as political capital is concerned.[27] On an issue of this sort the opposition can easily implant doubt. Doubt takes root and blossoms, the more the issue is discussed. For whatever reason the issue is raised for *public* discussion – whether it is because of a democratic debating tradition in the city's associations or a tradition of holding referenda – the opposition succeeds in arousing the citizenry to vote "no" and endless exhortations by proponents under the rubric of "educating" the public seem to fail, often rather badly.

[27] *Ibid.*

TABLE 11. *Party Structure, Form of Government and Outcome**

	Mayor-Council			
	Two-Party	Local Parties	Non-Partisan	One-Party
	%	%	%	%
Administrative adoption	38	28	23	20
Held referenda	10	19	43	20
No action	52	53	34	60
Total	100	100	100	100
N	(63)	(32)	(33)	(30)

	Manager			
	Two-Party	Local Parties	Non-Partisan	One-Party
	%	%	%	%
Administrative adoption	38	32	22	18
Held referenda	33	21	33	46
No action	29	47	44	36
Total	100	100	100	100
N	(21)	(34)	(90)	(11)

*The data are derived from the publishers' responses to a question: How many of the present members of the city council are supported by the local Republican organization? . . . The local Democratic organization? . . . Other local parties? . . . Independent?

Obviously we have not been able to produce "clean" measures for all the concepts we have put to use, but the very fact that some of the rude measures we did employ showed up relatively well indicates that there is considerable room for indices of community decision-making which take into account both formal structural factors related to the local polity and indicators which probe the various facets of the political values of a community.

While fluoridation has turned out to be an easier case than might have been anticipated, the possibility has been raised that the study of *issues* and decision-making structures as an adjunct to the city-by-city approach, can be advanced through the judicious use of survey devices to obtain useful insights into the nature of local political systems.

Part 3

POLICY MAKING AND THE FORMAL STRUCTURES OF GOVERNMENT

Students of politics have long disputed the various forms and structures of governments. Since ancient times, much of the writing we consider "political" has urged one form of government or another. Contemporary political science has not left these ancient questions behind. Such questions as "Who should have the power to make binding decisions?" and "How should the powers of decision makers be checked and made responsive to others?" are evident in the articles presented here.

The unifying theme of Part 3 is the formal structure of state and local governments and the powers of office holders. This theme is not treated in isolation from others. There is concern for the social and economic environments of policy making as well as for political participation and partisanship. The topics examined are the tendency of certain local governmental forms to appear together in the same communities; the social, economic, and political antecedents of those forms; the influence of those forms on the nature of local policies; the character of state legislative institutions and the influence of some legislative institutions on the policies enacted by state governments; the formal powers of state governors and their influence on the budget decisions that are made by the governor and legislature, and the actions of local government administrators who wish to influence the policies followed by their agencies.

The articles by Raymond E. Wolfinger and John Osgood Field and Robert L. Lineberry and Edmund P. Fowler form a thematic group with the selection by Wilson and Banfield in Part 2. These pieces are not without their inconsistencies and strong arguments among the authors, but they do show a progression from Wilson and Banfield's expression of a seminal idea, through a challenge by Wolfinger and Field, to a more precise reformulation and analysis by Lineberry and Fowler.[1]

Wolfinger and Field ask if elements of local governmental structure identified as components of the public- and private-regardingness syndromes actually do cluster together in individual communities. They also look for the origin of these elements in the ethnic compositions of communities. Their findings differ from what Wilson and Banfield lead us to expect. Individual localities do tend to adopt several features of the public-regarding model (that is, council-manager government; non-partisan elections; and at-large selection of aldermen). However, cities with elected mayors show no clear tendency to adopt the other features of the private-regarding syndrome. Wolfinger and Field conclude that different waves of structural reform swept over American cities, with individual communities making separate decisions about components of their structures instead of clearly committing themselves to public- or private-regardingness.

Looking to the ethnic correlates of governmental forms, Wolfinger and Field find the data even more sharply at variance with the hypotheses derived from Wilson and Banfield. Instead of ethnically determined choices of governmental structures, they find regional patterns to be sharper. As we have noted previously, "region" by itself is not a satisfactory explanation for political events. However, Wolfinger and Field cite historical experiences in the Northeast, South, West, and Midwest that seem to account for the structures of local government that evolved in each section. Wolfinger and Field show that public- and private-regardingness are not simple packages of commitments that translate into clear choices of governmental forms, and that each is not simply the product of a population's ethnic composition.

Notwithstanding the qualifications of the Wolfinger and Field essay, the article by Lineberry and Fowler shows that elements of local governmental structure seem to influence policies in ways consistent with the Wilson and Banfield models. As the authors themselves say, it is too early to "carve a headstone" for the theory that public- and private-regarding values have influenced the choice of reform elements in local governments, or that such values have structured the effect of those reforms on

[1] See the heated exchange of letters between Wolfinger and Field, and Lineberry and Fowler in the *American Political Science Review*, 62 (March, 1968), 227–231.

subsequent policies. Lineberry and Fowler work with a limited range of policies — measured by taxes and expenditures per $1,000 of personal income. Their most important finding — from the view of the Wilson and Banfield models — is that communities with public-regarding types of structures enact policies that are less responsive to the social and economic conditions of their communities. The structures seem to isolate decision makers from the demands of local groups and lead to policies that are "politically neutral." If the public-regarding reformers wanted to isolate local policies from the private-regarding values of recent immigrant groups, they have been at least partly successful.

Despite the conflicts and inconsistencies in the Wilson-Banfield, Wolfinger-Field, Lineberry-Fowler set of essays, it is possible to see them as adding to one another. First, Wilson and Banfield suggest a syndrome of ideas toward local policies that are related to the forms of government and the ethnic character of the local population. Second, Wolfinger and Field show that the process of building local governmental structures is more complex than the syndrome suggests, and that ethnicity is frequently less important than other features of a community's experience. Third, Lineberry and Fowler admit the need to refine the basic theory, about the development of governmental forms, but show that governmental structures thought to isolate policy makers from private-regarding demands do work that way — at least when certain measures of policy are considered.

The articles by Thomas R. Dye, Brett W. Hawkins, and John G. Grumm are concerned with similar questions at the state level. They examine the structures of state legislatures and the influence of those structures on the policies enacted. Dye compares the state legislatures' degree of urban-rural equity in apportionment (prior to the landmark *Baker* vs. *Carr* decision of 1962 and the subsequent wave of reapportionment) with the nature of policies in the fields of education, welfare, and taxation. Dye finds little association between apportionment equity and each state's position on the measures of policy; and he concludes that the association he does find reflects the level of social and economic development in the states. From his data, Dye predicts that "reapportionment is not likely to bring about any significant policy changes."

Some problems with Dye's mode of analysis suggest skepticism about his conclusions. First, several of his measures of policy reflect the actions of local as well as state officials and so might be expected not to show any close association with conditions in state legislature. And second, the level of apportionment equity in each state prior to 1962 was a product of many years' population movements that operated in different ways upon the legislatures of different states. In some states, malapportionment gave "liberal" cities more representation than was warranted by their population. Without a dynamic analysis undertaken after the massive wave of reapportionments, it is impossible to predict with certainty what would occur under conditions of rapid change.

Hawkins's report about the dynamics of reapportionment in Georgia suggests how several related changes can affect the nature of policies. Urban counties increased their share of the seats; incumbents showed an increase in "attitudinal liberalism" relevant to the demands of urban residents; and voting patterns changed in the direction of urban interests. Hawkins cannot say if these changes are the direct result of reapportionment instead of some other social or political processes. However, his findings suggest that policy changes will occur in Georgia and that changes in policy are being strengthened by reapportionment in the legislature.

John Grumm offers a general review of the literature dealing with the policy impacts of legislative structures. He finds it tentative in its conclusions, beset with conflicts, and incomplete. He then makes his own addition to the literature by developing an index of "legislative professionalism" and comparing the policies of states whose legislatures differ along that scale. A legislature that scores high on professionalism pays high salaries to legislators, makes high expenditures for staff assistance, processes a larger than average number of bills, and has lengthy sessions. Grumm finds professionalism more important for policies in the welfare field than elsewhere. Also, he finds that certain political traits are more important for welfare policies in those states at the middle range of economic development. Perhaps wealthy states have enough resources to assure generous levels of services, while the poorest states have so few resources that noneconomic traits are not likely, by themselves, to affect policies. Reformers who would alter the nature of state governments and politics may find their greatest influence in policies in concentrating in the middle range of states.

Sharkansky also deals with the actions of state legislatures. He examines the confluence of their decisions on agency budgets with those of the governor. The governor is usually the most prominent figure in this process; his decisions set the standard that the legislature is likely to follow. Yet these practices differ from one state to another. The formal powers of the governor are important in shaping his role in the budget process. Where the governor has strong powers of appointment and veto and where he is free from restrictive limitations against succeeding himself in office, he tends to take a more aggressive line in dealing with the agencies, and his recommendations tend to be more successful in the legislature. Yet the formal powers of the governor do not alone determine his actions. The level of economic resources available to a state and the existing commitments of debt and expenditures are also important. As in other essays in Part 3, Sharkansky finds that the formal powers of government officials operate in a complex mix with social, economic, and political features.

In the final article of Part 3, Wallace Sayre and Herbert Kaufman examine the activities of top administrators in New York City. These are the heads of "line" agencies, those departments that provide services and enforce regulations for the population. By a combination of general comments and case reports of individual agencies, Sayre and Kaufman demonstrate that the policy making process is not only a matter of legislative and executive action. Administrators do not simply "administer" the decisions made elsewhere. Each government department is a complex organization whose members pursue a variety of goals, and each exists in a complex environment whose participants desire a variety of activities from the agency. Agency heads must gain internal control of their organizations and manipulate their external environment. Like other actors in the political process, administrators must work to create a favorable climate of public opinion, cultivate a constituency that will support their programs, and bargain with other holders of political power.

POLITICAL ETHOS AND THE STRUCTURE OF CITY GOVERNMENT

RAYMOND E. WOLFINGER
JOHN OSGOOD FIELD

For years specialists in local politics have deplored the anecdotal quality of literature in the field and have called for theoretically based comparative research. One of the most stimulating and ambitious attempts in this direction is Edward C. Banfield and James Q. Wilson's theory of "public-regardingness" and "private-regardingness," which states that much of what Americans think about the political world can be subsumed under one or the other of these conflicting orientations and that the prevalence of one ethos over the other influences the style, structure, and outcome of local politics.[1] Banfield and Wilson attribute these two ethics to different elements in the population and hypothesize that a number of political forms and policies are manifestations of each ethos. We intend to examine the associations between these hypothesized consequences and the demographic characteristics that are said to be the bases of the two ethics.

I The Theory of the Two Ethics

Banfield and Wilson take their cue from a famous passage in Richard Hofstadter's *The Age of Reform* contrasting native and immigrant political values in the early twentieth century:

Reprinted by permission from Raymond E. Wolfinger and John Osgood Field, "Political Ethos and the Structure of City Government," *American Political Science Review*, 60 (June, 1966), 306–326.

We are grateful to Kuan Lee for writing programs and supervising computer runs for the data analysis, to Richard A. Brody, Jay Kadane, and Morris Zelditch, Jr. for advice on statistical matters, to James D. Barber, Martha Derthick, Heinz Eulau, Genevieve Knupfer, Sheilah R. Koeppen, Nelson W. Polsby, Alan Rosenthal, Gilbert Y. Steiner, Aaron B. Wildavsky, James Q. Wilson, and Barbara Kaye Wolfinger for their advice and comments at various stages of our research, and to the Graduate Division of Stanford University and the Stanford Computation Center for financial assistance.

[1] This is one of the major themes of their *City Politics* (Cambridge: Harvard University Press and the M.I.T. Press, 1963); see also James Q. Wilson and Edward C. Banfield, "Public-Regardingness as a Value Premise in Voting Behavior," [*American Political Science Review*], 58 (December, 1964), 876–887.

> Out of the clash between the needs of the immigrants and the sentiments of the natives there emerged two thoroughly different systems of political ethics. . . . One, founded upon the indigenous Yankee-Protestant political traditions, and upon middle-class life, assumed and demanded the constant, disinterested activity of the citizen in public affairs, argued that political life ought to be run . . . in accordance with general principles and abstract laws apart from and superior to personal needs . . . The other system, founded upon the European backgrounds of the immigrants, upon their unfamiliarity with independent political action, their familiarity with hierarchy and authority, and upon the urgent needs that so often grew out of their migration, took for granted that the political life of the individual would arise out of family needs, interpreted political and civic relations chiefly in terms of personal obligations, and placed strong personal loyalties above allegiance to abstract codes of law or morals. It was chiefly upon this system of values that the political life of the immigrant, the boss, and the urban machine was based.[2]

Many specialists in local politics have referred to this passage in one context or another, but it remained for Banfield and Wilson to develop from it a comprehensive and persuasive theory to explain many aspects of American municipal politics. They introduce their argument as follows:

> There is a tendency for [urban cleavages] to coalesce into two opposite patterns. These patterns reflect two conceptions of the public interest that are widely held. The first, which derives from the middle class ethos, favors what the municipal reform movement has always defined as "good government" — namely efficiency, impartiality, honesty, planning, strong executives, no favoritism, model legal codes . . . The other conception of the public interest (one never explicitly formulated as such, but one all the same) derives from the "immigrant ethos." This is the conception of those people who identify with the ward or neighborhood rather than the city "as a whole," who look to politicians for "help" and "favors," . . . and who are far less interested in the efficiency, impartiality, and honesty of local government than in its readiness to confer material benefits of one sort or another upon them.[3]

At first reading there are troublesome points in this passage, as in Hofstadter's. Is a strong executive part of the old American political ideal? Are these "public-regarding" old settlers the same people who are usually considered devotees of Adam Smith's very private-regarding doctrine that the individual should pursue his own interests and that the public good would be achieved from the sum of individual interests? Did the peasants who came here from the monarchies of 19th century Europe introduce graft and the spoils system to America, or did they learn their bad habits from the Yankees? Did the Yankees withdraw from local politics because

[2] (New York: Knopf, 1955), pp. 8–9.
[3] Banfield and Wilson, p. 46.

they could not stomach the newcomers' sordid political customs or because, outnumbered by the immigrants whom they had rebuffed and exploited, they wanted to avoid the consequences of the resulting hostility? Have Yankees led fights for municipal reform because they are more upstanding or because they find corruption a handy club with which to beat their opponents? [4]

It is well known, however, that many cities with large foreign-stock populations tend to have political orders in which good government is subordinated to favoritism and machine politics. Tammany Hall, the formidable Democratic organization in Chicago, and the confused crooked Boston scene come immediately to mind. Furthermore, reform campaigns in these cities tend to be led by upper-middle-class Yankees and Jews whose life styles and political perspectives are a world apart from the outlook of ward heelers and clubhouse politicians.

But then one can easily think of an equal number of cases on the other side of the argument. Until its recent reformation, was Kansas City (11 per cent foreign stock) any less tainted than Boston (46 per cent)? [5] The South and the border states have notoriously corrupt politics and are just as notoriously Anglo-Saxon. Farther north, in Indiana, only 8 per cent of the residents are of foreign stock, but state employees are "maced" 2 per cent of their pay for the benefit of the ruling political party. In Pennsylvania, dominated until a dozen years ago by a Republican party based on small-town, native-born Americans, at least 40,000 state jobs are at the disposal of the party that wins control of the state government.[6]

The most obvious fact that emerges from this recital is that such comparisons are idle. Attempts to verify the existence of the two ethics and analyze their political consequences will have to proceed beyond discussion of simple honesty and dishonesty. Fortunately Banfield and Wilson have elaborated their basic hypothesis by drawing from the general theory of conflicting ethics a number of propositions about specific mani-

[4] Here, with Banfield and Wilson, we refer not to the stylish young liberal club members of California and Manhattan, but to the more conservative "good government" forces in many cities.

[5] Throughout this article the "per cent foreign stock" or "per cent ethnic" refers to the proportion of a city's 1960 population that is foreign born or native born with at least one parent born abroad. Nineteen per cent of the total U.S. population is of foreign stock. Data on nativity and parentage are from U.S. Bureau of the Census, *County and City Data Book, 1962* (Washington: U.S. Government Printing Office, 1962).

[6] Perhaps because so much of the best scholarly research on local politics has been conducted close to the great universities of the Northeast and perhaps also because most serious nonacademic writers live in a few northeastern cities, political organizations in these cities have been described at great length, while very little is known about existing machines in other parts of the country.

festations of one ethos or the other. "The logic of the middle class ideal implies also certain institutional arrangements" conducive to government by experts in the interests of the city as a whole: the city manager plan, nonpartisan ballots, election of the city council at large, or, if wards are used, from large districts.[7] On the other hand, the private-regarding ethos favors mayors, partisan ballots, and election of councilmen from wards, preferably small ones. The differences between the two ethics are said to be reflected as well in various municipal policies. The public-regarding ethos favors complete civil service coverage of city employees in order to maximize the professional and impartial conduct of public business. On the other hand, the private-regarding ethos emphasizes favoritism and patronage and therefore opposes civil service. Because the public-regarding ethos is concerned with the city as a whole and with long-range attempts to manage and improve the local environment, it favors city planning and urban renewal. The private-regarding ethos opposes such policies because they interrupt neighborhood patterns and impose unwelcome restraints on the city's residents.

Other writers have seen much of this conflict as a clash between middle-class admiration of efficiency and the working-class' desires for representation of their interests.[8] Some critics of Banfield and Wilson say that the labels for the two ethics are much too value-laden and that preferences described as selfish or unselfish could more properly be interpreted in terms of the different interests of different social classes.[9] For example, the fact that poor people protest urban renewal projects may be due not so much to private-regardingness as to the fact that the houses demolished in such projects usually are the homes of the poor.

These caveats are not germane to this study. We are not concerned for the moment with either the morality or the consequences of any particular governmental form or policy, nor are we concerned with how and where particular legal forms can be subverted by local political styles. We are examining the relationship between various forms and policies and the social properties of the relevant cities. It is sufficient for this purpose only to assume that the differences between the alternative forms are worth talking about.

[7] Banfield and Wilson, p. 330; see also *ibid.*, pp. 92, 95, 154, 170.

[8] See, e.g., Leo F. Schnore and Robert F. Alford, "Forms of Government and Socioeconomic Characteristics of Suburbs," *Administrative Science Quarterly*, 8 (June, 1963), 1–17.

[9] See especially Herbert Kaufman's review of *City Politics* in [*American Political Science Review*], 58 (June, 1964), 422–423. Kaufman asks, "are those measures designated 'public-regarding' by Banfield and Wilson *really* manifestations of selfless fellow feeling or are they the self-serving policies of a particular group in society that is trying to hold on to what it has?" (p. 423).

A more important question remains: is the independent variable ethnicity or occupational status? Some parts of the country have scarcely any foreign-stock population, while the distribution of social classes is, of course, fairly even not only from one region to another, but also among most cities. Moreover, cities with large ethnic populations do not necessarily have small middle classes. The correlation coefficient between per cent ethnic and per cent in white collar occupations for all New England cities of over 50,000 population is −.04; it is faintly positive for other regions with appreciable ethnic populations: .20 in the Middle Atlantic states, .20 in the Midwest, and .24 in the West.[10]

Banfield and Wilson seem to consider the two dimensions interchangeable. Sometimes they attribute the two ethnics to ethnicity, sometimes to social class, and sometimes they mingle both explanations. The weight of evidence suggests that ethnicity is meant to be the controlling independent variable. The theme of two ethics is introduced in a discussion of cleavages between old settlers and immigrants.[11] In a more recent work they remark, "We do not think that income *per se* has this effect [making people private- or public-regarding]; rather it is the ethnic attributes, or culture, empirically associated with it." [12] But this interpretation is confounded by statements like this: "The assimilation of lower-class people into the middle class has, of course, entailed their assimilation to the political ethos of the Anglo-Saxon-Protestant elite . . ." [13]

Is a combination of ethnicity and working-class status the origin of the private-regarding ethos? If so, why would upward mobility produce a change? It might be argued that private-regardingness is a consequence of ethnic consciousness, which disappears when middle-class status is attained. But the available data indicate that social mobility often has little effect on ethnic consciousness.[14] Nor is it plausible that upward-mobile ethnics will readily abandon their political perspectives in favor of views more characteristic of the middle class.[15]

Some of these difficulties may be resolved if "middle class" is interpreted, for present purposes, as "upper middle class." Indeed, in some

[10] In these computations the Midwest includes Ohio, Indiana, Illinois, Iowa, Michigan, Minnesota, and Wisconsin.

[11] Banfield and Wilson, pp. 38–46.

[12] Wilson and Banfield, p. 885.

[13] Banfield and Wilson, p. 123; see also *ibid.*, p. 329.

[14] Raymond E. Wolfinger, "The Development and Persistence of Ethnic Voting," [*American Political Science Review*], 59 (December, 1965), 896–908.

[15] In other areas of political behavior the upward mobile tend to have characteristics midway between their old and new classes; see James A. Barber, Jr., *Social Mobility and Political Behavior* (Chicago: Rand McNally, forthcoming).

passages Banfield and Wilson indicate that the important line of demarcation is between professional and business people on the one hand and lower status groups on the other. But the bulk of their treatment of the two ethics contradicts this. In particular, their discussion of the likelihood that "the middle class will in the very long run assimilate the lower class entirely," [16] suggests that they include everyone in a white collar occupation in the "middle class" as far as the two ethics are concerned.

Banfield and Wilson do not explain why immigrants should be private-regarding. Their silence on this point is a source of numerous complications. Did the immigrants bring the private-regarding ethos with them from their former countries or was it a product of interaction between their predispositions and the conditions of life they found in the United States? Hofstadter seems to favor the latter interpretation, but Banfield and Wilson speak of the ethos that "the new immigrants brought with them." [17] If the immigrants came with the private-regarding ethos, one would expect to find it distributed around the country in proportion to the number of persons of foreign stock. (This assumes, of course, that immigrants from different countries have similar inclinations to private-regardingness. Banfield and Wilson do not consider this point, except to single out Polish-Americans as particularly likely to be private-regarding, for reasons that are not explained.[18]

On the other hand, if the ethos is a response to American life, one would expect that its distribution would be related not only to the proportion of immigrants in the population, but also to the character of their experience in America. Typical immigrant experiences differed considerably from one region to another. This was notably true of the West, where non-Anglo-Saxon immigrants arrived with or on the heels of the earliest settlers. All shared the rigors of pioneering and the profits and instabilities of boom economies.[19] Compared to those in the settled Eastern cities, immigrants to the West were better off and better educated; labor was scarcer, wages were higher, and class distinctions were weaker and more unstable.[20] Status and income were neither so fixed nor so strongly stratified. If private-regardingness is an acquired characteristic, it seems likely that different regional immigrant histories might produce different levels of attachment to the ethos or perhaps different manifestations of it.

These observations do not invalidate the ethos theory, but they do

[16] Banfield and Wilson, p. 123.
[17] *Ibid.*, p. 40.
[18] *Ibid.*, p. 235.
[19] See, e.g., Louis Berg, "Peddlers in Eldorado," *Commentary*, July, 1965, pp. 64–66.
[20] Earl Pomeroy, *The Pacific Slope* (New York: Alfred A. Knopf, 1965).

suggest some necessary modifications. In particular, since the quality of the immigrant experience differed from region to region, it appears that a given level of foreign-stock population in, say, California and New York might produce very different levels of private-regardingness in the two places.[21] Our findings support this inference.

Several pieces of published research bear on the ethos theory. John H. Kessel found that the mayor form was more common in cities with large ethnic populations.[22] Schnore and Alford report the same finding in their study of 300 suburbs, but the difference here is slight: 9.3 per cent foreign-born population in mayor cities compared to 8 per cent in manager cities.[23] Both studies also found that manager cities had larger proportions of residents in white-collar occupations.[24] Phillips Cutright suggests that partisan elections are more likely to be found where "community cleavages" are intense, because such divisions provide "political parties with the social basis necessary for effective organization and sufficient activity necessary for survival as a community force." [25] He used two measures of "high cleavage": more than 50 per cent of the population employed in manufacturing indicates economic cleavage; while more than 20 per cent Catholics indicates religious cleavage. By either measure, high-cleavage cities were more likely to use the partisan ballot.[26]

[21] Similarly, an analysis of local voting returns in the 1960 presidential election showed considerable regional variation in the responses of similar Protestant voting groups to President Kennedy's candidacy; see Lucy S. Davidowicz and Leon J. Goldstein, *Politics in a Pluralist Democracy* (New York: Institute of Human Relations Press, 1963).

[22] John H. Kessel, "Governmental Structure and Political Environment: A Statistical Note about American Cities," [*American Political Science Review*], 56 (September, 1962), 615–620.

[23] Schnore and Alford, *op. cit.*, p. 12.

[24] Edgar L. Sherbenou found that Chicago suburbs with higher priced homes are very likely to use the manager form, while more modest towns all have mayors; see his "Class, Participation, and the Council-Manager Plan," *Public Administration Review*, 21 (Summer, 1961), 131–135.

[25] Phillips Cutright, "Nonpartisan Electoral Systems in American Cities," *Comparative Studies in Society and History*, 5 (January, 1963), p. 218.

[26] One proposition of the ethos theory states that public-regardingness is manifested in support for expansion of many government services that do not benefit the individual, but that will increase his tax payments. In their own work Banfield and Wilson have found that, among homeowners subject to property taxes, support for such measures to be financed by property taxation rises with the median income and home value of the voting unit. They also found that voting units with large foreign-stock populations were less likely to support such measures. They believe that the controlling element in these relationships is ethnicity, and attribute the findings to the prevalence of the private-regarding ethos among ethnic group members; see Banfield and Wilson, pp. 237–240; and Wilson and Banfield.

These studies have severe limitations as sources of evidence for the ethos theory. They are concerned with only two of its dependent variables. More important, they do not include controls for third variables, particularly region. Since some parts of the country are almost devoid of foreign-stock residents (and Catholics), it is reasonable to try to separate the influence of region from that of local population characteristics. Furthermore, western and southwestern cities, whatever their economic bases, tend to have larger white-collar populations than cities in the Northeast and Midwest. Because of the historical development of land-use patterns, these cities usually have more extensive residential neighborhoods with suburban characteristics, and thus have suffered less from the postwar flight to the suburbs that has reduced middle class populations in core cities elsewhere.

II Research Design

The ethos theory states that the city manager form of government, the nonpartisan ballot, at-large election of city legislators, big wards, civil service coverage of municipal employees, city planning, and urban renewal are favored by the public-regarding ethos, which is a prominent aspect of the political perspectives of white Anglo-Saxon Protestants. The opposing private-regarding ethos, rooted in the immigrant experience, favors the mayor form, the partisan ballot, ward election of city legislators, and small wards; it is opposed to civil service, city planning and urban renewal.[27] We have treated all these features as dependent variables and examined their relationship to the key independent variable, the proportion of a city's population that is of foreign stock. Other independent variables include social class (measured by the percentage of the labor force employed in white collar occupations), median family income, and educational level (measured by the median school years completed by residents aged 25 or over). We examined the relationship between each independent and dependent variable within each major region of the United States. We also measured the degree of association between ethnicity and each dependent variable while controlling for social class, income, and education. The dependent variables and their hypothesized relationships to the two ethics are summarized in Figure 1.

This study includes all 309 incorporated cities with 1960 populations in excess of 50,000 persons, excluding Washington, D.C. Data on all dependent variables except urban renewal were taken from *The Municipal*

[27] A number of other political forms, styles, and policies are said to be favored by one or the other of the two ethics. Data permitting intercity comparisons are not available on these other variables.

FIGURE 1. The Dependent Variables

	Private-Regarding	Public-Regarding
Form of Government	Mayor	Manager
Type of Ballot	Partisan	Nonpartisan
Method of Electing Councilmen	Wards	At Large
Size of Council Districts	Small	Large
Civil Service Coverage	Less	More
City Planning Expenditures	Low	High
Urban Renewal	Low	High

Year Book 1963.[28] The magnitude of urban renewal programs was measured by capital grants per capita for each city. Raw data on capital grants were obtained from the *Urban Renewal Directory* for December 31, 1963.[29] A variety of demographic data for each city was obtained from the *County and City Data Book, 1962*.

Cities are not always free to make their own decisions on what governmental forms they will adopt and what policies they will follow. State constitutions and legislatures often interfere with home rule by requiring cities to conform to particular forms or preventing them from adopting others. We have investigated this problem at some length and consulted scholars and officials of several professional organizations in the field of municipal government.[30] Whenever state law imposes constraints on cities' free choice with respect to any dependent variable we have omitted such cities from the relevant analyses.

It might be argued that our index of ethnicity is both too exclusive and too inclusive. Foreign-stock population percentages exclude Negroes, who might be considered inclined to the private-regarding ethos.[31] But

[28] Orin F. Nolting and David S. Arnold (eds.), *The Municipal Year Book 1963* (Chicago: The International City Managers' Association, 1963).

[29] Urban Renewal Administration, *Urban Renewal Directory, December 31, 1963* (Washington: Urban Renewal Administration, 1964).

[30] For information on state restrictions on home rule we are grateful to, among others, David S. Arnold of the International City Managers' Association, William N. Cassella, Jr. of the National Municipal League, Eugene C. Lee of the Institute of Governmental Studies of the University of California (Berkeley), and Keith Ocheltree of the Public Personnel Association.

[31] Banfield and Wilson do not include Negroes in those groups they consider disposed to private-regardingness, although some political goals they attribute to Negroes, such as desires for representation and "recognition,"

1960 levels of Negro population in northern cities reflect recent migration. In most such cities Negroes were scarce and politically unimportant until the postwar years; as with all newcomers, they still have not mobilized themselves so as to exert political strength commensurate with their numbers. In the South, of course, Negroes have been disfranchised until recently. Most southern cities have now gone a long way toward removing impediments to Negro voting, but the recency and unevenness of this development make it difficult to use numbers as an index of Negro political influence.

The criterion might be considered too inclusive in that most Jews are first- or second-generation Americans, and Banfield and Wilson say that at least upper-middle-class Jews are public regarding.[32] Jews amount to three or four per cent of the total American population. Almost all of them live in northern cities; more than a quarter live in New York City, where they comprise almost 30 per cent of the population. Aside from New York and a few other places, Jews have not been sizable parts of most cities' populations. Since only some Jews are exempted from the charge of private-regardingness and since we exclude the very large cities where most of them live from many of our computations, this problem is not so great.

In recent years many Jews have moved to the cities of southern Florida, some of which now have foreign-stock populations as large as any northern community. (In fact, Miami Beach, 53 per cent of whose population is ethnic, leads the nation in this category.) Since most Jewish Floridians have lived in the state only a few years, they are unlikely to have political influence in proportion to their numbers, and so one would not expect that the political practices of Florida cities would fully reflect their preferences. These cities are the exceptions to the general rule that 1960 levels of ethnic populations are a fairly reliable index of each city's relative ethnicity over the past fifty years.*

---

might be thought to incline them in that direction (Banfield and Wilson, pp. 158–159, 293–294, 307–308). On the other hand, Negroes are described as disproportionately public-regarding in their voting on bond issues (*ibid.*, pp. 237–239).

[32] See, e.g., *ibid.*, pp. 42, 123, 330. While upper-middle-class Jews are often classified with Yankees as adherents of the public-regarding ethos, Banfield and Wilson do not say if they are any more likely to be public-regarding than Catholics of similar social status.

* [This statement was based on inspection of the relevant census reports. It can now be put in a more precise form as a result of a recent study of 268 American cities with populations in 1930 of 30,000 or more (all such cities except a few constrained by state law from changing their form of government): "The percentage of foreign-born persons in 1930 correlates (Pearsonian r) .96, .95, and .89 with the percentage of foreign born in

The ethos theory does not refer to the actual incidence of its various dependent variables, but to attitudes toward the variables.[33] Therefore, propositions specifying relationships between cities' population characteristics and their political forms and policies are inferences from the ethos theory, not parts of the theory itself. These inferences are based on the assumptions that the strength of the public- and private-regarding ethics is related to the magnitude of the population groupings that supposedly give rise to one ethos or the other, *and* that the two ethics are important causal factors in city politics. Banfield and Wilson seem to have made the same assumption: "Obviously the social and ecological structure of a city largely determines which view as to the proper role of government will prevail in it.[34]

How valid are these inferences? Obviously it would be unwise to assert that there is a simple causal relationship between public attitudes toward a particular governmental feature and the likelihood that that feature will be adopted. Many other considerations affect the nature of local political institutions. Some of these other factors, such as state law, can be identified. Others, such as the interrelationship of other demographic variables, can be controlled by statistical manipulation. The effect of city size and region can also be controlled. Other factors, such as different national origins of immigrants, can be partially and indirectly isolated by analyzing the data by region.

When all these other variables have been taken into account, we do not think it untenable to assume that if the two ethics: a) exist, b) have

---

1940, 1950, and 1960, respectively." See Daniel N. Gordon, "Immigrants and Urban Governmental Form in American Cities, 1933–1960," *American Journal of Sociology*, vol. 73 (September, 1968), p. 169. – Aus.]

[33] We think it unlikely that most individuals' political knowledge has developed to the point of having opinions about, say, the relative merits of ward and at-large elections. Thus the ethics may exist at two levels: as general value systems for most people and as a set of specific political preferences for their leaders.

[34] Banfield and Wilson, p. 55. Our interpretation of this statement is based on its context, Banfield and Wilson's citation of the Sherbenou and Schnore – Alford correlational studies in support of their proposition about public-regardingness and the city manager plan (*ibid.*, p. 169n), and passages like this:

> "Many council-manager cities are upper-class or middle-class in character; few if any are predominantly lower-class. In the Chicago area, for example, . . . eighteen of the twenty cities with the highest home values had the [manager] plan, whereas none of the thirty-one cities with the lowest home values had it. Its popularity with people of the upper and middle classes explains its popularity in small communities, which are more likely to consist predominantly of those classes than are large ones" (*ibid.*, p. 169).

the properties attributed to them, and c) are associated with the ethnic composition of urban populations, then this will be reflected in statistical associations between a specific hypothesized dependent variable and levels of ethnicity, when such associations are examined in large groups of cities. This assumption does not deny the existence of other independent variables, but it does require that the ethos be of sufficient importance so that, *in the aggregate*, its influence will be discernible. If the hypothesized relationship between ethnicity and a given political form is not found, three conclusions can be considered: a) a preference for that form is not part of the ethos; b) the ethos is not related to ethnicity; c) the two ethics are not translated into political reality.

We will explore three general questions in the following sections. First, to what extent do the structural dependent variables – form of government, type of ballot, and method of electing councilmen – go together? For example, do cities with mayors also use the partisan ballot and elect their councilmen from wards? Second, how do cities differ by size and region with respect both to ethnicity and to the structural dependent variables? Third, and most important, what are the relationships between ethnicity and the dependent variables?

III The Consistency of Political Forms

All the structural manifestations of public-regardingness were elements in the municipal reform movement that began with the 20th century. Civil service, nonpartisanship, at-large elections, and big districts were principal features of the National Municipal League's "municipal program," issued in 1900. Together with the manager plan and city planning, these measures were incorporated in the League's "Model City Charter," promulgated in 1916 and reissued several times subsequently.[35] Since these various features have all been part of a package, jointly promoted and presumably reflecting the same spirit, one might expect that they would be found together in practice.[36] This conclusion follows both from the logic of Banfield and Wilson's argument and from their statement that "people who are decidedly public-regarding or decidedly private-regarding on one matter tend to be so on all matters." [37]

[35] *Ibid.*, p. 141. The International City Managers' Association considers nonpartisanship and at-large election "main features" of the manager system (*ibid.*, p. 172).

[36] Cf. Banfield and Wilson, "The connection between the partisan and district systems, as between the nonpartisan and at-large systems, is of considerable significance, for, as we shall see later, the connected elements tend in both cases to produce the same style of politics and to reinforce one another" (p. 90).

[37] *Ibid.*, p. 235.

Of the 309 cities, 146 use the manager form, 126 have elected mayors, and 37 have commission government. We will omit the commission cities from consideration because this form does not figure in the ethos theory. Of the cities with mayors or managers, 85 use the partisan and 186 use the nonpartisan ballot (information on one city is missing); 153 cities elect their councilmen at large, 67 elect them from wards, and 49 cities use a combination of the two methods (data on two cities are missing).[38] How do these features go together? If a city follows one ethos in one structural feature, will it be consistent with the same ethos in the other two features? It is clear that there will be less than a perfect fit in this respect, since the number of cities with a particular private-regarding feature ranges from 126 (with mayors) to 67 (electing councilmen from wards).

Manager cities are fairly consistent in their adoption of the other two structural variables: 85 per cent of them use the nonpartisan ballot, 81 per cent elect their councilmen at large, and 70 per cent use both the nonpartisan ballot and at-large elections. Mayor cities are much less consistent: half of them have partisan elections, 41 per cent elect their councilmen from wards, and only 23 per cent follow both of these private-regarding practices. As Table 1 shows, cities with mayors seem to be very eclectic in their choice of governmental institutions. Less than a quarter of them are "pure" private-regarding types and almost as many cities have each of the five other possible combinations of type of ballot and method of electing councilmen.

Three out of four cities with partisan local elections have mayors, but less than half of these partisan mayor cities also elect councilmen from wards. Partisan manager cities overwhelmingly prefer at-large elections. Where local elections are nonpartisan, two out of three communities are on the manager plan; and most of these cities also elect their councilmen at large. These data are presented in Table 2.

Cities electing councilmen from wards are very likely to have mayors, as are cities with a combination of ward and at-large elections. Both of these groups of cities are rather evenly split between partisan and nonpartisan ballots. By a similar three-to-one ratio, at-large cities have managers, and most of these communities also have nonpartisan elections.

In short, there is a recognizable "public-regarding" structural syndrome in American cities. Most of the manager cities have followed the

[38] Cities that elect at least three-quarters of their municipal legislators from wards are classified as using the ward system; the same criterion is used with the at-large system. Cities that elect more even proportions by the two methods are classified as "combination" cities. Since all cities using the commission form elect the commission at large, they are omitted from these tabulations.

TABLE 1. *Type of Ballot and Method of Electing Councilmen in Manager and Mayor Cities*

Form of Government and Type of Ballot	Method of Electing Councilmen			
	Ward	At-large	Combination	Totals
Manager:				
Partisan	3% (4)	11% (16)	1% (2)	15% (22)
Nonpartisan	9 (13)	70 (101)	6 (9)	85 (123)
	12% (17)	81% (117)	7% (11)	100% (145)[a]
Mayor:				
Partisan	23% (28)	11% (14)	17% (21)	51% (63)
Nonpartisan	18 (22)	18 (22)	14 (17)	49 (61)
	41% (50)	29% (36)	31% (38)	100% (124)[b]

[a] Data on method of electing councilmen missing for one city.
[b] Data on method of electing councilmen or type of ballot missing for two cities.

TABLE 2. *Form of Government and Method of Electing Councilmen in Cities Using the Partisan and Nonpartisan Ballot*[a]

Type of Ballot and Form of Government	Method of Electing Councilmen			
	Ward	At-large	Combination	Totals
Partisan:				
Mayor	33% (28)	16% (14)	25% (21)	74% (63)
Manager	5 (4)	19 (16)	2 (2)	26 (22)
	38% (32)	35% (30)	27% (23)	100% (85)
Nonpartisan:				
Mayor	12% (22)	12% (22)	9% (17)	33% (61)
Manager	7 (13)	55 (101)	5 (9)	67 (123)
	19% (35)	67% (123)	14% (26)	100% (184)[b]

[a] Cities with the commission form of government have been excluded from this table.
[b] Data on method of electing councilmen are not reported for two cities.

TABLE 3. *Type of Ballot and Form of Government in Cities Electing Councilmen from Wards, at Large, and by a Combination of Methods*[a]

Method of Election and Type of Ballot	Form of Government		
	Mayor	Manager	Totals
By Wards:			
Partisan	42% (28)	6% (4)	48% (32)
Nonpartisan	33 (22)	19 (13)	52 (35)
	75% (50)	25% (17)	100% (67)
At Large:			
Partisan	9% (14)	10% (16)	20%[b] (30)
Nonpartisan	14 (22)	66 (101)	80 (123)
	23% (36)	76% (117)	100% (153)
By a Combination:			
Partisan	43% (21)	4% (2)	47% (23)
Nonpartisan	35 (17)	18 (9)	53 (26)
	78% (38)	22% (11)	100% (49)

[a]Cities with the commission form of government have been excluded from this table.

[b] Does not sum to 19% because of rounding.

advice of the National Municipal League and adopted nonpartisan ballots and at-large elections. But the opposite is not true; there is no "private-regarding" syndrome. Instead, cities with mayors have, in fairly equal proportions, every conceivable combination of the other two structural variables. Forty-eight per cent of all cities with mayors or managers are "pure types"; the others are hybrids of one sort or another.

Civil service coverage of municipal employees is another element in the "good government" package and in the public-regarding ethos. *The Municipal Year Book* reports civil service coverage of various classes of municipal employees. These data refer only to the formal regulations. Undoubtedly the prevailing political style in many cities subverts the personnel laws. In Chicago, for example, all municipal workers except those in public utilities are "covered" by civil service. In fact, of course, a great many jobs in the Chicago government can be used for patronage purposes with little difficulty. Nevertheless we assume that in the aggregate the extent of official civil service coverage gives some indication of the reality of public personnel policies.[39] We have used *The Municipal Year Book* reports to develop four levels of civil service coverage that apply to almost all cities:

Level 1. All employees covered; 106 cities.
Level 2. All employees except manual workers covered; 13 cities.
Level 3. Only firemen and policemen covered; 57 cities.
Level 4. No civil service coverage; 33 cities.

Iowa, New York, and Ohio require their cities to use merit systems; in Massachusetts all local employees come under the jurisdiction of the state civil service commission. Since cities in these four states are not free to make their own personnel policies, we have excluded them from all tabulations involving civil service coverage.

We have compared the civil service coverage of municipal employees in mayor and manager cities.[40] Table 4 shows the proportion of each type of city that has each of the four levels of coverage. A slightly larger share of manager cities has complete coverage and somewhat more mayor cities are at level 2. These differences are small, however, and equal proportions

TABLE 4. *Form of Government and Level of Civil Service Coverage*[a]

Level of Civil Service Coverage	Mayor	Manager
1. All employees covered	49%	56%
2. All but manual workers covered	10	2
3. Only policemen and firemen covered	25	25
4. No civil service coverage	16	17
Total	100%	100%
N	(61)	(110)

[a] Excludes cities in Indiana, Iowa, Massachusetts, New York and Ohio.

[39] "However important may be the evasions of the civil service system in particular cases, it is clear that in general the effect of the system everywhere has been to make it increasingly difficult for the parties to maintain effective discipline over their workers by giving and withholding jobs" (*ibid.*, p. 209).

[40] State law in Anglo-Saxon Indiana makes it almost impossible for cities there to deviate from the mayor form of government. Since form of municipal government is not subject to local choice, we have excluded the nine Indiana cities from the tabulation presented in Table 4. Several other states interfere with home rule in this respect, but their cities all use the commission form and on this ground are excluded from our tabulations.

of both groups are at levels 3 and 4. There is little more than a random chance that the two alleged manifestations of the public-regarding ethos, city manager government and civil service protection, will be found together.

The various hypothesized manifestations of the two ethics are often found in "inconsistent" combinations. This suggests that the two ethics may be somewhat less differentiated from each other than Banfield and Wilson say. The forces influencing a city's choice of any one of these variables probably differ considerably in strength and composition from the factors influencing choices of other variables. These data indicate the unevenness of the wave of structural reform that swept over American cities in the twentieth century. They also suggest that the pressures for and against different items in the catalogue of reform were not as similar as has been assumed.

IV City Size and Region as Independent Variables

The second general question is how cities of different size and in different regions vary in their formal governmental characteristics and in the ethnic level of their populations.

Size turns out to make surprisingly little difference with respect either to ethnicity or structural characteristics. Cities with more than half a million residents are much more likely to have mayors, but below this point there is only a slight trend toward use of the manager form as size declines further.[41] (Mayors become more popular again in cities below 50,000 population.) Only cities with more than a million inhabitants are much more likely to elect their council members from wards; below this level the trend is slightly and irregularly toward the at-large system. The pattern is more uneven with respect to type of ballot. Cities with populations of more than a million and those in the 100,000 to 250,000 category are most likely to have partisan elections (although the nonpartisan ballot is still preferred by 60 per cent of the cities in each category), and cities in the quarter to half million group are least likely to hold partisan elections. But these differences are not, by and large, very great, and there is no consistent relationship between size and use of one ballot or the other. These data are presented in Table 5.

[41] Cf. Banfield and Wilson, "The larger the city, generally speaking, the more is at stake politically, and consequently the greater the effort that professional politicians will put forth to avoid being displaced. This is certainly a factor that generally tends to prevent adoption of the [city manager] plan in a large city" (pp. 182–183).

TABLE 5. *Governmental Forms and City Size*

Size	Form of Government[a]		Type of Ballot[b]	Method of Election[c]		Number in Each Size Category
	Mayor	Manager	Partisan	Ward	At-large	
Over 1 million	100%	—	40%	60%	20	5
500,000 to 1 million	73%	27	33%	27%	53	15
250,000 to 500,000	43%	40	23%	17%	73	30
100,000 to 250,000	39%	48	40%	20%	67	79
50,000 to 100,000	37%	51	29%	22%	60	180
Mean for all cities over 50,000	41%	47	32%	22%	62	
N	(126)	(146)	(98)	(67)	(190)	(309)

[a] Cities with the commission form of government have been excluded from these columns but not from the base on which the percentages were computed.

[b] All other cities use the nonpartisan ballot, except for one city for which data on type of ballot are missing.

[c] Cities using a combination of the ward and at-large method have been excluded from these columns but not from the base on which the percentages were computed. Data on the method used in three cities are missing.

Similar findings hold with respect to the relationship between size and ethnicity. As Table 6 shows, small and medium-sized cities are just as likely as the country's biggest cities to have large foreign stock populations. Whatever its importance in other areas, a city's size is an unimportant variable either for ethnicity or (with the exceptions noted) governmental structure.

The major operational conclusion to be drawn from these findings is that size need not be controlled in examining relationships between ethnicity and the structural dependent variables, except to exclude cities of over half a million population when form of government is a variable, and cities of over a million when analyzing the method of electing councilmen. Controlling for size turned out to be unnecessary for another reason: when we did it, there was no change in the results that are presented later in this paper.

Tables 7 and 8 show the distribution of alternative forms of government, types of ballot, and methods of electing councilmen in different parts of the country. These tables demonstrate the striking regional variations in each of these characteristics. The mayor form is the predominant one in the Northeast, is somewhat favored in the Midwest, unpopular in

TABLE 6. *Foreign-Stock Population and City Size*

Proportion of Population of Foreign Stock	Population Size: Over 250,000	Population Size: 100,000 to 250,000	Population Size: 50,000 to 100,000
0% to 9.9%	30%	32%	26%
10% to 19.9%	16	15	21
20% to 29.9%	18	28	21
30% to 39.9%	28	10	14
40% to 49.9%	6	14	13
50% and over	2	1	6
	100%	100%	101%[a]
Per cent of cities with 20% or more foreign stock	54%	53%	53%

[a] Sums to more than 100% because of rounding.

TABLE 7. *Form of Government and Type of Ballot—By Region*

Region	Form of Government: Mayor	Form of Government: Manager	Form of Government: Commission	Type of Ballot: Partisan	Type of Ballot: Nonpartisan	Number of Cities in Region
Northeast	65%	18	17	61%	39	76
Midwest	55%	37	8	33%	67	84
West	15%	81	3	5%	95	59
South	22%	59	19	19%	81	74
Border	38%	56	6	44%	56	16
All cities over 50,000	41%	47%	12%	32%	68%	
N	(126)	(146)	(37)	(98)	(210)	(309)

the South, and even less popular in the West.[42] The distribution is similar for the type of ballot; partisan elections are preferred only in the

[42] The western cities are those in the conventionally defined eleven western states, plus Honolulu. The Northeast includes the six New England states plus New York, New Jersey, and Pennsylvania. The Midwest includes Ohio, Indiana, Illinois, Iowa, Michigan, Minnesota, Wisconsin, North Dakota, South Dakota, Nebraska, and Kansas. The South includes the eleven ex-Confederate states.

TABLE 8. *Method of Electing Councilmen by Region, Excluding Commission Cities*

Region	Ward	At-large	Combina-tion	Total %	N
Northeast	31%	38	31	100	61
Midwest	33%	46	21	100	76
West	18%	75	7	100	57
South	13%	73	13	99[a]	60
Border	33%	53	13	99[a]	15
All cities over 50,000	25%	57%	18%	100%	
N	(67)	(153)	(49)		(269)

[a] Does not sum to 100 because of rounding.

Northeast. There are, however, two quite different patterns in the two sub-regions of the Northeast. Mid-Atlantic cities (in New York, New Jersey, and Pennsylvania) use the partisan ballot by a ratio of more than four to one, while almost two-thirds of the New England cities have nonpartisan local elections. Elsewhere in the country the nonpartisan system is heavily favored; in the West only three cities have partisan elections.[43] Regional variations in methods of electing councilmen are much milder, as Table 8 shows. Midwestern and northeastern cities are most addicted to the "private-regarding" alternative; almost one third of each group elect legislators from wards. Three quarters of the cities in the West and South use the at-large system.

Just as regional variations in structure are immense, so are they in levels of ethnicity. As Table 9 demonstrates, the Northeast is the most ethnic part of the country, with 94 per cent of its cities having more than the national average (19 per cent) of first- and second-generation Americans, and more than half being over 40 per cent foreign stock. The New England sub-region has the heaviest concentration of immigrants and their children; 27 of the 33 New England cities in our sample are at least 40 per cent ethnic. The distribution is somewhat less skewed in the Mid-

[43] Most western cities examined here are in California, where all cities use the nonpartisan ballot. California law does *not* require nonpartisan local elections, however. In 1913 the legislature required "general-law" cities (those without charters) to use the nonpartisan ballot. This did not apply to charter cities, of which there were 70 in 1960, including the communities in our sample. Any California municipality of more than 3500 persons may adopt its own charter. See Eugene C. Lee, *The Politics of Nonpartisanship* (Berkeley and Los Angeles: University of California Press, 1960), pp. 13–15, 23.

TABLE 9. *Foreign-Stock Population of Cities—By Region*

Proportion of Population of Foreign Stock	North-east	Mid-west	West	South	Border
0% to 9.9%	3%	16%	2%	80%	69%
10% to 19.9%	4	31	31	11	19
20% to 29.9%	17	24	53	4	6
30% to 39.9%	24	24	12	3	6
40% to 49.9%	40	6	3	—	—
50% and over	13	—	—	3[a]	—
Totals	101%[b]	101%[b]	101%[b]	101%[b]	100%
Per cent of cities with 20% or more foreign stock	94%	54%	68%	10%	12%

[a] Miami Beach and Laredo.
[b] Does not sum to 100 because of rounding.

west. Just under half of the cities there are less than 20 per cent ethnic, with almost all the rest in the 20 to 40 per cent range. The western cities show a different pattern; 84 per cent of them fall between 10 and 30 per cent foreign stock. Almost all the southern and border cities are homogeneously native, except for a few towns on the Mexican border and in the Forida resort belt. The foreign-stock residents of the former cases are, of course, largely Mexicans who have not participated heavily in local politics.[44] In the latter case the ethnics are mostly Jews who have moved to Florida in recent years.

V Ethnicity and Political Structures

We come now to the central question, the relationship between cities' ethnic populations and political forms. It might be assumed that the preceding section has already answered the question with a resounding affirmation of the ethos theory, for those regions with the largest foreign stock populations have the highest proportion of cities with elements of the private-regarding ethic. There are some exceptions to this, notably in the popularity of nonpartisanship in New England and in the consistent deviation of the West, but by and large the pattern is as predicted by the ethos theory.

[44] For a description of Mexican-American political apathy in one Texas border city see Edward C. Banfield, *Big City Politics* (New York: Random House, 1965), pp. 76–78.

More precise measures produce the same result. Excluding cities with a commission form of government and comparing the mean foreign stock populations of cities with mayors and with managers, we find that mayor cities have a much higher mean ethnic population. All mayor cities have a mean foreign-stock population of 29 per cent; those with a manager form are 18 per cent foreign stock. This difference is significant at the .001 level of confidence.[45]

But since both ethnicity and types of governmental structure vary markedly from one part of the country to another, it is necessary to control for region when examining the relationships between these variables. The South, for example, has few foreign-stock residents and few institutional manifestations of the private-regarding ethos. Indeed, the relationship in the South is so strong that it probably accounts in large part for the nationwide findings described in the preceding paragraph. But it would be rash to attribute southern political patterns to the scarcity of immigrants there. (Southern and border cities are excluded from the following intra-region comparisons because there is so little variation in the level of their foreign-stock populations.)

When the relationship between ethnicity and form of government is examined *within* regions, this control eliminates most of the apparent relationship. (We have also controlled for size by eliminating all cities of more than 500,000 population.) Northeastern cities with mayors have a mean ethnic population of 39 per cent; those with managers are 40 per cent foreign stock. The predicted relationship is found in the Midwest,[46] where cities with mayors average 6 per cent more ethnic than cities with managers. This difference is significant at the .05 level. There is a similar finding in the West, although its importance is diminished by the fact that only six western cities have mayors.[47] It is noteworthy that the northeastern manager cities are much more ethnic than cities in other parts of the country that use the mayor form.[48] This suggests that there is no nationally relevant level of ethnicity above which one form of gov-

[45] The significance of differences between means was measured with a two-tailed t test.

[46] In this and all other analyses of relationships between form of government and socioeconomic variables, the nine Indiana cities have been omitted.

[47] Controlling for social class by means of analysis of covariance did not produce greater differences in ethnicity between the two types of city. Whenever relationships between a dependent variable and a demographic independent variable are described in this paper, we have also controlled for the possible influence of other demographic variables of covariance. Except where noted, this procedure did not increase or diminish the explanatory power of the independent variable being examined.

[48] The same is true for the other structural dependent variables; the "public-regarding" northeastern cities are more ethnic than "private-regarding" cities in other parts of the country (see Tables 11 and 12).

ernment is likely to predominate, i.e., there is no threshold level of ethnicity. These data are summarized in Table 10.

The only discernible variable distinguishing mayor and manager cities in the Northeast is the proportion of their populations in white-collar occupations, and even here the difference is neither large nor statistically significant. The residents of northeastern mayor cities average 42 per cent in white-collar jobs, compared to 46 per cent in manager cities. The same difference is true in the Midwest. No such relationship is found in western cities. The levels of median income in manager cities are somewhat higher in all three regions. The differences range from $128 in the Midwest to $494 in the West. In the West this probably reflects nothing more than variations in the cost of labor, since there is no difference in the mean size of the working-class populations of the two types of cities there. Northeastern manager cities tend to have somewhat higher levels of education: 11.0 median school years completed as opposed to 10.3 in the mayor cities. There are no such differences in the Midwest and West.

The *nationwide* pattern of distribution of partisan and nonpartisan ballots is quite similar to that of form of government. All cities using the partisan ballot have a mean ethnic population of 25 per cent; those using nonpartisan ballots have a mean ethnic population of 21 per cent. While this difference is considerably smaller than that for forms of government, it is still significant at the .01 level.

This faint relationship breaks down or even reverses when examined within regions. As Table 11 shows, northeastern cities using a nonpartisan ballot have considerably *larger* ethnic populations than those which use the partisan ballot: 43 per cent v. 34 per cent; this difference is significant at the .001 level. This striking negative finding is due largely to New England, which is the most ethnic part of the country and where 64 per cent of the cities use the nonpartisan ballot. There is no difference between those midwestern cities using the nonpartisan ballot and those that do not. There is a difference among western cities in the predicted direction. It is not statistically significant, perhaps because only three western cities have partisan elections.

Examination of other demographic indices reveals no consistent patterns. Neither class, income, nor education is related to use of one type of ballot or the other. Controlling for third variables such as occupation and income did not produce greater relationships between any demographic variable and the presence of party labels in municipal elections.

The method of electing city councilmen is also unrelated to the level of foreign-stock population. As Table 12 indicates, there are no differences in foreign-stock population between northeastern cities electing their legislators from wards and at large, nor are there differences with respect

TABLE 10. *Form of Municipal Government and Selected Population Characteristics of Cities under 500,000 Population—By Region*

Population Characteristic	Northeast			Midwest			West		
	Mayor	Manager	Sig.[a]	Mayor	Manager	Sig.	Mayor	Manager	Sig.
% foreign stock	39%	40%	n.s.	26%	20%	.05	26%	22%	n.s.
% white collar	42%	46%	n.s.	45%	49%	n.s.	51%	50%	n.s.
Median family income in 1959	\$6200	\$6395	n.s.	\$6755	\$6883	n.s.	\$6481	\$6975	n.s.
Median school years[b]	10.3	11.0	.05	11.2	11.4	n.s.	12.1	12.0	n.s.
Number of cities	(44)	(14)		(32)	(30)		(6)	(47)	

[a] The difference between mayor and manager cities for the relevant demographic variable, in a given region, is measured with a two-tailed t test.

[b] For adults 25 and older.

TABLE 11. *Type of Ballot and Selected Population Characteristics—By Region*

	Northeast			Midwest			West		
Population Characteristic	Partisan	Nonpartisan	Sig.[a]	Partisan	Nonpartisan	Sig.[a]	Partisan	Nonpartisan	Sig.[a]
% foreign stock	34%	43%	.001	23%	22%	n.s.	28%	23%	n.s.
% white collar	42%	41%	n.s.	45%	46%	n.s.	49%	50%	n.s.
Median family income in 1959	$6099	$6058	n.s.	$6689	$6607	n.s.	$6330	$6917	n.s.
Median school years[b]	10.3	10.4	n.s.	11.0	11.2	n.s.	12.1	12.0	n.s.
Number of cities	(46)	(29)		(28)	(56)		(3)	(56)	

[a] A two-tailed t test was used to measure the significance of the difference between partisan and nonpartisan cities with respect to the relevant demographic variable in a given region.

[b] For adults 25 years of age and older.

TABLE 12. *Method of Electing City Councilmen and Selected Population Characteristics of Cities With Less Than One Million Population—by Region*

Population Characteristic	Northeast			Midwest			West		
	Ward	At-large	Sig.[a]	Ward	At-large	Sig.	Ward	At-large	Sig.
% foreign stock	38%	38%	n.s.	25%	21%	n.s.	21%	23%	n.s.
% white collar	43%	43%	n.s.	45%	47%	n.s.	52%	50%	n.s.
Median family income in 1959	$6211	$6157	n.s.	$6643	$6758	n.s.	$6713	$6926	n.s.
Median school years[b]	10.4	10.5	n.s.	10.9	11.2	n.s.	12.3	12.0	n.s.
Number of cities	(18)	(25)		(24)	(35)		(9)	(43)	

[a] Significance measured with a two-tailed t test.
[b] For adults 25 and older.

to any other demographic measure.[49] In the Midwest at-large cities are 4 per cent less ethnic and also have slightly more middle class residents (2 per cent) and a higher median income ($115). While all these differences are in the predicted direction, none is statistically significant, much less of any substantive consequence. Western cities electing councilmen from wards have *fewer* ethnic residents and slightly larger middle-class populations, but these differences are even smaller than those in the Midwest.

The salient conclusion to be drawn from these data is that one can do a much better job of predicting a city's political forms by knowing what part of the country it is in than by knowing anything about the composition of its population. The reasons for this may lie in certain regional historical experiences related to the influx of immigrants and the responses to their needs reflected in municipal political systems. We will discuss the importance of regional differences in the concluding section of this paper. For the present, it is sufficient to note that only in the Midwest can we detect relationships in the direction predicted by the

[49] The five cities with populations of more than a million persons have been excluded from these tabulations involving methods of electing councilmen.

TABLE 13. *Mean Foreign Stock Population of Cities with Each Combination of Form of Government, Type of Ballot, and Method of Electing Councilmen—By Region*[a]

Governmental Combination	Northeast Per Cent Ethnic	Northeast N	Midwest Per Cent Ethnic	Midwest N	West Per Cent Ethnic	West N
Mayor-Partisan-Ward	40	16	26	7	23	1
Mayor-Partisan-At-Large	33	9	33	2	—	0
Mayor-Nonpartisan-Ward	37	2	27	12	25	5
Manager-Partisan-Ward	26	1	19	2	—	0
Manager-Nonpartisan-Ward	—	0	27	4	19	4
Manager-Partisan-At-Large	40	4	25	5	22	1
Mayor-Nonpartisan-At-Large	44	3	24	9	37	2
Manager-Nonpartisan-At-Large	43	7	18	18	22	40

[a] Cities using the commission form or a combination of ward and at-large election have been excluded from this table.

ethos theory with respect to two of the three dependent variables we have examined.

In addition to analyzing each of these dependent variables singly, we have combined them. There are eight possible combinations of form of government (we limit ourselves to mayor and manager), type of ballot, and method of electing councilmen (here limited to ward or at-large, omitting combinations), as shown in Table 13. Within each region we have computed the mean foreign stock populations of those cities with each combination of characteristics. Conceivably the "pure type" cities would be more likely to display the ethnic characteristics said to be related to one ethos or the other. We can also evaluate Banfield and Wilson's suggestion that:

> Among the modifications that might make the [city manager] plan more acceptable and more workable in cities (whether large or small) having a politically significant lower class are the following: partisan rather than nonpartisan elections, election of some councilmen on a ward rather than an at-large basis. . . .[50]

As Table 13 shows, there is no consequential difference in the ethnic populations of any of the groups of cities, in any region, except for "pure" public-regarding cities in the Midwest; these 18 cities have, on the average, fewer ethnic residents than do cities with any of the other seven

[50] Banfield and Wilson, pp. 183–184.

combinations. In the Northeast the "pure" public-regarding cities have, in the aggregate, slightly larger foreign-stock populations than the "pure" private-regarding cities. Combining the manager form with partisan voting and ward-elected councilmen does not seem to have had the appeal suggested by Banfield and Wilson.

The difference between the two ethics is also said to be reflected in the size of the districts represented by members of the municipal legislature where wards, in fact, exist. Small districts are thought to be a consequence of the dominance of the private-regarding ethos, while large districts, which force each councilman to respond to a more heterogeneous constituency, reflect the public-regarding ethic. This proposition can be tested by examining relationships between the size of cities' ethnic populations and the number of persons represented by their ward-elected councilmen. If the proposition were valid, one would find negative correlations – that is, the larger the districts, the fewer the ethnic residents in the city.

As usual, the proposition is confirmed on a nationwide basis. For all cities with at least some ward-elected councilmen, the correlation coefficient (Pearson's r) between the foreign-stock population and the number of persons represented by each ward-elected councilman is –.23. This is significant at the .05 level.[51] The coefficient remains at about the same level when a partial correlation is computed to control for social class; similar results are found when other variables are controlled.

The relationship persists when size is controlled. For cities with populations between 100,000 and 250,000 the coefficient is –.30; it falls only to –.26 when social class is partialled. Both of these values fall just short of the .05 level of confidence. In the smaller cities the coefficient is –.28 whether or not other variables are controlled; this is significant at the .05 level.

Once again, however, examining the data on a regional basis alters the picture drastically. In the Northeast the coefficient for all cities is .02; this vanishes entirely when class is controlled. In the Midwest the relationship is slightly in the predicted direction (–.16), and persists when other variables are controlled, but falls short of statistical significance. In the West the 14 cities with some ward-elected councilmen present a strikingly different pattern; the relationship is opposite to that predicted by the ethos theory. The simple correlation coefficient is .30, which falls to .24 when class is controlled. Neither of these values is significant at the .05 level. It appears that the confirmation of the proposition obtained by examining cities on a nationwide basis is primarily an artifact of regional differences.

[51] Significance of correlations is measured by the F value.

VI Ethnicity and Public Policy

The ethos theory states that the private-regarding ethic is hostile to civil service, city planning, and urban renewal. In this section we will test this proposition by examining the relationships between ethnicity and indices of these policies.

There is a strong relationship between a city's size and the likelihood that its municipal employees will be under civil service. As Table 14 shows, cities with more than 250,000 residents are very likely to have complete coverage; only one of the 28 cities in this group for which we have data does not have any coverage at all. A bare majority of cities with populations from 100,000 to 250,000 have total coverage, while more than 40 per cent either have none or protect only firemen and policemen. The trend continues for smaller cities.

Table 15 shows the foreign-stock populations of cities with different levels of civil service coverage, with size controlled. The data seem to contradict the ethos theory powerfully. Those cities with complete coverage have the highest foreign-stock populations in every size category except the largest, and even there the cities with minimal coverage are by far the least ethnic.

As with all our other nationwide findings, these striking relationships are an artifact of regional differences. Controlling for region makes it clear that the very low ethnic population of the cities with scanty coverage is due to the contribution of southern and border cities, which characteristically have neither extensive civil service coverage nor large foreign-

TABLE 14. *Civil Service Coverage and Size of City*[a]

Level of Civil Service Coverage	Over 250,000	100,000 to 250,000	50,000 to 100,000
1. All employees covered	75%	51%	45%
2. All but manual workers covered	14	6	5
3. Only policemen and firemen covered	7	25	32
4. No civil service coverage	4	18	18
Total	100%	100%	100%
N	(28)	(51)	(130)

[a] Cities in Indiana, Iowa, Massachusetts, New York, and Ohio are excluded from all tables concerning civil service coverage.

TABLE 15. *Civil Service Coverage and Foreign-Stock Population—By Size*

Level of Civil Service Coverage	Mean Per Cent Foreign-Stock in Population		
	Over 250,000	100,000 to 250,000	50,000 to 100,000
1. All employees covered	21%	23%	24%
2. All but manual workers covered	24	15	16
3. Only policemen and firemen covered	6	10	18
4. No civil service coverage	4	16	14

stock populations. Unfortunately for the ethos theory, however, data for the rest of the country do not support the hypothesis. The ethnic populations of western and midwestern cities do not differ appreciably from one level of coverage to the next. There are considerable differences among northeastern cities, but their impact is, if anything, contradictory to the theory. The eleven northeastern cities in which only policemen and firemen are protected have the fewest ethnic residents. The two cities with the least coverage have the highest mean ethnic populations, but this exceeds the mean for the 18 cities with complete coverage by only 5 per cent. In short, ethnicity does not make any difference in any region so far as civil service coverage is concerned. Relationships with other demographic variables are no more evident.

TABLE 16. *Civil Service Coverage and Foreign-Stock Population—By Region*

Level of Civil Service Coverage	Mean Per Cent Foreign-Stock in Population:							
	Northeast		Midwest		West		South	
	%	N	%	N	%	N	%	N
1. All employees covered	40	18	23	25	23	38	13	20
2. All but manual workers covered	38	3	22	3	—	—	7	6
3. Only policemen and firemen covered	23	11	23	16	21	4	7	23
4. No civil service coverage	45	2	21	6	21	8	4	13

TABLE 17. *Correlations between Per Cent Foreign-Stock and City Planning Expenditures Per Capita—By Size and Region*[a]

Size of City	Northeast	Midwest	West
Over 250,000	–.11	.22	–.10
	(8)[b]	(15)	(10)
100,000 to 250,000	–.22	–.25	.21
	(21)	(19)	(14)
50,000 to 100,000	–.04	.23	.09
	(47)	(50)	(35)

[a] The value in each cell is the Pearsonian *r* of the relationship between per cent ethnic population and city planning expenditures per capita, for the given group of cities. A negative correlation is in the direction predicted by the ethos theory.
[b] Numbers in parentheses are the number of cases in each cell.

City planning supposedly comes close to being anathema to the private-regarding ethos. We have correlated per capita city planning expenditures with foreign-stock percentages for cities of different sizes and in different regions. These data are summarized in Table 17. If the ethos theory were correct in this respect, we would find negative correlations, presumably at some level of statistical significance. No such pattern can be discerned in Table 17. Five of the nine cells show negative correlations, ranging from –.04 to –.25. Positive correlation coefficients range from .09 to .23. It is difficult to regard these results as due to anything but chance. These relationships do not change when partial correlations are computed to control for social class.

For somewhat the same reasons that they are believed to oppose city planning members of ethnic groups are said to be hostile to urban renewal. The amount of the federal capital grants reserved for a city is an accurate index of the extent of its commitment to urban renewal. We have used capital grants per capita as a comparative measure.[52]

While probably every city with more than 50,000 residents "needs" at least some urban renewal, it would be unsafe to assume that the need is equally important or recognized everywhere. The compact, aging cities of the industrial East and Midwest are losing residents and businesses to

[52] We counted all projects classified in the execution stage, or where a loan and grant contract was approved but not yet formally executed, in the December 31, 1963 directory. A renewal project in the execution stage at the end of 1963 is the product of prior decisions extending at least two or three years into the past.

the suburbs, while most southern and western cities are growing more prosperous and populous. Quasi-ideological opposition to urban renewal is stronger in the latter areas.[53]

Renewal activity is also a function of a city's size. While 86 per cent of cities with populations over 250,000 have at least one renewal project in the action phase, this is true of 71 per cent of cities with populations between 100,000 and 250,000, and only 47 per cent of cities in the 50,000 to 100,000 category.

For these reasons we have controlled for size and region when correlating ethnicity and urban renewal grants per capita. The findings, summarized in Table 18, resemble those for city planning. There is no consistent relationship, either in one region or in the country as a whole. Partial correlations to control for social class do not materially change this picture.[54]

The conventional wisdom holds that city governments headed by mayors are more responsible to the political preferences of ethnic groups. If this were the case and if ethnics were opposed to city planning and urban renewal, we would expect to find that while there was no relationship between ethnicity and the extent of these policies in all cities, such a relationship might appear in mayor cities. That is, in political systems where members of ethnic groups supposedly have more influence, this influence might be manifested in lower expenditures on city planning and urban renewal.[55] We can test this proposition by further subdividing the classes of cities in Tables 17 and 18 into mayor cities and manager cities (discarding those with the commission form). These tabulations are summarized in Tables 19 and 20.

[53] Several western and southern states were very slow to pass enabling legislation to permit their cities to undertake urban renewal projects; one or two states still impose severe restraints in this regard. We excluded southern states from our analysis; the western states that followed this policy do not, with one exception, contain cities with populations over 50,000.

[54] Amos H. Hawley has found an inverse relationship between the proportion of businessmen and professionals in a city's population and the likelihood that it has begun to carry out a renewal project. See his "Community Power and Urban Renewal Success," *American Journal of Sociology*, 68 (January, 1963), 422–431. Hawley's study does not take account of the magnitude of a city's program. It has been criticized on other grounds by Bruce C. Straits, "Community Action and Implementation of Urban Renewal," *ibid.*, 71 (July, 1965), 77–82. See also Hawley's rejoinder, *ibid.*, pp. 82–84.

[55] An earlier study found no relationship between form of local government and magnitude of urban renewal. See George S. Duggar, "The Relation of Local Government Structure to Urban Renewal," *Law and Contemporary Problems*, 26 (1961), 49–69.

TABLE 18. *Correlations between Percent Foreign-Stock and Urban Renewal Capital Grants Per Capita—By Size and Region*[a]

Size of City	Northeast	Midwest	West
Over 250,000	−.54	.12	.72[b]
	(8)	(15)	(10)
100,000 to 250,000	.05	−.16	.34
	(21)	(19)	(14)
50,000 to 100,000	−.10	.02	.17
	(47)	(50)	(35)

[a] The value in each cell is the Pearsonian *r* of the relationship between per cent ethnic population and urban renewal capital grants per capita for all federally-aided urban renewal projects in the execution stage. A negative correlation is in the direction predicted by the ethos theory.

[b] Significant at the .05 level. This is the only value to attain this level of confidence.

This manipulation of the data does not yield any greater relationships between ethnicity and city planning, as Table 19 demonstrates. There are no consistent tendencies in any part of the country for the correlation coefficients in mayor cities to be in the negative direction. Table 20, on urban renewal, provides one ray of hope for the ethos theory in the cell

TABLE 19. *Correlations between Percent Foreign-Stock and City Planning Expenditures Per Capita in Mayor and Manager Cities—By Size and Region*[a]

Size of City	Northeast		Midwest		West	
Over 250,000	mayor	−.11	mayor	.21	mayor	.75
	b		manager	−.44	manager	−.16
100,000 to 250,000	mayor	−.39	mayor	−.37	c	
	manager	.08	manager	−.65	manager	.23
50,000 to 100,000	mayor	.11	mayor	.23	mayor	.32
	manager	−.12	manager	.12	manager	.13

[a] The value in each cell is the product moment correlation coefficient of the relationship between per cent ethnic population and city planning expenditures per capita, for those cities with the indicated form of government and size and region. A negative correlation is in the direction predicted by the ethos theory, which also predicts larger negative correlations for the mayor cities.

[b] One manager city in group.

[c] No mayor cities in group.

TABLE 20. *Correlations between Percent Foreign-Stock and Urban Renewal Capital Grants Per Capita in Mayor and Manager Cities—By Size and Region*[a]

Size of City	Northeast		Midwest		West	
Over 250,000 population	mayor	−.55	mayor	.15	mayor	.60
	b		manager	−.08	manager	.90
100,000 to 250,000	mayor	.06	mayor	.21	c	
	manager	.24	manager	.41	manager	.34
50,000 to 100,000	mayor	−.05	mayor	−.43[d]	mayor	−.41[e]
	manager	−.14	manager	−.14	manager	.21

[a] The value in each cell is the product moment correlation coefficient of the relationship between per cent ethnic population and urban renewal capital grants per capita, for those cities with the indicated form of government and size and region. The ethos theory predicts negative correlations, greater in mayor cities than in manager ones.

[b] One manager city in group.

[c] No mayor cities in group.

[d] Almost significant at the .05 level; the only value in either Table 19 or 20 that comes this close.

[e] Four cities in this sub-group.

for small midwestern cities. Those cities with mayors have a correlation coefficient of −.43 between foreign-stock population and urban renewal capital grants per capita. This value is just short of significance at the .05 level. The coefficient for small western cities is almost as high, but there are only four cities in this group with mayors. Interpretation of Table 20 is, by and large, a matter of temperament. This one weak finding, in a mass of negative evidence, does not impress us as very important.

VII Conclusions

Several conclusions can be drawn from the foregoing findings: (1) Contrary to specific propositions in the ethos theory, some of the political forms and policies are not manifestations of either ethos. (2) The two ethics are not as ethnically differentiated as has been suggested. (3) The ethics, as described, do not exist. (4) The propositions about manifestations of the ethics and their ethnic roots are all correct, but there are so many other factors bearing on political outcomes that the prevailing ethos in a city is not very important. The data at hand do not permit us to evaluate these conclusions, but we can be fairly confident of one other assertion: the propositions of the ethos theory need to be modified to account for special circumstances that limit their validity. Regional variations are the most obvious examples of such circumstances; they are a good starting point for this discussion.

The ethos theory is irrelevant to the South, where most municipal institutions seem to be corollaries of the region's traditional preoccupation with excluding Negroes from political power. A one-party system removes temptations to appeal to Negro voters, as does the city manager plan. With only one party, the partisan ballot is not meaningful. At-large elections minimize Negro voting strength. In view of these considerations, the scarcity of immigrants in the South appears to be a superfluous explanation for its local governmental practices.[56]

For other special reasons the theory is also inapplicable to the West, where cities do have a considerable range of foreign-stock populations. We suggested one cause earlier: the immigrant experience in the West was different, hence the conditions that allegedly produce private-regardingness did not develop there. This different history also probably accounts for the relatively low levels of ethnic consciousness in the West. Inhabitants of the West have never been as fascinated as Easterners with national origins (except where Orientals and Mexicans are concerned), and therefore the region has not displayed the ethnic politics characteristic of the East.[57] Some manifestations of the private-regarding ethos are conducive to ethnic politics. The election of councilmen from wards, for instance, makes it much easier to bestow "recognition" on nationality groups. In the absence of civil service regulations it is easier to give every ethnic group its "fair share" of public jobs without having to worry about qualifications. Where politics is viewed as conflict among nationality groups for jobs, nominations, and spoils, institutional forms consistent with these aspirations are likely to flourish, *quite apart from any other prevailing view of the political world.* Obviously, ethnic salience is a pre-

[56] This southern concern with unity may also explain why Mexican-Americans in Texas have been so apolitical, in contrast to the political involvement of immigrants in the North. Perhaps the political participation of newly arrived minority groups is enhanced when the political environment is competitive. European immigrants to northern cities typically arrived in political arenas where partisan competition motivated both sets of contenders to appeal for their votes. As the immigrants acquired political skill, their prices rose until they had attained political influence at least somewhat in proportion to their numbers. But if immigrants come to a political system where the elites shun conflict with each other, they are likely to find that the interest of those elites is to exclude them from politics rather than appeal for their support. The impact of immigrant political values obviously would be far greater in the former case.

[57] Regional differences in ethnic politics and salience are discussed at greater length in Wolfinger, *op. cit.*, p. 898.

requisite of ethnic politics. A strategy of "recognizing" nationality groups is meaningless if most group members do not see politics in ethnic perspectives. To the extent that ethnic salience contributes to the strength of private-regardingness, one would expect that the ethos would be less evident in those places where ethnicity is not as prominent a feature of political life as it is in the Northeast.

Yet the theory also fares badly in the Northeast. It might be argued that this reflects a different kind of historical circumstance. Perhaps the Yankees there, anticipating their submergence in the rising tide of immigrants, took steps to minimize this trend by changing the political structure accordingly. This might, for instance, explain why northeastern cities that use the nonpartisan ballot are so much more ethnic than the region's cities that adhere to the partisan ballot. But this explanation presents several difficulties. Even those cities with, say, partisan elections, are highly ethnic. A generation ago ethnics must have been even more numerous in them. Why, then, did the Yankees in those cities not take steps to protect their interests? Why were the Yankees apparently most successful in those cities where the ethnics were most numerous? Why did the ethnics not change the system back when they took over?

When Yankees are as outnumbered as they are in the Northeast, they may prefer a system that gives them some minority representation. Perhaps any self-conscious minority prefers institutions that guarantee it representation and a chance to maximize its political resources, and there is no doubt that Yankees are a self-conscious minority in urban New England. When Boston city councilmen were elected from wards some Yankees and Jews won seats. But when Boston adopted the public-regarding at-large system only Italians and Irishmen could get elected.[58]

Possibly the politics of the Northeast, with its virulent ethnic tensions, produces in the Yankees the same orientations that the ethnics are said to have. They develop the same interests in recognition, representation of their parochial interests, favors from city hall, and so on. When the choice is between doing business with a private-regarding regime and political isolation, perhaps all but the stiffest Brahmins adapt to the private-regarding style. This would explain why ethnicity appears to be worthless as an independent variable in the Northeast: everyone there except possibly the cosmopolitan upper-middle-class has succumbed to private-regardingness.[59] The triumph of the immigrants is complete. The

[58] Banfield and Wilson, p. 95.

[59] As we noted earlier, the scanty scholarly knowledge of nonmetropolitan political machines may be due to the fact that most of the best research on local politics has been done at schools like Harvard, Columbia, and Chicago. These universities are located in cities where politics is conducted almost entirely by members of ethnic groups. From the vantage point of Hyde

outnumbered, affronted, overpowered Yankees go along with the immigrant political style both because they have to and because its values have replaced their own in the community.

The Midwest provides the best evidence for the ethos theory, but even there the differences between "public-regarding" and "private-regarding" cities are small and uneven.

Whatever the utility of these assorted speculations about the ethos theory, we still have not explained our striking positive finding, the great variations in each of the structural variables from one region to the next. Outside the South regional variations may reflect to some extent interaction between cities' natural histories and prevailing political enthusiasms at crucial periods in those histories. Most eastern and midwestern cities were important communities in the 19th century, before the National Municipal League's various structural reforms were seriously proposed. Their political institutions were well established and had seen hard service in the first generation of industrialization. Politicians generally had vested interests in maintaining the existing forms and most political actors had at least developed means of dealing with those forms. These attachments and accommodations were weaker and less developed in newer cities or cities undergoing tremendous growth. They were even more irrelevant when it came to deciding on governmental institutions for brand new communities. In such cases there was no presumption in favor of the status quo, and the writers of municipal constitutions were responsive to contemporary political fashions.

Most southwestern and western cities were villages, at best, until the early twentieth century, when the new municipal governmental forms were all the rage. We think that regional differences in the age of cities may explain a good deal of the striking regional variations in form of government, type of ballot, and method of electing councilmen.

While sudden growth is the most common occasion on which constitutions are written *de novo*, other conditions may present similar opportunities. This seems most likely to happen after a major political

---

Park or Harvard Square, almost everyone not connected with the university is an ethnic. Political practices in such cities typically are "private-regarding." Much of the opposition to these practices comes from people connected with or attracted to universities, that is, mostly from Jews and Protestants. College faculties and their social satellites are scarcely typical of the Protestant middle class. Banfield and Wilson may be overgenerous to the bulk of the Anglo-Saxon population. While professors and account executives are not particularly interested in patronage, ticket fixing, and the like, these and other elements of the private-regarding style may be quite congenial to people who have little in common with college faculties but nonmembership in the Catholic Church.

upheaval. For example, California's wholesale conversion to local nonpartisanship was a result of the Progressives' great victory over the Southern Pacific Railroad in the election of 1910. Anxious to capitalize on their triumph, the Progressives were extraordinarily receptive to the prevailing nostrums of reform. Twenty years before, these measures were not yet plausible alternatives. Twenty years later, sophisticated reformers would have placed far less faith in such changes.

In short, the ethos theory clearly needs a good deal of modification. Whether a revised version will have much explanatory power remains to be seen.

REFORMISM AND PUBLIC POLICIES IN AMERICAN CITIES

ROBERT L. LINEBERRY
EDMUND P. FOWLER

A decade ago, political scientists were deploring the "lost world of municipal government" and calling for systematic studies of municipal life which emphasized the political, rather than the administrative, side of urban political life.[1] In recent years, this demand has been generously answered and urban politics is becoming one of the most richly plowed fields of political research. In terms originally introduced by David Easton,[2] political scientists have long been concerned with inputs, but

Reprinted by permission from Robert L. Lineberry and Edmund P. Fowler, "Reformism and Public Policies in American Cities," *American Political Science Review,* 61 (September, 1967), 701–716.

The authors are indebted to Professor Robert T. Daland, James W. Prothro, William R. Keech and James Q. Wilson for comments on an earlier draft of this paper. For assistance in statistical and methodological questions, the advice of Professor Hubert Blalock and Mr. Peter B. Harkins has been invaluable. The authors, of course, assume responsibility for all interpretation and misinterpretation.

[1] Lawrence J. R. Herson, "The Lost World of Municipal Government," [*American Political Science Review*], 51 (June, 1957), 330–345; Robert T. Daland, "Political Science and the Study of Urbanism," *ibid.,* 491–509.

[2] David Easton, "An Approach to the Analysis of Political Systems," *World Politics,* 9 (April, 1957), 383–400.

more recently they have focused their attention on other system variables, particularly the political culture [3] and policy outputs of municipal governments.[4]

The present paper will treat two policy outputs, taxation and expenditure levels of cities, as dependent variables. We will relate these policy choices to socio-economic characteristics of cities and to structural characteristics of their governments. Our central research concern is to examine the impact of political structures, reformed and unreformed, on policy-making in American cities.

I Political Culture, Reformism and Political Institutions

The leaders of the Progressive movement in the United States left an enduring mark on the American political system, particularly at the state and municipal level. In the states, the primary election, the referendum, initiative and recall survive today. The residues of this *Age of Reform*,[5] as Richard Hofstadter called it, persist in municipal politics principally in the form of manager government and at-large and nonpartisan elections. The reformers were, to borrow Banfield and Wilson's phrase, the original embodiment of the "middle class ethos" in American politics. They were, by and large, White Anglo-Saxon Protestants reacting to the politics of the party machine, which operated by exchanging favors for votes.[6]

It is important that we understand the ideology of these reformers if we hope to be able to analyze the institutions which they created and their impact on political decisions. The reformers' goal was to "rationalize" and "democratize" city government by the substitution of "community oriented" leadership. To the reformers, the most pernicious

[3] Edward C. Banfield and James Q. Wilson, *City Politics* (Cambridge: Harvard University Press and the MIT Press, 1963); see also James Q. Wilson and Edward C. Banfield, "Public-Regardingness as a Value Premise in Voting Behavior,"[*American Political Science Review*], 58 (December, 1964), 876–887.

[4] See, for example, Thomas R. Dye, "City-Suburban Social Distance and Public Policy," *Social Forces*, 4 (1965), 100–106; Raymond Wolfinger and John Osgood Field, "Political Ethos and the Structure of City Government," [*American Political Science Review*], 60 (June, 1966), 306–326; Edgar L. Sherbenou, "Class, Participation, and the Council-Manager Plan," *Public Administration Review*, 21 (Summer, 1961), 131–135; Lewis A. Froman, Jr., "An Analysis of Public Policies in Cities," *Journal of Politics*, 29 (February, 1967), 94–108.

[5] (New York: Alfred A. Knopf, 1955.)

[6] John Porter East, *Council Manager Government: The Political Thought of Its Founder, Richard S. Childs* (Chapel Hill: University of North Carolina Press, 1965), p. 18.

characteristic of the machine was that it capitalized on socio-economic cleavages in the population, playing on class antagonisms and on racial and religious differences. Ernest S. Bradford, an early advocate of commission government with at-large elections, defended his plans for at-large representation on grounds that

> . . . under the ward system of governmental representation, the ward receives the attention, not in proportion to its needs but to the ability of its representatives to 'trade' and arrange 'deals' with fellow members. . . . Nearly every city under the aldermanic system offers flagrant examples of this vicious method of "part representation." The commission form changes this to representation of the city as a whole.[7]

The principal tools which the reformers picked to maximize this "representation of the city as a whole" were the commission, and later the manager, form of government, the nonpartisan election and the election at-large. City manager government, it was argued, produced a no-nonsense, efficient and business-like regime, where decisions could be implemented by professional administrators rather than by victors in the battle over spoils. Nonpartisan elections meant to the reformer that state and national parties, whose issues were irrelevant to local politics anyway, would keep their divisive influences out of municipal decision-making. Nonpartisan elections, especially when combined with elections at-large, would also serve to reduce the impact of socio-economic cleavages and minority voting blocs in local politics. Once established, these institutions would serve as bastions against particularistic interests.

Banfield and Wilson have argued that the "middle class ethos" of the reformers has become a prevalent attitude in much of political life. The middle class stands for "public regarding" virtues rather than for "private regarding" values of the ethnic politics of machines and bosses. The middle class searches for the good of the "community as a whole" rather than for the benefit of particularistic interests.[8] Agger, Goldrich and Swanson, in their study of two western and two southern communities have documented the rise of a group they call the "community conservationists," who "see the values of community life maximized when political leadership is exercised by men representing the public at large, rather than 'special interests.' "[9] Robert Wood has taken up a similar theme in his penetrating analysis of American suburbia. The "no-party

[7] Ernest S. Bradford, *Commission Government in American Cities* (New York: Macmillan, 1911), p. 165.

[8] Banfield and Wilson, *op. cit.*, p. 41.

[9] Robert Agger, Daniel Goldrich, and Bert E. Swanson, *The Rulers and the Ruled* (New York: John Wiley and Sons, 1964), p. 21.

politics of suburbia" is characterized by "an outright reaction against partisan activity, a refusal to recognize that there may be persistent cleavages in the electorate and an ethical disapproval of permanent group collaboration as an appropriate means of settling disputes."[10] This ideological opposition to partisanship is a product of a tightly knit and homogeneous community, for "nonpartisanship reflects a highly integrated community life with a powerful capacity to induce conformity."[11]

Considerable debate has ensued over both the existence and the consequences of these two political ethics in urban communities. Some evidence has supported the view that reformed governments[12] are indeed found in cities with higher incomes, higher levels of education, greater proportions of Protestants and more white-collar job-holders. Schnore and Alford, for example, found that "the popular image of the manager city was verified; it does tend to be the natural habitat of the upper middle class." In addition, manager cities were "inhabited by a younger, more mobile population that is growing rapidly."[13]

More recently, Wolfinger and Field correlated socio-economic variables – particularly ethnicity and region – to political structures. They concluded that "the ethos theory is irrelevant to the South . . . inapplicable to the West . . . fares badly in the Northeast . . ." and that support for the theory in the Midwest was "small and uneven."[14] Region proved to be a more important predictor of both government forms and of policy outputs like urban renewal expenditures than did the socio-economic composition of the population.

In our view, it is premature to carve a headstone for the ethos theory. It is our thesis that governments which are products of the reform movement behave differently from those which have unreformed institutions, even if the socio-economic composition of their population may be similar. Our central purpose is to determine the impact of both socio-economic variables and political institutions (structural variables) on outputs of city governments. By doing this, we hope to shed some additional illumination on the ethos theory.

[10] Robert C. Wood, *Suburbia: Its People and Their Politics* (Boston: Houghton Mifflin Co., 1959), p. 155.

[11] *Ibid.*, p. 154.

[12] We refer to cities characterized by commission or manager government, nonpartisan elections, and at-large constituencies as "reformed." Our use of the term is historical and no value position in reformism's merits is intended. To refer to reformed cities as "public regarding" or "middle class" is, it seems, to assume what needs to be proved.

[13] Leo Schnore and Robert Alford, "Forms of Government and Socio-Economic Characteristics of Suburbs," *Administrative Science Quarterly*, 8 (June, 1963), 1–17. See also the literature cited in Froman, *op. cit.*

[14] Wolfinger and Field, *op. cit.*, pp. 325–326.

II Research Design

Variables. The independent variables used in this analysis, listed in Table 1, consist of relatively "hard" data, mostly drawn from the U.S. census.[15] These variables were selected because they represent a variety of possible social cleavages which divide urban populations – rich vs. poor, Negro vs. White, ethnic vs. native, newcomers vs. old-timers, etc. We assume that such social and economic characteristics are important determinants of individual and group variations in political preferences. Data on each of these independent variables were gathered for each of the two hundred cities in the sample.[16]

Our principal theoretical concern is with the consequences of variations in the structural characteristics of form of government, type of constituency and partisanship of elections. The variable of government form is unambiguous. Except for a few small New England towns, all American cities have council-manager, mayor-council or commission government. There is, however, somewhat more ambiguity in the classification of election type. By definition, a "nonpartisan election is one in which no candidate is identified on the ballot by party affiliation." [17] The legal definition

TABLE 1. *Independent Variables*

1. Population, 1960
2. Per cent population increase or decrease, 1950-60
3. Per cent non-white
4. Per cent of native population with foreign born or mixed parentage
5. Median income
6. Per cent of population with incomes below $3000
7. Per cent of population with incomes above $10,000
8. Median school years completed by adult population
9. Per cent high school graduates among adult population
10. Per cent of population in white collar occupations
11. Per cent of elementary school children in private schools
12. Per cent of population in owner-occupied dwelling units

[15] The source for the first nine variables is *The City and County Data Book* (Washington: United States Bureau of the Census, 1962). For the last three variables, the source is Orin F. Nolting and David S. Arnold (eds.), *The Municipal Yearbook 1965* (Chicago: International City Managers' Association, 1965), pp. 98 ff.

[16] We used a random sample of 200 of the 309 American cities with populations of 50,000 or more in 1960. All information on the forms of government and forms of election is drawn from *The Municipal Yearbook, 1965, op. cit.*

[17] Banfield and Wilson, *op. cit.*, p. 151.

of nonpartisanship conceals the wide variation between Chicago's and Boston's nominal nonpartisanship and the more genuine variety in Minneapolis, Winnetka and Los Angeles.[18] We will quickly see, though, that formal nonpartisanship is not merely an empty legal nicety, but that there are very real differences in the political behavior of partisan and nonpartisan cities, even though we are defining them in legal terms only.[19]

Our classification of constituency types into only two groups also conceals some variation in the general pattern. While most cities use either the at-large or the ward pattern of constituencies exclusively, a handful use a combination of the two electoral methods. For our purposes, we classified these with district cities.

The dependent variables in this study are two measures of public policy outputs. A growing body of research on local politics has utilized policy measures as dependent variables.[20] The present research is intended to further this study of political outputs by relating socio-economic variables to expenditure and taxation patterns in cities with varying political structures.

The dependent variables are computed by a simple formula. The measure for taxation was computed by dividing the total personal income of the city into the total tax of the city, giving us a tax/income ratio. Similarly, dividing expenditures by the city's aggregate personal income gave us an expenditure/income ratio as the measure for our second dependent variable. These measures, while admittedly imperfect,[21] permit

[18] For Minneapolis, see Robert Morlan, "City Politics: Free Style," *National Municipal Review*, 48 (November, 1949), pp. 485–490; Winnetka, Banfield and Wilson, *op. cit.*, p. 140; Los Angeles, Charles G. Mayo, "The 1961 Mayoralty Election in Los Angeles: The Political Party in a Nonpartisan Election," *Western Political Quarterly*, 17 (1964), 325–339.

[19] At least one other variable may produce a given institutional form in a city – the legal requirements of a state government, which vary from state to state and may even vary for different kinds of cities within the same state. We have not taken account of this variable because systematic information on comparative state requirements in this area was unavailable to us. However, Wolfinger and Field consulted several experts and eliminated cities which are not given free choice over their institutions. Nevertheless, a comparison of our figures with theirs revealed no important differences.

[20] See footnote 4, *supra*.

[21] We recognize that these are only rough indicators of city finance policies. Definitions of taxation vary from city to city and what may be financed from taxes in one city may be financed from fees in another. Expenditures present a more complex problem because the types and amounts of state transfer payments vary from state to state according to state laws, the division of governmental labor in a state, the incomes and sizes of cities, not to mention political factors at the state level. We think it important, however, that our independent variables explain a large proportion of the variation in municipal outputs as we measured them. No doubt

us to ask how much of a city's income it is willing to commit for public taxation and expenditures.

HYPOTHESIS. Much of the research on city politics has treated reformed institutions as dependent variables. Although we shall briefly examine the social and economic differences between reformed and unreformed cities, our principal concern will be to explore the *consequences* for public policy of political institutions. From our earlier discussion of the political culture of cities we hypothesized that:

1. The relationship between socio-economic cleavages and policy outputs is stronger in unreformed than in reformed cities.

This hypothesis focuses on the intention of the reformers to minimize the role of particularistic interests in policy making.

III REFORMED AND UNREFORMED CITIES: A COMPARISON

The economic and social contrasts between reformed and unreformed cities have been the subject of much research,[22] and for our purposes we may be brief in our treatment. We divided the independent variables into three groups, one measuring population size and growth, a second containing social class indicators and a third including three measures of social homogeneity. The means and standard deviations for each variable by institutional category are found in Table 2.

It should initially be noted that population size and growth rate fairly clearly separate the reformed from the unreformed cities. As Alford and Scoble amply documented,[23] the larger the city, the greater the likelihood of its being unreformed; the faster its growth rate, the more likely a city is to possess manager government, nonpartisan and at-large elections. These differences are likely accounted for by the fact that very

---

one could explain an even larger proportion of the variation in measures which specify different functional responsibilities of cities. At least these measures constitute a starting point, and we hope others will improve on them.

The source of our output measures was the *County and City Data Book*, *op. cit*.

[22] See, for example, Robert Alford and Harry Scoble, "Political and Socio-Economic Characteristics of American Cities," *The Municipal Yearbook 1965*, *op. cit.*, pp. 82–97; Sherbenou, *op. cit.*; John H. Kessel, "Governmental Structure and Political Environment," [*American Political Science Review*], 56 (September, 1962), 615–620.

[23] Alford and Scoble, *op. cit*. The particularly large differences found between the populations of reformed and unreformed cities reflect the fact that New York City and several other urban giants are included in the sample.

large cities are most likely to (1) have unreformed institutions and (2) be stable or declining in population. Since neither of these variables emerged as particularly important predictors of our output variables, we relegated them to secondary importance in the rest of the analysis.

The data in Table 2 indicate that reformed cities (at least those over 50,000) do not appear to be "the natural habitat of the upper middle class." While reformed cities have slightly more educated populations and slightly high proportions of white collar workers and home ownership, unreformed cities have generally high incomes. In any case, whatever their direction, the differences are not large. What is striking is not the differences between the cities but the similarities of their class composition.

Homogeneity is easily one of the most ambiguous terms in the ambiguous language of the social sciences. We have followed Alford and Scoble who used three measures of homogeneity: for ethnicity, the per cent of population native born of foreign born or mixed parentage; for race, the per cent non-white; and for religious homogeneity, the per cent of elementary school children in private schools. The last measure, while indirect, was the only one available, since data on religious affiliation are not collected by the Census Bureau.

With the exception of race, reformed cities appear somewhat more homogeneous than unreformed cities. While the differences in homogeneity are more clear-cut than class differences, this hardly indicates that reformed cities are the havens of a socially homogeneous population. Although the average nonpartisan city has 16.9 per cent of its children in private schools, this mean conceals a wide range – from 2 to 47 per cent.

Our findings about the insignificance of class differences between reformed and unreformed cities are at some variance with Alford and Scoble's conclusions. There is, however, some support for the argument that reformed cities are more homogeneous. While we used cities with populations of over 50,000, their sample included all cities over 25,000; and varying samples may produce varying conclusions. The only other study to analyze cities over 50,000 was Wolfinger and Field's and our conclusions are generally consistent with theirs. We differ with them, however, on two important questions.

First, Wolfinger and Field argued that what differences there are between unreformed and reformed cities disappear when controls for region are introduced: "The salient conclusion to be drawn from these data is that one can do a much better job of predicting a city's political form by knowing what part of the country it is in than by knowing anything about the composition of its population." [24] Since regions have had different historical experiences, controls for region are essentially controls for

[24] *Op. cit.*, p. 320.

TABLE 2. *Comparison of the Means (and Standard Deviations) of Socio-Economic Characteristics of Reformed and Unreformed Cities*

Independent Variable	Government Type: Mayor-Council		Manager		Commission	
Population:						
Population (10^3)	282.5	(858.6)	115.7	(108.0)	128.6	(115.2)
% Change, 1950-60	36.4%	(118.8)	64.1%	(130.4)	18.5%	(36.7)
Class:						
Median Income	$6199.	(1005.0)	$6131.	(999.6)	$5425.	(804.4)
% under $3000	15.3%	(7.0)	17.3%	(6.9)	21.5%	(7.9)
% over $10,000	16.9%	(7.2)	17.5%	(6.7)	12.5%	(3.7)
% High school graduates	40.7%	(10.8)	48.1%	(8.9)	41.6%	(10.4)
Median Education (yrs.)	10.7	(1.1)	11.4	(.89)	11.0	(2.1)
% Owner-Occupied Dwelling Units	54.9%	(15.1)	57.3%	(13.6)	54.6%	(13.7)
% White collar	44.1%	(9.0)	48.1%	(7.1)	44.2%	(7.6)
Homogeneity:						
% Nonwhite	10.6%	(11.5)	11.6%	(10.8)	16.5%	(14.9)
% Native with Foreign Born or Mixed Parcentage	19.7%	(9.9)	12.4%	(8.3)	11.7%	(10.7)
% Private School Attendance	23.5%	(11.9)	15.3%	(11.8)	16.6%	(11.8)
	N = 85		N = 90		N = 25	

Independent Variable	Election Type: Partisan		Nonpartisan	
Population:				
Population (10^3)	270.8	(1022.1)	155.8	(198.7)
% Population Increase 1950-1960	17.1	(40.1)	58.3%	(136.1)
Class:				
Median Income	$5996.	(904.5)	$6074.	(1045.5)
% under $3000	16.8%	(7.1)	17.2%	(7.2)
% over $10,000	16.1%	(6.1)	16.7%	(7.0)
% High School Graduates	40.5%	(9.2)	45.3%	(10.6)
Median Education (yrs.)	10.6	(1.1)	11.2	(1.2)
% Owner-Occupied Dwelling Units	51.5%	(14.4)	57.7%	(13.8)
% White Collar	43.5%	(7.5)	46.7%	(8.3)

TABLE 2. *Comparison of the Means (and Standard Deviations) of Socio-Economic Characteristics of Reformed and Unreformed Cities (Continued)*

Independent Variable	Election Type (*Continued*)			
	Partisan		Nonpartisan	
Homogeneity:				
% Nonwhite	13.0%	(11.9)	11.5%	(11.8)
% Native with Foreign Born or Mixed Parentage	17.5%	(10.7)	14.7%	(9.6)
% Private School Attendance	24.1%	(13.6)	16.9%	(11.3)
	N = 57		N = 143	

Independent Variable	Constituency Type			
	District		At-large	
Population:				
Population (10^3)	246.9	(909.8)	153.6	(191.2)
% Population Increase 1950-1960	23.1%	(36.4)	59.1%	(143.7)
Class:				
Median Income	$6297.	(965.2)	$5942.	(1031.9)
% under $3000	14.7%	(6.5)	18.2%	(7.6)
% over $10,000	17.7%	(7.1)	16.0%	(6.6)
% High School Graduates	43.6%	(10.9)	44.4%	(10.4)
Median Education (yrs.)	10.9	(1.1)	11.2	(1.2)
% Owner-Occupied Dwelling Units	55.1%	(14.4)	56.9%	(14.5)
% White Collar	45.2%	(9.4)	46.3%	(7.5)
Homogeneity:				
% Nonwhite	9.8%	(10.6)	13.0%	(12.3)
% Native with Foreign Born or Mixed Parentage	18.9%	(9.4)	13.4%	(9.7)
% Private School Attendance	23.2%	(12.5)	16.6%	(11.7)
	N = 73		N = 127	

history, and more specifically, historical variation in settlement patterns. The problem with this reasoning, however, is that to "control" for "region" is to control not only for history, but for demography as well: to know what region a city is in *is* to know something about the composition of its population. Geographical subdivisions are relevant subjects of political inquiry only because they are differentiated on the basis of attitudinal or socio-economic variables. The South is not a distinctive political region because two surveyors named Mason and Dixon drew a famous line, but because the "composition of its population" differs from the rest of the country.

It is therefore difficult to unravel the meaning of "controlling" for "region" since regions are differentiated on precisely the kinds of demographic variables which we (and Wolfinger and Field) related to reformism. Cities in the Midwest, for example, have a much higher proportion of home ownership (64%) than cities in the Northeast (44%), while northeastern cities have more foreign stock in their population (27%) than the Midwest (16%). Hence, to relate ethnicity to political reformism and then to "control" for "region" is in part to relate ethnicity to reformism and then to control for ethnicity. Consequently, we have grave reservations that the substitution of the gross and unrefined variable of "region" for more refined demographic data adds much to our knowledge of American cities. "Controlling" for "region" is much more than controlling for historical experiences, because region as a variable is an undifferentiated *potpourri* of socio-economic, attitudinal, historical and cultural variations.[25]

We also differ with Wolfinger and Field in their assertion that their analysis constitutes a test of the ethos theory. As we understand it, Banfield and Wilson's theory posits that particular attitudes are held by persons with varying sociological characteristics (ethnic groups and middle class persons, in particular) and that these attitudes include preferences for one or another kind of political institution. But relating the proportion of middle class persons in a city's population to its form of government says nothing one way or another about middle class preferences. An important part of understanding, of course, is describing and it is certainly useful to know how reformed cities differ from unreformed cities.

[25] In statistical parlance, the problem with "region" as an independent variable might be described as treating a complicated background variable as the first variable in a specific developmental sequence. But, as Blalock argues, ". . . *one should avoid complex indicators that are related in unknown ways to a given underlying variable.* Geographical region and certain background variables appear to have such undesirable properties": Hubert M. Blalock, *Causal Inferences in Nonexperimental Research* (Chapel Hill: University of North Carolina Press, 1964), p. 164 (italics in original).

In our view, however, such tests as Wolfinger and Field used cannot logically be called explanations, in any causal sense. The most obvious reason is that they violate some important assumptions about time-order: independent variables are measured with contemporary census data, while the dependent variables are results of decisions made ten to fifty years ago. Moreover, this problem is multiplied by the difficulty of inferring configurations of political power from demographic data. Presumably, their assumption is that there is a simple linear relationship between sheer numbers (or proportions) of, say, middle class persons and their political power: the larger the size of a group in the city's population, the easier it can enforce its choice of political forms. At least one prominent urban sociologist, however, has found empirical support for precisely the opposite proposition. Hawley concluded that the smaller the proportion of middle class persons in a city, the greater their power over urban renewal policies.[26] Similarly, it may also be dubious to assume that the size of an ethnic population is an accurate indicator of influence of ethnic groups. Although we recognize the importance of describing the socio-economic correlates of political forms, the logical problems involved suggest the need for a good deal of caution in interpreting these differences as explanations.[27]

In any case, the question of why the city adopts particular structures is of less interest to us than their consequences for public policy. It is to this analysis that we now turn.

IV Policy Outputs and the Responsiveness of Cities

We are now in a position to take three additional steps. First, we can compare the differences in policy outputs between reformed and unreformed cities. Second, we can assess the cumulative impact of socio-economic variables on these policy choices. Finally, we can specify what variables are related in what ways to these output variables. In essence, we can now treat political institutions, not as dependent variables, but as factors which influence the *level* of expenditures and taxation and the *relationship* between cleavage variables and these outputs.

Differences between reformed and unreformed cities' outputs. Contrary to Sherbenou's conclusions about Chicago suburbs,[28]

[26] Amos Hawley, "Community Power and Urban Renewal Success," *American Journal of Sociology,* 68 (January, 1963), 422–431.

[27] See also the exchange between Banfield and Wilson and Wolfinger and Field in "Communications," [*American Political Science Review*], 60 (December, 1966), 998–1000.

[28] Sherbenou, *op. cit.*, pp. 133–134.

TABLE 3. *Mean Values of Tax/Income and Expenditure/Income Ratios, by Structural Characteristics*

Structural Variables	Taxes /Income	Expenditures /Income
Election type:		
Partisan	.032	.050
Nonpartisan	.030	.053
Government type:		
Mayor-Council	.037	.058
Manager	.024	.045
Commission	.031	.057
Constituency type:		
Ward	.036	.057
At-large	.027	.049

our data indicate that reformed cities both spend and tax less than unreformed cities, with the exception of expenditures in partisan and nonpartisan cities. It appears that partisan, mayor-council and ward cities are less willing to commit their resources to public purposes than their reformed counterparts. What is of more importance than the difference in outputs, however, is the relative responsiveness of the two kinds of cities to social cleavages in their population.

The responsiveness of cities. We have argued that one principal goal of the reform movement was to reduce the impact of partisan, socio-economic cleavages on governmental decision-making, to immunize city governments from "artificial" social cleavages – race, religion, ethnicity, and so on. As Banfield and Wilson put their argument, the reformers "assumed that there existed an interest ('the public interest') that pertained to the city 'as a whole' and that should always prevail over competing, partial (and usually private) interests." [29] The structural reforms of manager government, at-large, and nonpartisan elections would so insulate the business of governing from social cleavages that "private regarding" interests would count for little in making up the mind of the body politic. But amid the calls of the reformers for structural reforms to muffle the impact of socio-economic cleavages, a few hardy souls predicted precisely the opposite consequence of reform: instead of eliminating cleavages from

[29] *Op. cit.*, p. 139.

political decision-making, the reforms, particularly the elimination of parties, would enhance the conflict. Nathan Matthews, Jr., a turn-of-the-century mayor of Boston, issued just such a warning:

> As a city is a political institution, the people in the end will divide into parties, and it would seem extremely doubtful whether the present system, however illogical its foundation be, does not in fact produce better results, at least in large cities, than if the voters divided into groups, separated by property, social or religious grounds.[30]

Matthews recognized implicitly what political scientists would now call the "interest aggregation" function of political parties.[31] Parties in a democracy manage conflict, structure it, and encapsulate social cleavages under the rubric of two or more broad social cleavages, the parties themselves. "Parties tend to crystallize opinion, they give skeletal articulation to a shapeless and jelly-like mass . . . they cause similar opinions to coagulate . . ." [32] The parties "reduce effectively the number of political opinions to manageable numbers, bring order and focus to the political struggle, simplify issues and frame alternatives, and compromise conflicting interests." [33] Since parties are the agencies of interest aggregation, so the argument goes, their elimination makes for greater, not lesser, impact of social cleavages on political decisions.

Political scientists have recently confirmed Matthews' fears, at least with regard to electoral behavior in partisan and nonpartisan elections. Evidence points to the increased impact of socio-economic cleavages on voting when a nonpartisan ballot is used than when the election is formally partisan. Gerald Pomper studied nonpartisan municipal elections and compared them with partisan elections for the New Jersey State Assembly in Newark. He concluded that the "goal of nonpartisanship is fulfilled, as party identification does not determine the outcome. In place of party, ethnic affiliation is emphasized and the result is 'to enhance the effect of basic social cleavages.' " [34] If (1) this is typical of other Ameri-

[30] Quoted in Banfield and Wilson, *op. cit.*, p. 154.

[31] For a discussion of the concept of interest aggregation, see Gabriel Almond, "Introduction: A Functional Approach to Comparative Politics," in Gabriel Almond and James S. Coleman (eds.), *The Politics of Developing Areas* (Princeton: Princeton University Press, 1960), pp. 38–45.

[32] Maurice Duverger, *Political Parties* (New York: Science Editions, 1963), p. 378.

[33] Frank J. Sorauf, *Political Parties in the American System* (Boston: Little, Brown and Co., 1964), pp. 165–166.

[34] Gerald Pomper, "Ethnic and Group Voting in Nonpartisan Municipal Elections," *Public Opinion Quarterly*, 30 (Spring, 1966), p. 90; see also, J. Leiper Freeman, "Local Party Systems: Theoretical Considerations and a Case Analysis," *American Journal of Sociology*, 64 (1958), 282–289.

can cities and if (2) electoral cleavages can be translated effectively into demands on the government in the absence of aggregative parties, then we might assume that the reformed institutions would reflect cleavages more, rather than less, closely than unreformed ones.

Essentially, then, there are two contrasting views about the consequences of municipal reform. One, the reformers' ideal, holds that institutional reforms will mitigate the impact of social cleavages on public policy. The other argues that the elimination of political parties and the introduction of other reforms will make social cleavages more, rather than less, important in political decision-making.

THE MEASUREMENT OF RESPONSIVENESS. We have hypothesized that socio-economic cleavages will have less impact on the policy choices of reformed than unreformed governments. Thus, one could do a better job of predicting a city's taxation and expenditure policy using socio-economic variables in partisan, mayor, and ward cities than in nonpartisan, manager, and at-large cities. Operationally, we will test this hypothesis by using multiple correlation coefficients. Squaring these coefficients, called "multiple R's," will give us a summary measure of the total amount of variation in our dependent variables explained by our twelve independent variables.[35] The results of the correlation analysis are summarized in Diagrams 1 and 2.

On the whole, the results of the correlation analysis strikingly support the hypothesis, with the exception of commission cities. Thus, we can say, for example, that our twelve socio-economic variables explain 71 per cent of the variations in taxation policy in partisan cities, and 49 per cent of the variation in nonpartisan cities. In commission cities, however, socio-economic variables predict substantially more variation in both taxes and expenditures than in the unreformed mayor-council cities.[36] The anomaly of commission governments is interesting, for they present, as we will see, marked exceptions to virtually every pattern of relationships we found. The substantial explanatory power of these socio-economic

[35] It is possible that the difference between any two correlations may be a function of very different standard deviations of the independent variables. A quick look at Table 2, however, suggests that this is not likely to affect the relationship we find.

[36] Wolfinger and Field, *op. cit.*, p. 312, ". . . omit the commission cities from consideration since this form does not figure in the ethos theory." Historically, however, commission government was the earliest of the structures advocated by the Progressives and is quite clearly a product of the reform era. While history tells us that commission cities can not legitimately be excluded from the fold of reformism, they appear to be its black sheep, characterized by low incomes, low population growth and large proportions of nonwhites. In fact, they present a marked contrast to both mayor-council and manager cities.

DIAGRAM 1. Proportion of Variation Explained (R^2) in Taxation Policy with Twelve Socio-Economic Variables, by Institutional Characteristics[a]

Independent Variables	Structural Variables	Dependent Variable
	Reformed Institution:	
	Government: Commission	62%
	Government: Council-Manager	42%
	Election: Nonpartisan	49%
	Constituency: At-Large	49%
Twelve Socio-Economic Variables		Tax/Income Ratio
	Unreformed Institution:	
	Government: Mayor-Council	52%
	Election: Partisan	71%
	Constituency: Ward/Mixed	59%

[a] In the total sample, the twelve independent variables explained 52% of the variation in taxes.

variables is not altered, but confirmed, by examining the variables independently. The rest of the correlations show a consistent pattern: reformed cities are less responsive to cleavages in their population than unreformed cities.

If one of the premises of the "political ethos" argument is that re-

DIAGRAM 2. Proportion of Variation Explained (R^2) in Expenditure Policy with Twelve Socio-Economic Variables, by Institutional Characteristics[b]

Independent Variables	Structural Variables	Dependent Variable
	Reformed Institution:	
	Government: Commission	59%
	Government: Council-Manager	30%
	Constituency: At-Large	36%
	Elections: Nonpartisan	41%
Twelve Socio-Economic Variables		Expenditure/Income Ratio
	Unreformed Institution:	
	Government: Mayor-Council	42%
	Constituency: Ward/Mixed	49%
	Elections: Partisan	59%

[b] In the total sample, the twelve independent variables explained 36% of the variation in expenditures.

formed institutions give less weight to the "private regarding" and "artificial" cleavages in the population, that premise receives striking support from our analysis. Our data suggest that when a city adopts reformed structures, it comes to be governed less on the basis of conflict and more on the basis of the rationalistic theory of administration. The making of public policy takes less count of the enduring differences between White and Negro, business and labor, Pole and WASP. The logic of the bureaucratic ethic demands an impersonal, apolitical settlement of issues, rather than the settlement of conflict in the arena of political battle.

V To Spend or Not to Spend

If efforts to expand or contract the scope of government stand at the core of municipal political life,[37] they are nowhere better reflected than in the taxation and expenditure patterns of cities. A generation ago, Charles Beard wrote, "In the purposes for which appropriations are made the policies of the city government are given concrete form – the culture of the city is reflected. Indeed, the history of urban civilization could be written in terms of appropriations, for they show what the citizens think is worth doing and worth paying for." [38] Pressures to expand and contract government regulations and services are almost always reflected one way or another in the municipal budget. Labor, ethnic groups, the poor and the liberal community may press for additional services and these must be paid for; the business community may demand municipal efforts to obtain new industry by paring city costs to create a "favorable business climate"; or businessmen may themselves demand municipal services for new or old business. In any case, few political conflicts arise which do not involve some conflict over the budget structure.

Class variables and public policies. Part of the political rhetoric associated with the demand for a decrease in the scope of the national government is the argument that the initiative for policy-making should rest more with the state and local governments. Opposition to high federal spending levels, as V. O. Key has demonstrated, is found more often among persons with middle class occupations than among blue-collar workers.[39] It is not inconceivable that the middle class argument about state and local responsibility might be more than political rhetoric, and that at the local level, middle class voters are willing to undertake

[37] Agger *et al.*, *op. cit.*, pp. 4–14.

[38] Charles A. Beard, *American Government and Politics* (New York: Macmillan, 1924, 4th edition), p. 727.

[39] V. O. Key, *Public Opinion and American Democracy* (New York: Alfred A. Knopf, 1961), p. 124.

major programs of municipal services, requiring large outlays of public capital. Wilson and Banfield have argued that the "public regarding" upper-middle-class voters in metropolitan areas are often found voting for public policies at variance with their "self-interest narrowly conceived," and that "the higher the income of a ward or town, the more taste it has for public expenditures of various kinds." [40] Similarly a longitudinal study of voting patterns in metropolitan Cleveland found that an index of social rank was positively correlated with favorable votes on welfare referenda.[41] If these data reflect middle class willingness to spend on a local level, they might indicate that the "states' rights" argument was more than ideological camouflage: middle class voters stand foursquare behind public expenditures at the local level even when they oppose those expenditures from the national government. Therefore, we hypothesized that:

2a. The more middle class the city, measured by income, education and occupation, the higher the municipal taxes and expenditures.

In line with our general concern of testing the impact of political structures on municipal policies, we also hypothesized that:

2b. Unreformed cities reflect this relationship more strongly than reformed cities.

With respect to hypothesis 2a, the data in Table 4 on three middle class indicators are unambiguous and indicate a strong rejection of the hypothesis. However we measure social class, whether by income, education or occupation, class measures are negatively related to public taxes and expenditures.

It is possible, however, that income does not have a linear, but rather a curvilinear, relationship with municipal outputs. Banfield and Wilson argue that "In the city, it is useful to think in terms of three income groups – low, middle, and high. Surprising as it may seem to Marxists, the conflict is generally between an alliance of low-income and high-income groups on one side and the middle-income groups on the other." [42] If the relationships between income and expenditure are curvilinear, then we should expect to find that proportions of both low and high income groups were positively correlated with outputs. Our data, however, lend no support to this notion of a "pro-expenditure" alliance. Rather, the proportion of the population with incomes below $3000 is

[40] Wilson and Banfield, *op. cit.*, p. 876. Footnote 5 in the same article conveniently summarized research supporting this proposition.

[41] Eugene S. Uyeki, "Patterns of Voting in a Metropolitan Area: 1938–1962," *Urban Affairs Quarterly*, 1 (June, 1966), 65–77.

[42] Banfield and Wilson, *op. cit.*, p. 35.

TABLE 4. *Correlations between Middle Class Characteristics and Outputs in Reformed and Unreformed Cities*

Correlations of	Government Type			Election Type		Constituency Type	
	Mayor-Council	Manager	Commission	Partisan	Non-partisan	Ward	At-large
Taxes with:							
Median income	–.13	–.24	–.19	.03	–.19	–.17	–.22
White collar	–.23	–.12	–.62	–.21	–.33	–.30	–.32
Median education	–.36	–.22	–.08	–.45	–.24	–.48	–.18
Expenditures with:							
Median income	–.19	–.32	–.43	–.04	–.32	–.23	–.34
White collar	–.24	–.23	–.58	–.18	–.39	–.32	–.35
Median education	–.32	–.36	–.26	–.36	–.38	–.44	–.32

positively correlated with expenditures in all city types (although the relationships are small) and the proportion of the population in the above $10,000 bracket is negatively correlated with expenditures. Summing the two measures and correlating the combined measure with outputs produced no correlation greater than .15 and the relationships were as likely to be negative as positive. Tests for nonlinearity also suggested that no such coalition exists in the cities in our analysis.

To be sure, aggregate data analysis using whole cities as units of analysis is no substitute for systematic survey data on middle class attitudes, but it is apparent that cities with larger middle class population have lower, not higher expenditures. As we emphasized earlier, the "ethos theory" deals with attitudes and the behavior of individuals, while our data deal with cities and their behavior. The coalition suggested by Banfield and Wilson, however, is not discernible at this level of aggregation in these cities.

Hypothesis 2b is not consistently borne out by the data. In fact, the relationships between middle class variables and outputs are, if anything, stronger in the reformed cities than in their unreformed counterparts. One would not want to make too much of the data, but a large body of literature on city politics, which we discuss below, suggests that reformed institutions maximize the power of the middle class.

We originally assumed that the proportion of owner-occupied dwelling units constituted another measure of middle class composition, but it soon became apparent that it was only weakly related to income, occupation and education measures. Nevertheless, it emerged as the strongest single predictor of both expenditure and taxation policy in our cities. We hypothesized that:

3a. Owner-occupancy and outputs are negatively correlated, and
3b. Unreformed cities reflect this relationship more strongly than reformed cities.

Hypothesis 3a is consistently borne out in the data presented in Table 5. These relationships were only slightly attenuated when we controlled for income, education and occupation. No doubt self-interest (perhaps "private regardingness") on the part of the home owner, whose property is intimately related to the tax structure of most local governments, may account for part of this relationship. Moreover, home ownership is correlated (almost by definition) with lower urban population density. High density, bringing together all manner of men into the classic urban mosaic, may be itself correlated with factors which produce demands for higher expenditures – slums, increased needs for fire and police protection, and so on.

In confirmation of hypothesis 3a, the unmistakable pattern is for un-

TABLE 5. *Correlations between Owner Occupancy and Government Outputs in Reformed and Unreformed Cities*

Correlations of Owner Occupancy with:	Government Type			Election Type		Constituency Type	
	Mayor-Council	Manager	Commission	Partisan	Non-partisan	Ward	At-large
Taxes	−.57	−.31	−.73	−.64	−.45	−.56	−.48
Expenditures	−.51	−.23	−.62	−.62	−.40	−.50	−.40

reformed cities to reflect these negative relationships more strongly than the manager, nonpartisan and at-large cities, although commission cities show their usual remarkably high correlations.

HOMOGENEITY VARIABLES AND PUBLIC POLICIES. Dawson and Robinson, in their analysis of state welfare expenditures, found strong positive relationships between the ethnicity of a state's population and the level of its welfare expenditures.[43] If this is symptomatic of a generalized association of ethnic and religious minorities with higher expenditures, we might find support for the hypothesis that:

4a. The larger the proportion of religious and ethnic minorities in the population, the higher the city's taxes and expenditures.

And, if our general hypothesis about the impact of political institutions is correct, then:

4b. Unreformed cities reflect this relationship more strongly than reformed cities.

The correlations between ethnicity, religious heterogeneity and outputs (see Table 6) are, with one exception, positive, as predicted by hypothesis 4a. These associations may reflect the substantial participation by ethnic groups in municipal politics long after the tide of immigration has been reduced to a trickle.[44] The relatively intense politicization of ethnic groups at the local level,[45] the appeals to nationality groups through "ticket balancing" and other means, and the resultant higher turnout of ethnic groups than other lower status groups,[46] may produce an influence on city government far out of proportion to their number.

We found when we related all twelve of our independent variables to outputs in various city types that the associations were much weaker in cities we have labeled reformed. The correlations for ethnicity and religious homogeneity show a generally similar pattern, with commission cities exhibiting their usual erratic behavior. The data, then, show fairly clear support for hypothesis 4b.

The third variable of our homogeneity indicators – per cent of population non-white – had almost no relationship to variation in outputs,

[43] Richard E. Dawson and James A. Robinson, "The Politics of Welfare," in Herbert Jacob and Kenneth Vines (eds.), *Politics in the American States* (Boston: Little, Brown and Co., 1965), pp. 398–401.

[44] Raymond Wolfinger, "The Development and Persistence of Ethnic Voting," [*American Political Science Review*], 59 (December, 1965), 896–908.

[45] Robert E. Lane, *Political Life* (Glencoe, Ill.: The Free Press, 1959), pp. 236–243.

[46] *Ibid.*

TABLE 6. *Correlations between Ethnicity and Religious Heterogeneity and Outputs in Reformed and Unreformed Cities*

Correlations of	Government Type			Election Type		Constituency Type	
	Mayor-Council	Manager	Commission	Partisan	Non-partisan	Ward	At-large
Taxes with:							
Ethnicity	.49	.26	.57	.61	.43	.56	.40
Private School Attendance	.38	.15	.37	.33	.37	.41	.25
Expenditures with:							
Ethnicity	.36	.02	.21	.48	.21	.44	.13
Private School Attendance	.34	−.01	.07	.25	.24	.40	.05

regardless of city type. We found the same weak correlations for the poverty income variable, which was, of course, strongly related to the racial variable. An easy explanation suggests that this is a consequence of the political impotence of Negroes and the poor, but one should be cautious in inferring a lack of power from the lack of a statistical association.

We have dealt in this section with factors which are positively and negatively related to spending patterns in American cities. While social class variables are associated negatively with outputs, two measures of homogeneity, private school attendance and ethnicity are related to higher taxes and spending. Examining the strengths of these correlations in cities with differing forms, we found some support for our general hypothesis about the political consequences of institutions, especially for the homogeneity variables and the home ownership variable. Interestingly, however, this was not the case with class variables.

VI Reformism as a Continuous Variable

The central thrust of our argument has been that reformed governments differ from their unreformed counterparts in their responsiveness to socio-economic cleavages in the population. Logically, if the presence of one feature of the "good government" syndrome had the impact of reducing responsiveness, the introduction of additional reformed institutions should have an additive effect and further reduce the impact of cleavages on decision-making. We therefore decided to treat "reformism" as a continuous variable for analytic purposes and hypothesized that:

5. The higher the level of reformism in a city, the lower its responsiveness to socio-economic cleavages in the population.

We utilized a simple four-point index to test this hypothesis, ranging from the "least reformed" to the "most reformed." The sample cities were categorized as follows:

1. Cities with none of the reformed institutions (i.e., the government is mayor-council, elections are partisan and constituencies are wards).
2. Cities with any one of the reformed institutions.
3. Cities with two of the reformed institutions.
4. Cities with three reformed institutions (i.e., the government is either manager or commission, elections are nonpartisan and constituencies are at-large).

We can not overemphasize the crudity of this index as an operationalization of the complex and abstract concept of "reformism." Nonetheless, we think some of the relationships we found are strongly suggestive that reformism may in reality be a continuous variable.

To test this hypothesis, we took four variables which had moderate-to-strong correlations with our dependent variables and computed simple correlations in each reform category. If our hypothesis is correct, the strength of the correlations in Table 7 should decrease regularly with an increase in reform scores. While there are some clear exceptions to the predicted pattern of relationships, there is some fairly consistent support for the hypothesis. Even when the decreases in the strengths of the correlations are irregular, there is a clear difference between cities which we have labeled "most reformed" and "least reformed."

Again, we would not want to attach too much importance to the results of this rough-and-ready index. But, the patterns support our previous argument about the impact of reformism: the more reformed the city, the less responsive it is to socio-economic cleavages in its political decision-making.

VII A Causal Model and an Interpretation

A causal model. The implicit, or at times explicit, causal model in much of the research on municipal reformism has been a simple one: socio-economic cleavages cause the adoption of particular political forms. A more sophisticated model would include political institutions as one of

TABLE 7. *Correlations between Selected Independent Variables and Output Variables by Four Categories of Reformism*

Correlations of	Reform Scores			
	1 (Least Reformed)	2	3	4 (Most Reformed)
Taxes with:				
Ethnicity	.62	.41	.50	.34
Private School Attendance	.40	.32	.28	.25
Owner-Occupancy	–.70	–.39	–.54	–.44
Median Education	–.55	–.27	–.32	–.13
Expenditures with:				
Ethnicity	.51	.27	.41	.05
Private School Attendance	.46	.23	.16	.08
Owner-Occupancy	–.67	–.30	–.54	–.38
Median Education	–.49	–.19	–.38	–.37

the factors which produce a given output structure in city politics. We hypothesize that a causal model would include four classes of variables: socio-economic cleavages, political variables (including party registration, structure of party systems, patterns of aggregation, strength of interest groups, voter turnout, etc.), political institutions (form of government, type of elections and types of constituencies), and political outputs. Diagram 3 depicts one possible causal model.

This study has of necessity been limited to exploring the linkages between socio-economic cleavages, political institutions and political outputs. We found that political institutions "filter" the process of converting inputs into outputs. Some structures, particularly partisan elections, ward constituencies, mayor-council governments and commission governments, operate to maximize the impact of cleavage indicators on public policies. We conclude by discussing some of the reasons why different structures have varying impacts on the conversion process.

AN INTERPRETATION. Three principal conclusions may be derived from this analysis.

1. Cities with reformed and unreformed institutions are not markedly different in terms of demographic variables. Indeed, some variables, like income, ran counter to the popular hypothesis that reformed cities are havens of the middle class. Our data lent some support to the notion that reformed cities are more homogeneous in their ethnic and religious popu-

DIAGRAM 3. A Hypothesized Causal Model

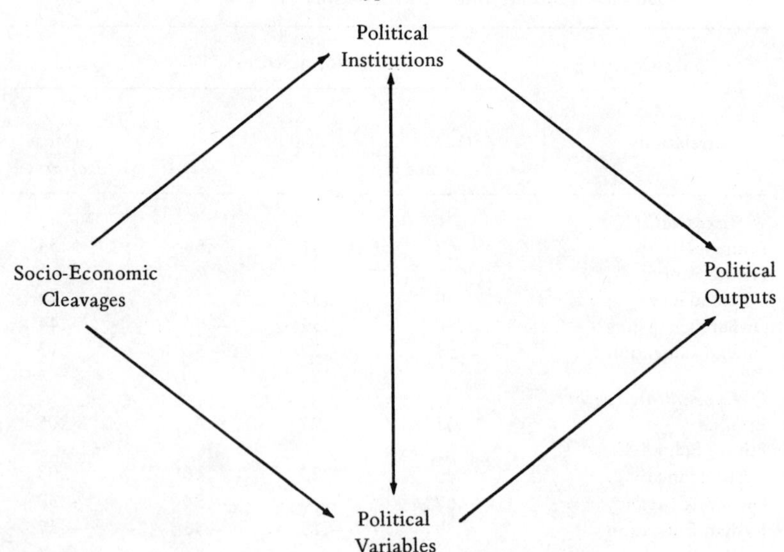

lations. Still, it is apparent that reformed cities are by no means free from the impact of these cleavages.

2. The more important difference between the two kinds of cities is in their behavior, rather than their demography. Using multiple correlation coefficients, we were able to predict municipal outputs more exactly in unreformed than in reformed cities. The translation of social conflicts into public policy and the responsiveness of political systems to class, racial, and religious cleavages differ markedly with the kind of political structure. Thus, political institutions seem to play an important role in the political process – a role substantially independent of a city's demography.

3. Our analysis has also demonstrated that reformism may be viewed as a continuous variable and that the political structures of the reform syndrome have an additive effect: the greater the reformism, the lower the responsiveness.

Through these political institutions, the goal of the reformers has been substantially fulfilled, for nonpartisan elections, at-large constituencies and manager governments are associated with a lessened responsiveness of cities to the enduring conflicts of political life. Or, as Stone, Price and Stone argued in their study of changes produced by the adoption of manager governments, the council after the reform "tended to think more of the community as a whole and less of factional interests in making their decisions." [47]

The responsiveness of a political institution to political conflicts should not be confused with the "responsibility" of a political system as the latter term is used in the great debate over the relative "responsibility" of party systems.[48] In fact, the responsiveness of political forms to social cleavages may stand in sharp contrast to "responsible government" on the British model. Presumably, in American cities, partisan elections, ward constituencies, and mayor-council governments maximize minority rather than majority representation, assuring greater access to decision-makers than the reformed, bureaucratized and "de-politicized" administrations.

Partisan electoral systems, when combined with ward representation, increase the access of two kinds of minority groups: those which are

[47] Harold Stone, Don K. Price and Kathryn Stone, *City Manager Government in the United States* (Chicago: Public Administration Service, 1940), p. 238.

[48] The standard argument for party responsibility is found in the works of E. E. Schattschneider, esp., *Party Government* (New York: Farrar and Rinehart, 1942) and in the report of the Committee on Political Parties of the American Political Science Association, *Toward a More Responsible Two-Party System* (New York: Rinehart, 1950).

residentially segregated, and which may as a consequence of the electoral system demand and obtain preferential consideration from their councilmen; and groups which constitute identifiable voting blocs to which parties and politicians may be beholden in the next election. The introduction of at-large, nonpartisan elections has at least five consequences for these groups. First, they remove an important cue-giving agency – the party – from the electoral scene, leaving the voter to make decisions less on the policy commitments (however vague) of the party, and more on irrelevancies such as ethnic identification and name familiarity.[49] Second, by removing the party from the ballot, the reforms eliminate the principal agency of interest aggregation from the political system. Hence, interests are articulated less clearly and are aggregated either by some other agency or not at all. Moreover, nonpartisanship has the effect of reducing the turnout in local elections by working class groups,[50] leaving officeholders freer from retaliation by these groups at the polls. Fourth, nonpartisanship may also serve to decrease the salience of "private regarding" demands by increasing the relative political power of "public regarding" agencies like the local press.[51] And when nonpartisanship is combined with election at-large, the impact of residentially segregated groups or groups which obtain their strength from voting as blocs in municipal elections is further reduced.[52] For these reasons, it is clear that political reforms may have a significant impact in minimizing the role which social conflicts play in decision-making. By muting the demands of private-regarding groups, the electoral institutions of reformed governments make public policy less responsive to the demands arising out of social conflicts in the population.

The structure of the government may serve further to modify the strength of minority groups over public policy. It is significant in this respect to note that commission governments, where social cleavages have the greatest impact on policy choices, are the most decentralized of the three governmental types and that manager governments are relatively the most centralized.[53] From the point of view of the reformer, commission government is a failure and their number has declined markedly

[49] See Pomper, *op. cit.*; and Freeman, *op. cit.*

[50] Robert Salisbury and Gordon Black, "Class and Party in Partisan and Nonpartisan Elections: The Case of Des Moines," [*American Political Science Review*], 57 (September, 1963), 584–592.

[51] One newspaperman said of nonpartisan politics that "You can't tell the players without a scorecard, and we sell the scorecards": Banfield and Wilson, *op. cit.*, p. 157.

[52] Oliver P. Williams and Charles Adrian, *Four Cities* (Philadelphia: University of Pennsylvania Press, 1963), pp. 56–57.

[53] Alford and Scoble, *op. cit.*, p. 84.

in recent years.[54] This greater decentralization of commission and of mayor-council governments permits a multiplicity of access points for groups wishing to influence decision-makers.[55] It may also increase the possibilities for collaboration between groups and a bureaucratic agency, a relationship which has characterized administrative patterns in the federal government. As a result of this decentralization, group strength in local governments may be maximized.

It is important in any analysis of reformism to distinguish between the factors which produce the *adoption* of reformed institutions and the *impact* of the new political forms once they have been established. We can offer from our data no conclusions about the origins of reformed structures, for it is obviously impossible to impute causation, using contemporary census data, to events which occurred decades ago. Once a city has institutionalized the reformers' ideals, however, a diffused attitude structure may be less helpful in explaining the city's public policy than the characteristics of the institutions themselves. With the introduction of these reforms, a new political pattern may emerge in which disputes are settled outside the political system, or in which they may be settled by the crowd at the civic club at the periphery of the system.[56] If they do enter the political process, an impersonal, "non-political" bureaucracy may take less account of the conflicting interests and pay more attention to the "correct" decision from the point of view of the municipal planner.

These conclusions are generally consistent with the ethos theory developed by Banfield and Wilson. If one of the components of the middle class reformer's ideal was "to seek the good of the community as a whole" and to minimize the impact of social cleavages on political decision-making, then their institutional reforms have served, by and large, to advance that goal.

[54] In our view, the failure of the commission government to achieve the intended reforms is more plausible as an explanation of its demise than its administrative unwieldiness – the conventional explanation.

[55] Williams and Adrian, *op. cit.*, pp. 30–31.

[56] Carol E. Thometz discusses the role of the "Civic Committee" in decision-making in Dallas: see *The Decision-Makers* (Dallas: Southern Methodist University Press, 1963).

MALAPPORTIONMENT AND PUBLIC POLICY IN THE STATES

THOMAS R. DYE

Commentators on state policy have often implied that malapportionment seriously affects the policy choices of state legislatures. In the literature on state politics it is frequently argued that there are important policy differences between urban and rural constituencies and that malapportionment, by over-representing rural interests, grants them a real advantage in policy-making.[1] It is also frequently predicted that reapportionment on a population basis will bring about noticeable shifts in many state policies.[2]

Malapportionment of state legislatures has been successfully challenged on the grounds that it denies to the citizens equal protection of the laws.[3] This challenge was essentially a normative one, stemming from deeply held values about political equality.[4] The merits of this type of challenge do not lend themselves to empirical verification. How-

Reprinted by permission from Thomas R. Dye, "Malapportionment and Public Policy in the States," *Journal of Politics*, 27 (August, 1965), 586–601.

[1] See Charles Adrian, *State and Local Governments* (New York: McGraw-Hill, 1960), pp. 306–307; Daniel Grant and H. C. Nixon, *State and Local Government in America* (Boston: Allyn and Bacon, 1963), pp. 204–205; Richard Frost, "On Derge's Metropolitan and Outstate Legislative Delegations," *American Political Science Review*, Vol. 53 (September, 1959), pp. 792–795; Commission on Intergovernmental Relations, A *Report to the President for Transmittal to Congress* (Washington: U.S. Government Printing Office, 1955), p. 39; Malcolm Jewell, *The State Legislature* (New York: Random House, 1962), pp. 30–33; V. O. Key, Jr., *American State Politics: An Introduction* (New York: Knopf, 1956), pp. 76–77.

[2] See "After Redistricting Decision – Where States May See Changes in Taxes, Welfare, Highways," *U.S. News and World Report*, July 6, 1964, pp. 34–36; and "A New Charter for State Legislatures," *Time*, June 26, 1964, pp. 22–23.

[3] *Baker* v. *Carr*, 369 U.S. 186 (1962); *Reynolds* v. *Sims*, 84 S.Ct. 1362 (1964).

[4] E.g., "The conception of political equality from the Declaration of Independence to Lincoln's Gettysburg Address, to the Fourteenth, Fifteenth, Seventeenth, and Nineteenth Amendments can mean only one thing – one person, one vote." *Gray* v. *Sanders*, 83 S.Ct. 801 (1963), p. 809.

ever, statements about the effect of malapportionment on public policy, and predictions about the policy consequences of reapportionment, can be tested empirically. Such tests, of course, in no way reflect upon the moral quality of the proposition "as nearly as practicable one man's vote should be equal to another's." [5] But they can help us to know what to expect in the way of policy changes in the wake of reapportionment. In the past, proponents of reapportionment have been very enthusiastic about its expected consequences. Having attributed a lack of party competition, unfair distributions of state funds, conservative tax schemes, unprogressive education policies, and penny-pinching welfare programs to rural over-representation, they naturally expect to see these conditions changed by reapportionment. Court-ordered reapportionment is viewed as a source of strength for state legislatures rather than an infringement of heretofore exclusive prerogative of these bodies. Reapportionment, it is said, will help states come to grips with important domestic problems in the nation and reassume their rightful place in our federal system.

In contrast, a few scholars have sounded a note of caution regarding the expected consequences of reapportionment. On the basis of roll call analyses in the Missouri and Illinois legislatures, David Derge concluded that metropolitan and non-metropolitan legislators seldom opposed each other in unified voting blocs.[6] It is difficult to see how reapportioning legislatures to reduce rural over-representation would have much effect on policy-making, if we accept Derge's conclusions that only infrequently do rural-urban divisions influence legislative decisions anyway. Duane Lockard also entered a caveat about the consequences of malapportionment. With specific references to conditions in Massachusetts and Connecticut he asked: "Do states with fair apportionment respond to urban appeals more readily? If anyone has made a systematic study of this, I am unaware of it, but limited evidence does not seem to indicate that the states with fair apportionment are any more considerate of urban problems than states with malapportionment." [7] Herbert Jacob was equally skeptical of the consequences of malapportionment. He computed rank-order correlation coefficients for the relationship between malapportionment and party competition, highway fund distributions, and certain welfare expenditures for the fifty states. On the basis of low coefficients, he concluded, "it is improbable that it (reapportionment) will substantially invigorate state

[5] *Wesberry* v. *Sanders*, 84 S.Ct. 526 (1964), p. 530.

[6] David Derge, "Metropolitan and Outstate Alignments in the Illinois and Missouri Legislative Delegations," *American Political Science Review*, Vol. 53 (December, 1958), pp. 1051–1065.

[7] Duane Lockard, *The Politics of State and Local Government* (New York: Macmillan, 1963), p. 319.

governments or dissolve the stalemates which sap public confidence in them." [8]

The purpose of the study reported here was to examine systematically the impact of malapportionment on party competition and public policy in all fifty states. If the policy choices of malapportioned legislatures are noticeably different from the policy choices of well-apportioned legislatures, and these differences in policies can be traced to malapportionment rather than some other condition, then reapportionment can be expected to have a significant impact on state policies. However, if the policy choices of well-apportioned and malapportioned legislatures do not differ significantly, or if differences which do occur are the product of some condition other than malapportionment, then more caution is warranted regarding the policy changes that reapportionment may bring. The same test applies to expectations about the impact of reapportionment on party competition. Only if there is significantly more party competition in well-apportioned legislatures than in malapportioned ones, and this increased competition is attributable to apportionment rather than some other condition, is one safe in predicting that reapportionment will bring about greater party competition.

Measuring Malapportionment

Several measures of the malapportionment of state legislatures are available. Perhaps the most common measure is the theoretical minimum percentage of a state's population that can elect a majority of each house.[9] The two minimum percentages for each chamber can be added to provide an index of malapportionment for the legislature as a whole. Percentages are additive in this case because the real denominator is the power of each house to influence policy and this is assumed to be real. In 1960 this index ranged from a low of 37 for Nevada with the least representative legislature to a high of 96 for Oregon with the most representative legislature. Hereafter this measure is referred to as the "index of representativeness."

Another index was devised by David and Eisenberg to focus on urban under-representation in state legislatures.[10] Because urban areas are most likely to be the subject of discrimination, the authors felt that urban

[8] Herbert Jacob, "The Consequences of Malapportionment: A Note of Caution," *Social Forces*, Vol. 43 (December, 1964), pp. 256–261.

[9] Manning J. Dauer and Robert G. Kelsay, "Unrepresentative States," *National Municipal Review*, Vol. 44 (December, 1955), pp. 571–575.

[10] Paul T. David and Ralph Eisenberg, *Devaluation of the Urban and Suburban Vote*, Bureau of Public Administration, University of Virginia, 1961.

under-representation should be a specific object of measurement, in addition to theoretical measures of representativeness. In order to determine the degree of discrimination against urban areas, David and Eisenberg computed the "value" of a vote cast in the largest urban counties of each state. First they computed the average population of a single member district in each state. Actual constituencies were then compared to these average constituencies: the "value" of a vote was represented by the ratio of an actual constituency to the average constituency in each state. For example, in a district with twice the population of the state's average district, the value of a vote would be .50. The "value" of a vote in the largest category of county in each state was computed for each house and then the measures for both houses were averaged to provide an "index of urban representation" for each legislature. In 1960 this index ranged from a low of .12 for Georgia, where the largest counties were most discriminated against in apportionment, to a high of 1.05 in Louisiana, where the largest counties were granted the greatest legislative representation.

A third measure of malapportionment is the technically sophisticated "apportionment score" proposed by Glendon Schubert and Charles Press.[11] The apportionment score combines inverted coefficients of variation for each state (divide the population of the average district by the standard deviation of all districts and subtract the quotient from 1.0) with statistical measures of skewness and kurtosis in the distribution of districts by size of population. The result is an index that measures the combination of variance, skewness, and kurtosis in the populations of legislative districts in each state. According to this scale, in 1962 Massachusetts, with the highest apportionment score, was technically the best apportioned legislature in the nation and Indiana, with the lowest score, was the worst.

All three of these measures – the index of representativeness, the index of urban under-representation, and the apportionment score – are used in this study. Each measure depicts a slightly different aspect of malapportionment; each results in a slightly different ranking of states.[12] The first measure focuses on the theoretical minimum proportion of a state's population that can control the legislature, the second measure focuses on urban under-representation, and the third measure focuses on the de-

[11] Glendon Schubert and Charles Press, "Measuring Malapportionment," *American Political Science Review,* Vol. 58 (June, 1964), pp. 302–327; and corrections published December, 1964, pp. 966–970.

[12] The simple correlation coefficients between these three measures are as follows: index of representativeness and urban under-representation: .45; index of representativeness and apportionment score: .52; urban under-representation and apportionment score: .65.

gree to which a state's apportionment scheme approaches the statistical concept of normality. In the analysis to follow we shall evaluate the political relevance of each of these measures.

Measuring Public Policy

Measuring state policy choices is an even more difficult task than measuring malapportionment. In the 1960–61 legislative biennium, more than 104,000 bills were introduced in the state legislatures throughout the nation. Each bill rejected or enacted represents a separate policy choice. What policies are to be selected in order to assess the impact of malapportionment? It was decided to select 30 measures of state policy in three of the most important subject matters of state politics – education, welfare, and taxation. Education is the largest category of state spending. In fact, with the exception of national defense, education is the nation's largest public undertaking. The responsibility for this undertaking rests with the fifty state governments. Twelve variables reflecting important attributes of state educational systems were selected for analysis:

Public School Expenditures Per Pupil in Average Daily Attendance, 1960–61
Average Annual Salary Per Member of Instructional Staff, 1961–62
Male School Teachers as a Per Cent of Total, 1961–62
Pupil-Teacher Ratio: Enrollment Per Member of Instructional Staff, 1961–62
Per Cent of Elementary Teachers with B.A. Degree, 1962
Per Cent of Secondary Teachers with M.A. Degree, 1962
Drop-out Rate: High School Grads in 1963 as Per Cent of 9th Graders in 1959
Per cent of Selective Service Examinees Disqualified for Failing Mental Test, 1962
Average Size of School District in Pupils, 1961–62
State Participation: School Revenues from State as Per Cent of Total School Revenue, 1961–62
Federal Participation: School Revenues from Federal Sources as Per Cent of Total School Revenues, 1961–62
Per Capita State Expenditures for Higher Education, 1961

Welfare expenditures are the second largest category of state expenditures. Although many state welfare efforts are federally assisted, responsibility for welfare programs and benefits rests with the fifty state governments. Ten welfare variables were selected for analysis:

Average Weekly Payment Per Recipient Unemployment Compensation, 1961
Average Monthly Payment, Old Age Assistance, 1961

Average Monthly Payment Per Family, Aid to Dependent Children, 1961
Average Monthly Payment, Aid to Blind, 1961
Average Monthly Assistance, Medical Assistance for Aged (Kerr-Mills), 1961
Per Capita State and Local Expenditures for Welfare, 1960
Per Capita State and Local Expenditures for Health and Hospitals, 1960
State Participation: Per Cent State Expenditures of Total Expenditures for Welfare, 1960
State Participation: Per Cent State Expenditures of Total Expenditures for Health and Hospitals, 1960
Federal Participation: Per Capita Federal Grants to the State for Health, Welfare and Related Purposes, 1960

Eight measures of tax burden and revenue structure in the states were also selected:

Total State and Local Tax Revenues Per Capita, 1960
State Revenues Per Capita, 1960
State Revenues as a Per Cent of Total State and Local Revenues, 1960
Per Cent of Total State and Local Revenues from Federal Sources, 1960
Income Tax Revenues as a Per Cent of Total Tax Revenues, 1961
Sales Tax Revenues as a Per Cent of Total Tax Revenues, 1961
Alcohol and Tobacco Tax Revenues as a Per Cent of Total Tax Revenues, 1961
Motor Fuel and Vehicle Tax Revenues as a Per Cent of Total Tax Revenues, 1961

All 30 variables were obtained for each of the fifty states.[13]

Measuring the Impact of Malapportionment on Public Policy

The method chosen to assess the impact of malapportionment on party competition as well as state education, welfare, and tax policies was that of linear regression analysis. First, simple correlation coefficients were computed for the relationships between the several measures of malapportionment and the selected measures of state policy. These simple coefficients show the extent to which differences in policies among the fifty states are associated with malapportionment, but they do not deal with the possibility that some other intervening variables and not mal-

[13] Sources of data on education, welfare, and tax variables were: U.S. Office of Education, *Statistics of School Systems 1961–62* (Washington: U.S. Government Printing Office, 1963); National Education Association, *Rankings of the States 1963* (Washington: National Education Association, 1963); U.S. Bureau of Census, *Statistical Abstract 1963* (Washington: U.S. Government Printing Office, 1963).

apportionment, might account for these differences. For example, if it is shown that, in general, wealthy states are better apportioned than poor states, it might be that differences in the policies of well-apportioned and malapportioned states are really a product of the fact that the former are wealthy while the latter are poor. If this were the case, policy differences between the states might be attributed to wealth rather than malapportionment. Other intervening variables might be urbanization, industrialization, or the educational level of the state's population. Several studies have shown these socio-economic variables, all of them interrelated, to be associated with variations in state policies.[14] In order to isolate the effect of malapportionment on state policies from the possible effects of socio-economic variables, it is necessary to control for these latter variables. This required that partial correlation coefficients be computed which would show the relationship between malapportionment and the several measures of state policies while controlling for the effect of urbanization, industrialization, income, and education. If relationships between malapportionment and state policies which appear in simple correlation coefficients disappear when socio-economic variables are controlled, then we may conclude that there is no independent relationship between malapportionment and public policy. On the other hand, if the correlation coefficients between malapportionment and state policies remain significant, even after the effects of socio-economic variables are controlled, then we may more readily conclude that malapportionment does have an independent effect on public policy.

In interpreting correlation coefficients in this study, it was decided to dismiss as insignificant those coefficients which might easily have occurred by chance. An analysis of variance test for the significance of r identifies those coefficients which could occur by chance more than 5 out of 100 times in the correlation of any set of random digits.[15] All calculations are made on the basis of observations about all 50 states (except

[14] See, for example, Jerry Minar, *Social and Economic Factors in Spending for Public Education* (Syracuse: Syracuse University Press, 1963); Richard E. Dawson and James A. Robinson, "Inter-party Competition, Economic Variables and Welfare Policies in the American States," *Journal of Politics*, Vol. 25 (May, 1963), pp. 265–289.

[15] The analysis of variance test determines the possibility that any coefficient might have been obtained by correlating sets of 50 random numbers from an imaginary infinite universe of states. It does not matter that the fifty states are a universe rather than a sample. The allusion to sampling in tests of significance is a hypothetical one. It helps us to determine whether the correlations which are obtained might have been obtained by correlating various columns of 50 digits found in a table of random numbers. See Hubert M. Blalock, *Social Statistics* (New York: McGraw-Hill, 1960), pp. 302–305.

with regard to party competition for which Nebraska and Minnesota are dropped from analysis because of their non-partisan character). Given a constant number of observations in all correlations, it is possible to state that only simple coefficients above .30 and partial coefficients above .35 are significant at the .05 level, and that all other coefficients can be dismissed as likely to be a product of chance.

Malapportionment and Party Competition

Before turning to a discussion of malapportionment and public policy, let us briefly consider the impact of malapportionment on party competition in state legislatures. Party competition in state legislatures is measured here by the percentage of total seats in each house of the legislature between 1954 and 1964 which were held by the majority party. Percentages are then inverted so that the competition scores in the house and senate of Alabama, Arkansas, Louisiana, Mississippi, and South Carolina, where the minority party did not hold a single seat during those years, are set at 0 and all other scores range upward. If it is true that malapportionment adversely affects party competition, then malapportioned legislatures should be less competitive than well-apportioned legislatures, and these differences in competition should be attributable to malapportionment rather than some other social or economic condition.

The simple correlation coefficients in Table 1 indicate a significant relationship between the index of urban under-representation and party competition in both upper and lower chambers. Discrimination against urban areas in representation is associated with decreases in party competition. However, this relationship noticeably weakens when the effects of urbanization, industrialization, income, and education are controlled. The apportionment score also appears related to party competition in simple correlations, but this relationship falls well below accepted significance levels once socio-economic variables are controlled.

Coefficients obtained with the index of urban under-representation are higher than those obtained with either the index of representativeness or the apportionment score. Both of these latter two indices measure malapportionment in an abstract sense and not its discrimination against a particular interest. We might conclude that malapportionment itself does not affect party competition except when it operates to discriminate against urban areas. However, none of the coefficients in Table 1 is very high. Urban under-representation at best can explain less than 25 per cent of the variation among the several states in party competition. Factors other than urban under-representation must be looked to in order to account for 75 per cent of the total variation in party competition among the states.

TABLE 1. *The Relationship between Malapportionment and Party Competition in State Legislatures, Controlling for the Effect of Four Socio-Economic Variables*

Party Competition 1954-1964	Malapportionment: Index of Representation		Urban Under-Representation		Apportionment Score	
	Simple	Partial	Simple	Partial	Simple	Partial
Lower Houses	.13	.28	.44	.35	.39	.27
Upper Houses	.06	.30	.50	.38	.43	.29

NOTE: Figures at the left under each heading are simple correlation coefficients for 48 states; figures at the right are fourth-order partial coefficients which control for the effect of urbanization, industrialization, income, and education.

Malapportionment and Public Policy

Table 2 shows the relationship between malapportionment and 30 separate measures of education, welfare, and tax policies in the fifty states. Simple correlation coefficients are shown at the left under each measure of malapportionment, while partial coefficients – controlling for the combined effect of urbanization, industrialization, income, and education in the states – are shown at the right. Perhaps the most striking feature of Table 2 is that none of the coefficients is very high. For the most part, variations in public policy among the states can *not* be explained by malapportionment.

In the field of education, it might be hypothesized that malapportionment results in lower per pupil expenditures, lower teachers' salaries, and higher pupil-teacher ratios, which in turn produce lower teacher qualifications, higher drop-out rates, and more selective service mental failures. The signs of the coefficients in Table 2 tend to bear out these relationships, but few of the coefficients obtain at a level of significance that would merit much confidence in these hypotheses. None of the coefficients under the index of representativeness or the apportionment score is statistically significant. This helps confirm our suspicion that malapportionment in its technical aspects has no policy relevance. Only six of the twelve simple coefficients under the index of urban under-representation are above the level of significance and only four of these hold up well once socio-economic variables are controlled. Urban under-representation is slightly related to higher pupil-teacher ratios, higher drop-out rates, and increased state and federal participation in public school

TABLE 2. *The Relationship between Malapportionment and State Education, Welfare and Tax Policies Controlling for the Effect of Four Socio-Economic Variables*

State Policy Measures	Malapportionment					
	Index of Representation		Urban Under-Representation		Apportionment Score	
	Simple	Partial	Simple	Partial	Simple	Partial
Education						
Per Pupil Expenditures	.12	.06	.36	.12	.09	.01
Average Teachers' Salaries	.28	.20	.30	–.17	.01	.27
Teachers With B.A.	.24	.18	.13	.29	.12	.24
Teachers With M.A.	.07	.10	.14	.07	.09	.04
Male Teachers	.22	–.01	.15	.01	.01	–.10
Pupil-Teacher Ratio	–.11	–.23	–.31	–.40	–.15	–.21
Drop-out Rate	.06	.29	.37	.53	.15	.29
Mental Failures	–.09	–.27	–.15	–.26	–.16	–.14
Size of School Districts	–.24	–.31	–.10	–.20	–.14	–.15
State Participation	–.25	–.34	–.32	–.42	–.23	–.28
Federal Participation	–.06	–.13	–.33	–.38	–.07	–.18
Higher Education Expenditures	–.07	–.07	–.15	–.07	–.16	–.20
Welfare						
Unemployment Benefits	.17	.20	.29	.09	.13	.03
Old Age Benefits	–.01	.07	.37	.04	.01	.06
ADC Benefits	.12	.11	.49	.06	.14	.09
Blind Benefits	–.08	.16	.32	.09	.01	.02
Kerr-Mills Benefits	.13	.18	.34	.27	.05	.05
Welfare Expenditures, Per cap.	.04	.05	.09	.01	–.17	.02
Health Expenditures, Per cap.	–.21	.03	–.01	.01	–.08	.05
State Participation, Welfare	–.12	–.17	–.26	–.11	–.08	–.05
State Participation, Health	.10	.06	.34	.31	.17	.18
Federal Participation	.01	–.08	–.31	–.18	–.28	–.29
Taxation						
Total Taxes Per capita	.15	.05	.26	.17	.01	.09
State Revenue Per capita	–.16	–.07	–.18	–.17	–.10	–.09
State Percent of Total Revenue	–.01	–.06	–.30	–.20	–.13	–.10
Federal Percent of Total Revenue	–.03	–.09	–.36	–.23	–.04	–.08
Income Taxes	.12	.07	.14	.01	.02	.05
Sales Taxes	–.14	–.15	–.20	–.20	–.14	–.09
Alcohol & Tobacco Taxes	.14	.04	.13	–.01	.02	.07
Motor Fuel Taxes	.22	.08	.01	.04	–.19	.14

NOTE: Figures at the left under each heading are simple correlation for 50 states; figures at the right are fourth-order partial coefficients which control for the effect of urbanization, industrialization, income, and education.

finance. Yet these relationships are not so close to warrant predictions about changes in these policies once urban areas are given better representation. Per-pupil school expenditures decline with increases in malapportionment, yet this relationship is clearly a product of the fact that pupil expenditures are greater in the rural, less wealthy, agricultural states; once socio-economic variables are controlled, the relationship between pupil expenditures and malapportionment disappears. Likewise the relationship between low teachers' salaries and malapportionment also disappears once socio-economic variables are controlled.

Few policy variables in the welfare field appear related to malapportionment. The closest relationship is between urban under-representation and state participation in the provision of health and hospital services. Yet urban under-representation accounts for only 11 per cent of the total variation among the states in the extent of their participation in the health field. The level of payments to recipients of unemployment compensation, old age assistance, aid to dependent children, and aid to the medically indigent aged under Kerr-Mills laws, appears to be slightly related to urban under-representation on the basis of simple coefficients. Most of these coefficients disappear, however, once socio-economic variables are controlled. In short, the relationship between urban representation and welfare policies among the fifty states is a product of intervening socio-economic variables. There is no evidence that reapportionment will bring any noticeable liberalization of welfare policies.

Not one of the relationships between malapportionment and the eight selected tax policies is statistically significant. It is doubtful, for example, that reapportionment will bring higher tax levies. Neither total state and local taxes per capita nor total state revenues per capita are significantly related to apportionment. While federal grants constitute a larger share of the revenue of malapportioned states, this is merely a product of the fact that these states tend to be less wealthy; the relationship between federal support and malapportionment disappears when socio-economic variables are controlled. State revenues are a larger share of total revenues in malapportioned states, but this relationship also appears as a product of socio-economic variables rather than malapportionment itself. It was hypothesized that well-apportioned states would place greater reliance in their tax structure on progressive income taxation, while malapportioned states would rely more on regressive sales taxation. The signs of the coefficients in Table 2 tend to confirm this hypothesis, but the coefficients are so low, the relationships so slight, that they might easily have occurred by chance. Certainly there is no evidence that reapportionment will bring about any substantial changes in state tax structures.

It is interesting to note that the few significant policy correlations obtained in this study, were obtained with David and Eisenburg's index of urban under-representation. This index measures the degree to which a particular political interest is affected by malapportionment rather than the existence of malapportionment in the technical sense. The failure to obtain any significant policy correlates with the index of representatives suggests that the theoretical minimum population which *could* control a legislature is not a relevant political variable. Nor does the extent to which the populations of legislative districts approach a normal statistical curve, as measured by the Schubert and Press apportionment score, appear to be a politically relevant variable. Schubert and Press rebuked earlier scholars for their technically unsophisticated measures of malapportionment ("the difference in the costs for the computation of precise and crude indices is . . . minimal").[16] Yet it turns out that David and Eisenburg with their less sophisticated measure came closer to identifying the relevant political aspect of malapportionment than Schubert and Press. For malapportionment becomes relevant when it operates to discriminate against specific political interests in a state.

Conclusion

On the whole, the policy choices of malapportioned legislatures are not noticeably different from the policy choices of well-apportioned legislatures. Most of the policy differences which do occur turn out to be a product of socio-economic differences among the states rather than a direct product of apportionment practices. Relationships that appear between malapportionment and public policy are so slight that reapportionment is not likely to bring about any significant policy changes. Of course, these conclusions are predicted on results obtained from analyzing 30 selected measures of public policy in three separate fields – education, welfare, and taxation. Conceivably malapportionment could have a more direct effect on some area of policy-making that was not investigated. However, expenditures for welfare and education, the liberality of welfare benefits, teachers' qualifications and salaries, the quality of public education, the tax burden, the revenue structure, and the extent of state participation in education, health, and welfare, are certainly among the most important issues in state politics. And apportionment practices seem to have little impact on the outcome of these issues.

At this point it seems appropriate to enter a caveat regarding the conclusions that can be drawn from these operations. All that has been shown is that reapportionment is not likely to have a direct impact on party competition or on certain policy outcomes. This is *not* to say that reapportionment will have no effect on state political systems or processes.

[16] Schubert and Press, *op. cit.*, p. 311.

Quantification necessitates a simplification of what may be a very complex question. The consequences of reapportionment may be so subtle and diverse that they defy quantitative measurement. Perhaps the consequences in each state will vary so much that direct interstate comparisons are inappropriate. Certainly we need more refined analyses of the impact of apportionment systems on state political processes and policy outcomes; we especially need more "before and after" studies of reapportionment. But these operations do succeed in challenging the easy assumptions and simple generalizations about the effects of malapportionment on public policy, and they caution us not to expect major policy changes in the wake of reapportionment.

How can we account for the bitter political battles fought over reapportionment in many states if malapportionment really has little effect on public policy? Perhaps the explanation lies in the distinction between the potential for power and the exercise of power. Certainly malapportionment overweights rural representation in legislatures. Malapportionment may give rural legislators a potential for power over their urban counterparts, *but* if they do not vote together with a high degree of unity to oppose urban interests on actual questions of public policy, their "power" may be more hypothetical than real. Legislative control can change hands and still leave policies unchanged if there are few policy differences between those placed in power and those dispossessed. Suburban voters, for example, may be just as conservative as the rural voters whose voice they may replace. In addition, divisions other than rural-versus-urban may characterize much of the legislative process: divisions between the parties, between a Governor's supporters and his opponents, between economic interests and organized groups, between liberals and conservatives, between labor and management, between regions of a state, and so forth. Reapportionment could change the distribution of power between rural and urban constituencies and yet have so subtle an effect on these other divisions that few policy changes would result. In short, even rural-urban divisions are affected by reapportionment, these divisions are only one of many types of legislative divisions.

These conclusions need not moderate enthusiasm for reapportionment. The moral case for equality of representation is as compelling as it ever was. The impact on reapportionment of public policy, however, may be somewhat less sweeping than many expect.

CONSEQUENCES OF REAPPORTIONMENT IN GEORGIA

BRETT W. HAWKINS

Comparative studies of the effect of reapportionment on state policies have dealt a major blow to reformist generalizations about reapportionment. Reformers have long argued that reapportionment would lead to policy changes, among them more spending for services benefitting city dwellers; but studies by Dye, Hofferbert, Jacob, and Brady and Edmonds indicate that variations in apportionment have little or no independent effect on state expenditure levels.[1] Since 1968 many single state studies – using roll call data, local observer perceptions, and legislator perceptions – also have suggested the unimportance of apportionment.[2] However, few if any comparative or single-state studies flatly conclude that apportionment has no effect on policy. Rather, they conclude that if apportionment has an effect it is slight, subtle, unquantifiable, not manifested in expenditures, or not yet shown. Nonetheless, the dominant

The research for this article was made possible by a grant from the National Municipal League as part of a twelve-state study of the impact of reapportionment. Additional financing was received from the Institute of Government, University of Georgia. Research reported here was conducted by Thomas R. Dye, Frank K. Gibson, Brett W. Hawkins, and Ira Sharkansky.

[1] Thomas R. Dye, "Malapportionment and Public Policy in the States," *Journal of Politics*, 27 (August, 1965), 586–601; Richard I. Hofferbert, "The Relation Between Public Policy and Some Structural and Environmental Variables in the American States," *American Political Science Review*, 60 (March, 1966), 73–82; Herbert Jacob, "The Consequences of Malapportionment: A Note of Caution," *Social Forces*, 43 (December, 1964), 256–261; and David Brady and Douglas Edmonds, *The Effect of Malapportionment on Policy Output in the American States* (Iowa City: Laboratory for Political Research, 1966).

[2] David Derge, "Metropolitan and Outside Alignments in Illinois and Missouri Legislative Delegations," *American Political Science Review*, 52 (December, 1958), 1051–1065; John G. Grumm, "The Means of Measuring Conflict and Cohesion in the Legislative," *Southwestern Social Science Quarterly*, XLIV (March, 1964), 337–388; William J. D. Boyd (ed.), *Compendium on Legislative Apportionment* (New York: National Municipal League, 1962); and Robert S. Friedman, "The Urban-Rural Conflict Revisited," *Western Political Quarterly*, XIV (June, 1961), 481–495.

theme of the recent political science literature conflicts with the dominant theme of the earlier reformist literature.

The implications of the recent literature are important to political science and political reform alike. Both scientists and reformers are interested in negative evidence concerning the impact of changes in political structure on the output of political systems. Indeed, some scientists and reformers appear to be trying to resurrect structural characteristics of political systems in explaining government performance and output. The Georgia reapportionment study is relevant to all such interests.

None of the published comparative studies have examined the same states before and after reapportionment. Instead they have compared well-apportioned with malapportioned states for policy differences. Emphasis has been on the association between interstate variations in apportionment and spending. Few single-state studies have appeared using a before-after research design.[3] Part of the reason for the scarcity of before-after studies, of course, is the short time since reapportionment. Using a before-after design, this within-state study of Georgia finds theoretically important policy consequences of reapportionment. Reapportionment increased the number of urban legislators, brought more city-oriented policy preferences into the legislature, resulted in more urban legislators in positions of influence, and further stimulated a trend toward the passage of urban-desired legislation. These results differ from most previous research, both comparative and within-state.

The Georgia study began with the assumption that because of its county-unit, malapportioned past,[4] Georgia is one state in which reapportionment might be expected to have a major policy impact. We expected that before-after analysis would show the direction of change manifested through the legislature, even though it is too early to fully assess all consequences of reapportionment since the Senate was reapportioned in 1962 and the House in 1965. Complications for analysis stem from other changes occurring at the same time that reapportionment has occurred.

[3] Exceptions are Allan Dines, "A Reapportioned State," *National Civic Review*, LV (February, 1966), 70–74, and Alvin D. Sokolow, "The First Session," *National Civic Review*, LVII (May, 1968), 243–248. While both note some changes consistent with reformist expectations, Dines does not conclude that reapportionment was the direct cause of them. And Sokolow concludes that the policies of the reapportioned California legislature do not indicate a major impact of reapportionment. In *The Missouri Legislature: A Preliminary Profile* (Columbia: University of Missouri School of Business and Public Administration, 1967) David A. Leuthold finds slightly increased support in the reapportioned house for four of five categories of policy.

[4] Albert B. Saye, "The County Unit Vote in Georgia," *Journal of Politics*, XII (February, 1950), 93–106 and V. O. Key, *Southern Politics in State and Nation* (New York: Knopf, 1951), Chapter 6.

These include urbanization, industrialization, rising incomes and education, increasing Negro political participation, a legislative independence movement, and the emergence of two-party competition. All of these system and environmental changes might be expected to affect the Georgia legislature and its policies. A single state, before-after analysis does not enable us to systematically disentangle the effect of one change compared with the other, but it does allow us to make informed inferences about reapportionment's direct and indirect consequences.

The data analyzed in the Georgia study concern reapportionment's impact on (1) the representation of political interests; (2) policy and other attitudes in the legislature; (3) the structure of power in the legislature; and (4) voting and policy output.[5]

Impact on the Representation of Political Interests

Apportionment systems affect the distribution of political power in a state by the way they give legislative access to different political interests. Key reformist expectations, moreover, concern increased representation for urban, Negro, and better educated constituencies. Equally important reformist expectations concern changes in the characteristics of legislators, such as the inclusion of more Negro, Republican, better educated, and big city legislators. Georgia's reapportionment altered the composition of the legislature in a way that carried certain policy implications.

The representation of various constituencies.[6] The main questions here are: What was the effect of Georgia's reapportionment on the representation of various kinds of constituencies? What increase in the representation of urban and metropolitan areas occurred with reapportionment? Did high income constituencies gain by reapportionment? Did constituencies with relatively well-educated adults gain by reapportionment? What was the effect of reapportionment on the representation of Georgia's Negro population?

The method for answering these questions was to compare the number of seats allocated to various types of constituencies in the last session before and the first session after reapportionment. As expected, the effect

[5] Background is provided in Doyle Mathis, "Georgia's Reapportionment History and Process," mimeo., Department of Political Science, University of Georgia, 1967; and Tim Ryles, "The 1965 House and Reapportionment in Georgia: An Appraisal," mimeo., Department of Political Science, University of Georgia, 1967.

[6] This section is based on Thomas R. Dye, "The Impact of Reapportionment on the Representation Afforded Various Constituencies in Georgia," mimeo., Department of Political Science, University of Georgia, 1967.

of reapportionment was to increase the representation of urban and metropolitan constituencies. In the House representation for constituencies in the 90 to 100 per cent urban category increased dramatically – from 6 to 57 legislators. In the Senate before reapportionment only 1 legislator was elected from a district where 90 to 100 per cent of the population lived in urban places; after reapportionment 21 senators were elected from such districts.

Before House reapportionment the five-county Atlanta SMSA [7] had only 13 members; after reapportionment it had 46. The Atlanta SMSA had 4 Senators before Senate reapportionment and 13 afterwards. And Georgia's other metropolitan areas – Albany, Augusta, Columbus, Macon, and Savannah – also gained by reapportionment. In all, House members from metropolitan areas increased from 31 to 81, while House members from non-metropolitan areas decreased from 174 to 120. In the 54-man Senate, reapportionment brought an increase in metropolitan representation from 9 to 26 and a decrease in nonmetropolitan representation from 45 to 28.

Reapportionment in Georgia thus had the expected effect on the representation of urban-rural constituencies. As for the representation of income and education groups, reapportionment again had the expected effect. It could be predicted that simply by increasing urban representation reapportionment would increase the representation of higher income and education groups, because on the whole Georgia's urban populations have higher income and education levels than rural populations. The most dramatic shift occurred in the highest income category (median family income over $4,500). House seats representing such districts jumped from 31 to 65, and Senate seats from 4 to 18. Reapportionment reduced the representation of poorer districts.

Reapportionment increased the representation of better educated adults and reduced the representation of poorer educated adults. In the House before reapportionment 147 legislators were from districts where the median school years completed was under 8.5. After reapportionment, only 113 legislators were from such districts. The representation of poorer educated constituencies in the Senate declined from 44 to 27 seats.

Perhaps the most interesting finding of the constituency study is that reapportionment reduced the representation of areas with more Negro population. (This result seems contradicted by the finding that reapportionment resulted in the seating of 8 Negro legislators in the House and 1 in the Senate – the first since Reconstruction. The seating of these

[7] A Standard Metropolitan Statistical Area (SMSA) is a county or group of contiguous counties containing at least one city with a population of 50,000 people or more.

legislators, however, was due to the increased representation given to Fulton County [Atlanta] and to the establishment of single-member districts within that county.) In the House, before reapportionment, 35 legislators were from districts with over 50 per cent of the population nonwhite; after reapportionment there were only 25. In the Senate before reapportionment there were 10 legislators from districts where over 50 per cent of the population was nonwhite; after reapportionment there were only 5. By shifting representation from rural to urban areas, reapportionment thus reduced Negro representation. In the constituency sense this decline in representation of black-belt counties led to the loss of Negro representation. Of course, Negroes in Georgia's black-belt counties are not as politically effective as Negroes in Georgia's cities, especially Atlanta, and so even though Negro populations lost representation in the constituency sense, Negroes gained political power. On the other hand, it is conceivable that in the long run Negroes would have gained still more power in a malapportioned legislature, when their numbers in rural areas became politically effective.

CHARACTERISTICS OF LEGISLATORS.[8] Another way to consider the impact of reapportionment on the representation of Georgia's political interests is to examine its effect on the characteristics of persons serving in the legislature. For example, did reapportionment result in the replacement of many veteran legislators? Did it bring men with different educational or occupational backgrounds to the legislature? Did it increase the representation of Republicans and of racial and religious minorities.

Comparing the characteristics of legislators before reapportionment with characteristics after spotlights differences that appear attributable to reapportionment. Of course, there is no foolproof way of knowing whether differences in legislator characteristics are caused by reapportionment or other changes occurring simultaneously in Georgia. For example, increased representation of Republicans may also be due to the growing strength of the Republican party. Furthermore, a legislator's social background does not necessarily determine his attitude or vote, although it does reveal the nature of influences to which legislators are subjected during their term in office. Also, background characteristics of legislators presumably tell something about elite political socialization patterns in Georgia and the criteria recruiters have in mind when they search for candidates.

Reapportionment lowered the average age of Georgia legislators, especially in the Senate, where the average age was reduced from 51 to 35

[8] This section is based on Thomas R. Dye, "The Impact of Reapportionment on the Characteristics of Georgia Legislators," mimeo., Department of Political Science, University of Georgia, 1967.

years. Such large changes in age levels are unlikely to occur from one session to the next without reapportionment. We conclude, therefore, that reapportionment produced the loss of many older legislators and brought younger ones.

Reapportionment did not significantly affect the predominance of business and professional men in the legislature. In both houses the proportion of legislators having these occupations was changed little after reapportionment. Reapportionment's most notable occupational consequence concerned farmers: It reduced the number of farmers from 11 to 7 in the Senate and from 41 to 29 in the House. Even so, farmers still form a larger proportion of the legislature than of the general population.

Reapportionment did have an effect on legislative turnover. In the Senate there were 33 freshmen in the session before reapportionment and 35 in the session after. The contrast is more apparent in the House where there were 35 freshman members in the session before reapportionment and 93 in the session after. This means that turnover in the House rose from 27 to 45 per cent. Thirty-three members of the House had over ten years experience in the session before reapportionment, but only 16 of these veterans were still there after reapportionment.

Reapportionment also resulted in better educated men serving in the House. The number of House members with college experience increased from 69 to 85 with reapportionment. The number of legislators with only high school education decreased from 56 to 45, and legislators with only elementary school education decreased from 13 to 4.

Perhaps the most striking change accompanying reapportionment was the increase in the number of Negroes in the legislature. The state's first Negro since Reconstruction was elected to the Senate after reapportionment in 1962. No Negro ever served in the House until reapportionment, when 8 were elected in 1966. At that time they represented the largest number of Negro legislators serving in any state legislature in the nation.

It is unlikely that any Negroes would have been elected to the Georgia legislature in the absence of reapportionment. All were elected from Fulton County (Atlanta) districts created by reapportionment. And their election cannot be attributed to increased Negro voting, or to federal voting laws, since Negroes had voted freely in Fulton County for many years before reapportionment. Rather their election must be attributed to the increased representation given to Fulton County with reapportionment and to the creation of single-member districts within the county. Prior to Senate reapportionment Fulton County was allotted one Senator. Reapportionment resulted in Fulton County getting 7 Senate seats and in the creation of 7 subcounty senatorial districts. One of these was the predominately Negro 38th District, which promptly elected a Negro Senator. Prior to House reapportionment Fulton County was allotted only 3 seats elected on a county-wide basis. Reapportionment resulted in Fulton County getting 24 House seats and in the creation of 22 single-member districts. Eight of these 22 districts promptly elected Negroes.

There is little doubt that reapportionment also added impetus to the growth of the Republican party in Georgia. While in northeastern and midwestern states Democratic strength is found principally in urban areas and Republican strength in rural areas, the opposite is true in Georgia. In Georgia, the GOP has been strongest in the Atlanta suburbs and in the cities of Augusta, Savannah, and Macon. When reapportionment granted additional seats to these areas, the Republican party picked up more seats than it had held since Reconstruction.

Prior to reapportionment, the Republicans held only 2 seats in the House, both in rural areas. After reapportionment they held 23 seats. All but 5 of these 23 House seats came from the metropolitan counties of Bibb (Macon), Richmond (Augusta), and Cobb, DeKalb, and Fulton (Atlanta). All these counties gained seats with reapportionment; and Republicans won most of the newly created seats.

Of course, not all of the Republican gains can be attributed to reapportionment alone. During the time that reapportionment was taking place, the Republican party was making giant strides in Georgia. In the 1964 presidential election, Barry Goldwater carried the state with 54 per cent of the popular vote. Republican Howard "Bo" Callaway was elected to the United States House of Representatives in 1964 and won a plurality in the governor's election in 1966 (although he did not win the necessary majority). Thus, it is very likely that the Republican party would have made some gains in the Georgia legislature without reapportionment.

However, by a conservative estimate, 11 out of 23 House Republican seats can be attributed directly to reapportionment. These are the Republican House seats that were created by reapportionment – 3 in Richmond County, 3 in Bibb County, 1 in DeKalb County, and 4 in Fulton County. In other words, without reapportionment Republicans could not have won more than 12 House seats in the 1965–66 session.

The religious composition of state legislatures, and both houses of Congress, is predominantly Protestant. The Georgia legislature is overwhelmingly Protestant, with Baptists constituting the largest denominational group. Reapportionment slightly increased the representation of non-Protestants. Catholic representation in the House rose from 3 to 6 seats with reapportionment and in the Senate it rose from 0 to 2. Jewish representatives increased from 1 to 2 in the House. All the newly seated non-Protestants came from districts in Atlanta and Savannah that were created by reapportionment. Thus, reapportionment, by increasing urban representation, also increased the representation of Catholics and Jews located in Georgia's two largest cities.

SUMMARY. Analysis of differences between the last session before reapportionment and the first session after shows changes generally consistent with reformist expectations. Urban constituencies and those with more educated and higher income people gained representation. On the other hand, constituencies with considerable Negro populations lost representation although this loss was perhaps offset by the election of several Atlanta area Negroes to the General Assembly. Besides the seating of several Negroes, other changes in the characteristics of legislators also occurred – most consistent with reformist expectations. These include more Republicans, fewer farmers, the loss of many veteran legislators, and an increase in the educational level of the House.

Thus, changes in the representation afforded various constituencies were directly caused by reapportionment. Also, reapportionment was a major factor in the loss of many veteran legislators and in the seating of Negroes and Republicans.

These data indicate that in the representation of Georgia's political interests reapportionment brought changes in a reformist direction. Although no consequences for legislative attitudes, organization, or output are revealed by these data, the potential for such changes is clear. Increases in the number of legislators from urban areas, and in the number of legislators having more typically urban social characteristics, offer the prospect of more legislative support for urban policies. It seems reasonable to assume that, sooner or later, the impact of a changed legislative composition may be translated into important decisions about leadership and policy. What form such decisions appear to have so far taken is the subject of the last three sections of this article.

IMPACT ON LEGISLATOR ATTITUDES [9]

The Georgia data supported reformist generalizations about reapportionment's impact on legislators' background and constituency characteristics. What about legislators' attitudes? Are there attitudinal manifestations of the changed composition of the Georgia legislature?

Because no data are available on legislators' attitudes in a before session, before-after comparisons are not possible. The alternative procedures used in this study were to inquire into (post reapportionment) legislators' perceptions of reapportionment's impact, and to find out

[9] This section is based on Frank K. Gibson and Brett W. Hawkins, "Reapportionment and the Political Attitudes of Georgia legislators," mimeo., Department of Political Science, University of Georgia, 1968.

whether legislators from urban districts, and those who favor reapportionment, have persistently different attitudes from their rural and reapportionment-resistant colleagues. If they do, inferences can be made about the impact of reapportionment.

In the 1967 session 87 of the 205 members of the House and 33 of the 54 Senators were interviewed personally or by mail. Results of direct interviews and mail questionnaires were systematically compared, and remarkably similar results were observed.[10] The two sets of results are therefore combined for the analysis reported here.

Personal interviews were conducted with legislators as they entered or left each chamber on the assumption that entering and exiting legislators would be thoroughly shuffled as to personal characteristics, although the sample may conceivably underrepresent the most inactive legislators. Only one legislator refused to be personally interviewed. A comparison of the personal characteristics of sample legislators with the universe of legislators further increased confidence in the sample. For these reasons we assume that the sample is largely free from self-selection.

Strictly speaking, however, the conclusions reached below apply only to the legislators included in the survey. On the other hand, the sample does provide the best available objective evidence of representative attitudes among contemporary Georgia legislators. Here emphasis is on whether relationships in the data support or contradict reformist generalizations about reapportionment's impact. Special stress is placed on whether district urbanism and legislator attitude toward reapportionment discriminate among policy preferences.

PERCEIVED IMPACT ON LEGISLATION AND POLICIES. Those individuals and groups that advocate reapportionment have at times suggested that a reapportioned legislature would produce different types of programs – more liberal legislation would be introduced and passed – and that state policies would thus be dramatically affected. In order to test this generalization against the perceptions of Georgia legislators, respondents were asked the following questions: (1) What do you think the effect of reapportionment will be on the nature of legislation introduced in the General Assembly? (2) What do you think the effect of reapportionment will be on state policies such as education, welfare, roads, taxes, etc.?

Concerning the perceived effect of reapportionment on the nature of legislation introduced, 45.5 per cent of the Senators and 41.1 per cent of the Representatives saw no change at all resulting from reapportionment,

[10] See Frank K. Gibson and Brett W. Hawkins, "Interviews versus Questionnaires," *American Behavioral Scientist*, XII (September–October, 1968), NS 9–11.

while 27.3 per cent of the Senators and 23.0 per cent of the Representatives replied that more "urban legislation" would be introduced. Relevant cross-classifications showed no relationship between position on reapportionment and perceived changes in legislation. Also, there was no relationship between district urbanism and perceived changes in legislation.

As for the perceived effect of reapportionment on policies (Question 2), the same general pattern prevailed. Combined "no effect" and "very little effect" responses indicate that at least in the opinion of legislators currently serving in the General Assembly the hopes of reformers supporting reapportionment as a means of changing state policies will not be borne out. Analyzing these data by district represented and attitude toward reapportionment brings forth no meaningfully patterned relationships.

Perceived impact on interest group activity. When asked if they received more pressure from urban interest groups since reapportionment, 54.5 per cent of the Senators and 41.1 per cent of the Representatives answered yes. However, there was no patterned relationship between these responses and level of district urbanism or position on reapportionment.

When asked to identify the interest groups responsible for the most pressure, the first choice was the Georgia Municipal Association. A slight relationship appears between this response and district urbanism – that is, legislators from urban districts are somewhat more likely to respond with "Georgia Municipal Association." Also, those who support reapportionment perceive GMA pressure to a greater degree than those who oppose it.

Policy attitudes. It is often assumed that support of reapportionment, the level of urbanism, and liberal policy preferences are related. One assumption is that the higher the district's urbanism and the more liberal the legislator, the more likely he is to regard reapportionment favorably. It is also assumed that legislators from urban districts and those supporting reapportionment are more likely to hold liberal policy views.

In order to test these hypothesized linkages among Georgia legislators, each respondent was shown a series of statements to which he was asked to agree or disagree. The questions were designed to distinguish liberal from conservative policy attitudes. The following paragraphs summarize the observed relationships between policy preference, the level of district urbanism, and position on reapportionment.

"The use of tax rolls to select jurors should be discontinued since it discriminates against non-property owners." Agreement indicated the liberal position. There was more agreement with this statement from House members representing highly urbanized areas, and there was agreement from supporters of reapportionment in both houses.

"That government is best which governs least." Agreement indicated the conservative position. In both houses supporters of reapportionment tended to disagree much more than opponents. House members representing districts over 50 per cent urban disagreed, and those from rural areas agreed. In the Senate no substantial relationship with level of urbanism appeared.

"Federal money brings federal control." Agreement indicated the conservative position. In general the hypothesized relationships held true. Supporters of reapportionment tended to disagree while opponents of reapportionment tended to agree. The strongest disagreement came from those representing the most urban districts.

"The state should increase aid to cities since they have inadequate revenues to meet their needs." Agreement indicated the liberal position. In this study those who supported reapportionment were more likely to agree. Also, the greatest agreement came from those representing the most urbanized districts.

"Raise sales tax if additional revenue is needed since this tax catches those who escape other forms of taxation." Agreement indicated the conservative position. The hypothesized relationship failed to materialize on this statement. No relationship appeared with reference to attitude on reapportionment or district urbanism. Unfortunately the data do not explain the deviation, but the basic conservatism of Georgia legislators, coupled with a large Negro population, may be part of the answer. Also, the question of increasing a sales tax puts the policy liberal in a difficult position. Liberals want increased governmental activity; increased governmental activity requires increased revenue; and the sales tax is an excellent producer of revenue.

"The state should refuse to raise taxes even if it means delaying needed programs." Agreement indicated the conservative position. In fact, respondents from both Georgia houses disagreed. While no relationship appeared with regard to position on reapportionment, district urbanism is related. The greatest disagreement, especially in the House, came from the most highly urbanized districts.

In general, the hypothesized relationship between reapportionment position, level of urbanism, and liberal policy attitudes does exist in the Georgia data.

SUMMARY. Patterns exist in the data that bear on generalizations about the impact of reapportionment. Positive relationships between support of reapportionment, district urbanism, and liberal policy attitudes are consistent with reformist generalizations. These relationships offer the prospect of more and more urban, liberal representatives coming into the General Assembly of Georgia. They suggest that the influx of urban, better educated legislators brings more liberal policy preferences. Of course, the policy outcomes (if any) of this influx are unknown, but reformist generalization-makers can at least cite evidence that reapportionment is bringing the proper mix among key variables.[11] In addition, sample legislators saw urban interest groups as becoming more vigorous in their activities since reapportionment. Finally, district urbanism and support of reapportionment are systematically related to the perceived need for a stronger, more independent legislature and for more legislative aids. (This finding is not reported above.) Reformers can point to this as evidence that reapportionment encourages a professionalized legislature.

On the other hand, the evidence in the data is that legislators typically expect reapportionment to produce no change in legislation or state policies. In addition, supporters and opponents of reapportionment, and legislators from both urban and rural districts, agree on this position. There is no encouragement here for the generalization that reapportioned legislatures will result in more liberal legislative programs and state policies.

Opinions on reapportionment's impact, however, are probably not as important for speculating about policy changes as data indicating positive relationships between district urbanism and attitudes.[12] Relationships in the data show that district urbanism discriminates among legislator attitudes in the direction suggested by reformers. Sixty-one per cent of all questions – some were not reported here – produced responses that are related to district urbanism in ways consistent with reformist generalizations. However, only 35 per cent of all questions produced results related to reapportionment positions in ways consistent with reformist generalizations. Thus, when all questions are weighted alike the data offer limited support of reformist generalizations about reapportionment's impact.

Impact on the Structure of Power in the Legislature[13]

The structure of political power within the legislature – including committee and leadership selections – may be affected by apportionment.

[11] Twenty-five per cent of Georgia legislators expect more urban legislation to be introduced.

[12] It may be that current legislators expect no policy consequence of the urban influx because they see great obstacles to cooperation among urban legislators and tenacious rural occupation of key legislative positions. The linking of these explanations to the perception of no policy change is plausible in view of the fact that sample legislators typically expect no change in leadership patterns and say, overwhelmingly, that city legislators have proven that they cannot work together. These findings are not reported above.

[13] This section is excerped from Brett W. Hawkins and Cheryl Whelchel, "Reapportionment and Urban Representation in Legislative Influence Positions: The Case of Georgia," *Urban Affairs Quarterly*, III (March, 1968), 69–80, with permission of the publisher, Sage Publications, Inc.

Malapportionment, it is said, tips the selection scales in favor of rural interests and thus gives them a major advantage in their defense of the status quo. In Georgia, reapportionment's champions argued that urbanization and reapportionment would combine to produce an urban-run legislature and, eventually, more urban-directed policies. Others suggested, however, that reapportionment would not change the operation and output of the legislature because (1) urban legislators are too diverse a group to act as a bloc: (2) no distinct urban-rural split ever existed in the legislature: and (3) more experienced rural legislators, representing less socially diverse and politically competitive districts, would continue to dominate in positions of influence. While political scientists and reformers have made many assumptions about these changes in influence positions, few, if any, systematic, empirical studies attempt to specify their nature and direction.

The statistics used in this analysis are indices of proportionate urban and metropolitan representation in the following influence positions: (1) major legislative leaders;[14] (2) key committee chairmanships and vice-chairmanships;[15] (3) key committee memberships. These positions are considered to have potential for influence. The focus is on the potential for influence inherent in key committee and leadership positions, and not on the direct exercise of influence. Such a positional study, however, provides a basis for inferences about the exercise of influence.

The statistics analyzed here are similar to those used by Matthews in his study of the United States Senate.[16] They measure proportionate position holding, or the degree to which urban representation is higher or lower than one would expect from the operation of chance. For example, if influence positions within the legislature were selected by chance, and without regard to residence, urban representation in such positions could be expected to be the same as the urban composition of the universe from which the selections were made; that is, the total membership of each house.

Our "population index" was based on the percentage of Georgia's population that is urban, according to the 1960 census:

$$\frac{\text{Percentage of influence positions held by urban legislators}}{\text{Percentage of urban population of Georgia}}$$

[14] Speaker of the House, Speaker Pro Tempore of the House, Administration Floor Leader of the House, President Pro Tempore of the Senate.

[15] Agriculture, Appropriations, Banks and Banking, Education, Highways, Judiciary, Rules, and Ways and Means. The last committee has no equivalent in the Senate.

[16] Donald R. Matthews, *U.S. Senators and Their World* (New York: Vintage Books, 1960).

Our "legislative index," in contrast, refers to index numbers based on the percentage of each house's membership that is urban:

$$\frac{\text{Percentage of influence positions held by urban legislators}}{\text{Percentage of urban members in house}}$$

We began with the assumption that urban position holding after reapportionment would necessarily lag behind because of the lack of seniority and experience of new urban members. A disproportionate number of veterans could be expected to be rural in the immediate post-reapportionment sessions. Such a lag would be reflected in the legislative index. For purposes of this analysis, however, we assumed that legislative indices that drop from *above* 1.0 (more than proportionate representation) to below it are important, because they show a significant loss in proportionate position holding. An index number of 1.0 indicates perfectly proportionate representation.

The adjective "urban" as used here refers to those legislators representing districts in which more than 50 per cent of the people live in urban places. "Metropolitan" is treated as a subcategory of "urban" and describes legislators from districts in which 75 per cent of the people live in urban places.[17]

In summary form, the findings are that urban-metropolitan gains occurred in absolute numbers and in relation to the proportion of the state's population living in urban-metropolitan places. These gains are important in themselves. On the other hand, there were losses in proportion to urban members in the legislature. Before reapportionment, urban legislators had more than proportionate representation in relation to their numbers in the legislature. After, they had much less than proportionate representation. Influence positions are now even more in rural hands (in proportion to their numbers) than they were before, especially in the Senate. And it seems that an additional post-reapportionment has not had a very great impact on this situation. After three post-reapportionment sessions, urban Senators hold no more influence positions, in proportion to total members, than their House counterparts, despite one more after session. This shows more tenacious rural position holding in the Senate, due in part, no doubt, to the fact that the lieutenant governor, who presides over the Senate, in all post-reapportionment sessions but the last (1967) was the same rural, county-unit-bred politician. His appointments, plus the alliances built up over the years, almost certainly continued to have an effect.

[17] These classifications are based on the urban composition of the entire legislative district, not the county of residence of the legislative position holder.

Reapportionment in Georgia has not yet resulted in urban legislators occupying influence positions in proportion to their numbers in the legislature. This appears to be due to the greater seniority and experience of rural legislators compared with urban legislators and to a rurally oriented presiding officer in the Senate. Still another factor is that with reapportionment urban-metropolitan delegations have become larger and more diverse in terms of status, life style, race, and urban-suburban residence. Diversity is especially great where subdistricting has occurred, as in Fulton County. Large, diverse urban delegations are less unified in pressing for key committee assignments than small, homogeneous delegations. Our findings are not due, however, to partisan discrimination against the small number of Republicans, most of whom represent metropolitan districts. Republicans have enjoyed generous committee assignments since reapportionment.

Impact on Voting and Legislation

Voting patterns and policy implications.[18] Roll call studies, of course, rely on recorded votes rather than attitudes to indicate differences between urban and rural legislators. Should any major differences appear between urban and rural legislators in roll calls, one might assume that they are important, because voting records probably minimize urban-rural differences where outnumbered or outpositioned urban legislators have had to accept half a policy loaf, or less. We assumed that roll calls are conservative indicators of urban-rural policy differences. Many political scientists have said that roll call analysis is important to propositions about the expected impact of reapportionment, for if legislators seldom vote in urban-rural blocs then greater representation for urban areas may have little effect on policy.

Attacks against rurally dominated legislatures – in Georgia and other states – drew their strength from a variety of sources. Some reformers wanted equal representation for its own sake, without clear expectations about the results. Others expected changes in policy.[19] Behind the expectations of policy change was the assumption that the urban-rural split was a fundamental political cleavage. To be an urban resident meant favoring expansion in programs for urban communities, and to be urban legislator

[18] This section is based on Ira Sharkansky, "Legislative Reapportionment in Georgia: Changes in Voting Patterns and Their Policy Implications," mimeo., Department of Political Science, University of Georgia, 1968.

[19] See, for example, Gordon E. Baker, *Rural versus Urban Political Power: The Nature and Consequences of Unbalanced Representation* (New York: Random House, 1955), 21–25.

meant voting with colleagues from one's own and other cities in support of benefits for urban voters and municipal governments.

The Georgia study looked at roll calls before and a short while after reapportionment and tried to discern if certain policy relevant changes have occurred. Because of the short time since reapportionment, it was not feasible to examine public services themselves to see if urban oriented policies have changed. There has not been enough time for a new era of planning, bill drafting, legislation, and administration to assert itself and counterbalance the generations of tradition and precedent formed under rural domination. However, it may be possible to gain insight into future events by examining decisions in the newly reapportioned legislature. In this study, we attempted to discover if reapportionment produced important changes in the voting patterns of Georgia legislators, and we tested some basic assumptions of those who predict that policy changes will result from reapportionment. Have Georgia's urban legislators actually voted together against rural legislators? Has bloc voting increased with the inclusion of more urban legislators since reapportionment? Has an urban bloc coalesced behind measures that have special meaning for urban residents?

In order to answer these questions, we examined 741 controversial roll calls from 1961 to 1966. By computing *chi* squares for votes on these bills against the percentage of each legislator's constituency that was urban, we determined the saliency of urbanism and ruralness for each controversial vote. Where urbanism and ruralness were salient (i.e., showed *chi* squares with at least a .05 level of statistical significance) we regarded the measure as producing an urban vs. rural division. The incidence of significant urban vs. rural votes during each legislative session served to measure any change in voting by urban-rural blocs. Emphasis was on changes after reapportionment. Also, by examining the titles of bills that set urban against rural legislators, we identified the nature of issues that produced bloc voting.

Admittedly, this study suffered from many problems that adhere to roll call analysis. Not all controversies are settled by recorded roll calls. Negotiations in committee sessions and in private meetings resolve many issues. Also, the recorded vote of a legislator can mask a wide variety of opinions; and urban legislators might not have voted as they did if the rural majority had been smaller. It requires an inferential leap to conclude that an "urban salient vote" represented the legislator's awareness that he has taken a position on an issue that is consistent with an urban or rural point of view. We used our roll call data with these limitations in mind. For our purposes, they indicated the extent to which legislators from urban districts vote together, the proportion of votes that urban legislators win against rural legislators, and the types of issues that generate urban-rural divisions.

Between 1961 and 1966 urban vs. rural voting in the Georgia legislature clearly increased; but the data do not indicate that this increase was a direct result of reapportionment. Table 1 shows a steady rise in the per cent of controversial bills that set urban against rural legislators – from 8 per cent in 1961 to 40 per cent in 1966. There was also a steady rise in the per cent of bills that urban representatives won – from 8 per cent in 1961 to 30 per cent in 1966. By themselves, these data suggest that reapportionment has affected bloc voting and that increased urban membership has raised the incidence of urban victories. However, a house by house breakdown rules out this interpretation. Table 2 presents the same data separated for House and Senate. (Recall that the Senate reapportioned in 1962 and the House in 1965. Thus, the first post-reapportionment session in the Senate was held in 1963; and in the House it was held in 1966.)

The Senate data show the expected eruption in urban vs. rural voting in the first *major* session (1964) after reapportionment. The incidence of bloc voting and urban success more than doubled from the last session before reapportionment. However, in the sessions of 1965 and 1966, bloc voting and urban success in the Senate returned to the level of the *status quo ante*.

The data for the House also fail to show a clear response to reapportionment. Although urban vs. rural voting and urban success increased from 1965 to 1966, this was part of a steady progression going back to 1961. Each year bloc voting and urban success increased in the House, even though reapportionment did not add to urban strength until 1966.

TABLE 1. *Incidence of Urban-Rural Bloc Voting, and Urban Successes: Georgia House and Senate Combined, 1961-1966*

	Total Controversial Bills*	Per Cent Urban-Rural Bloc Voting	Per Cent Urban Success
1961	48	8	8
1962 (Senate Reapportionment)	87	16	11
1963	78	19	14
1964	278	30	20
1965 (House Reapportionment)	94	30	23
1966	156	40	30

*Bills in which at least 10 per cent of the house voted on the losing side.

TABLE 2. *Incidence of Urban-Rural Bloc Voting, Urban Successes: Georgia Senate and House Computed Separately, 1961-1966*

	Total Controversial Bills*	Per Cent Urban-Rural Bloc Voting	Per Cent Urban Success
		Senate	
1961	18	11	11
1962 (Reapportionment)	13	15	8
1963	2	0	0
1964	71	34	20
1965	31	13	6
1966	45	13	13
		House	
1961	30	7	7
1962	74	16	12
1963	76	20	14
1964	207	29	20
1965 (Reapportionment)	63	38	32
1966	111	50	37

*Bill in which at least 10 per cent of the house voted on the losing side.

Different types of issues aroused urban vs. rural antagonisms between 1961 and 1966. After a preliminary inspection of the urban vs. rural roll calls, eight categories were selected to portray most of the votes. Because of the need to divide among these categories the small number of Senate votes before reapportionment, and the small number of House votes after reapportionment, it is not practical to discuss changes in the issue focus of blocs as a direct result of reapportionment. However, Table 3 shows the number of votes in each category over the 1961 to 1966 period.

Many of the urban vs. rural bloc votes appeared in categories that are important from the perspective of those who predict that policy changes will result from reapportionment: the structure of state government, the powers and state aids of local governments, the regulation of business, labor, and the professions, and taxes. Together these issues accounted for 46 per cent of the bloc votes. In the category labeled "State government structure," the most prominent issue was reapportionment itself. Four of the bloc votes in 1962 (the year of Senate reapportionment) and 11 in 1965 (the year of House reapportionment) dealt with this issue.

TABLE 3. *Issues Generating Urban-Rural Bloc Voting in the Georgia Legislature, by Category, 1961-1966*

	Number of Votes	Per Cent of Total	Number of Votes Won by Urban Side
Taxation	13	6	10
Elections	27	13	19
Auto and traffic	10	5	9
Criminal law other than traffic	11	5	9
Local government powers and state aids	22	11	20
Regulation of labor, business, professions	22	11	15
State government structure	38	18	35
Highways and other transportation	6	3	3
Other and ambiguous	57	28	30

The category covering local government powers and state aids amounted to 11 per cent of all bloc votes. Almost all of these (20 out of 22) were won by the urban bloc, which suggests that representatives of Georgia's cities may take command of this potentially important category of public policy. The 11 per cent of the votes dealing with regulation of business, labor, and the professions suggests that increased urban strength may have an impact on those residents affected by state business-labor policies. In a number of states it was alleged that many such policies had been thwarted by probusiness, antilabor legislators from small towns and rural areas.

Tax issues accounted for only 6 per cent of the urban-rural votes, but their presence in even a small number suggests that with the passage of more time, urban legislators may provide municipal governments with additional tools to help with their financial problems.

Our findings showed clear differences from earlier studies of the policy implications of legislative reapportionment. In contrast to Derge's study [20] we found that a significant number of roll calls produced a split between urban and rural legislators. The incidence of these splits and the incidence of urban success increased during the era of reapportionment. Moreover, a significant proportion of these splits occurred on policy issues that appear relevant for urban interests. In contrast to the suggestions of Jacob, Dye, and Hofferbert [21] that well-apportioned legislatures will not produce policies more urban oriented than those produced by poorly apportioned legislatures, we perceive policy implications in the reapportionment of Georgia. It is true that no evidence points to a change in voting resulting directly from reapportionment. In the Senate, bloc voting increased only temporarily after reapportionment. In the House, the increase in bloc voting was part of a clear trend that began four years prior to reapportionment. But no matter what the direct cause of the increase in urban vs. rural voting and urban success, reapportionment should benefit urban interests by adding to the members of the urban bloc. If this newly emerged bloc remains cohesive, and continues to focus its votes on issues having relevance for urban interests, then urban residents and municipal governments should benefit from reapportionment.

If the influx of urban legislators caused by reapportionment did not produce an increase in urban vs. rural voting in the Georgia legislature, what was the cause of this increase? Several explanations are tenable, although none can be validated with a single state study. Our findings may reflect a broad-gauged modernization of Georgia politics. This occurrence may be unique in Georgia, or it might be part of larger developments that are occurring among formerly rural states in the South. This modernization may be coupled with changes in several features of Southern politics: a decline in the prominence of rural whites in state government; increased participation of Negroes in political life; awakened concern among state elites for improving public services; and increased capital investment in industry. The migration of rural Negroes and whites into such cities as Atlanta, Birmingham, and Memphis, plus the attraction of outsiders to professional and managerial positions in these cities, may increase the prominence of urban problems throughout the South, facilitate the mobilization of popular support for urban spending, generate increased rapport among urban legislators, and, perhaps as a reaction against this increased urbanism, increase cohesion among rural legislators.

There may be an increasing awareness of urbanism among political actors throughout the country, perhaps in response to an increasing prominence of urban problems. The Supreme Court's decision in *Baker*

[20] Derge, *op. cit.*
[21] See footnote 1.

vs. Carr may itself be a product – as well as additional stimulant – of increased awareness of urbanism. That is, *Baker vs. Carr* and its legal consequences, and the increased urban awareness of Georgia legislators, may be separate responses to common urban oriented changes in values in the American political system.

LEGISLATION AFFECTING CITIES.[22] We operationally defined "legislation affecting Georgia's cities" as those bills and resolutions supported or opposed by the Georgia Municipal Association.[23] Bills and resolutions from the 1960 through 1967 sessions inclusive were analyzed with emphasis on their aggregate numbers annually, the houses in which they were introduced, whether they passed both houses, and changes in previous patterns. This was not a study of particular bills and their importance.

Since the Georgia Senate reapportioned in 1962 and the House in 1965, the first post-reapportionment sessions were in 1963 and 1966 respectively. Table 4 shows that the 1960, 1961, and 1962 sessions were successful in that 86 per cent of all GMA supported bills and resolutions passed both houses, and not one opposed bill or resolution emerged from the General Assembly. Very small numbers of bills and resolutions were involved, however. The Georgia Municipal Association program contained few items in these years, in part because GMA wanted to concentrate on a few much wanted bills.

Most supported bills and resolutions were introduced in the House of Representatives. This reflected a deliberate strategy of the Georgia Municipal Association, based on their perception of the House as the main obstacle to urban legislation. GMA officials perceived a greater general awareness of urban problems in the Senate, with its larger constituencies usually including at least small cities, even before it was apportioned on a population basis. They believed that the major fights would be in the House and that if desired measures cleared the House, they were home free.

In 1962, the United States Supreme Court announced the *Baker vs. Carr* decision and the Georgia Senate apportioned itself on a population basis. A year later the Supreme Court also struck down Georgia's county-unit system. The reaction among rural representatives was considerable.

[22] This section is based on Brett W. Hawkins, "Reapportionment Aids Georgia's Urban Bills," *National Civic Review*, LVII (March, 1968), 153–156. Used with the permission of the publisher, the National Municipal League.

[23] Two limitations of GMA bills and resolutions as indicators of legislation affecting cities should be noted. GMA represents small towns as well as large cities, and so its legislative program should not be regarded as a metropolitan or big-city program. Second, GMA has from time to time pushed a bill to get concessions on other highly favored bills. Such strategic ruses may or may not have been staged with a bill that GMA expected to pass. But it has always been a bill of interest to cities.

TABLE 4. *Outcome of Georgia Municipal Association Supported and Opposed Bills and Resolutions*

Supported Bills and Resolutions				Opposed Bills and Resolutions			
Year	Introduced	Passed	Failed	Year	Introduced	Passed	Failed
			A. Before Reapportionment				
Senate				Senate			
1960	3*	5*	0	1960	0	0	0
1961	0	8	0	1961	1	0	1
1962	0	5	0	1962	1	1	0
Totals	3	18	0	Totals	2	1	1
House				House			
1960	2*	5*	0	1960	0	0	0
1961	10	8	2	1961	1	0	1
1962	6	5	1	1962	2	0	3
1963	12	7	5	1963	2	0	2
1964	8	4	4	1964	1	0	1
1965	11	6	5	1965	0	0	0
Totals	49	35	17	Totals	6	0	7
			B. After Reapportionment				
Senate				Senate			
1963	0	7	0	1963	0	0	0
1964	0	3	1	1964	0	0	0
1965	2	8	1	1965	0	0	0
1966	14	14	0	1966	4	1	3
1967	14	13	1	1967	3	0	3
Totals	30	45	3	Totals	7	1	6
House				House			
1966	32	28	4	1966	12**	0	13**
1967	41	34	7	1967	8	0	8
Totals	73	62	11	Totals	20**	0	21**

*Excluding failures, the difference between bills introduced and passed is due to the fact that some passed bills were introduced in the other chamber. Such differences appear frequently in the table.

**In 1966 a total of 16 opposed bills and resolutions were introduced. All 16 failed, but for 3 of them the chamber of introduction could not be traced. The 3 are here recorded as introduced in the House—where most other bills were introduced. They are also recorded as having failed in the House.

Apparently out of fear of the urban vote and concern over their traditional advantages, representatives from the two-unit-vote counties even formed a "club of 121" as a protective device. (There were 121 small, essentially rural counties that had dominated not only the legislature but also the election of governor.)

The year 1963 witnessed a sharp break in the pattern of the previous three years. In 1963 12 bills and resolutions were introduced (all in the House), and 5 of them failed. The following year 5 of 8 failed (one in the Senate); and in 1965 6 of 13 failed. Thus from 1963 to 1965 only 55 per cent of all supported measures passed both houses – a large drop in the success rate of the previous three years. However, no opposed bills were enacted.

In 1965 the House of Representatives reapportioned itself on a population basis. The 1966 session was therefore the first with both houses reapportioned. That year witnessed an expansion of the GMA's program and therefore a big jump in the number of supported bills and resolutions introduced. For the first time several favored measures were introduced into the Senate. Their perfect success rate in the Senate, moreover, bore out the GMA's long standing belief that the Senate was the more urban-receptive body. By 1966, of course, the Senate had experienced three complete after sessions. In 1966 and 1967 the success rate was very much like the 1960 to 1962 period, but with many more bills and resolutions. Eighty-nine of the 101 measures introduced passed both houses (88 per cent), and none of the opposed measures got through the General Assembly. The main findings, then, are the three-period pattern and an uneven increase in the absolute number of urban-relevant bills and resolutions introduced and passed.[24]

What explains these findings? Reapportionment is part of the explanation, but not all of it. The three-period pattern of a high success rate, followed by a low rate, and finally by a high success rate again (with many more bills and resolutions) is illustrative. In the years before *Baker vs. Carr*, Georgia Municipal Association officials had painstakingly built up good relationships with rural legislators. By 1962 they had come to feel that progress had been made and that they could get a friendly hearing for some city bills. Then came *Baker vs. Carr*, a heightened rural conscious, and a drop in the success rate for GMA measures. Evidently, a rural protectivist mentality toward traditional prerogatives (such as rural roads) manifested itself in the form of urban legislative setbacks. The election in 1962 of a city-oriented governor, Carl Sanders, by popular vote rather than county unit vote may have heightened rural defensiveness.

[24] It is also interesting that throughout this entire period no opposed bill got through both houses of the General Assembly.

After *Baker vs. Carr* the Georgia Municipal Association had to work for a readjustment. In this effort they were aided by a reapportioned Senate where, even before reapportionment, the larger constituencies – (all with some urban areas) – produced more sympathy for urban legislation. And when, in 1966, a reapportioned House also became a reality, a breakthrough in legislative successes occurred. More urban legislators made the GMA's job easier. During these years of effort and readjustment by the GMA, plus reapportionment, there occurred a fairly steady rise in the number of bills and resolutions in the GMA's legislative program.

The point of this discussion is that the Georgia Municipal Association was better organizing itself and became more active at the same time that reapportionment on a population basis was bringing more urban representatives into the General Assembly. Throughout the reapportionment era there has developed an increasingly favorable consideration of bills and resolutions relevant to cities. In addition, after both houses were reapportioned a discernible jump occurred. However, with before-after data from a single state one cannot determine what part of the increase in legislation favorable to cities is directly attributable to reapportionment and what part to changes in the legislative environment, such as urbanization and a better organized, more active municipal association. It is possible of course that an unreapportioned legislature might have passed some, most, or all of the measures passed by the reapportioned legislature; but we think that few would have passed. Indeed, given the strategy of the GMA, few would even have been introduced.

Conclusions

Our data do not permit simple, unqualified conclusions about the impact of reapportionment on observed changes. One can still argue that reapportionment's policy impact seems more subtle than sharp, and less directly shown than inferred. But the Georgia data do indicate that reapportionment has brought changes. The increased representation of urban political interests is largely attributable to reapportionment. And since the attitude data show urban legislators to be more liberal in some policy preferences than their rural colleagues we conclude that reapportionment has increased attitudinal liberalism in the Georgia legislature. In other words, there are attitudinal manifestations of changes in composition, and in a direction consistent with reformist expectations. Also, the positional study indicates that urban position holding has sharply increased in absolute numbers and in relation to the state's urban population. Finally, theoretically interesting voting and policy changes have taken place during the reapportionment era.

However, we cannot confidently conclude that reapportionment is the direct or major cause of the increased success rate of municipal association measures, of increased urban-rural bloc voting, or of increased urban successes in urban-relevant policy areas. Some of these changes began before reapportionment; and all seem partially the result of such other variables as urbanization and the growing saliency of urban needs. Indeed, much in the data suggests that urbanization, an environmental factor, is an important explanatory variable in Georgia. But because reapportionment has brought in more urban representatives, who are more liberal, and who are voting together more often, and winning more often, we conclude that to some unknown degree reapportionment has been a factor in observed policy changes since reapportionment. The direction of these changes, moreover, is consistent with reformist generalizations. At least some policies seem partially dependent on the apportionment system for their enactment. Changes observable now, in addition, suggest that reapportionment will be an important factor in future policy choices.

Thus the results of our before-after, single-state legislative study differ from most previous comparative and single-state studies. Previous studies suggest that variations in apportionment do not affect policies to any important degree. The Georgia study suggests that variations in apportionment do affect policy, and that this influence is detectable when *intra*state variations in apportionment are studied. The true impact of apportionment systems may not be detectable when only *inter*state variations in apportionment are studied. Interestingly, the possibly critical importance of studying intrastate variations in apportionment is also suggested by other research. Before-after analysis in Michigan reached positive conclusions about reapportionment's impact,[25] and, even more importantly, other comparative before-after analysis is emerging that shows an impact of reapportionment.[26]

Being much less expansive in interpreting our data, it is possible that the difference between the Georgia study and most others is simply due to Georgia having been an extreme case of malapportionment. In other words, reapportionment will make a difference for policy but only under exceptional circumstances. On a scale designed to measure population equality in apportionment, Georgia ranked last among the states before

[25] David A. Leuthold, "The Effects of Legislative Reapportionment on Policy: Michigan and Missouri." Distributed by the Conference on the Measurement of Public Policy in the American States, July 28–August 3, 1969, Ann Arbor, Michigan.

[26] I am grateful to my colleague Roger Hanson for making known to me the preliminary results of his study of twenty-three states. They show a pattern of statistically significant changes in spending for states that had reapportioned, and very few such changes for states that had not reapportioned, at the time the data were collected.

reapportionment.[27] Extreme cases, of course, are often disregarded when the research goal is to generalize about the whole population of American states. It should be noted, however, that before-after analysis in Michigan – a state not on either extreme of the apportionment continuum [28] – reached conclusions similar to ours. This suggests that our findings are not due to Georgia being an extreme case, but even if they are it is important to learn that reapportionment following a high degree of malapportionment can have policy consequences.

Another possibility is that the difference between our findings and others is due to variables besides apportionment; in other words, apportionment systems may really not be important for policy. When it is discovered that a relationship holds for some states but not others, political scientists should consider the possibility that other, intervening variables explain the difference. The key intervening variable or variables may pertain to properties of Georgia's political system other than apportionment, or to Georgia's political culture. Systemic or cultural attributes not measured, perhaps even the collective system or culture, may account for the difference. Certainly Georgia can claim unique political and cultural attributes and has not hesitated to do so when it suited the purpose of the state's leaders.

[27] John T. Elliff, "Malapportionment Remeasured," *American Political Science Review*, LVIII (December, 1964), Table 4.

[28] Elliff ranks Michigan 30th. Earlier Dauer and Kelsay had ranked Michigan's Lower House 7th and its Upper House 29th. Elliff *op. cit.*; Manning J. Dauer and Robert G. Kelsay, "Unrepresentative States," *National Municipal Review*, XLIV (December, 1955), 571–575, 587.

THE EFFECTS OF LEGISLATIVE STRUCTURE ON LEGISLATIVE PERFORMANCE

JOHN G. GRUMM

What effects do the structures of political institutions have on the performance of these institutions? More specifically, what effects does structure have on the behavior of individuals in these institutions and the policies emanating from them? These questions really cannot be answered very fully since the total accumulated body of knowledge on the subject is, as yet, very small. A generation ago political scientists were concerned about such questions, and some of them thought they knew the answers, but either they did not have the tools for research or they did not think it was necessary to make the empirical investigations to support their assertions.[1] Some modern political scientists have tested several of the older propositions, but the results have appeared to be somewhat contradictory or inconclusive so far. It is important, however, to continue the quest and to sort out and expand our knowledge in this realm. Purposeful as well as accidental structural changes will continue to be made in political institutions and we ought to be able to predict what the consequences of these changes will be.

State legislatures in the United States have recently undergone some very profound changes largely as a result of *Baker* v. *Carr*. But reapportionment, only part of the picture, has served to focus attention on other aspects of state legislatures and in some cases has altered the political environment to the extent that other changes in the institutions could be more readily accomplished. These developments, therefore, present us with an exceptional opportunity to use our new and sharper tools of empirical analysis to study structural change and its effects in a political institution.

Model of the Political System

Studies on the interaction of structural factors with legislative performance or output have incorporated, either explicitly or implicitly, a model of the policy process that looks something like Figure 1.[2] This model, although highly simplified, is nevertheless reasonably appropriate considering the rather rudimentary development of the empirical basis for this research. The linkages shown in this model (a, b, c, and d) should serve to illuminate some of the possible explanations of policy outcomes as well as the possibility of a reciprocal effect of policy on inputs (feedback loop, d). This model also suggests that the relations between the environment and the system's output may be affected by specified characteristics of the political system. If route c is the main causal path, this indicates that the response of the system to a given

[1] Much of the literature in public administration was concerned with the effects of structural variation in administrative organizations on their performance. But it concentrated on efficiency to the exclusion of other aspects of performance. Furthermore, few of the studies in this field could lay claim to much scientific rigor, at least until recently. See Robert Golembiewski, *et al.*, *A Methodological Primer for Political Scientists* (Chicago: Rand McNally, 1969), 44–62.

[2] Adapted from Thomas Dye, *Politics, Economics, and the Public* (New York: Rand McNally, 1966), 4.

FIGURE 1

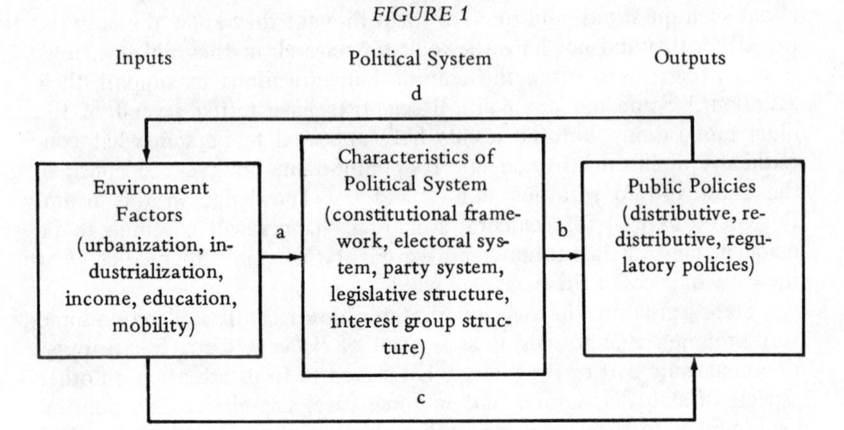

environmental stimulus is uniform across political systems with varying structural characteristics, or, alternatively, that environment variations produce variations in output that are independent of structural characteristics of the system. On the other hand, a route following paths a and b signifies that the response of the political system varies according to variations in the particular structural characteristics of the system under examination and that these characteristics are determined to a degree by some aspect of the environment. In such a case, the environmental factors being analyzed do not directly provide the stimulus for the output response but alter the response mechanism in such a way as to affect the output.

A mixed condition would exist if paths a, b, and c were all involved roughly to the same extent. This would indicate that the particular environmental influence was generating inputs tending to bring about a pattern of responses or outputs of a particular nature and direction, and that the manner in which the system responded to these was determined by a set of structural characteristics which themselves were affected by the same environmental influence. Interestingly, in this situation the joint effect of the structural and direct environmental influences may be either reinforcing or counteracting. If the relationships – which can be measured by regression or path coefficients – are all positive, then the joint effect is additive or reinforcing. This will also be the case if the coefficients for paths a and b are of opposite polarity and that for c is negative, or if a and b are both negative and c is positive.[3] Under these circum-

[3] The rule is to multiply path a times path b; if the sign is the same as that of path c, the effect is reinforcing; if the sign is different, the effect is counteractive.

stances the process is one in which the environmental factors produce pressures and demands for a particular output, and at the same time, help to create the structural conditions which facilitate the production of the designated output. A hypothetical example might involve urbanization as the environmental factor and the system of apportionment of legislative districts as the structural factor. A high degree of urbanization in a state might generate demands for increased state financial aid to large cities, and it might also create pressures that would lead to a more equitable apportionment of the state legislature, which, in turn, might make it easier to pass the desired legislation.

The joint effect of the upper and lower routes in figure 1 would be counteractive when all paths are negative, when a and b are of opposing polarities and c positive, or where a and b are both positive and c negative. In such instances, the net direct effect of environment would be partially or wholly counteracted by the tendency toward the maintenance of structural conditions that would be relatively inhibitory to the production of outputs commensurate with the environmental influences. This situation might prevail, for example, where increases in the relative size and deprivation of racial minorities had the net effect of enlarging pressures and demands for higher welfare and poverty expenditures and providing the incentive for distorting the representational system through gerrymandering or other means. If this distortion made it more difficult for the system to respond to these pressures and demands, the joint effect would be counteractive.

With these considerations in mind, it should be possible to determine under what conditions structural characteristics serve to reinforce or counteract the direct effects of inputs emanating from the environment. Where we can identify a causal connection between a set of environmental conditions and a set of policy outputs, and at the same time demonstrate a connection between these two and a structural variable, it should thus be possible to determine whether and in what way the structural variation affects the ability of the system to respond to demands. Carrying this one step further, we should also be able to assess structural characteristics in terms of their ability to enhance or diminish the responsiveness of the system, if such responsiveness is defined as the capability of responding in the same manner in which the average or typical unit responds under the same environmental conditions.

The best strategy for investigating these possibilities calls for first identifying the conditions under which structure has an impact on output, and then examining the interrelationships between these factors and the environment. We will take cognizance of three categories of structural variation: the system of apportionment, the professionalization of the legislature, and some general representational factors. Aggregate data from the American states provide the empirical foundation for the analyses.

Apportionment

Studies that have sought to determine the effects of apportionment on legislative performance or output have generally yielded negative or inconclusive results. Without much evidence to support the notion, it was often assumed that important substantive differences on public policy existed between urban and rural constituencies and that there would consequently be considerable differences between the outputs of the malapportioned legislatures, which were generally dominated by rural interests, and the well-apportioned legislatures, where urban interests had more influence. But my own findings and the findings of Herbert Jacob, Richard Hofferbert, David Brady and Douglas Edmonds, David Derge, and Thomas Flinn raise some doubts that variations in malapportionment account for any significant variations in policy.

Jacob studied the effects of malapportionment on party competition, highway funds distribution, and some welfare expenditures, and found that there were no important differences for these three factors between states with malapportioned legislatures and those with well-apportioned ones.[4] Hofferbert hypothesized that the amount of state aid received by large cities would be sensitive to the degree of malapportionment of state legislatures. But his data yielded a rank-order correlation coefficient of only .22 between these two variables, and he concluded that this did not indicate a significant relation. In addition, he correlated his apportionment ranking with a "welfare orientation" ranking, producing a coefficient of only .03, which caused him to reject the hypothesis that the greater the "imbalance in the state's apportionment, the less likely the legislature is to pass 'liberal' or welfare-orientated policies beneficial to urban groups."[5]

Brady and Edmonds examined four policy areas in relation to two indexes of malapportionment. The areas were Kerr-Mills plan adoptions, right to work laws, state liquor monopolies, and state income tax programs. They found no significant relationships with one of the malap-

[4] Herbert Jacob, "The Consequences of Malapportionments: A Note of Caution," *Social Forces,* XLIII (December, 1964), 256–261.

[5] Hofferbert's "welfare orientation" index is a combination of mean per-recipient expenditures for aid to the blind, old age assistance, unemployment compensation, aid to dependent children, and expenditures for elementary and secondary education. Averages for the bienniums in the period 1952–1961 were used. Richard Hofferbert, "The Relation Between Public Policy and Some Structural and Environmental Variables in the American States," *American Political Science Review,* LX (March, 1966), 74, 75.

portionment measures, the Schubert-Press Index, but did find a significant association between the other measure, the David-Eisenberg Index, and Kerr-Mills adoptions and right to work laws. Nevertheless, they were not able to attribute to malapportionment any substantial influence over policy output. At least, they concluded, it "is not as significant a factor as has been posited." [6]

Derge's findings support these others, although he used roll-call data rather than aggregate cross-sectional data. In his examination of over 19,000 roll-call votes in Missouri and Illinois over a ten-year period, he concluded that, at the voting stage, there was no evidence of rural-urban antagonism.[7] Flinn's study of urban-rural factionalism in Ohio produced results that coincided with Derge's.[8] My analysis of approximately 1,600 roll-call votes in two sessions of the Kansas legislature revealed only two bills on which there was a significant division between legislators from rural constituencies and those from urban districts.[9]

A rather rigorous analysis of the independent effects of malapportionment on policy output has been conducted by Thomas Dye. He examined five policy areas as measured by fifty-four indicator variables and correlated these data with three separate indexes of malapportionment.[10] Although he found significant correlations between some of the

[6] David Brady and Douglas Edmonds, *The Effects of Malapportionment on Public Output in the American States* (Iowa City: Laboratory for Political Research, 1966).

[7] David Derge, "Metropolitan and Outstate Alignments in Illinois and Missouri Legislative Delegations," *American Political Science Review*, LII (December, 1958), 1065.

[8] Thomas A. Flinn, "The Outline of Ohio Politics," *Western Political Quarterly*, XIII (September, 1960), 702–721.

[9] John G. Grumm, "The Means of Measuring Conflict and Cohesion in the Legislature," *Southwestern Social Science Quarterly*, XLIV (March, 1964), 377–388.

[10] The three apportionment measures used by Dye in *Politics, Economics, and the Public* were 1) an "index of representativeness," which was devised by Manning Dauer and Robert Kelsay ("Unrepresentative States," *National Municipal Review*, XLIV [1955], 551–575) and was based on the theoretical minimum percentage of a state's population that can elect a majority in each house; 2) an "index of urban representation" devised by Paul David and Ralph Eisenberg (*Devaluation of the Urban and Suburban Vote* [Charlottesville: Bureau of Public Administration, University of Virginia, 1961]) based on the value of a vote cast in the individual districts as represented by the ratio of each constituency to the average constituency in the state; and 3) an "apportionment score" based on a measure proposed by Glendon Schubert and Charles Press ("Measuring Malapportionment," *American Political Science Review*, LVII [June, 1964], 968–970) which combines inverted coefficients of variation for each state with statistical measures of skewness and kurtosis in the distribution of the districts by size of populations.

policy variables and some of the indexes of malapportionment, when he held a variable which he called "economic development" constant, most of these vanished.[11] Consequently, he concluded that the correlations between policy and malapportionment were spurious and a result of the joint effect of economic development and both factors. If we were to put this in terms of our model (figure 1), we would designate route c as the major causal path and conclude that this particular structural characteristic had little or no independent effects on legislative policy outcomes and therefore could not be related to the responsiveness characteristics of the legislation.

A demurrer needs to be entered at this point, however, because there is not a perfect correspondence between Dye's conclusions and his findings. There are, for example, significant partial correlations between one of his apportionment measures, the "index of urban representation," and two of his education policy variables, percentage of total school revenue from the state (−.43) and pupil-teacher ratio (−.41). Since both of these are negative and are partial coefficients, we can conclude that, regardless of the level of the state's economic development, the better apportioned legislatures tend to emit policy outputs that result in lower pupil-teacher ratios in the schools and a lower degree of state financial participation in the public schools.

Although Dye proposes a model similar to that shown in figure 1, he neglects to follow through with it. Had he incorporated his findings into such a scheme we might have the necessary conditions for assessing the responsiveness capabilities of this particular set of system conditions. Figure 2 represents an attempt to reconcile his findings with his model.

Unfortunately, Dye does not provide us with all of the necessary coefficients, although there is enough data to tell us that the "c" coefficients are moderately high and negative, and the "a" coefficient is fairly small and positive. We can still, however, make a tentative interpretation from the data. It appears that economic development "causes" more equitable urban representation, probably because it is associated with greater urbanization, which produces more urban representatives and eventually ends the rural domination of the legislature and causes the enactment of reapportionment legislation, further increasing urban representation. Economic development also results in a smaller pupil-teacher ratio as it creates the conditions whereby more public funds can be fed

[11] Dye used four measures of economic development: industrialization (one minus the percentage of the work force engaged in agriculture), urbanization (percentage of the population living in incorporated places of 25,000 or more or in urban fringes of cities of 50,000 or more), median family income, and median school years completed. *Politics, Economics, and the Public,* 28–34.

FIGURE 2

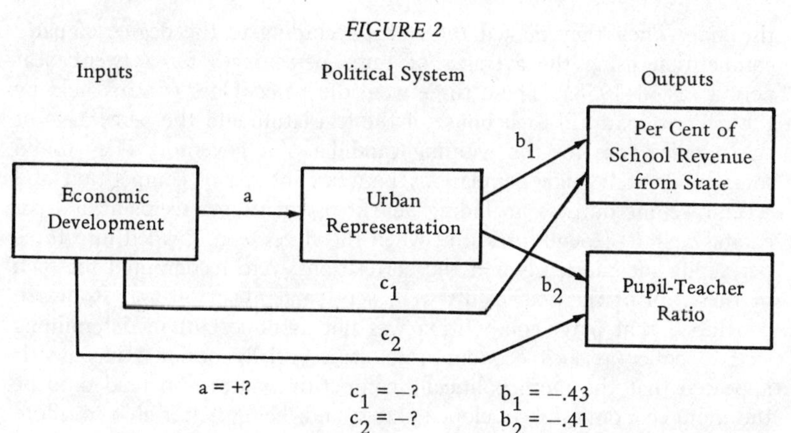

into the schools. But development seems to bring a larger increase in local contributions to public schools than in the state's contribution; thus, it results in a decrease in the percentage of state participation. It appears that the polarities of the relationships are such that the indirect effects of economic development operating through urban representation serve to reinforce the direct effects. We might say, then, that the operation of the structural variable urban representation is to enhance the responsiveness characteristics of the system. But even if we cannot go quite this far (and we cannot if the "a" coefficient in the above diagram is not significant and positive), at least the moderately high partial coefficients between the apportionment index and the two outputs tell us that the structural variable is a significant factor in determining educational policy.

Other Aspects of Representativeness

The system of apportionment is one element involved in the "representativeness" of the political system. Other elements include the party system, particularly the degree of party competition, and the electoral system. Several studies, taking policy output as the dependent variable, have analyzed the hypothetical effects of party competition as an independent variable. One of the first of these was that of Dawson and Robinson.[12] They were concerned only with welfare policy, which they measured by means of nine variables that included four revenue items and five expenditure items. They ranked the states according to each of

[12] Richard Dawson and James Robinson, "Inter-Party Competition, Economic Variables, and Welfare Policies in American States," *Journal of Politics*, XXV (May, 1963), 265–289.

the nine. Then they ranked the states according to the degree of party competition using the averages of three percentages for a twenty-year period (1938–1958). These three were the percentages of seats held by the majority party in each house of the legislature and the percentage of the popular vote for the winning candidate for governor. They found some moderately high correlations between interparty competition and several welfare outputs, including benefit payments per recipient and per capital welfare expenditures. But when the states were divided into three per capita income levels and the correlations were recomputed for each of these, all of the coefficients were very small. Dawson and Robinson concluded that party competition was not as important in determining welfare policy as socio-economic factors, especially personal income. It appeared that the more politically competitive states also tended to be the more economically developed states; and, being better able to afford it, they tended to be more liberal in their welfare allotments.

A cross-national study by Phillips Cutright provides some seemingly contradictory evidence to Dawson's and Robinson's study.[13] He constructed an index to measure the degree of social security coverage of a nation's population and related this to an index of "political representativeness." The latter was purportedly a measure of the amount of accessibility that the people have to the ruling elite in the parliament and executive bureaucracy. As in the Dawson-Robinson study, economic development (as measured by energy consumption, urbanization, and literacy) was held constant, in this case by analyzing the relationship between representativeness and the level of social security coverage at five different levels of development. Cutright found that, even with economic development controlled, the more representative governments generally introduced programs earlier than the less representative ones. Within the lowest levels of development, however, there was little relationship between representativeness and the social security index, presumably because these nations did not have the resources for such social programs; thus, regardless of how potentially responsive their governments might be, there was realistically little possibility of responding to demand for welfare legislation. At the highest levels of development, on the other hand, the social security index was quite closely and positively related to political representativeness.

Can we reconcile Cutright's results with those of Dawson and Robinson? Of course, one should not expect very close correspondence since different indicators of social security were used, and Cutright's

[13] Phillips Cutright, "Political Structure, Economic Development, and National Social Security Programs," *American Journal of Politics*, LXX (1965), 537–550.

representativeness index was composed not only of inter-party competition measures but measures relating to the electoral system and other aspects of the party system. Furthermore, his analysis was conducted across nations instead of states in a federal system that imposes a certain degree of uniformity on state welfare policies. Nevertheless, a reconciliation would still seem possible. While Dawson and Robinson divided the states into three groups to partial out the effects of economic development, as measured by per capita income in their case, Cutright divided his nations into five groups. Roughly speaking, the Dawson-Robinson middle and lowest groups correspond in terms of averages to about the highest and second highest Cutright groups. In both studies these groups showed some correlation between welfare policy and party competition in the one case and representativeness in the other. In Cutright's lowest economic groups and in Dawson's and Robinson's highest, there was virtually no correlation.

In an attempt to approach a higher degree of comparability between the two studies, I reanalyzed the state data on party competition and welfare policies by following Cutright in employing a single index of welfare orientation and using Dawson's and Robinson's three economic groupings. The index of welfare orientation constructed by Hofferbert for his study of the relationship between welfare policy and apportionment was used rather than Cutright's own index which was somewhat inappropriate for American states.[14] I also used Hofferbert's index of inter-party competition instead of Dawson's and Robinson's, since his was based on the votes for a larger number of offices and appeared to gauge better the underlying political competition within the electorate. My analysis showed a moderately high rank-order correlation between welfare policy and party competition (.68) for the states with the lowest per capita incomes and only a slightly smaller coefficient (.59) for the middle group of states. For the group with the highest incomes the correlation was quite small (.15).

It is really not feasible to insert these findings into our diagrammatic model of the political system because economic development is measured in terms of ordinal categories rather than on an interval scale, and we cannot very well assign coefficients to the paths connecting it to other variables or compute any partial coefficients where it is to be held constant. But, we can infer that there are causal connections going from economic development to the representativeness factor and to welfare policy, that there is also a connection between the latter two, and that the polarity of all these connections is positive. So, even though all of

[14] Hofferbert, "The Relation Between Public Policy and Some Structural and Environmental Variables," 75.

this cannot be represented diagrammatically very well, we can see that we have the requisite conditions for a reinforcing system.

The relationships here are more complex than those involved with apportionment. It appears that the level of economic development of a nation or a state in the federal system has a substantial position influence on the "representativeness" of the political institutions in the former and, at least, on the level of political competition in the latter. Economic development also creates the conditions under which "liberal" or extensive welfare programs are made possible. In the very poor nations of the world – and presumably no American state would fall in this group – these conditions have not reached the threshold level where any sort of social security program can be adequately financed. Thus, regardless of how responsive the nation's political institutions may be themselves, little is done to relieve the pressures for welfare legislation since the financial resources for it do not exist. Among the richest American states, the reverse conditions exist. Their fiscal resources are so abundant that liberal welfare programs can be adopted without much relative strain on the state budget. With the encouragement and financial participation of the federal government, even the most unresponsive of these states' governments will generally not fail to legislate relatively generous provisions in their welfare laws. This explains the lack of correlation between welfare policy and representativeness in the poorest nations and the richest states.

The middle group, on the other hand – that is, the wealthiest two-fifths of the nations and the remaining two-thirds of the American states – generally find themselves in a financial condition that will permit them to support social security programs of moderate magnitudes, but such programs will not be forthcoming or very generous where the legislature and executive are not responsive to popular demands. Where the public has poor access to the legislative and executive elite, the latter will hold out longer before instituting welfare programs and will be more parsimonious with the provisions of these programs. Presumably access is better and responsiveness is probably greater where there is a high degree of competition in the party system. One-party states and one-party nations, on the whole, respond less readily to the welfare demands of their publics. Therefore, we can conclude that, within a limited range of economic development, the system conditions described tend toward reinforcement, and the structural variables involved play a significant role in the responsiveness sensitivity of the system.

Legislative Professionalism

The institutional factors mentioned above are only partially within the control of the legislature (apportionment) or not directly within its control at all (party competition). The legislature itself, however, has comparatively direct control over its supporting services and the expenditures made in the operation of the legislative branch, including salaries of members. Some legislatures may be characterized as highly professional. By this I mean that their members and their committees are well staffed; good informational services are available to them; a variety of services and aids, such as bill drafting and statutory revision, are maintained and well supported; the legislators themselves are well paid, tend to think of their legislative jobs as full time or close to it, and regard their legislative role as a professional one. Other legislatures are poorly staffed, with little or nothing in the way of legislative services, and the members are poorly paid and regard their legislative work as encompassing a very insignificant part of their lives. It happens that most of these factors go together in syndromes of professionalism or amateurism. This dimension varies widely among state legislatures in the United States, but the long-term trend is generally toward the professional end of the continuum.

One might hypothesize that the legislatures that fell close to the professional end of the continuum – where the members devoted a great deal of their time to their legislative jobs, where they had good access to a wide variety of informational sources and were better able to gauge popular demands – would be more responsive to at least some kinds of demands than would legislatures that fell at the opposite end of the continuum. I have tested such a proposition.

In order to be as comprehensive as possible, I put into the analysis as many measures of environmental influence and policy outputs as were available and appeared relevant. The problem of handling all of these measures in an orderly or systematic manner was solved through the use of factor analysis. This technique provides a relatively objective means of establishing categories among a vast array of data, of selecting measures relating to these categories, and of combining or weighting these measures into a single index for each class. A basic proposition of factor analysis is that the relationships between a complex system of variables can be represented simply and economically by a small number of factors. Factors common to a number of variables can be thought of as either causing the relationships between the variables or as embodying the concept that represents these inter-relations.[15] Here, factor analysis is used

[15] Those interested in a basic understanding of this technique should see Benjamin Fruchter, *Introduction to Factor Analysis* (Princeton: D. Van Nostrand Co., 1954); or for a more thorough understanding see H. H. Harmon, *Modern Factor Analysis*, 2d ed. (Chicago: University of Chicago Press, 1967). The technique employed here is the "Alpha" method, the most distinguishing feature of which is the use of communality estimates

in the latter sense. Thus, a large number of measures of legislative output, environmental influence, or professionalism can be combined and reduced to a small number of factors.

When factor analysis is used in this manner – that is, as a method of index construction – the factors can be considered as composite indexes measuring the various dimensions of the domain being investigated. The factor loadings therefore provide the system of weights by which the relevant variables are combined in the construction of each index. The factor scores computed from these loadings provide an index score for each of the states or its legislature on each of the dimensions.[16]

Policy Output Factors

Thirty-one quantitative measures of policy output for the fifty states were factor analyzed into five factors. These can most readily be identified by the variables that are highly loaded on them, as shown in Table 1.

Factor I is labeled the welfare liberalism factor. Almost all of the measures that were highly related to this dimension concerned welfare policy although several variables connected with educational policy were also involved, which suggests that the two are closely connected. Table 2, which presents the state scores for the output factors, shows that the more affluent states of the North had the highest degrees of welfare liberalism, while the poorer states, primarily in the South, were usually quite conservative in this respect.

Factor II represents the magnitude of the state government's operations adjusted for the size of its population. The label government size may be somewhat misleading unless it is kept in mind that the variables loaded on this factor are essentially expressed in per capita amounts. The states that scored highest here were by no means the largest or the ones that had the greatest total expenditures. The ones with the highest scores appeared rather to be the smaller states that were probably unable to realize the "economies of scale" enjoyed by the larger states.

Factor III is related to revenue collection and distribution. It is labeled financial centralization because most of the variables loaded on it are measures of the relative magnitude of the state tax bite and of the

---

based on coefficients of multiple determination of each variable with every other variable. The original factor loadings are rotated orthogonally according to the "varimax" criteria. The sets of environmental and output factors selected for rotation each accounted for about two-thirds of the variance in the original correlation matrix of variables. The single factor used for the professionalism index accounted for 57 per cent of the original variance.

[16] See Henry F. Kaiser, "Formulas for Component Scores," *Psychometrika,* XXVII (March, 1962), 83–87.

TABLE 1. *Output Factor Loadings (Variables with Loadings > +.500 and < –.500)*

Variables	Factor Loadings
Factor I—Welfare Liberalism	
Old age assistance, ave. monthly payment per recipient (Dec., 1964)	.852
Aid to dependent children, ave. monthly payment per recipient (Dec., 1964)	.819
Aid to the blind, ave. monthly payment per recipient (Dec., 1964)	.785
Unemployment compensation, ave. weekly payment per recipient (1963)	.727
Average teachers' salaries (1964)	.695
Expenditures on police protection per capita (1963)	.661
Public school expenditures per capita (1963)	.642
Aid to permanently and totally disabled, ave. monthly payment per recipient (Dec., 1964)	.571
Average weekly earnings of full-time state employees (1964)	.565
Factor II—Governmental Size	
State expenditures for higher education per capita (1964)	.895
Total state expenditures per $1,000 personal income (1964)	.835
Full-time state government employees per 10,000 population (1964)	.754
General revenue of state government per capita (1964)	.677
Total state expenditures per capita (1964)	.646
Average weekly earnings of full-time state employees (1964)	.554
Public school expenditures per capita (1963)	.551
Factor III—Financial Centralization	
State taxes per $1,000 personal income	.833
Per cent of state and local revenue coming from the state (1963)	.772
Per cent of local school revenue from the state (1964-1965)	.713
State intergovernmental expenditures per capita (1964)	.697
General sales and gross receipts tax per $1,000 personal income (1964)	.649
Factor IV—Progressive Taxation	
Individual income tax as a per cent of total state taxes (1964)	.657
Individual income tax collections per $1,000 personal income (1964)	.650
Individual income tax rate range (highest rate minus lowest) (1964)	.618
Sales and gross receipt tax as a per cent of total state taxes (1964)	.583
Factor V—Governmental Expansion	
Expenditures for police protection per capita (1963)	.614
Increase in general expenditures per capita (1953-1963)	.604
State debt outstanding per capita (1963)	.549
Average teachers' salaries (1964)	.518
Public school expenditure per $1,000 personal income (1963)	–.506

TABLE 2. *Factor Scores for Five Output Factors (States with Scores > + 1.000 and < – 1.000)*

Factor I		Factor II		Factor III		Factor IV		Factor V	
Calif.	2.563	Alas.	4.304	N.M.	2.036	Del.	3.102	Nev.	2.298
Wisc.	1.894	Utah	1.740	Wisc.	1.944	Mass.	1.866	Del.	2.203
Mass.	1.773	R.I.	1.487	La.	1.637	Alas.	1.641	Alas.	1.022
N.Y.	1.671	N.M.	1.255	S.C.	1.525	N.D.	1.531	Conn.	1.816
Mich.	1.142	N.D.	1.162	N.C.	1.562	Ida.	1.245	Va.	1.282
Ill.	1.096	Colo.	1.066	Del.	1.453	W.V.	1.226	Fla.	1.230
Ind.	1.051			Miss.	1.301	Ore.	1.211	Mo.	1.185
Kan.	1.051			Wash.	1.264	N.C.	1.119	Ky.	1.161
N.J.	1.013			R.I.	1.197			R.I.	1.002
				Mich.	1.158				
Tex.	–1.073	S.C.	–1.093	S.D.	–1.147	Ind.	–1.085	Ala.	–1.017
Me.	–1.084	Md.	–1.148	Mont.	–1.273	Mich.	–1.218	Iowa	–1.106
Tenn.	–1.170	Ohio	–1.195	N.J.	–1.540	Tex.	–1.225	Mont.	–1.260
S.C.	–1.287	Pa.	–1.309	Va.	–1.593	Utah	–1.339	Ind.	–1.351
W.V.	–1.403	Mass.	–1.979	N.H.	–2.211	Ill.	–1.600	Okla.	–1.374
Ga.	–1.492			Nebr.	–2.758	Nev.	–1.940	Minn.	–1.463
Ark.	–1.613							S.D.	–1.667
Miss.	–1.798							N.D.	–1.719
Ky.	–1.887							Ark.	–1.745
Va.	–1.889							Kan.	–1.802

degree to which state-collected revenues predominate in the total state-local revenue system.

Factor IV is essentially a measure of the progressiveness of the state's tax structure. One of the highly loaded variables on this factor is the income tax-rate range, which is a reasonably direct measure of the progressiveness of this tax. Two other variables with high loadings on the factor are indicators of the degrees to which the state relies on the income tax as its major source of revenue. Since the income tax is the only important tax that tends to be progressive in its operation, this factor has been labeled the progressive taxation factor. The sales tax is also loaded on this factor, though not very highly, because states usually impose both taxes or neither.

Factor V is labeled governmental expansion although this was not very clearly delineated. The basis for this labeling was the loadings on the factor of two variables signifying expansion of the state budget, these two being "increase in general expenditures per capita (1953–1963)" and "state debt outstanding per capita (1963)." The factor might also have been called a police protection or public safety factor, since per capita expenditures for police protection had the highest loadings. For the purposes of the present analysis, however, it does not make a great deal of difference how this factor is labeled. Often in factor analysis one or two factors are difficult to identify simply and clearly.

Environmental Factors

On the input side of the legislative system forty-five environmental variables were factor analyzed with the result that four factors were extracted. As in the case of the five output factors, these four represented about two-thirds of the original variance. The variables with high loadings on these factors are shown in Table 3.

The first factor in Table 3 clearly relates to economic affluence, although the educational level of the population is inextricably involved in it. The variable with the highest loading (though negative) is "Per cent failures in draft board mental test." This is closely related to the level of education of the population, probably even more so than median number of school years completed. But, again, the label of the factor is not terribly important; it might be regarded as a combined economic and educational factor.

Table 4 shows the states with the highest scores on each of the environmental factors. What clearly stands out in regard to Factor I is its North-South orientation. States with the high positive scores are all from the northern part of the country. Those with the highest negative scores are all in the South with the exception of the border state of Kentucky.

Factor II clearly represents population expansion. In contrast to the first factor's North-South orientation, this one is aligned on an East-West basis. All of the states with high positive scores are in the West, with the exception of Florida, which is, after all, very similar demographically to a western state.

Factor III is the urbanization factor. The urban percentage of the population has the highest loading on this, and most of the other highly loaded variables are related to urbanism. This factor can be distinguished from Factor II in that the states with high scores on the latter have expanding populations and are probably becoming more urban as a result, but those with high scores on Factor III are already highly urbanized and have generally more stable populations.

Factor IV is another that presents some difficulties in defining. Since it includes a number of measures of the amounts of federal money entering the state, it was labeled the federal support factor.

TABLE 3. *Environmental Factor Loadings (Variables with Loadings* $> +.500$ *and* $< -.500$*)*

Variables	Factor Loadings
Factor I–Economic Affluence	
Retail sales per capita (1963)	.830
Median school years completed of persons over 25 (1960)	.782
Sound housing, per cent of total (1960)	.668
Increase in percentage of Negro population (1950-1963)	.655
Estimated market value of all property in state, per capita (1961)	.623
Foreign and mixed parentage as a per cent of total population (1960)	.616
Telephones per 1,000 population	.615
Income per capita	.586
College enrollment per 10,000 population (1964)	.531
Per cent failures in draft board mental test (1963)	–.943
Negro percentage of population (1960)	–.867
Increase in per capita income (1950-1960)	–.579
Population per lawyer (1963)	–.540
Factor II–Population Expansion	
Increase in urban percentage of population (1950-1960)	.761
Percentage population increase (1960-1963)	.743
Average value per farm (1959)	.722
Construction expenditures per capita (1963)	.716
Net migration, 1960-1963, as a percentage of 1960 population	.685
Increase in value added by agriculture (1950-1960)	.682
Increase in value added by manufacturing (1954-1963)	.677
Average acreage per farm (1959)	.640
Per cent of 1960 population residing in different county than in 1955	.637
Crime rate: offenses per 100,000 population (1965)	.573
Per cent of land in state owned by federal government (1963)	.522
Value added by manufacturing per capita (1963)	–.540
Factor III–Urbanization	
Urban percentage of population (1960)	.856
Physicians per 100,000 population (1962)	.740
Telephones per 1,000 population (1963)	.698
Federal income and employment tax collections per capita (1963)	.693
Income per capita (1963)	.665
Crime rate: offenses per 100,000 population (1965)	.664
Sound housing, per cent of total (1960)	.656
Value added by manufacturing, per capita (1963)	.639
Per cent of urban population in state's largest S.M.A. (1963)	.628
Total population of state (1963)	.596
Newspaper circulation per 1,000 population (1964)	.583
Median age (1960)	.521
Population per square mile (1963)	.502

TABLE 3. *Environmental Factor Loadings (Variables with Loadings* $> +.500$ *and* $< -.500$*) (Continued)*

Variables	Factor Loadings
Factor III—Urbanization (Continued)	
Workers who walked to work, per cent of total population (1960)	−.656
Per cent of state and local revenue from federal government (1963)	−.628
Per capita federal grants to state and local governments (1963)	−.507
Factor IV—Federal Support	
Increase in college enrollments (1950-1960)	.888
Total federal expenditures per capita (1963)	.857
Federal defense expenditures per capita (1963)	.793
Increase in expenditures for new plant and equipment (1954-1963)	.707
Per capita federal grants to state and local governments (1963)	.676
Per cent of 1960 population residing in different county than in 1955	.655
Per cent of land in state owned by federal government (1963)	.589
Per cent of state and local revenue from federal government (1963)	.504
Per cent increase in per capita federal grants to state and local government (1953-1960)	−.522
Per cent owner-occupancy of all housing (1960)	−.518

Professionalism Index

In constructing a "Professionalism Index" the first step was to define a small number of variables that were most obviously connected with this quality. Four were designated: (1) compensation of legislators;[17] (2) total length of sessions during the 1963–1964 biennium;[18] (3) expenditures for legislative services and operations during the same biennium;[19] and (4) a "legislative services" score. The latter was based on a study by

[17] This is the computed realized compensation of the average legislator in each of the states for the 1964–1965 biennium from data in the *Book of the States, 1966–1967* (Chicago: Council of State Governments, 1966), 43–49. Where pay was based wholly or partially on per diem amounts, these were multiplied by the number of days in session to produce total realized compensation.

[18] *Ibid.*, 62–63.

[19] These are the figures reported under "Expenditures on the Legislative Branch" in U.S. Bureau of Census, *Compendium of State Government Finance in 1964* (Washington, D.C.: Government Printing Office, 1964), less the total amount paid for legislative compensation. They include, therefore, all expenditures for the operation and maintenance of the legislature and its facilities and services, but do not include pay to legislators.

TABLE 4. *State Factor Scores for Four Environmental Factors (States with Scores $> +1.000$ and < -1.000)*

Factor I		Factor II		Factor III		Factor IV	
Iowa	1.676	Nev.	3.558	N.Y.	2.477	Alas.	6.061
Wyo.	1.494	Ariz.	2.986	Conn.	2.455	Haw.	1.714
Wash.	1.326	Fla.	2.129	Calif.	1.851	Ky.	1.572
Mont.	1.201	Colo.	1.586	Mass.	1.795	Conn.	1.370
Wisc.	1.123	Calif.	1.631	Ind.	1.744	Wyo.	1.234
N.D.	1.111	N.M.	1.609	R.I.	1.402	R.I.	1.100
Ill.	1.090			N.J.	1.253	Ind.	1.004
Minn.	1.059			Fla.	1.183		
				Pa.	1.142		
				Ky.	1.092		
				Nev.	1.007		
N.C.	−1.017	Pa.	−1.063	Miss.	−1.027	Minn.	−1.091
Ala.	−1.548	N.H.	−1.065	N.H.	−1.028	N.J.	−1.091
Va.	−1.577	Wisc.	−1.077	N.C.	−1.066	Iowa	−1.114
Ky.	−1.624	Conn.	−1.084	Me.	−1.085	Ill.	−1.120
La.	−1.655	Me.	−1.094	Mont.	−1.243	Tenn.	−1.277
Ga.	−1.809	Mass.	−1.231	Nebr.	−1.251	Okla.	−1.407
Miss.	−2.227			Alas.	−1.261	Nebr.	−1.464
Ark.	−2.293			Minn.	−1.417	Ala.	−1.578
S.C.	−2.941			Ida.	−1.424	W.V.	−1.848
				Wyo.	−1.716		
				Okla.	−1.944		
				N.D.	−1.970		
				W.V.	−2.013		

the Citizens Conference on State Legislatures of the legislative services provided by each of the fifty states.[20] The score was constructed by means of a "point system" by which state legislatures were graded according to such considerations as the extent of the services actually provided, the size of the staff involved, and the degree to which the services were used by the legislators.

The next step was to examine other variables relating to the legislative process and select those that were correlated with the other four. Twelve were scrutinized, but only one, the number of bills introduced in both houses during the biennium,[21] was deemed to have a sufficiently

[20] Calvin W. Clark, *A Survey of Legislative Services in the Fifty States* (Kansas City, Mo.: Citizens Conference on State Legislatures, 1967).
[21] *Book of States, 1966–1967*, 62–63.

high average correlation with the four original variables to be considered as an additional measure of this dimension. The five variables, then, were factor analyzed and the unrotated first factor loadings were used to compute factors scores for each of the states. These scores constituted the professionalism index. This unrotated first factor can be regarded as essentially representing the common denominator of all the variables. The index for each of the states is listed in Table 5 in the order of the most professional to the least. The factor loadings for the five variables were as follows:

1. Biennial compensation of legislators (1964–1966)	.814
2. Expenditures for legislative staff, services, operations, and printing (1963–1964)	.787
3. Number of bills introduced in 1963–1964 sessions	.787
4. Length of regular plus extra sessions, in calendar days (1963–1964)	.730
5. Legislative services score	.661

TABLE 5. *Professionalism Index*

Calif.	2.294	Ariz.	–.100
Mass.	2.185	Okla.	–.101
N. Y.	2.145	Nebr.	–.107
Pa.	1.715	Me.	–.114
Mich.	1.538	Miss.	–.122
N. J.	1.455	Ind.	–.150
Ill.	1.043	Colo.	–.173
Haw.	1.010	Alas.	–.188
Wisc.	.837	Ky.	–.218
Tex.	.795	Kansas	–.260
Ohio	.599	W. V.	–.366
Ore.	.396	Iowa	–.382
S. C.	.325	Va.	–.613
Dela.	.317	Nev.	–.697
Fla.	.279	Ark.	–.765
La.	.273	S. D.	–.821
Ga.	.248	N. M.	–1.006
Conn.	.226	Tenn.	–1.190
Md.	.219	Vt.	–1.203
Minn.	.203	N. H.	–1.357
Mo.	.202	N. D.	–1.364
Wash.	.142	Utah	–1.366
Ala.	.104	Ida.	–1.545
R. I.	–.065	Mont.	–1.827
N. C.	–.096	Wyo.	–2.355

TABLE 6. *Correlation Matrix: Environmental Factors, Professionalism Index, and Output Factors*

	Economic Affluence.	Population Expansion	Urbanization	Federal Support	Prof. Index
Prof. Index	–.090	–.159	.650	.003	——
Welfare-Liberalism	.630	–.016	.402	.048	.431
Gov'tal. Size	.293	.268	–.342	.514	–.369
Financial Central	–.260	.224	.098	.040	.206
Progressive Tax	.066	–.395	–.123	.175	.031
Gov'tal. Expansion	–.026	.026	.509	.422	.311

Causal Relationships

Table 6 presents the intercorrelations of the factor scores for the environmental factors with the output factors and each of these with the professional index. It appears from this that there may be some connection between professionalism and the first two outputs and possibly also the fifth. But it is also apparent that there are some interconnections between the professionalism index and the third environmental factor, and between the latter and these three outputs. To sort out the significant relationships among the many possible combinations, the techniques of causal modeling as developed by Simon and Blalock [22] were employed, and beta coefficients were computed for all of the significant connections. The results of this process are to be seen in figures 3 and 4. The numbers above each of the paths are the betas and indicate the relative strength of the paths. Only those that are significant at $P \leq .01$ are shown. There is no figure to represent the forces acting on the third output factor, financial centralization, since neither the professionalism index nor any of the environmental factors were significantly related to it. Coefficients of multiple determination with the output factor as the dependent variable are shown next to the corresponding output.

The relationships depicted in Figure 3 were extracted from the rest as these represented the only ones in which the structural variable was involved. This figure shows that legislative professionalism has an independent effect on legislative output, in this case on welfare policy. The effect is positive, which means that the more professional the legislature, the more liberal the policy. Professionalism itself is strongly affected by

[22] See Herbert A. Simon, *Models of Man* (New York: John Wiley and Sons, 1957), chaps. I–III; and Hubert M. Blalock, Jr., *Causal Inference in Non-experimental Research* (Chapel Hill: University of North Carolina Press, 1964), chaps. I–III.

urbanization – about 45 per cent of the variation in professionalism can be accounted for by urbanization. But the influence of urbanization on this policy output is not direct and is only made effective through legislative professionalism. This is to say that any ultimate effect that urbanization may have on welfare liberalism is due essentially to the impact of urbanization on legislative professionalism, which sequentially has the more direct effect on welfare policies.

Since the relationships in figure 3 do not exactly meet the criteria for our model of a reinforcing or counteracting system, we must hesitate to draw any conclusions about the effects of legislative professionalism on system responsiveness. What is missing in this respect is a c path between urbanization and output or an a path between economic affluence and legislative professionalism. It is possible, however, that we should not have rejected the c path. Even though legislative professionalism accounts for almost all of the correlation between urbanization and welfare liberalism, the partial correlation between these two (.20) is almost significant at the .01 level, and it is positive. It also seems reasonable that great pressures and demands would be built up in the more urbanized states for liberalization of welfare policies. So, on the basis of some rather weak statistical evidence and an intuitive feeling that urbanization leads to demands for welfare liberalization, we might tentatively conclude that this is an example of a reinforcing system and that this structural variable, legislative professionalism, works toward greater system responsiveness as herein defined.

Two observations might be made about the role of economic affluence. First, its effect on policy does not result from the creation of demands for more liberal welfare legislation. In fact, we would expect that these demands would be the greatest in the poorest states, although the most affluent have the most liberal policies. Rather, affluence provides the conditions under which demands resulting from other factors (i.e.,

FIGURE 3. Determinants of Welfare Liberalism

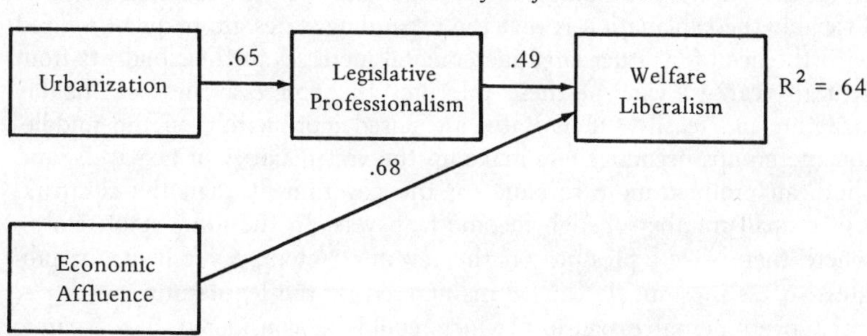

urbanization) can be met. Second, the indications from figure 3 are that economic affluence has no effect at all on legislative professionalism. Apparently a state does not have to be rich in order to provide adequate support for its legislature.

Because of their substantive imports, several observations ought to be made also regarding the relationship between environmental factors and outputs in Figure 4. Governmental size is dependent on four of the five environmental factors and is largely determined by these. Although there is a moderately high simple correlation between professionalism and this policy output, it turns out to be entirely spurious, primarily due to the effect of urbanization on both of these. The relationship between urbanization and governmental size is negative, which indicates that the most urbanized states tend to have smaller governmental operations in relation to their total population than the least urbanized ones. Undoubtedly, this is because the highly urbanized states are also the largest ones, and they apparently find it possible to enjoy some of the economics of size. Regardless of the size of the state, there are certain minimum requirements in the way of governmental structure, facilities, and services that must be provided; thus the less urbanized states find they must spend more money, on a per capita basis, than the big states. Evidence that economic affluence is an important environmental factor contributing to governmental size certainly confirms to expectations. Population expansion is related to this output factor because of the necessity to spend extraordinary amounts of money on capital construction in those states with rapidly growing populations. Federal support is related to the size of the state government operations probably because of the need for the state to match federal money in many of the federally initiated programs, and because of increased state overhead costs resulting from federal projects and installations located within the state.

Figure 4 indicates that population expansion is the only environmental factor having any influence on the progressiveness of a state's system of taxation. The negative coefficient means that rapidly expanding states tend to have less progressive tax policies than the more stable ones. Probably the explanation is that the expanding states are frequently faced with the need for rather large incremental increases in their budgets from year to year. In view of these pressures the progressiveness of the tax structure may easily suffer. Rates are raised inordinately on the middle-income groups because these make up the vast majority of taxpayers, and they can produce more revenue for the government than the comparatively small number of high income taxpayers. In the more stable states, where there is less pressure on the revenue system, a modicum of progressiveness presumably can be maintained by the legislature.

Governmental expansion, which could be considered the dynamic

FIGURE 4. Environmental Determinants of Three Policy Factors

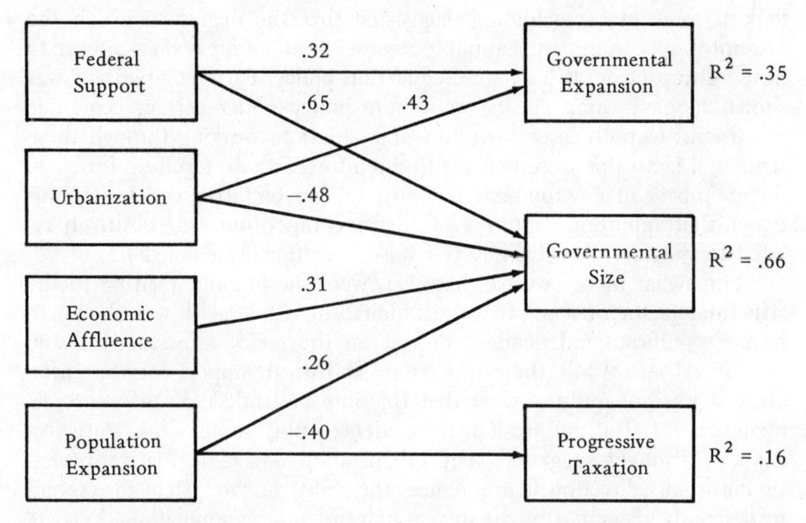

counterpart of governmental size, is moderately related to urbanization and weakly related to federal support. It appears that the highly urbanized states are expanding their general governmental outlays at a more rapid rate than the less urbanized. Welfare payments are, of course, part of this general expansion, but educational, public safety, health, highway, and correctional expenditures must also be involved. It is not clear why population expansion is not related to governmental expansion but probably whatever relationship existed was factored out by some of the statistical manipulations. This environmental factor is most closely related to *percentage* increase in population, and states which scored high on this often tended to be small states, which probably had small absolute gains in population but high percentage gains. The small states also had high per capita costs; thus they start from a high base and the percentage increase in their cost might not generally match their population increase.

Conclusions

The major question with which this study has been concerned is the effects of legislative structure on legislative performance. It was first necessary to determine if there were any effects at all and, then, if there were, to define how these contributed to or subtracted from the responsiveness characteristics of the system.

In the review of recent studies on the effects of reapportionment and other aspects of representation on policy output, it was seen that some of the original negative findings should probably be reconsidered. A closer look at some of these findings suggested that the degree to which the system of apportionment equitably represents urban areas does appear to have an impact on at least state education policy. Party competition was shown to have some effects on welfare policy under certain economic conditions. In both cases environmental variations working through these structural factors produced effects that reinforced those resulting from the direct impact of environment on output. The tentative conclusion was drawn that apportionment and inter-party competition were positively related to system responsiveness as I have operationally defined it.

Somewhat more positive, however, were the findings relating to the structural factor of legislative professionalism. At least it was shown to have a significant independent impact on the policy dimension of welfare liberalism. While there was strong statistical support for this inference, it was not quite so clear that this impact tended toward reinforcement or not. But impressionistic evidence, plus some weak statistical support, strongly suggested that urbanization affects legislative professionalism in a direction that enhances the ability of the system to respond to demands generated by an increasingly urbanized population. We are not warranted in going much beyond this, however. Surely we would not want to draw any conclusion about the general responsiveness of the system and its relation to professionalism in the legislature on the basis of these findings.

A more generalized conception of responsiveness would, indeed, be difficult to define and operationalize. There are quite a number of separate dimensions to it. Consider, for example, such matters as the rate of responses, the form and direction of responses, their timing, their adequacy in meeting demands, and the kinds of demands toward which they are directed. What does it mean therefore, to say that one legislature is more or less responsive than another? We cannot really say. So this study has attempted to look only at a rather narrowly defined aspect of responsiveness and to relate it to structural variables and a rather small range of policy outputs. We might expect that the non-financial policy outputs would show a greater dependence on structure than financial ones. But the former are very difficult to measure, and almost all studies, including the present one, have used financial indicators. Hopefully, some indicators of non-financial output will soon be developed so that we can extend our analyses into this realm.

Despite these limitations, we can conclude that structure does affect legislative performance in several specific ways, and that we have made a beginning, though only a small one, in defining the many complexities of the interrelationships involved.

AGENCY REQUESTS, GUBERNATORIAL SUPPORT AND BUDGET SUCCESS IN STATE LEGISLATURES

IRA SHARKANSKY

This is a study of the budget success of state administrative agencies. Although a number of recent studies provide valuable information about environmental influences on state and local government expenditures, relatively little is known about the factors that affect the budgets of individual administrative units.[1] Existing studies typically focus on the state as the unit of analysis, and report findings about the correlates of state (or state plus local) government expenditures in total and by the major fields of education, highways, public welfare, health, hospitals *et al.* The United States Bureau of the Census provides an invaluable service for this scholarship by collecting state and local government data and ordering it into categories that permit state-to-state comparisons. When political scientists and economists rely exclusively on Census Bureau publications, however, they preclude an attack on certain aspects of the expenditure process. In order to report data by the comparable fields of education, highways, public welfare etc., the Bureau of the Census re-

Reprinted by permission from Ira Sharkansky, "Agency Requests, Gubernatorial Support, and Budget Success in State Legislatures," *American Political Science Review*, 62 (December, 1968), 1220–1231.

The author wishes to thank the Social Science Research Council's Committee on Governmental and Legal Processes, and the University of Georgia's Office of General Research for their financial assistance; and Patricia Owens for her help in gathering the data.

[1] See, for example, Thomas R. Dye, *Politics, Economics and the Public: Policy Outcomes in the American States* (Chicago: Rand McNally, 1966); Glenn W. Fisher, "Interstate Variation in State and Local Government Expenditures," *National Tax Journal*, 17 (March, 1964), 57–64; Seymour Sachs and Robert Harris, "The Determinants of State and Local Government Expenditures and Intergovernmental Flow of Funds," *National Tax Journal*, 17 (March, 1964), 75–85; Elliott R. Morss, J. Eric Fredland and Saul H. Hymans, "Fluctuations in State Expenditures: An Econometric Analysis," *Southern Economic Journal* (April, 1967); Richard E. Dawson and James A. Robinson, "Interparty Competition, Economic Variables, and Welfare Politics in the American States," *Journal of Politics*, 25 (May, 1963), 265–289; and Ira Sharkansky, "Economic and Political Correlates of State Government Expenditures: General Tendencies and Deviant Cases," *Midwest Journal of Political Science*, 11 (May, 1967), 173–192.

arranges the expenditures made by individual state agencies.[2] As a result we know little about the factors that affect the budgets of individual agencies. And because it is the agency's budget that is the focus of budget-making, we have no systematic information about many of the influences that might affect government expenditures. Chief among the unknowns are the influence of each agency's budget request in the expenditure process, and the support given to the agencies by the governor.

Much of the existing literature on government budgeting suggests the importance of incremental decision rules. Officials who review agency requests in the executive and legislative branches are said to have too few resources for a comprehensive examination of each agency's program. Studies of federal budgeting reveal that appropriations committees generally accept each agency's "base" of previous expenditure, and focus their attention on the requests for new funds.[3] Congress holds down the growth rate of most agency budgets, typically to within 10 per cent of their existing budget.[4] The common explanation for incremental budgeting cites the difficulties associated with a comprehensive review of each agency. Legislatures have much else to do besides reviewing past and present expenditures. To reopen past budget decisions each year would broaden the scope of political controversy. Decision-makers can limit their task by accepting their own past evaluations about each existing program, and by focusing their current inquiries on those items that an agency seeks for the first time, or those which the agency hopes to increase well beyond the limit of past funding.[5]

A principal task of this study is to identify and measure some likely mechanisms of incremental budgeting in state governments. By looking at the *requests* of 592 agencies in 19 states, the *response of the governor* to agency requests, and the *action of the legislature*, it will assess the importance of incremental routines in each of these states. Then it identifies certain characteristics of each state that influence the nature of its budget procedures. The study proceeds at two levels of analysis. It first reports the results of 19 separate within-state analyses that show relationships between measures of agency success in the legislature and measures

[2] Most state governments have several administrative units with educational responsibilities, for example, and their titles and program responsibilities vary considerably from one state to another.

[3] Otto A. Davis, M. A. H. Dempster, and Aaron Wildavsky, "A Theory of the Budgetary Process" [*American Political Science Review*], 60 (September, 1968), 529–547.

[4] Richard F. Fenno, Jr., *The Power of the Purse: Appropriations Politics in Congress* (Boston: Little, Brown, 1966), Chapters 8 and 11.

[5] Charles E. Lindblom, "Decision-Making in Taxation and Expenditure," in *Public Finances: Needs, Sources and Utilization* (Princeton: National Bureau of Economic Research, 1961), pp. 295–333.

of budget size, agency acquisitiveness and gubernatorial support. Secondly, it uses these 19 states as the units of analysis, and defines the importance of certain environmental conditions for these relationships among agencies, the governor and the state legislature.

I Techniques and Expectations

The complexity and individuality of state government budgets represent formidable barriers to comparative analysis. Because state budgeting proceeds with a variety of separate funds whose labels and components vary from state to state, and because the official documents vary widely in the quality of information they contain, it is necessary to eliminate over half of the state governments from this analysis. The budget documents and financial reports of 19 state governments meet the essential criteria of providing an agency-by-agency record of current expenditures; the agencies' initial requests for the coming budget period; [6] the amount recommended by the governor for each agency; [7] and the sum appropriated by the legislature. The 19 states come from each major section of

[6] The states included in this study – and the nature of the findings – may be affected by the requirement of separate indications for the agency's budget request and the governor's recommendation. One tenet of certain administrative reformers prescribes that public agencies *not* submit their own budget requests to the legislature. Instead, they should submit their requests to the chief executive, who should then review each agency's budget in the light of his whole program, and submit his own recommendations for each agency to the legislature. Presumably the legislature will consider only these budget recommendations of the executive, and thereby force each agency to operate within the budget limits set by the leader of the "administration team." A number of states have adopted these budget procedures, and their budgets show only the governor's recommendation for each agency. Our sample, in contrast, may be overly representative of states with "unreformed" budget procedures.

The "budget period" employed is the fiscal year or the biennium, depending upon the usage prevailing within each state. Although the use of a single year or a biennium varies from one state to another, this should not have a material effect on the findings insofar as the principal findings grow out of correlation coefficients that are calculated separately for each state. The particular years employed in the analysis of each state are indicated with the name of each state in Table 1. In each case, the most recent budget period was employed for which complete data were available. A small number of additional states publish budgetary information that would qualify them for this type of analysis. They are not included here, however, because the appropriate documents were not available.

[7] In some cases it is a budget review board, rather than the governor *per se*, that is directly responsible for the recommendation to the legislature. In each case, however, it is reported by observers native to the state that the governor's role is critical in the recommendations.

the country and range in population size from Texas and Illinois to Vermont and Wyoming. They range in economic well-being (measured in per capita personal income) from Illinois and Indiana to West Virginia and South Carolina. For each major agency in these states two measures of budget success are defined. These are the dependent variables for the within-state analysis of agency budgets: [8]

Y_1: the percentage of the agency's request for the coming budget period appropriated by the legislature (short-term success)

Y_2: the percentage of current expenditures appropriated by the legislature for the coming budget period (success in budget expansion)

The first dependent variable is labelled short-term success because of its concern with one budget period. It simply measures the success of each agency in getting from the legislature what it announces as its goals. The second dependent variable measures the willingness of the legislature to provide each agency with an increase over its current budget. Thus, it measures the increment of growth enjoyed by each unit. In most of the states there is not a significant coefficient of simple correlation between the two measures of success, indicating that they are distinct aspects of the budgetary process.

The independent variables for the within-state analysis of agency budgets are:

X_1: agency request for the coming budget period (budget size)

X_2: agency request for the coming budget period as a percentage of current expenditures (agency acquisitiveness)

X_3: the governor's recommendation for each agency as a percentage of its request (short-term support)

X_4: the governor's recommendation for each agency as a percentage of its current expenditures (support for budget expansion)

[8] All of the findings reported below for the within-state analysis of agency budgets reflect data about the "general fund" for those states that segregate the "general" fund from the "total" fund. For most states, the designation of "general" fund pertains to those moneys subject to state legislative appropriation. For those states showing both general and total fund accounts, the correlation analyses were performed twice: once with each account. However, the findings from the two analyses were not so different as to warrant separate reporting here. For each state, agencies requesting at least $500,000 were included. These are considered the "major" agencies. Supplementary appropriations are excluded from the legislature's appropriation due to lack of data. In the case of one state for which supplementary appropriations were available, the within-state analysis of agencies was run with and without the supplementals; the differences in findings appear inconsequential.

Due to the alleged conservatism of governors and legislators who review agency budgets,[9] it is expected that measures of budget size and acquisitiveness will show negative relationships with the measures of short-term support and legislative success; incremental budget reviewers should cut budgets that threaten to grow. But because an expansionist request is probably a requirement for an increase in appropriations, there are likely to be positive relationships between the measure of acquisitiveness and gubernatorial support and legislative success in budget expansion; it is probably the agencies that ask for the largest increases that receive the largest increases, even though their final appropriation is reduced substantially below their request. Because state legislators have limited investigatory resources and are poorly prepared by training or background for budget reviews,[10] it is expected that the governor's recommendation will serve as an important cue for their decisions. The measures of gubernatorial support should therefore relate closely to the measures of legislative appropriations.

Coefficients of simple correlation are computed separately for each of the nineteen states, and provide measures of association between the dependent and independent variables.[11] With these correlations, we shall also perform a causal analysis to test for the relative importance of the agencies' requests and the governor's recommendations in the decisions of the legislature.

Once we have correlation coefficients that express the prevailing relationships between agency acquisitiveness, gubernatorial support and budget success for each state, we shall employ these coefficients as dependent variables in another inquiry that focuses on the state as the unit of analysis. There we shall consider several aspects of governmental structure, political characteristics and economic resources as potential influences on relationships between agencies, the governor and the legislature. The independent variables for the state-by-state analysis are: [12]

[9] Cf. Thomas J. Anton, *The Politics of State Expenditure in Illinois* (Urbana: University of Illinois Press, 1966), Chapters 5, 6.

[10] Malcolm E. Jewell and Samuel C. Patterson, *The Legislative Process in the United States* (New York: Random House, 1966), p. 251 ff.

[11] The data used in this study meet two of the primary assumptions of correlation analysis: the distribution of each variable approximates normality; and all two-variable relationships are linear.

[12] Several other variables were considered, but excluded in this report because of their failure to add anything of importance to the findings reported below. Those excluded are:

a. Schlesinger's index of the Governor's formal budget powers
b. Schlesinger's index of the Governor's formal powers of appointment
c. Schlesinger's aggregate index of the Governor's formal powers
d. Ranney's measure of Democratic party strength

S_1: Schlesinger's index of the Governor's potential for tenure in office [13]
S_2: Schlesinger's index of the Governor's veto power [14]
S_3: Ranney's measure of two-party competition [15]
S_4: number of elected state executive officials
S_5: percentage of voting-age population casting ballots in a recent state-wide election [16]
S_6: total state government expenditures per capita [17]
S_7: total state government debt per capita
S_8: per capita personal income of state residents

It is expected that a governor with long tenure potential and extensive veto powers will have a relatively strong position *vis a vis* the agencies and the legislature. Such governors may take a hard line in cutting agency budgets, and succeed in providing the legislature with its major budget cues. Intense party competition and high voter turnout often work in favor of high expenditures.[18] Under conditions of high turnout and competition, therefore, acquisitive agencies should be able to elicit the most support from the governor and the legislature. Where there is a large number of separately elected executive officials, it is expected that acquisitive agencies will use them as allies and have a better chance of getting the governor and legislature to approve their budgets. And because independent executives may compete with the governor in supporting agency budgets, the states with numerous elected officials may be those where the governor's recommendations are least potent in the legislature. Where state resources are as-yet uncommitted, agencies may draw on the "slack"

---

e. biennial compensation paid to members of the state Legislature
f. state expenditures per capita for personal services
g. total population of the state
h. number of state government departments with elected heads.

[13] Joseph A. Schlesinger, "The Politics of the Executive," in Herbert Jacob and Kenneth N. Vines, *Politics in the American States* (Boston: Little, Brown and Company, 1965), p. 229.

[14] *Loc. cit.*

[15] Austin Ranney, "Parties in State Politics," in Jacob and Vines, *op. cit.*, p. 65. The measure of competition used here equals the difference between each state's score on Ranney's index of Democratic Party strength and .5000, with the result inverted so that high scores indicate high interparty competition.

[16] The data pertain to the 1964 election for U.S. Representative.

[17] The figure used is total general state government expenditures per capita in 1966.

[18] See the works of Dye and Dawson and Robinson, cited in note 1.

for their budgets.[19] Therefore, the states with low per capita expenditures and debt, but high per capita personal income should offer the most hospitable environments for acquisitive agencies.

Recall that the dependent variables of the state-by-state analysis will be correlation coefficients determined by the within-state analysis of agency budgets. After describing the results of the within-state analysis, we shall specify the dependent variables for the second inquiry.

II Findings: The Correlates of Agency Budget Success

Administrative agencies and the governor play more consistent roles than the legislature in the state budget process. In each of the 19 states the major agencies requested a sizable increase (15–33 per cent) over their current appropriations for the coming year, and the governor pared down the increase in his recommendations (by 4–31 per cent). Table 1 shows the percentage changes occurring at each major stage of the budget process by states; it indicates that major agencies requested an average 24 per cent increase over their current budgets, and that the governor's recommendation trimmed an average 14 per cent from their requests. The legislature's final appropriation for these agencies typically remained close to the governor's recommendation, but varied from a cut of 8 per cent below his recommendation to an increase of 19 per cent above his recommendation. Six of the legislatures cut agency budgets below the governor's figure, and 11 appropriated more than the governor asked. In only one case, however, did a legislature (in Nebraska) give more money to the agencies than they had requested themselves. The average legislative grant for the coming period was 13 per cent below the agencies' request, but 13 per cent above the agencies' current budget.

The governor's support appears to be a critical ingredient in the success enjoyed by individual agencies in the legislature. In 16 states there is a significant positive correlation (shown in Table 2) between the governor's support and short term success,[20] and in 14 of the states there is a similar relationship between the governor's support and success in budget expansion. A contrary finding appears only in the case of Nebraska, where a negative coefficient of .54 links the governor's recommendation with

[19] The concept of "slack" is explained in Richard M. Cyert and James G. March, A *Behavioral Theory of the Firm* (Englewood Cliffs: Prentice-Hall, 1963), pp. 36 ff.

[20] A test for significance is not, strictly speaking, applicable because the units of analysis are not chosen at random to represent a larger population. Nevertheless, the tests for significance provide a convenient device to denote relationships that are "sizable."

TABLE 1. *Annual Percentage Changes by Stages in the Budget Process of Major Agencies, by State*

State, Showing Years of Budget Analyzed and Number of Agencies	Agency Request as Per Cent of Current Expenditure	Governor's Recommendation as a Per Cent of Agency Request	Legislature's Appropriation as a Per Cent of Gov's Request	Legislature's Appropriation as Per Cent of Agency's Current Expenditure	Legislature's Appropriation as a Per Cent of Agency Request
Florida 1965-67, $n = 39$	120	90	93	109	84
Georgia 1965-67, $n = 26$	153	86	100	139	87
Idaho 1967-69, $n = 23$	119	93	92	109	86
Illinois 1963-65* $n = 37$	118	83	102	108	85
Indiana 1965-67, $n = 47$	123	83	103	112	86
Kentucky 1966-68, $n = 28$	120	90	93	109	84
Louisiana 1966-67, $n = 32$	121	90	101	110	91
Maine 1965-67, $n = 17$	114	85	108	109	92
Nebraska 1965-67, $n = 10$	122	87	119	124	104
North Carolina 1965-67, $n = 61$	120	84	105	112	87
North Dakota 1965-67, $n = 21$	124	74	111	111	82
South Carolina 1966-67, $n = 29$	117	96	104	116	99
South Dakota 1967-68, $n = 25$	136	82	98	109	80
Texas 1965-67, $n = 41$	128	82	104	117	86
Vermont 1965-67, $n = 17$	121	87	106	115	91
Virginia 1966-68, $n = 57$	120	92	100	114	91
West Virginia 1966-67, $n = 43$	125	88	92	101	81
Wisconsin 1965-67, $n = 26$	115	96	98	111	94
Wyoming 1967-69, $n = 13$	133	69	109	112	75

* The Illinois data comes from the Appendix of Thomas J. Anton's *The Politics of State Expenditures in Illinois* (Urbana: University of Illinois Press, 1966). All other data come from the official budgets and financial reports of the states.

the legislature's appropriation. In 1965, the Nebraska Legislature was unique in acting consistently in opposition to the recommendations of Governor Frank B. Morrison. A reading of Nebraska newspapers during that period suggests that gubernatorial-legislative antagonism over the budget was part of a larger dispute that grew out of a tax conflict. The conservative Democratic Governor opposed any new taxes, while the Republican leadership of the legislature sought the establishment of a state income or sales tax. Perhaps in an effort to force the Governor's acceptance of a new tax, the legislators voted more funds than the governor recommended for the major agencies. (see Table 1). The legislature was especially generous with those agencies which had suffered a budget-cut in the Governor's office (see Table 2).

The acquisitiveness of agency requests plays an important role in the budget process. There is a significant negative relationship between ac-

TABLE 2. *Coefficients of Simple Correlation between Measures of Budget-Success in the State Legislature and Independent Variables, by State*

	Correlations between Short-Term Success and:			Correlations between Budget Expansion and:		
	Budget Size	Agency Acquisitive-ness	Governor's Short-Term Support	Budget Size	Agency Acquisitive-ness	Governor's Support for Expansion
Florida	.03	–.63*	.77*	–.04	.50	.71*
Georgia	.02	–.82*	.93*	–.12	–.09	.92*
Idaho	.04	–.80*	.72*	–.14	.74*	.79*
Illinois	.03	–.51*	.79*	–.04	.81*	.81*
Indiana	.04	–.27	.86*	–.04	.99*	.99*
Kentucky	.06	–.77*	.80*	–.14	.07	.19
Louisiana	.00	–.48*	.72*	–.09	.04	.54*
Maine	.24	.18	.75*	.25	.64*	.74*
Nebraska	–.09	.51	–.54	–.06	.79*	.43
North Carolina	–.04	–.20	.99*	–.05	.93*	.99*
North Dakota	.17	–.80*	.94*	–.16	.42	.87*
South Carolina	.00	–.17	.36	–.05	.81*	.75*
South Dakota	.00	–.70*	.63*	–.15	.58*	.48*
Texas	–.25	–.06	.52*	–.10	.95*	.89*
Vermont	–.12	–.61*	.58*	.24	.37	.46
Virginia	.07	–.27*	.19	–.02	.81*	.60*
West Virginia	.01	–.65*	.61*	–.09	.22	.26
Wisconsin	–.08	–.28	.67*	–.06	–.10	.16
Wyoming	–.18	–.70*	.94*	–.13	.18	.92*

* Significant at the .05 level (see note #20).

quisitiveness and short-term success in 12 states and a significant positive relationship between acquisitiveness and success in budget expansion in 11 states. The legislature is most likely to trim the budgets of agencies that ask for large increases, but it is only these acquisitive agencies that can hope for a large increase to remain after the legislature has acted. The acquisitiveness of the agencies is also a factor in the governor's recommendation. Table 3 shows significant negative relationships between acquisitiveness and the governor's short-term recommendation in 14 states, and significant positive relationships between acquisitiveness and the governor's recommendation for budget expansion in 14 states. Both the governor and the legislature may be using similar decision rules: do not cut the agencies that ask for little or no increase; but do not recommend a budget expansion for those agencies that ask for little or no increase. Short term cuts are made in the budgets of acquisitive agencies, but the acquisi-

TABLE 3. *Coefficients of Simple Correlation between Measures of Gubernatorial Support and Independent Variables, by State*

	Correlations between Short-Term Support and:		Correlations between Support for Expansion and:	
	Budget Size	Agency Acquisitiveness	Budget Size	Agency Acquisitiveness
Florida	.04	–.80*	–.03	.22
Georgia	.08	–.86*	–.05	–.11
Idaho	.45*	–.70*	–.03	.99*
Illinois	.07	–.52	.00	.85*
Indiana	.10	.13	–.04	.99*
Kentucky	.18	–.94*	.02	.04
Louisiana	.12	–.82*	–.05	.37*
Maine	.08	.22	.09	.75*
Nebraska	–.23	–.59	–.27	.76*
North Carolina	–.05	–.20	–.06	.94*
North Dakota	–.01	–.84*	–.34	.39
South Carolina	.06	–.30	–.02	.77*
South Dakota	.02	–.75*	–.11	.71*
Texas	–.10	–.63*	–.04	.93*
Vermont	–.16	–.67*	.36	.85*
Virginia	.12	–.56*	–.05	.71*
West Virginia	.16	–.57*	.03	.57*
Wisconsin	–.03	–.61*	.07	.88*
Wyoming	–.15	–.82*	–.09	.28

* Significant at the .05 level (see note #20).

tive agencies stand the best chance of enjoying a substantial budget increase.

The absolute size of agency budget requests does not appear to influence the decisions made by the governor or legislature. Tables 2 and 3 show generally weak or inconsistent correlations between budget size and the governor's recommendations or the legislature's appropriations. Budget reviewers in the governor's office and the legislature are using procedures that serve to minimize the increments of budget growth; they are more likely to respond to the increment of change that is requested (i.e., agency acquisitiveness) than to the sheer size of the request.

Because agency acquisitiveness shows similar relationships with both the governor's recommendation and the legislature's appropriation, one is tempted to ask if the legislature responds directly to the agencies' acquisitiveness, or merely to the governor's recommendations. The alternate explanations are conveniently depicted and analyzed with the techniques of causal inference.[21] The alternate linkages and the computations associated with them are reported in Figure 1 and Table 4. The results support the inference that the legislature responds more often to the governor's recommendations than directly to agency acquisitiveness. In the case of short-term success, the data support this for Florida, Georgia, Illinois, Louisiana, Nebraska, North Carolina, North Dakota, South Carolina and Wyoming. Only in the cases of South Dakota and Virginia does the legislature seem to respond primarily to agency acquisitiveness. In the remaining states the findings suggest that the legislature is responding to a combination of gubernatorial recommendations and agency acquisitiveness. Similar findings appear in the causal analysis of budget expansion. Georgia, Idaho, Kentucky, Maine, North Carolina, North Dakota, Vermont, West Virginia and Wyoming show legislative reliance primarily on the governor's recommendation while only South Dakota, Texas and Virginia show legislative response primarily to agency acquisitiveness.

For most of the 19 states, it is a combination of incrementalism and legislative dependence on the governor's recommendation that shapes the budgets of major agencies. Both the governor and the legislature respond to the agencies' request for increments above their present expenditures, and their response serves to minimize budget growth. Also, most legisla-

[21] The techniques are explained in Hubert M. Blalock, Jr., *Causal Inferences in Nonexperimental Research* (Chapel Hill: University of North Carolina Press, 1964), pp. 64 ff.; and demonstrated in Donald J. McCrone and Charles F. Cnudde, "Toward a Communications Theory of Democratic Political Development: A Causal Model," [*American Political Science Review*], 61 (March, 1967), 72–79. In this causal analysis, the author is following the convention of inferring a linkage to be absent if the difference between expected and actual findings is less than the difference for the alternative model, and if the difference between expected and actual findings is less than .10.

FIGURE 1. Alternative Causal Models for Relationships among Administrative Agencies, the Governor and the Legislature

Model 1: *No direct link between agency acquisitiveness and Legislature.*

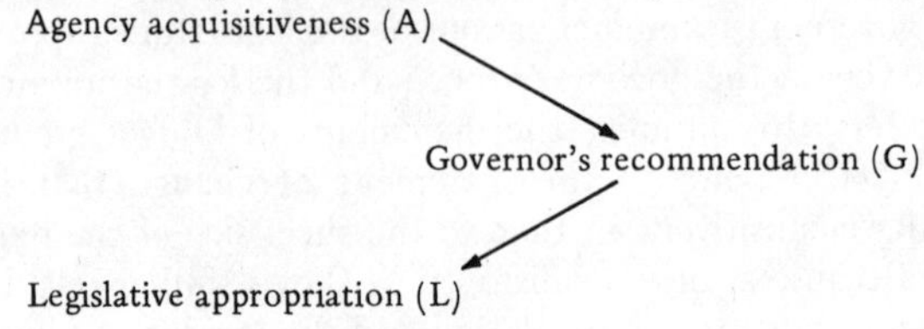

Model 2: *No direct link between Governor's recommendation and Legislature*

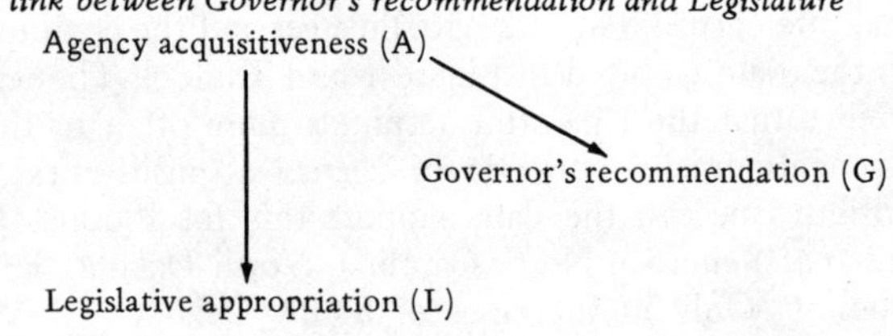

Model 3: *Links from both agency acquisitiveness and Governor's recommendation to the Legislature*

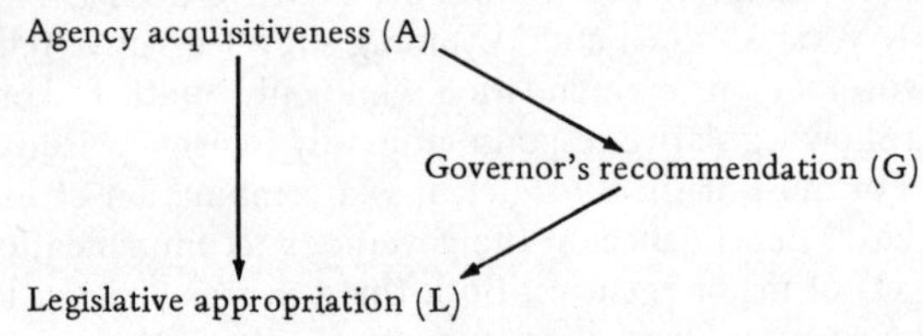

tures weigh the governor's recommendations heavily in their own decisions. Without a favorable recommendation from the governor, an agency is unlikely to enjoy any substantial increase in its appropriation.

III The Correlates of Agency-Governor-Legislature Relationships

An examination of the correlation coefficients in Tables 2 and 3 indicates that states vary in the nature of budget relations among agencies, the governor and the legislature. Although agency acquisitiveness and the

TABLE 4. *Differences between Relationships Expected on the Basis of Causal Inferences and Actual Relationships*

	Short-Term Success				Program Expansion			
	Expected	Actual	Differ-ence	Model Inferred	Expected	Actual	Differ-ence	Model Inferred
Florida								
$r_{AL} = r_{AG}r_{GL}$	–.62	–.63	.01	#1	.16	.50	.34	#3
$r_{GL} = r_{AG}r_{AL}$	.50	.77	.27		.11	.71	.60	
Georgia								
$r_{AL} = r_{AG}r_{GL}$	–.80	–.82	.02	#1	–.10	–.09	.01	#1
$r_{GL} = r_{AG}r_{AL}$	.71	.93	.22		.01	.92	.91	
Idaho								
$r_{AL} = r_{AG}r_{GL}$	–.50	–.80	.30	#3	.78	.74	.04	#1
$r_{GL} = r_{AG}r_{AL}$	.56	.72	.16		.73	.79	.06	
Illinois								
$r_{AL} = r_{AG}r_{GL}$	–.41	–.51	.10	#1	.69	.81	.12	#3
$r_{GL} = r_{AG}r_{AL}$	.41	.79	.38		.69	.81	.12	
Indiana								
$r_{AL} = r_{AG}r_{GL}$	–.11	–.27	.16	#3	.99	.99	.00	indeter-minate
$r_{GL} = r_{AG}r_{AL}$	.04	.86	.82		.99	.99	.00	
Kentucky								
$r_{AL} = r_{AG}r_{GL}$	–.75	–.77	.02	#1	.01	.07	.06	#1
$r_{GL} = r_{AG}r_{AL}$	.72	.80	.08		.00	.19	.19	
Louisiana								
$r_{AL} = r_{AG}r_{GL}$	–.59	–.48	.11	#3	.20	.04	.16	#3
$r_{GL} = r_{AG}r_{AL}$	.39	.72	.33		.01	.54	.53	
Maine								
$r_{AL} = r_{AG}r_{GL}$	.17	.18	.01	#1	.56	.64	.08	#1
$r_{GL} = r_{AG}r_{AL}$	.04	.75	.71		.48	.74	.26	
Nebraska								
$r_{AL} = r_{AG}r_{GL}$	.32	.51	.19	#3	.33	.79	.46	#3
$r_{GL} = r_{AG}r_{AL}$	–.30	–.50	.20		.60	.43	.17	
North Carolina								
$r_{AL} = r_{AG}r_{GL}$	–.20	–.20	.00	#1	.93	.93	.00	#1
$r_{GL} = r_{AG}r_{AL}$	.04	.99	.95		.87	.79	.12	

TABLE 4. *Differences between Relationships Expected on the Basis of Causal Inferences and Actual Relationships (Continued)*

	Short-Term Success				Program Expansion			
	Expected	Actual	Difference	Model Inferred	Expected	Actual	Difference	Model Inferred
North Dakota								
$r_{AL} = r_{AG} r_{GL}$	–.79	–.80	.01	#1	.34	.42	.08	#1
$r_{GL} = r_{AG} r_{AL}$	.67	.94	.27		.16	.87	.71	
South Carolina								
$r_{AL} = r_{AG} r_{GL}$	–.11	–.17	.06	#1	.58	.81	.23	#3
$r_{GL} = r_{AG} r_{AL}$	.05	.36	.31		.62	.75	.13	
South Dakota								
$r_{AL} = r_{AG} r_{GL}$	–.47	–.70	.23	#2	.34	.58	.24	#2
$r_{GL} = r_{AG} r_{AL}$	.53	.63	.10		.41	.48	.07	
Texas								
$r_{AL} = r_{AG} r_{GL}$	–.33	–.06	.26	#3	.83	.95	.12	#2
$r_{GL} = r_{AG} r_{AL}$	.04	.52	.48		.88	.89	.01	
Vermont								
$r_{AL} = r_{AG} r_{GL}$	–.39	–.61	.22	#3	.39	.37	.02	#1
$r_{GL} = r_{AG} r_{AL}$	.41	.58	.17		.31	.46	.15	
Virginia								
$r_{AL} = r_{AG} r_{GL}$	–.11	–.27	.16	#2	.43	.81	.38	#2
$r_{GL} = r_{AG} r_{AL}$	.15	.19	.04		.58	.60	.02	
West Virginia								
$r_{AL} = r_{AG} r_{GL}$	–.35	–.65	.30	#3	.15	.22	.07	#1
$r_{GL} = r_{AG} r_{AL}$	.37	.61	.24		.13	.26	.13	
Wisconsin								
$r_{AL} = r_{AG} r_{GL}$	–.41	–.28	.13	#3	–.09	.16	.25	#3
$r_{GL} = r_{AG} r_{AL}$	.17	.67	.50		.14	–.10	.24	
Wyoming								
$r_{AL} = r_{AG} r_{GL}$	–.77	–.70	.07	#1	.26	.18	.08	#1
$r_{GL} = r_{AG} r_{AL}$	.57	.94	.37		.05	.92	.87	

governor's recommendations generally show certain correlations with the legislature's appropriation, the strength (and occasionally the direction) of these relationships vary from state to state. By examining these variations it is possible to define the conditions under which the governor is severe or supportive in his review of agency budgets, and the conditions under which the legislature is particularly responsive to agency acquisitiveness and the governor's recommendations. The dependent variables of this inquiry are certain correlation coefficients from Tables 2 and 3:

$r_{X_2X_3}$: the stronger the *negative* correlation between agency acquisitiveness and the governor's short-term support, the more the governor appears to be restraining the agencies' budget development

$r_{X_2X_4}$: the stronger the *positive* correlation between agency acquisitiveness and the governor's support for budget expansion, the more the governor appears to accept agency-initiated budget expansions

$r_{X_2Y_1}$: the stronger the *negative* correlation between agency acquisitiveness and short-term success in the legislature, the more the legislature appears to be restraining agency budget development

$r_{X_2Y_2}$: the stronger the *positive* correlation between agency acquisitiveness and budget-expansion in the legislature, the more the legislature appears to accept agency-initiated budget expansions

$r_{X_3Y_1}$: the stronger the *positive* correlation between the governor's short-term recommendation and the legislature's short-term appropriation, the greater the gubernatorial-legislative rapport in short-term budget making

$r_{X_4Y_2}$: the stronger the positive correlation between the governor's budget-expansion recommendation and the legislature's budget-expansion appropriation, the greater the gubernatorial-legislative rapport in budget-expansion

The independent variables for this analysis are introduced above. By examining correlation coefficients between the measures of agency-governor-legislature relationships and the measures of government structure, political characteristics and economic resource, it is possible to define certain state characteristics that support these behaviors.

FINDINGS: THE ENVIRONMENT OF AGENCY-GOVERNOR-LEGISLATURE BUDGET RELATIONS. The impact of the environment on agency-governor-legislature budget relations does not appear to be strong. Only a few of the correlation coefficients reported in Table 5 are strong enough to pass a test for statistical significance. However, by combining these

TABLE 5. *Coefficients of Simple Correlation between Measures of Agency-Governor-Legislature Relationships and Independent Variables*

	S_1: Governor Tenure	S_2: Governor Veto	S_3: Party Comp	S_4: Elected Execs.	S_5: Voter Turnout	S_6: Expend/ Capita	S_7: Debt/ Capita	S_8: Personal Income/ Capita
$r_{X_2X_3}$: agency acquisitiveness and Gov short-term support	.15	–.52*	.16	–.08	.16	–.34	–.05	.14
$r_{X_2X_4}$: agency acquisitiveness and Gov support for expansion	–.04	–.20	.34	.07	.40	–.22	–.45	.33
$r_{X_2Y_1}$: acquisitiveness and Legis short-term appropriation	–.17	–.21	.07	.34	–.09	–.45	–.21	.15
$r_{X_2Y_2}$: acquisitiveness and Legis expansion appropriation	.09	–.27	.14	.20	.10	–.51*	–.50*	.24
$r_{X_3Y_1}$: Gov support and Legis short-term appropriation	.32	–.05	–.11	–.31	.08	.34	.21	–.06
$r_{X_4Y_2}$: Gov support and Legis expansion appropriation	.38	–.01	–.17	.18	–.11	–.07	–.45	.14

* Significant at .05 level (see note #20).

significant relationships with those showing a magnitude of at least .30, it is possible to speculate about certain conditions that give some support to certain budget behaviors.

Two environmental characteristics associated with the governor's restraint of agency budget development are substantial veto powers and high state government expenditures.[22] Perhaps the threat of veto permits the governor to impose a severe review on the agencies when they submit requests to him. And the already-high expenditures may incline the governor against further large increases in state spending. Where the governor accepts agency requests for budget expansion, there tends to be a low state debt, high personal income, relatively intense party competition and high voter turnout.[23] Perhaps low debt and high personal income permit the governor to support agency plans for expansion. And in a high participation-competitive party situation he may be inclined to seek electoral and legislative rewards by supporting innovative agencies.

Where the legislature restrains agency budget development there is relatively high state government expenditure and a low incidence of separately elected officials.[24] Like the governor, the legislature appears to resist an acquisitive agency in the face of already high expenditures. And with a scarcity of separately elected executives, agency heads may lack for politically independent allies who can promote their budget through the legislature. Where the legislature accepts agency-initiated budget expansions there tend to be low total state expenditures and state debt.[25] Thus, the condition of still-flexible resources seems to permit the legislature (like the governor) to give some support to acquisitive agencies.

Gubernatorial-legislative rapport on short-term success is high where the governor has considerable tenure potential, where there is a scarcity of separately elected executive officials, and where total expenditures are relatively high.[26] With high tenure potential the governor may be able to

[22] The correlations indicate that high scores on veto power and expenditures correspond with high *negative* relationships between agency acquisitiveness and the governor's short-term support.

[23] The correlations indicate that low scores on debt, but high scores on party competition, voter turnout, and per capita personal income correspond with high *positive* relationships between agency acquisitiveness and the governor's support for budget expansion.

[24] The correlations indicate that high state expenditures and a low number of elected officials correspond with high *negative* relationships between agency acquisitiveness and short-term success in the legislature.

[25] The correlations indicate that low expenditures and debt correspond with high *positive* relationships between agency acquisitiveness and budget-expansion success in the legislature.

[26] The correlations indicate that high tenure potential and expenditures, but a low number of elected officials correspond with high *positive* relationships between the governor's short-term recommendation and the legislature's short-term appropriation.

elicit legislative cooperation on the expectation that he will remain in office for some time to come. The scarcity of separately elected executives may reduce the governor's competition with other power-holders for the legislature's attention. And the already-high expenditures may encourage the legislators to accept the governor's cues on the agencies' budgets. Where the governor and legislature show rapport in budget-expansion there is a similar high tenure potential and there tends to be a low state debt.[27] Perhaps the low debt constraint permits the governor and legislature to cooperate in the support of agencies that seek to expand their budgets.[28]

IV Summary and Discussion

By means of separate correlation analyses within each of 19 states this article has defined certain relationships between administrative agencies, the governor and the legislature in state government budgeting. A

[27] The correlations indicate that high tenure potential and low debt correspond with high *positive* relationships between the governor's recommendation and the legislature's appropriation for budget expansion.

[28] An examination of simple correlation coefficients among variables $S_1 - S_8$ suggests that the relationships which appear most strongly in Table 5 are independent. Except for the expected relationships among turnout, competition and personal income, few of the variables show strong relationships with each other. Thus, the relationships in Table 5 involving the governor's veto, and tenure potential, and total per capita state expenditures and debt are not the product of any of the other independent variables considered in this study. The coefficients of simple correlation among the independent variables are reported here:

	S_1	S_2	S_3	S_4	S_5	S_6	S_7	S_8
S_1 governor's tenure	1.00	.06	−.34	−.32	.13	.19	.08	.30
S_2 governor's veto		1.00	.20	.22	−.24	.20	−.28	.13
S_3 party competition			1.00	.53*	−.87*	−.20	.15	−.65*
S_4 # elected executives				1.00	−.45	−.32	−.10	−.23
S_5 voter turnout					1.00	.35	−.19	.50*
S_6 expenditures/capita						1.00	.08	−.09
S_7 debt/capita							1.00	−.27
S_8 personal income/capita								1.00

* Significant at the .05 level (see note #20).

A test with regression analysis lends support to the importance of many elected officials for the legislature's short-term support of acquisitive agencies and the importance of few elected officials for governor-legislative rapport on short-term appropriations; this independent variable (S_4) shows a regression coefficient of at least 1.5 times the standard error with the appropriate dependent variables, in the presence of all other independent variables.

favorable recommendation from the governor seems essential for agency budget success in the legislature. The agency may influence both the governor's recommendation and the legislature's appropriation by the nature of its request. Acquisitive requests generally receive severe short-run treatment from the governor and the legislature, but an acquisitive strategy appears to be essential for a significant budget expansion. On the basis of separate causal analyses for each of the 19 states, it appears that the governor's recommendation is more directly important for the legislature of more states than is the acquisitiveness of agency requests.

The findings about the interaction of agency, gubernatorial and legislative behavior help to substantiate several observations that have been made previously about executive-legislative relations and the budgetary process in American governments.[29] The reluctance of governors and legislators to support an acquisitive agency in the short term reveals the conservative bias that is built into incremental budgeting. Agencies that request little or no increase over their current budget are generally treated well by the governor and the legislature, while those seeking large increases suffer the greatest reductions in their requests. Yet an acquisitive strategy appears to be a prerequisite for a substantial budget increase. It is a rare occurrence for the governor or legislature to provide an agency with a sum larger than that it had requested. In part, this is a function of incremental budgeting. Executive and legislative budget-makers concentrate on the inspection and reduction of increments; they leave the development of increments to the agencies. At its heart, the reluctance of governors and legislators to innovate may reveal the difficult position of the generalists in their relations with agency specialists. The highly trained professional personnel in the agencies are most intimately aware of current programs and the new services that an expanded budget might produce. Chief executives and legislators have surrendered much of their innovative potential for a more limited role as reviewers of administrators' requests. And state legislators seem to have accepted a more limited

[29] See, for example, Arthur MacMahon, "Congressional Oversight of Administration: The Power of the Purse," *Political Science Quarterly*, 58 (June and September, 1943), 161–190; and 380–414; Warner Schilling, "The Politics of National Defense: Fiscal 1950," in Schilling *et al.*, *Strategy, Politics and Defense Budgets* (New York: Columbia University Press, 1962), pp. 1–266; Elias Huzar, *The Purse and the Sword* (Ithaca: Cornell University Press, 1950); Aaron Wildavsky, *The Politics of the Budgetary Process* (Boston: Little, Brown and Company, 1964); Rufus Browning, "Innovative and Non-Innovative Decision Processes in Government Budgeting," a paper delivered at the Annual Meeting of the American Political Science Association, September, 1963; Richard Fenno, *The Power of the Purse*, *op. cit.*; John P. Crecine, "A Computer Simulation Model of Municipal Resource Allocation," a paper presented at the 1966 Midwest Political Science Association Meeting.

supervisory role than the governors. The findings of greater importance for the governor's recommendation (rather than the agency's request) in the legislature's decisions indicates the legislature's dependence on the governor's budget cues. Perhaps this reflects the greater staff resources of the governor and the typically amateurish character of state legislatures. When they are compared to the professional analysts in the governor's office, legislators appear to have little experience in public budgeting, no professional training in a relevant discipline, an impossibly brief time to consider agency budgets and inadequate staff and clerical assistance.[30] State legislators have a desperate need for cues that will guide their budget performance and the governor's recommendation is usually the best cue available.

When the 19 states are examined for the characteristics that support various styles of relationships between agencies, the governor and the legislature, the findings shed some new light on the influence of governmental and political characteristics of the states.[31] The veto and tenure powers of the governor help to strengthen his position with both the agencies and the legislature. Because of formal prerogatives, the governor appears to be in a more secure position when he reduces agency requests and makes recommendations to the legislature; the governors that have these powers are more likely to be severe in cutting agency requests and they are more likely to be successful in their recommendations to the legislature. In contrast, the presence of numerous separately elected executives appears to benefit agencies at the governor's expense. In the states where there are many elected officials, agencies are more likely to get their acquisitive requests approved by the legislature, and the governor's recommendation is most likely to be altered in the legislature. Party competition and voter turnout also seem to strengthen the agencies' position. In states with heavy turnout and intense competition the governor is most likely to support the agencies' acquisitive requests, perhaps in an effort to assert his own identity as a program innovator. High levels of state government expenditure and debt work in opposition to agency budget aspirations. Where spending and debt are already high, both the governor and the legislature are severe in reviewing agency requests. This may be an outgrowth of incremental budgeting. The principal reviewers are conservative in their attitudes toward increases in expenditures, and they may be particularly wary of acquisitive agencies when existing state resources are already heavily committed.

[30] See Malcolm E. Jewell and Samuel C. Patterson, *op. cit.*, p. 251 ff.

[31] See the works by Dye, Dawson and Robinson and Sharkansky cited in note 1; plus Richard I. Hofferbert, "The Relation between Public Policy and Some Structural and Environmental Variables in the American States" [*American Political Science Review*], 60 (March, 1966), 73–82.

ADMINISTRATORS OF THE LINE AGENCIES

WALLACE SAYRE
HERBERT KAUFMAN

Line Administrators, Governmental Decisions, and the Prizes of Politics

Many prizes of politics, it was noted earlier, are commonly contained and distributed in governmental decisions affecting public services, financial benefits, and costs to the people of the city. For this reason, many groups organize to participate in the governmental process, seeking by their strategies to determine the nature of the governmental decisions relevant to their own situations.

These participants are most often concerned with the official behavior of the line agencies – that is, the administrative agencies in direct contact with all or part of the populace that perform the regulatory, enforcement, and service functions of government. The immediate targets of the participants' efforts may be laws, executive orders, rules and regulations, or judicial judgments. The concrete objective usually is to influence the actions of tax collectors, policemen, or inspectors; to affect the location of schools, firehouses, health centers, libraries, traffic signals, or playgrounds; or perhaps to increase the size of salary checks or welfare payments. Statutes and other high-level decisions are means to concrete ends; it is the ends that seem to count most heavily in the contest for the stakes of politics. In the last analysis, the day-to-day actions of specific public officers and employees in the line bureaus and departments are the vehicles in which the stakes are carried.

The high commands of the line agencies – the Commissioners, their deputies and assistants, and their bureau chiefs – are key figures in the governmental process. They possess the formal legal powers of their agencies – the power to promulgate rules and regulations having the force of law; to fix the levels and quality of service; to set conditions for, or withhold, licenses and permits, and to suspend or revoke them; to deploy work forces and set project priorities; and to intervene in individual cases

Reprinted by permission from William Sayre and Herbert Kaufman, *Governing New York City*, 249–264, 269–272, 285, 287–292, 303–305.

handled by their agencies. In addition to their formal authority, they are often treated as experts in their particular areas of public policy. But perhaps most important of all is that many agency leaders have, or develop, powerful incentives to function actively and aggressively in the performance of their tasks and in defense of their agencies. For some, the motive is apparently simply pride in a job well done. For others, it is a desire to acquire reputations that will enable them to advance to higher positions, appointive or elective, in government, or to call their talents to the attention of others. In some cases it may be nothing more than a desire to avoid the discredit that is the lot of an administrator who fails to furnish leadership, and whose agency consequently falls into a state of disorganization and incompetence. A few seem simply to enjoy the exercise of power. Some have leadership thrust upon them by the pressures of their subordinates, their clientele, their political superiors, or by crisis. In any event, whatever the motivation, many agency chiefs are drawn into the center of the political arena.

Because they are legal repositories of authority and responsibility, widely regarded as experts in their fields, and often self-conscious and energetic leaders, line agency heads are foci of many efforts to influence governmental decision-making. It is to them that a great deal of legislative, executive, and court action is addressed. It is to them that other administrators, employees, and interest groups turn with demands of various kinds. While all claims and mandates and requests do not have the same standing or success, the attention paid the line officers by all kinds of participants in politics enhances their importance still further.

To be important, however, is not the same as to be a free agent. The very circumstances that draw the attention of the various participants, by subjecting the line administrators to batteries of pressures and legal requirements and suggestions and advice, in the end limit the administrators' discretion. Almost every move they make affects somebody, either favorably or adversely; almost every failure to move pleases some people and provokes others. Moreover, the administrators are vulnerable; the jurisdiction of their agencies is not immutably fixed, their appropriations are not guaranteed, their job tenure is generally far from secure. Scarcely a year goes by without the birth of a new municipal agency, the elimination or absorption of an old one, a major modification of an existing one. A line agency head is not in a risk-free situation. He cannot make decisions as he pleases, without reference to the field of forces in which he operates, if he does not wish to jeopardize the position of his agency, his own career, or the programs and projects to which he is personally, professionally, and organizationally committed. He cannot disregard decisions made elsewhere in the governmental system for the same reasons. To impress his own preferences on the decision-making process, or even merely to prevent policies unacceptable to him from being adopted, he must learn to deal with the world in which he lives. In other words, he must learn to use his considerable resources to produce the kinds of decisions he wants and needs. He must formulate strategies that make the most of his opportunities and minimize his hazards. He must be a manipulator, or he will become an instrument in the hands of others and possibly pay high costs as a consequence.

The Strategies of Line Administrators

Getting internal control. The *sine qua non* for the exercise of influence upon governmental decisions by line agency heads is to gain control of the subordinates in their departments and bureaus. To be sure, an administrator can live at peace with his subordinates by routinely ratifying their proposals for running the agency and managing its program. But their perceptions of the policies to be followed are, because they see things from a different vantage point, ordinarily narrower than the perceptions of their chiefs. The latter will be subject to ranges of pressures and sources of information and advice largely unknown to the men in the lower ranks or in exceedingly specialized occupations. Agency heads will be aware of opportunities and dangers, of complications and repercussions, that subordinates often do not realize exist. Frequently, the heads will be freer of the habits, traditions, and vested interests in the *status quo* that stifle not only innovation and inventiveness but even adaptiveness to changing conditions on the part of those at lower levels of the hierarchies. In the short run it may be more convenient to surrender to the hierarchies than to assume the taxing role of leader. In the long run, however, this may simply be courting disaster.

Gaining control of subordinates in city departments and bureaus is not a simple task. It is true that just being commissioner or bureau chief is a major aid in this respect, for the title and position invest the incumbent with the symbols of legitimacy, the formal signs that he has the "right" to demand and receive the allegiance and obedience of his staff. But this is seldom enough by itself.

In the first place . . . a commissioner usually finds he does not have a free hand in selecting his subordinates. Even his own deputies, assistants, and bureau chiefs, whose influence on his own actions every commissioner knows will be considerable, are not often selected for their loyalty to him. The Mayor and the leaders of the Mayor's party often have candidates of their own for these positions, and other officials, the bureaucracies, the press, and nongovernmental groups also generally offer counsel backed by the implied threat of sanctions if they are disregarded. Over other personnel in his department, the commissioner usually has still less choice; most are career civil servants who come from within the ranks of their own services. So a commissioner cannot easily surround himself with aides he knows will do his bidding and who will see that others in the agency do so also. On the contrary, he must often exert his leadership through subordinates who are at best neutral, at worst openly hostile, and who are always well aware of the limitations of his power. If he is clever and fortunate, he can make sufficient personnel changes to establish a fairly high degree of control. Commissioners of Police and Fire, in particular, attempt periodically to accomplish this by reassigning officers (at all levels down to the middle ranks) in what the newspapers customarily describe as "shake-ups." But this is not a managerial implement to be used frequently and in sweeping proportions, nor is its efficacy at all certain.

In the second place, commissioners normally cannot count on their own personal and professional reputations to produce enthusiastic receptivity to their proposals. Although they may be widely recognized as excellent administrators and experts in the subject matter of their agencies, they are apt to be regarded as novices and "laymen" by those who have spent their lives in the agencies – indeed, in a single bureau or division. If a commissioner comes from within the career ranks, as increasing numbers in recent years have done, he may enjoy the confidence of his staff only so long as he continues to behave like a career executive. If he is not from the ranks, he is likely to be considered a temporary outsider. Even Health Commissioners brought in from outside because of their outstanding professional reputations have on occasion been treated as virtual amateurs by the strongly entrenched permanent personnel of the bureaus under them.

Commissioners are also hampered, in the third place, by their comparatively rapid turnover. Under them, career civil servants continue indefinitely, and many of the permanent staff look on their formal chiefs (the commissioners and their deputies) as birds of passage. *Bureau* chiefs who have risen to their positions of command by promotion from within often enjoy the deference of their subordinates because they are viewed as true members of their units and because they know and control the details of large budgets. Their personnel identify with them and respect them. *Commissioners* who stay in office for a brief number of years, to be supplanted by other strangers to the bureaucracies under them, rarely know the advantages of these strong social and personal ties as wellsprings of zealous rank and file support.

In the fourth place, commissioners sometimes discover that bureaus in their departments develop independent sources of outside support – often, among the interest groups they regulate. To the outside observer, such groups appear to be part of the broad clientele of the department, but the department heads find that they furnish support to the particular bureau with which they are associated rather than to the department as a whole. Frequently this is reinforced by common professional identifications between the personnel of the bureau and the interests with which they are linked. Sanitarians and restaurant operators, for example, or health inspectors and commercial exterminators often have had similar training and experience, and a substantial part of the bureaus' staffs is either recruited from the regulated industry or has hopes of returning to it eventually.

Some commissioners try to ingratiate themselves with their bureaucracies by fighting to get for them the things they want – higher classifications, better pay scales, more liberal fringe benefits, and similar advantages. A commissioner who comes to be regarded as a champion of his staff can often count on more willing compliance with his innovations in substantive program. He achieves at least an approximation of the support an individual moved up from the ranks would receive for the same efforts. The commissioner who resorts to this strategy, however, runs the risk of being "captured" by his subordinates, and becoming a defender of the state of affairs to which they, by habit, are wedded. A few have avoided this pitfall and, after winning acceptance, have used this source of authority to work many changes of organization, procedure, and program. Others have been entrapped by their efforts to earn the confidence of the career personnel, and have become followers of the "insiders" rather than leaders and innovators.

This does not mean commissioners are often confronted with open defiance of their directives if they assert their formal powers. It does mean they can be thwarted by reluctance, persistence of old habits and customs, neglect, and resistance on the part of their subordinates. Commissioners therefore have their strongest impact on the decisions and behavior of their staffs only when they follow up instructions with personal inspection to make sure commands are executed as intended. Personal attention, backed by the legitimate authority of office and the possibility of official sanctions, is most likely to elicit the kind of action desired by a department head. That is why many department heads concentrate on only a restricted segment of the whole range of activities of their agencies when they want to introduce new emphases or new functions. And that is why they often leave the rest of the duties of their organizations to career people who perform them in the customary way.

MANIPULATION OF THE EXTERNAL ENVIRONMENT. If an agency head in the city government is not at least as energetic in protecting the jurisdiction and income of his organization as he is in winning control of its internal affairs, he may soon be left with little worth controlling. Manipulation of the external environment presumes a certain degree of internal control, but there is more to it than that. Agency survival also requires expertness in "external relations."

External relations on behalf of each agency has become the unique (but not the sole) function of its department head and bureau chiefs. They have evolved four basic techniques for performing it: (1) creation of a favorable climate of public opinion; (2) cultivation of active constituencies; (3) concessions to, or understandings with, actual or potential wielders of punitive sanctions against them; and (4) truces with other governmental agencies.

Creating a favorable climate of opinion. Like executives of all large organizations, commissioners of the city's line agencies conduct public relations programs beamed at the entire population with which they are concerned – in this case, usually all the people of the city. The methods are those traditionally employed in the public relations profession: news releases sent to newspapers and other mass media of communication when items of more or less routine interest are involved; newsletters and similar publications mailed to public opinion leaders; press conferences and conducted tours of physical installations for unusual achievements; and public relations officers, or their equivalent under other titles, who manage these matters, to whom reporters seeking information can turn for quick help when they need it, and who can ensure that the reporters understand the agencies' side of every question. The opening of a new facility, the inauguration of a new service, and even the expansion or improvement or intensification of an old one, generally get fairly conspicuous display in the local press, presumably because these things are of general community interest. They are welcomed by city reporters and editors. The newsworthiness of such items is enhanced by the appearance of prominent elected officials, from assemblymen up to the Governor, who wish to be identified with a new enterprise. Coverage by the mass media thus satisfies the needs and desires of many, among whom are the heads of departments and their subordinates.

And so it happens that there is a ceremony when ground is broken for any kind of city construction, and when the cornerstone is laid, and when the facility is opened. Some years ago there was a ribbon-cutting ceremony opening a new highway before the highway was completely paved since the paving could not be completed before Election Day. This also explains why the signs in front of big construction projects while they are going up normally bear the names of half a dozen or more officials. It indicates why a great deal of attention was given in the press to the Fire Commissioner's campaign against careless demolition practices and unsafe storage of inflammables following the spectacular fire in the old John Wanamaker building; to the project of the Department of

Buildings to compel all landlords to maintain their properties at the level required by law after housing groups in the city and a number of tenement house fires focused the public spotlight on the rapid spread of the slums; to the Department of Traffic's figures on time saved by the introduction of one-way avenues; to the Transit Authority's experiments with air-conditioned subway cars and buses; to the punishment of officers in the Fire and Police Departments convicted in departmental trials of accepting gifts and tips; and to many other similar developments treated saliently in the city's newspapers. It accounts for the play in the press for new schools, housing projects, bridges, reservoirs, sewage disposal units, and the like. By calling notice publicly to efforts to compensate for past shortcomings, and by playing up self-initiated accomplishments, department heads build their own reputations and followings as individuals; simultaneously, they strengthen the strategic positions of their departments.

As in merchandising, the product is often its own best advertisement. City and other government line agencies building and managing great public works are thus more fortunate than many. The reputations enjoyed by members of the Port of New York Authority and by Commissioner Robert Moses rest in considerable part upon the fact that people use, see, enjoy, and benefit from the facilities to which their names are attached. The tunnels and bridges, highways and parks, and playgrounds and beaches testify to millions of citizens that these are men who get things done. For the agencies, the use of their facilities thus serves a triple service – solidifying community support for them, maximizing their earnings, as well as providing New York City and the surrounding areas with needed services. In less dramatic fashion, and on a much smaller scale but with similar results, some other city agencies have adopted comparable tactics. The Transit Authority has expanded off-hour service on the subways in efforts to win back riders who turned to other means of transportation rather than wait twenty minutes to half an hour for trains, and it posts car-cards and distributes free baseball schedules to point up the number of places served by its lines. Museums and botanical gardens and zoological parks also post notices in public places and run special shows to attract clientele. The Public Library makes special vacation arrangements for the loan of books and thus maintains a brisk level of business during the summer, when its patronage ordinarily falls off. The Board of Education throws its facilities open to parents each year during Open School Week. It would be cynical to argue that these actions are taken for no other purpose than to benefit the administrative organizations or their leaders; in many cases, the measures doubtless spring from motivations to perform a social service. Whatever the motivations, however, one of the consequences is establishment of a friendly attitude on the part of the general public, of special constituencies, and of the organs that make the laws and control the budget.

Service functions lend themselves much more readily to "advertising" than regulatory or enforcement functions. New services and facilities are visible and usable; they speak for themselves of the proficiency of the agencies operating them, and they can ordinarily be instituted or constructed without need of widespread public cooperation. Regulation or enforcement, on the other hand, is generally out of sight of all but those affected, is likely to be taken for granted by the general population, and is sure to arouse some opposition and complaint from those regulated. Furthermore, regulatory agencies must secure compliance; their work does not depend on them alone but on the behavior of others. Now and then, an agency head promotes his cause with a spectacular regulatory campaign. Most of the time, he steers a course calculated to produce enough compliance with requirements to avoid scandalous or numerous violations without provoking storms of opposition from the regulated interests. A quiet state of affairs is often the most successful kind of public relations for regulatory and enforcement activities.

Another kind of public relations is the managed demonstration. One of the most spectacular of these was a recent intensive undertaking by the Police Commissioner to "saturate" high crime-rate areas with foot patrolmen. With policemen on every corner all through the day and night, and with roving patrols covering the areas between, he reported, all types of offenses dropped. He inferred from this that budget increases enabling him to expand the size of the police force would reduce crime throughout the city. With the news of the experiment prominently reported in all the major daily newspapers, the demonstration doubtless helped him obtain what he sought. A generation earlier, the Department of Health constructed health centers and stationed district health officers in neighborhoods with the highest disease and death rates in the city. The concentration and coordination of these health "shock troops" was declared to have brought down sharply both the incidence of disease and fatalities and was a prelude to the construction of additional health centers and the engagement of additional personnel to man them in other areas. More recently, the Fire Commissioner has received attention for his fire prevention campaign, which he reported to have cut sharply the number of fires and the amount of damage. In this way, line agency heads endeavor, and often succeed, in mobilizing public opinion behind them.

The impending crisis is also employed as a public relations method. One such instance in 1957 was a blistering condemnation of conditions in Bellevue Hospital by eight division heads of that institution; these officers, who numbered among them two Nobel Prize winners, released to the press expressions of alarm and approaching disaster and called for complete renovation and substantial new construction to bring the most famous of the city's hospitals up to satisfactory standards. In like fashion, Police Department crime statistics often give rise to newspaper headlines about crime waves. Toxic substances in the atmosphere were reported by the Department of Air Pollution Control to have reached deadly proportions in some areas. The Department of Buildings complains of the continued spread of urban blight despite its best efforts. The Board of Education itself points up local shortages of classroom space, unfavorable teacher-pupil ratios, and school overcrowding with the likelihood of even worse conditions if drastic remedial measures are not adopted. This is not to say these problems are not real or that the crises are deliberately invented or manufactured. In every case the facts tend to bear out the anxieties of the agencies. Nevertheless, the agency heads or their subordinates employ these situations to arouse public opinion. By well-timed self-exposure they proclaim their competence, their zeal, and their devotion to the public interest and, at the same time, indicate they are hampered by lack of funds and manpower in the performance of their jobs. No city department head has apparently ever gone quite so far as United States Postmaster General Summerfield, who slashed postal service and threatened not to restore it unless his budget requests were fulfilled. The difference, however, is one of degree rather than kind.

Finally, purely educational activities by line agencies often serve public relations purposes. Health Department posters on poison control, for example, not only alert the public to a real safety hazard, but also call attention to the department, its leaders, and its program. Similarly, widespread distribution of Fire Department leaflets on the dangers of kerosene heaters and training programs on methods of fire prevention offered in the public schools perform a valuable public service while also presenting the agency to the populace in a benevolent light.

Whatever the specific tactics of these public relations efforts by city commissioners, the results are not easily assessed. It cannot be proved that efforts put into public relations definitely protect the jurisdiction and income of line departments and bureaus. On the other hand, the evidence strongly suggests that the Mayor, the Board of Estimate, the City Council, the Bureau of the Budget, and other important legislative, executive, and financial institutions of the city government hesitate to refuse requests for appropriations and power by agencies in high popular favor. The political liabilities of such action, particularly in the case of an agency whose head would not hesitate to denounce his official superiors, are far too great. It could hurt the party in power badly at the following election. Moreover, on the reverse side of the coin is the fact that the achievements of the line agencies reflect credit on the elective as well as the administrative officers of government. Not only do the other officials fear to curtail the jurisdiction and expenditures of the better known and respected departments, but they are apt to want to aid them as far as possible in order to reap the benefits of their achievements. Unquestionably, the agencies with the greatest public relations attainments and programs have also been the ones to enjoy the greatest support from the general public, the press, and from the money-providing organs of the city government.

Cultivating active constituencies. Public opinion is amorphous, ambiguous, and apparently capricious a good deal of the time. Hence, while it is a valuable implement for most agency heads, it is not entirely reliable. That is why most commissioners and bureau chiefs foster continuing and helpful relations with nongovernmental groups, and often call upon these allies to aid them in their battles against contractions of jurisdiction and curtailment of appropriations, and to back their struggles to expand their powers or expenditures. Nongovernmental groups have many means of influencing the decisions and actions of government officials and employees; consequently, those agency heads who wish to influence other public officers seek to invoke the assistance of nongovernmental allies. The groups, in turn, seek to exercise influence over the agency heads. The groups that help and the groups that oppose the commissioner may be thought of as his "constituency."

By and large, nongovernmental groups are not created by city agencies for strategic purposes, nor are governmental decisions and actions the sole, or even the chief, concerns of such groups. They ordinarily have more than one purpose and more than a single origin. A few, to be sure, are encouraged by the departments with which they are associated; Parent-Teachers Associations, for example, owe much of their vigor to Board of Education support and help. But this is the exception rather than the rule as far as the allies of line agencies are concerned; agency heads make use of groups they are not instrumental in forming or leading (and are in turn used by the groups).

Although they will accept assistance from every quarter, agency heads depend most heavily on permanent and persistent sources, for these are the ones with the resources, the skills, the reputations, and the lines of access to make their weight felt in the topmost levels of government. Generally, these tend to be clientele groups (associations of people served or regulated by a given agency), professional groups (from whose ranks the agency's dominant professional work force is selected), and functional groups (whose social or economic activities parallel those of the agency), but others are also often involved. Some agency heads have constituencies composed of groups of all three kinds; no agency head is without at least one. Connected with the Board of Education, for instance, are the United

Parents Association (a clientele group), the local affiliates of the National Education Association (a professional group), the Public Education Association and the Citizens Committee for Children (functional groups). At times, the Board is also buttressed by teachers' trade unions and teachers colleges. In the cases of the Department of Health and the Department of Hospitals, there are many health and welfare organizations and their "peak association," the Community Council of Greater New York; the American Public Health Association; the medical societies in the city; the New York Academy of Medicine; and the American Nurses Association. The Department of Traffic is inevitably in close contact with bus companies, retail trade associations, labor unions, and the local units of the American Automobile Association. Welfare organizations and associations of welfare workers, as well as recipients of welfare benefits, constitute important segments of the constituencies of the Department of Welfare. Neighborhood groups and the Park Association of New York City keep in touch with the work of the Department of Parks. The businesses and trades licensed by the Department of Licenses follow its fortunes. Owners and drivers of taxis are linked to the Hack Bureau of the Police Department. No matter what the line agency, it is sure to have at least one, and usually several, nongovernmental groups whose interests are intertwined with its own in some way and thus constitute the agency's constituency.

Many times these nongovernmental groups need no prompting from the agency head to apply their own modes of influence in defense of the agency's powers, appropriations, and position. On their own initiative, and in pursuit of their own interests, they can be counted upon to take forceful action. At other times, agency heads let it be known that a struggle is impending and informally call their allies to the fore when they are needed. To be able to call them requires lines of communication, so the lines of communication are carefully kept open. Contacts are established and maintained; group leaders are assured of ready access to the department or bureau head; informal meetings and briefing sessions are arranged; the groups are consulted, given opportunities to appear at both closed and open hearings, and notified in advance of pending moves by their respective agencies. In every possible way, their "natural" attachment to the well-being of particular agencies is intensified by deliberately cultivated bonds, for the groups are often influential and invaluable friends to the agencies.

Concessions. They are also demanding ones. Although they may frequently come to the defense of a city agency, they do not invariably endorse whatever the agency does. On the contrary, they generally have notions of their own about what the contents of decisions ought to be and what courses of action should be followed. The lines of access kept open by agency heads for their own strategic purposes also serve the strategic purposes of the groups; they employ the channels of communication to let their own demands upon the agencies be known. Indeed, administrators dare not close these lines even if they want to, for every group that is a powerful ally could also be a formidable enemy. The department heads and bureau chiefs therefore listen; that is the minimum price of coalition.

Commissioners must make concessions, too. It is not just a matter of hearing the groups out in cathartic sessions but of keeping them sufficiently satisfied to retain their support. Sometimes commissioners will not make an appointment to a particular post without first clearing the choice with a group deeply interested in it. Rarely will a group be able to exercise a veto on more than a few positions, and rarely will its own direct representatives be appointed even to those. Power over choice of staff, where it exists at all, is more often negative and restricted. Sometimes commissioners will discuss forthcoming policy and program changes with various groups and adjust their ideas in the light of the groups' criticisms and recommendations. Sometimes an agency head will accept the advice of a "satellite" group with respect to an individual order or action. Occasionally, a group is virtually coopted into a department as an influential advisory body. Thus the decisions and actions of line agencies are commonly influenced strongly by the constellation of nongovernmental groups in which the agencies are placed. The influence of these groups is often salutary. Departmental and bureau programs are often improved because of nongovernmental group participation in their formulation. It is also clear that agency heads yield lukewarmly to these groups on many issues of substance in order to assure the survival and growth of the agencies they command.

Chiefs of regulatory and enforcement agencies are under special compulsions to work out adjustments with their constituencies, especially with their clientele groups. If administration is exceedingly severe and literal, the interests the agencies are charged with controlling and inspecting may resist by political action, or, even more drastically, by wholesale noncompliance. The collapse of administrative effectiveness may lead to the transfer of responsibility to other agencies, the abandonment of a program, and to the disgrace of the agency leader and his associates. By the same token, however, lax enforcement designed to placate clientele may give rise to conditions that threaten the safety or welfare of the public, to scandals, or to attacks from groups favoring enforcement. Deliberate ineffectiveness can often be as damaging as impotence. Agency heads in this position normally come to informal, often tacit, understandings with the people they regulate, conceding to them by displays of tolerance and "reasonableness," trying by this technique to secure enough compliance to satisfy also the interests insisting on regulation.

In addition, agency heads frequently make concessions to nongovernmental groups not closely identified with their particular agencies, groups that do not often intervene on behalf of those agencies, but that occasionally make claims and are in position to constitute powerful opposition if they are not somehow conciliated. The demands of the religious and ethnic groups fall into this classification. There is normally a balance among the Superintendent and Associate Superintendents of the Department of Education, with Catholic, Protestant, and Jewish segments of the population equally represented, and with the demands of Negro New Yorkers beginning to receive increasing attention here. When the Board of Education recently acceded to Catholic wishes for a policy statement encouraging the inculcation of spiritual values in pupils in the public schools, it was compelled to moderate the original version to make it acceptable to protesting Jewish and Protestant groups, who contended that the initial formulation threatened to permit sectarian religious training in the public school system.

Protestant and Jewish groups again joined to resist acquiescence by the Commission of Hospitals in Catholic objections to the dispensing of contraceptive devices in municipal hospitals. The insistence of some religious groups is also largely responsible for the Department of Welfare policy of assigning children's welfare cases to social workers of the same religion as the children. Negro criticisms of the boundary lines of areas served by public elementary and high schools stimulated a Department of Education survey to find ways of reducing virtual segregation created by the concentration of white and Negro populations in different neighborhoods. None of these groups rush to the aid of these departments when the departments press their pleas for funds and struggle to protect their jurisdiction, but they can make so much difficulty for agency heads that the administrators try to accommodate them whenever possible.

For the same reasons, agency heads often try to conciliate party leaders. Party hierarchies can be redoubtable foes of an administrator and his agency. Usually the influence they attempt to exert on administrative decisions and actions relates to the selection or advancement of personnel, or to individual concessions – such as exemptions from formal regulations, dropping prosecutions, hastening the processing of applications – for party followers, members, supporters, and workers. But they may sometimes intervene in broader policy matters as well.

Finally, concessions are made to the Mayor, the Board of Estimate, and the City Council. Jointly, and individually in varying degrees, as later discussion will show, these top city officials have extensive formal powers over budgets, jurisdiction, and personnel of all city departments and agencies. Consequently, the expected reactions of the citywide organs of government are taken into consideration in the formulation of decisions and courses of action by agency heads, at least to avoid instigation of punitive measures, and, positively, to win sympathy and friendship. Top-level intervention in the operations and internal affairs of the line agencies is far from continuous, and it often takes the form of informal requests like those of party functionaries. It is not unheard of for an administrator to refuse outright to comply with such unofficial demands, and it is fairly common for administrators to dilute or neutralize instructions from above by delay and inaction. For all that, though, no agency leader can afford persistently to ignore the wishes of the major political officers, whether these wishes are tacit or explicit, official or unofficial, general or specific. These desires therefore become important factors in what agency heads decide to do.

Cultivating constituencies is primarily a way of winning friends. Concessions are made for the purpose of avoiding antagonisms. Both are accomplished partly by submission to the will of individuals and groups outside the boundaries of the agencies *per se*.

Truces with other agencies. The fourth strategy of city agency heads is to stabilize their situations by reaching understandings with other line departments and bureaus. The lines of jurisdiction separating one agency from another are often blurred, and a good deal of administrative rivalry is generated by endeavors on the part of administrators to carve out areas of power in which their own organizations are indisputably in control.

There are many places in the government and politics of the city in which rivalries have occurred. The Board of Standards and Appeals, for instance, recently fought off an attempt by the City Planning Commission to acquire some of the Board's power over allowance of variations from zoning regulations. The Department of Traffic defeated the bid of a specially created New York City Parking Authority for control of parking meters and parking-meter revenues and off-street parking facilities. The Department of Marine and Aviation lost its fight to retain control of Idlewild and La Guardia Airports but has thus far fended off proposals to transfer municipally owned piers to the Port of New York Authority, to which the air terminals were leased. A more recent clash of opinion developed over whether to lodge authority to regulate and supervise private refuse collectors in the Department of Licenses or the Department of Sanitation. Agencies vie with each other for jurisdiction and appropriations. Sometimes they even compete to avoid program assignments that are especially difficult and controversial. The Commissioner of Hospitals and the Commissioner of Correction have both tried to prevent lodging responsibility for treatment of narcotics addicts in their departments, and the Department of Health has been restive under burdens of building inspection the Commissioner and the Board of Health would generally prefer to have placed entirely on the Department of Buildings.

However, there are many places in the city government in which rivalries might be expected but which have been stabilized by agreement. School physicians and nurses could be under the Department of Health or the Department of Education; by agreement, they are now under the former, although there is still some vestigial controversy over custody of pupils' health records. Social work services of the Department of Education and the New York City Youth Board overlap. Some aspects of housing are inspected by the Bureau of Sanitary Inspections of the Health Department, some by the Department of Buildings, some by the Division of Interior Electrical Inspections of the Department of Water Supply, Gas, and Electricity, and some by the Fire Department. The Department of Markets as well as the Department of Health has a hand in regulating some food-handling establishments. There are a number of parallels between the out-patient services of the Department of Hospitals and some of the clinics run by the Department of Health. The Department of Traffic relies on the Police Department to enforce its regulations (and does not have a force of inspectors of its own, as the Department of Sanitation does). The city Transit Authority, however, has its own police force. Many line departments besides the Department of Licenses issue licenses of different kinds. There are endless ambiguities of jurisdiction that could precipitate bitter battles. But most line administrators much prefer to work out understandings by negotiation and agreement. They have difficulty enough without being distracted by jurisdictional fights with their colleagues.

Similarly, they work out understandings with their state and federal counterparts. Many municipal agencies are bound closely to the administrative machinery of other levels of government. These sometimes provoke unrestrained hostilities, such as developed between the City Construction Coordinator and the Administrator of the Federal Housing and Home Finance Agency with respect to federal aid for the projected cultural center in Lincoln Square, but are more frequently adjusted quietly and amicably.

THE COUNTERPOISE OF FORCES. With so many factors to keep in mind and so many different kinds of demands to contend with, the life of a line agency chief in the city is not an easy one. Virtually every decision, every action, is a compromise, or reflects a past compromise, or is a compromise with anticipated alignments of forces. The factor preventing most line executives from completely losing control of the policies and programs of their agencies is the very pluralism of the forces with which they must deal. They play one off against the other, which permits them to follow their own preferences part of the time.

The configuration of claimants on each side of every controversy is often composed of quite disparate groups. On birth control questions, for example, Protestant and Jewish religious groups may be joined with medical associations and welfare groups, as well as with planned parenthood organizations. On the handling of child welfare cases, a professional society of social workers was at odds with Catholic groups. Increase of governmental medical services for the public may be backed by the American Public Health Association, yet opposed by medical societies. Traffic and parking regulations may set bus companies and truckers and taxicab operators and garage owners and the American Automobile Association against each other, and may possibly arouse businessmen in the areas affected. Neighborhood groups threatened with displacement by new roadways or civic improvements may battle with all their strength against planning and motorist and cultural groups. The divisions are not always neat and symmetrical. Any combination of elements, including parts of the bureaucracies involved, may form to support or oppose an agency on any question.

Agency heads usually become adept at calculating the gains and costs of various courses of action, and the opportunities for the satisfaction of their personal values, or they do not stay in office long. All kinds of things must be considered: the effect on public relations generally; the probabilities that a given contender feels strongly enough about an issue, and has enough staying power and skill, to be a useful ally or an opponent worth watching in subsequent agency tribulations; the other connections and modes of influence of the combatants; the reactions of other political officers of government; the chance that quiescent groups, assuming the decisions will go the way they prefer, may spring into action if their expectations are not realized; and many others. In the end, of course, a great deal depends on each administrator's intuition and experience, for there is no mathematical calculus to answer these questions. A good deal of the time, they yield to the forces they think will give them the strongest support in the long run – or at least provide the weakest resistance to other phases of the agency program. Frequently, they try to work out compromises. Sometimes they take refuge in inaction, and let the contending interests fight on until one or the other seems clearly to have the upper hand. Sometimes they act and then manage to convince the objectors that they had no other choice. Occasionally, they do exactly what they want and hope the antagonists will stalemate each other.

At bottom, what the governmental line agencies in the city do is a compound of customary routine, strategies for survival, and a small increment of periodic innovation. The first of these is sure to continue as long as the second is successfully accomplished. Accomplishment of the second hinges, in turn, on the third, for a static organization in the dynamic world of New York City politics is marked for eventual extinction. It is the second and third elements of the compound that fall within the personal province of the agency heads: hence their strategies directed at getting internal control of their agencies, winning external support and avoiding external attacks, and balancing the forces around them so that they can introduce innovations. These are some of the factors at work shaping the pattern of governmental services, regulation, and enforcement activities in New York. . . .

Selected Examples of Line Administrators in Action

Department of buildings. The Commissioner of Buildings heads a line agency of intermediate size (approximately 1,500 employees), but he faces a task of immense difficulty and his choices of strategy as an administrator are characterized by persistent dilemmas. The job of the Department of Buildings is to ensure by a system of inspections and certificates the safety for use and occupancy of every building and structure in the city, and by inspection and sanctions to secure safe and sanitary housing for all dwellers in tenements and other multiple dwellings. The agency thus has a regulatory assignment, a governmental role invariably surrounded by frustrations and risks for the officials involved.

The troubled evolution of the Department as an organization is itself testimony to the uncertainties of purpose and method which have accompanied the functions of the agency. When the charter of 1901 was adopted, the regulation of buildings was left with the five Borough Presidents, in recognition of the many "local" forces which demanded accommodation in the application of the Building Code (a part of the Administrative Code) and other regulatory controls. However, when the social reformers of a half century ago won a victory in their battle against "the tenements," they preferred to entrust the enforcement of the Multiple Dwelling Law not to the Borough Presidents, but to a new city department – the Tenement House Department. Thus matters stood until 1938, when the new charter established a Department of Housing and Buildings, transferring the functions of the Borough Presidents in this field, as well as the functions of regulating multiple dwellings, to the new department (renamed the Department of Buildings in 1957).

The Commissioner of Buildings and his two deputies accordingly administer an agency which has two quite distinctive assignments: first, the issuance of permits and certificates for all buildings and structures in the city under the terms of the city's Building Code, the state Labor Law, the rules and regulations of the city's Board of Standards and

Appeals, and other related statutes and rules; second, the enforcement of safety and sanitary standards in multiple dwellings under the terms of the state Multiple Dwelling Law, the more stringent city Multiple Dwelling Code (a part of the Administrative Code), and other related statutes and rules. These two main tasks of the Department have some common elements, but they also bring to the Commissioner the difficulties of working under two quite different sets of rules, dealing with two sets of constituencies, and competing or cooperating with two groups of other governmental agencies. One assignment does not strengthen his hand in performing the other. Further, the laws and rules under which his agency exercises its powers are highly complex and detailed. They are less the product of his predecessors' recommendations than they are of the ceaseless efforts of his constituencies to win points in statute or rule. And both the courts and the Board of Standards and Appeals show a decided tendency to review his agency's actions in detail. The Commissioner's instructions thus come less from the Mayor than they do from state and local law and rules written for him by others, and under which his exercise of discretion is subject to close and frequent review by the Board and the courts.

Moreover, the Commissioner does not find it easy to establish his leadership or control over the internal organization of his department. Until 1957 the charter required that there be "in each borough a branch office and a borough superintendent." The Borough Superintendent was made, for all practical purposes, an autonomous official, his actions being subjected to review only by the Board of Standards and Appeals – not by the Commissioner. This concession to borough autonomy, and to the interest groups accustomed to that arrangement, was also accompanied by a requirement that there should be a Division of Housing within the Department, its head to be one of the deputy commissioners. The Commissioner was able, in 1957, to gain greater control over his agency by reorganization, which placed Borough Superintendents under his supervision and permitted him to consolidate the functions and staff of the Housing Division with other functions of his agency. But the difficulties of internal control by the Commissioner persist. The attitudes and habits of the staff are set deep in the past arrangements, and the tenure and status of its members are protected by civil service law and rules enforced by the city's Personnel Department.

The Commissioner has no great assets when he deals with the other agencies of the city government. The organized groups in his constituency are in such matters more often hostile than helpful to him. His leverage with the Bureau of the Budget is accordingly slight, as it is also with the Personnel Department. He cannot often command high priority with the Law Department, upon whose staff he depends for assistance in the prosecution of housing violations. The Department of Investigation is not infrequently an inquisitor of his staff, as are also the District Attorneys, for the head of a regulatory agency soon learns that staff irregularities are an endemic phenomenon. Both the Fire Department and the Department of Air Pollution Control have inspectional and licensing powers that compete with their own. Inspections are also conducted by the Department of Health, partly under regulations of the Board of Health and partly under more general housing legislation; both the Department and the Board are said to be resentful of having to perform services they regard as more appropriate for the Department of Buildings, and they tend to be critical of every Buildings Commissioner. The State Department of Labor, too, is a critical observer of many of his actions. But most of all, the Commissioner of Buildings feels the supervisory weight of the Board of Standards and Appeals and of the courts: the Board not only makes rules for him to enforce, but it also has sweeping powers of review over the specific actions of his agency. The courts have equally extensive control over the sanctions (fines or imprisonment) which are his main reliance in the enforcement of safety and sanitary standards in multiple dwellings. In short, the Commissioner is not a favorably situated bargainer when he deals with the other agencies of the city government.

The Commissioner's difficulties arise in considerable part out of the nature of his interest group constituency. There are several elements in this constituency: the building and construction industry, the real estate owners and managers, the labor unions of the building and construction trades, the architectural and engineering professions, and the citizen and professional associations concerned with the housing conditions of the low-income population. Only the last-named – the housing groups – can be counted upon consistently by the Commissioner as defenders of his powers. All the others feel the pinch of his regulations and so are more inclined to limit than to expand his initiative and discretion. To the builders (for example, the Building Congress, the Building Trade Employers Association, the Metropolitan Builders Association), the permits and certificates of the Buildings Department are restraints which they prefer to minimize while acknowledging their necessity. The owners and managers of real estate (organized, for example, in the Real Estate Board of New York, the Commerce and Industry Association, and others) share these attitudes, as do the organizations of architects and engineers. To the interested labor unions (for example, the carpenters, bricklayers, electricians, plumbers, building employees), the Department of Buildings is a guardian of the gains which they have won in labor laws and building codes; they do not expect initiative and leadership from its leaders and staff.

The Commissioner of Buildings has few opportunities to cultivate active and helpful constituencies or to create a favorable climate of public opinion that would provide him with support and bargaining power. In this respect, he shares a common condition with most regulatory agencies: created often through the efforts of an aroused public opinion, they are gradually left to deal primarily with those whom they regulate. The Commissioner can expect occasional assistance from the civic groups (for example, the Citizens Union, the Citizens Housing and Planning Council), the charitable, religious, and social welfare groups (for example, the Community Council of New York), and from various tenant organizations (usually temporary in character). But these groups are more likely to be critical of his concessions to others than to give him consistent support. The press will take its main cues from these criticisms and from periodic investigations of alleged irregularities in the agency. No Commissioner of Buildings has ever been a hero to the city press.

The relations between the party leaders and the Department of Buildings have low visibility. Historically, these accommodations were arranged mainly in the semiautonomous borough offices and (except perhaps for multiple dwelling enforcement matters) seem still to be centered there despite the recent reorganization of the agency. In their dealings with the Department, the party leaders tend to share the views of the regulated groups that the Commissioner should be sympathetic and flexible in his use of the regulatory power. The party leaders have no disposition to encourage him in aggressive use or expansion of his jurisdiction. Only the Mayor has consistent tendencies to assist him in the vigorous exercise of his powers and duties, but the Mayor is isolated from the Department by the barriers of highly detailed statutes and rules, by the buffer of the autonomous Board of Standards and Appeals, and by the borough-centered traditions and loyalties of the staff.

Without other allies of weight and influence, without opportunities to form a broadly supporting public opinion, each Commissioner of Buildings is brought back, whatever his initial aspirations, to the necessity of a settlement with the groups whose activities he regulates. It is with them that he must make his peace. . . .

POLICE DEPARTMENT. The Police Commissioner heads the most visible, the most publicized, the most dramatic and controversial of the city's line agencies. His Department is also one of the city's largest, its staff numbering over 26,000 at the end of 1957, of which more than 25,000 were members of the uniformed force. Representing one of the oldest of the city government's functions, but confronted with constantly changing problems and pressures in its assignments, the Department presents to the Police Commissioner and his deputies complexities and dilemmas not often matched in difficulty in the city's other line agencies.

The Police Department has the broadest regulatory assignment among all the regulatory activities of the city government. From the charter alone, the Department derives a sweeping obligation and power to "preserve the public peace, prevent crime, detect and arrest offenders, . . . preserve order . . . , enforce and prevent the violation of all laws and ordinances . . . ," accompanied by a series of more specific assignments. But the greater body of the Department's assignments comes from state laws and local ordinances and codes containing extensive regulatory and law enforcement provisions which the Department is expected to apply to all violators. Still other provisions of charter and statute make the Police Commissioner the licensing, inspecting, or supervising authority over certain trades (for example, public dance halls, cabarets, taxicabs and taxi drivers, pawnbrokers, cartmen, and others). To all these regulatory assignments of the Department there must also be added the traditional and widespread expectations that the police force is a service agency, obliged to attend to the countless necessities and conveniences of an urban population for whom the police are a visible and available resource. The Commissioner can find few boundaries to his responsibilities; he has less difficulty in discovering the limits of his opportunities and resources.

The Police Commissioner's hopes for the exercise of personal leadership and initiative as the responsible head of his Department revolve around his capacity to secure internal control over his agency, his relations with the Mayor, with other city officials and the party leaders, and with the Department's complex constituency. These basic conditions of his leadership and initiative are rarely fully mastered by the Police Commissioner. Resolute outsiders and insiders, in their turn as Commissioners, have each expended great energies and varied strategies upon this dilemma without triumphant results. Other Commissioners have accepted the prevailing arrangements, expressing satisfaction in quite marginal increments of change; still others have moved quickly on to more responsible or less taxing environments.

Securing internal control of the Department is the insurmountable barrier to leadership, initiative, and innovation by Police Commissioners. The Commissioner is not lacking in formal power for this purpose. The charter declares that he "shall have cognizance and control of the government, administration, disposition and discipline of the department, and control of the police force of the department" and, further, that he "shall be the chief executive officer of the police force." But these formal powers must in reality be exercised in the context of a personnel system which blunts their use, in the face of the close-knit organized police bureaucracies determined to limit the Commissioner's initiative and discretion, and through an organization structure designed to preserve the traditions of the force and its settled patterns of operation. The Commissioner has few "civilian" helpers; they are mainly clerical and custodial. The personnel system dictates that every member of the uniformed police force must be first recruited and inducted as a patrolman, a "rookie" without special skills or knowledge who enters upon a long apprenticeship in the tradition-centered doctrines and practices of the force, rising slowly rank by rank through examinations which also emphasize seniority and mastery of the Department's established codes of police practice.

The police captains who emerge from this process of advancement by apprenticeship, indoctrination, and seniority constitute the pool of talent from which the Commissioner must select his officers for the command posts and the managerial tasks of the Department – the deputy inspectors, the inspectors, the deputy chief inspectors, the assistant chief inspectors, and the Chief Inspector who is the head of the uniformed force. In recent decades, Police Commissioners have increasingly chosen, or have been persuaded, to select their deputy commissioners from this group also. Thus the Commissioner is enclosed within (or ostracized by, if he does not conform) a personnel system which limits his choices of key personnel and provides him but rarely with fellow champions of innovation, or with experts and specialists in fields of knowledge (technological and sociological) which might transform police administration under his leadership, or even with that modicum of competition in ideas among different segments of his staff which might give him limited opportunities for catalytic action as Commissioner.

If the personnel system confronts the Commissioner with a tradition-centered top command – "the top brass," composed of approximately 100 inspectors at various grades and of not quite 200 captains – the organized police bureaucracies (lieutenants, sergeants, patrolmen) bring additional restrictive pressures to bear upon him. Mayor McClellan observed long ago that the Police Department was "run by the inspectors," not by the Commissioner; for the past several decades, he would have needed to add "and by the police bureaucracies." They have power inside the Department to mold the behavior of their members in such ways as will reduce the impact of any change in policy or procedure sponsored by the Commissioner. They have secured special protections for their members in both state statutes and city rules, which preserve their capacity to resist without much risk of reprisal or severe discipline. They have power in the more general political arena, where officials and party leaders have learned to listen to them and to act sympathetically. Police Commissioners may bristle at bureaucratic boldness and evoke the symbols of command and discipline, but the organized police groups are confident and persistent; they are on familiar ground and have often waited out these storms before. Their goal is self-direction in their accustomed ways, not an eager responsiveness to either the "top brass" or the current Commissioner.

The twin forces of the Department's closed personnel system and the organized police bureaucracies help to preserve a third barrier to leadership by the Commissioner – an organization structure awkwardly suited to the Commissioner's purposes of leadership and innovation. The basic structure is traditional and does not yield much to the requirements of changes in policies and in assignments, or of advances in police technology developed elsewhere. Organizationally, the Department is wedded to performing its work through geographical units – precincts, districts and divisions, borough commands – at the expense of greater specialization and mobility of its resources. The major concessions to specialization which have been made (the detective, traffic, and emergency service patrol groups) are themselves each organized geographically. In this and other ways specialized personnel is almost invariably squeezed into the geographical chains-of-command. Methods and procedures must also conform to the mold of geography, affecting adversely the attraction and feasibility of almost every proposed change in technology or policy. Police Commissioners are only occasionally aware of this tyranny of geography as an organizational vise; they have no managerial staff to develop for them the alternatives in police organization and procedures which might give them unsuspected opportunities for breaking the crust of custom and habits in police administration. For example, the Police Commissioner was forced in 1949 to yield the traffic planning assignment to a new city agency because his personnel system and his organizational arrangements could produce neither the specialized personnel (the traffic planners, traffic engineers, and statistical analysts) nor the specialized methods necessary to handle the traffic problem at a high level of experiment and innovation.

The closed personnel system, the power of the police bureaucracies, and the inflexible organization structure of the Department have an additional by-product for the Commissioner: he must expend a great part of his energies in attempts at "policing the police." His problems are concentrated in two phenomena: police corruption and police violence. However aggressively the Commissioner pursues the goal of police integrity by the use of special squads to investigate the force, by shake-ups and transfers of command, by swift suspensions and other forms of discipline, he accepts ultimately that police corruption is endemic to his organization, and that he is fortunate if he can prevent its reaching epidemic proportions. He lacks the resources to do more. On the score of police violence, he is compelled to yield in a different fashion: he must almost invariably take a tough line in justification of the use of force by the police, whether it be rationalizing the promiscuous use of the club, the gun, or the "third degree." His organization (and his own training, if he is a career Commissioner) does not permit him to depart from this doctrine.

Police Commissioners thus exercise formal but essentially peripheral control over the Police Department. They can dramatize the role of the Department in the life of the city; they can urge forcefully and often successfully the expansion of the Department in numbers and budget and thus win some internal support; they can lead crusades against selected targets ("round-ups" of alleged vagrants; raids on gamblers, narcotic "rings," houses of prostitution; arrests of alleged subversives); and they can be stern disciplinarians in dealing with individual members of the force who violate overtly the regulations of the Department. But these are the outer boundaries of their control. The more positive measures of leadership are beyond their reach.

Police Commissioners in New York City have long sought an autonomous status for their Department with freedom from supervision by the Mayor, from interventions by party leaders, and from jurisdictional invasions by other governmental agencies. "No outside interference" has been their uniform motto for several decades, and all external influences have usually been condemned as "politics." In seeking to maximize the self-directing capacity of the Department, Commissioners have presumably sought also to maximize their own opportunities for leadership and direction of the police agency. But autonomy for the Department has also meant isolation for the Commissioner from sources which might help him in his difficult task of securing internal control. The police bureaucracy seems to be the main beneficiary of the autonomy which the Police Commissioners have secured.

Freedom from supervision by the Mayor has been a special target of the drive for police autonomy. Mayoral interest in police policy and police administration has been consistently rebuffed by equating it with the interests of party leaders or, more ambiguously, with politics. In their acceptance of this formula for ostracizing Mayors from any opportunities to assume general responsibility for leadership in law enforcement, the Police Commissioners have had the support of the police bureaucracy, the civic groups, the communication media, and others. There is a general consensus that Mayors merit only the blame for police failures. The assistance which Mayors might give Police Commissioners in their efforts to acquire leadership within the Department has been forfeited in preference for the ambiguous formula of autonomy.

Removal of the influence of party leaders from police administration has also been a goal of most Police Commissioners, supported by the police bureaucracy and by almost all the articulate voices in the city. Several Commissioners have given this problem high priority, and the long-term trend in the Department has been to reduce steadily the opportunities of party leaders to intervene overtly either in the personnel system or in police policy. The most striking example is the neutralization of the police role in election administration. The upper limits of the trend are to be found, however, in the disposition of individual members of the force to build mutually useful relationships with party leaders. If party leaders have been largely excluded at headquarters, they are not yet ignored in the precincts or other local commands. One consequence of this development may be that the Commissioner is isolated from the party leaders in a way in which his lieutenants, detectives, captains, and inspectors are not.

Other governmental agencies give Police Commissioners less difficulty. The Police Commissioners are especially able to escape some of the tight controls of the overhead agencies – Budget, Personnel, Law, Investigation, and others – which so often burden the discretion of other department heads. With other line agencies, the relations are often more complex and sometimes characterized by jurisdictional friction, for example, with District Attorneys, and the Departments of Education, Fire, Health, Sanitation, Traffic, Welfare, the Youth Board, and the special authorities. In the main, however, the Police Department tends more often to have its own way, the other agencies yielding to its power, its autonomy, and its cohesiveness. The other side of the medal is the Police Commissioner's limited opportunities to offer firm cooperation with other agencies even when he wishes to do so. His control over his own Department is not sufficient for him to pledge its affirmative participation in programs involving important innovations in police attitudes or methods.

The Police Department has one of the most complex constituencies among the city's line agencies. It is the object of relatively constant attention from a wider range of nongovernmental groups than any other single agency. With such extensive attention directed at them, Police Commissioners have great difficulty in deciding to which voices they must listen most receptively, and on what subjects. The most relevant constituency elements are difficult to identify. Fragmentation in organization and ambivalence in attitudes toward the Department are their most distinctive characteristics. Police Commissioners never quite succeed in identifying the hard core either of their supporting groups or of the opposition groups with whom they must come to terms. The formations and their attitudes tend to be fluid and unpredictable.

There are a few certainties upon which the Police Commissioner can reasonably depend in his dealings with the Department's constituency, but the sum total of these several certainties is likely to confront him with as many inconsistencies as clarifications. He can usually expect more support than opposition for proposals to expand the size of the police force; the economy groups have a traditional tolerance for police budgets, and most other groups are regularly demanding more police services. He can count upon the groups licensed or inspected by the Department to attempt to capture the licensing and inspection units of his organization, thus threatening his control over policy and exposing him to the risks of unfavorable exposés. He can reasonably anticipate that the communication media, especially the press, will be ambivalent in their attitudes toward him and his agency, publicizing with equal zeal and emphasis the dramatic accomplishments of the police and the sordid chapters of police corruption and violence. He will note, too, that the merchant and automobile associations urging more effective traffic control are also inclined to condemn "arbitrary" or "rigid" enforcement techniques. Each religious group presses for its doctrines of law enforcement. Employer groups urge strict supervision of picketing; labor unions emphasize their hard-won standards of strict neutrality by the police in labor disputes. Some groups demand a hard line by police toward juvenile delinquents; others insist upon a subordinate role for the police in such matters. Some voices advocate wide use of the nightstick and the dragnet against gangsters, punks, and gamblers; others, such as bar associations, civil liberties groups, and some communication media, remind the Police Commissioner of the due process of law. There are no "peak associations" tying these groups together, either as support or opposition. The prime difficulty for the Police Commissioner is that, while his highly fragmented constituency can cause him much trouble, he cannot expect much help from it; he cannot, in fact, find even a stable and significant center of opposition with which he might reach long-term accommodations. Nor does his constituency furnish him with a lever which he might use to move the police bureaucracy toward greater responsiveness to his leadership.

The Police Commissioner – isolated from the Mayor and other elected officials, from the party leaders, and from other agencies, and confronted by an unstructured, fragmented constituency – is thus cut off from effective external alliances and thrust back upon his own limited resources in attempting to lead and direct the police bureaucracy. Autonomy for the Department spells isolation for the Commissioner. With energy and resolution, and some public relations skill, he may create a favorable public image of himself as an omnipresent, incorruptible, and determined administrator. He may exploit the competitive relation between the 300 members of "the brass" and the 24,000 members of the rank and file, in ways that may increase somewhat his influence with both; he may emphatically invoke the semimilitary command structure and vocabulary of the Department to make his purposes unambiguous. He may find tangible and intangible rewards to bestow as incentives for innovation and for responsiveness to his leadership, and he may exhort his officers and men to aspire to the status of a profession, to embrace the trends toward modernization, to take the lead among police systems. All these efforts will help him in his leadership, but their combined long-range increment is not strikingly large. In the end, whatever the dash and determination at the beginning, the Commissioners yield to the necessity of being more the spokesman and the advocate than the leader and the innovator. . . .

The Ordeals and Triumphs of Line Agency Leaders

Faced by awesome combinations of forces with vested interests in the existing situation, few commissioners are willing to invest the energy and take the risks required to make extensive changes in policy, organization, or procedure. They can easily create a general impression of vigor and drive by working assiduously to intensify prevailing activities – to add new policemen or firemen or teachers or other personnel, to increase the number of police stations or firehouses or schools or hospitals or parks or other installations, to augment services – in short, to do more and more of what has traditionally been done, and to do it in the customary way. In such efforts, they can normally count on the enthusiastic support of their career bureaucracies, partly because the bureaucrats, as specialists, believe ardently in the importance and desirability of the programs they administer, and partly because expansion of this kind opens additional opportunities for advancement without disturbing the settled arrangements and long-standing accommodations worked out in the past. They can depend on the backing of the clientele they serve or regulate, who hope for better service on the one hand and, on the other, suppression of violators of regulations whose violations give them competitive advantages over more conscientious business rivals, and on the approval of the party organizations who hope at least for benefits on Election Day, and perhaps for more immediate returns in the form of enlarged patronage opportunities. Economy-oriented tax-paying groups and the financial officers of the city may battle proposals for intensified activity, but they are less effective than their adversaries because the service-demanders are more numerous, and because each coalition of line administrators, bureaucrats, and associated nongovernmental groups concentrates on a narrow range of the spectrum of public functions while their opponents spread their resources over the entire field. The Mayor and the Board of Estimate, it will later be seen, tend to ratify the agreements reached by the contending factions. So line administrators are not idle, nor are they paralyzed by the powerful field of forces in which they find themselves. But the *courses* of action open to them are the traditional ones; they find it easiest to be active and dynamic, and to achieve successes, when they strengthen the ongoing system. The strategies available to them discourage departures from routine, introduction of extensive alterations, experiments in program or method, for the strategies are most effective within the established framework. The path of innovation is rocky, twisting, and full of pitfalls.

Another opportunity for dynamism is offered by dramatic "clean-ups" and managerial "improvements." Again, these rarely work profound transformations of policy, organization, or procedure; but they frequently add to the luster of the existing state of affairs by robbing complaints of corruption and inefficiency of their force. And they win the plaudits of reform and civic groups, professional organizations, and exponents of economy. Nothing really changes, but the familiar things are done better, more honestly, and perhaps more cheaply. Line agency chiefs are often able to accomplish a great deal of this nature by following their standard strategies.

Yet innovations do occur; the system is not static. The impetus may come from a scandal, an alarming deterioration of service, a higher level of government (especially through financial grants), a reform administration, or a singularly energetic administrator undaunted by the magnitude of the task he sets for himself. The innovations, however, are usually limited in scope; they strike at selected parts of a program or agency, not at everything simultaneously. They are incremental, not total.

Indeed, the scale of innovation, even under the pressures of crisis, can hardly be much greater than this. For the strategies of the line administrator – winning internal control of his agencies, and manipulating his environment – require, as we have seen, accommodations with all the participants in the contest for the stakes of politics who are concerned with the agency decisions. To render himself less vulnerable to all the conflicting and contradictory demands and instructions, and to all the forms of resistance and opposition to his will, the agency head has to muster the support of all the friends he can find and strike bargains with everyone around him. To preserve his discretion in some areas of his jurisdiction, he must surrender in others. He has to placate his allies to keep them on his side and pacify those who are rarely active in his aid lest they use their influence to injure him and his agency. He has to balance a welter of factors to survive, let alone to progress, for virtually everyone he deals with has an independent source of power.

In working out their adjustments, line agency chiefs often become so proficient in negotiating with other contestants that they achieve a high degree of immunity from the leadership of the central organs of government. Together with their friends and allies, and their professional and bureaucratic counterparts in other levels of government, they emerge as central – but not necessarily dominant – figures in functional islands of decision-making power. Their impress on the substance of governmental decisions is therefore considerable. Nevertheless, their freedom of action is sharply restricted. That is why the exceptional line agency chief who is so skilled at setting the pressures upon him against one another that he has numerous occasions to satisfy his creativity and his cravings for leadership towers over his fellows on the governmental scene.

Part

4

POLICIES AND THEIR SOCIOECONOMIC ENVIRONMENTS

All of the essays in this book deal with policies and the social and economic features in their environments that help to shape them. The essays in Part 4 stand apart by presenting some innovative conceptions of policy and a focused examination of the socioeconomic environment.

We have seen various conceptions of policy: the decisions of a population in referenda; the actions of local governments in deciding how to proceed with fluoridation decisions; the aggregate level of taxation; expenditures in total and for certain kinds of service; the average benefits provided to welfare recipients; factor analyses of several policy measures; gubernatorial and legislative decisions on agency budget requests; and roll call votes in a state legislature. The measures of social and economic determinants include individuals' income, education, and ethnic group membership; urban and rural residence patterns; residential mobility; valve systems; "region" as a surrogate for several cultural and historical features. Part 4 offers one conception of policy as the timing of state governments in adopting new programs; another that sees policy as an evolving, continuous process where earlier decisions are critical to subsequent decisions; and one that expands the conception of public policies to include the actions of local businessmen and attorneys in their pursuit of debtors. Finally, one study of socioeconomic characteristics reports on eight separate factor analyses ranging over the 1890–1960 time span. It finds two stable components of states' social and economic traits, shows how those components can be used to plot major changes in certain states over time, and shows that the salience of economic features for politics changes with historical conditions.

Jack L. Walker tries to capture one dimension of state policy by noting the time — relative to other states — when each state adopts certain programs. He wants to measure an important feature of policy that may not show up in aggregate levels of government expenditures or current levels of service. In various parts of his essay, he terms this phenomenon "innovation," or a state's willingness to make speedy adoptions of innovations developed elsewhere. By knowing how early a state begins a program, according to Walker, we can learn something about its policy process. Although Walker seems to be on the trail of an important feature of state policy, his article includes some implicit questions that remain unanswered: Do states making the later adoptions of programs named in his article simply copy the activities of the earlier states? Or are some later adopters being highly innovative in developing changes from programs earlier conceived? How often are major innovations (that is, programs that affect huge resources or numerous people) developed in states that score low on the average index of innovation? What conditions provoke these deviations? How can we explain the juxtaposition of California and Missouri in the same cluster of innovation, when California's reputation is that of a leader in state programs while Missouri's is that of a laggard?

The selection by Andrew T. Cowart uses simple measures of policy: per capita expenditures in several programs aided by the United States Office of Economic Opportunity. Yet his findings point to a conception of policy that has not been treated in earlier selections. In showing that previous commitments to welfare and education policies are the strongest determinants of early action in the "anti-poverty" field, Cowart points up the sequential, evolutionary processes that have been found elsewhere in policy making. A state's posture in welfare and education may reflect the support of the population for those services, or a feature of the "political culture." Or prior policy performance may signal the presence of dedicated and successful public officials who develop the legislative support necessary for strong programs and generous budgets. Whatever the source of strength and education in welfare, it transfers to newly available programs in related fields. The adoption of new programs is not a separate political act, but rather the assimilation of new opportunities into an existing fabric of policy. States that had created strong programs in the past move ahead with more speed and commitment than states that have weak programs. The strengths of existing programs are more important for the new developments than are other features of the states' economy, population, or politics.

Herbert Jacob expands our conception of public policy by his study of decisions made by local businessmen and their lawyers with respect to debtors. These form public policies insofar as they involve the decisions of state and federal courts. Jacob explains the several alternatives that face a creditor. He can use private means of persuasion or negotiation with debtors, or he can invoke either of two legal proceedings: garnishment of wages, a state enforced procedure for paying off debts over a two-year period that provides little protection to the debtor, or a federally enforced procedure for paying off debts that provides somewhat more protection for the debtor. Jacob reports marked differences in the use of these options in four Wisconsin communities. These differences are not conditioned by the kinds of social, economic, or political traits that have been cited as determinants of policy in other essays of this book. However, the procedures followed are consistent with community norms that have been identified by other scholars. Jacob suggests there may be other kinds of policy differences between jurisdictions that do not show themselves in gross measures of expenditures or taxation, but must be identified through a detailed inquiry into the decisions made by government officials or, as in this case, by those private citizens who serve as tangents to government officials.

Richard I. Hofferbert deals with many indicators of social and economic traits that other articles have considered. His contribution lies in defining the historical continuity of two principal dimensions. From 1890 to 1960, he finds that the traits of "Industrialization" and "Affluence" sum-up the social and economic features on which states differ. "Industrialization" includes such elements as the value of manufactured goods, the proportion of the work force in manufacturing, the value of agricultural land, population density, the proportion of foreign stock in the population, and urbanism. "Affluence" includes levels of education, property values, personal income, the incidence of motor vehicles and telephones, and the proportion of the population that is white. Hofferbert computes "factor scores" showing each state's relative position on these dimensions at each decade. With these scores he identifies changes in the economic status of individual states and entire regions during the twentieth century. He also shows that relationships between economic conditions and politics have not remained constant from one generation to the next. Like other essays in this book, Hofferbert points away from simple notions of economic determinism and cites the need of evaluating economic influences in the context of other historical features.

THE DIFFUSION OF INNOVATIONS AMONG THE AMERICAN STATES

JACK L. WALKER

We are now in the midst of a notable revival of interest in the politics of the American states. During the last decade studies have been conducted of the social, political and economic determinants of state policy outcomes.[1] Several of these writers have argued that the relative wealth of a state, its degree of industrialization, and other measures of social and economic development are more important in explaining its level of expenditures than such political factors as the form of legislative apportionment, the amount of party competition, or the degree of voter participation.[2] It has been claimed that such factors as the level of per-

Reprinted by permission from Jack L. Walker, "The Diffusion of Innovations among the American States," *American Political Science Review*, 63 (Sept., 1969), 880–899.

Thanks are due to the Committee on Governmental and Legal Processes of the Social Science Research Council, the Carnegie Corporation, the Michigan Legislative Intern Program, and the Rackham Faculty Research Fund of the University of Michigan for grants which made this study possible; to Mrs. Adarsh Trehan, Doyle Buckwalter, Michael Traugott, Mrs. Jennifer Drew Campbell, and Terry Bender who assisted in the collection and analysis of the data; and to H. Douglas Price, Rufus Browning, Warren Miller, Lawrence Mohr, Robert Friedman, Joel Aberbach, Robert Putnam, Ronald Brunner, Dennis Riley, Gail MacColl, and my wife, Linda Walker, whose criticisms and comments have helped me avoid several errors of inference and judgment.

[1] Beginning with Richard E. Dawson and James A. Robinson, "Inter-Party Competition, Economic Variables, and Welfare Policies in the American States," *Journal of Politics* (May, 1963), 265–289, there have been numerous articles and books on the subject. The most recent summary is: John H. Fenton and Donald W. Chamberlayne, "The Literature Dealing with the Relationships Between Political Processes, Socio-economic Conditions and Public Policies in the American States: A Bibliographical Essay," *Polity* (Spring, 1969), 388–394.

[2] For examples see: Herbert Jacob, "The Consequences of Malapportionment: A Note of Caution," *Social Forces* (1964), 260–266; the chapters by Robert Salisbury, Robert Friedman, Thomas Dye, and Dawson and Robinson in: Herbert Jacob and Kenneth Vines (eds.), *Politics in the American States: A Comparative Analysis* (Boston, 1965); Richard I. Hofferbert, "The Relation Between Public Policy and Some Structural and Environmental Variables in the American States," [*American Political Science Review*] (March, 1966), 73–82; and Thomas Dye, *Politics, Economics and the Public: Policy Outcomes in the American States* (Chicago, 1966).

sonal income or the size of the urban population are responsible *both* for the degree of participation and party competition in a state, *and* the nature of the system's policy outputs. By making this argument these writers have called into question the concepts of representation and theories of party and group conflict which, in one form or another, are the foundations for much of American political science.[3]

There is a growing awareness, however, that levels of expenditure alone are not an adequate measure of public policy outcomes. Sharkansky has shown, for example, that levels of expenditure and levels of actual service are seldom correlated; presumably, some states are able to reach given service levels with much less expenditure than others.[4] Besides establishing the appropriate level of expenditure for a program, policy makers must also decide about the program's relative scope, provisions for appeal from administrative orders, eligibility requirements, the composition of regulatory boards and commissions, and many other matters which have little to do with money. Before we can evaluate the relative importance of structural and political factors as determinants of policy, therefore, we need to investigate decisions outside the budgetary process. In order to advance that object this study will focus on one of the most fundamental policy decisions of all: whether to initiate a program in the first place.

States have traditionally been judged according to the relative speed with which they have accepted new ideas. Wisconsin, because of its leadership during the Progressive period and its early adoption of the direct primary, the legislative reference bureau, and workmen's compensation, gained a reputation as a pioneering state which it has never lost. Reputations of this kind are usually based only on random impressions and they may be inaccurate or misleading, but if it is true that some states change more readily than others a study of the way states adopt new ideas might lead to some important insights into the whole process of political change and development.

This essay is primarily an exercise in theory building. My aim is to develop propositions which might be used as guides to the study of the diffusion of innovations and which might also apply to budgeting and

[3] For an evaluation of the significance of this literature and its implications for political science see: Robert Salisbury, "The Analysis of Public Policy: A Search for Theories and Roles," in Austin Ranney (ed.), *Political Science and Public Policy* (Chicago, 1968), pp. 151–178.

[4] Ira Sharkansky, "Government Expenditures and Public Services in the American States" [*American Political Science Review*] (1967), 1066–1077. Sharkansky also identifies important political variables in his: "Economic and Political Correlates of State Government Expenditures: General Tendencies and Deviant Cases," *Midwest Journal of Political Science* (1967), 173–192.

other forms of decision making.[5] Limitations in the data I have collected do not allow empirical testing of all the explanations I propose; the currently untestable propositions are presented in the hope that they may help in preparing the ground for future research. The study begins with an effort to devise a measure of the relative speed with which states adopt new programs. Once a measure of this phenomenon is created efforts are made to discover its principal demographic and political correlates. The article concludes with an effort to devise an explanation for the adoption of innovations based on insights gathered from studies of decision making, reference group theory, and the diffusion of innovations. The major questions being investigated are: (1) why do some states act as pioneers by adopting new programs more readily than others, and once innovations have been adopted by a few pioneers, (2) how do these new forms of service or regulation spread among the American states?

I Definitions and Distinctions

Several terms have already been used here which have ambiguous meanings and it is important to make clear just how they are to be defined. The most important, and potentially misleading, is the term "innovation." An innovation will be defined simply as a program or policy which is new to the states adopting it, no matter how old the program may be or how many other states may have adopted it. Even though bureaucratic innovations or new departures by regulatory commissions or courts may be mentioned in the course of the discussion, the data used to measure the relative speed of adoption of innovations consists exclusively of legislative actions, simply because the data was readily available only in that form.

[5] There is a well established body of research on the diffusion of innovations from which I have drawn many insights. For general reviews of this literature see: Everett M. Rogers, *Diffusion of Innovations* (New York, 1962), Elihu Katz, Martin L. Levin, and Herbert Hamilton, "Traditions of Research in the Diffusion of Innovations," *American Sociological Review* (1963), 237–252. For early attempts to study the American states from this perspective see: Ada J. Davis, "The Evolution of the Institution of Mothers' Pensions in the United States," *American Journal of Sociology* (1930), 573–582; Edgar C. McVoy, "Patterns of Diffusion in the United States," *American Sociological Review* (1940), 219–227; and E. H. Sutherland, "The Diffusion of Sexual Psychopath Laws," *American Journal of Sociology* (1950–51), 144–156. Also see: Torsten Hagerstrand, *Innovation Diffusion as a Spatial Process* (Chicago, 1967); and Robert Mason and Albert N. Halter, "The Application of a System of Simultaneous Equations to an Innovation Diffusion Model," *Social Forces* (1968), 182–193.

We are studying the relative speed and the spatial patterns of *adoption* of new programs, not their invention or creation. Invention, or bringing into being workable, relevant solutions to pressing problems, is an important activity and has been the subject of fascinating research.[6] We will concentrate on the way in which organizations select from proposed solutions the one which seems most suited to their needs, and how the organizations come to hear about these new ideas in the first place.[7] We are not trying to specify the circumstances under which new ideas or programs will be conceived or developed; we are studying instead the conditions under which state decision makers are most likely to adopt a new program.

The object of this analysis is the process of diffusion of ideas for new services or programs. Sometimes new legislation is virtually copied from other states. The California fair trade law, adopted in 1931, "was followed either verbatim or with minor variations by twenty states; in fact, ten states copied two serious typographical errors in the original California law." [8] No assumption is being made, however, that the programs enacted in each state are always exactly alike or that new legislation is written in exactly the same way by every legislature. It is unlikely that the highway department established in Wisconsin in 1907 had the same organizational format as the one adopted by Wyoming in 1917, or that the council on the performing arts created in New York in 1960 bears an exact resemblance to the one created by Kentucky in 1966. In each case, however, a commitment was made to offer a new service, establish a new principle of regulation, or create an agency which had never existed before. Our concern is the origin and spread of the idea to provide public subsidies for the arts, not the detailed characteristics of institutions created in each state to implement the policy.

No ideological bias was employed in selecting issues for study. The patterns of diffusion for each issue have been treated equally, and no effort was made to develop any method of determining the relative im-

[6] For examples see: Gary A. Steiner (ed.), *The Creative Organization* (Chicago, 1965); and Tom Burns and G. M. Stalker, *The Management of Innovation* (London, 1961).

[7] There is much confusion over this distinction in the literature on diffusion. For an excellent discussion of the problem see: Lawrence B. Mohr, "Determinants of Innovation in Organizations," [*American Political Science Review*] (1969), 111–126.

[8] Once the mistake was discovered, the Arkansas statute, which reproduced a model prepared by the National Association of Retail Druggists, was copied either verbatim or with minor changes by seventeen states. Ewald T. Grether, *Price Control Under Fair Trade Legislation* (New York, 1937), pp. 19–20.

portance or desirability of the programs.[9] Programs are sometimes enacted only to provide symbolic rewards to groups within the population and once created are left with inadequate funds or otherwise disabled.[10] Oklahoma's legislature, for example, emulated other states by creating a state civil rights commission, but once the commission was established, only $2,500 was appropriated for its operation.[11] For the purposes of this study, however, all adoptions are equal. My goal is to provide an explanation of the relative speed of adoption and the patterns of diffusion of innovations; I am not interested in the effectiveness of Oklahoma's civil rights commission, but in where the legislature got the idea to create such a commission and why it acted when it did.

II The Innovation Score

My first aim is to explain why some states adopt innovations more readily than others. I assume that the pioneering states gain their reputations because of the speed with which they accept new programs. The study must begin, therefore, with an attempt to devise an innovation score that will represent the relative speed with which states adopt innovations.

The innovation score is based on the analysis of eighty-eight different programs (see the Appendix for a list) which were enacted by at least twenty state legislatures prior to 1965, and for which there was reliable information on the dates of adoption. In order to make the collection of programs as comprehensive and representative as possible, I adopted a list of basic issue areas similar to the one employed by the Council of State Governments in its bi-annual reports included in the *Book of the States*. I tried to study six to eight different pieces of legislation in each of these areas: welfare, health, education, conservation, planning, administrative organization, highways, civil rights, corrections and police, labor, taxes, and professional regulation. In the course of my analysis I studied issues ranging from the establishment of highway departments and the enactment of civil rights bills to the creation of state councils on the performing arts and the passage of sexual psychopath laws. Most of the programs

[9] In later work I will report the results of comparisons of the diffusion patterns of issues from different subject matter areas. Preliminary efforts at such comparisons, however, have not revealed significant variations. There does not seem to be much difference in the diffusion patterns of issues of different types.

[10] For a discussion of this phenomenon see: Murray Edelman, *The Symbolic Uses of Politics* (Urbana, 1964), chapters 2 and 9.

[11] Duane Lockard, *Toward Equal Opportunity* (New York, 1968), p. 23.

were adopted during the twentieth century, but sixteen of them diffused primarily during the latter half of the nineteenth century.

Once the eighty-eight lists of dates of adoption were collected they were used to create an innovation score for each state. The first step was to count the total number of years which elapsed between the first and last recorded legislative enactment of a program. Each state then received a number for each list which corresponded to the percentage of time which elapsed between the first adoption and its own acceptance of the program. For example, if the total time elapsing between the first and last adoption of a program was twenty years, and Massachusetts enacted the program ten years after the first adoption, then Massachusetts received a score of .500 on that particular issue. The first state to adopt the program received a score of .000 and the last state received a 1.000. In cases in which all the states have not yet adopted a program, the states without the program were placed last and given a score of 1.000.[12] The innovation score for each state is simply 1.000 minus the average of the sum of the state's scores on all issues. The larger the innovation score, therefore, the faster the state has been, on the average, in responding to new ideas or policies. The issues may be divided into groups according to subject matter areas or time periods, and separate scores can be created for these smaller groupings of issues by following the same procedure. The results of this scoring procedure, using all eighty-eight issues, are presented in Table 1.

A note of caution should be sounded before the results of this exercise are analyzed. We are endeavoring to measure a highly complex process in which an enormous number of idiosyncratic influences are at work; an official with an unusually keen interest in a particular program, a chance reading of an article or book by a governor's aide, or any number of other circumstances peculiar to any one issue might lead to the rapid adoption of a piece of legislation by a state which is usually reluctant to accept new programs. Mississippi, which has the lowest average score and ranks last among the states in relative speed of adoption, was nonetheless the first state to adopt a general sales tax.

If this reservation is kept in mind, the data in Table 1 provide a crude outline of the standard or typical pattern of diffusion of new programs or policies among the American states. The states at the top of the list tend to adopt new programs much more rapidly than those at the

[12] The beginning point for the existence of each state was the date upon which it was officially organized as a territory. Using this system, Oklahoma is the last state to come into being, having been organized in 1890. If a program began its diffusion before a state came into existence, that issue was not included in figuring the innovation score for the state.

TABLE 1. *Composite Innovation Scores for the American States*[13]

New York	.656	New Hampshire	.482	Idaho	.394
Massachusetts	.629	Indiana	.464	Tennessee	.389
California	.604	Louisiana	.459	West Virginia	.386
New Jersey	.585	Maine	.455	Arizona	.384
Michigan	.578	Virginia	.451	Georgia	.381
Connecticut	.568	Utah	.447	Montana	.378
Pennsylvania	.560	North Dakota	.444	Missouri	.377
Oregon	.544	North Carolina	.430	Delaware	.376
Colorado	.538	Kansas	.426	New Mexico	.375
Wisconsin	.532	Nebraska	.425	Oklahoma	.368
Ohio	.528	Kentucky	.419	South Dakota	.363
Minnesota	.525	Vermont	.414	Texas	.362
Illinois	.521	Iowa	.413	South Carolina	.347
Washington	.510	Alabama	.406	Wyoming	.346
Rhode Island	.503	Florida	.397	Nevada	.323
Maryland	.482	Arkansas	.394	Mississippi	.298

[13] Alaska and Hawaii were omitted from the analysis because data for their years of adoption were often missing.

bottom of the list. Having provided a preliminary measurement of this phenomenon, we must now try to explain it. Why should New York, California and Michigan adopt innovations more rapidly than Mississippi, Wyoming and South Dakota?

III The Correlates of Innovation

Demographic factors. After studying the acceptance of technological innovations by both individuals and organizations, several writers have concluded that the decision maker's relative wealth, or the degree to which "free floating" resources are available, are important determinants of the willingness to adopt new techniques or policies.[14] If "slack" resources are available, either in the form of money or a highly skilled, professional staff, the decision maker can afford the luxury of experiment and can more easily risk the possibility of failure.[15] Other studies, especially in the areas of agriculture and medicine, have also shown organiza-

[14] Everett M. Rogers, *Diffusion of Innovations* (New York, 1962), pp. 40, 285–292. Also see: S. N. Eisenstadt, *The Political Systems of Empires* (New York, 1963), p. 27, 33–112.

[15] For a discussion of "slack" resources and innovation see: Richard M. Cyert and James G. March, *A Behavioral Theory of the Firm* (Englewood Cliffs, N.J., 1963), pp. 278–279.

tional size to be a strong correlate of innovation.[16] Given these results from prior studies in other fields we might expect to find that the larger, wealthier states, those with the most developed industrial economies and the largest cities, would have the highest innovation scores. It would seem likely that the great cosmopolitan centers in the country, the places where most of the society's creative resources are concentrated, would be the most adaptive and sympathetic to change, and thus the first to adopt new programs.

In order to test these assumptions several measures of social and economic development were correlated with the innovation score. As we can see in Table 2, there is evidence that the larger, wealthier, more industrialized states adopt new programs somewhat more rapidly than their smaller, less well-developed neighbors. Fairly strong relationships exist between the innovation score and the value added by manufacturing, the average per acre value of farms, the size of the urban population, and the average per capita income. These relationships remain virtually unchanged in all time periods. In fact, the only relationship which changes substantially over time is that between innovation and the percentage of illiterates in the population which declines steadily across the three time periods. This declining relationship and the low correlation between innovation and the median school year completed is caused primarily by the states in the Rocky Mountain region which have the highest rankings on median school years completed and yet are among the slowest to adopt new programs.[17] The median of educational attainment in the

[16] Rogers, *op. cit.*, Mohr, *op. cit.*; and also: Edwin Mansfield, "The Speed of Response of Firms to New Techniques," *Quarterly Journal of Economics* (1963), 293–304; Jerald Hage and Michael Aiken, "Program Change and Organizational Properties: A Comparative Analysis," *American Journal of Sociology* (1967), 516–517; and Richard J. Hall, S. Eugene Haas, and Norman J. Johnson, "Organizational Size, Complexity and Formalization," *American Sociological Review* (1967), 903–912.

[17] Regional affects of this kind appear frequently in analyses of data from the American states. In many studies, especially those which involve measures of political participation or party competition, strong relationships appear which are actually only a result of the distinctive nature of the southern states. In order to insure that the correlations in this analysis were not merely a result of the social and political peculiarities of the South, the eleven states of the confederacy were removed from all distributions. Since the Southern states do not cluster at one extreme of the innovation scale, no great changes occurred in correlation coefficients based upon data from the thirty-nine states outside the South. Within the eleven Southern states, however, almost all the relationships were substantially reduced in size. Because only eleven states are involved, this fact is difficult to interpret, but will be treated more fully in later work. For an example of this problem discussed in another context see: Raymond Wolfinger and John Osgood Field, "Political Ethos and the Structure of City Government," [*American Po-*

TABLE 2. *Correlations between Innovation Scores and Five Social and Economic Variables, by Time Periods*

Social-Economic Variables	Innovation Scores* 1870–1899	1900–1929	1930–1966	Composite Score
Per Cent Population Urban:	.62**	.69	.62	.63
Total Population:	.52	.40	.50	.59
Average Income, Per Capita:	—***	.62	.50	.55
Value Added Per Capita by Manufacturing	.46	.55	.57	.66
Average Value, Per Acre, of Farms:	.70	.52	.52	.54
Per Cent Population Illiterate:	−.58	−.44	−.12	−.23
Median School Years Completed:	—***	—***	—***	.26

*In order to insure that the innovation score and the social and economic variables came from comparable periods, separate innovation scores were calculated for three time periods: 1870-1899, 1900-1929, and 1930-1966. In constructing this table each innovation was placed in the time period during which the first ten states adopted it. Thus, if a program was adopted by only four states during the 1800's, and completed its diffusion during the 1900's, the program is placed in the second time period: 1900-1929, even though its first adoption took place during the nineteenth century. Social and economic data are taken from the years 1900, 1930, and 1960. The composite score is correlated with social and economic data from 1960.

**The table entries are Pearson product-moment correlations.

***Measures of these phenomena corresponding with these time periods do not exist.

states with the highest innovation scores is pulled down by the presence of a large, poorly educated, lower class, living primarily in the inner cities. The highly industrialized states with large urban concentrations are characterized by great inequality of social status and attainment. It would seem, however, that the elements necessary to foster innovation are present in these states even though they do not have highest average level of educational achievement.

Political factors. Although students of policy making have be-

litical Science Review] (1966), 306–326. For a more extensive discussion of the methodological implications see the discussion of "interaction effects" in Hugh Donald Forbes and Edward R. Tufte, "A Note of Caution in Causal Modelling," *ibid.* (1968), pp. 1261–1262; and the communication from Dennis D. Riley and Jack L. Walker, *ibid.* (September, 1969), pp. 880–899.

gun to doubt the importance of the political system as an independent determinant of the behavior of decision makers, it seems likely that both the degree of party competition and a state's system of legislative apportionment would affect its readiness to accept change. It would seem that parties which often faced closely contested elections would try to out-do each other by embracing the newest, most progressive programs and this would naturally encourage the rapid adoption of innovations. Lowi argues that new departures in policy are more likely at the beginning of a new administration, especially when a former minority party gains control of the government.[18] If this tendency exists it would also seem likely that state political systems which allow frequent turnover and offer the most opportunities to capture high office would more often develop the circumstances in which new programs might be adopted.[19]

Another prerequisite for the rapid adoption of new programs might be a system of legislative apportionment which fully represented the state's urban areas and which did not grant veto power to groups opposed to change. Such a system might be expected to allow consideration and debate of new policies and programs in all areas. Some recent findings, such as Barber's study of legislators in Connecticut,[20] lead us to speculate that representatives from newly developing urban and suburban areas would be more cosmopolitan, better informed, and more tolerant of change. If nothing else, urban legislators would probably be more willing to deal with problems of sanitation, planning, transportation, and housing peculiar to large metropolitan areas.

No matter what the composition of the legislator's constituency, however, it would seem that the presence of competent staff, superior clerical facilities, and supporting services would allow him to give serious consideration to a larger number of new proposals. Several studies of the diffu-

[18] Theodore Lowi, "Toward Functionalism in Political Science: The Case of Innovation in Party Systems," [*American Political Science Review*] (1963), 570–583. Evidence which seems to confirm Lowi's theory may be found in: Charles W. Wiggens, "Party Politics in the Iowa Legislature," *Midwest Journal of Political Science* (1967), 60–69; and Frank M. Bryan, "The Metamorphosis of a Rural Legislature," *Polity* (1968), 191–212.

[19] Joseph A. Schlesinger has developed an index of the "general opportunity level" in each state. The index measures the relative number of chances which exist in each state to achieve major political office. See: *Ambition and Politics: Political Careers in the United States* (Chicago, 1966), pp. 37–56.

[20] James D. Barber, *The Lawmakers: Recruitment and Adaptation to Legislative Life* (New Haven, 1965). For testimony from legislators about the importance of reapportionment see: Frank M. Bryan, "Who is Legislating," *National Civic Review* (December, 1967), 627–633; Allan Dines, "A Reapportioned State," *National Civic Review* (February, 1966), 70–74, 99.

sion of technological innovations have demonstrated that the best informed individuals are most likely to pioneer in the use of new techniques or tools,[21] and so the states which provide the most extensive staff and research facilities in their legislatures ought to pioneer in the adoption of new programs.[22]

In Table 3 efforts to test some of these hypotheses in different time periods are displayed. Measures of political variables are usually based on evidence only from contemporary periods because data are seldom available on state and local elections or the operation of legislatures in earlier decades. Measures are available, however, for the degree of party competition and the extent of legislative malapportionment.[23] As we can see in Table 3 party competitiveness does not seem to be consistently related to the innovation score, at least as it is measured here.[24] Legislative apportionment is not correlated with the innovation score in the 1900–1929 period, but is related in the 1930–1966 period. Since legislatures steadily became less representative of urban populations after 1930, it may be that we have here some empirical evidence of the impact of malapportionment on policy making in the states.

Recent studies of state expenditures have shown that the explanatory effects of political variables could be eliminated if statistical controls for social and economic variables were applied. Therefore, in Table 4 I have presented both the zero-order correlations of the composite innovation score with measures of party competition, turnover in office, legislative

[21] Rogers, *op. cit.* Also see: Mansfield, *op. cit.;* James S. Coleman, Elihu Katz, and Herbert Menzel, *Medical Innovation: A Diffusion Study* (Indianapolis, 1966); and John W. Loy, Jr., "Social Psychological Characteristics of Innovators," *American Sociological Review* (1969), 73–82.

[22] For a somewhat different view see: Norman Meller, "Legislative Staff Services: Toxin, Specific, or Placebo for the Legislature's Ills," *The Western Political Quarterly* (June, 1967), 381–389.

[23] There is one other index in existence which deals with political phenomenon: Rodney Mott's Index of Judicial Prestige. The Mott index measures the degree to which state supreme courts were used as models by the legal profession. It is based on a study of citations in federal Supreme Court decisions and all state supreme court decisions, the number of cases reprinted in standard textbooks, and the opinion of a panel of prominent legal scholars; it covers the period 1900 to 1930. The Mott index and the innovation score from the same time period are correlated at .62. This finding might be interpreted to mean that emulative behavior in the judicial arena is not much different from that in the legislative arena. For details of the Judicial Prestige Index see: Rodney L. Mott, "Judicial Influence," [*American Political Science Review*] (1936), 295–315.

[24] Data for this table were derived from Richard Hofferbert's collection, "American State Socio-economic, Electoral, and Policy Data: 1890–1960" which he has graciously allowed me to use.

TABLE 3. *Correlations between Innovation Scores and Measures of Political Variables, by Time Periods*

Political Variables*	Innovation Scores 1870–1899	1900–1929	1930–1966	Composite Score
Party Competition for Governorship:	.36	.02	.14	.24
David-Eisenberg Index of Malapportionment:	**	.07	.55	.65

*The Index of party competition used in this table is the per cent of the total vote going to the gubernatorial candidate coming in second, times 2. This yields a scale from 0 to 100. It was created by Richard Hofferbert. The apportionment Index appears in Paul T. David and Ralph Eisenberg, *Devaluation of the Urban and Suburban Vote* (Charlottesville: Bureau of Public Administration, University of Virginia, 1961).

**Measures of this phenomenon corresponding with this time period do not exist.

apportionment, and legislative professionalism,[25] and also partial correlations with four social and economic variables controlled. The control variables are value added by manufacturing, per cent urban population, total population size, and per capita personal income, all of which earlier proved to be independently related to the innovation score. In Table 4 the effect of each control variable is displayed separately along with the combined impact of all four. The results tend to corroborate earlier analyses which minimize the independent effects of these political variables on policy outcomes. The Schlesinger index of opportunity, which measures the difference among the states in the average number of times major offices have changed hands, and the Hofferbert index of inter-party competition seem to have some independent impact on innovation, although it is greatly weakened when all four control variables are combined. This finding lends some credence to Lowi's argument that turnover in office fosters change.

Certainly, the most important result depicted in this table is the con-

[25] The sources are: Richard Hofferbert, "Classification of American State Party Systems," *Journal of Politics* (1964), 550–567; Dennis Riley and Jack L. Walker, "Problems of Measurement and Inference in the Study of the American States" (paper delivered at the Institute of Public Policy Studies, University of Michigan, 1968); David and Eisenberg, *op. cit.*; Glendon Schubert and Charles Press, "Measuring Malapportionment," [*American Political Science Review*] (1964), 302–327, and corrections, 968–970; Schlesinger, *op. cit.*; and John Grumm, "Structure and Policy in the Legislature" (paper presented at the Southwestern Social Science Association Meetings, 1967).

TABLE 4. *Relationships between the Composite Innovation Score and Measures of Legislative Apportionment and Party Competition*

	Zero-Order	Value Added Manu-facturing	Per Cent Urban	Total Population	Per Capita Income	Four Factors Combined
Apportionment						
David-Eisenberg Index	.65	.47	.64	.67	.60	.58
Schubert-Press Index	.26	.12	.34	.31	.26	.21
Party Competition						
Hofferbert Index	.54	.35	.34	.50	.26	.12
Riley-Walker Index —Gov.	.40	.33	.22	.47	.09	.17
Riley-Walker Index —Legis	.31	.24	.17	.34	.04	.07
Turnover in Office						
Schlesinger Index of Opportunity	.53	.40	.39	.32	.34	.24
Legislative Services						
Grumm's Index of Legislative Professionalism	.63	.38	.33	.41	.51	.11

sistent strength of the correlation between innovation and the David and Eisenberg index of urban representation.[26] Earlier studies, using expenditures as a measure of policy outcomes, have consistently found that apportionment has little importance as an explanatory variable.[27] Our findings indicate that apportionment does make a difference where innovation is

[26] Although much simpler than the Schubert and Press measure, the David and Eisenberg index seems to have more relevance to political outcomes. Thomas Dye had the same experience. See Dye, *op. cit.*, pp. 19–20, 63–69, 112–114, 146–148, 174–177, 236–237, 270–281.

[27] Herbert Jacob, "The Consequences of Malapportionment: A Note of Caution," *Social Forces* (1964), 260–266; Thomas R. Dye, "Malapportionment and Public Policy in the States" *Journal of Politics* (1965), 586–601; Richard I. Hofferbert, "The Relation Between Public Policy and Some Structural and Environmental Variables in the American States," [*American Political Science Review*] (1966), 73–82; David Brady and Douglas Edmonds, "One Man, One Vote – So What?" *Trans-action* (March, 1967), 41–46. A recent article calls some of the conclusions of this research into question: Alan G. Pulsipher and James L. Weatherby, Jr., "Malapportionment, Party Competition, and the Functional Distribution of Governmental Expenditures," [*American Political Science Review*] (1968), 1207–1219.

concerned. Although the other political factors do not have great independent impact on innovation, the clear implication arising from Tables 3 and 4 is that those states which grant their urban areas full representation in the legislature seem to adopt new ideas more rapidly, on the average, than states which discriminate against their cities.

Given the results of this correlational analysis, we might conclude that New York, California and Michigan adopt new programs more rapidly than Mississippi, Wyoming, and South Dakota primarily because they are bigger, richer, more urban, more industrial, have more fluidity and turnover in their political systems, and have legislatures which more adequately represent their cities. Although these findings are important, they leave many important questions unanswered. The political system does not react automatically in response to the growth of manufacturing industries or to the increase in the percentage of the population living in cities. Developments of this kind obviously cause problems which public officials might try to solve, but the mere presence of such a stimulant does not cause public officials to act, nor does it determine the form the solution will take, or which state might act first to meet the problem. Our analysis has provided us with evidence that change and experimentation are more readily accepted in the industrialized, urban, cosmopolitan centers of the country, but we have not improved our understanding of the institutions and decision-making processes which cause strong statistical relationships between industrial output and innovation. Also, we have not explained the way innovations spread from the pioneering states to those with lower innovation scores. In order to develop explanations of these processes we must go beyond the search for demographic correlates of innovation and develop generalizations which refer to the behavior of the men who actually make the choices in which we are interested.

IV Political Science and Innovation

In one form or another, interest group theories, based on self-regulating systems of countervailing power, are at the heart of much of the recent research into American politics.[28] Studies of the legislative process in the United States, for example, have been strongly influenced by theories which emphasize the importance of the group basis of politics.

[28] Examples of this general approach to policy making are: David B. Truman, *The Governmental Process* (New York, 1960); Edward Banfield, *Political Influence* (New York, 1961); and Richard E. Neustadt, *Presidential Power* (New York, 1960). For an excellent critique of theories which employ concepts of power as a major explanatory variable see: James G. March, "The Power of Power," in David Easton (ed.), *Varieties of Political Theory* (Englewood Cliffs, 1966), pp. 39–70.

Beginning with the efforts of A. Lawrence Lowell [29] political scientists have worked to discover the basic factions within the legislature and have striven to develop operational definitions of power or influence.[30] Extensive efforts have been made to isolate and measure the various influences which come to bear on the individual legislator and motivate him to join one or another legislative bloc: what is a legislator's most important source of cues; is it a lobbyist with whom he has close connections, his party leaders, members of his constituency, the governor, or members of his own family? What impact on his attitudes does the legislative institution itself have; do its informal rules and traditions affect the legislator's decisions, and if so, in what way? [31] Great emphasis has been placed on the analysis of roll-call votes and several sophisticated research techniques have been developed to pursue this work, ranging from Beyle's cluster bloc analysis and Guttman scaling to the more complex, computerized routines presently in use.[32] But all this machinery is useful only in studying those roll-calls which cause divisions in the house; all unanimous votes, nearly eighty per cent of the total in most legislatures, are ignored. Riker has devised a technique in which he uses the percentage of the total membership which is present for the vote and the closeness of the division to determine the relative significance of roll-call votes in legislatures. The more legislators present and the closer the vote, the more significant the issue involved.[33] The full attention of the researcher is thus focused on the relatively small number of decisions which cause significant disagreements, because it is assumed that these are the most important votes; at least, they are the only ones which will provide clues to "the conflicting forces and pressures at work in the legislative systems," [34] and the discovery of those forces and pressures, according to the group theory of politics, is the principal object of political science.

One of the main purposes in this study is to develop an approach to governmental policy making which will serve as a guide in the analysis of

[29] A. Lawrence Lowell, "The Influence of Party Upon Legislation," *Annual Report of the American Historical Association* (1901), pp. 321–543.

[30] The best example is: Robert Dahl, "The Concept of Power," *Behavioral Science* (1957), pp. 201–215.

[31] For the best general review of the results of research on the legislative process, see: Malcolm E. Jewell and Samuel C. Patterson, *The Legislative Process in the United States* (New York, 1966).

[32] For a discussion of these techniques see: Lee F. Anderson, Meridith W. Watts, Jr. and Allen R. Wilcox, *Legislative Roll-Call Analysis* (Evanston, 1966). Also see Jewell and Patterson, *op. cit.*, pp. 528–550.

[33] William H. Riker, "A Method for Determining the Significance of Roll Calls in Voting Bodies," in John C. Wahlke and Heinz Eulau (eds.), *Legislative Behavior* (Glencoe, 1959), pp. 337–383.

[34] Jewell and Patterson, *op. cit.*, p. 416.

all legislative decisions, the unanimous as well as the contested ones, and which will lead as well to a better understanding of decisions made by bureaucrats, political executives and other governmental officials. Rather than focus upon the patterns of conflict among factions within the legislature or the administrative agencies, I will search for the criteria employed by legislators and administrators in deciding whether a proposal is worthy of consideration in the first place. This search rests on the belief that whoever the decision maker may be, whether administrator, lobbyist, party leader, governor or legislator, and however controversial a particular issue may become, a set of general criteria exists in every state which establishes broad guidelines for policy making. Regardless of the interests supporting an innovation, no matter whether the decision system is primarily monolithic or pluralistic, if a proposal for change does not fall within those guidelines its chances for acceptance are slim. Many of the propositions I will develop cannot be verified until they are tested with evidence from individual decision makers; [35] they are presented here only as a first, tentative step toward a more comprehensive theory of governmental policy making.

V Emulation and Decision Making in the States

We are searching for answers to three major questions: 1) why do certain states consistently adopt new programs more rapidly than other states, 2) are there more or less stable patterns of diffusion of innovations among the American states, and 3) if so, what are they? Our answers to these questions will be founded, in part, on the theories of organizational decision making developed in recent years by writers like Simon, March, Cyert and Lindblom.[36] At the heart of these theories is the concept of the decision maker struggling to choose among complex alternatives and constantly receiving much more information concerning his environment than he is able to digest and evaluate. An ordinary decision maker, required to make frequent choices and faced with an inconclusive flood of reports, programs, suggestions and memos, must simplify his task in some way. According to Simon, he does not – cannot – search in every case for the best possible solution to the problems he faces; he has neither the time nor the energy. Instead, he makes decisions by searching until he finds an alternative which he believes is good enough to preserve whatever

[35] Thanks to a grant from the Carnegie Corporation I have been able to launch a pilot study involving interviews in several states.

[36] I refer to: Herbert Simon, *Administrative Behavior*, Second Edition (New York, 1957); Richard M. Cyert and James C. March, A *Behavioral Theory of the Firm* (Englewood Cliffs, N.J., 1963); and Charles E. Lindblom, *The Intelligence of Democracy* (New York, 1965).

values are important to him. The limits of rationality imposed by human capacities prevent him from maximizing his benefits in every situation; rather, he "satisfices," or chooses a course of action which seems satisfactory under the circumstances.

The individual in a complex organization, therefore, does not deal directly with all the sources of information potentially available to him, nor does he evaluate every conceivable policy option. In place of the debilitating confusion of reality he creates his own abstract, highly simplified world containing only a few major variables. In order to achieve this manageable simplicity he adopts a set of decision rules or standard criteria for judgment which remain fairly stable over time and which guide him in choosing among sources of information and advice. A decision maker decides both where to look for cues and information and how to choose among alternatives according to his decision rules; these rules also embody the current goals and aspirations of his organization, or the values which the organization is designed to advance and protect. Hence, if we wish to predict the decision maker's behavior, we should try to discover these rules of thumb, or "heuristics" as they are sometimes called, which shape his judgment. His choices could then be explained in terms of the alternatives he considers, his knowledge of each alternative, the sources of his knowledge, and the standard decision rules he applies in cases of this kind.[37]

Taking cues from these theories of human choice and organizational decision making our explanation of the adoption of innovations by the states is based on the assertion that state officials make most of their decisions by analogy. The rule of thumb they employ might be formally stated as follows: *look for an analogy between the situation you are dealing with and some other situation, perhaps in some other state, where the problem has been successfully resolved.*[38]

We are looking to what has been called the "inter-organizational context," [39] or the *horizontal* relationships among the states within the federal system, for the principal influences which regulate the speed of

[37] For a comprehensive review of the literature on decision making see: Donald W. Taylor, "Decision Making and Problem Solving," and Julia Feldman and Herschel E. Kanter, "Organizational Decision Making," in James G. March (ed.), *Handbook of Organizations* (Chicago, 1965), pp. 48–86, 614–649. Also see: W. Richard Scott, "Theory of Organizations," in Robert E. L. Faris (ed.), *Handbook of Modern Sociology* (Chicago, 1964), pp. 485–529.

[38] Decision rules of this kind are mentioned in both Taylor, *op. cit.*, pp. 73–74; and Cyert and March, *op. cit.*, especially pp. 34–43.

[39] William M. Evan, "The Organization-Set: Toward a Theory of Inter-Organizational Relations," in James D. Thompson (ed.), *Approaches to Organizational Design* (Pittsburgh, 1966), pp. 173–191.

adoption and the patterns of diffusion of innovations. Most of the existing work on intergovernmental relations and federalism concentrates on the question of centralization within the American system of government. In line with the general interest of most political scientists in the factors which affect the access of organized groups and the lines of authority within a political system, many writers are concerned with the virtues of centralization or decentralization and try to determine how much of either exists in the system. They have studied primarily the *vertical* relationships among national, state and local governments, and have usually identified the party system and its demands as the institutional influence most responsible for maintaining the present, decentralized, federal relationships.[40] I want to focus attention on the mutual perceptions and relationships among state governments and to show how these relationships affect the behavior of state decision makers.[41]

One of the most common arguments used in state legislatures against raising taxes or passing measures designed to regulate business is the fear that such measures might retard industrial development or force marginal plants to leave the state. Lawmakers often are called upon to deal with the problems which arise when one or two states establish extremely per-

[40] Some recent examples are: William Anderson, *The Nation and the States, Rivals or Partners?* (Minneapolis, 1955); M. J. C. Vile, *The Structure of American Federalism* (London, 1961); William Riker, *Federalism: Origin, Operation, Significance* (Boston, 1964); Daniel J. Elazar, *American Federalism: A View From the States* (New York, 1966); Morton Grodzins, *The American System* (Chicago, 1966). For a general critique see: A. H. Birch, "Approaches to the Study of Federalism," *Political Studies* (1966), 15–33.

[41] This is not the first study to discover the important role of emulation and competition in the development of public policy. Richard Hofferbert in: "Ecological Development and Policy Change in the American States," *Midwest Journal of Political Science* (1966), p. 485; and Ira Sharkansky in: "Regionalism, Economic Status and the Public Policies of American States," *Southwestern Social Science Quarterly* (1968) both mention the influence of other states in the calculations of state decision makers. Several earlier students of local government complained that sparsely populated, arid Western states had blindly copied from the heavily populated Eastern states forms of local government which were inappropriately suited for the conditions prevailing in the Great Plains. See: A. Bristol Goodman, "Westward Movement of Local Government," *The Journal of Land and Public Utility Economics* (1944), pp. 20–34; Herman Walker, Jr. and Peter L. Hansen, "Local Government and Rainfall," [*American Political Science Review*] (1946), 1113–1123. Robert L. Crain has recently used emulation as a principal explanatory variable in his study of the spread of water fluoridation programs among American cities: "Fluoridation: The Diffusion of an Innovation Among Cities," *Social Forces* (1966), 467–476; as did Thomas M. Scott in his: "The Diffusion of Urban Governmental Forms as a Case of Social Learning," *The Journal of Politics* (1968), 1091–1108.

missive standards for the granting of licenses, such as the corporation laws in New Jersey and Delaware, or the divorce laws in Nevada. However, interstate competition does not always drive standards down; it has a positive side as well. State decision makers are constantly looking to each other for guides to action in many areas of policy, such as the organization and management of higher education, or the provision of hospitals and public health facilities. In fact, I am arguing that this process of competition and emulation, or cuetaking, is an important phenomenon which determines in large part the pace and direction of social and political change in the American states.[42]

Uncertainty and the fear of unanticipated consequences have always been formidable barriers to reform. Proponents of new programs have always had to combat the arguments of those who predict dire consequences if some innovation is adopted. Even though American history is full of cases where the opponents of change have later had to admit that the dangers they feared never materialized, inertia and the unwillingness to take risks have prevented a more rapid rate of change.

Inertia can more easily be overcome, however, if the proponent of change can point to the successful implementation of his program in some other similar setting. If a legislator introduces a bill which would require the licensing of probation officers, for example, and can point to its successful operation in a neighboring state, his chances of gaining acceptance are markedly increased. As Harsanyi has asserted:

> . . . it is not an overstatement to say that a very considerable part of the social values of most societies is based on sheer ignorance. . . . One of the reasons why other persons' example is so important in encouraging changes in people's values and behavior lies in the fact that it tends to dispel some groundless fears about the dismal consequences that such changes might entail. Another reason is of course that people can more easily face the possible hostility of the supporters of the old values if they are not alone in making the change.[43]

In fact, once a program has been adopted by a large number of states it may become recognized as a legitimate state responsibility, something which all states ought to have. When this happens it becomes extremely

[42] This set of hypotheses is consistent with more general theories concerning the manner in which human beings formulate judgments and establish expectations in all areas of life. See: Leon Festinger, "A Theory of Social Comparison Processes," *Human Relations* (1954), 117–140; and Robert Merton, *Social Theory and Social Structure* (rev. ed.; Glencoe, 1957), pp. 225–420.

[43] John C. Harsanyi, "Rational Choice Models v. Functionalistic and Conformistic Models of Political Behavior" (Paper delivered at American Political Science Association Meetings, 1967), p. 17.

difficult for state decision makers to resist even the weakest kinds of demands to institute the program for fear of arousing public suspicions about their good intentions; once a program has gained the stamp of legitimacy, it has a momentum of its own. As Lockard found in studying the passage of Fair Employment Practices laws the actions of other states are sometimes key factors in prompting reluctant politicians to accept controversial programs.

> Pressure mounted in New Jersey during 1944 and 1945 for some stronger policy, and when New York passed its FEP law certain key politicians in New Jersey decided to act. Governor Walter E. Edge concluded, apparently reluctantly, that he had to commit himself to such a law. "As the session drew to a close," Edge wrote in his autobiography, "minority racial and religious groups pressed for adoption of an antidiscrimination program. While it was a subject which I would have preferred to give greater study, politically it could not be postponed because New York had passed a similar measure and delay would be construed as a mere political expedient."[44]

For similar reasons there have been numerous efforts to enact a program of homesteading in Hawaii as a way of disposing of its arable public lands even though the circumstances there are quite different from other states where homesteading was successfully introduced.[45] And in Connecticut one of the most powerful arguments in favor of introducing the direct primary system during the 1950's was simply that all the other states had adopted one.[46]

The Connecticut case neatly illustrates some of the generalizations we are developing. Lockard points out that the leaders of both political parties privately opposed the introduction of a primary system but felt that an endorsement of the idea had to be put into their platforms to avoid having their opponents charge them with "bossism." Demands for the primary came for the most part from small groups in the state's suburban areas which were interested in the issue as "a consequence of the influx of migrants from states with primaries." [47] Speaking as a professional political scientist as well as a legislator, Lockard was well suited to counter the extreme fears expressed by the party leaders who predicted that party organizations would be completely destroyed if primaries were introduced. Lockard reasoned by analogy to the experience in other states

[44] Duane Lockard, *Toward Equal Opportunity* (New York, 1968), pp. 20–21.

[45] Allan Spitz, "The Transplantation of American Democratic Institutions," *Political Science Quarterly* (1967), 386–398.

[46] Duane Lockard, *Connecticut's Challenge Primary: A Study in Legislative Politics* (Eagleton Case #7, New York, 1959).

[47] *Ibid.*, p. 2.

both in countering the opponents of change and in shaping his own moderate position:

> I expressed my considerable doubts about the effect of party primaries on party organization. From observations of politics in some of the most thoroughgoing party primary states, [however,] it seemed that party organizations had been shattered with many undesirable consequences. In my campaign I expressed support only for a limited form of a primary and not one calculated to wreck the party system.[48]

Events like these illustrate the way in which the agenda of controversy in a state is determined, at least in part, by developments in other states, and they also show how experiences and examples from outside the system help to overcome the natural reluctance of any institutional structure to risk the consequences of change. The constituent units of any federal system are under considerable pressure to conform with national and regional standards or accepted administrative procedures. These norms result primarily from the processes of emulation and competition we have described and also from the efforts of nationally organized interest groups. They are affected also by the growth and development of professional organizations and other forms of communication among state administrators, and the natural circulation of active, politically involved citizens among the states, such as the Connecticut suburbanites who began agitating for a primary system in their adopted political home.

VI Regional Reference Groups and Standards of Evaluation

Nationally accepted standards or norms provide a convenient measure which can be used by interested citizens or political leaders to judge the adequacy of services offered in their own states. But these norms have an ambiguous influence on the performance of state governments. On the one hand, the existence of national standards probably encourages *higher* performance among the *poorer* members of the federation than we could expect if functions and service levels were established independently within each unit of government, solely as a result of internal demands. An example of this tendency was discovered by May in his study of Canadian federalism:

> Newfoundland chose for a long time to remain outside the Canadian federation, thus not subjecting itself to the forces of national reorientation, and when, after joining the Dominion, a royal commission reported on its financial position, the commission observed that Newfoundland's public

[48] *Ibid.*, p. 22.

services were very backward in relation to those of the other provinces, including even the maritimes. . . .[49]

In the United States, Mississippi, Vermont, and North Dakota are good examples of relatively poor states which are making unusually large efforts to bring their public services into closer approximation of national standards. But, on the other hand, national standards and norms can have a *conservative* impact, especially in the richer, industrial states which are able to provide services somewhat above the national averages with relatively little effort.[50] Hansen complains of this tendency when he points out that:

> Some northern states fall considerably below their northern neighborhood states in public service standards. . . . Their fiscal problems arise not because they are poor but because their tax levels are low by northern standards. This is notably true for example of a tier of large industrial states – Illinois, Indiana, Ohio and Pennsylvania. . . . These states are not excessively hard pressed by tax burdens relative to the country as a whole.[51]

This statement by Hansen is drawn from an essay in which he expresses disapproval of what he considers the inadequate public services of large industrial states which have relatively low tax burdens. But the statement we have cited contains several ambiguities. For example, Hansen charges that "some northern states fall considerably below their northern neighboring states in public service standards," but then he specifically points as examples to Illinois, Indiana, Ohio, and Pennsylvania, states which border on each other. It is not clear whether we are being asked to compare these states to their neighbors, to other northern states with higher tax burdens, or to "the country as a whole." Within Illinois, however, the states' decision makers are probably comparing their own performance with their counterparts in Indiana, Ohio, Pennsylvania or New Jersey. Officials in Illinois may know of the procedures and performance levels in New York or California, but they are unlikely to think of events in these states as legitimate guides to action.[52]

When examining the public policy of any state, therefore, it is important to discover in which "league" it has chosen to play. For example,

[49] Ronald J. May, *Financial Inequality Between States in a Federal System* (unpublished doctoral dissertation submitted to Nuffield College, Oxford University, 1966), p. 168.

[50] For a somewhat similar argument concerning government spending see: Anthony Downs, "Why the Government Budget is too Small in a Democracy," *World Politics* (July, 1960), 541–563.

[51] Alvin H. Hansen, *The Postwar American Economy: Performance and Problems* (New York, 1964), pp. 30–31.

[52] For evidence of this perspective, see Thomas J. Anton, *The Politics of State Expenditure in Illinois* (Urbana, 1966), p. 263.

Salisbury, in a statement much like Hansen's, reasons by analogy in arguing that Missouri does not provide as much aid for its schools as its potential resources might warrant. He points out that in 1959 the "state ranked 18th in per capita income but 38th in per capita expenditure for local schools." [53] This relatively low level of support seems to result from the correspondingly low aspirations of the officials of the Missouri State Teachers Association who, according to Salisbury, "have chosen to get what they can with a minimum of agitation or conflict rather than attempt broader public campaigns in behalf of larger objectives." [54] The officials of MSTA "are fully conscious of the gap between the Missouri school aid level and that of, say, neighboring Illinois," but they are quick to point out "that by comparison with other neighboring states – Arkansas, Oklahoma, or Nebraska, for example – Missouri's record is much more impressive." [55] It would seem from this example that Missouri's leaders, at least those concerned with public education, are emulating and competing primarily with the states to their south and west, rather than with the Great Lakes states to their north and east, or the Rocky Mountain states, the Deep South or the Far West. The choice of relatively poor states like Arkansas and Oklahoma as the principal, legitimate reference groups establishes an upper limit of aspirations which is considerably below that which might exist if Missouri's accepted basis for comparison were the public services of Illinois, Wisconsin or Michigan.

VII Regional Groupings Among the States

We have come far enough in our analysis to see that our original presentation of the innovation scores in Table 1 as a linear distribution masked some pertinent information. A more useful representation of the data, which would conform more closely to the actual patterns of diffusion, would have to be in the form of a tree. At the top of the tree would be a set of pioneering states which would be linked together in a national system of emulation and competition. The rest of the states would be sorted out along branches of the tree according to the pioneer, or set of pioneers, from which they take their principal cues. States like New York, Massachusetts, California, and Michigan should be seen as regional pace

[53] Nicholas A. Masters, Robert Salisbury, and Thomas H. Eliot, *State Politics and the Public Schools* (New York, 1964), p. 12.

[54] *Ibid.*, p. 25.

[55] *Ibid.*, p. 21. For a similar discussion of the importance of aspirations in determining the speed with which innovations are adopted see: Rufus P. Browning, "Innovative and Noninnovative Decision Processes in Government Budgeting," in Robert T. Golembiewski (ed.), *Public Budgeting and Finance* (Itasca, Illinois, 1968), pp. 128–145.

setters, each of which has a group of followers, usually within their own region of the country, that tend to adopt programs only after the pioneers have led the way. For example, Colorado, which ranks ninth in Table 1, might be seen as the regional leader of the Rocky Mountain states. The rest of the states in that region are found much further down the list: Utah is twenty-second, Idaho is thirty-third, Arizona is thirty-sixth, Montana is thirty-eighth, New Mexico is forty-first, Wyoming is forty-sixth, and Nevada is forty-seventh. All of these states, with the possible exception of Utah which may share in the leadership of the region, might be seen as Colorado's followers who usually pick up new ideas only after the regional pioneer has put them into practice.

If we are right about the general patterns of competition and emulation, we should discover in our data some evidence of the existence of regional clusters among the states. In an effort to find such groupings, a varimax factor analysis was performed, using a matrix of pair-wise comparisons of all state innovation scores on all eighty-eight issues. If states in the same region are adopting programs in a similar order or pattern over time, a factor analysis should uncover several underlying dimensions in the matrix along which all states would be ordered according to their responses to the programs upon which the innovation score is based. The results of the factor analysis are presented in Table 5.

As we can see, the regional groupings we expected to find do exist, although the patterns are not as neat and clear as we might have hoped. To produce each factor I recorded all loadings which were over .400. The five factors which result bring the states into generally recognizable, contiguous groupings. The states with the largest loadings in each region are not necessarily those with the highest innovation scores. Instead, they are states like Connecticut, Florida, or New Mexico whose innovation scores are closer to the average for their regions. The presence of Nebraska, Iowa and South Dakota on Factor 1, which otherwise identifies Southern states, may indicate that more than one regional cluster is being identified on that factor.

There are several ambiguities in the data. For example, New York, Pennsylvania, West Virginia, Arkansas, and Illinois are loading on more than one factor. The easiest explanation of this may be that the states actually have connections with more than one region. This is especially true of New York, the state with the highest innovation score, which displays fairly strong connections in this analysis with the New England, Mid-Atlantic, and Great Lakes states. I believe that this finding reflects the fact that New York actually serves as a model for states in all three areas. Certainly New York is formally involved in interstate compacts with all three regions, and, if nothing else, enjoys a perfect geographical position from which to carry on relations over such a large area. If the findings concerning New York seem explainable, those concerning Cali-

TABLE 5. *Varimax Factor Analysis of Innovation Scores for Forty-Eight States*

Factor Loading	State
FACTOR I (South)	
.756	Florida
.711	Tennessee
.663	Alabama
.661	Virginia
.656	Georgia
.630	Mississippi
.621	Delaware
.600	North Carolina
.590	South Carolina
.576	Arkansas
.543	Texas
.517	Nebraska
.464	West Virginia
.460	Louisiana
.459	Iowa
.454	South Dakota
.433	Nevada
7.8 Total Factor Contribution	
FACTOR II (New England)	
.795	Connecticut
.766	Massachusetts
.758	New Hampshire
.659	Rhode Island
.536	New York
.512	Vermont
.434	Maine
.404	Pennsylvania
4.1 Total Factor Contribution	
FACTOR III (Mountains and Northwest)	
.791	New Mexico
.719	Idaho
.702	Montana
.694	Utah
.638	Washington
.620	North Dakota
FACTOR III (Mountains and Northwest) *(Continued)*	
.610	Wyoming
.569	Oklahoma
.516	Louisiana
.503	South Dakota
.432	Oregon
.419	Maryland
.410	Arkansas
.407	West Virginia
6.7 Total Factor Contribution	
FACTOR IV (Mid-Atlantic and Great Lakes)	
.795	New Jersey
.637	Wisconsin
.605	New York
.577	Minnesota
.536	Illinois
.516	Pennsylvania
.451	Indiana
4.0 Total Factor Contribution	
FACTOR V (Border, Great Lakes and California)	
.698	California
.610	Missouri
.584	Kentucky
.577	Michigan
.548	Ohio
.515	Nebraska
.458	Illinois
4.1 Total Factor Contribution	

fornia do not. I cannot explain why California loads on Factor V, especially since many of its neighbors load on Factor III. These ambiguous findings concerning New York and California might be merely a reflection of ambiguity in the data. Factor analysis will identify regional groupings in the data only if the regions respond to new programs as a unit, adopting some new ideas with haste and lagging behind on others. Since New York and California consistently lead the country in the adoption of new programs, they may not be members of the cohesive regional group or "league" of states, a fact which may prevent their neat categorization through factor analysis.

There is no accounting at all in this analysis for the behavior of three states: Arizona, Colorado, and Kansas. Both Colorado and Arizona load at the .300 level on Factor III, the one which includes most of the rest of the Rocky Mountain states. Colorado and Nevada both load strongly (.577 and .485 respectively) on a separate factor which was not reported since no other state scored higher than .300 on the factor and its contribution score was only 1.7. The same is true for Kansas which was the only state loading strongly (at .658) on a factor whose contribution score was only 1.9.

VIII Specialized Communications Among the States

Our analysis has provided evidence that a continuum exists along which states are distributed from those which are usually quick to accept innovations to those which are typically reluctant to do so; we also know something about the correlates of innovation and have evidence of regional groupings among the states; but it is not always easy to identify a regional pioneer or to know exactly which states make up each "league" or sub-system of cue-taking and information exchange. Some states seem to have connections with more than one region and may regularly receive cues from states in both groupings. As the American political system has developed, an increasing number of specialized communication systems have been created which cut across traditional regional lines and bring officials from many different regions into contact with each other and with federal and local officials, journalists, academic experts, and administrative consultants.

Several organizations now exist, such as the Council of State Governments, the Federal Commission on Intergovernmental Relations, and the recently established Citizen's Conference on State Legislatures, whose primary function is to improve communications among the states. Most important of these specialized communications networks are the professional associations of state officials, such as the National Association of State Budget Officers, or the National Association of State Conservation

Officers. Associations of this kind were first created late in the nineteenth century and more seem to be forming each year. There were only five formed prior to 1900, but by 1930 there were approximately thirty-one, and by 1966 there were at least eighty-six in existence.[56]

These groups serve two general purposes: first, they are sources of information and policy cues. By organizing conferences or publishing newsletters they bring together officials from all over the country and facilitate the exchange of ideas and knowledge among them, thus increasing the officials' awareness of the latest developments in their field. Secondly, these associations serve as "occupational contact networks" which expedite the interstate movement or transfer of personnel. Through the efforts of these groups officials become aware of desirable job openings in other states and are able to create professional reputations that extend beyond the borders of their own states.[57]

By rapidly spreading knowledge of new programs among state officials and by facilitating the movement of individuals to jobs in other states, professional associations encourage the development of national standards for the proper administration and control of the services of state government. Just as in other sectors of American life such as the business, the military and the academic world, as individuals increase their mobility, their role perceptions are likely to change; they are likely to adopt a more cosmopolitan perspective and to cultivate their reputations within a national professional community rather than merely within their own state or agency.[58]

Since general awareness of new developments is achieved much more quickly now than ever before, we would expect that the time which elapses from the first adoption of an innovation by a pioneering state to its complete diffusion throughout all the states would be greatly reduced. Certainly, several recent innovations, such as educational television or state councils on the performing arts, have diffused rapidly. In Table 6 we have measured the average speed of diffusion in years for three periods of time: 1870–1899, 1900–1929, and 1930–1936. The results shown in

[56] Unpublished memo from the Council of State Governments, Chicago, Illinois.

[57] For a discussion of the role of professional organizations in determining career lines see: Fred E. Katz, "Occupational Contact Networks," *Social Forces* (1958), 52–58. Also see: Jack Ladinsky, "Occupational Determinants of Geographic Mobility Among Professional Workers," *American Sociological Review* (1967), 253–264.

[58] Merton, *op. cit.* Also see: Alvin W. Gouldner, "Cosmopolitans and Locals: Toward an Analysis of Latent Social Roles," *Administrative Science Quarterly* (1957), 281–306; and Harold L. Wilensky, *Intellectuals in Labor Unions* (Glencoe, 1956).

TABLE 6. *Average Elapsed Time of Diffusion in Years for Innovation in Three Time Periods*

Time Periods	For All Adoptions	First Twenty Adoptions
1870-1899:	52.3	22.9
1900-1929:	39.6	20.0
1930-1966:	25.6	18.4

the first column of this table make it very plain that the speed of diffusion has been constantly increasing as time has passed. This measurement, however, is somewhat misleading. The second column of the table indicates the average number of years it took the first twenty states to adopt the programs in each time period. The same trend toward increased speed of diffusion is evident here, but the differences among the three time periods are much smaller.[59] This evidence suggests that the pioneering states, those with high innovation scores, adopted new programs about as quickly in the early part of this century, prior to the development of many specialized communication links, as they did in the 1900's. The total elapsed time of diffusion, however, has decreased primarily because the laggard states, those with low innovation scores, are now reacting more quickly to pick up new programs adopted by the pioneers. This development results partly from the efforts of the federal government to stimulate state action through grants-in-aid, and partly from the increasing professional development in state government. Both these tendencies seem to have had a larger impact on the behavior of the more parochial states than the more cosmopolitan, pioneering states.

IX The Persistence of Regionalism

Improved communications and greatly increased contacts of all kinds among state officials seem to be accelerating the process of diffusion, but this does not necessarily mean that the regional clusters or "leagues" of

[59] A small portion of the difference between the two columns in Table 6 is an artifact of measurement. Since not all the programs in this analysis have been adopted by all forty-eight states, laggard states sometimes remain. As time passes and programs receive widespread acceptance these laggard states slowly fall into line and adopt the programs. Since the programs in the first two time periods have been around longer, they have more likely completed their spread among the states and thus, given our scoring procedure, are also more likely to have a longer period of diffusion.

states to which we have referred have been destroyed.[60] In order to investigate this question the innovation scores in the time periods from 1870 to 1929 were combined, and two matrices of innovation scores of almost equal size were created, one for 1870–1929 and the other for 1930–1966.[61] Within each of these matrices each state's set of innovation scores (issue by issue) was correlated with the set of innovation scores for each other state. A varimax factor analysis was performed on each matrix, just as was done earlier to produce Table 5.

The results of this analysis are presented in Table 7. The factors derived from 1870–1929 are presented in the left column of the table and those from 1930–1966 are presented in the right column. The factors from each time period are arranged with the highest loadings first and the rest following in descending order. As we can see, the factors from the two time periods are not completely comparable. Some states change their relative rankings on the two factors, and some appear on a factor during only one of the time periods. The state of Georgia, for example, is found at the bottom of Factor 1 during 1870–1929 and moves all the way to the top of the same factor during 1930–1966. Some regional groupings, such as New England, seem to be disintegrating, while others, such as the Middle Atlantic states, seem to be more clearly defined in the later period. The factors for the later period include more states, on the average, and have slightly higher contribution scores, but they are not quite as distinct as those in the early period and include more inappropriate loadings. These data do not contain evidence of any large scale erosion of regionalism in the United States, but a drift away from clearly defined clusters of states is apparent.

During the last thirty years many new professional associations have been formed and more inter-state and federal agencies have begun facilitating communications and encouraging national uniformity. The diffusion process is operating much faster today than ever before, especially among those states which have traditionally lagged behind in adopting new ideas. The older, established modes of communication and evalua-

[60] The best recent analysis of long-term changes in the American political system is: Donald Stokes, "Parties and the Nationalization of Electoral Forces," in William N. Chambers and William D. Burnham (eds.), *The American Party Systems: Stages of Political Development* (New York, 1967), pp. 182–202. Also see: Norval D. Glenn and J. L. Simmons, "Are Regional Cultural Differences Diminishing?" *Public Opinion Quarterly* (1967), 196–205; and Ira Sharkansky, "Economic Development, Regionalism and State Political Systems," *Midwest Journal of Political Science* (1968), 41–61.

[61] When the data are combined in this manner the 1870–1929 matrix contains 42 issues and the 1930–1966 matrix contains 46 issues.

TABLE 7. *Varimax Factor Analysis of Innovation Scores for Forty-Eight States in Two Time Periods*

1870-1929		1930-1966	
Factor Loading	State	Factor Loading	State
	FACTOR I (South)		
.762	Tennesseee	.793	Georgia
.748	Mississippi	.759	Virginia
.745	Florida	.649	Delaware
.705	North Carolina	.629	Tennessee
.662	West Virginia	.623	Florida
.646	Kentucky	.593	Texas
.521	Louisiana	.570	North Carolina
*.499	Arizona	*.541	Utah
.465	Delaware	.524	Alabama
.426	Virginia	.494	Maryland
.425	South Carolina	*.493	Nebraska
*.424	Iowa	.493	South Carolina
.404	Georgia	*.451	Arizona
		*.432	Montana
5.7 Total Factor Contribution		*.426	Kansas
		*.415	Iowa
		*.415	Maine
		.413	Louisiana
		*.410	New Hampshire
		7.1 Total Factor Contribution	
	FACTORS II AND III (New England–Mid-Atlantic–Great Lakes)		
.851	Connecticut	.800	Connecticut
.814	New Hampshire	.702	Massachusetts
.707	Vermont	.629	New Hampshire
.705	Massachusetts	*.564	Colorado
.670	Rhode Island	*.498	Oregon
.576	Maine	.467	Rhode Island
.509	Delaware		
.487	New York	1.7 Total Factor Contribution	
.467	Pennsylvania		
.467	Virginia		
.405	Maryland		
*.405	Alabama		
5.3 Total Factor Contribution			

TABLE 7. *Varimax Factor Analysis of Innovation Scores for Forty-Eight States in Two Time Periods (Continued)*

1870-1929		1930-1966	
Factor Loading	State	Factor Loading	State
FACTORS II AND III (New England–Mid-Atlantic–Great Lakes) (Continued)			
.808	Kansas	.778	New York
.694	Indiana	.686	Pennsylvania
.643	Wisconsin	.684	New Jersey
.622	Illinois	.666	Wisconsin
.601	Minnesota	.537	Illinois
*.448	Texas	.491	Michigan
4.5 Total Factor Contribution		.486	Indiana
		.474	Minnesota
		.448	Maryland
		4.8 Total Factor Contribution	
FACTOR IV (Plains and Mountains)			
.769	North Dakota	.710	North Dakota
.762	New Mexico	.683	New Mexico
.722	Montana	.682	Kansas
.709	Utah	.641	Wyoming
.665	Idaho	.633	Oklahoma
.639	Washington	.598	Washington
.567	South Dakota	.572	Oregon
*.494	Maine	.557	Utah
4.7 Total Factor Contribution		*.494	Alabama
.751	Arizona	.462	Idaho
.588	Nevada	*.457	Vermont
.578	Wyoming	*.439	West Virginia
*.469	Arkansas	*.416	Wisconsin
2.5 Total Factor Contribution		.410	Montana
.730	Oregon	*.406	Mississippi
.611	California	6.5 Total Factor Contribution	
.645	Colorado		
*.433	Maryland		
2.9 Total Factor Contribution			

TABLE 7. *Varimax Factor Analysis of Innovation Scores for Forty-Eight States in Two Time Periods (Continued)*

1870-1929		1930-1966	
Factor Loading	State	Factor Loading	State
FACTOR V (Mid-America)			
.885	Missouri	.726	Missouri
.767	Nebraska	.614	Mississippi
*.639	Michigan	*.600	South Carolina
.519	Ohio	*.589	Idaho
*.400	California	.573	Arkansas
		.530	Tennessee
3.4 Total Factor Contribution		.432	Illinois
		.426	West Virginia
		*.409	South Dakota
		*.409	Montana
		4.5 Total Factor Contribution	

*States which are loading on inappropriate factors are marked with an asterisk.

tion, based on traditional ties of region and common culture, are persisting, but there are indications in these data that the system is slowly changing. Decision makers in the states seem to be adopting a broader, national focus based on new lines of communication which extend beyond regional boundaries.

X Conclusions

This essay began as an effort to explain why some states adopt innovations more rapidly than others, but in order to explain this aspect of American tederalism, we have had to make a more extensive investigation of the complex system of social choice by which we are governed. The approach to policy making which has emerged from our investigation is founded on the perceptions and attitudes of individual state decision makers. Of course, as I have already mentioned, the theory cannot be fully elaborated or put to a test until data can be gathered directly from legislators, bureaucrats, governors, and other officials in several states, on a comparative basis. Enough evidence has been presented already, however, to make apparent the major theoretical and practical implications of this approach.

The theory presented here directs our attention to the rules for decision employed by policy makers, rather than their formal group affiliations or their relative power or authority, and thus enables us to offer useful explanations of all policy decisions, not merely those which generate controversy. Emphasis is placed on those factors which lead to the establishment of parameters or guidelines for decision, not on the groups or interests supporting one policy over another. In Figure 1 the outlines of the diffusion process are depicted as it operates in a single state. There are undoubtedly many other influences on the level of agitation for change than the ones presented here, and many other secondary effects stemming from the enactment of new programs; this simple diagram is only meant to summarize the fundamental process operating in most cases of diffusion. Relationships are characterized by plus and minus signs but no effort has been made to estimate their relative importance in the system.

The process we have been describing is extremely complex; many influences shape decisions to adopt innovations and no two ideas diffuse in exactly the same way. In all cases, however, the likelihood of a state adopting a new program is higher if other states have already adopted the idea. The likelihood becomes higher still if the innovation has been adopted by a state viewed by key decision makers as a point of legitimate comparison. Decision makers are likely to adopt new programs, therefore, when they become convinced that their state is relatively deprived, or that some need exists to which other states in their "league" have already responded.

Before states may respond to new programs adopted in other states their political leaders must be aware of these developments, so interstate communications are an important factor in the process of diffusion. We have mentioned that many specialized systems of communication among the states have grown up during the last thirty years, mainly through the creation of professional associations among state administrators. These new information networks are spreading into all the states, but even today the isolation of some state capitals from the major cosmopolitan centers of the country is a major obstacle to the adoption of new ideas.[62]

Emerging from this study is the picture of a national system of emu-

[62] See Alan L. Clem's description of the isolation of Pierre, the capital of South Dakota, in his: *Prairie State Politics: Popular Democracy in South Dakota* (Washington, 1967), p. 137; and Norton E. Long's emphasis on the importance of information sources in his: "After the Voting is Over," *Midwest Journal of Political Science* (1962), 183–200. For a general review of communications theory and its application to politics see: Richard R. Fagen, *Politics and Communication* (Boston, 1966), especially pp. 34–69, 88–106. Also see: Karl W. Deutsch, *The Nerves of Government*, Second Edition (New York, 1966), especially pp. 145–256.

FIGURE 1. Factors Affecting the Adoption of Innovations *

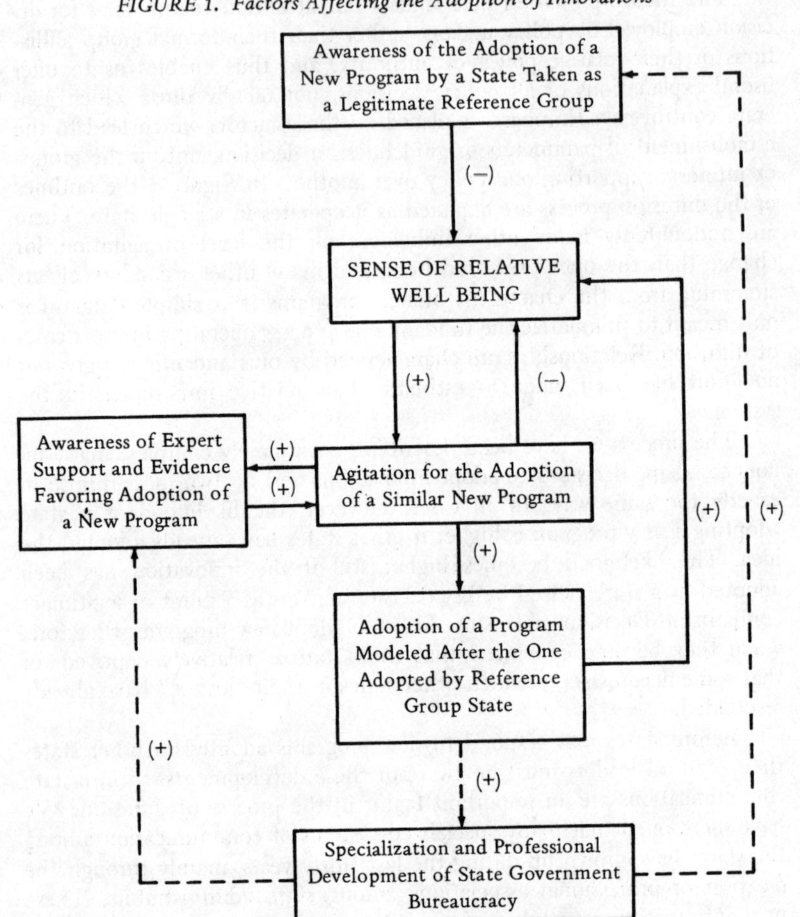

*Secondary effects depicted by broken lines.

lation and competition. The states are grouped into regions based on both geographical contiguity and their place in the specialized set of communication channels through which flow new ideas, information and policy cues. Through this nationwide system of communications a set of norms or national standards for proper administration are established. This system links together the centers of research and generation of new ideas, national associations of professional administrators, interest groups, and voluntary associations of all kinds into an increasingly complex network which connects the pioneering states with the more parochial ones.

Because of the limitations of the data presently available to us we can only outline each regional grouping of states, and we cannot yet construct an elaborate theory of the interactions among professional associations, federal officials, private interest groups, and political leaders in setting the agenda of politics within a state. Normative questions arise, which cannot be considered here, concerning the responsiveness of this system and the degree to which it is subject to the control of democratic, representative institutions.[63] Much more investigation will be necessary before we can gain a full understanding of this system and its function as a device for controlling the pace and direction of policy development in the American states. Once we know more, it might be possible to prescribe with confidence some changes in the decision-making system, or the creation of some new governmental institutions, which might accelerate or redirect the process of innovation.

Appendix

Note: Following are the eighty-eight programs upon which the innovation score is based.

1. Accountants Licensing
2. Advertising Commissions
3. Agricultural Experiment Stations
4. Aid for Roads and Highways
5. Aid to the Blind (Social Security)
6. Aid to Dependent Children (Social Security)
7. Aid to Permanently and Totally Disabled (Social Security)
8. Air Pollution Control
9. Alcoholic Beverage Control
10. Alcoholic Treatment Agencies
11. Anti-Age Discrimination
12. Anti-Injunction Laws
13. Architects Licensing
14. Australian Ballot
15. Automobile Registration
16. Automobile Safety Compact
17. Beauticians Licensing
18. Board of Health
19. Budgeting Standards
20. Child Labor Standards
21. Chiropractors Licensing
22. Cigarette Tax
23. Committee on the Aged
24. Compulsory School Attendance
25. Conservation of Oil and Gas
26. Controlled Access Highways
27. Council on the Arts

[63] Questions of this kind have been raised already in: Daniel P. Moynihan, "The Professionalization of Reform," *The Public Interest* (1965), 6–16; Theodore J. Lowi, "The Public Philosophy: Interest Group Liberalism," [*American Political Science Review*] (1967), 5–24; and Philip Green, "Science, Government, and the Case of RAND: A Singular Pluralism," *World Politics* (1968), 301–326.

28. Court Administrators
29. Debt Limitations
30. Dentists Licensing
31. Direct Primary
32. Education Agencies
33. Education Television
34. Engineers Licensing
35. Equal Pay for Females
36. Fair Housing – Private
37. Fair Housing – Public Housing
38. Fair Housing – Urban Renewal Areas
39. Fair Trade Laws
40. Fish Agency
41. Forest Agency
42. Gasoline Tax
43. Geological Survey
44. Highway Agency
45. Home Rule – Cities
46. Human Relations Commissions
47. Initiative and Referendum
48. Integrated Bar
49. Junior College – Enabling Legislation
50. Juveniles Supervision Compact
51. Labor Agencies
52. Legislative Pre-Planning Agencies
53. Legislative Research Agencies
54. Library Extension System
55. Mental Health Standards Committee
56. Merit System
57. Migratory Labor Committee
58. Minimum Wage Law
59. Normal Schools – Enabling Act
60. Nurses Licensing
61. Old Age Assistance (Social Security)
62. Parking Agencies – Enabling Act for Cities
63. Park System
64. Parolees and Probationers Supervision Company
65. Pharmacists Licensing
66. Planning Board – State Level
67. Development Agency
68. Police or Highway Patrol
69. Probation Law
70. Public Housing – Enabling Legislation
71. Real Estate Brokers – Licensing
72. Reciprocal Support Law
73. Retainers Agreement
74. Retirement System for State Employees
75. Right to Work Law
76. School for the Deaf
77. Seasonal Agricultural Labor Standards
78. Slaughter House Inspection
79. Soil Conservation Districts – Enabling Legislation
80. Superintendent of Public Instruction
81. Tax Commission
82. Teacher Certification – Elementary
83. Teacher Certification – Secondary
84. Urban Renewal – Enabling Legislation
85. Utility Regulation Commission
86. Welfare Agency
87. Workmen's Compensation
88. Zoning in Cities – Enabling Legislation

ANTI-POVERTY EXPENDITURES IN THE AMERICAN STATES: A COMPARATIVE ANALYSIS

ANDREW T. COWART

Though the focus of this paper is specifically on the Federal Anti-Poverty Program, it seeks generalizations about the impact of politics, economics, and past experiences on new public policies in American states and communities. Recent literature in the field of public policy provides various explanations for the level of expenditures of welfare-oriented programs in the states. Dawson and Robinson conclude that public welfare policies in the states are a function of socio-economic phenomena rather than the competitiveness of state partisan politics. Similarly, Dye argues that strong relationships which appear between political system characteristics and public policy actually disappear when measures of economic development are held constant. Conversely, Sharkansky's analysis of state government expenditures, as distinct from state and local expenditures, shows significant simple and partial correlations between political variables and state expenditures per capita. Sharkansky also argues that the political variable of previous expenditures exhibits the strongest relationship to state government expenditures per capita and serves as the most reliable predictor of present state spending.[1] The foci of these studies have been primarily on the explanation of public

Reprinted from Andrew T. Cowart, "Anti-Poverty Expenditure in the American States: A Comparative Analysis," *Midwest Journal of Political Science*, 13 (May, 1969), 219–236, by permission of the Wayne State University Press.

The author is indebted to Ira Sharkansky for helpful comments and criticisms of the original draft. The Office of General Research and the Computer Center of the University of Georgia provided welcomed financial and technical assistance, respectively. A list of variables and sources used in this study may be obtained from the author.

[1] See: Thomas R. Dye, *Politics, Economics, and the Public* (Chicago: Rand McNally and Company, 1966); Ira Sharkansky, "Economics and Political Correlates of State Government Expenditures: General Tendencies and Deviant Cases," *Midwest Journal of Political Science*, Vol. XI, No. 2 (May, 1967); Richard E. Dawson and James A. Robinson, "Inter-Party Competition, Economic Variables, and Welfare Policies in the American States," *Journal of Politics*, Vol. [XXV, No. 2 (May, 1963)]; Ira Sharkansky, "Some More Thoughts About the Determinants of Government Expenditures," *National Tax Journal*, Vol. XX, No. 2 (June, 1967).

policies which have become well-established in the states. Indeed, while the phenomenon of incrementalism, if narrowly conceived as intra-program variations in spending, is a reliable predictor of government expenditures, it is, by definition, not useful in predicting expenditures for new and innovative programs.

The present study, focusing on spending for and participation in Economic Opportunity Act Programs in the states, differs from previous examinations of welfare-oriented public policies in that its primary concern is with a program at its inception. In addition, it allows an assessment of the response of localities within the state political system rather than focusing upon welfare policies which, for the most part, are allocated by and channelled from federal and state governmental units to local communities.[2] Response is conceptualized in terms of degrees of action, that is, in terms of variations in the extent to which state and local governments and private organizations seek Anti-Poverty funds. Relatively high expenditures for aggregates of governmental and private units within the state indicate extensive response to federal Anti-Poverty Programs, while low expenditures per poor person suggest that state and local governments and private organizations have not responded to the needs of the poor by maximizing participation in EOA Programs.

Measurement and Techniques of Analysis

The designation of the states as the primary units of analysis is not intended to ignore the prominent role of local governments and private organizations in the expenditure of funds for the Anti-Poverty Program. Indeed, the contacts between the federal government and local governments and organizations far exceed similar contacts between federal and state governments in the administration of funds. The focus on the state conceptualizes the state, not simply as a governmental institution, but as a political system. Though most federal Anti-Poverty funds do not pass through the hands of state officials, they are administered by individuals who are products of the state political culture. Environmental stimuli (politics, economics, and past experiences) may interact and condition decision-makers within the state to respond, or not to respond, in varying

[2] Though the Economic Opportunity Act requires a non-Federal contribution of 10 per cent of the costs of most EOA programs, that percentage may be provided in cash or in-kind. Localities most often meet this requirement by supplying equipment, space, et cetera, rather than through a direct commitment of financial resources. Through April, 1966, estimates of local contributions to the Community Action Programs indicate approximately 2 per cent local support. See: Advisory Commission on Intergovernmental Relations, *Intergovernmental Relations in the Poverty Program* (April, 1966), pp. 179–180.

ways. The demands made upon political leaders may influence the ways in which they respond to federal public policy. This kind of conceptual focus provides a means for examining relationships between state system characteristics and the application of national public policy in the states.

The following dependent variables allow an analysis of the relationships between independent variables and response to the Anti-Poverty Program as well as a comparison of state government response to that of localities: [3]

1. Anti-Poverty expenditures per poor person, by state, through April, 1966
2. Initial Community Action Program allotment per poor person, by state, FY 1966
3. Reallocated Community Action Program allotment per poor person, by state, FY 1966
4. Technical Assistance allocation per poor person, by state, FY 1966
5. Technical Assistance grant per poor person, by state, FY 1966
6. State share of Technical Assistance funds per person, by state, FY 1966

Variable #1 provides a measure of response for state governments, local governments, and private organizations. Variables #2 and #3 focus upon the Community Action Program (CAP), to which 67 per cent of all Office of Economic Opportunity funds are allocated. Almost totally a federal-local enterprise, CAP expenditures provide a basis for analyzing response by localities within the state, while excluding the funds allocated to the state government.[4] Variables #4 through #6 measure only state

[3] EOA expenditures are based upon a per poor person measure developed by the Social Security Administration in 1965. This definition of being poor is based upon a minimum, nutritionally sound food plan designed by the Department of Agriculture. The food costs in this subsistence plan are used to determine the minimum total income requirements for different sized families. Budget levels for farm families are reduced by 30 per cent to allow for lower cash expenditures required where home-grown food is available and to recognize the lower cost of farm housing. On this basis, the poverty income line for nonfarm families of four persons was $3130; for farm families of this size, $2190. Nonfarm individuals were defined as poor if their money income was below $1540; for farm individuals, $1080. See: Advisory Commission on Intergovernmental Relations, *op. cit.*, p. 5.

[4] Federal grants to Community Action agencies are reasonably representative of expenditures in the Anti-Poverty Program because: (1) 67 per cent of all EOA funds are allocated to Community Action Agencies, and (2) the broad range of activities which Community Action Programs encompass includes some functional aspect of practically every program in the Economic Opportunity Act.

government initiative in seeking funds from the Office of Economic Opportunity. Technical Assistance expenditures are grants made to state governments which are used to stimulate and encourage local governments and organizations to actively seek Anti-Poverty funds from the federal government. These three kinds of measures allow comparisons of state and local unit response to EOA Programs.[5]

Independent variables which might be expected to influence the extent of state and local government and private group response to the needs of the poor are listed below. The electoral process, the level of economic development, and established policy norms are operationally defined by the following three groups of indices:

A. Measures of Economic Development:
   1. per cent families in 1960 with incomes less than $3000 in 1959
   2. per capita personal income, 1965
   3. per cent poor population (incomes less than $3000) which is urban, 1960
   4. per cent male civilian labor force unemployed, 1960
   5. per cent non-white population, 1960
   6. non-white population in 1940 as a percentage of that in 1960
   7. per cent adult population 25 years old and over with high school education, 1960
   8. per cent persons 5 and 6 years old enrolled in school, 1960
   9. number of high school graduates in 1962–63 as percentage of ninth graders in 1959–60

B. Measures of the Electoral Process:
   1. Ranney measure of inter-party competition
   2. average per cent turnover in gubernatorial and senatorial elections in non-Presidential years, 1952–60
   3. Schubert and Press apportionment equity score, 1962

[5] Both initial allocations and actual grants were utilized as measures of response. The initial allocation for FY 1966 was based in part, on actual spending during FY 1965; thus, it is a measure of response though less precise than the reallocation or grant figure. The reallocation figure was computed by the Office of Economic Opportunity in the following way: Initial allocations were made at the beginning of FY 1966; however, at the midpoint during the fiscal year, as it became apparent that some states would not request all the funds allocated, those allocations were reallocated to other states who were requesting more than their initial allocation. Thus, funds initially allocated to unresponsive states were reallocated to the more responsive states. Apparently, this procedure was followed for both CAP allocations and Technical Assistance allocations.

C. Measures of Established Policy Norms:
1. state and local expenditures for education per capita, 1964–65
2. state and local expenditures for health and hospitals per capita, 1964–65
3. state and local expenditures in federally aided vocational programs per capita, 1964–65
4. Old Age Assistance expenditures per poor person, 1966
5. Aid to Families with Dependent Children expenditures per poor person, 1966
6. Aid to the Blind expenditures per poor person, 1966
7. Aid to the Permanently and Totally Disabled expenditures per poor person, 1966

An analysis of relationships between the dependent variables and those in category A involves such questions as: If a high percentage of families in the state are poor, is poverty likely to become an identifiable issue and thus provoke greater response? Or, are states whose populations sustain higher incomes more likely to exhibit a concern over the conditions of poverty? Are states and communities with large concentrations of urban poor more likely to respond to the needs of the poor, due in part to organizational advantages of mobilization for community action? Do high unemployment rates produce a greater interest in EOA Programs concerning job training? Do states that respond to the educational programs of EOA contain highly educated or poorly educated populations? Are large concentrations of non-whites in the state likely to induce states and communities to seek the elimination of the impact of racial discrimination through EOA Programs; or is the Anti-Poverty Program perceived as a "gravy train" for low income Negroes with white political leaders remaining unresponsive in areas with large aggregates of Negro Americans? Linkages between the independent variables in Category B and the dependent variables suggest other questions: Do highly competitive political systems require decision-makers in those systems to actively seek the support of low income groups? Do high levels of participation in the system and equitable apportionment increase the likelihood of response to the needs of low income groups?

An examination of relationships between the dependent variables and those in the third category, established policy norms, focuses upon present response to the problems of poverty as a function of previous experiences in related welfare programs. Variables #1 through #7 indicate a willingness of the state to combine its own resources in varying degrees with extra-system resources to solve the problems associated with welfare. These variables reflect established or institutionalized patterns of participation by state and local governments. Admittedly, expenditures for federal categorical assistance programs do not strictly measure decisions of local governmental leaders to participate in those programs. However, as state participation becomes established over a period of time, these kinds of programs are likely to become the focus of both state and local welfare norms. Individuals who are products of the local political culture are likely to administer federal categorical assistance programs at the local level. As these funds are continually spent in local communities, they may independently influence local values concerning welfare programs. This kind of influence may be especially potent in the case of the federal welfare program, Aid to Families with Dependent Children, for which expenditures continue to rise annually. With repeated attacks on AFDC as a promoter of illegitmacy, the program itself is likely to have an impact upon the response of communities to new policies which benefit similar clientele groups. Thus, it is expected that these kinds of established norms concerning welfare-related programs directly influence the ways in which states and communities respond to new, welfare-oriented programs, such as those of the Office of Economic Opportunity.

Coefficients of simple correlation are useful indicators of the strength of relationships between measures of EOA spending and the independent variables. In addition, coefficients of multiple determination will indicate the proportion of variance in the dependent variables explained by any one grouping of independent variables. Multiple-partial coefficients will show the proportion of variance in the dependent variable explained by several independent variables, controlling for one or more independent variables.[6] In this way, it will be possible to isolate the independent impact of electoral politics, economics, and established policy norms on Anti-Poverty expenditures in American states and communities. Figure 1 symbolizes the conceptual framework through which these kinds of questions will be analyzed.

Findings: Simple Relationships

It is evident from an examination of Table 1 that Linkage A-4 in the model can be eliminated. The linkage suggests that federal public policy is formulated and executed in a centralized and systematic manner, with individual states influencing marginally or not at all the nature of federal spending in the states. Clearly, the diversity of response among the states to EOA Programs is great, ranging from $9.93 per poor person spent in Kansas to $96.80 per poor person for Oregon. However, what are the factors associated with high or low levels of response in the states?

[6] Hubert M. Blalock, Jr., *Social Statistics* (New York: McGraw-Hill Book Company, 1960), pp. 350–351.

FIGURE 1. A Model for the Analysis of Federal Public Policy in the States

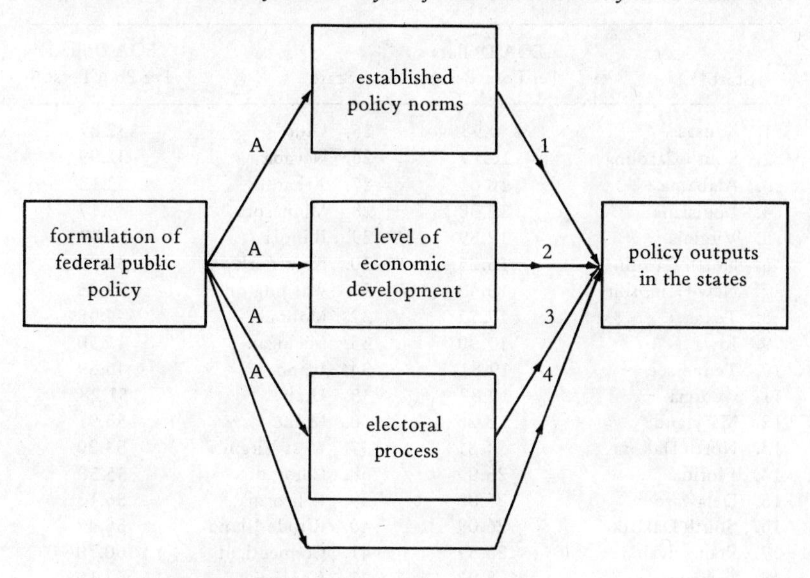

As expected, response to EOA Programs is related to the state's level of economic development. It is evident from Table 2 that states whose populations sustain relatively high incomes with few aggregates of poor people are more likely to respond positively to the Anti-Poverty Program. In those states where the poor are primarily urban rather than rural, Anti-Poverty funds are more likely to be sought.

The racial phenomenon has long been associated with welfare policies in the states. In those states where racial discrimination has been a salient feature in the development of the state political culture, the population may perceive the Anti-Poverty Program as primarily beneficial to Negroes. Table 2 suggests that both those states which have high percentages of Negro population and those states which exhibit significant Negro migration out of the state are likely to be low responders to the Anti-Poverty Program. This relationship is considerably influenced by the impact of the Southern states where perception of any public policy as a program benefiting Negroes substantially minimizes potential support for the policy. Finally, the relationships between the three measures of educational attainment of the population and response to poverty support the contention that a more highly educated population is a more socially concerned population. In those states where educational systems appeared to be meeting the needs of the population, as measured by the three inde-

TABLE 1. *EOA Dollars Per Poor Person and State Rankings (Lowest to Highest)**

State**	EOA Dollars Per Poor Person	State	EOA Dollars Per Poor Person
1. Kansas	$ 9.93	25. Ohio	$32.87
2. South Carolina	10.19	26. Nevada	32.99
3. Alabama	10.61	27. Arkansas	33.12
4. Louisiana	12.38	28. Minnesota	36.17
5. Virginia	12.89	29. Illinois	36.89
6. North Carolina	16.25	30. New York	38.20
7. New Hampshire	16.43	31. Washington	39.45
8. Texas	17.77	32. Montana	44.05
9. Iowa	17.90	33. Michigan	46.30
10. Tennessee	19.81	34. Idaho	46.69
11. Georgia	19.82	35. Utah	51.28
12. Maryland	23.26	36. Maine	53.91
13. North Dakota	24.81	37. West Virginia	54.20
14. Florida	25.09	38. Colorado	55.58
15. Delaware	25.80	39. California	56.13
16. South Dakota	26.09	40. Rhode Island	56.47
17. Pennsylvania	28.59	41. Connecticut	60.70
18. Indiana	28.93	42. Kentucky	63.10
19. Nebraska	29.18	43. Massachusetts	65.85
20. Wisconsin	29.52	44. New Jersey	68.41
21. Oklahoma	30.05	45. New Mexico	72.29
22. Missouri	31.10	46. Arizona	75.12
23. Mississippi	31.77	47. Oregon	96.80
24. Vermont	32.61		

*From *Intergovernmental Relations in the Poverty Program.*

**Alaska and Hawaii were excluded due to particularly difficult problems of adjusting expenditures to inflationary problems in those states. Wyoming was also excluded from the analysis because of the absence of a state Technical Assistance Agency in that state. Thus, meaningful comparisons of state-local response would have been influenced by this factor.

pendent variables, response to the Anti-Poverty Program was significantly greater.

The response of states and communities to EOA Programs also appears to be significantly related to the characteristics of the electoral process in the states. Coefficients of simple correlation provided in Table 2 indicate positive relationships between measures of state and local response to the Anti-Poverty Program and indices of partisan competitiveness and participation in the political system. However, an equitably apportioned legislative body does not appear to be characteristic of those states which are high responders to federal Anti-Poverty Programs.

TABLE 2. *Relationships between Economic Development and Electoral Process Variables and Response to EOA Programs: Coefficients of Simple Correlation*

Independent Variables	Dependent Variables					
	EOA Expend/ pp	Initial CAP Allotment/ pp	Reallocated CAP Allotment/ pp	TA Allocation/ pp	TA Grant/ pp	State Share TA Funds/ pp
percentage families with incomes less than $3,000	–.40	–.58	–.57	–.34	–.42	–.42
PCPI	.27	.62	.63	.39	.40	.44
percentage poor population urban	.36	.65	.68	.45	.24	.31
percentage unemployed	.33	.19	.17	–.07	.03	.04
percentage non-white	–.48	–.28	–.25	–.08	–.28	–.25
non-white population 1940 as percentage that 1960	–.41	–.45	–.40	–.17	–.36	–.36
percentage high school education	.35	.43	.35	.09	.33	.29
percentage 5 to 6 year olds in school	.24	.52	.55	.38	.33	.38
high school grads as percentage 9th graders	.22	.38	.34	.16	.10	.08
Ranney measure of inter-party competition	.52	.60	.54	.25	.37	.32
average percent turnout in Gov.' and Sen.' elections in non-Presidential years, 1952-1960	.47	.45	.39	.16	.33	.32
Schubert-Press apportionment equity score, 1962	.26	.14	.13	.14	.05	.18

The measures of previous participation in welfare-related programs were selected on the basis of three criteria: (1) functional similarity – that is, each is a measure of public policy which is functionally directed toward problems associated with low income groups (e.g. public expenditures for education, vocational training, health, welfare); (2) similar clientele groups – each is expected to substantially benefit the poor; (3) program differentiation – no measures were employed which would indicate relationships between previous expenditures for one program and present expenditures for the same program. Though educational expenditures are not directed solely toward low income groups, it can be argued that the relative benefit of high educational expenditures is greater for lower income groups than for higher income groups, who retain the alternative of private school enrollment. At any rate, all programs selected were expected to substantially benefit the poor. Utilization of independent variables based upon the above criteria allow broader generalizations about welfare-oriented environments where state and local governmental response becomes habitualized and reflects established patterns of participation in functionally similar programs directed toward certain clientele groups within the state.

Expenditures for federally aided categorical assistance programs vary from state to state. These programs are directed toward the needy aged, the blind, the disabled, and dependent children. The use of expenditures for these programs is facilitated by computing a "per poor person" figure rather than a "per recipient" figure to establish comparability with the dependent variables.

Table 3 provides evidence of significant relationships between response to EOA Programs and previous participation in other governmental programs directed toward the needs of the poor. Where state and local governments spend more per capita for health, hospitals, and education, they are significantly more likely to seek funds for instituting Community Action Programs. Somewhat stronger relationships occur between CAP expenditures and funds from federal categorical assistance programs. Spending per poor person for Old Age Assistance, Aid to Families with Dependent Children, Aid to the Blind, and Aid to the Permanently and Totally Disabled exhibits significant relationships with the dependent variables. This finding suggests that spending for well-established welfare programs in local communities may influence attitudes toward the levels of response to new programs. Although participation in federal categorical assistance programs does not represent local governmental decisions to do so, the level of spending in the locality established over a period of time may influence the community's response to similar programs. Relationships between spending for federal categorical assistance programs and the dependent variables were somewhat higher for measures of local

TABLE 3. *Relationships between Measures of Established Policy Norms and Response to EOA Programs: Coefficients of Simple Correlation*

Independent Variables	Dependent Variables					
	EOA Expend/pp	Initial CAP Allotment/pp	Reallocated CAP Allotment/pp	TA Allocation/pp	TA Grant/pp	State Share TA Funds/pp
state and local expend for health and hospitals per capita	.02	.47	.43	.12	.23	.54
state and local expend per capita in federally-aided vocational programs	.19	.24	.27	.41	.58	.34
state and local expend per capita for education	.35	.34	.33	.02	.26	.26
OAA expend/pp	.06	.34	.30	–.02	.02	.00
AFDC expend/pp	.51	.83	.84	.43	.25	.47
AB expend/pp	.10	.52	.49	.09	.27	.24
APTD expend/pp	.51	.68	.65	.22	–.05	.03

response than for similar measures of state government response, suggesting that the influence of previous experiences and established policy norms in welfare programs is more salient at the local level than at the state level.

Findings: Independent Influences on Response to Poverty

Levels of economic development, characteristics of the electoral process, and established welfare policy norms have been found to be significantly related to response to EOA Programs. However, the independence of each of the relationships has not been tested. The following generalizations can be made thus far: The higher the level of economic development, the more competitive and participatory the electoral process, and the greater the previous levels of participation in welfare programs, the more likely are American states and communities to respond to the needs of the poor through participation in EOA Programs. Which group of factors, however, contribute most to the explanation of the dependent variables? In addition, does the relationship between any one group of variables disappear when other variables are held constant?

Table 4 provides evidence that established welfare policy norms explain a greater proportion of the variance in all of the dependent variables than do economic or electoral phenomena. The proportion of variance explained by these variables, indicated by coefficients of determination, ranges from 34 per cent to 74 per cent, while similar percentages for economic phenomena and electoral phenomena are 20 per cent to 51 per cent and 8 per cent to 38 per cent, respectively. Table IV also presents multiple-partial coefficients between the dependent variables and each grouping of independent variables, controlling for the remaining independent variables. For every dependent variable except one, multiple-partial coefficients are significantly higher for the measures of previous levels of participation in welfare-related programs than are similar coefficients for economic and electoral variables. When the impact of the electoral process and the level of economic development are held constant, established welfare policy norms continue to explain a significant proportion of the variance in the dependent variables. However, when measures of established policy norms are held constant, relationships decrease considerably for both economic and electoral phenomena. Thus, it is not the level of economic development or the nature of electoral politics that directly influences response to the Anti-Poverty Program. It is, rather, an established and institutionalized pattern of participation in functionally related public policies which structures the nature of response to new policies directed toward similar goals in the system. It may be that economic and/or electoral characteristics of the states influence initial decisions of governments to participate in specific functional areas of public policy (in this case, welfare). However, once extensive involvement becomes accepted as legitimate, that established level of involvement is likely to independently influence response to new but similarly oriented policies in the states.

The finding that there is stability in response to welfare-oriented programs does not mean that some states do not deviate from the general pattern. A few states spend considerably more than expected on the basis of participation in other welfare-related programs, while the response of other states has been less. The use of regression analysis allows the identification of those deviant cases. The analysis employs a regression formula, $Y = a + bX$, where Y is the dependent variable (EOA expenditures), X is the independent variable (measures of established welfare policy norms) most powerful for explanatory purposes, and a and b are constants. After having shown above that established and institutionalized policy norms concerning the value of participation in welfare-related pro-

TABLE 4. *Coefficients of Multiple Determination and Multiple Partial Coefficients between the Dependent Variables and the Level of Economic Development, Characteristics of the Electoral Process, and Established Welfare Policy Norms*

	Coefficients of Multiple Determination			Multiple Partial Coefficients					
	Economic Variables	Electoral Process Variables	Policy Norm Variables	Economic Variables Controlling for Electoral Process Variables	Economic Variables Controlling for Policy Norm Variables	Electoral Process Variables Controlling for Economic Variables	Electoral Process Variables Controlling for Policy Norm Variables	Policy Norm Variables Controlling for Electoral Process Variables	Policy Norm Variables Controlling for Economic Variables
EOA expend/pp	.38	.29	.42	.24	.41	.13	.09	.26	.45
Technical Assistance allocation/pp	.20	.08	.34	.15	.12	.03	.08	.34	.28
Technical Assistance grant/pp	.31	.14	.48	.23	.08	.04	.02	.41	.31
CAP initial allocation/pp	.51	.38	.74	.26	.19	.06	.04	.60	.57
CAP grant/pp	.50	.32	.73	.29	.11	.04	.07	.63	.52
State share TA funds/pp	.35	.12	.57	.36	.30	.14	.28	.65	.54

grams explain a greater proportion of the variance in the dependent variables than do economic or electoral phenomena, it is now possible to identify those states for which this generalization does not hold. By predicting each state's EOA expenditures on the basis of previous participation in welfare programs, it is then possible to compare real expenditures with predicted expenditures according to the formula:

$$\frac{\text{real expenditures}}{\text{predicted expenditures}}$$

The closer to 1.00 the results are, the more a state fits the prevailing pattern. If the value is considerably greater than 1.00, then the state is responding to the Anti-Poverty Program more than would have been expected on the basis of its previous level of involvement in other welfare programs; if the result of the formula is significantly less than 1.00, the response of the state is below that predicted on the basis of spending for other welfare programs.[7] A 50 per cent deviation for the ratio of real expenditures to predicted expenditures was arbitrarily selected to designate a state as a deviant case.

The data presented in Table 5 indicate that eight states qualify as deviants which spend more than would be expected for all EOA Programs on the basis of past experience with welfare-oriented programs, while five states spend less than that predicted by the formula. What factors account for that deviation? Four of the five states which spend less than expected are Southern states, where expenditures for welfare functions are below those of the majority of other states. Perhaps the explosive political nature of welfare spending in the South, coupled with a perception that Negroes are the principal beneficiaries, influences political leaders to respond with considerable caution and delay to new, functionally similar programs. The perception by Southern whites that AFDC is a federal welfare program which substantially benefits Negroes and increases illegitimacy rates among them may caution restraint in the acceptance of new federal programs directed toward similar clientele groups. This may be the case even in Louisiana which has traditionally maintained high levels of spending for welfare functions. In 1961, the state ranked second among the states in total welfare expenditures per capita, although its rank for AFDC payments per recipient was 34th. Thus, perceptions in local communities in Southern states (in this case, Louisiana) that Negroes are the principal beneficiaries of AFDC payments may further depress response to programs directed toward similar

[7] For use of this technique, see: Ira Sharkansky, "Economic and Political Correlates of State Government Expenditures: General Tendencies and Deviant Cases," *op. cit.*

TABLE 5. *Measures of Previous Response as Predictors of EOA and CAP Expenditures per Poor Person: Ratios of Real to Predicted*

State**	Ratio EOA	CAP	State	Ratio EOA	CAP
1. Alabama	.50*	.62	25. Nebraska	.94	.50*
2. Arizona	1.79*	1.12	26. Nevada	1.52*	1.51*
3. Arkansas	1.66*	1.06	27. New Hampshire	.61	.91
4. California	.85	.92	28. New Jersey	1.23	.93
5. Colorado	1.32	1.00	29. New Mexico	1.42	.93
6. Connecticut	.86	1.10	30. New York	.84	.84
7. Delaware	.61	.88	31. North Carolina	.52	1.06
8. Florida	1.16	1.05	32. North Dakota	.57	.98
9. Georgia	1.00	1.06	33. Ohio	.99	1.04
10. Idaho	1.10	.48*	34. Oklahoma	.71	.96
11. Illinois	.80	1.03	35. Oregon	1.64*	1.01
12. Indiana	.97	.78	36. Pennsylvania	.85	1.00
13. Iowa	.63	.77	37. Rhode Island	1.23	1.19
14. Kansas	.25*	.86	38. South Carolina	.49*	1.13
15. Kentucky	2.34*	1.07	39. South Dakota	.72	1.05
16. Louisiana	.48*	1.05	40. Tennessee	.88	1.04
17. Maine	1.51*	.85	41. Texas	.77	1.03
18. Maryland	.58	.92	42. Utah	.82	1.13
19. Massachusetts	1.28	1.04	43. Vermont	.76	1.12
20. Michigan	1.32	1.10	44. Virginia	.43*	.97
21. Minnesota	1.14	1.04	45. Washington	.72	1.35
22. Mississippi	1.55*	1.48	46. West Virginia	1.62*	1.16
23. Missouri	1.17	1.04	47. Wisconsin	.95	.88
24. Montana	1.08	1.06			

* Deviates 50 per cent or more.

** Alaska, Hawaii, and Wyoming excluded; see footnote, Table 1.

clientele groups, even though other kinds of welfare programs have been strong in the state. Kansas is a deviant case for which the explanation of its low level of response is not readily apparent.

It is significant that both Kentucky and West Virginia were among the states which deviated by spending more than expected. Both states have experienced the particularly acute employment and income problems of the Appalachian region. Caudill notes the propensity of people in this area to pursue aggressively funds from the federal government for welfare programs to relieve their depressed economic conditions.[8] Thus,

[8] Harry M. Caudill, *Night Comes to the Cumberlands* (Boston: Little, Brown and Company, 1962).

with almost total federal financing of the Anti-Poverty Program, West Virginia and Kentucky have sought EOA funds to a greater extent than for other welfare programs. The case of Mississippi is an interesting deviant where response to EOA Programs has been significantly greater than expected on the basis of past experience in welfare programs. A substantial part of the explanation lies in attempts by the federal Office of Economic Opportunity, six months after the Program's inception in 1964, to directly induce response by sending OEO organizers to Mississippi which, at that time, appeared to exhibit a low level of interest in the Anti-Poverty Program. Other deviant cases remain for which the explanation is not readily apparent. It may be necessary to analyze intrastate variations for those remaining cases which do not fit the general pattern.

Table 5 provides additional evidence that past levels of participation in welfare-oriented programs are reliable predictors of response to EOA Programs. Community Action expenditures, a more precise measure of funds actually going to localities in the state, are substituted in the regression formula as the dependent variable in place of EOA expenditures per poor person. The closeness of the fit is greater than that for total EOA expenditures, with only three deviant cases identified. The ratios contribute to the substantiation of earlier findings that in states and communities where high levels of participation in welfare programs have become institutionalized and habitualized, response to the needs of the poor through participation in EOA Programs is significantly greater.

Conclusion

Levels of economic development, characteristics of the electoral process, and established patterns of participation have been found to be significantly related to response to EOA Programs in American states and communities. However, through the techniques of controlling, it has been shown that the most salient influence on response to EOA Programs is previous experience with other welfare programs. Once participation in certain kinds of welfare programs becomes established in the state or locality, the associated level of spending may become a frame of reference for community evaluation of new programs, such as the federal Anti-Poverty Programs. However, four of the five states which responded less than expected to EOA Programs were Southern states, where experiences with previous welfare programs may depress response to new but similar programs, when those programs are perceived as primarily benefiting Negroes. These findings suggest a feedback influence of established public policies on newly formulated policies.

Theoretically interesting is the suggestion of an even broader interpretation of the phenomenon of incrementalism than that indicated in previous studies. Not only are increases in intra-program expenditures likely to be incremental; new programs involving policies functionally similar to well-established policies may be substantially influenced by the prior level of activity in that policy area. Thus, inter-state variations in the level of welfare expenditures for welfare policies become established over a period of time. Future responses may be influenced and structured by these kinds of past experiences which contribute to the internalization of norms concerning the value of welfare spending in American states and communities.

WAGE GARNISHMENT AND BANKRUPTCY PROCEEDINGS IN FOUR WISCONSIN CITIES

HERBERT JACOB

In recent years political scientists have focused most of their political participation research on the acts of voting, of running for political office, of campaigning for others, and of expressing demands through interest groups. These acts constitute in the main our image of political man. This characterization emphasizes his roles as a demander of governmental services and as a controller of public officials. Another role, intertwined with these, as a consumer of governmental services or as a user of public facilities, has not been much studied by us.[1]

The citizen's role as a consumer of governmental services has become more prominent with the growth of the welfare state. Many needs, if

Reprinted by permission from Jacob Herbert, "Wage Garnishment and Bankruptcy Proceedings in Four Wisconsin Cities," in James Q. Wilson, ed., *City Politics and Public Policy* (New York: John Wiley and Sons, 1968), 197–214.

The research on which this paper is based was supported by a grant from the Walter E. Meyer Research Institute of Law and by funds granted to the Institute for Research on Poverty at the University of Wisconsin by the Office of Economic Opportunity pursuant to the provisions of the Economic Opportunity Act of 1964. Donald Pienkos, Mary Ann Allin, and William Fisher aided considerably in the processing of the data. The conclusions are the sole responsibility of the author.

[1] Almond and Verba discuss one phase of the citizen's role as a consumer when they examine the concept of subject competence. Gabriel Almond and Sidney Verba, *The Civic Culture* (Princeton: Princeton University Press, 1963), pp. 214–257.

satisfied at all, were previously met mostly by private rather than public means. Education was provided mostly by private academies and denominational colleges. Private philanthropy furnished most welfare and health services. Insurance was supplied entirely by private enterprise and fraternal organizations.

Today these services are predominantly provided by the government. In addition, new public services are designed to meet a broad variety of needs for almost every citizen. Consequently, the public now consumes public services more frequently than ever before. For many citizens their principal contact with government is not through the suffrage but through public agencies which service their needs. Thus in 1960, there were 22.7 million people who obtained a large part or most of their income from government pensions; another 6.3 million received various kinds of public assistance payments. In addition, an estimated 26 million parents had children attending public schools or colleges. In these categories alone, 55 million people, or half the adult population, were consuming public services which were central to their life style.

Among the oldest agencies providing services for the general public are courts of law. They provide forums for airing private and public conflicts and for settling them according to established custom and law. Even such a traditional service has increased relevance to contemporary Americans. The provision of more public services and the extension of statutory law to many fields previously governed by private custom have made it possible to bring more issues to courts for settlement. More permissive attitudes toward divorce, the greater frequency of injuries from auto accidents, and higher urban crime rates have increased citizen contact with the courts. Available evidence suggests that the volume of litigation is now higher in most parts of the country than it was in the past.[2]

[2] See for example the following statistics and cases filed:

	Year	Cases per 100,000 pop.
Iowa District Court Cases Commenced	1956	845
	1965	1062
California Superior Court	1951–1952	2117
	1961–1962	2163
New Jersey Law Division and County Court Civil Cases	1949–1950	229
	1959–1960	332
Connecticut Superior Court and Court of Common Pleas	1929–1930	981
	1959–1960	995
Only Michigan Showed a Decline: All Trial Courts	1932	1370
	1960	1241

Sources.

Iowa: Judicial Department Statistician, 1965 Annual Report Relating to Trial Courts of the State of Iowa, pp. 15 and 18.

Citizen contact with the courts is likely to be as significant as contact with most agencies. In criminal matters the courts may deprive men of their liberty for long periods of time and brand them as convicts. In other cases the courts do more than provide a forum and the rules for settling private conflict or challenging the action of another government agency. Courts lend governmental power to the victor of a suit and enable him to force the loser to abide by the court decision. Many private conflicts are thus transferred to the public domain. Litigants may contend about private affairs but at the end both winner and loser find that the government has become intimately involved in their dispute.

The political consequences of the consumption of court services by various segments of the public are not at all obvious and have not been subjected to systematic empirical analysis. A few dramatic cases have changed the course of public policy [3] but most cases involve the application of existing policy.[4]

Court application of existing norms is likely to have several kinds of politically relevant consequences. The systematic application of norms may produce social and economic results that generate demands for legislative action to change the norms or the rules of their application. This is most likely to occur when the norms originated under different social or economic circumstances, but courts continue to enforce them without significant changes.[5] Court actions also frequently strike at the core of people's personal behavior, their life-style, or fortune. Such contact

---

California:	Judicial Council of California, 19th Biennial Report, 1962, p. 143.
New Jersey:	Annual Report of the Administrative Director of Courts, 1961–62, Supp. p. 5.
Connecticut:	17th Report of the Judicial Council of Connecticut, March, 1961, pp. 20–21.
Michigan:	Office of the Court Administrator, Annual Report and Judicial Statistics for 1961, p. 80.

[3] A few such dramatic decisions by the Supreme Court have been examined. See the many studies of the aftermath of *Brown vs. Board of Education* and Frank Sorauf, "Zorach vs. Clausen: The Impact of Supreme Court Decision," *American Political Science Review*, 53, 777–91 (1959).

[4] See H. Jacob, *Justice in America* (Boston: Little, Brown & Co., 1965), pp. 17–36 for this distinction and Joel Grossman, "Judicial Policy Making," paper presented in 1966 Midwest Conference of Political Scientists (mimeographed) for a critique.

[5] Some examples are: (1) The workmen's compensation laws which arose after attempted application of the fellow-servant rule to industrial accidents where the rule was inappropriate; (2) 19th century divorce laws in New York, the application of which finally provoked new legislation in 1966; and (3) current dissatisfaction with contributory negligence rules applied to auto accidents when the facts are usually too complicated for a just application of the rule.

with government about personally significant matters is likely to color people's impressions of their government. Insofar as their impressions remain distinctive to the courts, they may bear little relevance to their evaluation of the political regime in general. If their impression of the courts colors their preception of government or the political regime in general, such contacts with the courts may become highly significant elements in the generation of support for the regime or alienation from it.

In this paper we will concern ourselves only with the conditions under which different groups avail themselves of legal remedies. In subsequent reports of this research project, the impact of involvement in litigation and its political significance will be explored.

A definitive answer to the general question of the conditions under which judicial action becomes relevant to potential litigants cannot be given at this stage of our knowledge. Since court actions may involve a broad array of conflicts and potential litigants, each type of conflict requires separate examination. Considerable attention has recently been given to comparable questions in the sphere of criminal law [6] and in the use of litigation to settle disputes arising from automobile accidents.[7] I have limited my research to the area of creditor-debtor relations and, within that, to the use of court action to collect delinquent debts by attaching the debtor's wages and the use of several judicial proceedings by the debtor to delay immediate payment or avoid payment altogether.

Debtor-Creditor Conflicts

Debtor-creditor conflicts arise out of a variety of situations. They almost always involve a refusal by the debtor to pay his creditor what the latter thinks is due him. Such a refusal may be based on the debtor's feeling that he has been cheated or that the creditor did not fully live up to his end of the bargain. A refusal may also arise from a sudden inability to repay because of unemployment, ill health, a family emergency, or pressure from other creditors to repay them first. Sometimes, debtors fail to repay simply because they forget or no longer want to repay. In each of these cases, the probability of conflict between creditor and debtor is high because most creditors will pursue the debtor until he has repaid as fully as they can reasonably expect. Their judgment of reasonable repayment may be based on a number of factors; the most important, how-

[6] See Jerome Skolnick, *Justice Without Trial* (New York: Wiley, 1966); Wayne R. Lafave, *Arrest* (Boston: Little, Brown & Co., 1965); and Donald Newman, *Conviction* (Boston: Little, Brown & Co., 1966).

[7] Roger B. Hunting and Gloria S. Neuwirth, *Who Sues in New York City* (New York: Columbia University Press, 1962).

ever, is likely to be the cost of obtaining repayment judged against the amount of probable payment. When the cost of obtaining payment rises far above the amount owed, most creditors will write off the loan as uncollectible.

The range of individuals involved in these conflicts is immense in the kind of credit economy the United States has. Almost everyone in retail business, in service enterprises, and in the professions extends credit; in addition we have a multimillion dollar consumer finance industry. Thus, among creditors in such conflicts, we find finance companies, department stores, service stations, television repair shop proprietors, landlords, hospitals, doctors, and even lawyers.

With credit cards in almost every adult's wallet, the range of individuals involved as debtors in these conflicts is even wider. The only persons systematically excluded are the very poor who are without attachable incomes and who are unlikely to be extended credit.[8] Not every debtor is equally likely, however, to be involved in a credit dispute which will reach the courts.

A great variety of private actions may be undertaken in efforts to collect debts. When these fail, the courts stand ready to help creditors through a number of legal remedies. If an article was purchased through a conditional sales contract, the creditor may repossess it, sell it, and then collect from the debtor the difference between what it brought in the sale and what he still owes. Such proceedings frequently leave debtors owing substantial amounts for items they no longer possess because the resale value of many items bought on credit is less than the amount owed at the time of repossession. Creditors may also go to court to obtain a judgment against the debtor; such a judgment constitutes an official statement of the debt and authorizes the creditor to obtain the sheriff's assistance in collecting the amount due him. The sheriff may inspect the debtor's possessions and seize for sale any articles which are neither exempt from execution under the state's laws nor serving as security for another debt. When – as in many cases – the debtor owns no goods which may be seized to satisfy the judgment, creditors in many states have a final judicial remedy: they may attach the debtor's wages through a wage garnishment.[9] A summons is sent to the debtor's employer who is obligated to report whether he owes the debtor any wages; if he does, he must send those wages to court. The debtor may recover a token amount for living expenses, but the bulk of the funds so caught are used to satisfy

[8] But note the marginal credit exposed by David Caplovitz, *The Poor Pay More* (New York: Free Press, 1963).

[9] A recent summary of wage garnishment laws may be found in George Brunn, "Wage Garnishment in California: A Study and Recommendations," *California Law Review*, 53, 1222–27, 1250–53 (1965).

the debt. A creditor may garnishee his debtor's wages as often as necessary to obtain full payment.

Debtors, in turn, also have a number of extralegal and legal remedies to which they may turn. In a country where there is free movement and different laws in each state regarding creditor-debtor relations, the easiest thing for a debtor to do may be to move away from where he incurred his debts.[10] Alternatively, he may defend his nonpayment in the judgment suit although that is expensive and rarely successful. Increasingly, debtors make use of a much more successful legal maneuver – promising repayment through a court-approved amortization plan. Court-approved amortization plans may be available under state law (as they are in Wisconsin) or through Chapter 13 of the federal bankruptcy statute. Under the Wisconsin statute,[11] a debtor earning less than $7500 per year may agree to repay his debts in full within a two-year period. During this interim, the debtor is protected from wage garnishments and other court actions seeking to collect the debts listed in the amortization plan. Debts not listed and new debts may be collected as before through judgments or wage garnishments. Amortization under Chapter 13 of the Bankruptcy Act[12] allows the debtor to repay over a three-year period; during this time, interest accumulation is stopped and all creditor actions against the debtor are prohibited. New debts as well as old ones may be included in the repayment plan although the debtor may incur new debts only with the approval of a court-appointed trustee. Chapter 13 plans may also provide for partial payment in satisfaction of the debt.

Bankruptcy provides the final legal escape for the debtor. Bankruptcy is equally available under federal law to the business and nonbusiness debtor. A debtor need not be penniless; he need only have debts which he cannot pay as they fall due. Under bankruptcy proceedings, the debtor makes available to the court all nonexempt assets that he possesses for repayment to his creditors. The definition of exempt assets depends upon state law; in Wisconsin they include the equity in the individual's home up to $5000 or $1000 in savings accounts, life insurance up to $5000, equity in a car up to $1000, one television set and radio, personal clothing, jewelry up to $400, beds and stoves used by the family, other furniture up to a value of $200, one firearm up to a value of $50, plus assorted miscellany such as a Bible, pew, cemetery lot, library, sewing machine, and

[10] The extent of debtor mobility is indicated by the proportion of debtors in our study who had moved away within 12 months of court action involving them. This proportion ranged from 11% in Kenosha to 21% in Green Bay.

[11] Wis. Stat. 128.21.

[12] The statutory provisions for bankruptcy and Chapter 13 proceedings are found in 11 U.S.C. 1–1103.

tools of trade.[13] Consequently, almost all nonbusiness bankruptcies turn out to involve no assets that can be distributed to creditors. After this has been established, the federal court (through a special official, the Referee in Bankruptcy who handles these cases in place of the District Judge) discharges the debts of the bankrupt; he is therefore no longer legally obligated to repay. The single limitation to this remedy for debtors is that they may exercise it only once every six years.

Conditioning Factors

Only a tiny proportion of all credit transactions turn into conflicts between creditor and debtor and only a small proportion of those eventually are brought to court. It is therefore important to identify the conditions under which some people seek to invoke governmental sanctions in their efforts to collect or evade their debts. Five sets of conditions are readily identifiable.

First is the need of people to use the courts to resolve their conflicts. Creditors will not use the courts unless losses from credit transactions are high enough to reduce profits and cannot be recouped through extralegal means. Debtors will not seek refuge in court remedies unless their debts become burdensome because of creditor pressure. The threshold for creditors and debtors is different. For creditors it varies with the organizational structure of the firm and its sensitivity to customer relations. For debtors it depends upon their financial and psychological resources, their information about court remedies, and the size of their debt.[14]

A second conditioning factor is the availability of court action. In some communities, court action is unlikely because no court is sitting in the town – all actions must be started in a distant town making litigation inconvenient as well as expensive. Other factors, however, also make legal remedies variably available. Some courts are more stringent about requiring representation by lawyers than others; in some towns, attorneys are more readily available for collection work than in others; in some, attorneys charge more for collection work than in others. Finally, the cost of litigation varies from town to town, because local judges interpret state laws differently regarding fees, and local practices evade some of the more costly items.

Third is the ability of potential litigants to use remedies that are

[13] Wis. Stat. 128.21.

[14] "The Consumption of Governmental Services: Usage of Wage Garnishment and Bankruptcy Proceedings in Four Wisconsin Cities," paper prepared for delivery at the 1966 Annual Meeting of the American Political Science Association (mimeographed); a fuller analysis will appear in a monograph to be published by Rand McNally in 1969.

available. They need to know about them; they need the requisite financial resources; they must be convinced that court action is really appropriate in their situation; they need to be free of the psychological restraint of shame and the social restraint of retaliation. Different members of a community are likely to vary considerably in their ability to use available remedies.

The socioeconomic conditions prevailing in an area is a fourth factor. A recession (even if slight and local) following a period of prosperity when credit was freely extended is likely to be more productive of creditor-debtor conflicts than a continued period of prosperity or a long recession. Likewise, the type of economy an area has is likely to be important. Subsistence economies (either in rural or urban slums) are not likely to involve much consumer credit. Factory workers whose employment or earnings are erratic are more likely to be caught in credit difficulties than are white collar workers whose employment is steadier and whose wages, although lower, are also more regular. The availability of credit is also significant; those living in small towns or in cities with few banks and lending institutions may find it more difficult to obtain credit and may also find themselves less frequently tempted to borrow than those living among a plethora of lending institutions and constantly being bombarded by an invitation to borrow.

Finally, the "civic" or "public" culture of a community is likely to be important. Some communities may be more conservative in lending policies than others; in some, large blocs of citizens may refrain from borrowing, either because they are older and not used to it or because they come from ethnic groups which are unaccustomed to living on credit. Alternatively, some communities are composed of groups who borrow heavily. In some communities, resort to court action comes easily without cultural constraints; in others, it involves a morally and culturally difficult decision. Thus court action may be much more frequent in some communities than others.

In this paper I shall discuss only the last variable. The others are investigated elsewhere.[15]

The Research Design

The research on which this paper is based was designed to obtain an empirical description of the conditions under which wage garnishments, court-supervised amortization plans and bankruptcy proceedings were used. Four middle-sized cities in Wisconsin were chosen as research sites.

[15] *Ibid.*

The four were chosen because they had been the sites for previous studies into their community power structures and therefore extensive background materials were available for them. Since all the cities examined were located in one state, the available legal remedies were held constant. In each city, court files were searched for wage garnishments and bankruptcy cases. In one city, Green Bay, where the number of such proceedings was small, the entire population of such cases for a 12 month period was recorded; in the others (Kenosha, Madison, and Racine) a systematic random sample was taken for a similar period. After checking for current addresses, a subsample of the remaining names was taken and hour-long interviews were obtained with debtors whose wages had been garnished, who had gone through Chapter 13 proceedings, or who had declared themselves bankrupt. A total of 454 interviews with debtors were obtained. In addition, a random sample of creditors and employers were sent questionnaires. Finally, personal interviews were held with selected attorneys, creditors, collection agents, and court officials. In addition to these interview and questionnaire materials, information available on the court records was recorded and used as a check against the survey data and a supplement to it.

A second phase of the research (not reported here) involved the use of a state-wide survey to provide a control group against which to measure behavior and attitudes of debtors.

Findings

Neither creditors nor debtors use the courts to the same extent in the four cities we studied. Instead, gross variations in court usage are evident when we count the number of garnishment and bankruptcy actions initiated in a 12 month period (see Table 1).

Data for other court cases in these areas are also available, although

TABLE 1. *Garnishment and Bankruptcy Actions for 12 Month Period: Gross Totals and Actions per Population by City*

	Madison	Racine	Kenosha	Green Bay
Total Garnishments per	2860	2740	813	130
1000 pop.	22.6	30.7	12.0	2.1
Bankruptcies	112	100	63	32
Chapter 13's	37	18	5	7
Total BK-13 per				
1000 pop.	1.2	1.3	1.0	0.6

only on a county not a city basis.[16] The frequency with which all civil cases except garnishments are initiated in the four counties (See Table 2) follows the same pattern as the garnishment and bankruptcy rates. The highest rate occurs in Racine with Madison, Kenosha, and Green Bay following. Criminal case rates do not follow the same pattern except that Brown County (Green Bay) ranks low there as it does in civil litigation. The distinctive pattern of criminal rates seems to reflect a different set of causal factors as we might expect, since criminal cases are initiated by public officials while civil cases are initiated by private citizens for the most part.

Some of the recent efforts to explain such differences in the output of governmental agencies have sought to explain them in terms of social, economic, and (where appropriate) partisan characteristics of the area.[17] Our four cities do vary considerably on important socioeconomic indicators as is shown in Table 3. Madison is the largest city. The high education and mobility of its population reflect the impact of the state university on Madison; the presence of the university and of the state government offices also depresses the per cent of the population employed by manufacturing firms. Racine, Kenosha, and Green Bay are much more similar but not identical. Green Bay has only a small portion of its labor force engaged in manufacturing; it has a relatively high retail sales volume. Kenosha, the home of American Motors, has the highest proportion of its labor force in manufacturing but low retail sales volume and low per capita bank deposits.

These differences, however, do not help us explain the varying litigation rates. Madison's high garnishment and bankruptcy rate is incongruent with the high proportion of its population which is well educated, in

[16] The proportion of the city population to county population is not strikingly different for the four cities, except for Kenosha: The per cent of the county population in the city in 1960 was 57.2% for Madison, 59% for Racine, 67% for Kenosha, and 50.2% for Green Bay. The proportions of the population classified as urban in these counties were even more similar: Dane (Madison) 75%, Racine 73%, Kenosha 72%, and Brown (Green Bay) 80%. Consequently, the court data presented here should not reflect biases due to significant differences in size of urban population.

[17] *Cf.* the chapters by Richard Dawson and James Robinson, Robert Friedman, and Robert H. Salisbury in Herbert Jacob and Kenneth N. Vines, *Politics in the American States* (Boston: Little, Brown & Co., 1965); Richard I. Hofferbert, "The Relation between Public Policy and Some Structural and Environmental Variables in the American States," *American Political Science Review*, 60, 73–82 (1966); Robert R. Alford and Harry M. Scoble, "Political and Socio-economic Characteristics of American Cities," *1965 Municipal Yearbook* (Chicago: International City Managers' Association, 1965).

TABLE 2. *Civil and Criminal Cases in Four Counties, July 1, 1964–July 1, 1965*

	Dane (Madison)	Racine	Kenosha	Brown (Green Bay)
Civil Cases				
County and circuit court	1691	817	1203	803
Small Claims Court (minus garnishment)	4203	3024	743	233
All civil cases per 1000 pop.	18.9	21.3	7.4	1.9
Criminal cases				
(excluding ordinance)	3195	1020	867	722
All criminal cases per 1000 pop.	15.8	7.2	8.6	5.8

Source: Table 1, 1965 Annual Report of the Wisconsin Judicial Council; Table 10, 1965 Annual Report of the Wisconsin Judicial Council.

white collar rather than blue collar occupations, and with large bank deposits. Green Bay's low garnishment and bankruptcy rate is all the more surprising with its relatively high proportion of people in the income bracket most prone to these difficulties – the $3000 to $10,000 range; likewise, its high retail sales volume and relatively high bank deposit rate would indicate a garnishment and bankruptcy rate like Racine's. Instead, Green Bay's garnishment and bankruptcy rate is half of Racine's.

Other studies have also shown that cities [18] and states [19] which have similar socioeconomic characteristics nevertheless have different patterns of political behavior. This may be because they have reached their presently similar position by different developmental paths and acquired distinctive styles of public action and evaluations of public activity. There are aspects of a city's culture which are likely to permeate its decision-making processes and also affect the likelihood of citizens bringing cases to court.

The relevant cultural characteristics of our four cities have been sug-

[18] See for example: Oliver Williams and Charles Adrian, *Four Cities* (Philadelphia: University of Pennsylvania Press, 1963) and Robert E. Agger, Daniel Goldrich, and Bert E. Swanson, *The Rulers and the Ruled* (New York: Wiley, 1964).

[19] All studies examining expenditures by states show a considerable residual remaining after socioeconomic characteristics are entered into the regression equations. See the studies cited in footnote 17.

TABLE 3. *Selected Socioeconomic Indicators for the Four Cities*

	Madison	Racine	Kenosha	Green Bay
Population, 1960	126,706	89,144	67,889	62,888
Per cent nonwhite, 1960	1.9	5.4	0.5	0.4
Per cent with income between $3000 and $10,000, 1960	68.9	71.6	69.1	76.1
Per cent with high school or more education, 1960	65.3	40.6	36.8	46.3
Per cent migrants from different county, 1960	28.1	11.5	13.4	13.0
Per cent of labor force in manufacturing, 1960	15.1	49.0	50.6	26.9
Per cent in one unit structures, 1960	55.9	63.2	61.7	67.3
Per cent dwelling units owner occupied, 1960	54.2	65.0	65.7	65.0
Number of manufacturing establishments with more than 20 employees, 1958	45	82	37	42
Per capita retail sales, 1958	$1520	$1345	$1199	$1892
Per capita bank demand deposits, 1960	$931	$724	$558	$742

Source: Bureau of the Census, County-City Data Book, 1962, pp. 566-574

gested by Alford and Scoble's examination of their decision-making processes. Alford and Scoble [20] hypothesize that these cities represent four cultures: (1) *traditional conservatism* (Green Bay) where "government is seen as essentially passive, as a caretaker of law and order, not as an active instrument either for social goals or private goals"; (2) *traditional liberalism* (Kenosha) where "the bargaining process may even extend to traditional services. . . ."; (3) *modern conservatism* (Racine) where "government is seen as legitimately active, but furthering private economic interests which are regarded as in the long range public interest"; and (4) *modern liberalism* (Madison) where "a high level of political involvement . . . may itself exacerbate conflicts . . ." Alford and Scoble concentrate their analysis on the liberal-conservative dimensions of the

[20] Robert R. Alford and Harry M. Scoble, "Urban Political Cultures," paper delivered at the meeting of the American Sociological Association, September, 1964 (mimeographed), pp. 1–5. Quoted by permission of the authors. Elsewhere (in a yet unpublished draft of a book) they defined traditionalism in terms of low professionalization with consequent informality in decision-making and highly specialized leadership groups.

four cities because they focus on the kinds of public decisions made and the range of participation in the decision-making process. The data in Tables 1 and 2 suggest, however, that the cities cluster on the traditional-modern dimension when we examine civil litigation rates. Thus it appears that Green Bay and Kenosha share low litigation rates because of their more traditional public cultures while Racine and Madison share higher litigation rates because of their more modern public culture.

What are the possible linkages between political culture and the civil litigation rates? Civil litigation requires decisions by individual plaintiffs and their lawyers to transfer a private dispute into the public domain of the judiciary. Of course, the propensity to litigate depends on the expected pay-off; few people will sue if the chances of winning judgment are small or if there are no funds to recover. But holding that consideration constant, we may hypothesize that in some cultures, commonly held values become social constraints against litigating; in the absence of such values, people are more likely to sue. Where a high level of government activity is valued and where publicity is not particularly feared because social relationships are at a bureaucratic rather than personal level, conflicts are more likely to ripen into litigation than where these conditions do not exist. Both a high valuation of government activity and bureaucratized relationships are associated with a modern rather than traditional culture. Data from our interviews indicate that these cultural conditions in fact exist in the four cities and are associated with the variation in litigation rates.

Taking a debtor to court in order to collect a loan is a highly impersonal proceeding involving the use of public officials as intermediaries (the sheriff serves the papers) and arbiters. Interviews with attorneys indicate that in Green Bay and Kenosha, creditors depend more on private means than do their counterparts in the modern cities, Madison and Racine. Green Bay and Kenosha creditors make more use of personal contacts, telephone calls to the debtor or informal arrangements with employers. In addition, fewer creditors in Green Bay and Kenosha thought that eliminating garnishment would make a difference to their operations. Moreover, in Green Bay where the garnishment rate is lowest, attorneys and creditors often asserted that the city was small enough for everyone to know everyone else, making court action unnecessary. In fact, Green Bay has only 5000 fewer inhabitants than Kenosha (where no respondents mentioned the intimacy of the town) and is only one third smaller than Racine with its high garnishment rate. Nevertheless, the exaggeration of its small size is significant, since the perception of Green Bay as a small town fits our characterization of its culture as traditional.

Further, the lower garnishment rate also fits Alford's description of these traditional cities as ones in which the business elite does not look upon government as an instrument to obtain its private objectives. If those businessmen who extend credit take their cue from the leaders of the business community, we would expect that they would not be as ready to use the courts to collect their accounts as their counterparts in cities where the business community frequently invokes government power to attain its objectives. Passive government and informal bargaining, typical of many public situations in Green Bay and Kenosha, also typify the debt collection process more frequently than in Madison and Racine. In Madison and Racine creditor-debtor conflicts, like public disputes, more frequently reach official government agencies (in this case, the courts) for formal adjudication.

The traditionalism we have spoken of spills over to the legal culture. The way in which attorneys handle garnishment cases in Green Bay is one indication of it. In Green Bay most of the attorneys who handle garnishment cases send letters to the debtors prior to initiating court action, even though cases referred to attorneys have already been extensively worked over by the creditor's collection department or a collection agency. Attorneys in no other city took this precaution or were as concerned to avoid formal court action. In other cities, most attorneys reported that when a file was given them they immediately filed court action unless they knew that no one else had tried to collect. The distaste of the Green Bay attorneys for court action appears to reflect a more traditional, as well as conservative, attitude toward litigation. Attorneys in the other cities reflect more the modern view of litigation as a legitimate instrument to meet their objectives.

Alford's characterization of these four cities also leads us to look for differences in the degree to which people in these cities are fiscally traditional. In the two traditional cities, we might expect that even the debtor population would show greater distrust of finance companies than in the other two cities and that they would prefer, both in words and deed, such a respectable source of money as banks. In addition, we might expect the debtors of the two cities to express more conservatism in favoring borrowing for particular purposes than their counterparts in the "modern" cities.

These inferences are only partially supported by our data, as Table 4 indicates. Only in the traditional and conservative city (Green Bay) do debtors exhibit all the characteristics we expected: they are most approving of banks and least approving of finance companies as sources of loans; they actually used banks the most and finance companies the least when they borrowed money. They were the most conservative in approving borrowing for a wide range of items. They most frequently could indicate the interest rates they thought they were paying for their loans. The pattern in the other cities is not so clear. Debtors in Kenosha are like those

TABLE 4. *Measures of Fiscal Conservatism Among Debtors in the Four Cities: Per Cent of Debtors in Each City Indicating . . .*

	Madison	Racine	Kenosha	Green Bay
Best source of loans				
Banks	47.9	48.9	43.5	54.4
Finance company	2.1	5.3	4.6	1.5
Worst source of loans				
Finance company	46.5	44.0	45.8	61.8
Largest source of credit				
Finance company	43.4	63.8	50.5	33.3
Banks	23.1	13.8	16.5	30.4
Knows interest rate for all or some loans	70.9	42.2	54.2	76.8
Approved borrowing for a large range of items	37.1	37.0	34.5	30.0

in Green Bay only in evaluation of borrowing; in their attitudes toward finance companies and banks, in their borrowing behavior, and in their knowledge of interest rates, Kenosha debtors are more like those in their sister city, Racine. On the other hand, debtors in Madison are more like those in Green Bay except in their approval of borrowing.

These inconsistencies warn us not to explain all differences by the political culture of these cities. The differences in Chapter 13 rates, for instance, are more clearly related to differences in perceived accessibility to Chapter 13 trustees as the result of advice given debtors by attorneys. Where Chapter 13 proceedings are most frequent (Madison and Racine), lawyers mention this alternative more frequently, thus giving the debtors a real choice between it and bankruptcy. In the other cities, lawyers rarely speak about Chapter 13 to their bankruptcy clients; since few clients hear of Chapter 13 from other sources, fewer debtors in those cities used Chapter 13 proceedings.

The reason that more attorneys "push" Chapter 13 in some cities than in others is related to the pressure they feel from the Referee in Bankruptcy and the accessibility of a trustee. In Madison, the Referee was a strong advocate of Chapter 13 and the trustee was exceptionally vigorous in making his services available. Racine's higher Chapter 13 rate (in contrast to Kenosha's, where the same Referee is operating) reflects the fact that the trustee for those cases was a fellow Racine attorney, readily available on the telephone for consultation. Kenosha attorneys also had to use the Racine trustee, but they hesitated to incur the long-distance charge for a call to neighboring Racine. In addition, they felt that Chapter 13 cases were beyond their control; they expressed a strong preference for amortization under state law (although it provided less protection for the debtor), because they could maintain control over the proceedings and because they could keep in close contact with the debtor who might bring them higher fees when he brought an accident case or a divorce case. Green Bay, Racine, and Madison attorneys almost never used state amortization proceedings and did not speak of them as a lure to attract clients in better paying cases. In this instance, a characteristic of the legal structure of the communities plays an important role in the frequency of debtor actions.

With four cities, it is statistically impossible to estimate how much of the variation is explained by the political culture, by the legal structure, and by what appear to be accidental variations. Four cases are sufficient to discern variation without establishing the distribution of these variations. Nevertheless, it is significant that the wide variations we discovered should exist among four cities which (although not identical) are much alike in their size, economic base, and social structure. If our analysis is correct, variation in the use of courts by debt collectors and by debt evaders is closely related to rather subtle cultural and normative factors, when gross socioeconomic indicators are held relatively constant as they were in this study. Our analysis does not indicate whether still larger differences in court usage might occur if we were to examine cities with grossly different socioeconomic characteristics. However, if large metropolitan areas are more like Madison than Green Bay in possessing a modern political culture with impersonal and bureaucratized relationships, we would expect that court usage would be still greater than in Madison and Racine.

Conclusions

This exploration of court usage in wage garnishment and consumer bankruptcy actions has not shown any of the usual political linkages between governmental action and private demands. This is because the usual linkages are missing. If we were to look for partisan biases of the judges (or referees), for evidence of other attitudinal biases in their decisions, for the linkage between the judicial selection process and court decisions, for the role of other political activities in this process, we would come away convinced that this is a totally nonpolitical process. Only an examination of patronage would evidence the existence of the usual political processes at work, since the referees may appoint at will Chapter 13 trustees and trustees for all bankrupt estates. However, Chapter 13 cases do not generate a great deal of revenue for the trustees and most bankruptcies by consumers involve no assets or very nominal assets so that the lawyers appointed to these cases benefit little from their appointment. In the usual *partisan* sense, the processes we have been examining are indeed nonpolitical.

Nevertheless, I would urge that such a view is erroneous. Garnishment and bankruptcy cases involve invocation of governmental power for private ends. The rules for these proceedings (as provided by the state legislatures and by Congress) invite invocation of governmental power to all who meet quite minimal conditions. The fact that only a few of all those eligible to use these proceedings do so is significant to the political system. In the first instance, it brings to the courts far fewer actions than might otherwise be the case. Secondly, it has consequences that may not have been intended by the authors of the laws which make court usage possible or which, when apparent, are unacceptable to concerned political leaders. Wage garnishments are used by buoy the socially least desirable form of consumer credit, that extended by finance companies. Bankruptcy is in fact used only by some of the debtors who might benefit from its provisions. The law is applied unevenly, even though the variation is unintended by legislator and judge alike. Third, the variation in court usage is likely to result in deepening disaffection among the disadvantaged.[21] Those most likely to be disaffected, the debtors who are socially not well integrated, perceive the courts only as an instrument of the creditor not as a source of relief from their own troubles. Where garnishments are more common or more concentrated among a particular segment of the population, they may therefore become a significant source of political alienation.

The political process I have been describing is beyond doubt quite different from the electoral or legislative political processes which political scientists ordinarily describe. However, it may bear a significant resemblance to a portion of the administrative process which is becoming increasingly important: the conditions of usage of governmental agencies or consumption of government-provided services. The degree to which governmental action penetrates into the general social system depends to a great extent on the kinds of considerations we have examined wherever usage is voluntary rather than compulsory. In some administrative agencies the same kind of problem arises as in use of court services; this is true of the use of agricultural extension services, the use of counselling and educational services by the poor, and the use of higher-education facilities by the young – to name a few. None of these, however, involves the dramatic use of governmental coercive power over others for private objectives as does use of the courts.

[21] This problem will be the focus of later reports of this research. Data about political efficacy were collected in the debtor interviews. However, see the speculation about the association between garnishments and the 1965 riots in the Watts area of Los Angeles: Ralph Lee Smith, "Saga of the Little Green Pigs," *The Reporter*, 35, 39–42 (1966).

As this study indicates, governmental power can be invoked through much more routine ways than campaigning in elections. This invocation is based on different objectives, and varies according to different characteristics of the invoker, than the ordinary use of governmental power through partisan means.

SOCIOECONOMIC DIMENSIONS OF THE AMERICAN STATES: 1890–1960

RICHARD I. HOFFERBERT

Introduction

The study of American state political systems has, in recent years, increasingly been concerned with the impact of socioeconomic environmental characteristics upon various political features of the states. Recent studies have employed state data and relatively powerful statistical methods to examine the relationship between social rigidity and economic development,[1] the dimensions of social change,[2] the impact of socioeconomic variables upon public policy,[3] and the effect of various structural

Reprinted from Richard I. Hofferbert, "Socioeconomic Dimensions of the American States: 1890–1960," *Midwest Journal of Political Science*, 12 (August, 1968), 401–418, by permission of the Wayne State University Press.

I am grateful to the Social Science Research Council for financial support of the project of which this research is a part. Helpful criticism has been received from Professors Ira Sharkansky, Thomas R. Dye, and Samuel C. Patterson. Any errors of substance or interpretation are, of course, entirely my own.

[1] Ruth C. Young and Jose A. Moreno, "Economic Development and Social Rigidity: A Comparative Study of the Forty-Eight States," *Economic Development and Cultural Change*, 13 (July, 1965), 439–452.

[2] Francis R. Allen and W. Kenneth Bentz, "Toward the Measurement of Socio-cultural Change," *Social Forces*, 43 (May, 1965), 522–532.

[3] Richard E. Dawson and James A. Robinson, "Inter-Party Competition, Economic Variables, and Welfare Policies in the American States," *Journal of Politics*, 25 (May, 1963), 265–289; Thomas R. Dye, *Politics, Economics, and the Public* (Chicago: 1966, Rand McNally); Richard I. Hofferbert, "The Relation Between Public Policy and Some Structural Environmental

features of state government as they relate to policy and social composition.[4] In each of these studies, particular lists of environmental variables have been correlated in one fashion or another with some dependent political variables of particular relevance to the specific piece of research. Each author has used a somewhat different list of environmental variables, with no one offering an especially convincing or comprehensive rationale for his or her particular list. Such experimentation is to be expected and is quite healthy in an area of research blessed with a large amount of data and yet denied the benefits of relatively mature theory.

The absence of any fairly precise theory in these studies has left two major questions unresolved. First, there has been little by way of specification of linkages in the cases where social variables are found to correlate highly with the dependent political characteristics. Secondly, once the effect of environment has been measured, the amount of variance left unexplained is substantial. The theory necessary for a specification of linkage would also be likely to point the direction in which we might move in beginning to chip away at the unexplained variance.[5]

Sophistication of techniques, however, need not await full refinement of theory. The former frequently facilitates the latter. One of the major technical problems of this body of research, and one which has obvious theoretical and conceptual implications, is the identification of significant dimensions of independent social variables. The independent variables employed, for example, in the comparative study of determinants of state policy have been variously labeled "economic development," "social structure," "social environment," "ecological systems," etc. Little consideration has been given to the likely multi-dimensionality of these various lists which have been employed to represent such concepts. Yet there is no *prima facie* reason why one should assume that a single dimension would necessarily encompass, for example, urbanization, literacy, income, em-

---

Variables in the American States," *American Political Science Review*, 60 (March, 1966), 73–82; *ibid.*, "Ecological Development and Policy Change in the American States" [*Midwest Journal of Political Science*], 10 (November, 1966), 464–483; Ira Sharkansky, "Economic Development, Regionalism and State Political Systems," *ibid.* (February, 1968), and "Regionalism, Economic Status and Public Policies of the American States," *Southwestern Social Science Quarterly* (June, 1968).

[4] Thomas R. Dye, "Malapportionment and Public Policy in the States," *Journal of Politics*, 27 (August, 1965), 586–601; Hofferbert, *op. cit.*, "The Relation . . ."; Herbert Jacob, "The Consequences of Malapportionment: A Note of Caution," *Social Forces*, 43 (December, 1964), 256–261.

[5] An example of one successful attempt in this reduction of the unexplained variance in state variables is Sharkansky's studies of the independent impact of region, in addition to a variety of economic development features, in explaining the patterns of policy followed by the states. Sharkansky, *op. cit.*

ployment patterns, and population migration. Rather it seems sensible to assume at this point in the development of inquiry that we need an identification of the major dimensions of these variables and an indication of where each state falls in terms of the extent to which it shares features of these dimensions. The need is for valid, comprehensive, internally consistent indices. The most appropriate tool for this kind of index construction is factor analysis. It will be one purpose of this paper to present the results of several factor analyses of the types of data employed in the studies noted above.

Once one has conducted a factor analysis of such data from any single point in time, however, there is still no overpowering reason to assume that the dimensions so discovered are features of a durable social structure. Without a consideration of the stability of social dimensions over time, what may be mistaken for features of "social structure," in some systemic sense, may be nothing more than the transient confluence of peripherally related characteristics of the states.

The problem of longitudinality, therefore, reaches beyond the relatively mechanical task of index construction and raises some questions about the likely directions to be pursued in the development of theory. One of the main implications of studies such as those of Dawson and Robinson, Dye, Sharkansky, and my own earlier work is that something about the processes of "modernization" or "economic development" (as measured by income, urbanization, employment, etc.) creates a set of circumstances which require or at least facilitate the passage of policies providing more public funds for services within the states. With few exceptions, the data which have been employed in this mode of investigation have been drawn from a single point in time or from a very limited number of proximate years. Longitudinal considerations have not been confronted in any direct manner in most of these studies.[6] If the crude theory implicit in most of them is correct, longitudinal considerations

[6] There have been a few exceptions. One notable instance is Sharkansky's "Economic and Political Correlates of State Government Expenditures: General Tendencies and Deviant Cases," *Midwest Journal of Political Science*, 11 (May, 1967), 173–192.

The article employs only state level indicators (as opposed to state and local), and thus is not directly comparable to many of the other studies in the field. But it does raise interesting questions about the relevance of socioeconomic variables when compared to the relevance of past state policy activities.

In another study, I also considered the longitudinal dimension of socioeconomic policy correlations, but only between two points in time. The findings of the present study, however, cast considerable doubt upon the explanations offered at that time. See my "Ecological Development . . . ," *op. cit*.

should not affect the type of correlations that have been discovered, beyond a somewhat random variation due to differential fluctuation in overall magnitudes of some measures. Yet there is reason to believe not only that magnitudes have changed, but also that there are very marked variations in the strength of relationship between independent (social) and dependent (political) variables.[7] And this may be the case even where one can demonstrate the internal stability of social dimensions.

If longitudinal elements are to be considered, therefore, and if we are to check the multidimensionality of the independent variables being studied, some method must be devised for specifying change and stability in the infrastructure of the dimensions of social characteristics employed as independent variables. The latter objective is the second purpose of this paper. If this purpose is served successfully, and if reasonably stable structural dimensions are discovered, then the indices so devised may be employed to test the longitudinal consistency of social structural-political correlations.

To summarize my objectives, then, I am seeking first to identify some of the major dimensions of socioeconomic structure within the states. Secondly, I am examining data from specific periods over an extended span of time to see whether or not the dimensions identified at one point are comparable to those found at a different time such that we may legitimately refer to the dimensions of state social systems as aspects of social "structure," i.e., patterns of interrelationships that are durable over time. This latter objective is pursued not only because it might be interesting to plot the change and consistency of detail in the major dimensions of state social systems, but also out of a high expectation that when these factors are employed as independent variables the relationships discovered will prove substantively interesting and helpful in the construction of comparative theory.

Method and Findings

The first step in the construction of indices is to find and select data which are likely to produce valid and useful pictures of the characteristics being represented. In the case of any longitudinal analysis, there are a number of obstacles to the accumulation of optimum data. Although there is a wealth of quantitative material on the states for recent years, it is difficult to obtain consistent and comparable records for very many social indicators back into the last century. I have found and selected 21

[7] Richard I. Hofferbert, "Stability and Change in Some Social Correlates of Political Participation and Policy Outputs in the American States" (Paper presented at the annual meeting of the Southwestern Social Science Association, Dallas, Texas, March, 1967).

ecological variables which did, with few exceptions, seem to meet these requirements (both in definition and in mode of recording). (See Table 1 and note.)

One could complain that this list, like the others cited earlier, contains no readily apparent theoretical rationale for the particular variables employed. I suppose that I could construct some *post hoc* rationale that might be moderately adequate as a beginning theory. And, of course, the list could have been extended by using a variety of subdivisions of some of the items, for example – different breakdowns of occupational information, extensive lists of commercial and agricultural figures, etc. But the test of this particular list, either in terms of its cohesiveness or its inclusiveness, must be the same as for any alternative. Namely, how much promise does it hold for relating in a theoretically interesting manner to the dependent variables we seek to explain?

The 21 variables, or at least all of them that were available on or near each decade, were subjected to a factor analysis for each census year from 1890 to 1960. In some cases, data were not listed in available sources for the particular decennial year. In those instances, the data were included in the factor analysis for the nearest census year.[8] In all cases, the technical conditions of the factor analyses were the same for the analysis of each of the 8 decades.

The first question which I sought to investigate was: is there any consistency in N dimensions of social structure from decade to decade? That is, do the patterns of each variable's loadings on the major factors have any similarity from one period to the next and on through time?

The analyses indicated that the fewer the number of factors I extracted from the data, the more the consistency in loading patterns from decade to decade.[9] This is, of course, as might be expected given the

[8] The technique employed was a principle component analysis with a Kaiser Varimax rotation of the original matrix and an oblique rotation to maximize high and minimize low loadings on each of the two principle factors. Factor scores were then estimated and assigned to each state as a weighted summation of the original scores of each variable for each state. A straightforward and insightful discussion of these techniques is presented in the *IBM, 1130 Statistical System (1130–CA–06X): User's Manual,* 31–42.

A listing of sources for all data used in this article may be obtained from the author.

[9] It should be emphasized that I am not attempting to explicate the full implications of a theoretically comprehensive matrix of state characteristics. Rather, bearing in mind the limitations of the data which are available, I am trying to isolate only a few dimensions indicative of important features of the states – important in the sense that they hold high promise of having consequential capacity to explain or at least guide efforts to explain some of the dependent variables which are of interest to students of the states' political systems.

logic of factor analysis. But I found that by specifying two factors for oblique rotation, factors were produced which maintained a high degree of longitudinal consistency and still managed together to account for roughly 60 per cent of the variance in the matrix. (See Tables 1 and 2.) [10]

Maintaining two factors, therefore, the oblique rotation yields the results seen in Tables 1 and 2. A visual examination of the factor loadings, from decade to decade, indicates that there is a low amount of variation in the infrastructure of these two major dimensions.

Identification of the factors is also fairly easily accomplished by a brief examination of the pattern of factor loadings. It is even more clearly revealed by looking at the manner in which the states are arrayed by their factor scores. Tables 3 and 4 present ordinal data with the states arrayed according to their 1960 ranks.[11]

In labeling Factor I, it is as interesting to note what is not heavily loaded as it is to specify the principle components of the factor. Whereas in Factor II, the indicators of wealth, incidence of Negroes and illiteracy are prominent by their heavy loadings, the factor featured in Table 1 is not ethnicity; it is not predominantly wealth; it is not education or population change. Rather the factor is indicative of patterns of economic and occupational activity, thereby justifying the label "Industrialization." The proportion of the population in manufacturing employment and the value added per capita by manufacturing distinguish this dimension on the positive end of the scale.[12] And, although the negatively loaded variables are not as heavily or consistently related as those at the top of the scale, states with large average form size tend to be at the opposite pole from those with high manufacturing activity. The same holds true with owner occupancy of homes. Although the value of their homes may be low, a high percentage of the householders in Montana, New Mexico, North Dakota, and the other states at the bottom of the Industrialization factor own their own homes.

An examination of relative positions of the states on Factor I over time shows that Industrialization has not occurred at a uniform rate

[10] Inclusion of a third factor in the rotation would have increased the amount of the variance explained by about 10% at each of the eight time periods. This third factor, however, was found to be of little value in explaining the dependent variables which have been considered in this research.

[11] Although only ordinal ranks given in Tables 3 and 4, factor scores were employed in all calculations. A complete listing of factor scores may be obtained from the author.

[12] In assessing the changes in degree of relevance of several variables in 1930, one should bear in mind that much of the data in the 1930 factors may be for years somewhat after 1930, thereby reflecting the early impact of the Depression. The various indicators of manufacturing activity, for example, are actually 1931 data, although they are included in the 1930 factor analysis.

TABLE 1. *Loadings of 21 Variables on Factor 1 (Industrialization): 1890-1960**

1890		1900		1910		1920	
				Pop. in Mfg.	.918		
		Pop. in Mfg.	.914	Value Mfg.	.916	Pop. in Mfg.	.939
		Urban	.882	#Employees	.878	Value Mfg.	.935
Pop. in Mfg.	.938	Value Mfg.	.880	Density	.853	Urban	.881
Value Mfg.	.928	Density	.878	Urban	.841	Density	.861
Urban	.928	#Employees	.823	Population	.396	#Employees	.728
Density	.889	Farm Value	.701	Foreign	.379	Foreign	.517
Farm Value	.889	Population	.449	Farm Value	.228	Population	.482
#Employees	.756	Foreign	.328	Failures	.138	Telephones	.229
Population	.381	Income	.237	Telephones	.022	Failures	.212
Foreign	.334	Failures	.009	Mot. Veh.	.016	Farm Value	.139
—		—		+		—	
+		+		—		+	
Failures	.030	Property	.124	Illiteracy	.024	Pop. Incr.	.006
Property	.116	Negro	.127	Negro	.044	Property	.032
Divorce	.234	Illiteracy	.173	Tenancy	.106	Illiteracy	.071
Pop. Incr.	.310	Pop. Incr.	.323	Property	.253	Negro	.113
Negro	.342	Divorce	.492	Pop. Incr.	.479	Mot. Veh.	.243
Acreage	.357	Acreage	.502	Acreage	.579	Tenancy	.245
Illiteracy	.390					Own. Occup.	.490
						Acreage	.563
% Total Variance	36.67		36.13		26.67		26.55

* The abbreviations are as follows: Acreage–mean acreage per farm; Density–population per square mile; Divorce–divorce rate; # Employees–mean number of employees per manufacturing establishment; Failures–percent failures of business and commercial establishments; Farm Value–mean value per acre of farm land and buildings; Foreign–percent foreign (1890-1930, percent foreign born; 1940-1960, percent foreign born plus foreign or mixed parentage); Illiteracy–percent illiterate; Income–per capita personal income; Mot. Veh.–motor vehicle registrations per 1,000 population; Negro–percent Negro; Own. Occup.–percent housing owner occupied; Population–total population; Pop. in Mfg.–percent population employed in manufacturing; Property–estimated value of real property per capita; School Yrs.–median school years completed, age 25 and over; Telephones–telephones per 1,000 population; Tenancy–percent farms operated by tenants; Urban–percent urban; Value Mfg.–value added by manufacturing per capita.

In some instances there have been minor changes in the census definitions. These are not of such a nature, however, to be likely to affect the pattern of relationship between variables within any particular year. The data are not all from the specific decennial year, but every effort has been made to include variables from the nearest

1930		1940		1950		1960	
						Value Mfg.	.907
Urban	.893	Pop. in Mfg.	.914			Pop. in Mfg.	.877
Pop. in Mfg.	.853	Farm Value	.877			Farm Value	.831
Density	.825	Density	.854			Density	.775
Value Mfg.	.718	Value Mfg.	.805	Value Mfg.	.927	Foreign	.703
Income	.690	#Employees	.749	Pop. in Mfg.	.920	Population	.672
Foreign	.645	Urban	.741	Farm Value	.854	Urban	.657
Farm Value	.641	Population	.530	Density	.820	Telephones	.650
Failures	.632	Failures	.478	Urban	.759	#Employees	.638
Population	.557	Income	.434	#Employees	.731	Income	.573
#Employees	.520	Property	.389	Foreign	.665	Failures	.421
Telephones	.459	Foreign	.306	Population	.622	Property	.132
Pop. Incr.	.306	Telephones	.275	Income	.492	Negro	.066
Property	.232	Negro	.085	Failures	.462	Illiteracy	.039
—		—		—		—	
+		+		+		+	
Negro	.077	School Yrs.	.177	Telephones	.002	Pop. Incr.	.006
Mot. Veh.	.119	Tenancy	.271	Negro	.017	School Yrs.	.026
Illiteracy	.125	Mot. Veh.	.278	Pop. Incr.	.025	Tenancy	.266
Own. Occup.	.139	Pop. Incr.	.301	School Yrs.	.038	Own. Occup.	.316
Divorce	.209	Divorce	.313	Illiteracy	.070	Divorce	.325
Tenancy	.377	Own. Occup.	.438	Divorce	.282	Acreage	.503
Acreage	.526	Acreage	.639	Tenancy	.326	Mot. Veh.	.568
				Mot. Veh.	.342		
				Own. Occup.	.364		
				Acreage	.511		
% Total Variance	22.31		24.36		32.23		32.36

census year. Where there was a gap of several years, the variable was dropped. This accounts for the occasional lapse between decades. Also some data were simply not available for the earlier years.

Although the pattern of factor loadings in this and the following table is relatively consistent from decade to decade, the direction of this sign changes occasionally. This is a function of the technique of principle component analysis and may, in terms of the present analysis, be ignored between decades. Obviously the fact of opposite signs is crucial in interpreting the pattern of variable loadings at any single point in time. A comparison of the percent of the variance accounted for by each factor will also reveal that the principle factor is Industralization in some decades and Affluence in others. (Compare Tables 1 and 2.) Again, this is a function of "early decisions" in the processes of factor extraction and is of relatively minor consequence in making longitudinal comparisons.

TABLE 2. *Loadings of 21 Variables On Factor 2 (Affluence): 1890-1960**

1890		1900		1910		1920	
						Property	.852
						Telephones	.826
		Income	.893			Mot. Veh.	.780
		Property	.874	Mot. Veh.	.859	Foreign	.672
		Foreign	.816	Property	.852	Own. Occup.	.610
Property	.860	Acreage	.619	Telephones	.834	Acreage	.455
Foreign	.855	Divorce	.536	Foreign	.751	Urban	.360
Divorce	.637	Urban	.389	Farm Value	.530	Farm Value	.309
Pop. Incr.	.577	Value Mfg.	.340	Acreage	.463	Value Mfg.	.273
Acreage	.516	Farm Value	.205	Urban	.422	Pop. Incr.	.248
Urban	.308	Pop. Incr.	.200	Pop. Incr.	.352	Failures	.148
Value Mfg.	.254	Pop. in Mfg.	.148	Value Mfg.	.294	Pop. in Mfg.	.125
Farm Value	.170	Failures	.081	Pop. in Mfg.	.086	Population	.080
Pop. in Mfg.	.050	Density	.061	Density	.045	Density	.021
—		—		—		—	
+		+		+		+	
Density	.060	Population	.164	Population	.017	#Employees	.369
Failures	.166	#Employees	.187	Failures	.159	Tenancy	.710
#Employees	.258	Illiteracy	.748	#Employees	.265	Illiteracy	.860
Population	.286	Negro	.848	Tenancy	.694	Negro	.923
Illiteracy	.739			Illiteracy	.845		
Negro	.842			Negro	.903		
% Total Variance	26.90		26.16		36.16		33.43

for all states. The upper New England states of New Hampshire, Maine, and Vermont are illustrative in this regard. Their ranks in 1960 were, respectively, 16, 26 and 30. Yet these same states had ranks of 7, 12 and 13 in 1890. To be sure, some of this may be accounted for by the exodus of industrial concerns from that region. However, more to the point has been the greater rate of industrialization in regions formerly near the bottom of the scale. Texas has moved from forty-second to twenty-ninth, North Carolina improved its position by 16 ranks. Other examples could be selected to illustrate the usefulness of this index in plotting relative socioeconomic change.

It seems reasonable to label Factor II "Affluence." This dimension is obviously heavily regional, along North-South lines. Although the eleven states of the Confederacy scored relatively low on the Industrialization

1930		1940		1950		1960	
		School Yrs.	.926			School Yrs.	.909
Telephones	.820	Mot. Veh.	.900			Property	.792
Mot. Veh.	.819	Telephones	.832			Income	.730
Own. Occup.	.719	Foreign	.720	School Yrs.	.903	Mot. Veh.	.703
Property	.707	Income	.665	Income	.725	Telephones	.675
Foreign	.651	Property	.630	Mot. Veh.	.654	Pop. Incr.	.551
Income	.648	Own. Occup.	.595	Pop. Incr.	.535	Urban	.522
Urban	.417	Urban	.450	Failures	.490	Acreage	.488
Acreage	.409	Acreage	.441	Urban	.470	Divorce	.430
Divorce	.289	Divorce	.357	Acreage	.460	Failures	.287
Farm Value	.207	Failures	.242	Divorce	.392	Own. Occup.	.240
Value Mfg.	.169	Value Mfg.	.210	Own. Occup.	.350	Foreign	.230
Pop. in Mfg.	.123	Farm Value	.130	Foreign	.223	Population	.045
Pop. Incr.	.086	Density	.060	Value Mfg.	.082	Farm Value	.024
Failures	.080	Pop. Incr.	.051	Farm Value	.019	Value Mfg.	.015
Density	.073	Pop. in Mfg.	.027	Density	.014	Density	.008
+		−		+		−	
−		+		−		+	
Population	.032	Population	.068	Population	.017	Pop. in Mfg.	.132
#Employees	.335	#Employees	.443	Pop. in Mfg.	.033	#Employees	.351
Tenancy	.728	Tenancy	.682	Telephones	.125	Tenancy	.468
Illiteracy	.839	Negro	.902	#Employees	.331	Illiteracy	.737
Negro	.929			Illiteracy	.711	Negro	.752
				Tenancy	.716		
				Negro	.817		
% Total Variance	35.76		37.73		23.29		25.25

See note to Table 1. [Factor 2, "Affluence," was labelled "Cultural Enrichment" in the originally published version of this table.—Eds.]

dimension, they were by no means unique in this respect. The mean rank of these eleven states is 27.3 on the eight Industrialization indices, whereas it is 41.2 on the Affluence indices.

Aside from this distinct clustering of southern states at the bottom of Factor II, it is clear that the features which are heavily loaded are characteristics of modern, affluent cultures. The high loading of per cent Negro is indicative of the general cultural deprivation of non-white

TABLE 3. *Factor 1 (Industrialization): Ordinal Rankings by Factor Scores 1890-1960**

State	1890	1900	1910	1920	1930	1940	1950	1960
New Jersey	4	4	4	4	3	3	1	1
Connecticut	3	3	2	3	4	2	2	2
New York	5	5	6	5	5	5	5	3
Massachusetts	2	2	3	2	2	4	4	4
Illinois	11	9	9	10	6	7	6	5
Pennsylvania	6	7	7	7	7	6	9	6
Rhode Island	1	1	1	1	1	1	3	7
Delaware	8	8	8	11	14	13	13	8
Ohio	10	11	10	9	10	9	7	9
California	15	17	23	16	8	18	15	10
Michigan	14	15	13	6	9	8	8	11
Maryland	9	10	12	12	11	10	11	12
Indiana	17	16	16	13	15	12	10	13
Wisconsin	16	14	15	14	16	15	12	14
Missouri	18	20	21	21	18	20	17	15
New Hampshire	7	6	5	8	12	11	14	16
Washington	20	23	22	17	13	24	21	17
North Carolina	34	27	27	19	29	14	18	18
Virginia	24	24	24	28	27	19	20	19
Tennessee	36	31	33	29	28	21	24	20
Minnesota	23	25	28	30	26	30	25	21
Georgia	27	22	20	25	23	23	28	22
South Carolina	25	19	19	20	25	17	19	23
Louisiana	21	21	18	18	19	25	22	24
Iowa	31	32	40	40	32	27	29	25
Maine	12	12	11	15	21	16	16	26
West Virginia	32	30	34	26	30	22	23	27
Oregon	33	37	36	22	20	29	27	28
Texas	42	41	38	34	33	35	31	29
Vermont	13	13	14	23	35	28	30	30
Alabama	35	28	26	24	22	26	26	31
Florida	19	18	17	27	17	31	33	32
Kentucky	28	29	29	33	36	32	32	33
Kansas	37	40	39	41	40	36	34	34
Colorado	22	26	31	37	31	38	35	35
Utah	29	36	35	32	24	37	36	36
Nebraska	30	38	41	45	41	39	37	37
Oklahoma	—	44	45	42	37	40	40	38
Mississippi	39	35	32	31	34	33	38	39
Arkansas	41	39	37	38	38	34	41	40
Arizona	38	33	25	35	42	44	43	41
Nevada	44	48	47	44	39	42	44	42
Idaho	46	46	43	39	45	41	39	43

TABLE 3. *Factor 1 (Industrialization): Ordinal Rankings by Factor Scores: 1890-1960* (Continued)*

State	1890	1900	1910	1920	1930	1940	1950	1960
Montana	26	34	30	43	44	45	42	44
New Mexico	43	42	44	46	47	48	45	45
South Dakota	45	43	46	48	46	43	47	46
Wyoming	40	45	42	36	43	47	46	47
North Dakota	47	47	48	47	48	46	48	48

*The direction of the signs in this and Table 4 have been adjusted to conform between decades (see note to Table 1).

Americans, and is consistent with the correspondingly heavy loading of property values at the other end of the spectrum. Factor II is similarly reflective of high educational attainment, measured either negatively in terms of illiteracy or positively by median school years completed. Some may balk at the inclusion of per cent foreign born as a positive part of Affluence. Aside from the esthetic considerations of what constitutes "affluent," it should be noted that the major portion of the immigrants into the United States, at least in the earlier decades covered by this data, settled in the states which already were well off in terms of wealth, educational attainment, etc.

Although the Affluence factor has a heavy regional cast, it is interesting to examine the extent to which it has become less and less a specifically North-South dimension. While the South still brings up the bottom on this index, there have been significant changes in the relative Cultural Enrichment of some southern states. Florida, for example, has moved from forty-first in 1900 to fourteenth in 1960. Rhode Island, in the same period, dropped from eleventh to thirty-sixth. The universalizing tendencies of modern society and the declining uniqueness of particular cultural pockets of the country may be plotted by examining the breakdown in geographic contiguity of the states through time in respect of Affluence.

One of the charms of factor analysis is that it can take a particular set of phenomena which is widely thought to be unidimensional and demonstrate that it is, in fact, multidimensional. Conventional wisdom tends to assume that those features of cultural deprivation which are heavily concentrated in the South are virtually synonymous with the low industrialization of that area. Yet the technique employed here allows us to measure the distinction between these factors and to check the extent of their interrelationships. Interpretations of each factor, either descriptive

TABLE 4. *Factor 2 (Affluence): Ordinal Rankings by Factor Scores: 1890-1960*

State	1890	1900	1910	1920	1930	1940	1950	1960
Nevada	1	1	3	1	1	2	1	1
California	7	4	1	4	2	1	2	2
Wyoming	4	3	20	7	7	5	4	3
Colorado	5	5	11	13	11	10	7	4
Oregon	13	10	6	6	4	3	6	5
Washington	6	6	7	10	5	6	5	6
Montana	2	2	12	11	12	11	9	7
Nebraska	14	19	5	5	3	16	16	8
Kansas	20	27	14	12	10	19	14	9
Utah	12	17	22	17	24	4	3	10
Connecticut	22	15	16	26	23	7	15	11
Delaware	37	35	35	35	29	32	17	12
Idaho	8	14	26	15	20	20	12	13
Florida	40	41	39	39	39	37	24	14
Iowa	17	21	2	2	14	14	28	15
Arizona	9	7	30	29	31	27	8	16
Minnesota	11	16	8	8	8	13	27	17
New York	19	9	10	18	17	22	11	18
New Jersey	29	20	21	28	27	12	19	19
Massachusetts	21	12	17	21	22	8	10	20
Illinois	18	13	9	16	25	24	22	21
Ohio	28	26	19	24	21	21	21	22
Michigan	16	25	15	19	18	15	13	23
New Mexico	32	33	36	32	33	35	25	24
South Dakota	10	18	13	3	9	28	31	25
Oklahoma	—	32	32	33	35	36	37	26
Texas	33	36	37	38	37	34	34	27
Indiana	30	31	23	25	26	26	32	28
Maryland	35	34	33	34	34	33	35	29
New Hampshire	25	23	27	23	16	18	20	30
North Dakota	3	8	4	9	13	29	30	31
Wisconsin	15	22	18	14	6	17	29	32
Pennsylvania	31	24	28	31	32	30	33	33
Missouri	27	30	31	27	30	31	36	34
Vermont	23	29	24	20	15	23	26	35
Rhode Island	24	11	25	30	28	9	23	36
Maine	26	28	29	22	19	25	18	37
Virginia	41	42	41	41	40	40	39	38
Kentucky	36	38	38	37	38	39	38	39
West Virginia	34	37	34	36	36	38	40	40
Georgia	45	46	45	45	45	44	43	41
Tennessee	39	39	40	40	41	41	41	42
Louisiana	43	43	44	44	44	45	45	43
Arkansas	38	40	42	42	43	43	42	44
Alabama	44	45	46	46	46	46	46	45
North Carolina	42	44	43	43	42	42	44	46
South Carolina	47	48	48	48	48	47	48	47
Mississippi	46	47	47	47	47	48	47	48

or explanatory, should always keep clearly in mind that the scores on one factor are, in effect, "holding constant" the influence of the other.

The fact that Affluence and Industrialization can be separated, however, does not necessarily mean that there is no sharing of these features by particular states. The procedure of oblique rotation, unlike orthogonal rotation, allows for and calculates the correlation of factors. But the method of simple structure analysis isolates the underlying dimensions to the extent possible given the actual values of the original variables, with the result that inter-factor correlations are as low as possible.[13] In this case, the correlations of Affluence and Industrialization actually range from a −.114 to .143, indicating virtually complete isolation. The correlation coefficients for the two factors at each time are given in Table 5.

The utility of the indices which I have presented here, of course, can be appreciated only in the context of a few examples. Tables 6 and 7 give the simple correlations between Industrialization and Affluence, respectively, and selected indicators of policy and political behavior in the states.[14]

The correlation coefficients in Table 6 and the changing strength of relationship, to choose an example, between Industrialization and the various policies indicate clearly that there is marked variation in the ability of this particular environmental dimension to explain the patterns of state and local spending. A correlation between Industrialization and welfare spending taken in 1930 ($r = .613$) would lead to rather different interpretations of the relationship of this feature of the states' environments and welfare policies than would the same correlation taken with 1960 data

TABLE 5. *Correlations of Industrialization and Affluence Factors: 1890-1960*

Year	Correlation
1890	−.114
1900	−.002
1910	−.056
1920	−.005
1930	−.082
1940	.143
1950	−.024
1960	.023

[13] For a technical discussion of this procedure, see Benjamin Fruchter, *Introduction to Factor Analysis* (Princeton: D. Van Nostrand, 1954), 140–148.

[14] A fuller explication of the pattern of variation in such social structural-political relationships as these is the subject of a larger project of which the present article is a product.

TABLE 6. *Product Moment Correlations of Industrialization and Selected Political Variables*: 1890-1960*

Year	Total Spending	Spending for Education	Spending for Highways	Spending for Welfare	Vote Democratic for President**	Voter Turnout for President**
1890	.3081	.2082	.4438	.1690	–.0437	.1357
1900	.3395	–.0789	.3775	.3566	–.3767	.0508
1910	.2702	.0529	.3818	.0628	–.1147	.0506
1920	——	——	——	——	.2213	.2681
1930	.3778	–.0303	.1176	.6130	–.3574	.0653
1940	.1865	.0717	–.2560	.0568	–.1258	.1692
1950	.1403	.0024	–.0907	–.0679	.1528	.2272
1960	–.0396	–.1261	–.5037	.0082	.3520	.2065

* All spending figures are total state and local and are computed on a per capita basis. The spending figures are for the year 1890, 1902, 1913, 1932, 1942, 1957, and 1962 respectively.

** The data employed are percent of the total vote cast for the Democratic presidential candidates and the percent of the population over voting age casting ballots for president. Account has been taken of the different times at which suffrage was made available to women.

(r = .0082). And one certainly should take account of the complete change of direction of correlation between Industrialization and per cent Democratic for president which occurs over the 70 years encompassed by the data. Industrialization is fairly volatile in terms of its relation to all of

TABLE 7. *Product Moment Correlations of Affluence and Selected Political Variables*: 1890-1960*

Year	Total Spending	Spending for Education	Spending for Highways	Spending for Welfare	Vote Democratic for President**	Voter Turnout for President**
1890	.8006	.8296	.4388	.6214	–.7822	.0877
1900	.8161	.8680	.6080	.6670	–.6115	.3577
1910	.5994	.6152	.5212	.5879	–.8229	.6083
1920	——	——	——	——	–.2275	.5664
1930	.7190	.6992	.5248	.5900	–.7704	.7081
1940	.7009	.6476	.4606	.6555	.7792	.8390
1950	.5086	.4532	.3495	.0395	–.6399	.7398
1960	.7964	.7650	.3748	.0560	–.4055	.6354

* See note to Table 6.

** See note to Table 6.

the indicators of policy. It is less so in relation to partisan preferences and voter turnout. However, even in the latter instance, some interesting analyses are suggested by the variation in strength of relationship which does take place. The dramatic shift between the 1920 and 1932 presidential elections in the impact of Industrialization upon per cent Democratic is illustrative of the extent to which different factors were related to the partisan preferences of the states' electorates.

Affluence is much less volatile than Industrialization in terms of its relation to policy outputs. Unlike Industrialization, the effects of Affluence are seen uniformly in all policy areas over time. Whereas Industrialization – highway spending correlations, for example, vary considerably and independently of the relationships between Industrialization and other policy indicators, the pattern for Affluence – policy correlations is much more cohesive and consistent. This would indicate that Affluence is more pervasive and comprehensive in its impact upon the decision of policy makers within the states than is Industrialization. Only in the later years does Affluence have a differential impact upon the various substantive areas of policy. Probably in response to federal prodding and assistance, welfare spending seems no longer to be particularly dependent upon economic resources, but differences in total spending and educational spending are still very much a function of the economic environment in which decisions are made. Examining the pattern of Affluence – political behavior correlations shows that, although there is a general decline in the relevance of this dimension to voter turnout and partisan preference between 1940 and 1960, affluence considerations were at their lowest on the road back to Normalcy in 1920. And anyone familiar with 19th century voting in the South will recall that the Confederacy has not always been characterized by its present low level of voter turnout, despite its consistently low scores on the affluence dimension. I would assume that the rise in the correlation of Affluence and turnout between 1890 and 1910 reveals the success of the Jim Crow laws in limiting voter participation by significant numbers of southern residents.

A good deal more attention could be given to the implications of Tables 6 and 7, along with the various figures. However, the point here is to demonstrate the potential for this mode of analysis rather than to conduct the actual analyses of the data yielded by such techniques.

Conclusion

In addition to providing the specific scores on the two major indices of social structure in the American states for a period of three generations, the data in this article lead to two important conclusions.

First, there are indeed multiple dimensions to be found in the types of social characteristics which have been used most frequently in comparative state studies. The composition of these dimensions is sufficiently consistent over time to allow one to consider them major, enduring elements of social structure.

A second objective has been to suggest that static social structural-political correlations are likely to yield misleading results. When employed as independent variables in the analysis of certain features of state political systems, the explanatory power of the major social dimensions changes considerably. At least this is the conclusion suggested by a sketchy examination of a few political variables commonly the object of explanation with the types of independent variables represented in the data I have used.

The implication for theory of this second finding would seem to be that we must think beyond explications of political "responses" to modernization, economic development, socioeconomic advancement, or whatever our conceptualization of the independent social variables. Evidently a simple linear theory linking policy outcomes to levels of socioeconomic development is inadequate to explain the pattern of policy over time. Rather than setting up the major contours of a "theory of the policy process," the patterns of correlation between socioeconomic characteristics and policy outcomes are themselves variables to be explained. Improved theory must take account of other historical and, perhaps, transient, contextually related phenomena which "activate" social structure vis-a-vis public policy or political behavior. This, in turn, will contribute to and is partially dependent upon a refinement of our knowledge of the linkages between aggregate social characteristics and the parameters of the states' political systems which may be of interest to us.

Conclusion

THE NATIONALIZATION OF STATE POLITICS

Someone unfamiliar with the history of inquiry into American state and local politics would probably find nothing particularly startling in the general approach of the readings presented in the preceding sections.[1] Taken in their historical and methodological context, however, they represent a common and significant break with past ways of studying subnational politics. In one way or another, as noted in the introduction, they all help us understand why policies are the way they are in American states and communities. The authors represented here are able to advance our understanding of policy because they ask particular kinds of questions and because they seek answers by comparative analysis. They compare policies and sociopolitical systems. They view the policy process as a part of the social setting in which it operates. This social setting includes value systems and a propensity to innovate. All of these aspects of the sociopolitical system, when viewed comparatively, can be compared to policy performance and tested as to their particular relevance.

One conclusion that emerges from these studies, admittedly in refined and qualified form, is that the nature of the sociopolitical setting has measurable consequences for the pattern of policy followed by state and community decision makers. A question that remains, however, concerns the future direction of change within these combinations of social settings and policy making activities. We stated in the introduction that students

[1] This section relies heavily upon a discussion contained in Richard I. Hofferbert's *Social Structure and Public Policy in the American States* (Wadsworth Publishing Company, forthcoming).

of comparative policy studies make a basic assumption when they choose their units of analysis. They assume that the things they are studying differ sufficiently to make comparison possible but are enough alike to make comparison meaningful. American states and communities qualify on both counts. The question that remains with respect to the future is: "What is happening to the comparative patterns of social and policy change within the states and their communities?"

Theorizing about the future of American society is a widely indulged journalistic and scholarly activity. Estimating the direction and change in magnitude of governmental activity is not quite as popular a pastime, but it is still pursued with substantial vigor. Clearly we are getting richer in material goods. Suburbs grow, cities change and suffer, rivers get dirtier, the population increases, and through it all, the real per capita income goes up. The number of televisions, automobiles, electric toothbrushes, and brands of detergent all increase faster than the population. Governmental activities, too, extend to an ever enlarging portion of social life. Beautification and the arts are now accepted areas of government policy at all levels. And in the process of this extension, many would argue, it is getting harder and harder to tell the difference between one town and another, between one state and another, or between one person and another.

One of the arguments put forth by the founders of our federal system was that the arrangements between central and state governments would prevent the emergence of what we might call a single dominant life style,[2] and semi-autonomous enclaves within the various states could preclude the "tyranny of the majority." Perhaps we have evolved precisely such a tyranny. Some call it conformity, others call it "mass society,"[3] but the thesis is not new. Tocqueville saw in the American political system a process whereby the general patterns of life and political activity would tend toward a low common denominator.[4] The patterns of policy emulation and innovation found by Jack Walker may not be entirely salutary in their effects. If we can assume that governmental actions have some effect on the life styles of people within a political system, the diffusion found by

[2] The most succinct and well known statement is contained in *The Federalist*, Number 10.

[3] See, for example, William Kornhauser, *The Politics of Mass Society* (Glencoe: Free Press, 1959).

[4] See his essay "The Unlimited Power of the Majority in the United States and Its Consequences" in *Democracy in America*.

Walker may be yet another brick in the wall between an interesting and diverse society and a society characterized by mediocre sameness. The question being asked here, however, does not concern the esthetic or moral evaluation of the state of being in American states and communities. We are concerned rather with the nature and facts of increasing similarity or continued diversity in social structures and patterns of policy.

If patterns of fairly constant change can be demonstrated, we may hazard a prediction that future developments will be along the same general lines. We show in this concluding chapter that there have been common patterns of social development taking place within the states, and that the states are becoming more alike in their socioeconomic and political features. There is a process of sociopolitical "nationalization" in the American federal system.[5]

General Socioeconomic Development

A major organizing concept of much comparative political analysis, as we have seen in many of the preceding essays, is "development." This concept has an appropriate place in the comparative study of the American states, which are developing in two ways. They are, first of all, advancing in their absolute levels of economic affluence, industrialization, urbanization, and educational attainment. This economic and social development accompanies dramatic expansion of the scope and level of public activity that has characterized our history. Second, the states are becoming more alike in socioeconomic and policy terms.

These assertions can be made and supported. But one must not play fast and loose with such ideas as "development." In order to be able to label a particular set of affairs as somehow "developed" or "developing," it has to be shown that: (1) the set of affairs so labeled had a prior state of existence in which it possessed different key characteristics or fewer or less of them than it now possesses; and (2) other sets of affairs demonstrably akin to the former have a similar history or show clearly that they are somehow bent in the same direction. That is, things have to be changing, and the nature of the change has to be a feature of more than just one or a few isolated instances.

[5] See Richard I. Hofferbert, "Ecological Development and Policy Change in the American States," *Midwest Journal of Political Science*, 10 (November, 1966), 464–483.

We have to be careful with "development" in another sense. When we note the directions of change in the states over the past several decades, and when we label this change, "development," it is making no assessment of the quality of life within the states. That New York City has more automobiles now than it had in 1890 is not necessarily an indicator of improved life. The horses of the 1890's moved faster in rush hour than the automobiles of today. As it is being used here, then, "development" is a neutral, descriptive term. It means simply that change is taking place, and the same kind of change can be shown to be a feature of life in all the states.

No matter what indicator of socioeconomic life we pick, there are noticeable differences between the states. Yet the scores for all states are changing. The direction of change, furthermore, is similar for all states — even for those somehow "behind" in earlier years. Table 1 illustrates the nature of socioeconomic change in sample states between 1890 and 1960. All the states are becoming urban, industrialized, literate, and rich. Increases in literacy were temporarily set back between 1920 and 1930 in some states due to large numbers of immigrants, and the Depression interrupted the progress toward ever larger incomes. But generally, the directions of change are consistent and upward.

The one variable that deviates most from the pattern is manufacturing employment. Although in all cases the per cent of the population working in industry increased between 1899 and 1958, the rate of change does not appear quite as dramatic as with the other indicators in Table 1. Part of this is due to the declining proportion of the population in the work force as an increasing per cent of the population is either in school or retired. This itself is a sign of increasing wealth. Furthermore, the proportion of the actual work force in manufacturing has declined relative to other sectors in recent years. Automation, the growth of service trades, and a general shift to a white collar society are involved here. Nevertheless, there is sufficient difference in the magnitudes of change with respect to manufacturing employment to suggest we are measuring a somewhat different process of social change than with the other items in the table.

Overall, however, the direction of change among the states is common. But what is not revealed by these data is the relative rate of change among the states. Is the relative distance between the states along these socioeconomic lines increasing, decreasing, or holding constant? Are the rich states getting richer at a rate faster than the poor states? Or is social change taking place more rapidly in those states furthest behind?

TABLE 1. *Socioeconomic Development in Selected States*: 1890-1960*

State	1890	1900	1910	1920	1930	1940	1950	1960
% Urban								
Alabama	10.1	11.9	17.3	21.7	28.1	30.2	43.8	55.0
Arizona	9.4	15.9	31.0	35.2	34.4	34.8	55.5	74.5
California	48.6	52.4	61.8	68.0	73.3	71.0	80.7	86.4
Connecticut	83.5	87.2	89.7	67.8	70.4	67.8	77.6	78.3
Iowa	21.2	25.6	30.6	36.4	39.6	42.7	47.7	53.1
New Jersey	60.7	70.6	75.2	78.4	82.6	81.6	86.6	88.6
Ohio	41.0	48.1	55.9	63.8	67.8	66.8	70.2	73.4
Oklahoma	3.7	7.4	19.3	26.6	34.3	37.6	51.0	62.9
West Virginia	10.7	13.1	18.7	25.2	28.4	28.1	34.6	38.2
% Illiterate								
Alabama	**	24.2	16.4	16.1	12.6	**	6.2	4.2
Arizona		22.1	16.1	15.3	10.1		6.2	3.8
California		3.9	3.1	3.3	2.6		2.2	1.8
Connecticut		4.7	4.8	6.2	4.5		3.1	2.2
Iowa		1.8	1.3	1.1	.8		.9	.7
New Jersey		4.3	4.4	5.1	3.8		2.9	2.2
Ohio		3.1	2.6	2.8	2.3		2.3	1.5
Oklahoma		3.7	4.0	3.8	2.8		2.5	1.9
West Virginia		8.3	6.1	6.4	4.8		3.5	2.7
% Population Employed in Manufacturing								
		(1899)	(1909)	(1923)	(1931)	(1939)	(1947)	(1958)
Alabama	**	2.8	2.5	4.4	3.1	4.0	6.9	7.2
Arizona		2.5	1.5	2.4	1.3	1.2	2.0	3.4
California		5.2	3.2	5.8	3.5	3.9	6.5	8.1
Connecticut		17.5	14.3	18.0	11.9	13.6	20.5	16.1
Iowa		1.9	2.0	3.1	2.4	2.5	5.7	6.1
New Jersey		10.7	8.4	12.9	8.2	10.4	16.4	13.4
Ohio		7.4	6.5	11.5	7.6	8.6	15.3	12.5
Oklahoma		.6	.2	1.1	.9	1.1	2.5	4.1
West Virginia		3.4	2.7	5.4	3.7	3.8	6.6	6.3
Per Capita Personal Income (1929)								
Alabama	**	$ 88	**	**	$ 324	$282	$ 869	$1,462
Arizona		321			591	497	1,295	2,019
California		365			995	840	1,839	2,722
Connecticut		278			1,029	917	1,900	2,854
Iowa		202			577	501	1,449	2,024
New Jersey		277			931	822	1,790	2,652
Ohio		222			781	665	1,612	2,335
Oklahoma		114			454	373	1,146	1,841
West Virginia		117			462	407	1,098	1,671

* Selected on the basis of closest approximation of mean percent urban, 1920 in the United States Census regional groups.

** No data available

Comparative Rates of Social and Economic Development

To the extent that regional and state identity is an important feature of the operating American federal system, and to the extent that this identity has some recognizable roots in social differences, students of American politics must be concerned about the nature of inter-state social and political differences and what is happening to them. Furthermore, those concerned with social justice and the disparities in the quality of life in the United States quite naturally have an interest in the equity with which the fruits of development reach the various parts of the country. Table 2 presents the coefficients of relative variation between 1890 and 1960 for the four socioeconomic variables discussed in the preceding section.[6] The most striking feature of Table 2 is the marked and consistent tendency for the variation between the states to decline over the years. No doubt, several factors operate to bring about the increasing similarity of the social features of the states. But certainly a few processes command themselves to our attention.

The major feature of American society to strike the eyes of Alexis de Tocqueville, perhaps the most astute nineteenth-century observer of our collective lives, was our commitment to equality. No single aspect of public policy more clearly manifests this commitment than the spread of free public education. Compulsory school attendance was initiated in Massachusetts in 1852. The last state to follow the trend was Mississippi in 1918.[7] Illiteracy, a negative measure of schooling, is universally accepted as a social evil to be eliminated by public means. The value always attached to education in American society is such that even

[6] For an elementary discussion of this particular device, see John H. Mueller and Karl F. Scheussler, *Statistical Reasoning in Sociology* (Boston: Houghton Mifflin Company, 1961), 159–161. The computation formula for the Coefficient of Relative Variation is:

$$CRV = \frac{SD}{\overline{X}} \times 100,$$

where SD is the standard deviation and $\overline{X}$ is the mean. Mueller and Scheussler say, "The Coefficient of Relative Variation is simple to compute, and particularly useful in comparative work, since it has the effect of norming for differences in absolute magnitudes and in substantive units of measure. It makes comparable sets of small and large values of the same kind, as well as values that are qualitatively different." *Ibid.*, 161.

[7] Thomas R. Dye, *Politics, Economics, and the Public* (Chicago: Rand McNally & Company, 1966), 75.

TABLE 2. *Coefficients of Relative Variation in Selected Socioeconomic Characteristics of the States: 1890-1960*

Year	% Population Employed in Manufacturing*	% Population Urban	% Population Illiterate	Per Capita Personal Income
1890	**	68.3	88.9	**
1900	86.1	67.6	89.4	**
1910	92.3	57.4	83.9	**
1920	74.7	50.7	84.4	**
1930	71.9	43.3	84.4	36.2***
1940	73.7	38.7	**	37.2
1950	66.1	28.8	64.7	23.4
1960	51.6	24.0	60.6	20.8

*1899, 1909, 1923, 1931, 1939, 1947, 1958
**No data available
***1929

the least affluent states view the diffusion of minimum educational opportunity as a first priority of public policy.

The decline in variation in manufacturing employment measures many things. First, it reflects the decentralization of American industry and the movement of manufacturing concerns out of the industrial North and into the formerly agricultural regions of the South and, to a lesser extent the Plains. The statistics are also affected by the processes of automation and the consequent movement of people from manufacturing to white collar, tertiary employment in various service trades. This "post industrial" phase of economic development has been most impressive in the former manufacturing centers of the North and East, thereby reducing the difference between them and the areas that used to have few people producing manufactured goods.

Both the diffusion of education and the spread of moderately well-paying employment in manufacturing has contributed to the decline in personal income differentials between the states.

The closing of the gap in per capita income between the states is shown by the sample states displayed in Figure 1. This graph presents rates of increase. Bearing in mind that the vertical axis on the graph shows relative differences, it is clear that the states are moving closer to one another. Whereas in 1900 Alabama had a per capita income of only 31.49 per cent of Connecticut's, by 1967, it had risen to 56.04 per cent. (See Table 1.)

It is clear, therefore, that the poorer, less industrialized states are getting richer and more industrial at a faster rate than the states that have been in the lead. This "nationalization of social situations" plus the overall, common directions discussed in the preceding pages clearly allow us to speak of at least two aspects of "development" in the socioeconomic composition and relationships of the states.

From the general tenor of many of the essays in the preceding chapters, we might next want to ask whether or not the

FIGURE 1. Rates of Change in Per Capita Income for Four States: 1929 – 1967

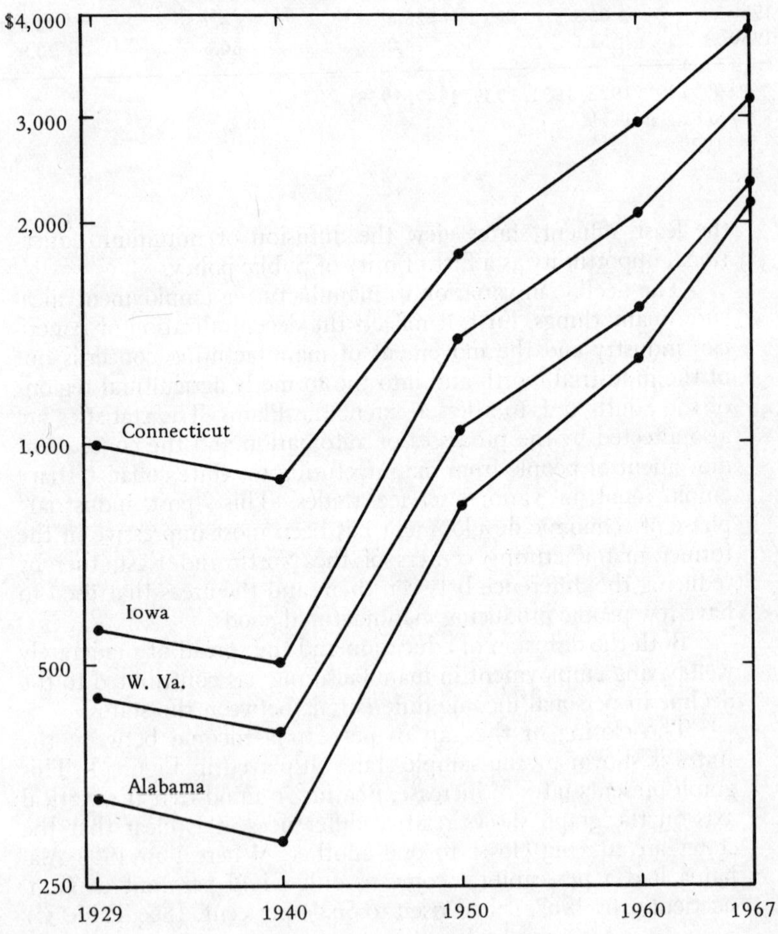

policies of the states — which have been seen to be, in some degree, tied to socioeconomic development — manifest similar developmental patterns.

Comparative Rates of Policy Change

It seems pointless to duplicate for public expenditures the same points made earlier with respect to social development. It is common knowledge that the levels of policy activity and public spending for all jurisdictions is upward. Few, if any, public functions are scaled down. With the exception of the depression years for local governments, all levels of government have increased steadily their levels of public expenditure since the early nineteenth century. But we may still wonder about the relative changes between different jurisdictions.

As Table 3 illustrates, the coefficients of relative variation in state and local expenditures have been steadily declining over the past several decades. The states that provide the lowest levels of services are increasing these activities at a faster rate than the states at higher absolute levels. Undoubtedly a number of forces are at work bringing about what might be called the "nationalization" of state policy. The centralizing tendencies accompanying an increased federal role would have this result as a function both of direct redistribution and of the program definitions that accompany grant-in-aid activities. But we should not overestimate the impact of federal redistributive formulas in the grant-in-aid programs. Most federal grant programs do not include an equalization formula. Of the policy areas plotted in Table 3, three are heavily affected by federal aid: health and hospitals, highways, and welfare. But, of these three, only welfare has a major portion of the aid distributed according to a concept of inter-state wealth redistribution. And there the formula provides federal assistance in accordance with the number of people on the welfare rolls rather than according to the level of assistance provided. The states with large numbers of needy people are encouraged by the formula to lower both the requirements for enrollment in their program and also the average level of assistance provided each recipient.[8]

If redistribution of financial resources from rich states to poor were the chief objective of federal aid, one would expect a strong inverse correlation between per capita federal assistance

[8] *Ibid.*, 120–121.

TABLE 3. *Coefficients of Relative Variation in Expenditures by State and Local Governments for Selected Policies: 1890-1962*

Year	Total State & Local	Education	Highways	Health & Hospitals	Police	Welfare
1890	54.69	48.43	83.66	141.06	106.82	81.74
1902	51.07	52.25	53.95	55.86	94.46	68.40
1913	49.45	62.58	48.63	75.76	59.04	59.88
1930	34.54	42.13	56.82	109.09	101.19	65.30
1947	29.21	26.24	41.75	47.13	52.94	55.64
1957	21.27	21.47	33.53	33.39	36.85	40.86
1962	19.21	21.50	35.16	30.84	35.28	35.84

and various indicators of state wealth, that is, the poorer states would receive a relatively greater amount of federal aid than their more affluent counterparts. The actual correlations with a number of socioeconomic indicators is shown in Table 4. These relationships make it apparent that federal money does bring about some redistribution of resources and probably contributes to the increasing similarity of state policy patterns. But this element hardly offers a major or key explanation of the trend.

There is no definitive explanation for the "nationalization" of state policy. The most appealing explanation is Walker's emulation thesis. An adequate test of this hypothesis would need to show such things as the frequency and nature of interstate communication and interaction between planners, administrators, and other policy makers in functionally comparable areas. As Walker notes, there are growing opportunities for professional contact across state lines. There are frequent national or regional meetings held between state welfare administrators, commissioners of natural resources, highway personnel, budget officers, correctional officials, and others. It is difficult to believe that such events do not lead the participants to become more alike in their policy aspirations, particularly since the agendas of such gatherings are commonly arranged around specific problem areas and focus on methods of attempted solution in one or another state.

The actuality of invidious comparisons with the policy performance of other states, added to existing internal claims, may be serving as a goad to the less affluent states. This increases as the career aspirations of administrators shift to a national professional constituency from aspirations of upward mobility within each state's bureaucracy. Although it has not yet been adequately

TABLE 4. *Relationship between Selected Socioeconomic Variables and Per Capita Federal Aid (by State) to States, Local Units, and Individuals: 1963**

Socioeconomic Variable	Correlation with Per Capita Federal Aid	Socioeconomic Variable	Correlation with Per Capita Federal Aid
	r =		r =
Per cent Urban, 1963	–.377	Per cent Literate, 1960	–.082
Per Capita Income, 1963	.000	Per cent Owner Occupancy of Housing, 1960	–.197
Per cent Population in Non-Agricultural Employment, 1963	–.290		

* Source: Richard I. Hofferbert, "Ecological Development and Policy Change in the American States," *Midwest Journal of Political Science,* 10 (November, 1966), 473

documented, we strongly suspect that the incidence of inter-state movement of upper level state administrators is increasing over time. The identification of administrators with the performance standards of their graduate schools and their national professions may lead them to pressure other policy makers in their states to commit revenues to social services "beyond their means," in a sense. That is, the poorer states will tend to devote a higher proportion of their available resources to social services than is the pattern in economically more well-off states. That this tendency is present, but hardly overpowering, is evident in the various measures of policy effort shown in Table 5 correlated with per capita personal income.

Although the correlations in Table 5 are not especially spectacular, they do all tend in the same direction. That governments in the less advantaged states seem to commit a larger portion of their available resources to social services indicates, of course, that there are more people in need of assistance in these states. But it also might make one wonder if there is not, in the minds of state and local policy makers throughout the country such a thing as a "natural" level of support for the disadvantaged or for particular public activities. No matter how rich a state may be in revenue resources, public demands, or technical skills, the salaries of teachers in the public schools or the amount of monthly payments to the economically unfortunate are not likely to go very much beyond certain absolute levels followed in the rest of the nation. Policy is "nationalized."

TABLE 5. *State Commitment to Selected Public Policies as Percent of Personal Income, Correlated with Per Capita Personal Income**

Policy Commitment as Per Cent of Personal Income	Correlated with Per Capita Income	Policy Commitment as Per Cent of Personal Income	Correlated with Per Capita Income
	r =		r =
State and Local Taxes, 1963	–.222	State and Local Spending for Welfare, 1963	–.471
State and Local Spending for Education, 1963	–.347	State and Local Spending for Health and Hospitals, 1963	–.105

* Source: Richard I. Hofferbert, "Ecological Development and Policy Change in the American States," *Midwest Journal of Political Science,* 10 (November, 1966), 479.

That they are becoming more alike is by no means to suggest that the states are becoming amorphous units in a mass system. To assert such a thesis would entail either incredible optimism on the part of those who see our federal system as a bulwark of parochialism or else to indulge in undue pessimism by one who happens to admire the diversity the structure seems to encourage. If one is willing occasionally to wander off the turnpikes and super highways he will soon discover there is considerable tenacity with which the people of our states and communities cling to that which is uniquely theirs. Policy makers will ignore this tenacity at their own political peril. Moreover, the regions of America still present viable differences in state and local politics and public policy. Indeed, a study of change, by regions, over the course of this century shows that the states of each region are becoming more like their neighbors in politics and policy. Interstate communications and emulation proceed on a regional as well as a national basis. The process of copying that leads to national similarities also leads to regional uniformities that are even more pronounced and more distinct from national norms than they were in the past.[9] Plenty of diversity remains in the American states, and they continue as fascinating subjects of comparative analysis.

[9] Ira Sharkansky, *Regionalism in American Politics* (Indianapolis: Bobbs-Merrill, 1969), chapter 4.